discover AUSTRALIA

LINDSAY BROWN
JUSTINE VAISUTIS, JAYNE D'ARCY, KATJA GASKELL,
PAUL HARDING, VIRGINIA JEALOUS, ROWAN MCKINNON,
CHARLES RAWLINGS-WAY, ROWAN ROEBIG, TOM SPURLING,
REGIS ST LOUIS, PENNY WATSON, MEG WORBY

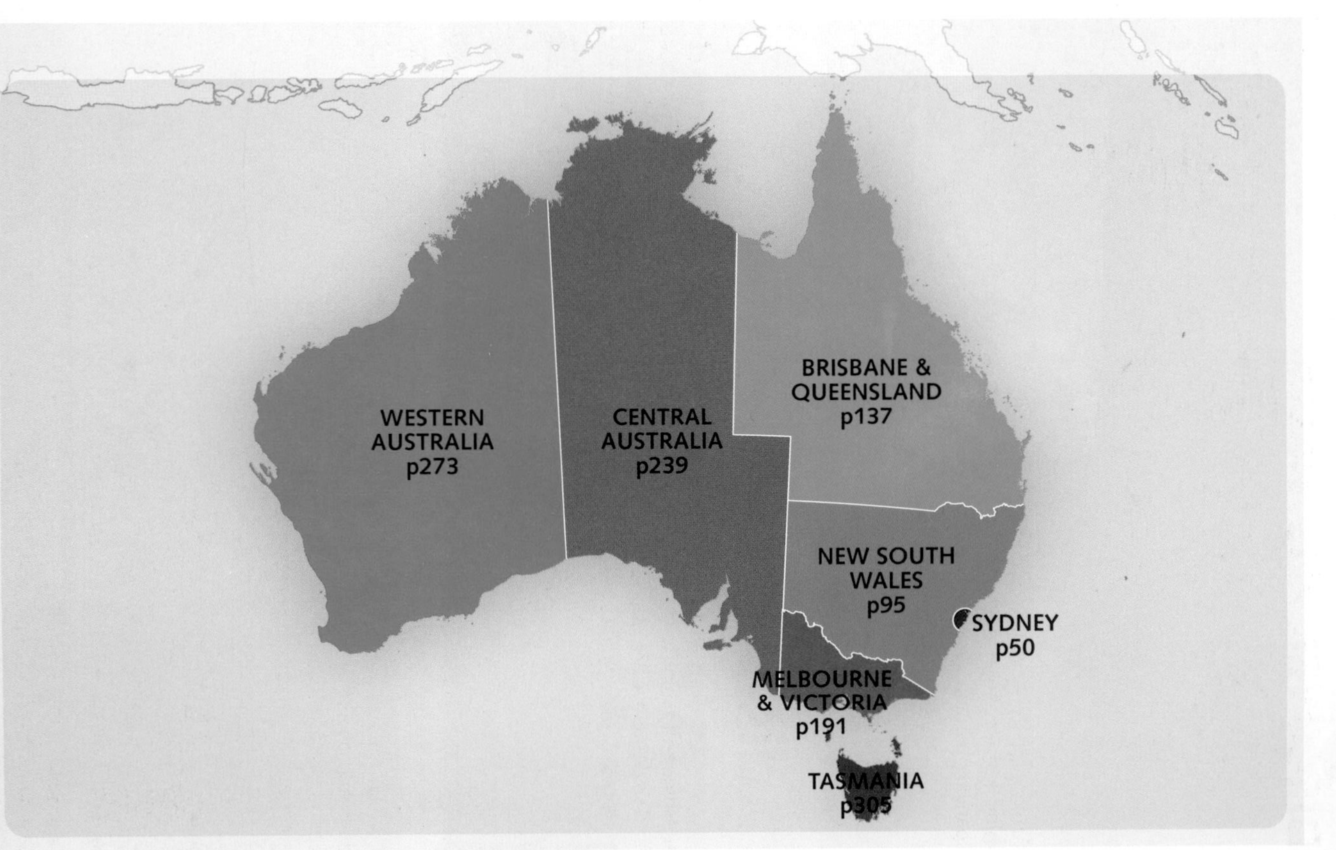
WESTERN
AUSTRALIA
p273
CENTRAL
AUSTRALIA
p239
BRISBANE &
QUEENSLAND
p137
NEW SOUTH
WALES
p95
SYDNEY
p50
MELBOURNE
& VICTORIA
p191
TASMANIA
p305

DISCOVER AUSTRALIA

Sydney (p50) Brash, bronzed and brimming with confidence, this city, with its sparkling harbour, won't be ignored.

New South Wales (p95) From southern snowfields to subtropical northern beaches, this state has all the action covered.

Brisbane & Queensland (p137) Beaches, sunshine and a mighty coral reef; Queensland sizzles above and dazzles below.

Melbourne & Victoria (p191) In a compact state of surprises, the multicultural capital blends coffee ritual, nightlife and sportlife.

Central Australia (p239) A quintessential blend of vineyards, mesmerising Red Centre landforms and tropical Top End.

Western Australia (p273) Majestic forests and vineyards down south; camel trains and marine-life spectacle in the tropical north.

Tasmania (p305) A premier bushwalking destination that's also epicurean hub, font of fresh air and antidote to city stress.

↘ CONTENTS

WESTERN AUSTRALIA p273
CENTRAL AUSTRALIA p239
BRISBANE & QUEENSLAND p137
NEW SOUTH WALES p95
SYDNEY p50
MELBOURNE & VICTORIA p191
TASMANIA p305

INDONESIA
TIMOR SEA
Melville Island
Cobourg Peninsula
Bathurst Island
DARWIN
Jabiru
Kakadu NP
KAKADU NATIONAL PARK p257
Encounter Indigenous culture and rock art in a stunning ancient landscape pulsing with wildlife
INDIAN OCEAN
Cape Londonderry
Joseph Bonaparte Gulf
Daly
Katherine
Mataranka
Wyndham
Kununurra
Collier Bay
Cape Leveque
The Kimberley
Lake Argyle
Victoria
Elliott
NINGALOO MARINE PARK p300
Accessible coral reef and the opportunity to swim with whale sharks and manta rays
Derby
Fitzroy Crossing
Ord
Broome
Fitzroy
Halls Creek
Eighty Mile Beach
Tennant Creek
Great Sandy Desert
Port Hedland
ULURU (AYERS ROCK) p263
Experience the allure of this timeless and truly divine monolith in a profoundly spiritual land
NORTHERN TERRITORY
Barrow Island
Dampier
Karratha
Marble Bar
The Pilbara
North-West Cape
Onslow
Fortescue
Exmouth
Tom Price
MacDonnell Ranges
Alice Springs
Ningaloo Marine Park
Paraburdoo
Newman
Tropic of Capricorn
Little Sandy Desert
WESTERN AUSTRALIA
Yulara
Uluru
Uluru-Kata Tjuta National Park
Gascoyne
Carnarvon
Shark Bay
Wiluna
Lake Carnegie
Marla
Denham
Meekatharra
Dirk Hartog Island
SOUTH AUSTRALIA
Great Victoria Desert
Kalbarri
Mt Magnet
Leonora-Gwalia
Laverton
SHARK BAY p294
Mingle with Monkey Mia's dolphins and discover an amazing World Heritage marine park
Kalgoorlie-Boulder
Nullarbor Plain
Southern Cross
Eucla
Ceduna
Kambalda
Northam
Merredin
Streaky Bay
PERTH
York
Norseman
Fremantle
Mandurah
Narrogin
Great Australian Bight
Cape Naturaliste
Bunbury
Esperance
Busselton
Manjimup
Margaret River
Walpole
Cape Leeuwin
Albany
Walpole-Nornalup NP
ELEVATION
1200m
900m
600m
300m
0
LEGEND
Freeway
Primary Road
Secondary Road
Railway
0 400 km
0 250 miles
SOUTHERN FORESTS p294
Tread lightly among forest giants or climb the canopy for a bird's-eye view
SOUTHERN OCEAN
10°S
15°S
20°S
25°S
35°S
40°S
105°E
110°E
115°E
120°E
125°E
130°E

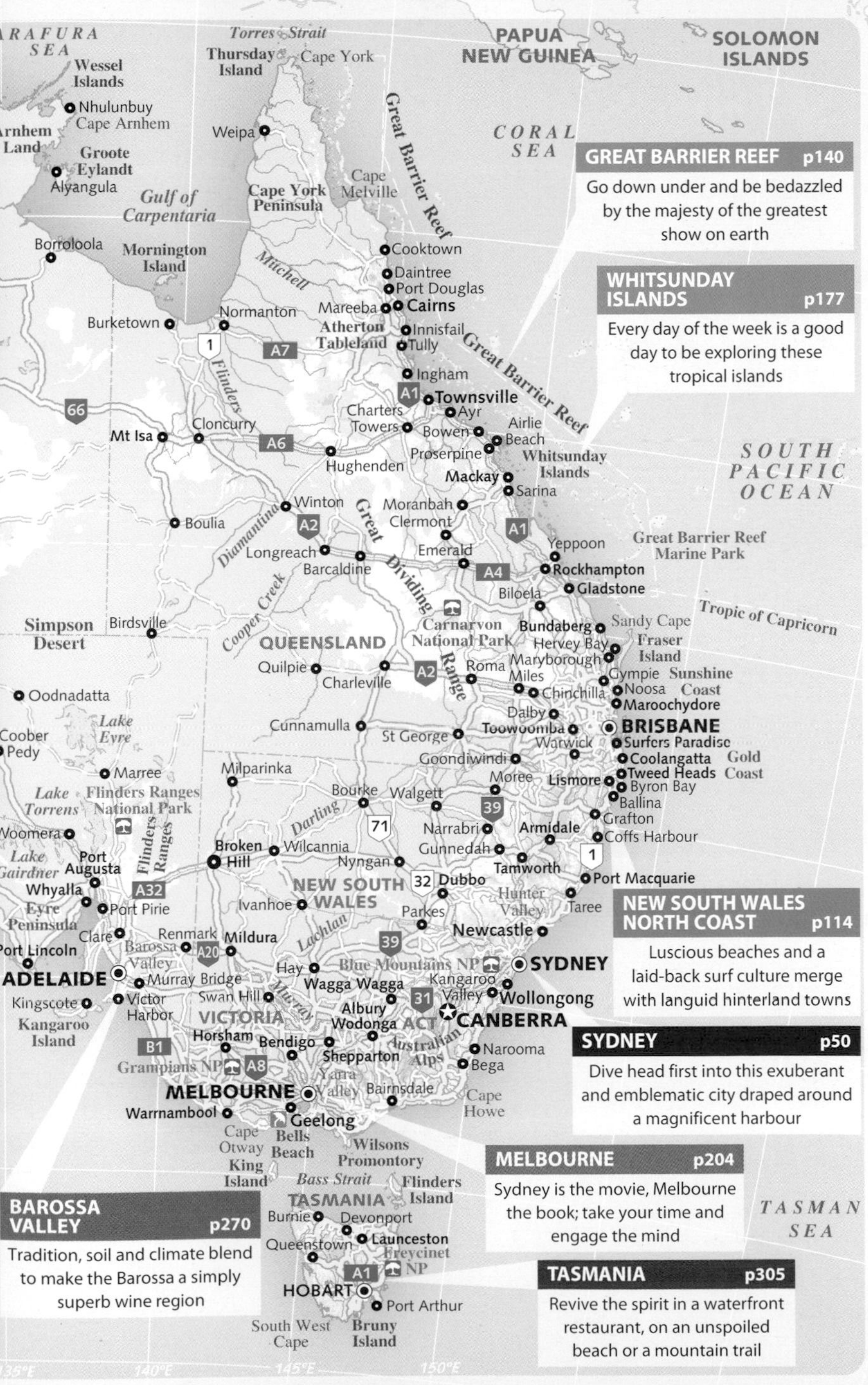
GREAT BARRIER REEF p140
Go down under and be bedazzled by the majesty of the greatest show on earth
WHITSUNDAY ISLANDS p177
Every day of the week is a good day to be exploring these tropical islands
NEW SOUTH WALES NORTH COAST p114
Luscious beaches and a laid-back surf culture merge with languid hinterland towns
SYDNEY p50
Dive head first into this exuberant and emblematic city draped around a magnificent harbour
MELBOURNE p204
Sydney is the movie, Melbourne the book; take your time and engage the mind
BAROSSA VALLEY p270
Tradition, soil and climate blend to make the Barossa a simply superb wine region
TASMANIA p305
Revive the spirit in a waterfront restaurant, on an unspoiled beach or a mountain trail
ARAFURA SEA
Torres Strait
PAPUA NEW GUINEA
SOLOMON ISLANDS
CORAL SEA
SOUTH PACIFIC OCEAN
TASMAN SEA
Gulf of Carpentaria
Great Barrier Reef
Great Barrier Reef Marine Park
Tropic of Capricorn
Great Dividing Range
QUEENSLAND
NEW SOUTH WALES
VICTORIA
ACT
TASMANIA
Bass Strait
Thursday Island
Cape York
Wessel Islands
Nhulunbuy
Cape Arnhem
Arnhem Land
Groote Eylandt
Alyangula
Weipa
Cape York Peninsula
Cape Melville
Borroloola
Mornington Island
Cooktown
Daintree
Port Douglas
Mareeba
Cairns
Atherton Tableland
Innisfail
Tully
Normanton
Burketown
Ingham
Townsville
Ayr
Charters Towers
Bowen
Airlie Beach
Proserpine
Whitsunday Islands
Mackay
Sarina
Mt Isa
Cloncurry
Hughenden
Winton
Boulia
Moranbah
Clermont
Emerald
Longreach
Barcaldine
Yeppoon
Rockhampton
Gladstone
Biloela
Carnarvon National Park
Simpson Desert
Birdsville
Bundaberg
Sandy Cape
Hervey Bay
Fraser Island
Maryborough
Roma
Miles
Quilpie
Charleville
Gympie
Sunshine Coast
Noosa
Maroochydore
Chinchilla
Dalby
Oodnadatta
Lake Eyre
Cunnamulla
St George
Toowoomba
BRISBANE
Warwick
Surfers Paradise
Coolangatta
Gold Coast
Tweed Heads
Coober Pedy
Marree
Goondiwindi
Moree
Lismore
Byron Bay
Ballina
Milparinka
Lake Torrens
Flinders Ranges National Park
Bourke
Walgett
Grafton
Woomera
Narrabri
Armidale
Coffs Harbour
Broken Hill
Wilcannia
Gunnedah
Lake Gairdner
Port Augusta
Flinders Ranges
Nyngan
Tamworth
Whyalla
Port Macquarie
Dubbo
Hunter Valley
Eyre Peninsula
Port Pirie
Ivanhoe
Taree
Parkes
Clare
Renmark
Mildura
Newcastle
Port Lincoln
Barossa Valley
Blue Mountains NP
SYDNEY
ADELAIDE
Murray Bridge
Hay
Kangaroo Valley
Wagga Wagga
Wollongong
Kingscote
Victor Harbor
Swan Hill
Albury
Wodonga
CANBERRA
Kangaroo Island
Horsham
Bendigo
Australian Alps
Narooma
Shepparton
Bega
Grampians NP
MELBOURNE
Yarra Valley
Bairnsdale
Cape Howe
Warrnambool
Geelong
Cape Otway
Bells Beach
Wilsons Promontory
King Island
Flinders Island
Burnie
Devonport
Launceston
Queenstown
Freycinet NP
HOBART
Port Arthur
South West Cape
Bruny Island
Mitchell
Flinders
Diamantina
Cooper Creek
Darling
Lachlan
Murray
A1
A2
A4
A6
A7
A8
A20
A32
B1
1
66
71
32
39
31
135°E
140°E
145°E
150°E

➘ THIS IS AUSTRALIA

This immense island continent is a rare place of space on an increasingly crowded planet. As well as room to move and clean air, it has a relaxed lifestyle, fine weather, a big bridge and an even bigger, redder rock.

Australia is so vast and diverse it fulfils the full spectrum of holiday adventure, from active escapade to peaceful retreat. A well-developed tourism infrastructure provides options and opportunities for travellers on all budgets and allows you to land in any city with little more than your first night's accommodation sorted.

Australia's greatest enigma is its extremes. The driest and flattest inhabited continent on earth is also home to dripping wet rainforests in Tasmania and Queensland. The world's largest coral reef adorns 2300km of an immense coastline, golden sand and surging surf fringe gleaming modern cities as well as pristine forests, and at its heart, the iconic Uluru (Ayers Rock) overwhelms visitors with its spiritual presence.

Australians' love for home is matched by an intense interest in the foreign; their cities are in constant flux, absorbing fresh influences from far corners of the globe.

Former colonies were fused over a century ago during Federation, yet the cities retain distinct personalities: Sydney is a glamorous entertainer with a bounty of natural magnetism, Melbourne a European-inspired, caffeine-enriched artiste, and Brisbane a blithe and blossoming playmate, while the personalities of Adelaide, Perth, Darwin and Hobart are as dissimilar as their climates. In between are deserts, coastal villages, beaches, forests and outback communities, each adding definition to the ever-changing Australian portrait.

'Australia is big – *really* big – so planning is of the essence'

An important thing to remember is that Australia is big – *really* big – so planning is of the essence. An intrepid road trip through the outback or tropical Top End will require an extra level of investigation and planning. The state capitals and most regional centres, on the other hand, are well connected by airlines, so with a little groundwork you can cover a good portion of the country in just a few weeks.

AUSTRALIA'S TOP 25 EXPERIENCES

1

BONDI BEACH BUMS

Sydney's **Bondi Beach** (p75) is as famous for its lifeguards as it is for its swell. A T-shirt from Bondi will have you going home looking like you've just stepped off the set of *Baywatch,* but with a touch more class.

Kate West, Traveller, Australia

FOOTY IN MELBOURNE

2

Some things can become addictive. That warm sense of camaraderie, where everyone is equal regardless of actual nationality, race or religion. The welcoming faces and friendly greetings of complete strangers. The siren goes and battle commences. This is the beauty of **footy** (p358) in Melbourne.

Edward Hanby, Traveller, UK

3

SNORKELLING THE REEF

Snorkelling the **Great Barrier Reef** (p140) is like entering another world; it is like swimming in earth's womb. The colours of the reef and fish take your breath away, and when the reef ends and there is a sheer drop into deep ocean, it feels like you're skydiving from the highest mountain.

Ursula Hogan, Traveller, Austria

1 RODNEY HYETT; 2 JEFF YATES; 3 ROBERT HALSTEAD

1 Bondi Beach (p75); 2 Australian Rules football, Melbourne Cricket Ground (p212); 3 Diver and cuttlefish, Great Barrier Reef (p140)

SAILING THE WHITSUNDAYS

4

The **Whitsundays** (p176) is one of the best areas to visit in the world. The best way is to get onto a boat and cruise around. And if you go at the right time of year you will see whales migrating, dolphins swimming, turtles cruising by. It is truly paradise!

Jimmy Barnes, Musician

5

CHILLING IN BYRON

Byron Bay (p122) certainly has its fair share of interesting characters, a large proportion left over from the Age of Aquarius. The beaches are beautiful, the shopping is great and the pace is chilled out. It's the perfect gateway to the hinterland towns that surround this magnetic place.

Victoria Downey, Traveller, Australia

TOP DROPS

Australia produces brilliant wines for you to sip, swish and swallow. There are numerous picturesque wine-producing regions with cellar door sales, romantic accommodation and fine dining, including the **Barossa Valley** (p270), **Yarra Valley** (p224) and **Hunter Valley** (p116).

Lindsay Brown, Lonely Planet Author, Australia

6

4 HOLGER LEUE; 5 MICAH WRIGHT; 6 GLENN VAN DER KNIJFF

4 Hardy Reef, near Whitsunday Islands (p176); 5 Byron Bay (p122); 6 Fergusson winery, Yarra Valley (p224)

➘ TOURING TASMANIA

Motoring around **Tasmania** (p305), enjoying good food and wine with the family. Such a laid-back relaxed atmosphere… OK, it sometimes resembles the '80s but that period brings back fond memories to me.

Julie Bicknell, Traveller, Australia

7

8 SURFING THE SUNSHINE COAST

The **Sunshine Coast** (p167) is brilliant for catching waves. Noosa has a reputation for the best point breaks in Queensland and the strip from Sunshine Beach to Coolum has world-class beach breaks.

Rowan Roebig, Lonely Planet Staff

9 KANGAROO VALLEY

My favourite place out of the water is somewhere I go to relax and take a complete break from the demands of life. **Kangaroo Valley** (p132) slows you down, encourages you to take a deep breath and appreciate the incredible beauty of the environment.

Layne Beachley, World Champion Surfer

7 ROB BLAKERS; 8 OLIVER STREWE; 9 DAVID HANCOCK / ALAMY

7 Walls of Jerusalem National Park, Tasmania (p305); 8 Body surfing in Tea Tree Bay (p170), Noosa; 9 Kangaroo River, Kangaroo Valley (p132)

10

VALLEY OF THE GIANTS

The locals in **Walpole** (p294) say ancient tingle trees make you 'tingle all over', and it's true. Walk among trees so tall that people used to take pictures of cars sitting in hollow trunks, and see the sapphire flash of an iridescent fairy wren, small and surprising like the strange native orchids that arrive in spring.

Moira Finucane, Writer & Performer

TASMANIA'S FAVOURITE HAUNTS

11

Tasmania is haunted. It's no secret, ask any of the locals and they'll be happy to share their favourite ghost story. Take a ghost tour of historic Battery Point in **Hobart** (p322) for a spine-tingling experience, or test your courage with a ghost tour at **Port Arthur** (p326). Beware the Parsonage…

Kate Slomkowski, Traveller, USA

ESPRESSO MELBOURNE

12

The great thing about **Melbourne** (p204) is that at almost any place you go, you're sure to find a happening cafe hub. Cafe culture is part of the scenery in Melbourne. Well-known restaurant and cafe locations in the inner city include the CBD and Southbank, as well as Lygon St in Carlton.

Sandra Taranto, Traveller, Australia

13

SYDNEY PARTY CENTRAL

This city has everything! Beautiful **beaches** (p56), loads of cool **shopping** hot spots (p89) and everything else for having a good time.

'Turbz', Traveller

10 ANDREW BAIN; 11 WIBOWO RUSLI; 12 PHIL WEYMOUTH; 13 GLENN BEANLAND

10 Tree Top Walk, Valley of the Giants (294); 11 Port Arthur (p326), Tasmania; 12 Cafe at Centre Pl (p218), Melbourne; 13 Sydney Opera House (p68)

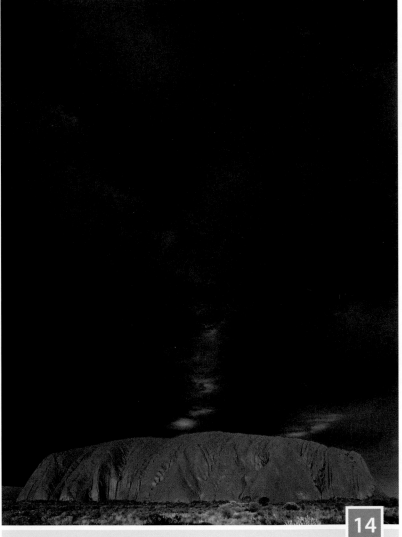

14

ULURU IN THE RAIN

It rarely rains in the outback, but while walking around **Uluru** (Ayers Rock; p262) we were suddenly deluged with one heck of a storm. We noticed waterfalls beginning to form and, as the rain got harder, the waterfalls grew bigger and we experienced something even most locals don't get to see.

Sherree Worrell, Traveller, USA

WILSONS PROMONTORY, VICTORIA

Only 2½ hours drive from Melbourne is the pristine wilderness of **Wilsons Promontory National Park** (p237). Book a couple of nights at one of the historic lighthouse cottages and enjoy the walk in with friends, followed by a glass of red while you watch the sun set. Or take a lighthouse tour.

Marg Haycroft, Traveller, Australia

15

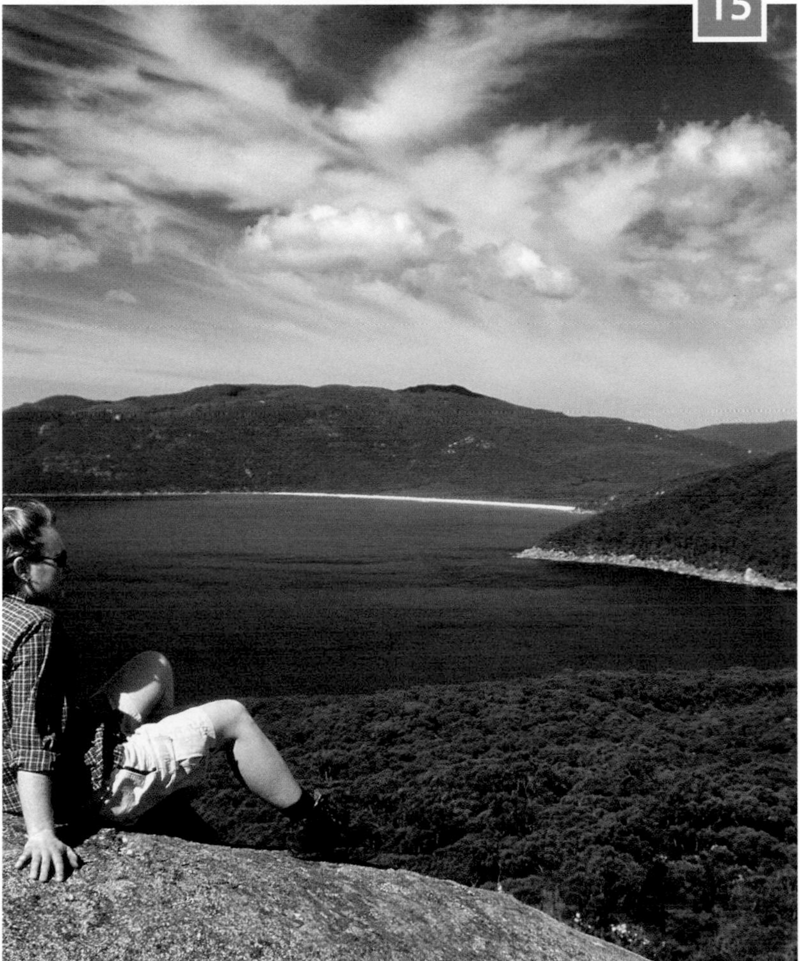

14 CHRIS MELLOR; 15 ANDREW BAIN

14 Uluru (Ayers Rock; p262); 15 Kersop Peak and Waterloo Bay, Wilsons Promontory (p237)

OUTBACK ROADS

Driving through the **outback** (p250) as the sun set, looking out across expanses of seemingly uninhabited land, was breathtaking. A curtain of burning horizon signified an end to the day's driving, and provided a slideshow of nature for which we always had the best seats.

Neil Foster, Traveller, UK

16

17

BLUE MOUNTAINS ESCAPE

Stock up on trail mix and head to the **Blue Mountains** (p106), a wilderness escape just a stone's throw from Sydney. If the hazy blue vistas of this ancient range lull you too deeply, smarten up with an adrenalin-stirring rock climb.

'Peskyfeminist', Traveller

TRAVELLING WITH CHILDREN

Travelling with children (see p342) opened a world of experiences for me. I travelled with a one year old and a three year old. We hired a campervan and saw a lot of the 'sunburnt country'. We spent four months there and the children were able to experience the beaches, deserts, and cities...brilliant!

Caite Khan, Traveller, UK

18

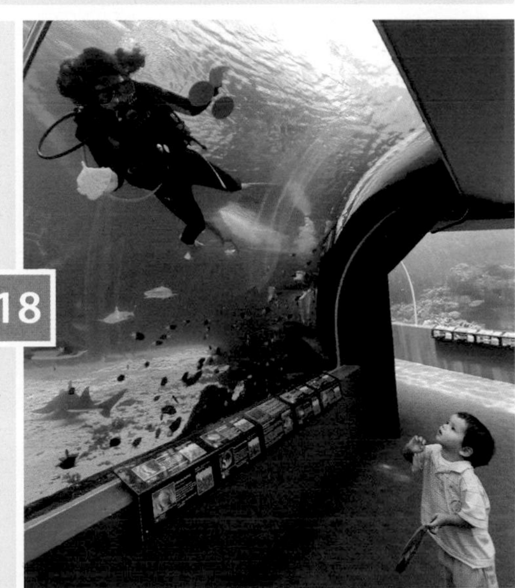

16 RICHARD I'ANSON; 17 RACHEL LEWIS; 18 PAUL DYMOND

16 Kakadu National Park (p257); 17 Three Sisters (p98), Blue Mountains; 18 A Queensland aquarium

↘ BRIDGE CLIMB, SYDNEY

Afraid of heights? Not a problem! The guides on this particular activity (p81) are trained to put you instantly at ease and get you through the three-and-a-half-hour trek to the top of what is surely one of the most iconic landmarks in the world.

Debbie Black, Traveller, UK

19

20

KAKADU ROCK ART

Entering the Nourlangie and Nanguluwur art sites in **Kakadu National Park** (p257), Northern Territory, just before sunset was a magic experience. Ending up at the Gunwarddehwarde lookout just as the sun was setting, we enjoyed stunning views of the plains below and the most colourful sunset ever.

Jan Erling Stordal, Traveller, Sweden

19 HOLGER LEUE; 20 HOLGER LEUE

19 Climbers on Sydney Harbour Bridge (p69); 20 Indigenous rock paintings at Nourlangie, Kakadu National Park (p257)

21

GRAMPIANS (GARIWERD) NATIONAL PARK

We saw amazing ancient rock formations, stunning panoramic views and loved the wildlife: emus, cockatoos and kookaburras, and a large group of kangaroos grazing in the dusk with babies peering out of pouches – magic! We learnt so much at the Indigenous cultural centre in **Hall's Gap** (p233).

Kim Conway, Traveller, New Zealand

MARGARET RIVER

22

The southwest coast of Australia is amazing! Remote, but not too much. I particularly enjoyed Yallingup, which is a beautiful beachside village in the **Margaret River** region (p292). This area is famous for its surfing and has the most beautiful beaches and wineries.

Nikki Sinclair, Traveller, UK

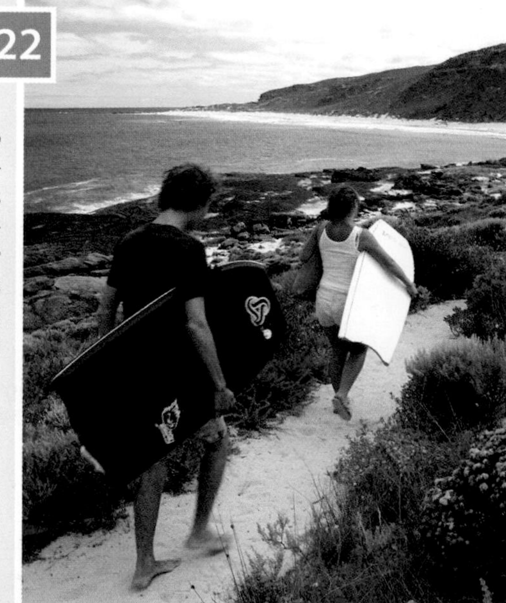

GREAT OCEAN ROAD

23

This is really a great trip with some spectacular views along the way. Let the surfers blow your mind catching massive waves on **Bells Beach** (p228), enjoy the pretty villages along the way, or take a helicopter ride over the **Twelve Apostles** (p232) to get the best photo.

Fiona O'Sullivan, Traveller, Ireland

24

CAMPING KANGAROO ISLAND

While on **Kangaroo Island** (p269) we were sitting round the campfire, enjoying the beauty of the place and reflecting on the day. Then our tour guide got out a didgeridoo and started playing before each of us tried it out too. A great ending to a wonderful day.

Julia Ramforth, Traveller, Germany

21 PAUL SINCLAIR; 22 ORIEN HARVEY; 23 RODNEY HYETT; 24 ROSS BARNETT

21 Grampians (Gariwerd) National Park (p232); 22 Contos Beach, Margaret River (p292); 23 Twelve Apostles (p232), Great Ocean Road; 24 Remarkable Rocks, Kangaroo Island (p269)

CULTURAL BRISBANE

Check out the best of Brisbane's indoor attractions. The **Queensland Museum** South Bank and the newly constructed **Gallery of Modern Art** (p154) are just two that are free to enjoy all year round (except for some exhibitions of course).

Kelly Tohill, Traveller, Australia

25

OLIVER STREWE

Miro sculpture, Gallery of Modern Art (p154), Brisbane

➘ AUSTRALIA'S TOP ITINERARIES

CITY, SURF & BUSH

FIVE DAYS SYDNEY ROUND TRIP

With only a week and your jet lag to consider, you may prefer to stick around Sydney, explore the harbour, relax on a beach and get a taste of the Australian bush in the nearby Blue Mountains.

❶ SYDNEY CBD

Arriving in **Sydney** (p50) after the almost-inevitable long-haul flight, you will need time to adjust, orientate to life down under and get acquainted with Australia's first city. Take a **city tour** (p80) and wander across the **Sydney Harbour Bridge** (p69). If you have planned ahead spend a few hours on a **bridge climb** (p81) before roaming the historic **Rocks** (p69) and **Circular Quay** (p70). Take dinner in a harbour-side restaurant and perhaps a show in the renowned **Sydney Opera House** (p68).

❷ SYDNEY HARBOUR

Get your sea legs on a **harbour cruise** (p80) to discover the delightful coves, colonial history and inevitable celebrity gossip that accompanies prime harbour-front real estate. Spend part of the day at **Manly** (p76) taking a leisurely swim or even a lesson in surfboard technique. Explore the parks and harbour beaches of the **eastern suburbs** (p75) and wander out to the **Gap** (p75) for excellent cliff-top views at the entrance to Sydney Harbour.

MARK PARKES

Seawater pool at Narrabeen beach (p77), Sydney

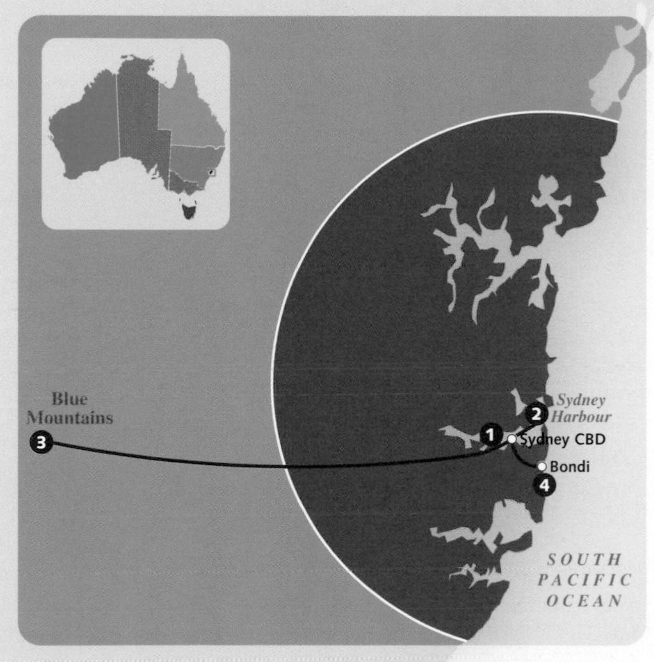

❸ BLUE MOUNTAINS

You could hop on a tour, catch a train, or hire a car for maximum flexibility to explore the **Blue Mountains** (p106) in Sydney's backyard. Stop in **Glenbrook** (p107), at the base of the mountains, inspect Aboriginal hand stencils and get the camera out for views of Jamison Valley and Wentworth Falls. Continue to the Blue Mountains hub of **Katoomba** (p108), where you can indulge in gourmet delights and charming and romantic accommodation. Suck in the mountain air and enjoy the tremendous views at **Echo Point** (109), and if you're feeling energetic, jump into some mountain activities, such as canyoning and rock climbing (p109).

❹ BONDI

Back in Sydney cruise out to world-famous **Bondi Beach** (p75) for a relaxing day of sun and surf. If you are feeling active you could take a lesson in surfboard riding or embark on one of the best short walks in New South Wales: the **Bondi to Coogee Coastal Walk** (p75) features stunning coastal views and plenty of opportunities to stop for a cooling swim or refreshing drink.

EAST COAST CRUISER

TEN DAYS MELBOURNE TO CAIRNS

This classic coastal run takes in thousands of kilometres of coastline. It could take a lifetime or, with just 10 days and a handful of airline tickets, you could taste a few of the east coast's highlights.

❶ MELBOURNE

Start this itinerary in the southern capital of **Melbourne** (p204), a city famous for its nightlife, multicultural mix and diverse dining experiences. Rather than wander far and wide, we suggest you delve into the inner city's bohemian and mainstream art scenes, linger in the cafe-colonised laneways, go shopping and take in a show.

❷ SYDNEY

Your next stop is the bright and breezy harbour city of **Sydney** (p50). You really need a couple of days to do this city justice. Must-dos include a **Sydney Harbour cruise** (p80) to get your bearings and a sense of how geography influences this city's personality. No visit to Sydney would be complete without a plunge in the famous waves of **Bondi Beach** (p75). On your final night book a restaurant with views of the spotlit Harbour Bridge and Opera House.

❸ BRISBANE

Move north to **Brisbane** (p150), Queensland's fast-paced capital, where you can board a river cruise to go cuddle a koala or catch a ferry to **Moreton Island** (p164) and hand-feed a wild dolphin.

LEONARD ZELL

Gorgonian fans at the base of Mantis Reef, Great Barrier Reef (p182)

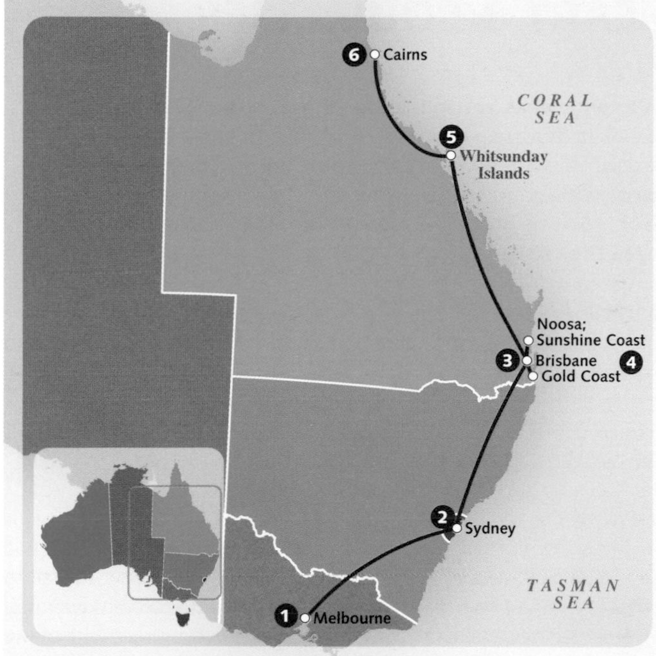

❹ THE GOLD & SUNSHINE COASTS

From Brisbane there are options to head to the **Gold Coast** (p164) with its glamorous beachside developments, great surf and over-the-top **theme parks** (p165). Alternatively, head to the **Sunshine Coast** (p167) via the famous **Australia Zoo** (p168), and then on to the stylish beach resort town of **Noosa** (p168).

❺ WHITSUNDAY ISLANDS

To get to the magnificent **Whitsunday Islands** (p177) you can fly to the party town of **Airlie Beach** (p174) or directly to **Hamilton Island** (p178). Here you can opt for tropical cruising under a billowing sail, fabulous coral reef diving or snorkelling, or just lazing by the resort's pool.

❻ CAIRNS

Perhaps as an alternative to the Whitsundays, or if you still have the time and energy to go further north, move on to Far North Queensland's tourism mecca. **Cairns** (p179) has something for everyone. There are fabulous excursions to rainforest hinterland and tropical beaches but best of all Cairns is the base for exploring the **Great Barrier Reef** (p182). Once out on the reef, join a dive, strap on a snorkel or just hop on a glass-bottom boat.

HEART & SOUL

TWO WEEKS BRISBANE TO SYDNEY

With two weeks you will need to hop, skip and jump using domestic flights to cover the vast distances that take you through Australia's heart and soul. This journey runs from the coastal cities and surf beaches up to the magnificent tropical north, then through the astonishing Red Centre before returning to the coast.

❶ BRISBANE

Start this journey in the Queensland capital of **Brisbane** (p150). Within reach of this booming city is the relaxing seaside town of **Noosa** (p168), a perfect spot to work on a tan and catch a wave. Another option is to head down to the **Gold Coast** (p164), where there are excellent beaches, dazzling nightlife and kid-friendly **theme parks** (p165).

❷ CAIRNS

Moving north, your next stop is tropical **Cairns** (p179), the base for all the amazing sights and activities of Far North Queensland. Take time to visit the rainforest town of **Kuranda** (p189) and explore the nearby tropical beaches. Make the most of your submarine excursions of the **Great Barrier Reef** (p182) by donning a snorkel or scuba gear.

❸ DARWIN & KAKADU

Keeping to the tropics, fly to **Darwin** (p250), where you can learn the art of the didgeridoo, peruse the markets and even swim with a crocodile. Darwin is also the base for Top End excursions featuring

DAVID WALL

Uluru (Ayers Rock; p263)

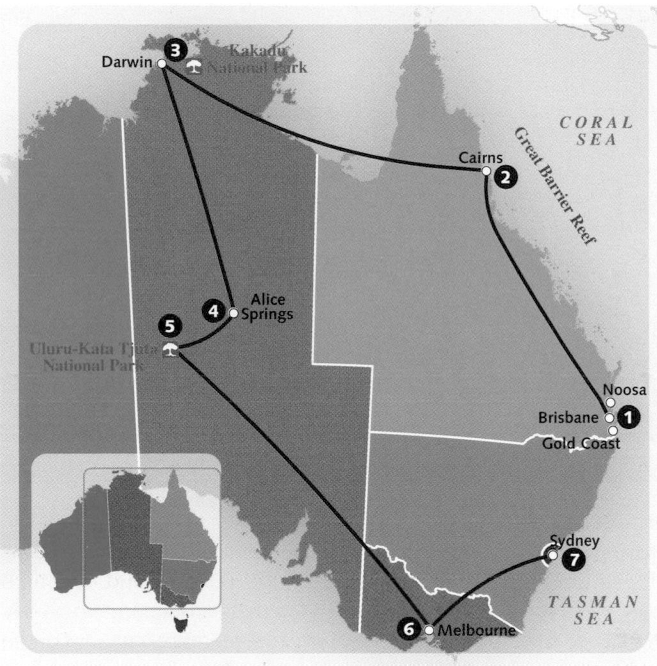

Indigenous culture and wildlife. The main destination is the amazing **Kakadu National Park** (p257), but other options include **Litchfield National Park** and **Katherine Gorge** (both p258).

❹ ALICE SPRINGS

Heading south, the next leg of the journey takes you to the heart of the continent. **Alice Springs** (p259) is the only large town in a vast swathe of the country. Its isolation is palpable but the grand scenery and oases of the **MacDonnell Ranges** (p258) surprise many visitors. Alice is also the best place to see and buy the mesmerising dot paintings from the Central Desert school of art (p261).

❺ ULURU-KATA TJUTA NATIONAL PARK

From Alice we move to the spiritual heart of the country: **Uluru-Kata Tjuta National Park** (p262). Be moved by the commanding bulk of **Uluru (Ayers Rock)** (p263) and be introduced to the country by the traditional owners on an Anangu tour. Don't miss the radiance of Uluru at sunset. Nearby **Kata-Tjuta** (p264) is just as impressive and also holds a special spiritual place in the traditions of the local Indigenous people. Take the time to walk among the imposing domes.

GREG ELMS

Federation Square (p205), Melbourne

❻ MELBOURNE

Leaving the desert country, we continue south to the Victorian capital of **Melbourne** (p204). Melbourne is on one side a sophisticate, with leafy parks and gardens, elaborate Victorian architecture and a distinguished suite of theatres, museums and galleries. But there is also a more street-wise side to the city's personality, with world-famous street art, a vibrant independent music scene and a laneway coffee culture all its own.

❼ SYDNEY

The last leg of the journey through the heart and soul of this vast country is the show-stopping city of **Sydney** (p50). You may want to rest your travel-weary legs but the city lights beckon; there are options galore in the harbour city. One of the most relaxing activities is a leisurely **harbour cruise** (p80) to get a feel for the landscape. History buffs will enjoy a stroll through the **Rocks** (p69), while those looking for a little surf and sand action will head straight to the beaches. As well as the famous **Bondi Beach** (p75), check out the cafes and waves at **Manly** (p76), and from there the other **northern beaches** (p77).

↘ PLANNING YOUR TRIP

AUSTRALIA'S BEST...

BEACHES

- **Bondi** (p75) An iconic stretch of sand peopled by a melting pot of sun worshippers
- **Whitehaven** (p178) Bedazzling swathes of white sand caressed by azure tropical waters
- **Wineglass Bay** (p327) Crystal-clear waves lap the sensuous curve of Tasmania's most photogenic beach
- **Byron Bay** (p122) This famous town is a magnet for travellers
- **Bells** (p228) The rugged Victorian surf coast beats to the rhythm of the Southern Ocean

WILDLIFE ENCOUNTERS

- **Great Barrier Reef** (p182) The largest coral reef in the world is home to thousands of species
- **Ningaloo Marine Park** (p300) Seasonal show of massive whale sharks and manta rays
- **Monkey Mia** (p296) The locals and the dolphins have been friends for decades
- **Kakadu National Park** (p257) Amazing birds as well as prehistoric crocodiles
- **Phillip Island** (p225) The nightly parade of little penguins has a giant reputation

PLACES TO LEARN TO SURF

- **Sydney** (p78) There are no shortage of options; you can even learn at Bondi
- **Yamba and Angourie** (p122) Angourie Point is epic but gentle Yamba has beaches of room for beginners

LEFT: CHRISTOPHER GROENHOUT; RIGHT: CHRIS MELLOR

Left: Wineglass Bay (p327), Tasmania; Right: Fairy penguins, Phillip Island (p225)

- **Byron Bay** (p125) The breaks are accommodating and you can even mix it with a little yoga
- **Surfers Paradise** (p166) It's all in the name; there are plenty of options and expert instructors
- **Noosa** (p171) Relaxed and stylish – that's Noosa – but now let's work on your technique

RELAXING RETREATS

- **Margaret River** (p292) A fertile gourmet region of forest drives, vines and wines
- **Blue Mountains** (p106) So close to the city yet a world away from its stress, traffic and air
- **Noosa** (p168) The climate, the beaches and the cafe lifestyle
- **Freycinet Peninsula** (p327) Cosy accommodation, elegant coastline and abundant wildlife
- **Barossa Valley** (p270) Australia's premier wine-producing region boasts romantic accommodation and dining options

CULTURAL JOURNEYS

- **Uluru-Kata Tjuta National Park** (p262) Share the spiritual significance of country with an Anangu guide
- **Kakadu National Park** (p257) Join a bush tucker tour to get a taste of local culture
- **Multicultural Melbourne** (p204) Mingle in one of the world's most harmonious multicultural cities
- **Shark Bay** (p294) See this exceptional region with the help of an Indigenous guide
- **Sydney** (p62) What makes contemporary Australia tick? Sydney is as good a place as any to start your investigation

SCENIC TRIPS

- **Great Ocean Road** (p227) A classic road trip with curves and fabulous coastal views
- **Grand Pacific Drive** (p130) Drive over the water on the spectacular Sea Cliff Bridge
- **Kuranda** (p189) Take the scenic way above Cairns and into the rainforest
- **Southern Forests** (p293) Drive through amazing tall forests
- **Blue Mountains** (p106) Great views and fresh mountain air

WALKS IN THE BUSH

- **Blue Mountains** (p106) So close to the big smoke yet with an abundance of scenic trails
- **Freycinet Peninsula** (p326) Energetic walks are rewarded with stupendous coastal views
- **Overland Track** (p329) Australia's iconic bushwalk in Tasmania's high country
- **Wilsons Promontory** (p237) Squeaky sand, wandering wombats and peaceful forests
- **Grampians National Park** (p232) Spectacular wildflowers, rock formations and Indigenous rock art

THINGS YOU NEED TO KNOW

AT A GLANCE

- **ATMs** Omnipresent in large cities and most towns
- **Credit cards** Visa and MasterCard are widely accepted
- **Currency** The Aussie dollar
- **Electricity** Three pin, 240 V AC, 50Hz
- **Language** English
- **Tipping** Not required, but expectation is creeping in in restaurants and taxis (about 10%)
- **Visas** Required (see p379)

ACCOMMODATION

- **B&Bs** (p364) These homey choices can be great for getting local insights and can be either hosted or nonhosted; in the latter you have more privacy. Regional tourist offices have lists of B&Bs.
- **Camping** Camping grounds abound in Australia. They vary from basic national park clearings to luxury resorts.
- **Hostels** Hostels or backpackers are highly social, low-cost affairs, usually packed with under-30 patrons.
- **Hotels** (p364) Three- to five-star hotels with high-standard amenities can easily be found in the major cities and towns as well as in foremost tourist locations.
- **Motels** (p364) Cookie-cutter sameness is tempered by value for money, convenience, dependable mattresses, security and cleanliness.
- **Pubs** (p364) Also known as hotels, but not to be confused with three-, four- and five-star hotels, these vary from friendly country hubs to inner city dives. Always inspect the room before you commit.
- **Resorts** Miniworlds boasting swimming pools and restaurants, providing all your holiday needs, usually for a range of budgets.

ADVANCE PLANNING

- **Three months before** Look into visa requirements and shop around for the best deal on flights
- **One month before** Book accommodation and regional flights, trains etc
- **One week before** Book a surfing lesson, reef dive or tour
- **One day before** Reserve a table at a Sydney harbour-side restaurant or equivalent

COSTS

- **$100 per day** A well-planned budget traveller staying in hostels could still have some fun and get around on public transport
- **$150–200 per day** More midrange accommodation, more activities and tours, and better restaurants
- **More than $200 per day** Hire cars and petrol become available, as do a few luxuries

EMERGENCY NUMBERS

- **Ambulance, fire & police** ☎ 000

GETTING AROUND

- **Walk** the bush trails for fresh air and pristine views, and city streets and laneways for cafes and shopping
- **Tram** the streets of Melbourne
- **Bus** on midrange, intrastate coastal travel
- **Train** across the continent on legendary trains such as the east–west *Indian Pacific* and the north–south *Ghan*
- **Boat** to tropical islands, coral-reef diving platforms and Tasmania
- **Fly** to the far-flung state capitals and regional centres with one of several domestic carriers

TRAVEL SEASONS

- **Tropical north** Winter (June to August) is the peak period and ideal travelling climate for exploring the tropics
- **Red Centre** Alice Springs and Uluru are also at their best in the winter months but don't underestimate the cold desert nights
- **Temperate south** Summer (December to February) is the peak when the locals are on holiday and the beaches are packed. The shoulder seasons of spring and autumn are very amenable to travel, while the ski season is from July to September.

RICHARD I'ANSON

Catseye Bay, Hamilton Island (p178)

WHAT TO BRING

- **Sunscreen** And don't forget sunglasses and a hat to deflect the harsh UV rays
- **Insect repellent** To fend off the merciless flies, sandflies and mosquitoes
- **Travel insurance** Make sure it covers any planned high-risk activities such as scuba diving
- **Visa** (p379) Confirm the latest visa situation
- **Electricity adapter** For all your digital gadgets

WHEN TO GO

- **Beat the crowds** The peak summer school-holiday season, when families are on the move and accommodation and transport can be booked out, starts at Christmas and continues throughout January
- **Catch the festivities** Football codes (p358) have their finals in September, October and February, and many other festivals cram the summer calendar (see p46)

LEFT: SIMON FOALE; RIGHT: MARK DAFFEY

Left: Local band the Cat Empire perform at a festival (see p46); Right: Melbourne Cricket Ground (p212)

GET INSPIRED

BOOKS

- **The Songlines** (Bruce Chatwin, 1986) Combines a fictional and nonfictional account of the author's trip to Australia; filled with his insights into outback and Indigenous culture.
- **Breath** (Tim Winton, 2008) A surfie recounts his coming of age in this novel, which is filled with Winton's typically evocative imagery.
- **The Rip** (Robert Drewe, 2008) A collection of powerful short stories based on and around the Australian coast. Like the sea, it's easy to dip in and out of, making for great beach reading.
- **Vertigo** (Amanda Lohrey, 2008) A couple decide on a sea change and move to the country. Their expectations of a quiet life are stretched when they encounter fire, drought and their own emotional quandaries.

FILMS

- **Two Hands** (1999, director Gregor Jordan) Heath Ledger at his vulnerable best, with Rose Byrne: Ledger's character finds himself spiralling into a world far more foreboding than his innocence could possibly imagine.
- **Ten Canoes** (2006, director Rolf de Heer) On a hunt for magpie geese, a young man is told the story of his ancestors. Spoken in the Ganalbingu language of Arnhem Land.
- **Little Fish** (2005, director Rowan Woods) Tracy (Cate Blanchett) is a former addict trying to stay straight in the midst of the Cabramatta (Sydney) drug scene.
- **Australia** (2008, director Baz Luhrmann) A grandiose period romance set in remote northern Australian cattle country.

MUSIC

- **Cold Chisel** *Circus Animals* (1982); key track 'You Got Nothing I Want'
- **GANGgajang** *GANGgajang* (1985); key track 'Sounds of Then (This is Australia)'
- **The Go Betweens** *16 Lovers Lane* (1988); key track 'Streets of Your Town'
- **Hunters & Collectors** *Human Frailty* (1986); key track 'Say Goodbye'
- **Paul Kelly** *Gossip* (1986); key track 'Before Too Long'
- **Yothu Yindi** *Tribal Voice* (1991); key track 'Treaty'
- **The Whitlams** *Undeniably* (1994); key track 'I Make Hamburgers'

WEBSITES

- **Australian Newspapers Online** (www.nla.gov.au/npapers) Listing of Australian newspaper websites
- **Australian Tourist Commission** (www.australia.com) Official site with nationwide info for visitors
- **Department of the Environment & Heritage** (www.environment.gov.au/parks/index.html) Information on Australia's national parks and reserves

CALENDAR

JAN FEB MAR APR

GREG ELMS

Sydney Gay & Lesbian Mardi Gras (see below)

JANUARY

BIG DAY OUT

This huge open-air concert tours Sydney, Melbourne, Adelaide, Perth and the Gold Coast, attracting big-name international acts and dozens of local bands and DJs; see www.bigdayout.com.

TOUR DOWN UNDER

The world's best cyclists compete in six races through South Australian towns, with the grand finale in Adelaide; see www.tourdownunder.com.au.

AUSTRALIA DAY 26 JAN

This national holiday commemorates the arrival of the First Fleet in 1788.

TROPFEST

The world's largest short-film festival is held in Sydney but is broadcast at events throughout the country; see www.tropfest.com.au.

ST JEROME'S LANEWAY FESTIVAL

An iconic indie festival crammed into laneways in Melbourne, Sydney, Brisbane, Perth and Adelaide, featuring a local and international music line-up; see www.lanewayfestival.com.au.

SYDNEY FESTIVAL

This calendar highlight (see www.sydneyfestival.org.au) floods the city streets and parks with art and includes free outdoor concerts in the Domain.

FEBRUARY–MARCH

SYDNEY GAY & LESBIAN MARDI GRAS

The highlight of this world-famous festival is the flamboyant Oxford Street parade; see www.mardigras.org.au.

ADELAIDE FRINGE

This annual independent arts festival (see www.adelaidefringe.com.au) in February and March is second only to the Edinburgh Fringe.

PERTH INTERNATIONAL ARTS FESTIVAL

Several weeks of multi-arts entertainment from early February to early March, including theatre, dance, music, film and visual arts; see www.perthfestival.com.au.

AUSTRALIAN WOODEN BOAT FESTIVAL

Biennial event (odd-numbered years only) that coincides with the Royal Hobart Regatta. The festival showcases Tasmania's boat-building heritage and maritime traditions; see www.australianwoodenboatfestival.com.au.

QUICKSILVER PRO & ROXY PRO SURFING COMPETITIONS

From late February to mid-March some of the world's best surfers compete for big waves and big prize money on the Gold Coast; see www.quiksilverpro.com.au.

MARCH–APRIL

TEN DAYS ON THE ISLAND

A major biennial Tasmanian cultural festival held in odd-numbered years in venues around the state; see www.tendaysontheisland.org.

WOMADELAIDE

An annual festival (www.womadelaide.com.au) of world music, arts and dance, held over three days in Adelaide.

APRIL

ANZAC DAY 25 APR

A national holiday commemorating the Australian and New Zealand Army Corps (Anzacs), who served in previous wars, and soldiers who are currently serving in the armed forces.

MELBOURNE INTERNATIONAL COMEDY FESTIVAL

Locals are joined by a wealth of international acts performing all over the city; see www.comedyfestival.com.au.

MAY

SORRY DAY 26 MAY

Each year concerned Australians acknowledge the continuing pain and suffering of Indigenous Australians affected by Australia's one-time child-removal practices and policies. Events are held in most cities countrywide; see www.nsdc.org.au.

JUNE

ANTARCTIC MIDWINTER FESTIVAL

A 10-day festival in Hobart celebrating the winter solstice and Tasmania's

CALENDAR

connection with the Antarctic; see www.antarctic-tasmania.info.

JULY

NAIDOC WEEK

Communities across Australia celebrate the National Aboriginal and Islander Day of Celebration (inaugurated in 1957), from local street festivals to the annual Naidoc Ball (held in a different location each year; see www.naidoc.org.au).

BEER CAN REGATTA

An utterly insane and typically Territorian festival that features races in boats made out of beer cans. It takes place at Mindil Beach, Darwin; see www.beercanregatta.org.au.

AUGUST

CITY TO SURF RUN

This 14km fun run in Sydney takes place on the second Sunday in August and attracts 40,000 nutcases who run from Hyde Park to Bondi Beach; see http://city2surf.sunherald.com.au.

DARWIN FESTIVAL

A two-week, mainly outdoor arts and culture festival (www.darwinfestival.org.au) that reflects Darwin's large Indigenous and Asian populations.

SEPTEMBER

AUSTRALIAN FOOTBALL LEAGUE (AFL) GRAND FINAL

The two best teams left standing in the Australian Rules football competition (www.afl.com.au) meet at the

RICHARD I'ANSON

Flemington Racecourse (p214), Melbourne

Melbourne Cricket Ground (MCG; p212) to decide who's best.

RUGBY LEAGUE GRAND FINAL

The two best teams left standing in the National Rugby League (NRL; www.nrl.com) meet in Sydney to decide who's best.

BRISBANE RIVER FESTIVAL

Brisbane's major festival of the arts is held over 10 days. Don't miss the spectacular Riverfire sky show on the Brisbane River; see www.riverfestival.com.au.

OCTOBER

INDYCAR

The streets of Surfers Paradise are transformed into a motor racing circuit every October, attracting up to 250,000 spectators; www.indy.com.au.

PERTH ROYAL SHOW

It's the west's biggest agriculture, food and wine show – with rides and show bags for the kids; see www.perthroyalshow.com.au.

NOVEMBER

SCULPTURE BY THE SEA

In mid-November the Bondi to Coogee Coastal Walk (p75) is transformed into an outdoor sculpture gallery; see www.sculpturebythesea.com.

SPRING RACING CARNIVAL

In October to November there are two feature races: the **Caulfield Cup** and the **Melbourne Cup** (at Flemington Racecourse). See www.springracingcarnival.com.au.

DECEMBER

SYDNEY TO HOBART YACHT RACE

Sydney Harbour is a fantastic sight on Boxing Day as hundreds of boats farewell competitors in the gruelling Sydney to Hobart Yacht Race. Yachts start arriving in Hobart around 28 to 29 December, just in time for New Year's Eve (yachties sure can party…). See http://rolexsydneyhobart.com.

BOXING DAY TEST 26 DEC

Held at the MCG (see p212), the first day of this annual international test match is Boxing Day, when the G is packed.

TASTE FESTIVAL

This week-long event, held on either side of New Year's Eve, is a celebration of Tasmania's gastronomic prowess, and features theatre, kids' activities, concerts, buskers and New Year's Eve shenanigans. See www.tastefestival.com.au.

NEW YEAR'S EVE 31 DEC

Sydney's Rocks, Kings Cross and Bondi Beach heave with alcohol-fuelled celebrations; the Harbour Bridge goes off with a bang; and cities and towns across Australia party.

SYDNEY

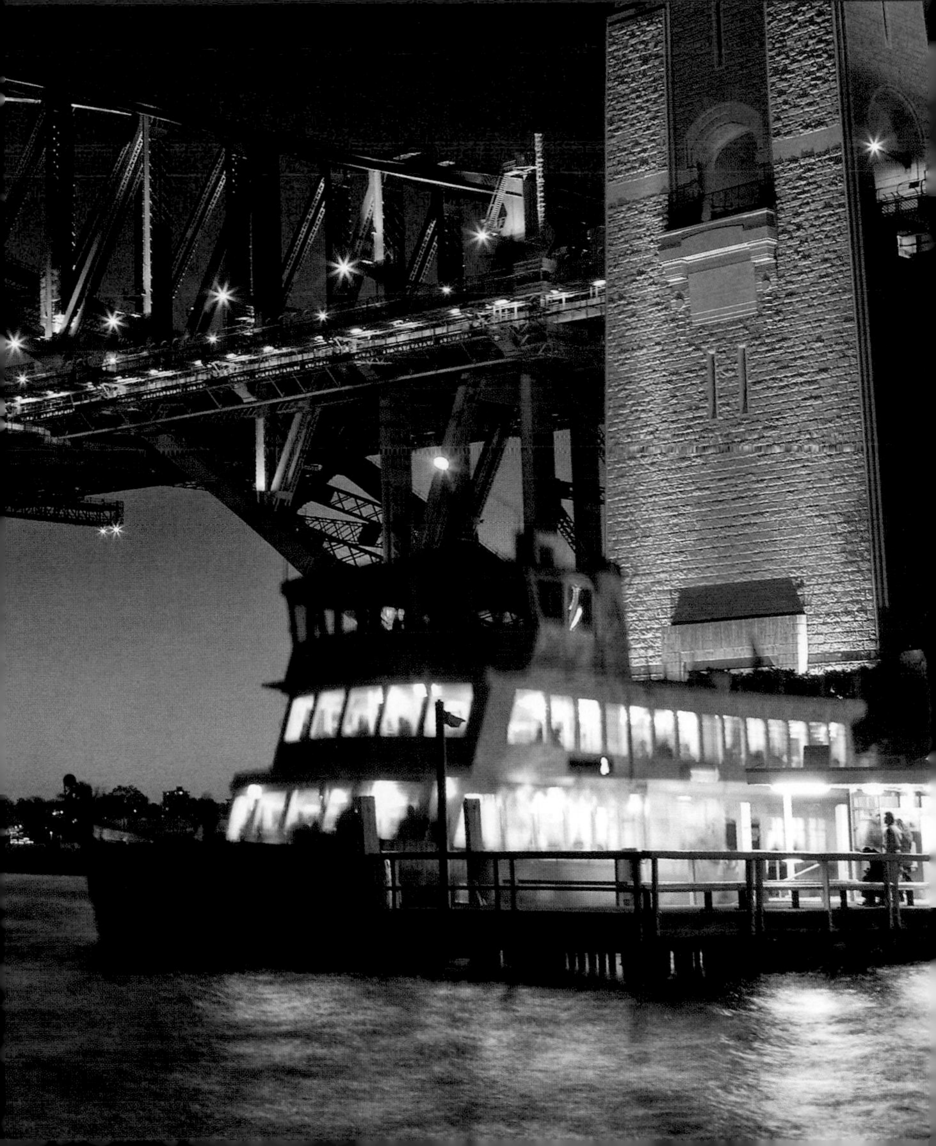

GREATER SYDNEY

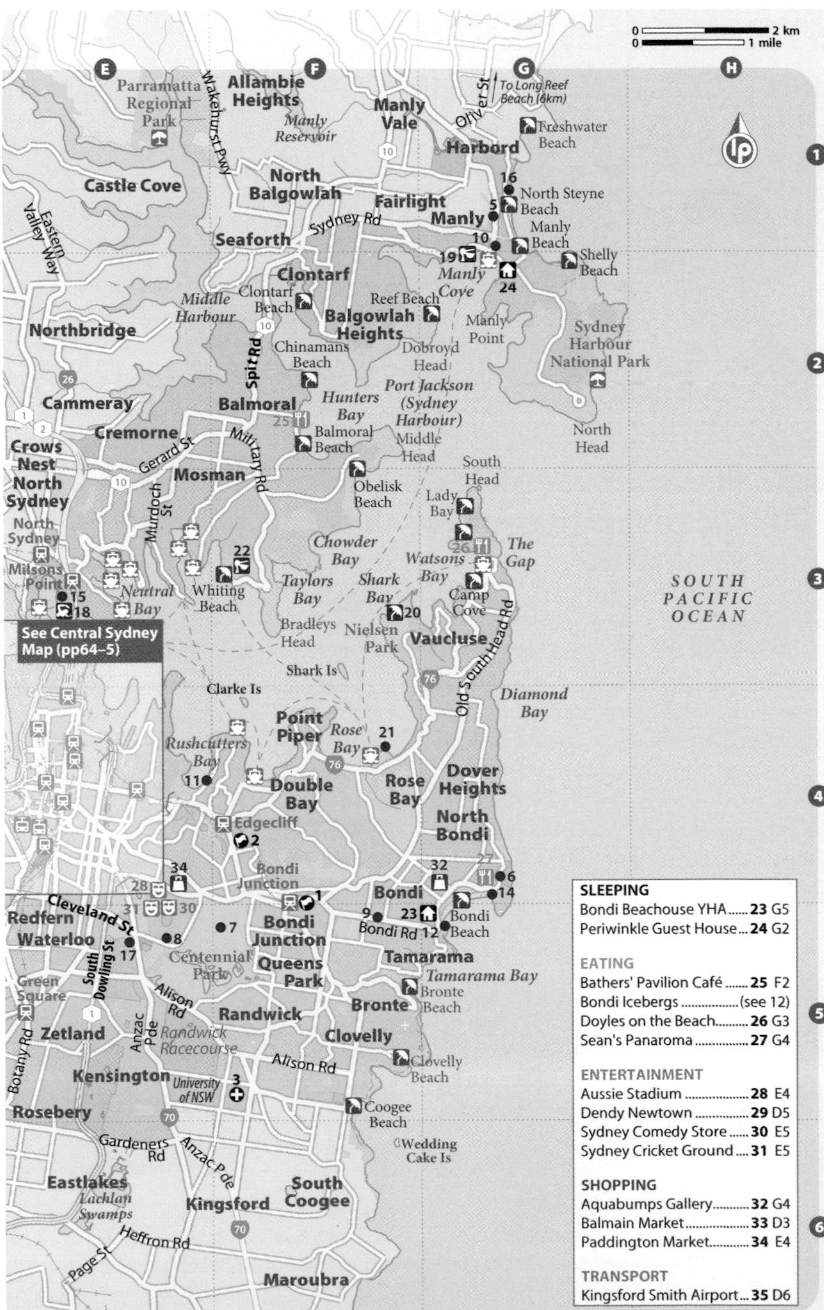
SLEEPING
Bondi Beachouse YHA...... 23 G5
Periwinkle Guest House... 24 G2

EATING
Bathers' Pavilion Café....... 25 F2
Bondi Icebergs................(see 12)
Doyles on the Beach.......... 26 G3
Sean's Panaroma................ 27 G4

ENTERTAINMENT
Aussie Stadium.................... 28 E4
Dendy Newtown................... 29 D5
Sydney Comedy Store...... 30 E5
Sydney Cricket Ground.... 31 E5

SHOPPING
Aquabumps Gallery........... 32 G4
Balmain Market.................. 33 D3
Paddington Market............ 34 E4

TRANSPORT
Kingsford Smith Airport... 35 D6

See Central Sydney Map (pp64–5)
SOUTH PACIFIC OCEAN
To Long Reef Beach (6km)

SYDNEY HIGHLIGHTS

1 SYDNEY HARBOUR

BY TONY ZRILIC, HOSPITALITY MANAGER, CAPTAIN COOK CRUISES

Sydney Harbour is the shimmering heart of our great city. Whether you are sitting in a waterfront restaurant, walking through one of many shore-side parks, taking a ferry to Manly or being spoilt aboard a leisurely harbour cruise, there just is no better way to experience the real beauty of our city.

↘ TONY ZRILIC'S DON'T MISS LIST

❶ FERRY TO MANLY

The Manly Ferry departs Circular Quay every half hour or so. For an unforgettable experience, take the ferry when big seas are rolling in through the entrance to Sydney Harbour, known as the Heads. When you get to **Manly** (p76), walk the Corso from the harbour beach to the ocean beach. Buy a gelato or have a cold beer watching the mass of sun lovers enjoying this unique part of Sydney.

❷ FORESHORE WALK FROM BRADLEY'S HEAD

The harbour is lined with fabulous foreshore walks. Take the ferry from Circular Quay to **Taronga Zoo** (p76), and then walk around the headland to Chowder Bay. Stop for breakfast or lunch at a foreshore brasserie.

❸ WATSON'S BAY PUB & GAP

Catch a hop-on hop-off cruise to **Watsons Bay** (p75) and have fish and chips at world famous **Doyles on the**

Clockwise from top: Shark Beach at Nielsen Park (p67); Passenger ferry on Sydney Harbour; Sydney Opera House from a ferry (p68); The Gap (p75); Beach at Manly (p76)

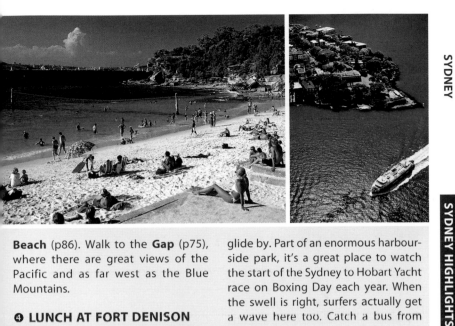

Beach (p86). Walk to the **Gap** (p75), where there are great views of the Pacific and as far west as the Blue Mountains.

❹ LUNCH AT FORT DENISON

One of my favourites is to take the ferry from Circular Quay to the heritage-listed island in the middle of the harbour, **Fort Denison** (p67). There's a great restaurant serving modern Australian cuisine – you can enjoy a meal while sitting in the midst of Sydney's amazing icons: the Opera House and the Harbour Bridge.

❺ SWIM AT NIELSEN PARK

Nielsen Park (p67) is one of the many netted harbour beaches where you can actually swim and snorkel as yachts glide by. Part of an enormous harbour-side park, it's a great place to watch the start of the Sydney to Hobart Yacht race on Boxing Day each year. When the swell is right, surfers actually get a wave here too. Catch a bus from Circular Quay.

➘ THINGS YOU NEED TO KNOW

Best photo opportunity On perfectly still early mornings or nights, catch magical reflections of the emblematic cityscape in the placid waters **Only two hours?** Board a lunch cruise (p80) and refuel the batteries while getting a running commentary of harbour-side sights **See our author's review on p67**

SYDNEY HIGHLIGHTS

2 SYDNEY'S NORTHERN BEACHES

BY MATT GRAINGER, HEAD COACH & OWNER, MANLY, LONG REEF & PALM BEACH SURF SCHOOLS

You can't beat being in the water on a board and seeing dolphins swimming around you. Surfing is pure magic. It's fun. It's healthy. Anyone can learn. We've taught students from five to 70 years old and students who have disabilities. They all love it.

MATT GRAINGER'S DON'T MISS LIST

❶ MANLY

Manly (p76) is the place to learn to surf. Gentle waves can almost always be found for frothing beginners, and during winter surfers are often treated to a pod of dolphins who roam the waves from the Bower to Queenscliff. Drinking holes also abound in 'Mantown': there are beers to be had on the beachfront, and on the harbour one of the best pubs is the **Manly Wharf Hotel** (☎ 02-9977 1266; www.manlywharfhotel.com.au; Manly Wharf, East Esplanade; 🕒 11.30am-midnight Mon-Fri, 11am-midnight Sat, 11am-10pm Sun).

❷ LONG REEF BEACH

Longy pumps, both in and out of the water. After a workout in the water, head down for Sydney's best pies at the legendary **Upper Crust Pie Shop** (1003 Pittwater Rd) in Collaroy for a range of hearty gourmet pastries. When the swell is flat, golf is a good option at Longy's great links course, **Long Reef Golf Club** (☎ 02-9971 8113; www.longreefgolfclub.com.au; Anzac Ave, Collaroy).

Clockwise from top: Freshwater Beach (p77); Whale Beach (p77); Palm Beach (p77); Long Reef Beach; Manly Beach (p76)

❸ FRESHWATER BEACH

If you walk through the 'wormhole' at low tide from Queenscliff you'll come out at Freshie (off Map pp52–3), famed for the surfing exhibition by Duke Kahanamoku, who showed Aussies how to surf back in 1914. You can revisit surfing history at **Freshwater Surf Club** (☎ 02-9905 3741; www.freshwaterslsc.com; Kooloora Ave, Harbord), where Kahanamoku's board is on show. There is also a statue of Duke on the headland at nearby McKillop Park.

❹ WHALE & PALM BEACHES

Book a seaplane from **Rose Bay** (see Scenic Flights, p78) and digest some awesome scenery on the way to Whaley. Lunch at **Jonah's** (☎ 9974 5599; www.jonahs.com.au; 69 Bynya Rd, Whale Beach; 🕑 Wed-Mon), which boasts one of the world's best views. You can stay the night here, but if you do, pack your board because there're some great waves at **Whale Beach** (p77). Inexperienced surfers can cruise around the headland to **Palm Beach** (p77). Here you'll find lifestyles of the rich and famous and a perfect little surf break for beginners.

➘ THINGS YOU NEED TO KNOW

Best learners' beaches Manly (p76) and Palm Beaches (p77) **Best time to visit** Manly hosts the Festival of Surfing in November and the Manly Food and Wine Festival in June **See our author's review on p77**

SYDNEY HIGHLIGHTS

3

↘ SYDNEY HARBOUR BRIDGE

Big and purposeful, the 'coathanger' dominates Sydney and is great to look up at and down from. Capture the soaring arch and immense bulk of the **bridge** (p69) from the ground, zip underneath in a ferry, climb the southeastern pylon for a view of the city skyline, jog the eastern walkway or cycle the western cycleway. Mind you, the ultimate experience is the **bridge climb** (p81).

4

↘ SYDNEY OPERA HOUSE

Sydney's most recognisable icon is the **Sydney Opera House** (p68) with its shell-like 'sails' shimmering on the blue harbour waters on a sunny Sydney day. Perfectly positioned on Bennelong Point, this curvy creation delights the eye from almost any angle and always makes a good photo. Get up close and examine the self-cleaning tiles or explore the interior on a guided tour. Better still, take in a show.

5

↘ THE ROCKS

The site of Australia's first European settlement and the birthplace of modern Australia, the **Rocks** (p69) is no longer the squalid slum of yore. Redevelopment in the 1970s restored remaining colonial buildings and renewed cobbled streets to create a pleasant, if touristy, ghetto of museums, galleries, shops and restaurants.

6

↘ CENTRAL SYDNEY

The synthetic canyons created by the modern business district of **central Sydney** (p70) shelter colonial-era sandstone buildings and magnificent churches and commercial edifices of the booming Victorian and Edwardian times. History students, theatregoers, architecture buffs, foodies and shopaholics will all find a central city ramble a rewarding time.

7

↘ DARLING HARBOUR

The erstwhile industrial waterfront of docks, factories and warehouses at **Darling Harbour** (p72) has been spruced up into a tourism focal point with attractions, restaurants and futuristic streetscapes. It's just a short stroll or monorail ride from the CBD and there's enough going on here to spend a fruitful day, especially if you have kids in tow.

3 HOLGER LEUE; 4 OLIVER STREWE; 5 MTMEDIA; 6 GREG ELMS; 7 HOLGER LEUE

3 Sydney Harbour Bridge climbers (81); 4 Sydney Opera House (p68); 5 The Rocks (p69); 6 Central Sydney (p70) from Darling Harbour; 7 Darling Harbour (p72)

SYDNEY'S BEST...

FRESH AIR FACTORIES

- **Manly Ferry** (p76) Step out on to the deck and suck in the sea air.
- **Hyde Park** (p71) This formally laid-out park with avenues of stately trees and swathes of lawn is Sydney's lungs.
- **Royal Botanic Gardens** (p72) Bordering Farm Cove, these enchanting gardens offer educational botany lessons.

PLACES TO LOOK DOWN & OUT

- **Sydney Harbour Bridge** (p69) The view from the southeastern pylon is good, and from the bridge climb (p81) it is unbelievable.
- **Sydney Tower** (p70) Take in all of Sydney Harbour, the Blue Mountains and Botany Bay. For an extra buzz take the alfresco Skywalk.
- **The Gap** (p75) An epic cliff-top lookout on the rugged south head at the entrance to Sydney Harbour.

PLACES TO COOL OFF

- **Bondi Beach** (p75) Join the crowd and catch a wave at Sydney's famous surf beach.
- **Camp Cove** (p75) A lovely family-friendly harbour beach.
- **Northern beaches** (p77) Choose from several delightful sandy surf beaches from Manly to Palm Beach.

PLACES TO STROLL

- **The Rocks & Circular Quay** (p69) Between the sails of the Opera House and the girders of the Harbour Bridge there's enough history and attractions to fill many hours.
- **Bondi to Coogee Coastal Walk** (p75) Before or after a surf take a stroll along this delightful patch of sandy beaches and seaside cliffs.
- **Royal Botanic Gardens** (p72) Wander the gardens in search of a shady picnic spot or scrub up on your botanical knowledge on a free guided walk.

LEFT: CAROL WILEY; RIGHT: TRAVIS DREVER

Left: North Cronulla Beach, south of Sydney; Right: Royal Botanic Gardens (p72)

THINGS YOU NEED TO KNOW

VITAL STATISTICS

- **Population** 4.4 million
- **Telephone code** ☎ 02
- **Best time to visit** October to June

NEIGHBOURHOODS IN A NUTSHELL

- **Central Sydney and the Harbour** (p67) Iconic Sydney embraces its famous harbour
- **Kings Cross and Darlinghurst** (p74) Bohemian, red-light and gay-friendly neighbourhoods
- **Eastern suburbs and beaches** (p75) Golden sand beaches and promenading bathers
- **Manly** (p76) Carefree and permanently on holiday
- **Northern beaches** (p77) Stunning beach after stunning beach

ADVANCE PLANNING

- **One month before** Book a place on the very popular bridge climb (p81)
- **Two weeks before** Book tickets for a Sydney Opera House performance (p88)
- **One week before** Book tickets for a harbour cruise (p80) and a table one of Sydney's premier restaurants (p84)

RESOURCES

- **City Host Information Kiosks** (9am-5pm) Circular Quay (Map pp64-5; cnr Pitt & Alfred Sts, Sydney); Martin Place (Map pp54-5; btwn Elizabeth & Castlereagh Sts, Sydney); Town Hall (Map p64-5; cnr Druitt & George Sts, Sydney)
- **Sydney Visitor Centre** (www.sydneyvisitorcentre.com); Darling Harbour (Map pp64-5; ☎ 02-9240 8788; Palm Grove; 9.30am-5.30pm) Information on *everything;* also acts as an accommodation agency; The Rocks (Map pp64-5; ☎ 02-9240 8788; www.sydneyvisitorcentre.com; cnr Argyle & Playfair Sts, The Rocks; 9.30am-5.30pm Mon-Fri).
- **Tourism New South Wales** (☎ 02-9931 1111; www.visitnsw.com.au; 9am-5pm Mon-Fri); airport (Map pp52-3; ☎ 02-9667 6050; International Arrivals, Terminal 1; 5am-11pm) State-wide accommodation and travel advice.

EMERGENCY NUMBERS

- **Police, fire and ambulance** (☎ 000)
- **National Roads & Motorists Association** (NRMA; Map pp64-5; ☎ 13 11 22; www.nrma.com.au; 74-6 King St, Sydney; 9am-5pm Mon-Fri) Car insurance and roadside service.

GETTING AROUND

- **Walk** around Circular Quay from the Rocks to the Opera House
- **Bus** (p92) all around the city
- **Ferry** (p91) to Taronga Zoo, Manly, Darling Harbour and other harbour-side destinations
- **Monorail** (p93) from the CBD to Darling Harbour and back
- **Train** (p93) around the suburbs
- **Airport Link** (p91) runs to/from the airport

DISCOVER SYDNEY

Sydney is the capital that all other cities love to hate; with stunning surf and buttery beaches, glorious weather and glamorous people, world-class restaurants and outrageously fashionable bars, the city seemingly has it all. And, damn it, doesn't it know it.

Built around one of the most beautiful natural harbours in the world, Sydney's shimmering soul reveals an iconic landscape that to many signifies 'Australia'. The Harbour Bridge, the Opera House, myriad sandstone headlands, lazy bays and scalloped shorelines are breathtakingly beautiful. But while its neighbours might snipe that Sydney is all about fleeting physical fun, Sydneysiders know that there's more to this city than its good looks (even if Bondi Beach on a Saturday afternoon argues otherwise). It's Australia's oldest, largest and most diverse city, with captivating monuments, urban galleries, magnificent museums, a vivacious performing arts scene and an edgy multiculturalism that injects colour into its outer suburbs.

SYDNEY IN...

Three Days

Start your time in Sydney the way that all Sydneysiders begin their day with a flat white and breakfast. Fortified, head to the harbour and get blown away by the stunning views on a **bridge climb** (p81). Ramble around **The Rocks** (p69) and wind your way over to the **Sydney Opera House** (p68), stopping in at the **Museum of Contemporary Art** (p70) on your way. Kick back in the Royal Botanic Gardens (p72), but keep an eye out for the flying foxes.

On day two goofy-foot it over to **Bondi** (p75) for a surf lesson followed by the **Coastal Walk** (p75) to Coogee. Fill up on fish for lunch at the **Sydney Fish Market** (p74) and then wander the arty streets of Glebe or Balmain, both of which offer ample opportunities for an early evening drink or two.

Start day three with some window shopping along **Oxford Street** (p75) followed by a bike ride and picnic in **Centennial Park** (p75).

One Week

It's easy to fill another four days in Sydney – lunch, beaches, swimming and views in **Manly** (p75) alone will take up one. Don't miss **Taronga Zoo** (p76), the **Sydney Aquarium** (p73) or the history-rich **Australian Museum** (p72).

ORIENTATION

At the heart of the city is Sydney Harbour (Port Jackson); the city centre runs from The Rocks and Circular Quay to Central Station in the south. The harbour divides Sydney into north and south, with the Sydney Harbour Bridge and the Harbour Tunnel connecting the two shores. Immediately west is Darling Harbour, while to the east lies Darlinghurst, Kings Cross and Paddington.

Head further southeast along the coast and you'll find the archetypal beach suburbs of Bondi and Coogee. Sydney's Kingsford Smith Airport is 10km south of the city centre.

INFORMATION

MEDICAL SERVICES

St Vincent's Hospital (Map pp64-5; ☎ 02-8382 1111; www.stvincents.com.au; 390 Victoria St, Darlinghurst; 🕑 24hr emergency)

Sydney 's Hospital (Map pp52-3; ☎ 02-9382 1111; www.sch.edu.au; High St, Randwick; 🕑 24hr kids' emergency)

MONEY

There are plenty of ATMs throughout Sydney; and both **American Express** (Map pp64-5; ☎ 1300 139 060; 50 Pitt St, Sydney; 🕑 9.30am-4pm Mon-Thu, to 5pm Fri) and **Travelex** (Map pp64-5; ☎ 02-9264 1267; Shop W64, Queen Victoria Building, George St, Sydney;

CLOCKWISE FROM TOP: CAROL WILEY; JULIET COOMBE; KARL BLACKWELL; GILLIANNE TEDDER

Clockwise from top: Sydney Harbour Bridge (p69) from Observatory Park; Taronga Zoo (p76); Sydney Opera House (p68); Bondi to Coogee Coastal Walk (p75)

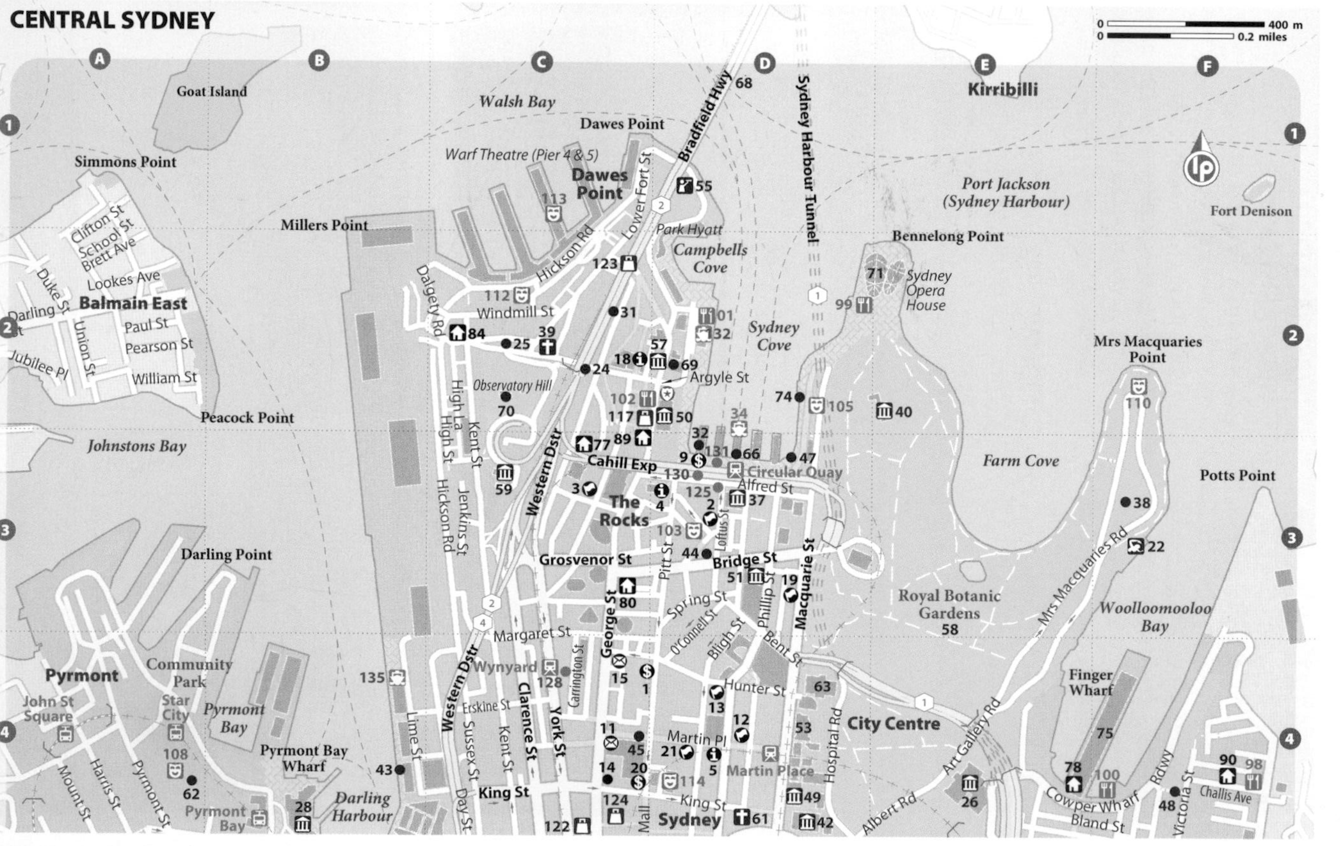
CENTRAL SYDNEY
0 400 m
0 0.2 miles
Goat Island
Walsh Bay
Dawes Point
Kirribilli
Fort Denison
Simmons Point
Warf Theatre (Pier 4 & 5)
Dawes Point
Port Jackson (Sydney Harbour)
Millers Point
Park Hyatt
Campbells Cove
Bennelong Point
Sydney Harbour Tunnel
Bradfield Hwy
Lower Fort St
Hickson Rd
Clifton St
School St
Brett Ave
Lookes Ave
Duke St
Darling St
Balmain East
Union St
Paul St
Pearson St
William St
Jubilee Pl
Windmill St
Dalgety Rd
Sydney Opera House
Sydney Cove
Mrs Macquaries Point
Argyle St
Observatory Hill
High La
High St
Kent St
Peacock Point
Johnstons Bay
Cahill Exp
Circular Quay
Alfred St
Western Dstr
The Rocks
Farm Cove
Potts Point
Loftus St
Pitt St
Jenkins St
Hickson Rd
Darling Point
Grosvenor St
Bridge St
Phillip St
Macquarie St
Spring St
O'Connell St
Bligh St
Bent St
Royal Botanic Gardens
Mrs Macquaries Rd
Woolloomooloo Bay
George St
Margaret St
Wynyard
Carrington St
Pyrmont
Community Park
Hunter St
Finger Wharf
John St Square
Star City
Pyrmont Bay
Erskine St
Clarence St
York St
Lime St
Sussex St
City Centre
Art Gallery Rd
Hospital Rd
Martin Pl
Martin Place
Pyrmont Bay Wharf
King St
Sydney
Mall
Mount St
Harris St
Pyrmont St
Darling Harbour
Day St
Albert Rd
Cowper Wharf Rdwy
Bland St
Victoria St
Challis Ave

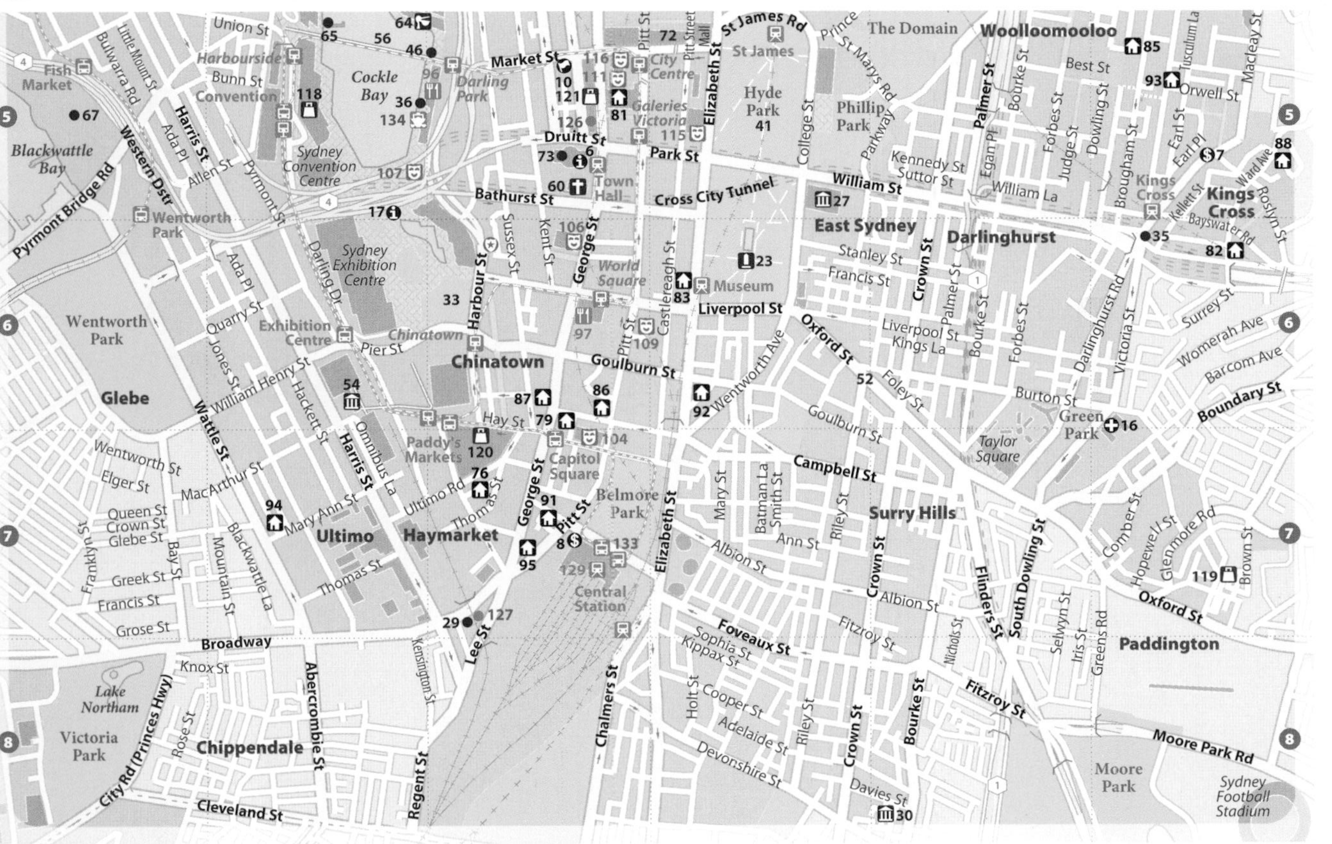
Woolloomooloo
Kings Cross
Darlinghurst
East Sydney
Surry Hills
Paddington
Moore Park
Sydney Football Stadium
The Domain
Phillip Park
Hyde Park
St James
Museum
Town Hall
World Square
Chinatown
Haymarket
Ultimo
Glebe
Chippendale
Cockle Bay
Darling Park
Sydney Convention Centre
Sydney Exhibition Centre
Exhibition Centre
Paddy's Markets
Capitol Square
Belmore Park
Central Station
Taylor Square
Green Park
Wentworth Park
Victoria Park
Lake Northam
Blackwattle Bay
Fish Market
Harbourside
Convention
City Centre
Galeries Victoria
Macleay St
Roslyn St
Ward Ave
Bayswater Rd
Kellett St
Earl Pl
Earl St
Orwell St
Tusculum La
Brougham St
Dowling St
Best St
Judge St
Forbes St
Bourke St
Palmer St
Egan Pl
William La
William St
Kennedy St
Suttor St
Parkway
St Marys Rd
Prince Albert Rd
College St
St James Rd
Elizabeth St
Pitt Street Mall
Pitt St
Castlereagh St
Park St
Cross City Tunnel
Market St
Druitt St
Bathurst St
Kent St
Sussex St
George St
Harbour St
Liverpool St
Goulburn St
Hay St
Oxford St
Wentworth Ave
Campbell St
Crown St
Riley St
Foley St
Stanley St
Francis St
Kings La
Burton St
Darlinghurst Rd
Victoria St
Surrey St
Womerah Ave
Barcom Ave
Boundary St
Brown St
Glenmore Rd
Hopewell St
Comber St
Greens Rd
Iris St
Selwyn St
South Dowling St
Flinders St
Nichols St
Fitzroy St
Davies St
Albion St
Ann St
Smith St
Batman La
Mary St
Foveaux St
Sophia St
Kippax St
Holt St
Cooper St
Adelaide St
Devonshire St
Chalmers St
Lee St
Regent St
Kensington St
Thomas St
Ultimo Rd
Omnibus La
Harris St
Pier St
Darling Dr
Mary Ann St
Hackett St
William Henry St
Jones St
Quarry St
Ada Pl
Pymont St
Wattle St
Blackwattle La
Mountain St
MacArthur St
Abercrombie St
Broadway
Knox St
Cleveland St
Rose St
City Rd (Princes Hwy)
Bay St
Wentworth St
Elger St
Queen St
Glebe St
Greek St
Grose St
Franklyn St
Union St
Bunn St
Allen St
Western Dstr
Little Mount St
Bulwarra Rd
Pyrmont Bridge Rd

8am-6pm Mon-Wed & Fri, to 7.30pm Thu, 11am-4pm Sat, noon-5pm Sun) have city branches.

Seven-day exchange bureaus can be found at **Central Station** (Map pp64-5; Coach Terminal; 9am-4pm), **Circular Quay** (Map pp64-5; Wharf 6; 8am-9.30pm) and **Kings Cross** (Map pp64-5; cnr Springfield Ave & Darlinghurst Rd; 8am-midnight).

INFORMATION

American Express 1 C4
British Consulate 2 D3
Canadian Consulate 3 C3
City Host Information Kiosk (Circular Quay) 4 D3
City Host Information Kiosk (Martin Place) 5 D4
City Host Information Kiosk (Town Hall) 6 C5
Exchange Bureau 7 F5
Exchange Bureau (Central Station) 8 C7
Exchange Bureau (Circular Quay) 9 D3
French Consulate 10 C5
General Post Office 11 C4
Japanese Consulate 12 D4
New Zealand High Commission 13 D4
NRMA 14 C4
Poste Restante Service 15 C4
St Vincent's Hospital 16 F6
Sydney Visitor Centre (Darling Harbour) 17 B5
Sydney Visitor Centre (The Rocks) 18 C2
Thai Consulate 19 D3
Travelex 20 C4
US Consulate 21 D4

SIGHTS & ACTIVITIES

Aboriginal Heritage - Walk the Rocks (see 18)
Aboriginal Heritage Tour (see 58)
Andrew 'Boy' Charlton Pool 22 F3
Anzac Memorial 23 D6
Argyle Cut 24 C2
Argyle Place 25 C2
Art Gallery of NSW 26 E4
Australian Museum 27 D5
Australian National Maritime Museum 28 B4
Bicycle NSW 29 C7
Bounce Walking Tours (see 71)
Brett Whiteley Studio 30 E8
BridgeClimb 31 C2
Cadman's Cottage (see 69)
Captain Cook Cruises 32 D3
Chinese Garden of Friendship 33 C6
Circular Quay 34 D2
Coca-Cola Sign 35 F6
Cockle Bay Wharf 36 B5
Customs House 37 D3
Domain 38 F3
Garrison Church 39 C2
Government House 40 E2
Hyde Park 41 D5
Hyde Park Barracks Museum 42 D4
King St Wharf 43 B4
Macquarie Place 44 D3
Martin Place 45 C4
Matilda Cruises 46 C5
Matilda Cruises 47 D3
McElhone Stairs 48 F4
Mint 49 D4
Museum of Contemporary Art 50 D2
Museum of Sydney 51 D3
Oxford Street 52 D6
Parliament House 53 D4
Powerhouse Museum 54 B6
Pylon Lookout 55 D1
Pyrmont Bridge 56 B5
Queen Victoria Building (see 121)
Rocks Discovery Museum 57 D2
Royal Botanic Gardens 58 E3
SH Ervin Gallery 59 C3
St Andrew's Cathedral 60 C5
St James' Church 61 D4
Star City Casino 62 A4
State Library of NSW 63 D4
State Theatre (see 111)
Strand Arcade (see 124)
Sydney Aquarium 64 B5
Sydney Architecture Walks (see 51)
Sydney by Sail 65 B5
Sydney Ferries 66 D3
Sydney Fish Market 67 A5
Sydney Harbour Bridge 68 D1
Sydney Harbour National Park Information Centre 69 D2
Sydney Observatory 70 C2
Sydney Opera House 71 E2
Sydney Tower 72 D5
Town Hall 73 C5
Tribal Warrior 74 D2
Woolloomooloo Wharf 75 F4

SLEEPING

Aaron's Hotel 76 C7
B&B Sydney Harbour 77 C3
BLUE Sydney 78 E4
Capitol Square Hotel 79 C6
Establishment Hotel 80 C3
Hilton 81 C5
Hotel 59 82 F6
Hyde Park Inn 83 D6
Lord Nelson Brewery Hotel 84 C2
Mariners Court 85 F5
Metro Hotel Sydney Central 86 C6
Pensione Hotel 87 C6
Pink House 88 F5
Russell 89 C3
Simpsons of Potts Point 90 F4
Sydney Central YHA 91 C7
Vibe Hotel 92 D6
Victoria Court Hotel 93 F5
Vulcan Hotel 94 B7
Wake Up! 95 C7

EATING

Blackbird 96 C5
Cafe Sydney (see 37)
Din Tai Fung 97 C6
Fratelli Paradiso 98 F4
Guillaume at Bennelong 99 D2
Harry's Café de Wheels 100 F4
Quay 101 D2
Rockpool 102 C2

ENTERTAINMENT

Basement 103 D3
Capitol Theatre 104 C7
Dendy Opera Quays 105 D2
George Street Cinemas 106 C6
IMAX 107 B5
Lyric Theatre 108 A4
Moshtix 109 C6
Open Air Cinema 110 F2
State Theatre 111 C5
Sydney Opera House (see 71)
Sydney Theatre 112 C2
Sydney Theatre Company 113 C1
Theatre Royal 114 D4
Ticketek 115 D5
Ticketmaster 116 C5

SHOPPING

Flame Opals 117 C2
Gavala 118 B5
Hogarth Galleries 119 F7
Paddy's Markets 120 C7
Queen Victoria Building 121 C5
RM Williams 122 C4
Rocks Market 123 C2
Strand Arcade 124 C4

TRANSPORT

Bus TransitShop (Circular Quay) 125 D3
Bus TransitShop (QVB) 126 C5
Bus TransitShop (Railway Sq) 127 C7
Bus TransitShop (Wynyard Station) 128 C4
Central Station 129 C7
CityRail Information Booth 130 D3
Countrylink Travel Centre (see 129)
Ferry Information Office 131 D3
Overseas Passenger Terminal 132 D2
Sydney Coach Terminal 133 C7
Watertours 134 B5
Yellow Water Taxis 135 B4

POST

Stamps are sold at post offices, Australia Post retail outlets in most suburbs and most newsagencies.

General Post Office (GPO; Map pp64-5; ☎ 13 13 18; www.auspost.com.au; 1 Martin Pl, Sydney; ⏲ 8.15am-5.30pm Mon-Fri, 10am-2pm Sat)

Poste Restante Service (Map pp64-5; ☎ 13 13 18; www.auspost.com.au; 310 George St, Sydney; ⏲ 8.15am-5.30pm Mon-Fri, 10am-2pm Sat) Bring identification to collect mail.

SIGHTS

Sydney's jam-packed with things to see and do, much of which doesn't cost a cent. But if you're planning to see an exceptional number of museums, attractions and tours, check out the **Smartvisit card** (☎ 1300 661 711; www.seesydneycard.com).

SYDNEY HARBOUR

Sydney's stunning harbour (officially Port Jackson) is the city's heart and soul. Stretching 20km inland to the mouth of the Parramatta River, it's peppered with islands, coves, beaches and bays, some insanely busy and others virtually deserted.

North Head and **South Head** form the gateway to the harbour. Close to South Head at the harbour entrance, **Camp Cove** (Map pp52–3) is a particularly photogenic swimming beach and is where Arthur Phillip first landed. The fortunately shark-netted **Shark Beach** at **Nielsen Park** (Map pp52–3) is similarly sublime. For the most part the harbour beaches tend to be far calmer than their frenzied ocean cousins. On the North Shore try **Manly Cove**, **Reef Beach**, **Clontarf Beach**, **Chinamans Beach** and **Balmoral Beach** (all Map pp52–3).

SYDNEY HARBOUR NATIONAL PARK

This **park** (Map pp52–3) protects scattered pockets of harbour-side bushland

GREG ELMS

Taronga Zoo (p76)

with magical walking tracks, lookouts, Aboriginal engravings and historic sites. Its southern side incorporates South Head and Nielsen Park; on the North Shore it includes **North Head**, **Dobroyd Head**, **Middle Head** and **Bradleys Head**.

Five harbour islands also form part of the park: **Clark Island** off Darling Point, **Shark Island** off Rose Bay, **Rodd Island** in Iron Cove (all Map pp52–3), **Goat Island**, and the small fortified **Fort Denison** (Map pp64–5) off Mrs Macquaries Point.

Except for Goat Island, which is currently off limits, the harbour islands are open to visitors. The NPWS runs a number of tours, including hour-long Fort Denison **heritage tours** (adult/child $27/17; ⏲ 12.15pm & 2.30pm daily, 10.45am Wed-Sun) – book at the **Sydney Harbour National Park**

MARK NEWMAN

Sydney Opera House

↘ SYDNEY OPERA HOUSE

Millions over budget, years overdue and a scandalous political affair that forced architect Jørn Utzon to resign before the building's completion: it's fair to say that **Sydney Opera House** had a troubled youth. Today, however, this visionary building is Australia's most recognisable icon and since its official opening in 1973 millions have admired its soaring shell-like exterior.

The building is said to have drawn inspiration from orange segments, snails, palm fronds, sails and Mayan temples. Less poetically it's been likened to a 'nun's scrum' and Clive James called it an 'Olivetti Lettera 22 typewriter full of oyster shells left after an office party'. He quickly changed his mind, however, when he saw it 'for what it is: an epic poem'.

However you view the building, there's no denying that it's impressive: the 67m-high roof features 27,230 tonnes of Swedish tiles – 1,056,000 of them in total. Sadly, Jørn Utzon died in 2008 having never seen the finished design in person.

There are four main auditoriums for dance, concerts, opera and theatre events, plus the left-of-centre Studio for emerging artists; get your tickets at the **box office**.

One-hour Opera House **tours** take you from 'front of house' to backstage, excluding theatres in rehearsal use. Let them know in advance if you require wheelchair access. Public transport to Circular Quay is the best way to get here, but if you're driving there's a **car park** under the building (enter via Macquarie St).

Things you need to know Sydney Opera House (**Map pp64-5; ☎ 02-9250 7111; www.sydneyoperahouse.com; Bennelong Pt, Circular Quay E, Sydney**); box office (**☎ 02-9250 7777; 🕑 9am-8.30pm Mon-Sat, 2hr pre-show Sun**); tours (**☎ 02-9250 7250; adult/concession $23/16; 🕑 9am-5.30pm**); car park (**☎ 02-9247 7599; nightly rate $32; 🕑 6.30am-1am**)

Information Centre (Map pp64-5; ☎ 02-9247 5033; www.environment.nsw.gov.au/nationalparks; 110 George St, The Rocks; ⌚ 9.30am-4.30pm Mon-Fri, 10am-4.30pm Sat & Sun).

Matilda Cruises (Map pp64-5; ☎ 02-9264 7377; www.matilda.com.au; adult/child $17/15; ⌚ every 45min from 9.45am departing Circular Quay & Pier 26, Darling Harbour) runs ferries to Shark Island.

SYDNEY HARBOUR BRIDGE

Sydneysiders adore their **bridge** (Map pp64–5). Dubbed the 'coat hanger' this colossal steel-arch bridge, held together by almost six million hand-driven rivets, links the CBD with the North Sydney business district. It took eight years to build and was completed in 1932 – at a cost of $20 million. The city took 60 years to pay it off.

There are many ways to experience this favourite Sydney icon – you can drive over it, climb up it, travel by train across it or sail underneath it – but the best way to fully appreciate the bridge is on foot. Staircases climb up from both shores leading to a footpath running the length of the eastern side. A cycle way wheels along the western side. You can climb the southeastern pylon to the **Pylon Lookout** (Map pp64-5; ☎ 02-9240 1100; www.pylonlookout.com.au; adult/child $10/4; ⌚ 10am-5pm), or ascend the great arc on a bridge climb (see p81).

On New Year's Eve the bridge takes centre stage with an impressive kaleidoscopic fireworks display.

THE ROCKS

The site of Sydney's first European settlement has evolved unrecognisably from its squalid origins. Early residents lived cheek by jowl in filthy alleyways festering with disease, prostitution and crime. Sailors, whalers and street gangs roamed the streets, boozing and brawling in the grimy harbour-side pubs.

The Rocks remained a commercial and maritime hub until shipping services sailed from Circular Quay in the late 1800s. A bubonic plague outbreak in 1900 furthered the decline and when construction began on the Harbour Bridge in the 1920s, entire streets were demolished.

It wasn't until the 1970s that The Rocks' cultural and architectural heritage was recognised and efforts were made to preserve and redevelop the area. Some argue that the result is a sanitised, 'olde worlde' tourist trap, but there's no denying that the area holds a certain charm, especially once you leave the main drag for the narrow backstreets.

Built in 1816, **Cadman's Cottage** (Map pp64-5; ☎ 02-9247 5033; www.environment.nsw.gov.au; 110 George St, The Rocks; ⌚ 9.30am-4.30pm Mon-Fri, 10am-4.30pm Sat & Sun) is Sydney's oldest house. Its namesake, John Cadman, was the government coxswain. Water police detained criminals here in the late 1840s and it was later converted into a home for retired sea captains. Today it is home to the Sydney Harbour National Park Information Centre (p68). Further along George St is the tourist-oriented weekend Rocks Market (see p89).

In a restored 1850s sandstone warehouse, the **Rocks Discovery Museum** (Map pp64-5; ☎ 1800 067 676; www.rocksdiscoverymuseum.com; Kendall Lane, The Rocks; admission free; ⌚ 10am-5pm) delves into the area's history and provides a sensitive insight into the lives of the Cadigal people, The Rocks' original inhabitants.

Beyond the **Argyle Cut** (Map pp64–5), an impressive tunnel excavated by convicts, is **Millers Point**, a relaxed district of early colonial homes. **Argyle Place** (Map pp64–5) is an English-style village green overlooked by the 1840 **Garrison Church**, the colony's first military church.

The 1850s, copper-domed, Italianate **Sydney Observatory** (**Map pp64-5; ☎ 02-9921 3485; www.sydneyobservatory.com.au; Watson Rd, Millers Point; admission free; 🕑 10am-5pm**) stands atop Observatory Park. Inside there's a 3-D **Space Theatre** (**adult/child/family $7/5/20; 🕑 2.30pm & 3.30pm daily, plus 11am & noon Sat & Sun**) and an interactive Australian astronomy exhibition. Squint at galaxies far, far away during night viewings (adult/child/family tickets cost $15/10/45); bookings are required.

In the old military hospital building nearby, the **SH Ervin Gallery** (**Map pp64-5; ☎ 02-9258 0173; www.nsw.nationaltrust.org.au/ervin.html; Watson Rd, Millers Point; adult/child $6/4; 🕑 11am-5pm Tue-Sun**) exhibits Australian art, including the fun and oft-controversial annual Salon des Refusés, an alternative collection from the hundreds of entries to the annual Archibald and Wynne art prizes.

The wharves around Dawes Point have emerged from prolonged decay into a cultural hub. Walsh Bay's Pier 4 houses the renowned Sydney Theatre Company (p87), the excellent **Bangarra Dance Theatre**, the **Australian Theatre for Young People (ATYP)** and the **Sydney Dance Company**.

CIRCULAR QUAY

Built around Sydney Cove, Circular Quay is one of the city's main focal points, as well as a major public transport hub, with ferry quays, bus stops, a train station and the Overseas Passenger Terminal. European settlement grew around the Tank Stream, which now trickles underground into the harbour near Wharf 6. For many years Circular Quay was also Sydney's port, but these days it's more of a recreational space, with harbour walkways, grassy verges, outstanding restaurants and buskers of unpredictable merit.

MUSEUM OF CONTEMPORARY ART

In 2008 Sydney's Chamber of Commerce recognised the **MCA** (**Map pp64-5; ☎ 02-9245 2400; www.mca.com.au; 140 George St, The Rocks; admission free; 🕑 10am-5pm**) as the city's most popular museum. Innovative and challenging, the ever-changing exhibitions from Australia and overseas are hip, thought provoking and often controversial. There are also excellent permanent exhibitions of Indigenous art.

CENTRAL SYDNEY

Central Sydney stretches from Circular Quay in the north to Central Station in the south. The business district has traditionally sat at the northern end, but is gradually creeping southwards. For a lofty city view, take a trip up **Sydney Tower** (**Map pp64-5; Centrepoint, 100 Market St, Sydney; adult/child/student $25/15/20; 🕑 9am-10.30pm**).

Sydney lacks a true civic centre, but **Martin Place** (Map pp64–5) comes close. This grand pedestrian mall extends from Macquarie St to George St and is lined with monumental financial buildings and the Victorian colonnaded General Post Office. In the centre is a cenotaph commemorating Australia's war dead.

Sydney's elaborate 1874 **Town Hall** (Map pp64–5) is a few blocks south of here on the corner of George and Druitt Sts. Currently undergoing major renovations, the building is due to reopen in late 2009. Next door, the Anglican **St Andrew's Cathedral** (Map pp64–5), was consecrated in 1868, making it Australia's oldest cathedral. Across the road from the Town Hall, and taking up an entire city block, is the Queen Victoria Building (QVB; p89), Sydney's most sumptuous shopping complex. Running a close second is the ornate Strand Arcade (p90) between Pitt St Mall and George St.

The grand **State Theatre** (Map pp64-5; ☎ 02-9373 6862; www.statetheatre.com.au; 49 Market St, Sydney; adult/child $12/8; ⏲ 11.30am-3pm Mon-Fri) was built in 1929. There are 45-minute tours, but even a quick peek at the glittering foyer is worthwhile.

Breathing life into the city's lacklustre southwestern zone are Sydney's blink-and-you'll-miss-it **Spanish Quarter**, along Liverpool and Kent Sts, and thriving **Chinatown** (Map p64–5), a tight bundle of restaurants, shops and barbecue-duck-scented alleyways around Dixon St. Chinatown goes berserk during Chinese New Year (late January/early February), when dancing lions roam the lantern-covered streets and dragon-boat races take over Darling Harbour.

On the eastern edge of the city centre is the formal **Hyde Park** (Map p64–5), which has a grand avenue of trees, delightful fountains and a giant public chess-board. Wander into the dignified **Anzac Memorial** (Map pp64-5; ☎ 02-9267 7668; www.anzacmemorial.nsw.gov.au; admission free; ⏲ 9am-5pm), with an interior dome studded with one star for each of the 120,000 NSW citizens who served in WWI.

MACQUARIE PLACE & AROUND

At the corner of Loftus and Bridge Sts is **Macquarie Pl** (Map p64–5), a leafy public square proudly displaying a cannon and an anchor from the First Fleet flagship, HMS *Sirius*, and an 1818 obelisk (cleverly positioned to disguise a sewer vent) etched with road distances to various points in the nascent colony.

MUSEUM OF SYDNEY

Built on the site of Sydney's first (and infamously pungent) Government House (1788), this thoroughly engaging **museum** (Map pp64-5; ☎ 02-9251 5988; www.hht.net.au; cnr Bridge & Phillip Sts, Sydney; adult/child/family $10/5/20; ⏲ 9.30am-5pm) brings the city's early history to life through whispers, arguments, gossip, artefacts and state-of-the-art installations. The sculpture in the forecourt symbolises the meeting of cultures that occurred when Cook and co first dropped anchor.

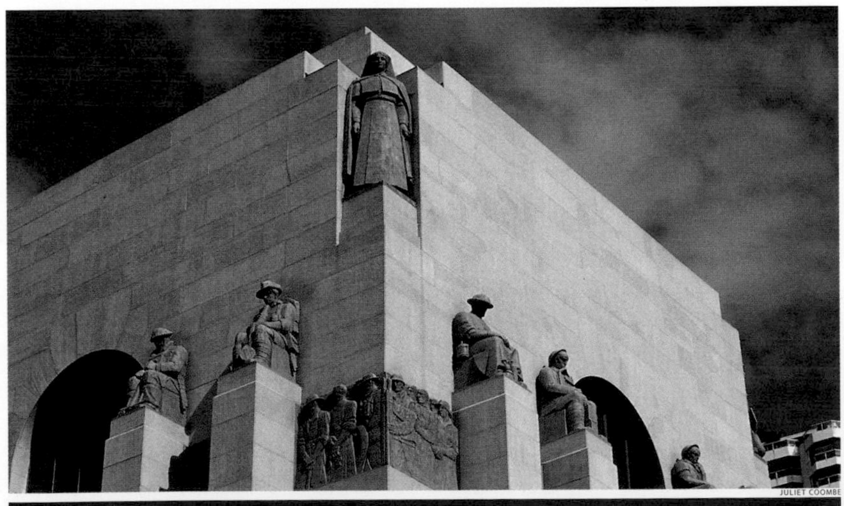

JULIET COOMBE

Anzac Memorial, Hyde Park

MACQUARIE STREET

A crop of early public buildings graces Macquarie St, defining the city's edge from Hyde Park to the Opera House. Many of these buildings were commissioned by Lachlan Macquarie, the first NSW governor to have a vision of Sydney beyond its convict origins. He enlisted convict architect Francis Greenway to help realise his plans.

Two Greenway gems front onto Queens Sq at Hyde Park's northern end: built in 1819 **St James' Church** (Map pp64–5) is Sydney's oldest church; the **Hyde Park Barracks Museum** (Map pp64-5; ☎ 02-8239 2311; www.hht.net.au; adult/child/family $10/5/20; 9.30am-5pm), was also built in 1819. The barracks functioned as convict quarters for Anglo-Irish sinners (1819–48), an immigrant depot (1848–86) and government courts (1887–1979) before its current incarnation: a window into everyday convict life.

Nearby are the deep verandahs and formal colonnades of the twin 1816 buildings of the **Mint** (Map pp64-5; ☎ 02-8239 2288; www.hht.net.au; admission free; 9am-5pm Mon-Fri) and **Parliament House** (Map pp64-5; ☎ 02-9230 2111; www.parliament.nsw.gov.au; admission free; 9.30am-4.30pm Mon-Fri).

Next to Parliament House, the **State Library of NSW** (Map pp64-5; ☎ 02-9273 1414; www.sl.nsw.gov.au; 9am-8pm Mon-Thu, to 5pm Fri, 10am-5pm Sat & Sun) holds over five million tomes, the smallest being a tablet-sized Lord's Prayer, and hosts innovative exhibitions in its **galleries** (9am-5pm Mon-Fri, 11am-5pm Sat & Sun).

Built between 1837 and 1845, the regal **Government House** (Map pp64-5; ☎ 02-9931 5222; www.hht.net.au; admission free; 10am-3pm Fri-Sun, grounds to 4pm daily, 45min tours from 10.30am) was designed by British architect Edward Blore, who was also involved in the design for Buckingham Palace. Unless there's an official event happening, you can tour the fussy furnishings.

AUSTRALIAN MUSEUM

Come face to face with some of Australia's deadliest creatures, including funnel webs (spiders) and salties (estuarine crocodiles), at this natural history **museum** (Map pp64-5; ☎ 02-9320 6000; www.amonline.net.au; 6 College St, Sydney; adult/child/family $12/6/30, extra for special exhibits; 9.30am-5pm); fortunately they're all behind glass. There are also excellent Indigenous exhibitions, and Indigenous performances on Sunday (noon and 2pm), plus good wheelchair access.

ART GALLERY OF NSW

This **gallery** (Map pp64-5; ☎ 02-9225 1744; www.artgallery.nsw.gov.au; Art Gallery Rd, The Domain; admission free, varied costs for touring exhibitions; 10am-5pm Thu-Tue, to 9pm Wed, free guided tours 11am, 1pm & 2pm) plays a prominent and gregarious role in Sydney society. Highlights include outstanding permanent displays of 19th- and 20th-century Australian art, Aboriginal and Torres Strait Islander art, 15th- to 19th-century European and Asian art, and blockbuster international touring exhibitions.

ROYAL BOTANIC GARDENS

The **gardens** (RBG; Map pp64-5; ☎ 02-9231 8111; www.rbgsyd.nsw.gov.au; Mrs Macquaries Rd; admission free; 7am-sunset) were established in 1816 as the colony's vegetable patch and are now Sydney's favourite communal backyard. Signs encourage visitors to 'smell the roses, hug the trees, talk to the birds and picnic on the lawns'. Take a free **guided walk** (10.30am daily & 1pm Mon-Fri), departing from the **Gardens Shop**. A trackless train does a circuit if you're feeling weary.

DARLING HARBOUR

What was once industrial docklands is today a rambling, purpose-built water-

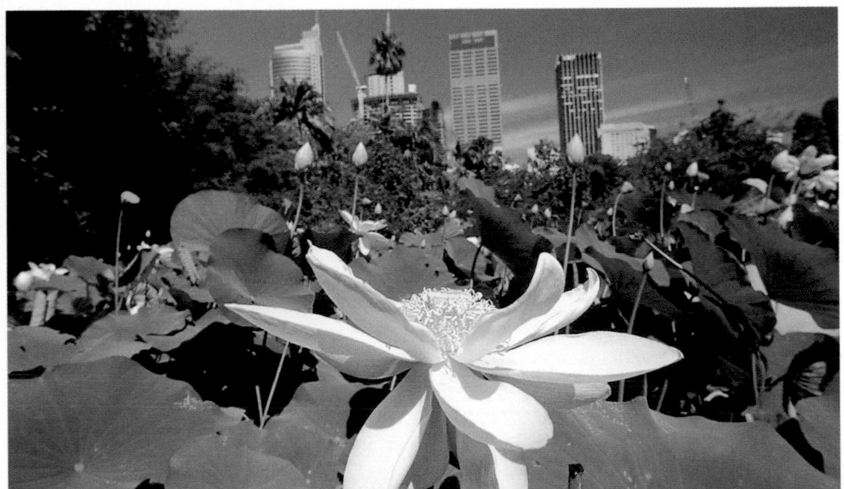
GILLIANNE TEDDER

Royal Botanic Gardens

front tourist park on the city's western edge. Although slick – think fountains, sculptures and sailcloth – the rejuvenation has scrubbed away much of the area's charm and character (and greenery). That said, the snazzy cafes and bars of the **Cockle Bay Wharf** and **King St Wharf** (Map pp64–5) precincts have injected some much-needed 'oomph' into the area.

A stroll across **Pyrmont Bridge** (Map pp64–5), the world's first electric swing bridge, leads you into Pyrmont, home of the overrated Harbourside Shopping Centre and the Sydney Fish Market (p74). Nearby bigger fish play at the **Star City Casino** (Map pp64-5; ☎ 02-9777 9000; www.starcity.com.au; 80 Pyrmont St, Pyrmont; 24hr).

Darling Harbour and Pyrmont are serviced by ferry, monorail, Metro Light Rail (MLR) and the Sydney Explorer bus. A dinky people-mover **train** (adult/child $5/4; 10am-6pm) connects the sights; the Sydney Visitor Centre (p61) is underneath the highway, next to the Imax cinema.

SYDNEY AQUARIUM

Kids and adults wander goggle-eyed through underwater glass tunnels at this ever-popular **aquarium** (Map pp64-5; ☎ 02-8251 7800; www.sydneyaquarium.com.au; Aquarium Pier, Darling Harbour; adult/child/family $30/14/63; 9am-10pm, last admission 9pm), celebrating the rich and colourful diversity of Australian marine life. Don't miss the kaleidoscopic colours of the Great Barrier Reef exhibit, the platypuses and crocodiles at the Southern and Northern Rivers display, and Pig and Wuru, two orphaned – and very cute – dugongs that now call the aquarium home.

AUSTRALIAN NATIONAL MARITIME MUSEUM

Play out your naval battle fantasies at this thematic **museum** (Map pp64-5; ☎ 02-9298 3777; www.anmm.gov.au; 2 Murray St, Pyrmont; admission free, special exhibits adult/child/family from $10/6/20; 9.30am-5pm) that explores Australia's inextricable relationship with the sea – from Aboriginal canoes to surf culture and the navy.

POWERHOUSE MUSEUM

This excellent and progressive **museum** (Map pp64-5; ☎ 02-9217 0111; www.powerhousemuseum.com; 500 Harris St, Ultimo; adult/child/family $10/5/25, extra for special exhibits; 10am-5pm) whirs away inside the former power station for Sydney's defunct tram network, and celebrates science, design, history, fashion, space, innovation and sustainability.

CHINESE GARDEN OF FRIENDSHIP

Built according to the balanced principles of yin and yang, these **gardens** (Map pp64-5; ☎ 02-9281 6863; www.darlingharbour.com; adult/child/family $6/3/15; 9.30am-5pm) are an oasis of tranquillity in the otherwise built-up Darling Harbour.

SYDNEY FISH MARKET

This cavernous **market** (Map pp64-5; ☎ 02-9004 1100; www.sydneyfishmarket.com.au; cnr Pyrmont Bridge Rd & Bank St, Pyrmont; 7am-4pm) is where Sydneysiders head to buy their Christmas lunch: in 2008 120,000 dozen oysters, 200 tonnes of snapper and 170 tonnes of prawns were purchased over the festive period. But this market is always busy – over 15 million kilograms of seafood are shipped through here annually. There are plenty of fishy restaurants, a deli, a wine centre, a sushi bar and an oyster bar.

KINGS CROSS

Stylish and sleazy, decadent and depraved, colourful Kings Cross rides high above the CBD under the neon glare of the oversized **Coca-Cola sign** (Map pp64–5), which is as much a Sydney icon as LA's Hollywood sign. It's an intense, densely populated domain that prompted notorious artist and writer Donald Friend to comment: 'In the Cross, everyone is wicked'.

Today the streets retain an air of seedy hedonism, but along with the strip joints and shabby drinking dens there are classy restaurants, cool bars and boutique hotels. Sometimes the razzle-dazzle has a sideshow appeal; sometimes walking up Darlinghurst Rd promotes pity. Either way, it's never boring.

Possibly the only word in the world containing eight 'o's, **Woolloomooloo**, down

OLIVER STREWE

Sydney Fish Market

McElhone Stairs (Map pp64–5) from the Cross, was once a slum full of drunks, sailors and drunk sailors. Things are begrudgingly less pugilistic these days – the pubs are relaxed and **Woolloomooloo Wharf** (Map pp64–5) contains some excellent restaurants. Nearby, the infamously lowbrow and exceedingly popular Harry's Café de Wheels (p85) dishes up pie floaters and more.

It's a 15-minute walk to the Cross from the city, or you could jump on a train. Buses 324 to 327 and 311 from the city also pass through here.

INNER EAST

The spirited backbone of the inner east is **Oxford Street** (Map pp64–5), a string of shops, cafes, bars and clubs that exudes a flamboyance largely attributable to Sydney's gay community. The Sydney Gay & Lesbian Mardi Gras (p46) gyrates in late February or early March each year.

South of Darlinghurst is **Surry Hills**, home to a raffish mishmash of style-conscious urbanites and a swag of great restaurants and bars. Preserved as a temple to rock-and-roll artistry, the **Brett Whiteley Studio** (Map pp64-5; ☎ 02-9225 1881; www.brettwhiteley.org; 2 Raper St, Surry Hills; admission free; 🕑 10am-4pm Sat & Sun) exhibits some of Whiteley's most raucous paintings. Surry Hills is a short walk east of Central Station or south from Oxford Street. Catch bus 301, 302 or 303 from Circular Quay.

Next door to Surry Hills, gentrified **Paddington** (Map pp64–5), aka 'Paddo', is an elegant suburb of restored terrace houses on steep leafy streets. Just southeast is Sydney's biggest park, the leafy 220-hectare **Centennial Park** (Map pp52–3), which has running, cycling, skating and horse-riding tracks, duck ponds, barbecue sites and sports pitches.

EASTERN SUBURBS

Handsome **Rushcutters Bay** (Map pp52–3) is a five-minute walk east of Kings Cross; its harbour-side park is a great place to stretch your legs and a family-friendly spot for the New Year's Eve fireworks.

At the entrance to the harbour is **Watsons Bay** (Map pp52–3), a snug community with restored fisherfolk's cottages, a palm-lined park and a couple of nautical churches. Nearby **Camp Cove** (Map pp52–3) is one of Sydney's best harbour beaches. **South Head** (Map pp52–3) has great views across the harbour entrance to North Head and Middle Head. The **Gap** (Map pp52–3) is an epic cliff-top lookout where sunrises, sunsets and suicide leaps occur with similar frequency.

Buses 324 and 325 from Circular Quay service the eastern suburbs via Kings Cross. Grab a seat on the left heading east to snare the best views.

EASTERN & SOUTHERN BEACHES

Bondi (Map pp52–3) lords it over every other beach in the city, despite not being the best one for a swim, a surf or a place to park. Still, there are many reasons why this is Sydney's most popular beach, and the crashing waves, flashy cafes and beautiful people are just some of them.

The stunning 6km **Bondi to Coogee Coastal Walk** leads south from Bondi Beach along the cliff tops to Coogee via Tamarama, Bronte and Clovelly Beaches, interweaving panoramic views, swimming spots and foodie delights.

Catch bus 333, 380 or L94 from the city or bus 381 from Bondi Junction to get to the beach.

NORTH SHORE

On the northern side of the Harbour Bridge is North Sydney, a high-rise office

PAUL BEINSSEN

Bondi Beach (p75)

↘ IF YOU LIKE...

If you like the sun, sand and water of **Bondi Beach** (p75), we think you might like these other beaches:

- **Balmoral** (Map pp52–3) Split in two by an unfeasibly picturesque rocky outcrop, Balmoral is a popular North Sydney haunt for swimming, kayaking and windsurfing. There are also some fabulous fish and chip shops. Catch bus 246 from Wynyard, then bus 257 from Spit Junction.
- **Bronte** (Map pp52–3) Norfolk Island pines and sandstone headlands hug the bowl-shaped park behind Bronte, a small family-oriented beach that has a playground, rock pool and sandy cafes. Catch bus 378 from Railway Sq.
- **Clovelly** (Map pp52–3) More like a giant ocean pool, the crystal clear waters of Clovelly is heaven for snorkellers. Keep an eye out for Bluey, the resident blue groper. Catch bus 339 from Central Station.

centre with little to tempt the traveller. On the eastern shore of Lavender Bay, the maniacal grin of the **Luna Park** (Map pp52-3; ☎ 02-9922 6644; www.lunaparksydney.com; 1 Olympic Pl, Milsons Point; admission free, multiride passes from $20; ⏲ 10am-9pm Sun-Thu, to 11pm Fri & Sat Dec-Feb, 11am-4pm Mon, to 10pm Fri & Sat, 10am-6pm Sun Mar-Nov) clown is the gateway to all manner of nausea-inducing fairground rides.

In a superb setting, **Taronga Zoo** (Map pp52-3; ☎ 02-9969 2777; www.zoo.nsw.gov.au; Bradleys Head Rd, Mosman; adult/child/family $39/19/99; ⏲ 9am-5pm) has some 4000 critters (from seals, tigers and monkeys to koalas, echidnas and platypuses), all well cared for and in decent habitats, although none can compete with the harbour views from the giraffe enclosure. Twilight concerts take place in the zoo during February and March.

Zoo ferries depart Circular Quay's Wharf 2 half-hourly from 7.15am on weekdays and from 8.45am on Saturday and Sunday. The zoo is on a fairly steep slope, so if you arrive by ferry, take the **Sky Safari cable car** (included in admission) or bus 238 to the top entrance and work your way downhill. A **Zoo Pass** (adult/child/family $44/22/117), sold at Circular Quay and elsewhere, includes return ferry rides and zoo admission.

MANLY

Laid-back Manly may only be a 30-minute ferry ride from Sydney's CBD, but it feels like another world. This narrow peninsula near North Head boasts ocean and harbour beaches, excellent surfing and a distinct personality all of its own.

On the harbour side, the **Manly visitor centre** (Map pp52-3; ☎ 02-9976 1430; www.manlyaustralia.com.au; Manly Wharf, Manly; ⏲ 9am-5pm Mon-Fri, 10am-4pm Sat & Sun), just outside the ferry wharf, has free pamphlets along with information on the Manly Scenic Walkway. There is also a range of cafes, pubs and restaurants here. West of the wharf is **Oceanworld** (Map pp52-3; ☎ 02-8251 7877; www.oceanworld

.com.au; W Esplanade, Manly; adult/child/family $19/10/46; 10am-5.30pm), where you can get up close and alarmingly personal with giant stingrays, turtles, shoals of fish and Maia the shark in the underwater tunnels.

Manly's harbour is separated from the ocean by the **Corso**, a pedestrianised strip of surf shops, burger joints, juice bars and cafes that have not been entirely kind to the strip's heritage character. At the southern end of the beach, a footpath follows the ocean shoreline around a small headland to tiny **Fairy Bower Beach** and lovely **Shelly Beach**, which is great for snorkelling.

To get to Manly, catch the ferry, bus E69 from Wynyard, or bus 169 or 151 from the QVB.

NORTHERN BEACHES

Extending north from Manly, Sydney's northern **beaches** form a continuous 30km stretch of sleepy 'burbs, craggy headlands and over 20 beaches, including **Freshwater** (off Map pp52–3), **Curl Curl**, **Dee Why**, **Collaroy**, **Narrabeen** and **Warriewood** beaches. At the end of the line is well-heeled **Palm Beach**: *Home and Away* fans will definitely recognise the area. Of the more spectacular beaches, **Whale**, **Avalon** and **Bilgola** rank highly. Buses 169 and 136 run from Manly Wharf to Dee Why and Curl Curl respectively. Bus L90 runs from Wynyard station to Palm Beach.

ACTIVITIES

CYCLING

The best spot to get some spoke action in this bike-unfriendly city is Centennial Park. **Bicycle NSW** (**Map pp64-5; ☎ 02-9281 5400; www.bicyclensw.org.au; fl 5, 822 George St, Sydney**) publishes *Cycling Around Sydney*, which details 30 classic city rides.

Many cycle-hire shops require a hefty deposit on a credit card.

Centennial Park Cycles (**Map pp52-3; ☎ 02-9398 5027; www.cyclehire.com.au; Centennial Park; per hr/day from $15/50; 9am-5pm, last hire 4pm**) Located 100m past the intersection of Grand and Hamilton Drs.

CHRIS MELLOR

Sydney Harbour National Park (p67)

Inner City Cycles (Map pp52-3; ☎ 02-9660 6605; www.innercitycycles.com.au; 151 Glebe Point Rd, Glebe; per day/week $33/88; 🕑 9.30am-6pm Mon-Wed & Fri, to 7pm Thu, to 4pm Sat, 11am-3pm Sun)

DIVING

Sydney's best shore dives are to be found at Gordons Bay north of Coogee, Shark Point in Clovelly, and Ship Rock in Cronulla. Popular boat-dive sites include Wedding Cake Island off Coogee (Map pp52–3), The Heads, and off Royal National Park.

Dive Centre Bondi (Map pp52-3; ☎ 02-9369 3855; www.divebondi.com.au; 198 Bondi Rd, Bondi; 🕑 8.30am-6pm Mon-Fri, from 7.30am Sat & Sun) Four-day PADI course from $425; shore and boat dives.

Dive Centre Manly (Map pp52-3; ☎ 02-9977 4355; www.divesydney.com.au; 10 Belgrave St, Manly; 🕑 8.30am-6pm Mon-Fri, from 7.30am Sat & Sun) Similar rates and offerings as its sister office in Bondi.

GOLF

There are more than 80 golf courses in the metropolitan area, though many are members only. Book to play on public courses (especially at weekends).

Bondi Golf Club (Map pp52-3; ☎ 02-9130 1981; www.bondigolf.com.au; 5 Military Rd, North Bondi; 18 holes $20; 🕑 7am-sunset Mon, Tue, Thu & Fri, from 10.30am Wed, 12.30pm-sunset Sat & Sun)

Moore Park Golf Course (Map pp52-3; ☎ 02-9663 1064; www.mooreparkgolf.com.au; cnr Anzac Pde & Cleveland St, Moore Park; 18 holes Mon-Fri $45, Sat & Sun $55; 🕑 6am-10pm)

HORSE RIDING

Centennial Stables (Map pp52-3; ☎ 02-9360 5650; www.centennialstables.com.au; Pavilion B, cnr Cook & Lang Rds, Centennial Park; per hr incl equipment $95; 🕑 9am-5pm) Conducts one-hour horse rides around leafy Centennial Park. Other stables at the centre also conduct rides; equine familiarity is not required.

Eastside Riding Academy (☎ 02-9360 7521; www.eastsideriding.com.au)

Moore Park Stables (☎ 02-9360 8747; www.mooreparkstables.com.au)

SAILING

Sydney has dozens of yacht clubs and sailing schools. Even if you have wobbly sea legs, an introductory lesson is a super way to see the harbour.

Eastsail Sailing School (Map pp52-3; ☎ 02-9327 1166; www.eastsail.com.au; D'Albora Marina, New Beach Rd, Rushcutters Bay; 3hr cruise per person from $109; 🕑 9am-6pm) A sociable outfit offering cruises and introductory courses from $500.

Sydney by Sail (Map pp64-5; ☎ 02-9280 1110; www.sydneybysail.com.au; Festival Pontoon, National Maritime Museum, Darling Harbour; 3hr tour $150, course $425; 🕑 9am-5pm) Daily harbour sailing tours and introductory sailing courses.

SCENIC FLIGHTS

See Sydney's sights from up high with **Sydney Seaplanes** (Map pp52-3; ☎ 02-9388 1978, 1300 732 752; www.seaplanes.com.au; Lyne Park, Rose Bay; 15min scenic flights per person from $160; 🕑 times vary according to flights & weather conditions).

SURFING

On the eastern beaches hang ten at Bondi, Tamarama and Coogee, or Maroubra and Cronulla in the south. The North Shore is home to a dozen gnarly breaks between Manly and Palm Beach, including Curl Curl, Dee Why, Narrabeen, Mona Vale and Newport.

Aloha Surf (Map pp52-3; ☎ 02-9977 3777; www.aloha.com.au; 44 Pittwater Rd, Manly; board hire half/full day $20/40; 🕑 9am-6pm) Longboards, shortboards, bodyboards.

Let's Go Surfing (Map pp52-3; ☎ 02-9365 1800; www.letsgosurfing.com.au; 128 Ramsgate Ave, Bondi; 2hr lesson incl board & wetsuit adult/child from $79/40; 9am-6pm) Excellent small-group lessons. Board and wetsuit hire is $25 for two hours.

Manly Surf School (Map pp52-3; ☎ 02-9977 6977; www.manlysurfschool.com; North Steyne Surf Club, Manly; lessons per hr incl board & wetsuit adult/child $55/45; 9am-6pm) Small-group surf lessons.

SWIMMING

There are over 100 public swimming pools in Sydney and many beaches have protected ocean swimming pools. The harbour beaches offer sheltered and shark-netted swimming, but nothing beats (or cures a hangover faster than) being pounded by Pacific Ocean waves. Always swim within the flagged lifeguard-patrolled areas and be wary of rips: they can be lethal.

There are several spectacular outdoor city pools around town. Here are three of the best.

Andrew 'Boy' Charlton Pool (Map pp64-5; ☎ 02-9358 6686; www.abcpool.org; 1c Mrs Macquaries Rd, The Domain; adult/child $6/4; 6am-8pm Sep-Apr) A 50m outdoor heated saltwater pool, one of Sydney's best.

Icebergs (Map pp52-3; ☎ 02-9130 4804; 1 Notts Ave, Bondi Beach; adult/child $5/3; 6am-6.30pm Mon-Wed & Fri, from 6.30am Sat & Sun) Watch the sunrise over Bondi while swimming laps in this 50m ocean pool.

North Sydney Olympic Pool (Map pp52-3; ☎ 02-9955 2309; www.northsydney.nsw.gov.au; Alfred St South, Milsons Point; adult/child $6/3; 5.30am-9pm Mon-Fri, 7am-7pm Sat & Sun) Next to Luna Park, right on the harbour.

SYDNEY FOR CHILDREN

Sydney is heaven for ankle-biters. There are plenty of activities on offer, particularly during the school holidays (December, January, April, July and September). Check www.sydneyforkids.com.au and the kids' section of *Time Out* magazine. The free *Sydney's Child* and *Kid Friendly* magazines also have listings.

HOLGER LEUE

Bondi Icebergs pool and Bondi Beach

Beach-wise there are plenty of options, but some of the best include Balmoral Beach, Shelly Beach and Dee Why on the north shore and Clovelly Beach, Bronte Beach and the North Bondi Children's Pool on the eastern beaches.

Otherwise, Sydney Aquarium (p73), Taronga Zoo, Oceanworld and Luna Park (all p76) are sure-fire crowd pleasers, as are the twisting, turning water slides at **Manly Waterworks** (Map pp52-3; ☎ 02-9949 1088; www.manlywaterworks.com; cnr West Esplanade & Commonwealth Pde, Manly; per hr/day $15/20; 10am-5pm Sat & Sun).

TOURS

There are countless tours available in Sydney. You can book most of them at the visitor centres (p61).

CITY BUS TOURS

Bondi Explorer (☎ 13 15 00; www.sydneybuses.info; adult/child/family $39/19/97; 8.45am-4.15pm) Hop-on, hop-off 19-stop loop (two hours) from Circular Quay to Kings Cross, Double Bay, Rose Bay, Vaucluse, Watsons Bay, the Gap, Bondi Beach and Coogee, returning to the city along Oxford Street. Buses depart every 30 minutes; buy your ticket on board or at STA offices.

Sydney Explorer (☎ 13 15 00; www.sydneybuses.info; adult/child/family $39/19/97; 8.40am-5.20pm) The red hop-on, hop-off explorer bus visits 27 of Sydney's best attractions starting from Circular Quay through Kings Cross, Chinatown, Darling Harbour, The Rocks and across the Harbour Bridge. Tickets include discounted entry to attractions. Buses depart every 20 minutes.

HARBOUR CRUISES

Captain Cook Cruises (Map pp64-5; ☎ 02-9206 1111; www.captaincook.com.au; Jetty 6, Circular Quay; adult/child/family from $28/15/59; 8.30am-6pm) Range of harbour cruise options; also at Aquarium Wharf, Darling Harbour.

Matilda Cruises (Map pp64-5; ☎ 02-9264 7377; www.matilda.com.au; Pier 26, Aquarium Wharf, Darling Harbour; adult/child from $35/30; 9.30am-5.30pm) Hop-on hop-off harbour explorer trips plus catamaran, yacht and ferry cruises. Cocktail dinner cruises also available.

Sydney Ferries (Map pp64-5; ☎ 02-9246 8363; www.sydneyferries.info/cruises.htm; Wharf 4, Circular Quay; adult/child $30/15; 1.30pm Mon-Sat) Ninety-minute harbour cruises that come with live commentary and a souvenir badge.

Tribal Warrior (Map pp64-5; ☎ 02-9699 3491; www.tribalwarrior.org; Eastern Pontoon, Circular Quay; adult/child $55/45; 12.45pm Tue-Sat) See Sydney through Indigenous eyes; includes authentic cultural performances.

WALKING TOURS

Aboriginal Heritage Tour (Map pp64-5; ☎ 02-9231 8134; www.rbgsyd.nsw.gov.au; adult/child $25/13; 1hr tours 2pm Fri) Discover the Botanic Garden's rich Indigenous heritage and get to sample Australian bush foods on tours led by the garden's Aboriginal Education Officer.

Aboriginal Heritage – Walk The Rocks (Map pp64-5; ☎ 0403 686 433; adult/child $23/12) Walkabouts exploring Sydney's Aboriginal history. One hour tours depart from The Rocks Visitor Centre; check there for times.

Bounce Walking Tours (Map pp64-5; ☎ 1300 665 365; www.bouncewalkingtours.com.au; adult/concession from $25/20; 2-3hr tours daily, times vary according to tour) Fun guided walks departing from the Opera House. The Crimes & Passions Tour (Kings Cross) is especially popular.

GREG ELMS

Climbers on Sydney Harbour Bridge

BridgeClimb (Map pp64-5; ☎ 02-8274 7777; www.bridgeclimb.com; 5 Cumberland St, The Rocks; adult $179-295, child $109-195; 🕐 3½hr tours 7am-7pm) Choose between the original (over the top) and the Discovery Climb, which walks through the bridge's inner workings.

Sydney Architecture Walks (Map pp64-5; ☎ 02-8239 2211; www.sydneyarchitecture.org; adult/concession $25/20; 🕐 2hr walks) Four themed walks guided by young archi-buffs. Tours depart from the Museum of Sydney.

SLEEPING

Booking through an accommodation agency such as Tourism New South Wales (p61) can sometimes land you a discount.

BUDGET

Pink House (Map pp64-5; ☎ 02-9358 1689, 1800 806 385; www.pinkhouse.com.au; 6-8 Barncleuth Sq, Kings Cross; dm/d incl breakfast from $24/75; 💻) Travellers love the Pink House (yep, it's a pink house) with its laid-back hippy vibe more akin to student digs than a Kings Cross hostel. It has welcoming communal areas, generous dorm rooms and three leafy patios perfect for dealing with the effects of the night before.

Bondi Beachouse YHA (Map pp52-3; ☎ 02-9365 2088; www.bondibeachouse.com.au; 63 Fletcher St, Bondi; dm/d from $28/70; P 💻) The ever-excellent YHA outdoes itself with a fabulous rooftop terrace that comes complete with spa. The staff are great, there's free snorkelling and surfboards, and you're only a hop, skip and splash from the surf.

Wake Up! (Map pp64-5; ☎ 02-9288 7888; www.wakeup.com.au; 509 Pitt St, Sydney; dm from $28, d & tw from $98; ❄ 💻) A perennial favourite with backpackers is this mammoth hostel housed within a converted 1900s department store. Convivial, colourful and with the best backpacker bar in town, visitors inevitably find themselves staying far longer than they had originally planned.

Sydney Central YHA (Map pp64-5; ☎ 02-9218 9000; www.yha.com.au; 11 Rawson

Pl, Haymarket; dm from $36, d & tw from $102;) Sydney's biggest hostel is also one of the city's most popular. But it's not the bright rooms and excellent kitchen that draw the crowds (although these certainly help) – it's the fabulous rooftop pool that's perfect for making faces at the office workers in the tower across the street.

MIDRANGE

CITY CENTRE, THE ROCKS & CIRCULAR QUAY

Lord Nelson Brewery Hotel (Map pp64-5; ☎ 02-9251 4044; www.lordnelson.com.au; 19 Kent St, The Rocks; d with/without bathroom $190/130;) Built in 1841, this boutique sandstone hotel claims to be the oldest in Sydney. It's been beautifully renovated and each bedroom showcases a slice of history, with either the original stone wall or dormer window on display.

B&B Sydney Harbour (Map pp64-5; ☎ 02-9247 1130; www.bedandbreakfastsydney.com; 140-142 Cumberland St, The Rocks; s/d incl breakfast from $140/155;) Occupying a lovely corner in The Rocks is this gorgeous guest house that dates back to the late 1800s. The nine bedrooms are named after famous Australians and are charming without being twee. Breakfasts are served in the leafy courtyard garden.

Russell (Map pp64-5; ☎ 02-9241 3543; www.therussell.com.au; 143a George St, The Rocks; d incl breakfast from $150, with bathroom $235;) We love a hotel with a story and the Russell has one of the best in town – room 8 is reportedly haunted by a 19th-century sea captain! The other rooms might not receive paranormal visitors, but don't let that deter you: this is an excellent hotel in a brilliant location.

Vibe Hotel (Map pp64-5; ☎ 02-8272 3300; www.vibehotels.com.au; 111 Goulburn St, Sydney; d from $165;) In a city where hushed tones and minimalist decor are the norm, Vibe stands out (literally) thanks to its neon-pink sofas, lime-green armchairs and bold, stripy bed linen. The 'Vibe Out' space (complete with lava lamp) is positively Austin Powers. Good weekend rates.

PAUL BEINSSEN

Street performer, Circular Quay

CHINATOWN & DARLING HARBOUR AREA

Pensione Hotel (Map pp64-5; ☎ 02-9265 8888; www.pensione.com.au; 631-635 George St, Haymarket; s/d/tr/f $99/115/140/170;) Run by the group that owns ubertrendy Kirketon, this is budget boutique chic. Housed within an elegantly reworked post office, the rooms are small (some are *very* small) but comfortable. Aim for a rear room – George St traffic grumbles at night.

Capitol Square Hotel (Map pp64-5; ☎ 02-9211 8633; www.rydges.com/capitolsquare; cnr George & Campbell Sts, Haymarket; d from $105; P) The colour scheme may be unnervingly similar to a certain Swedish super store, but don't let that put you off. Rooms are tidy and bright and the deluxe rooms come with balconies. Wheelchair access is available; the hotel offers frequent internet deals.

Aaron's Hotel (Map pp64-5; ☎ 02-9281 5555; www.aaronshotel.com.au; 37 Ultimo Rd, Haymarket; s/d from $115/135;) Deceptively large is this renovated 19th-century building that features spacious, clean and light-filled rooms. It's a hit with backpackers, families and groups, particularly the courtyard rooms that look and feel positively penthouse-esque.

Metro Hotel Sydney Central (Map pp64-5; ☎ 02-9281 6999; www.metrohospitalitygroup.com; 431-439 Pitt St, Haymarket; d from $135; P) Centrally located, the courteous Metro has newly refurbished, modern deluxe rooms and Brett Whiteley prints along the corridors. The open-air rooftop pool should clinch the deal.

Vulcan Hotel (Map pp64-5; ☎ 02-9211 3283; www.vulcanhotel.com.au; 500 Wattle St, Ultimo; d from $139; P) If you like your design contemporary then the Vulcan is sure to please. An old pub and a row of terraced houses have been woven to form a grey-and-white boutique bolthole that channels a cool vibe minus any pretensions.

KINGS CROSS & AROUND

Hotel 59 (Map pp64-5; ☎ 02-9360 5900; www.hotel59.com.au; 59 Bayswater Rd, Kings Cross; s/d/f incl breakfast $88/110/132;) Without doubt one of the friendliest places in town is this lovely family-run hotel. The nine rooms may hark back to a time when Wham! and crimped hair were in vogue, but they are spotless and oddly charming. The central location only adds to the appeal.

Victoria Court Hotel (Map pp64-5; ☎ 02-9357 3200; www.victoriacourt.com.au; 122 Victoria St, Potts Point; d incl breakfast $99-330; P) Decorated to within an inch of its life, this welcoming guest house fills a pair of three-storey 1881 brick terrace houses. The 25 rooms have private bathrooms, TV and plenty of flowery soft furnishings. The deluxe rooms come with a leafy private terrace.

Mariners Court (Map pp64-5; ☎ 02-9358 3888; www.marinerscourt.com.au; 44-50 McElhone St, Woolloomooloo; d/tr/f incl breakfast $154/174/198; P) Shipshape rooms and a stellar location around the corner from celeb hangout Woolloomooloo Wharf make this hidden gem a winner. There are lots of other added bonuses, too: the espresso machine at breakfast and the harbour glimpses from the 3rd-floor terrace.

Simpsons of Potts Point (Map pp64-5; ☎ 02-9356 2199; www.simpsonshotel.com; 8 Challis Ave, Potts Point; d incl breakfast $175-330; P) This handsome building had been carved up into apartments until it was painstakingly restored in the late 1980s. Today the heritage-listed building offers 14 luxurious rooms with fireplaces, balconies and antique prints.

Enjoy complimentary port in the elegant lounge and delicious breakfasts in the sunny conservatory.

MANLY

Periwinkle Guest House (Map pp52-3; ☎ 02-9977 4668; www.periwinkle.citysearch.com.au; 18-19 East Esplanade, Manly; s/d incl breakfast from $115/139; P) In a quiet corner of Manly, two Federation-style houses have been combined to create this relaxed guest house with 17 pretty bedrooms. Plump for a room on the top floor facing Manly Cove or our favourite, room 7, which is perfectly positioned for catching the winter sun.

TOP END

CITY CENTRE

Hyde Park Inn (Map pp64-5; ☎ 02-9264 6001; www.hydeparkinn.com.au; 271 Elizabeth St, Sydney; s/d/f incl breakfast from $176/193/209; P) The Hyde Park Inn has had a makeover and what a transformation: the 1980s colour palette has been replaced with neutral tones, contemporary furnishings and all manner of high-tech gadgets. The deluxe rooms have balconies overlooking Hyde Park.

Hilton (Map pp64-5; ☎ 02-9266 2000; www.sydney.hilton.com; 488 George St, Sydney; d from $270; P) This Hilton is a whole lot classier than the one who regularly graces the pages of celebrity magazines. The rooms are contemporary, chic and surprisingly spacious, while the fabulous Zeta Bar is reason alone to check in.

BLUE Sydney (Map pp64-5; ☎ 02-9331 9000; www.tajhotels.com/sydney; 6 Cowper Wharf Rd, Woolloomooloo; d from $360; P) Stay here for the night and boast that you slept next to Russell Crowe (he owns one of the apartments at the end of the wharf). But even if he's not your cup of tea, you're sure to enjoy the boutique sensibilities of this Taj-owned hotel.

Establishment Hotel (Map pp64-5; ☎ 02-9240 3100; www.establishmenthotel.com; 5 Bridge Lane, Sydney; d from $365;) Still one of the hippest hotels in town, Establishment continues to lure the superstars, supermodels and those who just wish they were. The guest rooms are all beautifully decorated but the New York-style penthouse suites are simply sublime.

EATING

If there's one thing Sydney does well it's food. Brunches, lunches, morning tea, high tea, pre-dinner appetisers, get-me-through-the-afternoon snacks or just plain old dinner, this city knows how to eat and you will rarely (and we mean hardly ever) have a bad meal.

CITY CENTRE, THE ROCKS & CIRCULAR QUAY

You'll find everything in the city centre from frenzied lunchtime sandwich shops to some of Sydney's best culinary experiences.

Cafe Sydney (Map pp64-5; ☎ 02-9251 8683; 5th fl, Customs House, 31 Alfred St, Sydney; mains $32-39; lunch Mon-Fri & Sun, dinner Mon-Sat) The amazing rooftop location above Customs House is spectacular, but if views of the harbour don't sell Cafe Sydney the food definitely will. The seasonal menu reflects a strong seafood theme, with freshly shucked oysters, seared scallops and tandoori-roasted blue-eye cod all making regular appearances.

Guillaume at Bennelong (Map pp64-5; ☎ 02-9241 1999; Sydney Opera House, Bennelong Point, Sydney; mains $35-42; lunch Thu & Fri, dinner Mon-Sat) Indulge in master chef Guillaume Brahimi's delectable creations under the sails of the city's most famous landmark. Snuggle into a banquette or sit yourself next to the window, and don't leave without trying the basil-infused tuna with mustard seed and soy vinaigrette.

Rockpool (Map pp64-5; ☎ 02-9252 1888; 107 George St, The Rocks; mains $52-59; 🕑 dinner Tue-Sat) Chef Neil Perry's innovative take on cooking results in modern seafood creations that consistently wow the critics. Even those on a budget can enjoy his work: grab a seat at the bar and order the Moroccan fish burger ($15) or half a dozen oysters.

Quay (Map pp64-5; ☎ 02-9251 5600; Level 3, Overseas Passenger Terminal, The Rocks; 4-course menu $145; 🕑 lunch Tue-Fri, dinner daily) Peter Gilmore's cooking is imaginative, delicate and beautifully executed. Add to this the iconic Sydney views and outstanding wine list and you've got a dining experience to remember. The two-course set lunch ($75 per person) is an excellent deal.

CHINATOWN & DARLING HARBOUR

Head to Chinatown for cheap and cheerful yum cha, noodles and barbecue duck, and to Darling Harbour for views and good (but pricier) food.

Din Tai Fung (Map pp64-5; ☎ 02-9264 6010; World Square Shopping Centre, 644 George St, Sydney; mains $4-16; 🕑 lunch & dinner) The immensely popular Taipei-based global chain has set up shop in Sydney and not surprisingly there are queues day and night. But the wait is worth it especially if you choose the expertly crafted *xiaolongbao* ('little dragon buns'). Ridiculously delicious.

Blackbird (Map pp64-5; ☎ 02-9283 7385; Cockle Bay Wharf, Darling Harbour; mains $16-33) This place is fun, funky and a little quirky with hearty bowls of pasta, New York-style pizzas and big burgers on the menu. Popular with students for the daily $12 specials, it's a great place to fill up before a night out.

KINGS CROSS, POTTS POINT & WOOLLOOMOOLOO

Cool cafes, even cooler restaurants and late-night fast-food joints populate the Cross.

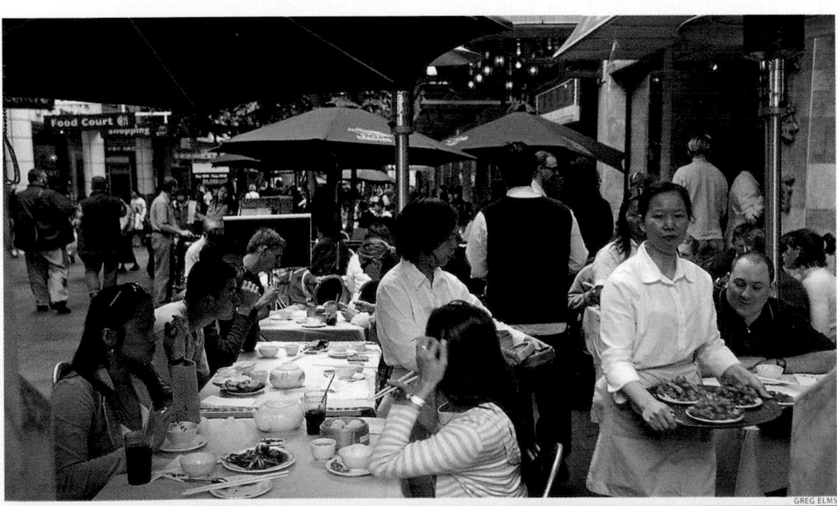

GREG ELMS

Eating yum cha, Chinatown

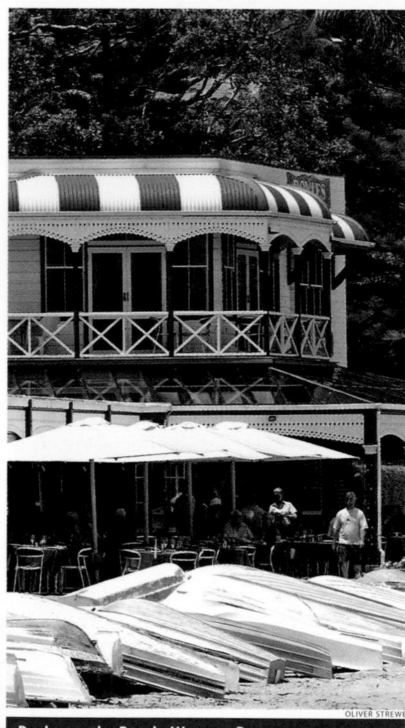
OLIVER STREWE
Doyles on the Beach, Watsons Bay

Harry's Café de Wheels (Map pp64-5; ☎ 02-9357 3074; Cowper Wharf Roadway, Woolloomooloo; mains $5-10) You've not been to Australia until you've had a pie, and Harry's serves up some of the best. For over 50 years, cabbies, sailors and Saturday night party people have slurred orders over Harry's famous counter.

Fratelli Paradiso (Map pp64-5; ☎ 02-9357 1744; 12 Challis Ave, Potts Point; mains $17-29; ⏰ breakfast & lunch daily, dinner Mon-Fri) This stylish banquette-lined trattoria is so Italian it should be in Rome. The menu is in Italian, the staff are Italian and the food is so damn tasty it can only be Italian. Try the melt-in-your-mouth calamari or the ravioli with veal, but be prepared to queue: locals love this spot.

PADDINGTON, WOOLLAHRA & EASTERN SUBURBS

Sean's Panaroma (Map p52-3; ☎ 02-9365 4924; 270 Campbell Pde, Bondi; mains $25-36; ⏰ lunch Fri-Sun, dinner Wed-Sat) Sean Moran's ever-changing menu hangs on swinging squares of chalked blackboard in this modest but romantic diner with ocean views, hearty seasonal dishes and friendly service.

Doyles on the Beach (Map pp52-3; ☎ 02-9337 2007; 11 Marine Pde, Watsons Bay; mains $30-60; ⏰ lunch & dinner) There may well be better places for seafood, but few can compete with Doyles' location or its history – this restaurant first opened in 1885. Catching the harbour ferry to Watsons Bay for a seafood lunch is a quintessential Sydney experience.

Bondi Icebergs (Map pp52-3; ☎ 02-9365 9000; 1 Notts Ave, Bondi; mains $38-97; ⏰ lunch & dinner Tue-Sun) When Hollywood A-listers come to town they head immediately to Icebergs. Something of a Sydney institution, this snazzy restaurant has phenomenal views across Bondi Beach, an excellent menu specialising in seafood and wagyu steaks, and a superb wine list.

NORTH SHORE

Bathers' Pavilion Café (Map pp52-3; ☎ 02-9969 5050; 4 The Esplanade, Balmoral; mains $16-34; ⏰ lunch & dinner) Gazing out over Balmoral Beach from within this iconic Spanish Mission–style restaurant is a true Sydney experience. The well-heeled North Shore crowd favours the restaurant next door, but the cafe section serves equally tasty food with a more affordable price tag.

ENTERTAINMENT

Sydney has an energetic and often underrated arts, entertainment and music scene. It's vibrant, eclectic and constantly changing, with innovative and eclectic theatre, a healthy live music scene (rock, jazz, classical and everything in between) and numerous showcases for the city's visual and performing arts. Outdoor cinemas and sports stadiums cater to families.

Tickets for most shows can be purchased directly from venues or the following distributors:

Moshtix (Map pp64-5; ☎ 02-9209 4614; www.moshtix.com.au; Red Eye Records, 370 Pitt St; 9am-6pm Mon-Wed & Fri, to 9pm Thu, to 5pm Sat, 11am-5pm Sun) Servicing alternative music venues.

Ticketek (Map pp64-5; ☎ 13 28 49; www.ticketek.com.au; 195 Elizabeth St; 9am-5pm Mon-Wed, to 7pm Thu & Fri, to 4pm Sat)

Ticketmaster (Map pp64-5; ☎ 13 61 00; www.ticketmaster.com.au; State Theatre, 49 Market St; 9am-5pm Mon-Fri)

CINEMAS

Unless otherwise stated, tickets generally cost $15 to $17 for an adult and $10 to $13 for a child. Most cinemas have a cheap night when tickets are discounted by around a third.

Dendy Opera Quays (Map pp64-5; ☎ 02-9247 3800; www.dendy.com.au; Shop 9, 2 Circular Quay E) Right on the harbour is this classy cinema where you can enjoy a glass of wine with your art-house flick. There's also a Dendy cinema in Newtown (Map pp52–3; ☎ 02-9550 5699; 261–263 King St).

George Street Cinemas (Map pp64-5; ☎ 02-9273 7333; www.greaterunion.com.au; 505-525 George St) Three huge complexes screening nonstop Hollywood fare.

IMAX (Map pp64-5; ☎ 02-9281 3300; www.imax.com.au; 31 Wheat Rd, Darling Harbour; adult/child $20/15) Watch supersized films on an eight-storey screen with both kid-friendly docs (sharks, space, haunted castles etc) and grown-up films (U2, Batman). Many are in 3-D.

Open Air Cinema (Map pp64-5; ☎ 1300 366 649; www.stgeorge.com.au/openair; Mrs Macquaries Point, Royal Botanic Gardens; adult/concession $24/22; box office 6.30pm, screenings 8.30pm Jan & Feb) This three-storey screen rises from the harbour with the bridge as its backdrop. Book tickets early: the season sells out within days.

THEATRE

Many theatres have cheap midweek pay-what-you-can (minimum price $10 per ticket) and under-30 deals.

Sydney Comedy Store (Map pp52-3; ☎ 02-9357 1419; www.comedystore.com.au; Entertainment Quarter, 122 Lang Rd, Moore Park; tickets $15-30; box office 10am-6pm Mon, to midnight Tue-Sat) This purpose-built comedy hall lures big-time Australian and overseas comics, including Edinburgh Festival stand-ups, and nurtures new talent with open-mic and 'New Comics' nights.

Sydney Theatre (Map pp64-5; ☎ 02-9250 1999; www.sydneytheatre.org.au; 22 Hickson Rd, Walsh Bay; tickets $35-130; box office 9am-8.30pm Mon-Sat, 3-5.30pm Sun) The resplendent Sydney Theatre at the base of Observatory Hill puts 896 bums on seats for specialist drama and dance. Wharf 1 stages reliably good theatre; Wharf 2 is more experimental.

Sydney Theatre Company (Map pp64-5; ☎ 02-9250 1777; www.sydneytheatre.com.au; Pier 4, Hickson Rd, Walsh Bay; tickets from $30; box office 9am-7pm Mon, to 8.30pm Tue-Fri, from 11am Sat, 2hr pre-show Sun) Working in tandem with the Sydney Theatre across the road, Artistic Directors Cate Blanchett and Andrew Upton lead the way for Sydney's premier theatre company.

Major theatres hosting West End and Broadway musicals, opera and concerts (tickets from $50 to $150):

Capitol Theatre (Map pp64-5; ☎ 02-9320 5000; www.capitoltheatre.com.au; 13 Campbell St, Haymarket; box office 9am-5pm Mon-Fri)

Lyric Theatre (Map pp64-5; ☎ 02-9657 8500; www.lyrictheatre.com.au; Star City Casino, 80 Pyrmont St, Pyrmont) Bookings through Ticketmaster (p87).

State Theatre (Map pp64-5; ☎ 02-9373 6655; www.statetheatre.com.au; 49 Market St; box office 9am-5pm Mon-Fri, to 8pm performance nights)

Theatre Royal (Map pp64-5; ☎ 02-9224 8444; www.theatreroyal.net.au; MLC Centre, 108 King St) Bookings through Ticketek (p87).

LIVE MUSIC

CLASSICAL

Sydney Opera House (Map pp64-5; ☎ 02-9250 7777; www.sydneyoperahouse.com; Bennelong Point, Circular Quay E; ticket prices vary with shows; box office 9am-8.30pm Mon-Sat) As well as theatre and dance, the Opera House (p68) regularly hosts the following classy classicists: **Australian Chamber Orchestra** (☎ 02-8274 3800; www.aco.com.au); **Musica Viva** (☎ 02-8394 6666; www.mva.org.au); **Opera Australia** (☎ 02-9699 1099; www.opera-australia.org.au); **Sydney Philharmonic Choirs** (☎ 02-9251 2024; www.sydneyphilharmonia.com.au); and **Sydney Symphony** (☎ 02-8215 4600; www.sydneysymphony.com).

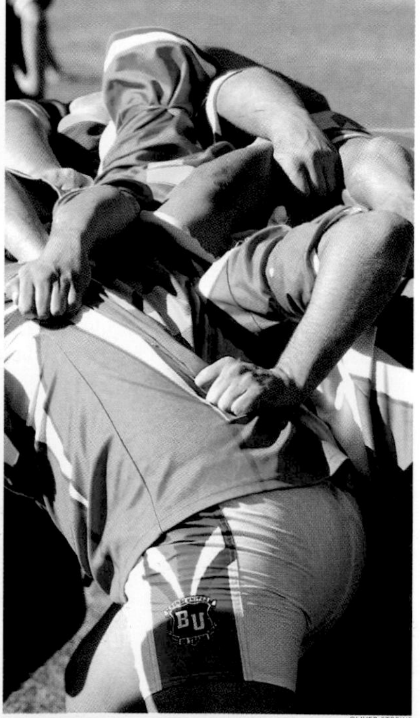
OLIVER STREWE

Under-17s play Rugby League

JAZZ & BLUES

Basement (Map pp64-5; ☎ 02-9251 2797; www.thebasement.com.au; 29 Reiby Pl, Circular Quay; tickets from $39; noon-1.30am Mon-Thu, to 2.30am Fri, 7.30pm-3am Sat, 7pm-1am Sun) Sydney's premier jazz venue has played host to all the greats from Dizzy Gillespie to Herbie Hancock, but it's not all scat – funk, blues, rock and reggae also feature on the musical menu with big international and local names. Book a table by the stage.

SPECTATOR SPORTS

Like most Australians, Sydneysiders are passionate about sport. But nothing gets the red-blooded Aussie male going (or grabs newspaper headlines) quite like the **National Rugby League** (NRL; www.nrl.com.au; Ticketek tickets $10-55). The season unfolds at suburban stadiums and **Aussie Stadium** (Map pp52-3; ☎ 02-9360 6601; www.aussiestadium.com; Driver Ave, Moore Park), with September finals. The fever-inducing NSW versus Queensland State of Origin series is played annually.

From March to September, the 2005 premiers Sydney Swans play in the **Australian Football League** (AFL; www.afl.com.au; Ticketmaster tickets $20-40) at the **Sydney Cricket Ground** (Map pp52-3; ☎ 02-9360 6601; www.sydneycricketground.com.au; Driver Ave, Moore Park) and **ANZ Stadium** (off Map pp52-3; ☎ 02-8765

2000; www.anzstadium.com.au; Olympic Blvd, Homebush Bay).

The **cricket** (www.cricket.com.au) season runs from October to March. The Sydney Cricket Ground plays host to Sheffield Shield (interstate competition) matches and sell-out international Test, one-day and Twenty20 matches.

SHOPPING

Shopping in Sydney is a mixed bag: fast and furious among the department, chain and high-end shops of the city centre, while neighbourhoods such as Paddington and Newtown offer a distinctly more leisurely (and enjoyable) retail experience.

Head to Oxford Street (Paddington) for upmarket boutiques and high-street shops, Queen St (Woollahra) for art and antiques, Transvaal Ave (Double Bay) for high-end labels, King St (Newtown) for independent designers and arty bookshops, and the streets of Surry Hills for off-beat designer furniture and fashion.

ART

Aquabumps Gallery (Map pp64-5; ☎ 02-9130 7788; 151 Curlewis St, Bondi) Photographer/surfer Eugene Tan has been snapping photos of Sydney's sunrises, surf and sand for 10 years and his colourful prints hang in this cool space, a splash from Bondi Beach.

Gavala (Map pp64-5; ☎ 02-9212 7232; Shop 131, Harbourside Centre, Darling Harbour) Aboriginal-owned store sells only authentic Indigenous products that are licensed, authorised or purchased directly from artists and communities. It stocks paintings, weavings, didgeridoos, boomerangs, masks, jewellery and more.

Hogarth Galleries (Map pp64-5; ☎ 02-9360 6839; 7 Walker Lane, Paddington) This privately run gallery has been supporting and promoting Aboriginal art for over 30 years, in addition to exhibiting works by Australian artists including Sidney Nolan.

AUSTRALIANA

Flame Opals (Map pp64-5; ☎ 02-9247 3446; 119 George St, The Rocks) Shimmering opals are sold in all shapes and sizes at this outlet, and prices range from about $20 to 'If you have to ask, you can't afford it'. There's a tax-free concession for overseas customers.

RM Williams (Map pp64-5; ☎ 02-9262 2228; 389 George St, Sydney) The unofficial uniform for urban cowboys and country folk, this hard-wearing outback gear is so quintessentially Australian it even has its own starring role in Baz Luhrmann's epic *Australia*. Favourites include oilskin jackets, leather work boots and Nicole Kidman-inspired blouses and jackets.

MARKETS

Paddington Market (Map pp52-3; ☎ 02-9331 2923; St John's Church, 395 Oxford St, Paddington; ⏲ 10am-4pm Sat) Born in 1973, Sydney's most attended weekend market has been the launching pad for some of Australia's high-profile fashion labels. Some 250 stalls flog jewellery, homewares, beauty products, art, palmistry and more. Parking is miserable – take public transport.

Rocks Market (Map pp64-5; ☎ 02-9240 8717; George St, The Rocks; ⏲ 10am-5pm Sat & Sun) Under a canopy of white sails, 150 stalls vie for tourists' attention with homemade jams, frames, photography, Indigenous artwares and other presents for folks back home.

SHOPPING CENTRES & DEPARTMENT STORES

Queen Victoria Building (QVB; Map pp64-5; ☎ 02-9264 9209; 455 George St, Sydney)

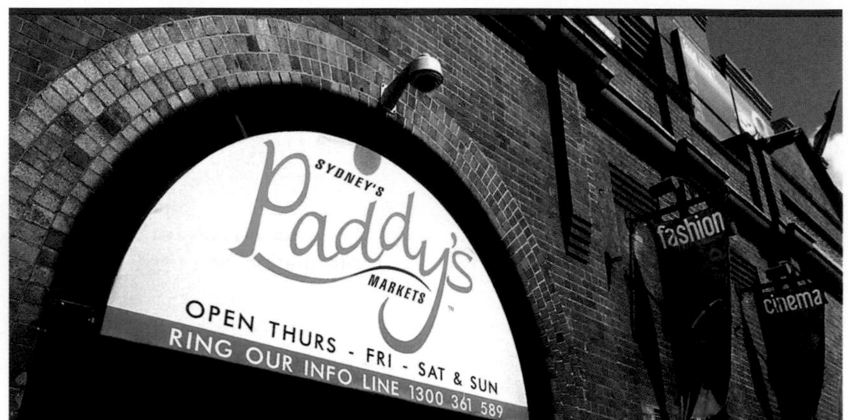

GREG ELMS

Paddy's Markets

IF YOU LIKE...

If you like poking around market stalls, such as the weekend market at the Rocks (p89), we think you might like these other markets:

- **Balmain Market** (Map pp52-3; ☎ 0418 765 736; 223 Darling St, Balmain; 8am-4pm Sat) Set in the shady grounds of St Andrews Congregational, stalls sell art, crafts, books, clothing, plants, and fruit and veg.
- **Bondi Markets** (☎ 02-9315 8988; Bondi Beach Public School, cnr Campbell Pde & Warners Ave, Bondi; 10am-4pm Sun) When school's out the yard fills up with stalls selling everything from vintage clothing and bric-a-brac to wooden frames and jewellery. It's great for grabbing a bargain from up-and-coming fashion designers.
- **Glebe Markets** (☎ 0419 291 449; Glebe Public School, cnr Glebe Point Rd & Derby Pl, Glebe; 10am-4pm Sat) Inner-city hippies flock here for vintage duds, new designers, arts and crafts, a chai latte and restorative massage. Live bands add to the festival vibe.
- **Paddy's Markets** (Map pp64-5; ☎ 1300 361 589; cnr Hay & Thomas Sts, Haymarket; 9am-5pm Thu-Sun) Among the dozens of stalls selling flashing toys, cheap backpacks and mobile phone covers, you'll find Ugg boots and other Aussie sheepskin memorabilia for a fraction of the price asked in shops.

Completed in 1898 this Victorian masterpiece occupies an entire city block. Die-hard shoppers will no doubt find something to buy, but we say forget the shops and focus instead on the intricate tiled floors, stained-glass windows and magnificent central dome.

Strand Arcade (Map pp64-5; ☎ 02-9232 4199; 412-414 George St, Sydney) The last remaining arcade of the five originally built in Sydney, the Strand matches the QVB in terms of splendour but wins in the style stakes; the shopping options here are much better.

GETTING THERE & AWAY

AIR

Sydney's Kingsford Smith Airport (Map pp52-3; ☎ 02-9667 9111; www.sydneyairport.com.au) is Australia's busiest. It's only 10km south of the city centre, making access easy, but this also means that flights cease between 11pm and 5am due to noise regulations. The T1 (international) terminal is a 4km bus ($6) or train ($14, or $6 if you are transferring between flights) ride from the T2 (domestic) and T3 (Qantas domestic) terminals.

You can fly into Sydney from all the usual international points and from within Australia. **Qantas** (☎ 13 13 13; www.qantas.com.au), **Jetstar** (☎ 13 15 38; www.jetstar.com.au) and **Virgin Blue** (☎ 13 67 89; www.virginblue.com.au) have frequent flights to other capital cities. Smaller Qantas-affiliated airlines fly to smaller Oz destinations.

For air travel to/from Australia, see p380.

BUS

All private interstate and regional bus travellers arrive at **Sydney Coach Terminal** (Map pp64-5; ☎ 02-9281 9366; Central Station, Eddy Ave; 6am-10.30pm).

The government's CountryLink rail network is also complemented by coaches. Most buses stop in the suburbs on the way in and out of Sydney. If you hold a VIP or YHA discount card, shop around the major bus companies with offices here: **Firefly** (☎ 1300 730 740; www.fireflyexpress.com.au); **Greyhound** (☎ 13 14 99; www.greyhound.com.au); **Murrays** (☎ 13 22 51; www.murrays.com.au); or **Premier** (☎ 13 34 10; www.premierms.com.au).

TRAIN

Sydney's main rail terminus for CountryLink interstate and regional services is **Central Station** (Map pp64-5; ☎ 13 22 32; www.countrylink.info; Eddy Ave; staffed ticket booths 6am-10pm, ticket machines 24hr). Call for information, reservations and arrival/departure times. CountryLink discounts often nudge 40% on economy fares – sometimes cheaper than buses!

GETTING AROUND

For information on buses, ferries and trains call the **Transport Infoline** (☎ 13 15 00; www.131500.com.au).

TO/FROM THE AIRPORT

One of the easiest ways to get to and from the airport is with a shuttle company such as **Kingsford Smith Transport** (KST; ☎ 02-9666 9988; www.kst.com.au; one way/return $13/22; 5am-11pm), which services hotels in the city, Kings Cross and Darling Harbour. Bookings are essential.

The **Airport Link** (☎ 02-8337 8417; www.airportlink.com.au; one way/return from Central Station to domestic terminal $15/22, to international terminal $15/23; 5am-midnight) train runs to and from the airport terminals every 10 to 15 minutes.

Taxi fares from the airport are approximately $25 to $35 to Circular Quay, $40 to $50 to North Sydney and Bondi, and $60 to Manly.

BOAT

FERRY

Sydney's most civilised and popular transport option, harbour ferries and RiverCats depart from Circular Quay. Most ferries operate between 6am and midnight; those servicing tourist attractions operate shorter hours. The **Ferry Information Office** (Map pp64-5; ☎ 13 15 00; www.sydneyferries.info; 7am-5.45pm Mon-Sat, 8am-5.45pm Sun) at Circular Quay has details. Many ferries have connecting bus services. A one-way inner-harbour ride on a ferry costs $5/3 adult/concession. A

GREG ELMS
A Circular Quay–bound ferry (p91), Sydney Harbour

one-way RiverCat ride to Parramatta (50 minutes, every 50 minutes) costs $8/4 adult/concession.

WATER TAXI

Water taxis ply dedicated shuttle routes; rides to/from other harbour venues can be booked.

Watertours (**Map pp64-5; ☎ 02-9211 7730; www.watertours.com.au; 9.30am-late**) Opera House to Darling Harbour $15/10 adult/child; one-hour harbour tours $35/20; Nightlights tours $20/15.

Yellow Water Taxis (**Map pp64-5; ☎ 02-9555 9778, 1300 138 840; www.yellowwatertaxis.com.au; 9am-late**) Circular Quay to Darling Harbour $15/10 adult/child; 45-minute harbour tours $30/20.

BUS

Sydney buses run almost everywhere; Bondi Beach, Coogee and parts of the North Shore are serviced only by bus. Nightrider buses operate skeletally after regular services cease around midnight.

The main city bus stops are Circular Quay, Wynyard Park (York St) and Railway Sq. Buy tickets from newsagents, 7-Elevens, Bus TransitShops and on some buses. Pay the driver as you enter, or dunk prepaid tickets in ticket machines by the doors. Fares start at $2. There's a **Bus TransitShop** (**Map pp64-5; www.sydneybuses.info; cnr Alfred & Loftus Sts; 7am-7pm Mon-Fri, 8.30am-5pm Sat & Sun**) at Circular Quay, and there are others at the Queen Victoria Building, Railway Sq and Wynyard Station (all Map pp64–5).

CAR & MOTORCYCLE

Cars are good for day trips out of town, but drive in the city and you'll spend more time looking for somewhere to park (and pay through the nose for it) than you will anything else.

RENTAL

Major rental agencies with offices in Sydney:

Avis (**☎ 13 63 33; www.avis.com.au**)
Budget (**☎ 1300 362 848; www.budget.com.au**)
Europcar (**☎ 1300 131 390; www.europcar.com.au**)
Hertz (**☎ 13 30 39; www.hertz.com.au**)
Thrifty (**☎ 1300 367 227; www.thrifty.com.au**)

ROAD TOLLS

Driving around Sydney can be expensive owing to the plethora of toll roads. There's a $4 southbound toll on the Sydney Harbour Bridge and Tunnel. If you're heading from the North Shore to the eastern suburbs, it's easier to take the tunnel. There's a $5 northbound toll on the Eastern Distributor and the Cross

City Tunnel costs $4 one way. Sydney's main motorways (M2, M4, M5 and M7) are also tolled ($3 to $6), as are the Lane Cove Tunnel and Flacon St Gateway.

You can pay cash on the Eastern Distributor, M4, M5 and M2, but all other roads are electronically operated. Look into getting an **e-Pass** (www.roamexpress.com.au), a temporary toll pass. Check www.rta.nsw.gov.au for the latest info.

FARE DEALS

The **SydneyPass** (www.sydneypass.info) offers three, five or seven days' unlimited travel over eight days on STA buses, ferries and within the rail network's Red TravelPass zone (inner suburbs). Passes include the Airport Express, Sydney and Bondi Explorer buses, RiverCats and three STA-operated harbour cruises. They cost $110/55/275 per adult/child/family (three days), $145/70/365 (five days) and $165/80/410 (seven days). Buy passes from STA offices, train stations, Bus TransitShops, the Sydney Ferry ticket offices at Circular Quay and Manly Wharf, and from Airport Express and Explorer bus drivers.

MONORAIL & METRO LIGHT RAIL (MLR)

The privately operated **Metro Monorail** (☎ 02-8584 5288; www.metrotransport.com.au; circuit $5, day pass adult/family $10/23; 🕒 every 3-5min 7am-10pm Mon-Thu, to midnight Fri & Sat, 8am-10pm Sun) is an elevated electronic worm circling around Darling Harbour and the city. The full loop takes about 14 minutes.

Run by the same company, the futuristic **Metro Light Rail** (MLR; Zone 1 adult/concession $3/2, Zone 1 & 2 adult/concession $4/3, day pass adult/concession $9/7; 🕒 24hr, every 10-15min 6am-midnight, every 30min midnight-6am) glides between Central Station and Pyrmont via Chinatown and Darling Harbour. The Zone 2 service beyond Pyrmont to Lilyfield stops at 11pm Sunday to Thursday, midnight Friday and Saturday. Purchase tickets on board.

Note that the SydneyPass isn't valid on the monorail or the MLR.

TAXI

Taxis and cab ranks proliferate in Sydney. Flag fall is $3.10, then it's $1.85 per kilometre (plus 20% from 10pm to 6am). The waiting charge is 80c per minute. Passengers must also pay bridge, tunnel and road tolls (even if you don't incur them 'outbound', the returning driver will incur them 'inbound').

The four major taxi companies offering phone bookings ($2 fee):

Legion (☎ 13 14 51)
Premier Cabs (☎ 13 10 17)
Silver Service (☎ 13 31 00)
Taxis Combined (☎ 13 33 00)

TRAIN

Sydney's vast suburban rail network bumbles along, providing good service for some areas and absolutely none whatsoever for the northern and southern beaches, Balmain or Glebe. All suburban trains stop at Central Station, and usually one or more of the other seven City Circle stations, too.

For train information, visit the **CityRail Information Booth** (Map pp64-5; ☎ 13 15 00; www.131500.com.au; Wharf 5, Circular Quay; 🕒 9.05am-4.50pm).

AROUND SYDNEY

Sydney's extensive urban sprawl eventually dissolves into superb national parks and historic small towns. North of Sydney, where the Hawkesbury River meets the sea, lies **Ku-Ring-Gai Chase National Park**, a dense cluster of forests, creeks and sheltered coves with a rich Aboriginal heritage. To the south, Royal National Park hides lost-to-the-world beaches, rainforest pockets and precipitous cliffscapes. The wooded foothills of the Great Dividing Range sit to the west of Sydney and climb to the magnificent Blue Mountains.

BOTANY BAY

In May 1787 the First Fleet left Britain for Australia, bound for Botany Bay. However, the sandy infertile soil was unsuitable for settlement and they moved to the natural harbour of Port Jackson to the north.

Today Botany Bay, on the city's southern fringe, is a smoke-stacked industrial heartland. Despite the refineries it still has scenic stretches and continues to hold a special place in Australian history. Joseph Banks, Cook's expedition's naturalist, named the bay for the many botanical specimens he found here.

Botany Bay National Park (**cars $7, pedestrians & cyclists free; 7am-7.30pm Sep-May, to 5.30pm Jun-Aug**) occupies both headlands of the bay – 458 hectares of bushland and coastal walking tracks, picnic areas, sheltered coves and beaches. A sandstone obelisk marks Cook's landing place in Kurnell, on the southern side of the park.

ROYAL NATIONAL PARK

The 15,080-hectare **Royal National Park** (**cars $11, pedestrians & cyclists free; gates to park areas locked at 8.30pm daily**) was established in 1879, making it the oldest national park in the world after Yellowstone in the USA. Here you'll find pockets of subtropical rainforest, windblown coastal scrub, sandstone gullies dominated by gum trees, fresh- and saltwater wetlands, and isolated beaches. Traditionally the home of the Dharawal people, there are also numerous Aboriginal sites and artefacts.

The national park begins at Port Hacking, 30km south of Sydney, and stretches 20km further south. Its main road detours to Bundeena, a small town on Port Hacking, the starting point for kayaking tours of the park and the 17km-long **Bundeena-Maianbar Heritage Walk**.

Within the park there's sheltered swimming at Wattamolla and Bonnie Vale, and good surf at Garie Beach, Era and Burning Palms.

The **visitor centre** (**02-9542 0648; www.environment.nsw.gov.au/nationalparks; Farnell Ave, Audley; 9am-4pm**) can assist with camping permits, maps and bushwalking details.

From Sydney, take the Princes Hwy south and turn off at Farnell Ave, south of Loftus, to the park's northern end – it's about a 45-minute drive from the city.

HAWKESBURY RIVER

Less than an hour from Sydney the slow-roaming Hawkesbury River is a favourite weekend destination for stressed-out city folk. The river – one of the longest in eastern Australia – flows past honeycomb-coloured cliffs, historic townships and riverside hamlets into bays and inlets and between a series of national parks.

The **Riverboat Postman** (**02-9985 7566; www.hawkesburyriverferries.com.au; Riverboat Postman Wharf, Brooklyn; adult/child/family $50/30/130; 9.30am Mon-Fri**), Australia's last operating mail boat, chugs 40km up the Hawkesbury as far as Marlow, near Spencer. There are additional 'coffee cruises' during summer.

If you feel like exploring, rev the river in an outboard dinghy from the **Berowra Waters Marina** (**02-9456 7000; www.barbecueboat.info; 199 Bay Rd, Berowra Waters; per half day $75; 8am-5pm**). Nearby, elegant **Berowra Waters Inn** (**02-9456 1027; www.berowrawatersinn.com; 4/5/6 courses $125/135/150; lunch Fri-Sun, dinner Thu-Sat**) is one of the region's best restaurants. The restaurant is only accessed by boat.

➘ NEW SOUTH WALES

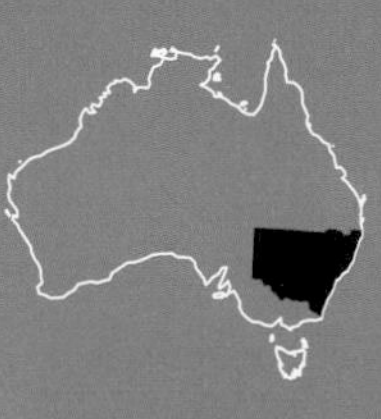

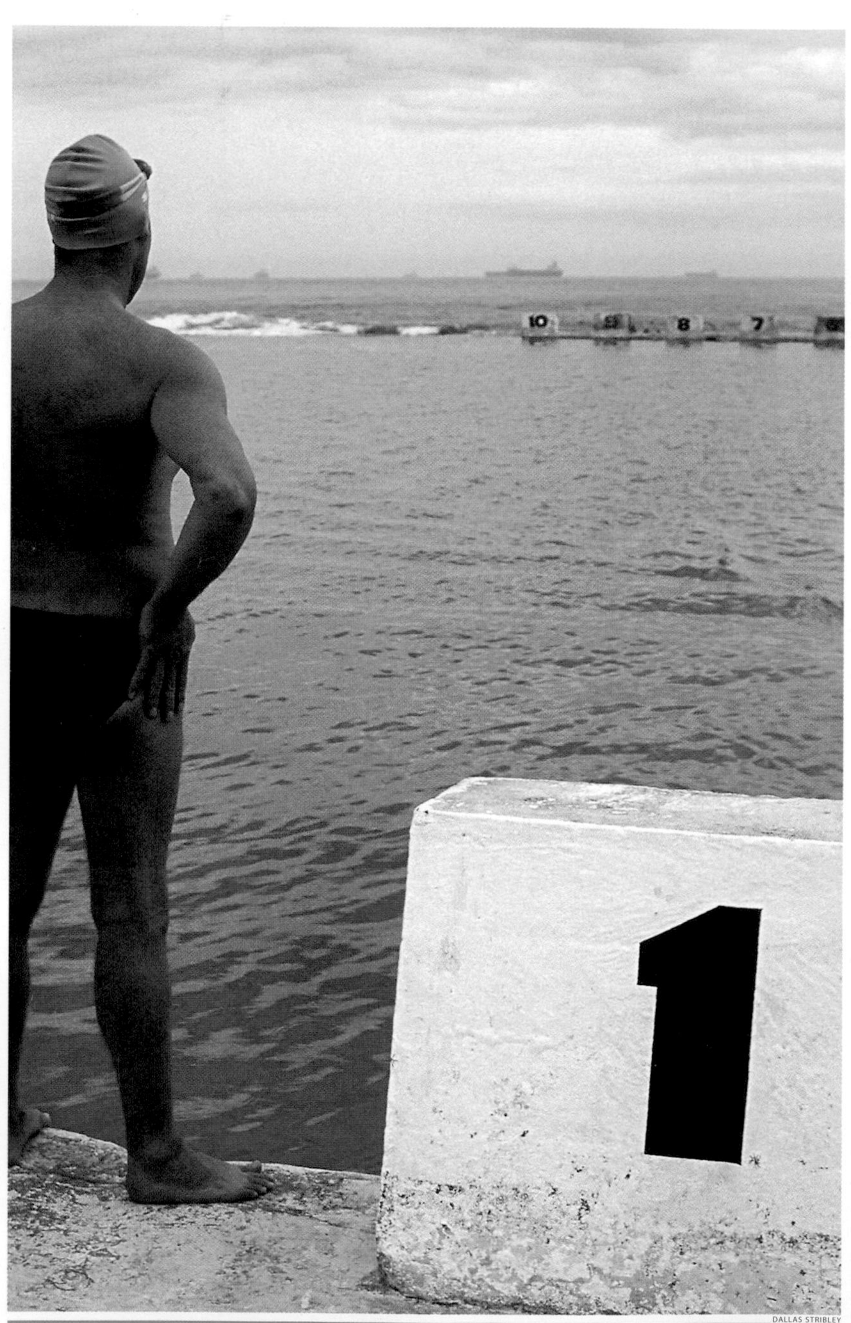

DALLAS STRIBLEY

Merewether Ocean Baths, Newcastle (p114)

NEW SOUTH WALES

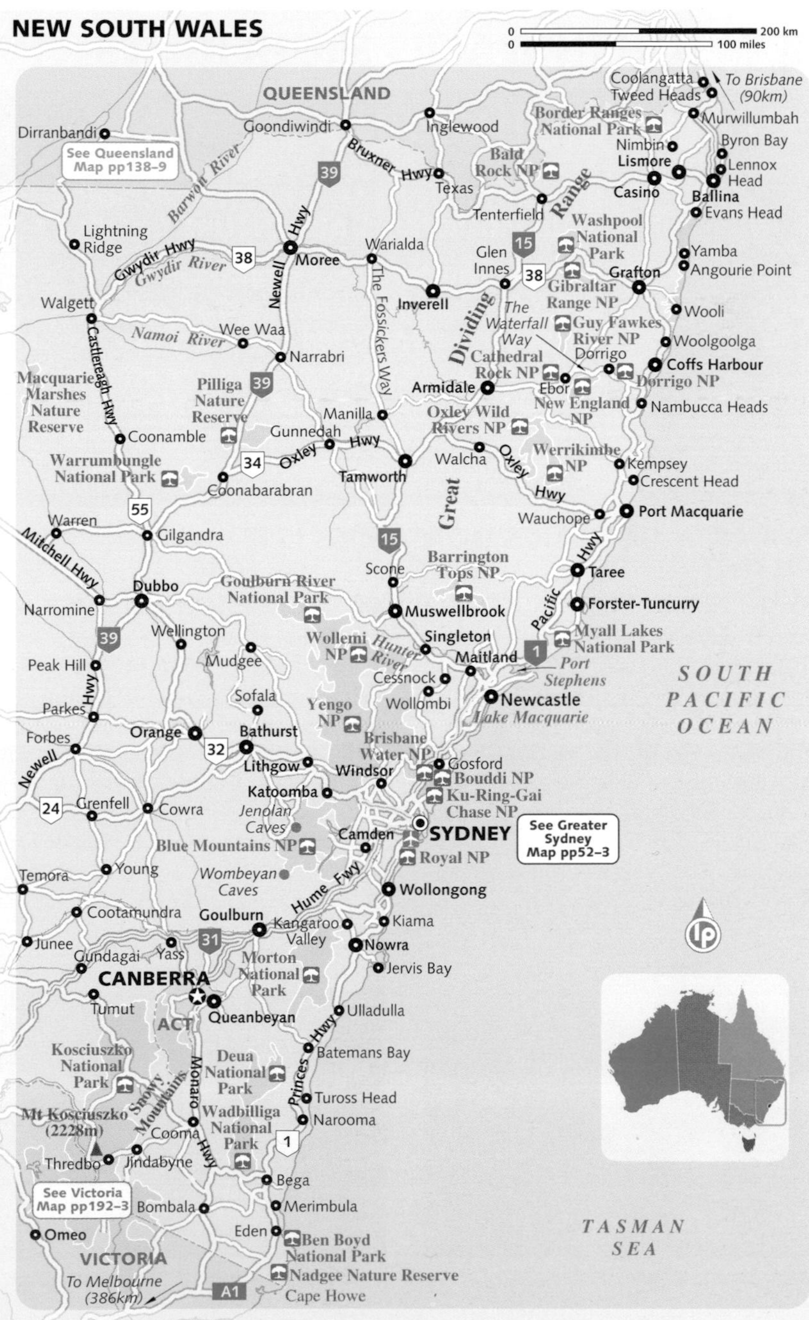

NEW SOUTH WALES HIGHLIGHTS

1 BLUE MOUNTAINS

BY MARTY DOOLAN, ADVENTURE GUIDE – BLUE MOUNTAINS ADVENTURE COMPANY

The Blue Mountains are a magnificent natural creation with endless stretches of sandstone cliffs, spectacular waterfalls and canyons. It's an awesome environment to experience adventure activities such as abseiling, canyoning, rock climbing, mountain biking and bushwalking – a lifetime's worth of adventuring to be had in Sydney's backyard!

↘ MARTY DOOLAN'S DON'T MISS LIST

❶ THREE SISTERS

An absolute must for all. The Three Sisters is a famous rock formation on the edge of the Jamison Valley. **Echo Point** (p109), the viewing platform for the Three Sisters, is one of the best lookouts in the Blue Mountains and is easily accessed from the town of Katoomba. If you can make it there after sundown you will see the Three Sisters spectacularly floodlit.

❷ CANYONING IN SUMMER

Canyoning is a terrific experience with plenty of thrill, excitement and adventure. Abseil down waterfalls, jump into deep pools of water, slide down natural water slides, swim and wade through geological treasures. These outdoor activities have a remarkable effect on people: after returning to their day-to-day lives refreshed and revived, most people experience a sense of renewed confidence in themselves.

Clockwise from top: Blue Mountains at dusk; Three Sisters; Narrow Neck and Megalong Valley from Cahills lookout; Waterfall; Another view from Cahills lookout

CLOCKWISE FROM TOP: GLENN VAN DER KNIJFF; ROSS BARNETT; HOLGER LEUE; CHRISTOPHER GROENHOUT; MTMEDIA

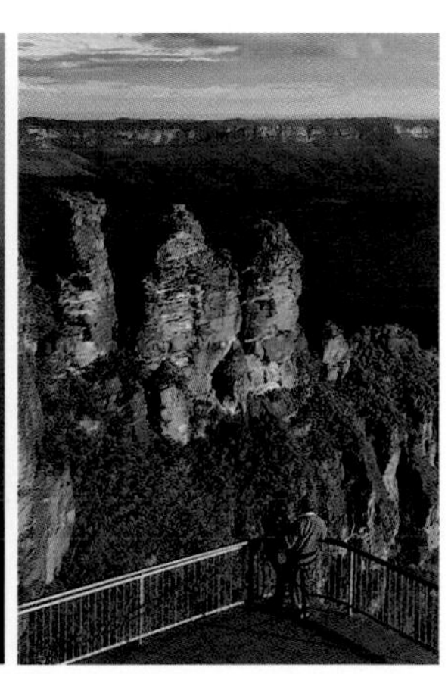

❸ SUNSET AT CAHILLS LOOKOUT

Cahills lookout is a lesser known lookout near Katoomba. It has amazing views of the Megalong and Jamison Valleys as well as Narrow Neck plateau and the remarkable Boars Head rock formation. Watch the mineralised sandstone cliffs gradually change colour as the sun dips towards the horizon.

❹ KATOOMBA

Katoomba St is a great place for a leisurely lunch or an uplifting coffee after a big day out. Loads of options abound. And don't miss the **Edge Cinema** (p112), which screens a fascinating documentary about the Blue Mountains on a six-storey-high screen – a great way to learn more about the Blue Mountains, and a good wet weather option.

❺ ROCK CLIMBING AT MT VICTORIA

The Blue Mountains has a long tradition of rock climbing; some of the first rock climbs in Australia were done in the Blue Mountains. Mt Victoria boasts several excellent rock climbing areas, each with a range of climbs and grades.

➘ THINGS YOU NEED TO KNOW

Best photo opportunity Sunrise or sunset at your pick of dozens of vertigo-inducing, cliff-top lookouts with waterfalls, rock formations and misty distant views **Avoid** The herd of tour buses expelling crowds at Echo Point; arrive early or late in the day **See our author's review on p106**

NEW SOUTH WALES HIGHLIGHTS

2

➘ KOSCIUSZKO NATIONAL PARK

New South Wales' largest national park, **Kosciuszko National Park** (p135), covers 690,000 hectares of high plains, weather-beaten mountains and contorted snow gums. It also encompasses the country's top ski resorts and is a winter playground. The rest of the year it entertains bushwalkers, fly-fishers and horse riders, and produces a showy display of wildflowers in spring and summer.

3

➘ BYRON BAY

Though its reputation precedes it, luckily beautiful **Byron Bay** (p122) mostly delivers on the high expectations. This is one of Australia's finest coastal towns, with a gorgeous setting of surf and sand backed by rolling green hinterland, all lazing in an idyllic subtropical climate. Byron's celebrated laid-back atmosphere is fully tested at peak holiday time, but outside this period the town is in full relaxation mode.

4

HUNTER VALLEY WINERIES

The Australian wine industry really got off the ground when free settler George Wyndham planted vines in the **Hunter Valley** (p116) in 1828. Now there are over 140 wineries producing award-winning Shiraz, Semillon and Chardonnay, among others. Along with the tasting rooms and cellar-door sales you'll find romantic escapes and fine dining.

5

WATERFALL WAY

The **Waterfall Way** (p128) is a diverting country road that wanders up the hills between the delightful villages of Bellingen and Dorrigo, to lead you to Armidale. True to name, numerous plunging streams are the feature of this drive, and protecting this area of spectacular gorges and waterfalls is a sequence of World Heritage–listed national parks.

6

GRAND PACIFIC DRIVE

Leave Sydney's snarling traffic behind and take a cliff-hugging trip to **Wollongong** (p130) on the Grand Pacific Drive, where the Great Dividing Range touches the Pacific. The route features the spectacular Sea Cliff Bridge, a ribbon of road sweeping out from the cliff over the water. It even has a footpath perfect for dolphin and whale watching.

2 Wombat, Kosciuszko National Park (p135); 3 Surfing the Pass (p123), Byron Bay; 4 Hunter Valley (p116); 5 Never Never Creek, near Bellingen (p128); 6 Coast road near Wollongong (p130)

NEW SOUTH WALES' BEST...

PLACES WITH A VIEW

- **Echo Point** (p109) A selection of cliff-top viewing platforms with Blue Mountain and valley views plus the famous Three Sisters.
- **Cape Byron** (p122) Spectacular coastline views and a sunrise from the continent's most easterly point.
- **Illawarra Fly Tree Top Walk** (p132) Swaying cantilevered springboards take you to the edge of the escarpment for spectacular sea views.

BEACHES TO HANG TEN

- **Wollongong** (p130) The industrial-but-relaxed city has good breaks.
- **Coffs Harbour** (p120) Clean beach breaks and a surfing museum.
- **Yamba & Angourie** (p122) Something for everyone (longboards and short), including Australia's first National Surfing Reserve.
- **Byron Bay** (p122) The beaches range from crowded to deserted in this iconic surf centre.
- **Crescent Head** (p119) The longboarding capital of Australia.

PLACES TO WORK UP A SWEAT

- **Katoomba** (p108) Clamber up a cliff; abseil or slither down a canyon.
- **Snowy Mountains** (p135) For year-round outdoor excursions: summer or winter, skiing or bushwalking.
- **Cape Byron** (p122) Climb the track from Clarkes Beach for a hard-earned view.

COUNTRY ESCAPES

- **Hunter Valley** (p116) Bucolic scenes, vineyards, wineries and restaurants a few hours from Sydney.
- **South Coast** (p130) Detour to pretty coastal towns, country backwaters and idyllic hinterland.
- **Blue Mountains** (p106) Although it's a popular area, it's easy to find a quiet and cosy corner of this bushland escape.

LEFT: RICHARD I'ANSON; RIGHT: JOHN BORTHWICK

Left: Lighthouse, Byron Bay (p122); Right: Crescent Head (p119), on the north coast

THINGS YOU NEED TO KNOW

VITAL STATISTICS

- **Population** 6.9 million
- **Telephone code** ☎ 02
- **Best time to visit** All year

LOCALITIES IN A NUTSHELL

- **Blue Mountains** (p106) Spectacular mountain and bushland scenery
- **North Coast** (p114) Superb beaches plus the Hunter Valley wineries
- **Far North Coast Hinterland** (p128) Rainforests, pastoral scenes and alternative culture
- **New England** (p129) More verdant countryside with rainforests, national parks and waterfalls
- **South Coast** (p130) The uncrowded coast with room to explore
- **Snowy Mountains** (p135) An all-year destination for active outdoor pursuits

ADVANCE PLANNING

- **One month before** If it is summer holiday season try to book everything this far in advance
- **Two weeks before** Enquire about, or book, a surfing/skiing lesson
- **One week before** Book a Blue Mountains activity or a table at that special restaurant

RESOURCES

- **National Roads & Motorists Association** (NRMA; Map pp64-5; ☎ 13 11 22; www.nrma.com.au; 74-6 King St, Sydney; 9am-5pm Mon-Fri) If you're hiring or buying a car, find out about insurance, road maps and guides. You can also book accommodation and tours online.
- **New South Wales National Parks** (☎ 02-9931 1111; www.nationalparks.nsw.gov.au) Information about national park access (including access for mobility-impaired visitors), camping permits, walking tracks, conservation, Indigenous heritage and children's activities.
- **Tourism New South Wales** (☎ 02-9931 1111; www.visitnsw.com.au) A good source for information, ideas and contacts.
- **www.nsw.gov.au** Bypass the boring parliamentary information and check out the leads to festivals, markets, galleries, Indigenous heritage and more.

EMERGENCY NUMBER

- **Police, fire and ambulance** (☎ 000)

GETTING AROUND

- **Hire Car** for ultimate flexibility; take a coastal drive
- **Bus** up and down the coast on a budget
- **Train** to the Blue Mountains from Sydney

NEW SOUTH WALES ITINERARIES

BLUE MOUNTAINS RAMBLE Three Days

Go west from Sydney, via the Western Motorway, to **(1) Glenbrook** (p107), at the base of the Blue Mountains, for Aboriginal hand stencils and the Norman Lindsay gallery.

Work the camera at Wentworth Falls and take in the view over the Jamison Valley. Admire the quaint gardens and buildings of **(2) Leura** (p108) as well as the sublime cliff-top views.

Continue west to the Queen of the Hills, **(3) Katoomba** (p108), where you can spend your first night. Catch the Three Sisters under a spotlight and relish the gourmet offerings in Katoomba St. Take in a leisurely breakfast, experience The Edge cinema and Scenic World or don a helmet for an active abseil.

Take to the Great Western Hwy again and move north to **(4) Blackheath** (p112) for some of the Blue Mountains' best lookouts. Check out sleepy **(5) Mt Victoria** (p113) and the ghost town of **(6) Hartley** (p113) before considering the out-and-back troglodyte excursion to **(7) Jenolan Caves** (p115).

After taking in a movie at Mount Vic Flicks, spend the second night in Blackheath. Train buffs simply must check out the **(8) Zig Zag Railway** (p114) before heading back to Sydney.

SOUTHERN COMFORT Five Days

With an early start, head south of Sydney on the spectacular **(1) Grand Pacific Drive** (p130) to the bustling port of **(2) Wollongong** (p130), where beaches, beds and restaurants abound.

Continue south to the pretty coastal region around **(3) Kiama** (p131), visit the famous blowhole, and then head inland to the spectacular Illawarra Fly Tree Top Walk, before retreating to the serenely relaxed **(4) Kangaroo Valley** (p132).

There's plenty to see and do on the south coast so take your time and spend a few days exploring. Cruise with dolphins at **(5) Jervis Bay** (p132) and look for whales at **(6) Narooma** (p133) and **(7) Eden** (p134).

Go back on the Princes Hwy to Bega and turn inland on the Monaro Hwy to the **(8) Snowy Mountains** (p135), where you can bunk down in **(9) Thredbo** (p135) and partake in winter or summer outdoor activities.

BYRON BECKONS One Week

With a tan, a board and a surf lesson or two under your belt, it's time to leave the fair city of Sydney and its hype and city lights and head

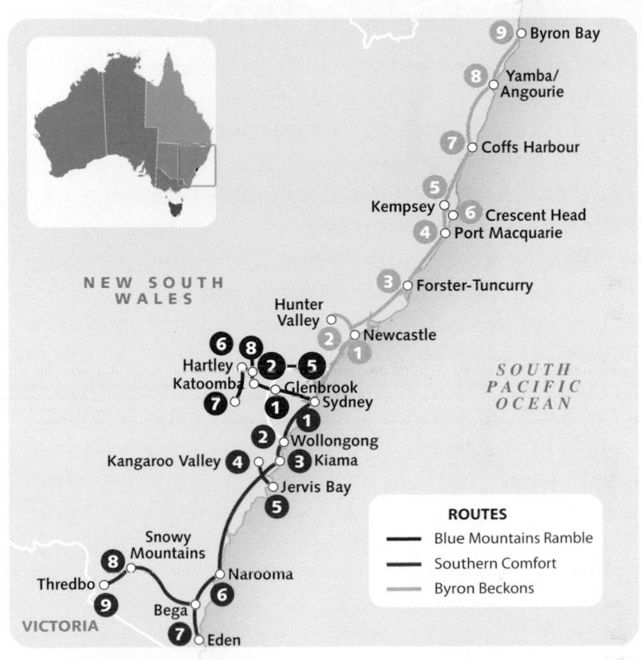

north on this classic north-coast run. First stop is the industrial port city of **(1) Newcastle** (p114), where there are fine beaches and restaurants. West of Newcastle the vineyards and wineries of the **(2) Hunter Valley** (p116) demand attention and offer a pleasant rural overnight stay.

Head back to the coast and up to the quiet beachside twins of **(3) Forster-Tuncurry** (p117), before staying in pretty **(4) Port Macquarie** (p118). Pick up an Akubra hat in **(5) Kempsey** (p119), detour to **(6) Crescent Head** (p119) to hang ten, or continue north to the Big Banana at **(7) Coffs Harbour** (p120), another great coastal base to spend a night.

Explore the coast north of Coffs for empty beaches and quiet towns such as **(8) Yamba** and **Angourie** (p122) before arriving at the continent's eastern apex, the chilled-out coastal mecca of **(9) Byron Bay** (p122).

DISCOVER NEW SOUTH WALES

Sometimes reserved, more often outrageously outgoing, but always welcoming, New South Wales (NSW) is endlessly fascinating. The country's most populous state and the birthplace of the modern nation, it's a state rich in history (both Indigenous and European), geography and contrasts. And of course it's home to stunning Sydney, the nation's capital in all but name.

Diversity reigns supreme here. South of the enchanting harbour, languid coastal towns hug the rugged coastline and deliver increasingly deserted and beautiful beaches. Still further south the Snowy Mountains lure ski bunnies in winter and ramblers in summer. Towns founded by gold miners and graziers pepper the heart of the state, and to the far west the arid lunar landscape of the outback beckons and beguiles. In the north, the classic Aussie surf culture dominates and alternative hinterland lifestyles rub shoulders with million-dollar beach houses. And in almost every corner you'll find incredible national parks to explore: some World Heritage listed and some that look like they should be.

BLUE MOUNTAINS

Within striking distance of Sydney is the spectacular wilderness area of the Blue Mountains. The slate-coloured haze that gives the mountains their name comes from a fine mist of oil exuded by eucalyptus trees.

For years these mountains formed an impenetrable barrier to colonial expansion from Sydney as numerous attempts to find a route through failed. It wasn't until 1813 that European explorers Blaxland, Lawson and Wentworth successfully traversed the mountains. Today the Great Western Hwy follows their route through the hilltop towns of – surprise, surprise – Blaxland, Lawson and Wentworth Falls.

There are three beautiful national parks in the area, the most accessible of which is the **Blue Mountains National Park**, which protects large tracts of gullies and gums north and south of the Great Western Hwy. Absorb the park's jaw-dropping scenery at the numerous drive-up lookouts, or get among the greenery on established bushwalking trails.

Entry to these national parks is free unless you enter the Blue Mountains National Park at Bruce Rd, Glenbrook ($7 per car, walkers free). For more information (including camping) contact the **NPWS Visitor Centre** (☎ **02-4787 8877; www.nationalparks.nsw.gov.au; Govetts Leap Rd, Blackheath; 🕑 9am-4.30pm**), about 2.5km off the Great Western Hwy and 10km north of Katoomba.

GETTING THERE & AWAY

If travelling by car follow the signs from the city to Parramatta. At Strathfield turn onto the Western Motorway tollway (M4; $3), which becomes the Great Western Hwy west of Penrith.

CityRail trains regularly service Leura, Katoomba, Blackheath, Mt Victoria and Lithgow.

SIMON RICHMOND

Blue Mountains National Park

IF YOU LIKE...

If you like **Blue Mountains National Park** (p106), we think you might like these other national parks (or see www.nationalparks.nsw.gov.au):

- **Wollemi National Park** North of Bells Line of Road, this is the state's largest forested wilderness area, with rugged bushwalking.
- **Kanangra Boyd National Park** (cars $7, pedestrians & cyclists free) Southwest of Katoomba, this park is accessible from Oberon or Jenolan Caves. Launch into a bushwalk, descend into limestone caverns or check out the amazing Kanangra Walls plateau, encircled by sheer cliffs.
- **Royal National Park** (cars $11, pedestrians & cyclists free; sunrise to 8.30pm daily) Bordering southern Sydney, the wilderness areas of Royal National Park hide dramatic cliff-top walks, including a 28km coastal walking trail.
- **Ku-Ring-Gai Chase National Park** (cars $11, pedestrians & cyclists free; sunrise to sunset) There are short bushwalks in this park, around the inlets of Broken Bay.
- **Myall Lakes National Park** (cars $7, pedestrians & cyclists free) The Myall Lakes form the largest natural freshwater system in New South Wales. Pooling in deep blue basins, they weave around clumps of forest and small settlements.
- **Morton National Park** (cars $7 at Bundanoon, $3 at Fitzroy Falls, pedestrians & cyclists free) There's a visitor centre (☎ 02-4887 7270; Nowra Rd) at Fitzroy Falls in the north and a great 'hard' walk to the top of Pigeon House Mountain in the south (access from Ulladulla).

GLENBROOK TO WENTWORTH FALLS

From **Marge's Lookout** and **Elizabeth's Lookout** near Glenbrook there are super views back to Sydney. The section of the Blue Mountains National Park south of Glenbrook contains **Red Hands Cave**, an old Aboriginal shelter with hand stencils on the walls. It's an easy 7km return walk southwest of the **Glenbrook NPWS**

centre (☎ 02-4739 2950; ⌚ Sat & Sun) on the Great Western Hwy.

Celebrated artist, author and bon vivant Norman Lindsay, famed for his racy artworks and children's tale *The Magic Pudding,* lived in Faulconbridge from 1912 until his death in 1969. His home and studio is now the **Norman Lindsay Gallery & Museum** (☎ 02-4751 1067; www.normanlindsay.com.au; 14 Norman Lindsay Cres, Faulconbridge; adult/child/family $9/6/24; ⌚ 10am-4pm), with a significant collection of his paintings, watercolours, drawings and sculptures. There is a very good **cafe** (☎ 02-4751 9611; mains $12-25; ⌚ breakfast & lunch) on site and you can overnight in the grounds in a cosy **cottage** (d $120-150).

As you head into Wentworth Falls, you'll get your first real taste of Blue Mountains scenery: views to the south open out across the majestic Jamison Valley. **Wentworth Falls** itself launches a plume of fraying droplets over a 300m drop – check it out from Falls Rd. This is also the starting point for a network of walking tracks that delves into the sublime Valley of the Waters, with waterfalls, gorges, woodlands and rainforests.

LEURA

Leura, with its pretty tree-lined streets, art deco houses and grand Victorian verandahs, is one of the most charming and attractive villages in the Blue Mountains. The **Leura Visitors Gateway** (☎ 02-4784 3443; www.bluemountainsway.com.au; 121 The Mall; ⌚ 9am-5pm) books accommodation and tours, organises car hire and has a local art gallery next door.

Sublime Point is a dramatic clifftop lookout south of Leura offering alternative (albeit distant) views of the Three Sisters. Further north is **Gordon Falls Reserve**, an idyllic picnic spot. From here you can trek the steep Prince Henry Cliff Walk, or take the Cliff Drive 4km west past Leura Cascades to Katoomba's Echo Point.

KATOOMBA

Grand old Katoomba has long been a popular holiday destination. During the 1920s and '30s the steep streets were lined

GLENN VAN DER KNIJFF

A view of Mt Solitary from Cahills Lookout, near Katoomba

with handsome residences, splendid art deco buildings and wealthy Sydneysiders seeking fun and frivolity.

Katoomba's crowning glory is **Echo Point**, where a series of sensational viewing platforms transport your gaze out over the Jamison Valley. The impressive **Three Sisters** rock formation towers over the scene. Legend has it that a sorcerer turned the Three Sisters to stone in order to protect them from the unwanted advances of three young men.

To the west of town is the very good **Scenic World** (☎ 02-4780 0200; www.scenicworld.com.au; cnr Cliff Dr & Violet St; cable-car return adult/child $19/10; 9am-5pm), with an 1880s railway descending the 52-degree incline to the valley floor and an elevated boardwalk through the rainforest. The eco-certified venue also has a glass-floored **Scenic Skyway** cable car floating out across the valley.

INFORMATION

Blue Mountains Accommodation Booking Service (☎ 02-4782 2652; www.bluemountainsbudget.com; 157 Lurline St; 10.30am-5.30pm) Free accommodation-booking service.

Echo Point Visitor Centre (☎ 1300 653 408, 02-4739 6787; www.visitbluemountains.com.au; Echo Point; 9am-5pm)

ACTIVITIES

The following offer climbing, hiking and cycling; prices indicate easy or beginner grades (more advanced equals more dollars):

Australian School of Mountaineering (☎ 02-4782 2014; www.asmguides.com; 166 Katoomba St; 8.30am-5.30pm) Full-day abseiling ($145) or canyoning ($165), plus two-day bush-survival courses ($425).

Blue Mountains Adventure Company (☎ 02-4782 1271; www.bmac.com.au; 84a Bathurst Rd; 9am-5pm) Abseiling (from $145), canyoning (from $165) and rock climbing (from $175).

High 'n' Wild Mountain Adventures (☎ 02-4782 6224; www.high-n-wild.com.au; 3/5 Katoomba St; 9am-5pm) Half-/full-day abseiling (from $99/145) and climbing

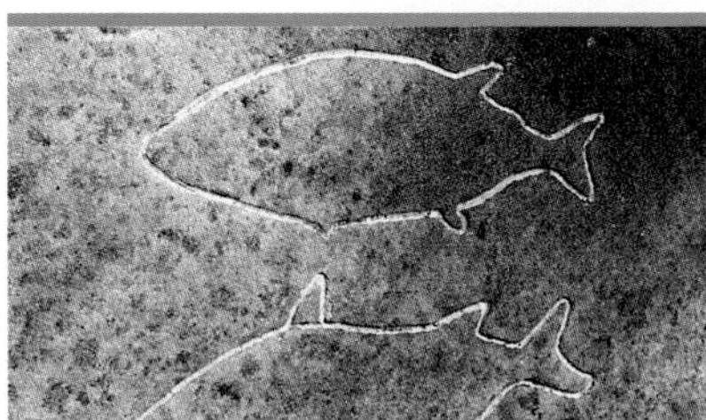

PAUL BEINSSEN

Aboriginal rock engravings, North Bondi headland

IF YOU LIKE...

If you like the art at **Red Hands Cave** (p107), you might like these other opportunities to view Indigenous rock art and engravings in New South Wales:

- **Bondi** There are some very faint Eora Aboriginal rock engravings north of the beach near the cliffs at the Bondi Golf Club – the name 'Bondi' derives from an Aboriginal word for the sound of the surf.
- **Ku-Ring-Gai Chase National Park** (cars $11, pedestrians & cyclists free; sunrise to sunset) The Aboriginal Heritage Track, an easy 1km path, leads past a fantastic Aboriginal engraving site.
- **Brisbane Water National Park** (cars $11, pedestrians & cyclists free; sunrise to sunset) The park is west of Gosford, the Bulgandry Aboriginal Engraving Site is 3km south of the Pacific Hwy on Woy Woy Rd.

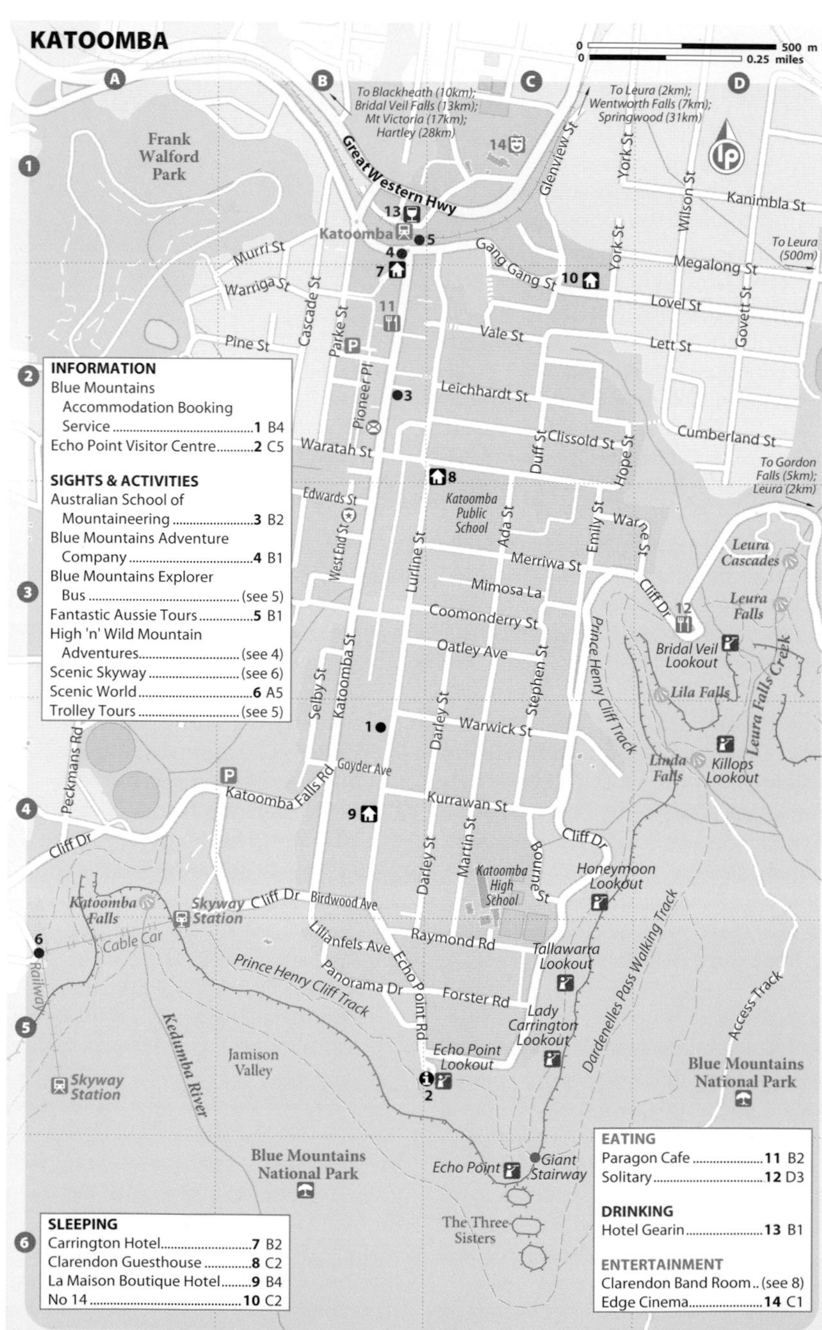
KATOOMBA
0 500 m
0 0.25 miles
A
B
C
D
1
2
3
4
5
6
To Blackheath (10km); Bridal Veil Falls (13km); Mt Victoria (17km); Hartley (28km)
To Leura (2km); Wentworth Falls (7km); Springwood (31km)
Frank Walford Park
Great Western Hwy
Katoomba
Glenview St
York St
Wilson St
Kanimbla St
To Leura (500m)
Megalong St
Gang Gang St
Lovel St
Lett St
Govett St
Murri St
Warriga St
Cascade St
Parke St
Pine St
Vale St
Pioneer Pl
Leichhardt St
Cumberland St
Clissold St
Duff St
Hope St
Waratah St
To Gordon Falls (5km); Leura (2km)
Edwards St
West End St
Katoomba Public School
Ada St
Emily St
Warne St
Lurline St
Merriwa St
Mimosa La
Coomonderry St
Oatley Ave
Cliff Dr
Prince Henry Cliff Track
Leura Cascades
Leura Falls
Bridal Veil Lookout
Lila Falls
Leura Falls Creek
Selby St
Katoomba St
Darley St
Stephen St
Warwick St
Linda Falls
Killops Lookout
Peckmans Rd
Goyder Ave
Katoomba Falls Rd
Kurrawan St
Martin St
Bourne St
Katoomba High School
Honeymoon Lookout
Katoomba Falls
Skyway Station
Birdwood Ave
Cable Car
Railway
Lilianfels Ave
Raymond Rd
Tallawarra Lookout
Dardenelles Pass Walking Track
Panorama Dr
Echo Point Rd
Forster Rd
Lady Carrington Lookout
Access Track
Kedumba River
Jamison Valley
Echo Point Lookout
Blue Mountains National Park
Echo Point
Giant Stairway
The Three Sisters
INFORMATION
Blue Mountains Accommodation Booking Service 1 B4
Echo Point Visitor Centre 2 C5
SIGHTS & ACTIVITIES
Australian School of Mountaineering 3 B2
Blue Mountains Adventure Company 4 B1
Blue Mountains Explorer Bus ....(see 5)
Fantastic Aussie Tours 5 B1
High 'n' Wild Mountain Adventures ....(see 4)
Scenic Skyway ....(see 6)
Scenic World 6 A5
Trolley Tours ....(see 5)
SLEEPING
Carrington Hotel 7 B2
Clarendon Guesthouse 8 C2
La Maison Boutique Hotel 9 B4
No 14 ....10 C2
EATING
Paragon Cafe 11 B2
Solitary 12 D3
DRINKING
Hotel Gearin 13 B1
ENTERTAINMENT
Clarendon Band Room ....(see 8)
Edge Cinema 14 C1

($159/179), and full-day canyoning ($179).

TOURS

Australian Eco Adventures (☎ 02-9971 2402; www.ozeco.com.au; adult/child $170/130; ⏲ 7am) Eco-certified luxury day tours of the Blue Mountains departing from Sydney (maximum 16 people). Includes breakfast, buffet lunch and champagne.

Blue Mountains Explorer Bus (☎ 02-4782 1866, 1300 300 915; www.explorerbus.com.au; 283 Main St; adult/child/family $34/17/85; ⏲ 9.45am-5.15pm) Hop-on hop-off service on an hourly Katoomba-Leura loop, stopping at 30 attractions.

Fantastic Aussie Tours (☎ 02-4782 1866; www.fantastic-aussie-tours.com.au; 283 Main St; adult/child/family $70/49/189; ⏲ tours 11.15am-5.15pm Mon-Sat, office 9am-5pm) Coach tours to the Jenolan Caves; price includes entrance to caves.

Trolley Tours (☎ 02 4782 7999, 1800 801 577; www.trolleytours.com.au; 258 Main St; adult/concession $20/15; ⏲ hourly 9.15am-4.15pm Mon-Fri, 9.45am-3.45pm Sat & Sun) A bus masquerading as a trolley, with piped commentary.

SLEEPING

our pick **No 14** (☎ 02-4782 7104; www.bluemts.com.au/no14; 14 Lovel St; dm $22, d with/without bathroom $69/59) This adorable yellow-painted weatherboard house has been operating as a guest house since it was built in 1913. The dorms are cute and cosy, and there's a well-equipped kitchen and a couple of inviting living areas. More like staying with your best mate than in a hostel.

Clarendon Guesthouse (☎ 02-4782 1322; www.clarendonguesthouse.com.au; 68 Lurline St; d $90-176; 💻 🚭) The rambling old Clarendon is as much a part of the Blue Mountains as the Three Sisters...almost. This wonderfully eccentric hotel has budget rooms (with shared bathroom) chock-full of heritage in the main house and spotless modern rooms in the annexed new building.

La Maison Boutique Hotel (☎ 02-4782 4996; www.lamaison.com.au; 175-177 Lurline St; s incl breakfast $90-230, d incl breakfast $98-300) Not as 'boutique' as the name might suggest, it's a good midrange option nevertheless. The rooms are pleasant with decent bathrooms and occasionally mismatched furniture. The hallways are eerily quiet during the day but things liven up at night.

Carrington Hotel (☎ 02-4782 1111; www.thecarrington.com.au; 15-47 Katoomba St; d incl breakfast $125-490) The Grand Old Lady of the mountains has a long and colourful history, having provided accommodation to road-weary travellers since 1880. Beautifully refurbished in the 1990s she now offers a wide range of indulgent heritage-infused rooms. The ballroom and dining room are equally splendid.

EATING

Paragon Café (☎ 02-4782 2928; 65 Katoomba St; mains $10-20; ⏲ breakfast & lunch Tue-Sun) Established in 1916, Paragon has been serving drinks and selling homemade chocolates to the blue rinse brigade for almost a century. The original booths, wood panelling and framed photos of movie stars make this charming cafe a compulsory Blue Mountains experience.

Solitary (☎ 02-4782 1164; 90 Cliff Dr; 2/3 courses $55/66; ⏲ lunch Sat & Sun, dinner Wed-Sun) The weatherboard cottage now called Solitary has been serving refreshments to Blue Mountain visitors since 1913. Today this oh-so-pretty restaurant offers the same amazing views but with a Mod Oz menu. The adjoining kiosk offers all-day brunches and lunches that are easier on the wallet.

DRINKING & ENTERTAINMENT

Hotel Gearin (☎ 02-4782 4395; 273 Great Western Hwy; admission free; 🕑 7am-2am Mon-Thu, to 3am Fri & Sat, 10am-10pm Sun) This art deco watering hole is one of the liveliest in town, with trivia nights, live music, pool comps and Sunday afternoon jazz. It's owned by actor Jack Thompson – reason enough for a beer and a $5 steak.

Clarendon Band Room (☎ 02-4782 1322; 68 Lurline St; admission $15-50; 🕑 live music Wed-Sat night) Everything from Australian folk and pop to jazz and rock is performed on the Clarendon stage. Dinner-and-dance shows are usually double the ticket price.

Edge Cinema (☎ 02-4782 8900; www.edgecinema.com.au; 225 Great Western Hwy; adult/child $14/10; 🕑 10am-late) A giant screen shows mainstream flicks plus a 40-minute Blue Mountains documentary (adult/child $15/10). Budget Tuesdays features flicks for $9 per person.

GETTING THERE & AROUND

CityRail runs to Katoomba from Sydney's Central Station (one way adult/child $12/6, two hours, hourly).

The Blue Mountains Bus Company services Katoomba en route from Mt Victoria to the north (one way adult/child $7/4, 40 minutes, three daily Monday to Friday) and Springwood to the east (one way adult/child $9/5, 50 minutes, nine daily Monday to Saturday). The Blue Mountains Explorer Bus and Trolley Tours (both p111) track the highlights through Katoomba and Leura.

BLACKHEATH AREA

Leura may be more affluent and Katoomba definitely sees more crowds, but neat and petite Blackheath is simply lovely. It's also a good base for visiting the Grose and Megalong Valleys.

SIGHTS & ACTIVITIES

East of town are lookouts at **Govetts Leap** (comparable to the Three Sisters in terms of 'wow' factor), **Bridal Veil Falls** (the

ROSS BARNETT

Hanging Rock, near Blackheath, Blue Mountains National Park

highest in the Blue Mountains) and **Evans Lookout**. To the northeast, via Hat Hill Rd, are **Pulpit Rock**, **Perry's Lookdown** and **Anvil Rock**.

There are steep walks into the Grose Valley from Govetts Leap; Perry's Lookdown is the start of the shortest route (five hours one way) to the magical **Blue Gum Forest**. From Evans Lookout there are tracks to Govetts Leap (1½ hours one way) and to **Junction Rock**, continuing to the Blue Gum Forest (six hours one way).

To the west and southwest lie the **Kanimbla** and **Megalong Valleys**, with spectacular views from **Hargreaves Lookout**. Register your walk and get trail-condition updates from the **Blue Mountains Heritage Centre** (☎ 02-4787 8877; www.nationalparks.nsw.gov.au; Govetts Leap Rd; 9am-4.30pm) near the entrance to Govetts Leap.

SLEEPING & EATING

Glenella Guesthouse (☎ 02-4787 8352; www.glenellabluemountainshotel.com.au; 56-60 Govetts Leap Rd; d incl breakfast $100-160) Gorgeous Glenella has long played an important – and lively – part in Blackheath's history. Today it's run by a friendly Welsh couple who have refreshed and restored this celebrated home to create seven comfortable bedrooms. There's also a large living area and a restaurant (dinner Thursday to Sunday, lunch Saturday and Sunday).

Gardners Inn (☎ 02-4787 6400; www.gardnersinn.com.au; 255 Great Western Hwy; s/d incl breakfast with bathroom $160/250, without bathroom $130/180) Across from Blackheath Station, this is the oldest licensed hotel (1831) in the Blue Mountains. It's just benefited from a $6 million refurbishment, which means that the rooms are modern and bright, although a smidgen of heritage charm remains. Good online deals.

Jemby-Rinjah Eco Lodge (☎ 02-4787 7622; www.jembyrinjahlodge.com.au; 336 Evans Lookout Rd; standard/deluxe cabins from $170/219) These eco-cabins are lodged so deeply in the bottlebrush you'll have to bump into one to find it. One- and two-bedroom weatherboard cabins are jauntily designed; the deluxe models have Japanese plunge-style spas.

Ashcroft's (☎ 02-4787 8297; 18 Govetts Leap Rd; 2/3 courses $68/80; dinner Wed-Sun, lunch Sun) This multi-award-winning restaurant experiments with European, Middle Eastern, Asian and Australian cuisine in a gallery-like setting. There's an excellent wine list, and the paintings and photography on display are all for sale.

MT VICTORIA, HARTLEY & LITHGOW

With a charming alpine air, **Mt Victoria** (population 828) sits at 1043m and is the highest town in the mountains. Historic buildings dominate and include **St Peter's Church** (1874) and the **Toll Keepers Cottage** (1849).

Nothing is far from the train station, where the **Mt Victoria Museum** (☎ 02-4787 1210; Mt Victoria Railway Station; adult/child $3/50c; 2-5pm Sat & Sun) is chock-full of quirky Australiana including old farm equipment, taxidermy and Ned Kelly's sister's bed. Inside an old public hall, the 130-seat **Mount Vic Flicks** (☎ 02-4787 1577; www.bluemts.com.au/mountvic; Harley Ave; adult/child $10/8; noon-8.30pm Fri-Sun, from 10.30am Thu) is a wonderful step back in time. With ushers, a piano player and door prizes you'll soon forget what you came to see.

The best pub in the area by a mountain mile, the 1878 **Imperial Hotel** (☎ 02-4787 1878; www.hotelimperial.com.au; 1 Station St, Mt

Victoria; d with/without bathroom incl breakfast from $99/60), has budget and basic downstairs rooms and grand ones above. The bar has live music and log fires, and the kitchen (mains $17 to $24) cooks solid pub grub.

About 12km past Mt Victoria, on the western slopes of the range, is the tiny, sandstone 'ghost' town of **Hartley**, which flourished from the 1830s but declined when bypassed by the railway in 1887. It's been well preserved and a number of historic buildings remain, including several private homes and inns.

The **NPWS Information Centre** (☎ **02-6355 2117; www.nationalparks.nsw.gov.au; 10am-1pm & 2-4.20pm**) is in the old Farmer's Inn (1845). You can explore Hartley for free or take a 20-minute guided tour of the 1837 **Greek Revival Courthouse** (**tours $6; hourly 10am-3pm**).

A further 14km on from Hartley in the western foothills of the Blue Mountains is **Lithgow** (population 11,298), a sombre coal-mining town popular with trainspotters for its **Zig Zag Railway** (☎ **02-6355 2955; www.zigzagrailway.com.au; Clarence Station, Bells Line of Road; adult/child/family $25/13/63; 11am, 1pm, 3pm & 4.45pm**), which sits just 10km east of town. Built in the 1860s to transport the Great Western Railway tracks down from the mountains into Lithgow, today it zigzags tourists gently down the precipice (1½-hour return trip).

CityRail trains run to Mt Victoria from Sydney's Central Station (one way adult/child $14/7, 2½ hours, hourly). The Blue Mountains Bus Company runs to Mt Victoria from Katoomba (one way adult/child $6/3, 15 minutes, four daily Monday to Friday). CityRail trains run to Lithgow from Sydney's Central Station (one way adult/child $18/9, three hours, hourly).

NORTH COAST

It's no wonder that the NSW north coast is one of the most celebrated road trips in Oz. This idyllic stretch of coastline from Sydney to Tweed Heads is a magical blend of sea and sand, sparkling lakes, enchanting national parks, rootsy towns and alternative lifestyles.

NEWCASTLE

pop 493,466

Sydney may possess the glitz and the glamour, but Newcastle has the down-to-earth larrikin charm. Swim or surf at the popular beaches and soak in ocean baths, explore the outstanding heritage architecture in the CBD and window shop along funky Darby St. Dine on fish and chips, watch the tankers chug along the horizon and catch some live music. Whatever you do, however, don't just pass through – Newcastle is easily worth a couple of days or more.

INFORMATION

Visitor Information Centre (☎ **02-4974 2999; 361 Hunter St; 9am-5pm Mon-Fri, 10am-3pm Sat & Sun**)

SIGHTS

Get your bearings (and your heart racing) with a climb up 180 steps to the top of the 40.3m-high **Queens Wharf Tower** (**Queens Wharf; admission free; 8am-dusk**) for a 360-degree view of the city.

From here, hot foot it along the **Bathers Way**, a 5km coastal walk that stretches from the lighthouse at Nobbys Head to Glenrock Reserve and includes Fort Scratchley (p116).

BEACHES

At the northeastern tip, the gentle curve of **Nobby's Beach** makes this one of the city's prettiest stretches of coast. Surfers

RICHARD I'ANSON

Pool of Cerberus, Jenolan Caves

JENOLAN CAVES

The story behind the discovery of **Jenolan Caves** is the stuff of legends: local pastoralist James Whalan stumbled across the prehistoric caves while tracking the escaped convict and cattle rustler James McKeown, who is thought to have used the caves as a hideout.

Originally named Binoomea or 'Dark Places' by the Gundungurra people, these spellbinding caves took shape more than 400 million years ago and are one of the most extensive and complex limestone cave systems in the world.

There are over 350 caves in the region, although only a handful is open to the public. You must take a tour to see them; the most comprehensive tours include the two-hour **Legends, Mysteries & Ghosts Tour**.

The caves are 30km from the Great Western Hwy. The narrow Jenolan Caves Rd becomes a one-way system between 11.45am and 1.15pm daily, running clockwise from the caves out through Oberon.

Things you need to know Jenolan Caves (☎ 02-6359 3911; www.jenolancaves.org.au; Jenolan Caves Rd; admission with tour adult/child/family from $25/18/59; 9.30am-5.30pm); Legends, Mysteries & Ghosts Tour (per person $38; 8pm Sat)

should head to the northern end to tackle the fast left-hander known as the Wedge. Around the corner a wonderful multicoloured art deco facade hides the ocean baths, perfect for those paranoid about sharks.

Newcastle Beach satisfies swimmers and surfers, the chugging cargo ships on the horizon provoking some interesting holiday snaps. South of here, below King Edward Park, the convict-carved **Bogey Hole** is Australia's oldest ocean bath. Scramble around the rocks and under the headland to **Susan Gilmore Beach**, where swimwear is optional (and not encouraged).

FORT SCRATCHLEY

Occupying one of Newcastle's best vantage points, the recently reopened **Fort Scratchley** (☎ 02-4974 5000; www.fortscratchley.com.au; Nobbys Rd; admission free; 10am-4pm Wed-Mon) played a vital role in defending the city when a Japanese submarine attacked Newcastle on 8 June 1942. A free map will guide you around the barracks and defence structures, but if you want to delve into the underground maze of tunnels then you must join a tour (adult/child $8/4, one hour).

SLEEPING

Newcastle Beach YHA (☎ 02-4925 3544; www.yha.com.au; 30 Pacific St; dm/s/d from $28/47/67;) In a heritage-listed old gentlemen's club is this excellent hostel with large light-filled rooms, a grand, old wood-panelled living room and more organised activities than there are days in the year. Almost.

Clarendon Hotel (☎ 02-4927 0966; www.clarendonhotel.com.au; 347 Hunter St; d $150-180;) The Clarendon does boutique chic in this old art deco building. Rooms feature contemporary hues with bold artwork and modern furnishings; some even have balconies. The bar downstairs is less stylish but equally convivial.

Crowne Plaza (☎ 02-4907 5000; www.crowneplaza.com.au; Wharf Rd; d incl breakfast from $270;) This is your best top-end bet in a city sadly lacking in high-end options. Located on the foreshore, many rooms have lovely views but the best one is from the outdoor swimming pool that overlooks the harbour.

GETTING THERE & AWAY

AIR

Newcastle's main **airport** (☎ 02-4928 9800; www.newcastleairport.com.au) is at Williamtown, about 15km north of the city.

Virgin Blue (☎ 13 67 89; www.virginblue.com.au) and **Jetstar** (☎ 13 15 38; www.jetstar.com.au) fly to Brisbane and Melbourne, and **Qantas** (☎ 13 13 13; www.qantas.com.au) flies to Sydney as well.

BUS

All local and long-distance buses leave from Newcastle Station. **Greyhound** (☎ 13 14 99) goes to Byron Bay (adult/child $106/92) and Sydney (adult/child $49/41).

TRAIN

All CountryLink trains stop at Broadmeadow, just west of town, and run up and down the coast to Coffs Harbour (adult/child $55/36). Change at either Casino or Grafton for Byron Bay (adult/child $75/54).

LOWER HUNTER VALLEY

Wine first arrived in Australia in 1788 when Captain Arthur Phillip planted the first vines in Sydney (no doubt he thought that establishing the first European settlement at Port Jackson might be an easier task with a glass of red in hand). In the Hunter Valley it was a free settler by the name of George Wyndham who first got things going; in 1828 he cleared some land, planted some vines and Wyndham Estate was born.

Today there are over 140 wineries in the area and the best-known varietals are the Hunter Semillon and Shiraz.

ORIENTATION & INFORMATION

The **Hunter Valley Wine Country Visitor Centre** (☎ 02-4990 0900; www.winecountry.com.au; 455 Wine Country Dr; 9am-5.30pm Mon-Fri, to 5pm Sat, to 4pm Sun) has oodles of local information and can book accommodation.

OLIVER STREWE

Winery, Hunter Valley

SIGHTS

The following are just a handful of the many Hunter wineries with welcoming cellar doors.

It's where it all began back in 1828, – **Wyndham Estate** (☎ 02-4938 3444; 700 Dalwood Rd, Dalwood; 9.30am-4.30pm) is the birthplace of Australian Shiraz. The 'Shiraz Experience' tasting plate is essential to a full understanding of the drop. Tours through the winery leave at 11am.

First planted in 1866, the **Audrey Wilkinson Vineyard** (☎ 02-4998 7411; www.audreywilkinson.com.au; DeBeyers Rd; 9am-5pm Mon-Fri, from 9.30am Sat & Sun) is believed to be one of the first in Pokolbin; ironically the vines were planted by a lifelong teetotaller.

The name of **Bimbadgen Estate Wines** (☎ 02-4998 4650; www.bimbadgen.com.au; 790 McDonalds Rd; 10am-5pm) derives from the Aboriginal term meaning 'a place of good view', although 'spectacular' might have been more apt. Its wines are equally impressive.

Legend has it that the hanging tree of **Hanging Tree Wines** (☎ 02-4998 6601; www.hangingtreewines.com.au; 294 O'Connors Rd, Pokolbin; 11am-5pm Fri-Sun) was once used to dangle the carcasses of animals as well as the odd bushranger. Today this gem of a winery offers one of the most welcoming cellar doors housed within an old cowshed.

Pressed for time and can't decide which winery to visit? Head to the **Small Winemakers Centre** (☎ 02-4998 7668; www.smallwinemakerscentre.com.au; McDonalds Rd, Pokolbin; 10am-5pm), which showcases the best of the bunch from smaller, lesser-known wineries.

NEWCASTLE TO PORT MACQUARIE

Separated by the sea entrance to Wallis Lake, the twin towns of **Forster-Tuncurry** have 'waterfront potential' stamped all over them: they're just waiting for a cash injection and the right town planner. In the meantime it's a great hub for exploring not only the lakes, but also a string of spectacular beaches along an unhurried and unpretentious coastline.

Forster (*fos*-ter), on the southern side of the entrance, is the big brother of the pair. The helpful **visitor centre** (☎ 02-6554 8799; Little St, Forster) is on the pretty street that runs beside the lake.

Beaches are of the highest quality in this area, with **Nine Mile Beach** the pick of the surf spots, **Forster Beach** a good family option with its swimming pools, and **One Mile Beach** also popular. The **Surf School** (☎ 02-6554 7811; 33 Wharf St, Forster; 1-5 lessons $50-180) meets at the surf club on One Mile Beach.

PORT MACQUARIE

pop 39,508

If Port, as it's affectionately known, had a 'big banana' or a 'big pineapple' like other Australian cities, it would probably have a bigger tourist profile. Mercifully, on both counts, the city has never had to manufacture its appeal, reclining as it does over a spectacular headland at the entrance to the subtropical coast.

SIGHTS & ACTIVITIES

Port Macquarie shares its beautiful gum trees with one of Australia's icons, the koala. Unfortunately, many end up at the **Koala Hospital** (☎ 02-6584 1522; www.koalahospital.org.au; Roto House, Lord St; admission by donation; feeding 8am & 3pm), which you can visit.

Billabong Koala & Wildlife Park (☎ 02-6585 1060; www.billabongkoala.com.au; 61 Billabong Dr; adult/child $18/11; 8am-4.30pm, feeding 3pm) is a wonderful family experience.

Sea Acres Rainforest Centre (☎ 02-6582 3355; Pacific Dr; adult/child $8/4; 9am-4.30pm) protects 72 hectares of coastal rainforest alive with birds, goannas, brush turkeys and, unfortunately, mosquitoes. There is a wheelchair-accessible boardwalk, a leafy rainforest cafe and excellent guided tours.

SLEEPING

our pick **Observatory** (☎ 1300 888 305, 02-6586 8000; www.observatory.net.au; 40 William St; apt from $129;) Soft tones,

MTMEDIA

Nobby's Beach, Port Macquarie

suede couches and glass doors that open onto beach-view balconies make these apartments and hotel rooms extremely comfortable.

Beachcomber Resort (☎ 02-6584 1881; www.beachcomberresort.com.au; 54 William St; apt from $130;) This low-rise condo-block has spiffy apartments with kitchenettes and bright, open living spaces. There's a barbecue courtyard, and Town Beach is across the way.

Rydges (☎ 02-6589 2888; www.rydges.com; 1 Hay St; r from $155;) With a day spa and coffee bar to hand, this hotel is a home-away-from-home for folk used to the good things in life. It's right on the water in the middle of town and the room rates increase with the better views. The rooftop swimming pool enables many laps of luxury.

PORT MACQUARIE TO COFFS HARBOUR

KEMPSEY

About 45km north of Port Macquarie, Kempsey is a large rural town serving the farms of the Macleay Valley.

It is home to the fabled **Akubra** (www.akubra.com.au) hat, the headwear of choice for a swag of Aussie icons – from Paul 'Crocodile Dundee' Hogan and singer John 'Whispering Jack' Farnham to former prime minister John Howard (when he wanted to bond with little Aussie battlers).

The factory is not open to the public, but the local department store will happily fit out those wanting an iconic Aussie souvenir.

The turn-off to Crescent Head is near the visitor centre in Kempsey. Or if you are coming from the north take the very scenic Belmore Rd, which leaves the Pacific Hwy at Seven Oaks and follows the Macleay River.

CRESCENT HEAD & AROUND

This little hideaway, 18km southeast of Kempsey, is the kind of sleepy place you'd come to write a book. Failing that, how about learning to ride a longboard? The town is the surf longboarding capital, and it's here that the Malibu surfboard gained prominence in Australia during the '60s. Today many come just to watch the longboard riders surf the epic waves of **Little Nobby's Junction**. There's also good shortboard riding off Plomer Rd.

our pick **Bush 'n' Beach Motel** (☎ 1800 007 873; www.surfaris.com; 353 Loftus Rd; dm/d $25/60;), better known as Surfari Central, is the perfect place for keen surfers to stay. These guys started the original Sydney–Byron surf tours and have now based themselves in Crescent Head because 'the surf is guaranteed every day'. The rooms are clean and comfortable with bathrooms and some wicked wall murals. Surf-and-stay packages are a speciality.

HAT HEAD NATIONAL PARK

This coastal **park** (per car per day $7) of 6500 hectares runs north from near Hat Head to **Smoky Cape** (south of Arakoon), protecting scrubland, swamps and some excellent beaches backed by one of the largest dune systems in NSW. Rising from the generally flat landscape is **Hungry Hill**, near Hat Head, and sloping Hat Head itself, where there's a walking track.

The wonderfully isolated village of **Hat Head**, surrounded by the national park, is much smaller and quieter than Crescent Head, with its own natural beauty. At the end of town, a picturesque wooden footbridge crosses the aqua-green salt marsh ocean inlet. The water is so clear you can see fish darting around. **Hat Head Coastal Café** (☎ 02-6567 7555; 40 Straight St) is the go-to spot for holiday-house rentals and information. **Hat Head Holiday**

Park (☎ 02-6567 7501; campsites/cabins $21/80) is close to the sheltered bay and footbridge. You can camp (adult/child $5/3) at **Hungry Head**, 5km south of Hat Head.

Hat Head and the national park are accessible from the hamlet of Kinchela, on the road between Kempsey and South West Rocks.

NAMBUCCA HEADS

Map reading around Nambucca's labyrinth of streets might be nauseating but that's a minor pay-off in a town idyllically strewn over a dramatically curling headland interlaced with the estuaries of the Nambucca River. It is spacious, sleepy and unspoilt with one of the coast's prettiest foreshores.

Nambucca Heads visitor centre (☎ 02-6568 6954; cnr Riverside Dr & Pacific Hwy) doubles as the main bus terminal and has a nice spot on the estuary.

Computing Innovations (☎ 02-6568 5411; Shop 4, Nambucca Plaza; per hr $8; 9am-5pm Mon-Fri, to noon Sat) has internet.

SIGHTS & ACTIVITIES

From the visitor centre, the newly extended **Gulmani Boardwalk** stretches 3km along the foreshore, through parks and bushland, and over pristine sand and waterways. It's the perfect introduction to the town.

Of the numerous lookouts, **Captain Cook Lookout**, with its 180-degree vista, best exploits the staggering views.

The only patrolled beach in town is **Main Beach**. **Beilby's** and **Shelly Beaches** are just to the south, closer to the river mouth – where the best surf is – and can be reached by going past the Captain Cook Lookout.

GETTING THERE & AWAY

Between Nambucca Heads and Coffs Harbour, detour off the highway onto the Waterfall Way (p128) to explore beautiful Bellingen and Dorrigo (both p128). A partly sealed road continues north from Dorrigo and swings east into Coffs Harbour via beautiful winding rainforest roads and a huge tallow wood tree, 56m high and more than 3m in diameter.

COFFS HARBOUR

pop 64,910

Coffs Harbour has always had to work hard to tart up its image. Where other coastal towns have the ready-made aesthetic of a main street slap-bang on the waterfront, Coffs has an inland city centre, a town 'jetty' (albeit with some great restaurants) that isn't actually on the water, and a semi-enclosed marina. On the flipside, the city has a string of fabulous beaches and a preponderance of water-based activities, action sports and wildlife encounters, making it hugely popular with families and the 'middle-Australian' market.

SIGHTS

Coffs Harbour boasts a ferrous-concrete **Big Banana** (☎ 02-6652 4355; www.bigbanana.com; Pacific Hwy; 9am-4.30pm) that's hailed by many as a national icon. This joint, built in 1964, actually started the craze for 'Big Things' in Australia (just so you know who to blame or praise).

The harbour's northern breakwater runs out onto **Muttonbird Island**, named for more than 12,000 pairs of birds who migrate here from late August to early April, with cute offspring visible in December and January. It marks the southern boundary of the **Solitary Islands Marine Park**, where warm tropical currents meet temperate southern currents, attracting unusual varieties of fish and great scuba diving.

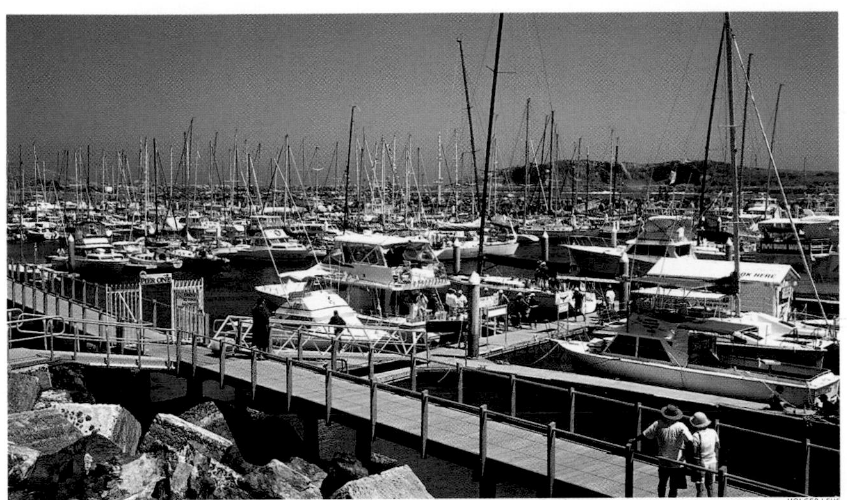

Marina, Coffs Harbour

At **Legends Surf Museum** (☎ 02-6653 6536; 18 Gaudrons Rd; adult/child $5/2; 10am-4pm), over 160 boards are on display as well as hundreds of surfing photos. It's 100m off the Pacific Hwy 10km north of Coffs; look for signs.

Sweeping **Park Beach** attracts plenty of swell along with punters and lifeguards from October to April. **Jetty Beach** is just south and a safer option. **Diggers Beach** – to the north – is partly nudist and sensational (for the surf), and **Macauleys Headland** also offers good surf. **Moonee Beach** lies 14km further north and **Emerald Beach** is a further 6km.

SLEEPING & EATING

The Jetty and the Promenade boast the best dining options. Most of the CBD closes down around 6pm. Kitchens start closing around 8.30pm, so come early or make a reservation.

our pick **Coffs Harbour YHA** (☎ 02-6652 6462; www.yha.com.au; 51 Collingwood St; dm/d with bathroom from $29/85) With service and amenities like these, it's a wonder hotels don't go out of business. The dorms and doubles with bathrooms are spacious and modern, and the TV lounge and kitchen are immaculate.

Aanuka Beach Resort (☎ 02-6652 7555; www.aanuka.com.au; 11 Firman Dr; r from $123) It might be out of town, but this luxurious resort, set amid luscious foliage, has excellent studios and apartments, all with spas and dishy interiors. It sits on a quiet neck of Diggers Beach and has tennis courts and an award-winning restaurant.

Novotel Pacific Bay Resort (☎ 1300 363 360, 02-6659 7000; cnr Pacific Hwy & Bay Dr; r from $149) The colossal Novotel is lavishly sprawled around a nine-hole golf course. The penthouse suites each have a rooftop eating area and outdoor spa tub.

COFFS HARBOUR TO BYRON BAY

If you want to avoid big city centres such as Coffs, **Woolgoolga** (also known as Woopi; population 4715), a coastal town just north of Coffs, is a good option. It's known for its surf-and-Sikh community.

As you drive by on the highway you're sure to notice the impressive **Guru Nanak Temple**, a Sikh *gurdwara* (place of worship).

YAMBA & ANGOURIE

Once a sleepy little fishing town, **Yamba** (population 6464) is slowly distancing itself from this reputation by attracting a fan base that has cottoned on to the merits of beaches on three fronts, a relaxed pace and excellent food without encroaching development.

Its southern neighbour **Angourie** (population 169) is home to NSW's first National Surfing Reserve and has always been a hot spot for experienced surfers (the type who were born on a board, wear helmets and leap off rocks). It complements Yamba's can-do attitude by remaining a small chilled-out place.

Surfing for the big boys is at **Angourie Point** but Yamba's beaches have something for everyone else. When the surf is flat **Pippi's** is decent, especially when dolphins hang around. **Yamba-Angourie Surf School** (☎ 02-6646 1496; 2hr lessons $50) has classes run by a former pro surfer.

BALLINA

At the mouth of the Richmond River, Ballina is spoilt for white sandy beaches and crystal-clear waters. If it were not so close to Byron it would be a tourist haven in its own right.

LENNOX HEAD

Recently classified as a protected National Surfing Reserve – à la the surfing mecca of Angourie – Lennox Head is home to picturesque coastline with some of the best surf on the coast, including long right-hander breaks. Its blossoming food scene combined with a laid-back atmosphere makes it an alternative to its boisterous well-touristed neighbour Byron, 17km north.

Stunning **Seven Mile Beach** runs along parallel to the main street. The best places for a dip are at the north end near the surf club or at the southern end in The Channel. **Port Morton lookout** is a whale- and dolphin-spotting high point.

BYRON BAY

Byron Bay's reputation precedes it like no other place in Australia: it's a gorgeous town where the trademark laid-back, New Age populace lives an escapist, organic lifestyle against a backdrop of evergreen hinterland and never-ending surfable coastline.

INFORMATION

Visitor centre (☎ 02-6680 9271; 80 Jonson St) A wealth of information.

SIGHTS

CAPE BYRON

The views from the summit are spectacular, particularly if you've just burnt breakfast off on the climbing track from Clarkes Beach. Ribboning around the headland, it dips and (mostly) soars its way to the lighthouse. The surrounding ocean also jumps to the tune of dolphins and migrating humpback whales in June and July.

Towering over all is the 1901 **lighthouse** (☎ 02-6685 6585; Lighthouse Rd; 8am-sunset), Australia's most easterly and powerful. The Cape Byron Walking Track continues around the northeastern side of the cape, delving into **Cape Byron State Conservation Park**, where you'll stumble across bush turkeys and wallabies.

WILL SALTER

The Pass, Byron Bay

BEACHES

Main Beach, immediately in front of town, is terrific for people watching and swimming. At the western edge of town, **Belongil Beach** is clothing optional. **Clarkes Beach**, at the eastern end of Main Beach, is good for surfing, but the best surf is at the next few beaches: the **Pass**, **Wategos** and **Little Wategos**.

ACTIVITIES

ALTERNATIVE THERAPIES

Byron is the alternative-therapy heartland. The *Body & Soul* guide, available from the visitor centre, is a handy guide to therapies on offer.

Buddha Gardens (☎ 02-6680 7844; www.buddhagardensdayspa.com.au; Arts Factory Village, 15 Gordon St; treatments from $80; 10am-6pm) Balinese-style day spa.

Byron Ayurveda Centre (☎ 02-6680 8788; www.ayurvedahouse.com.au; Shop 6, Middleton St; treatments from $45; 9am-6pm Mon-Sat) Indian medicinal therapies and organic products.

Byron Yoga Lounge (☎ 0402 770 441; www.byroniyengaryoga.com; 1 Banksia Dr; classes from $8) Daily classes.

Relax Haven (☎ 02-6685 8304; Belongil Beachouse, Childe St; 10am-8pm) Flotation tanks (one hour $35) and massage (one hour $55). Female therapists.

Shambala (☎ 02-6680 7791; www.shambala.net.au; 4 Carlyle St; treatments from $45; 9am-7pm) Massage, reflexology and acupuncture.

DIVING & SNORKELLING

About 3km offshore, Julian Rocks Marine Reserve blends cold southerly and warm northerly currents, attracting a profusion of marine species and divers alike.

Reputable diving companies:

Dive Byron Bay (☎ 1800 243 483, 02-6685 8333; www.byronbaydivecentre.com.au; 9 Marvell St) PADI courses from $395, dives from $90.

Sundive (☎ 1800 008 755; www.sundive.com.au; Middleton St) PADI courses from $395, snorkelling $50.

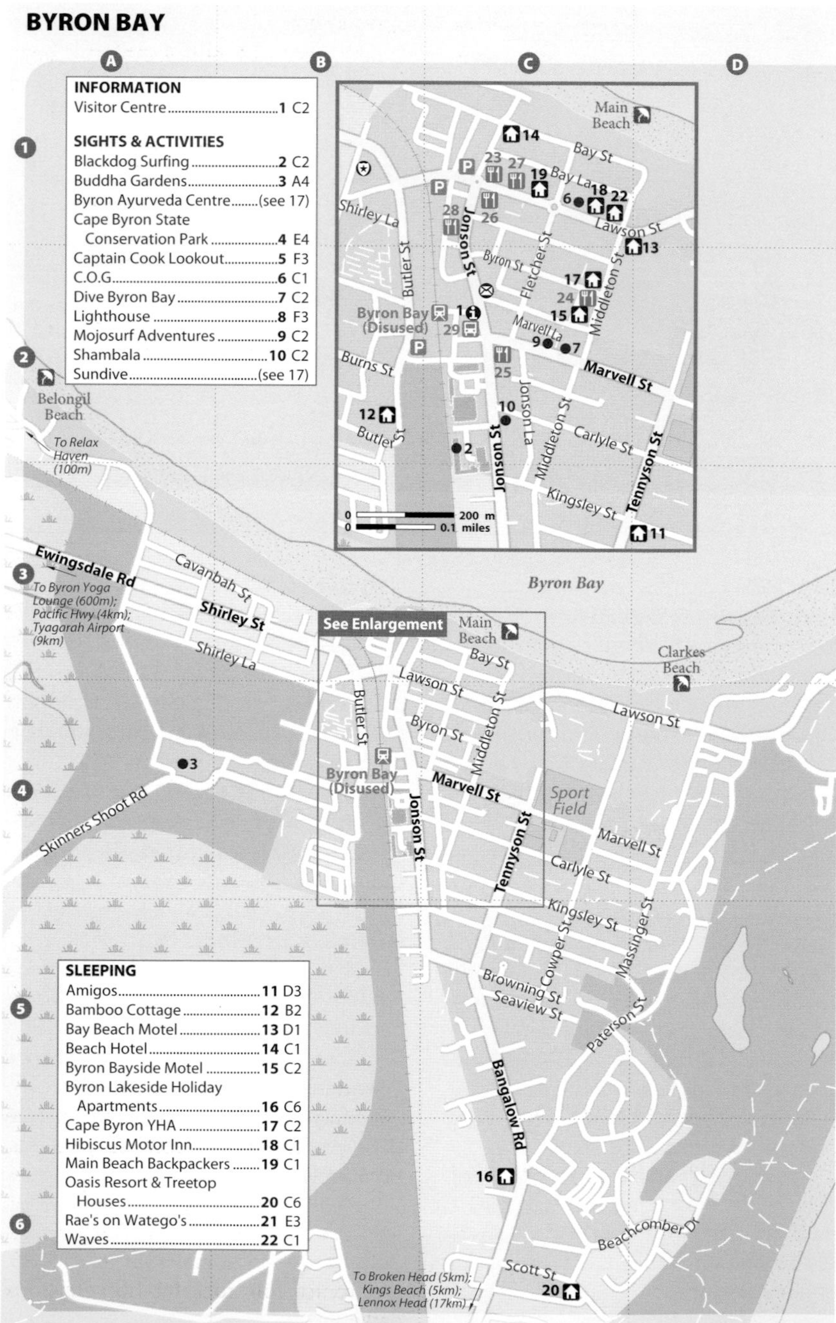
BYRON BAY
A
B
C
D
1
2
3
4
5
6
INFORMATION
Visitor Centre 1 C2
SIGHTS & ACTIVITIES
Blackdog Surfing 2 C2
Buddha Gardens 3 A4
Byron Ayurveda Centre .... (see 17)
Cape Byron State Conservation Park 4 E4
Captain Cook Lookout 5 F3
C.O.G 6 C1
Dive Byron Bay 7 C2
Lighthouse 8 F3
Mojosurf Adventures 9 C2
Shambala 10 C2
Sundive .... (see 17)
SLEEPING
Amigos 11 D3
Bamboo Cottage 12 B2
Bay Beach Motel 13 D1
Beach Hotel 14 C1
Byron Bayside Motel 15 C2
Byron Lakeside Holiday Apartments 16 C6
Cape Byron YHA 17 C2
Hibiscus Motor Inn 18 C1
Main Beach Backpackers 19 C1
Oasis Resort & Treetop Houses 20 C6
Rae's on Watego's 21 E3
Waves 22 C1
Main Beach
Bay St
Bay La
Shirley La
Lawson St
Butler St
Jonson St
Byron St
Fletcher St
Middleton St
Byron Bay (Disused)
Marvell La
Marvell St
Burns St
Jonson La
Carlyle St
Tennyson St
Kingsley St
0 200 m
0 0.1 miles
Belongil Beach
To Relax Haven (100m)
Ewingsdale Rd
Cavanbah St
Shirley St
To Byron Yoga Lounge (600m); Pacific Hwy (4km); Tyagarah Airport (9km)
Byron Bay
See Enlargement
Clarkes Beach
Skinners Shoot Rd
Sport Field
Cowper St
Massinger St
Browning St
Seaview St
Paterson St
Bangalow Rd
Beachcomber Dr
Scott St
To Broken Head (5km); Kings Beach (5km); Lennox Head (17km)

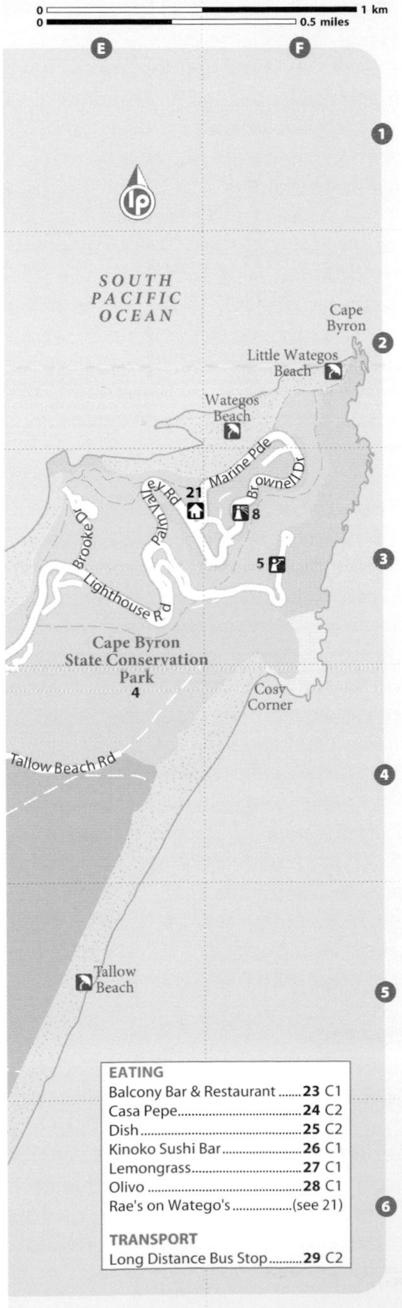

KAYAKING

Exhibitionist dolphins enhance scenic, half-day kayaking tours in and around Cape Byron Marine Park. Tours generally go for $50 to $60 per adult, less for children.

Cape Byron Kayaks (☎ 02-6680 9555; www.capebyronkayaks.com)

Dolphin Kayaking (☎ 02-6685 8044; www.dolphinkayaking.com.au)

Gosea Kayaks (☎ 0416 222 344; www.goseakayakbyronbay.com.au; 9.30am & 2pm)

SURFING

Byron Bay waves are often quite mellow. Most hostels provide free boards to guests.

Blackdog Surfing (☎ 02-6680 9828; www.blackdogsurfing.com; Shop 8, The Plaza, Jonson St) Three-hour lesson $60, three days $135.

C.O.G (☎ 02-6680 7066; 31 Lawson St) Rents boards for $25 per day.

Kool Katz (☎ 02-6685 5169; www.koolkatzsurf.com) Half-day lesson $49, three days $115.

Mojosurf Adventures (☎ 1800 113 044; www.mojosurf.com; Marvell St) Half-day lessons $65; two-to-five day, all-inclusive surf trips $195 to $635.

Samudra (☎ 02-6685 5600; www.samudra.com.au) Surf-and-yoga retreats.

FESTIVALS & EVENTS

East Coast International Blues & Roots Music Festival (☎ 02-6685 8310; www.bluesfest.com.au) Held over Easter, this international jam attracts high-calibre international performers and local heavyweights. Book early.

Splendour in the Grass (www.splendourinthegrass.com) Held in July, this popular indie music festival treats punters to funk, electronica, folk, rock, hip hop etc. Book early.

Taste of Byron (www.atasteofbyron.com) This celebration of produce from the Northern Rivers region rumbles the tummy in September.

SLEEPING

It's essential to book accommodation in advance for school holidays and summer, when rooms are full and tariffs increase by around 30%.

BUDGET

Cape Byron YHA (☎ 1800 652 627, 02-6685 8788; www.yha.com.au; cnr Byron & Middleton Sts; dm $25, d with/without bathroom from $90/80;) This purpose-built hostel is one tidy ship and has five-bed, uncramped dorms with lockers and fans. The doubles and twins are also spacious, and one has a bathroom. The kitchen and TV room are tight, but there's a sunny courtyard to compensate.

our pick **Main Beach Backpackers** (☎ 1800 150 233, 02-6685 8695; cnr Lawson & Fletcher Sts; dm $33, d $70-80;) This small and personable hostel makes guests feel like more than a number with friendly staff, a sunny lounge, and dorms and doubles reminiscent of comfy bedrooms.

MIDRANGE

Amigos (☎ 02-6680 8622; www.amigosbb.com; 32 Kingsley St; s/d from $88/108) Soaked in south-of-the-border flavours, this cute TV-free B&B has three bedrooms with crisp white linen and South American spreads. There are hammocks out the back.

our pick **Bamboo Cottage** (☎ 02-6685 5509; www.byron-bay.com/bamboocottage; 76 Butler St; r from $99) Featuring global charm and wall hangings, Bamboo Cottage treats guests to individually styled rooms with Asian overtones in a home-away-from-home atmosphere. It's on the quiet side of the tracks.

Byron Bayside Motel (☎ 02-6685 6004; www.byronbaysidemotel.com.au; 14 Middleton St; s/d $110/115) These spotless rooms have small kitchenettes and full laundries; ideal for campers looking for downtime. It's central, comparatively cheap and takes security seriously.

Oasis Resort & Treetop Houses (☎ 1800 336 129, 02-6685 7390; www.byronbayoasisresort.com.au; 24 Scott St; apt from $135, treetop apt from $205;) This compact resort is engulfed by palms and has sizeable one- and two-bedroom apartments with big balconies. Even better are the apartments sitting atop the tree canopies with outdoor spas and ocean views. All units are immaculate and kitted out in cheery decor.

Bay Beach Motel (☎ 02-6685 6090; www.baybeachmotel.com.au; 32 Lawson St; r $155-180, 2-bed apt from $235;) Unpretentious but smart, this white-brick hotel with contemporary furnishings is close to town, but not so close that party-goers keep guests awake.

More midrangers:

Byron Lakeside Holiday Apartments (☎ 02-6680 9244; www.byronlakeside.com; 5 Old Bangalow Rd; 4-night apt from $540;) Stylish holiday village with superb apartments.

Hibiscus Motor Inn (☎ 02-6685 6195; 33 Lawson St; d $155;) A basic but central motel with friendly owners.

TOP END

Beach Hotel (☎ 02-6685 6402; www.beachhotel.com.au; Bay St; r incl breakfast from $260;) This classy beachfront joint has garden-view rooms doused in forest greens and polished wood, with marble bathrooms and Thai silk cushions. Top of the food chain are the ocean-view loft rooms and the 'east coast suite'.

More top-enders:

Rae's on Watego's (☎ 02-6685 5366; www.raes.com.au; 8 Marine Pde, Wategos Beach; price on application;) One of Australia's best.

Waves (☎ 1800 040 151; www.wavesresorts.com.au; Lawson St; d apt from $250;) Cushy, boutique penthouse and studio apartments in the heart of Byron.

EATING

Lemongrass (☎ 02-6680 8443; Lawson Arcade, 3/17 Lawson St; mains $13-20; lunch Mon-Fri, dinner daily) All your favourite Vietnamese dishes, from rice-paper rolls and beef *pho* to green pawpaw salad and prawn fried rice.

Kinoko Sushi Bar (☎ 02-6680 9044; 7/23 Jonson St; lunch & dinner) Choo choo choose something from the sushi train or let the Japanese chef slice up a plate of fresh sashimi. This is a lively place where the Asahi also goes down well.

Casa Pepe (☎ 02-6685 7121; cnr Byron & Middleton Sts; mains $18-26; dinner Tue-Sat) It's strictly vegetarian, but this cosy restaurant is worthy of all dietary persuasions. Happy patrons sit in the sheltered courtyard and tuck into pizzas, pies, soups and tofu burgers for lunch and smart pastas for dinner.

our pick **Balcony Bar & Restaurant** (☎ 02-6680 9666; cnr Lawson & Jonson Sts; mains $20-30) Amid voyeuristic seating or cosy, obese cushions, the Balcony dishes up Ottoman overtones and fabulous fare for breakfast and lunch, and midnight tapas to soak up the cocktails.

Olivo (☎ 02-6685 7950; 34 Jonson St; mains $27-31; dinner) Chic and snug with global flavours such as baked eggplant stuffed with tomato, raisins and cinnamon, and duck confit with wild rice, grape and pistachio pilaf.

Dish (☎ 02-6685 7320; cnr Jonson & Marvell Sts; mains $27-38; dinner) Ivy-clad walls and floor-to-ceiling glass create an atrium atmosphere at this dishy restaurant. The equally sophisticated cuisine includes pan-roasted eye fillet with potato, onion and bacon croquette.

Rae's on Watego's (☎ 02-6685 5366; Marine Pde, Wategos Beach; entrées $32, mains $45;

GREG ELMS
Eating in Jonson St, Byron Bay

RICHARD I'ANSON

Ebor Falls, Guy Fawkes River National Park

↘ THE WATERFALL WAY

If you're into touring, point the car in this direction. The **Waterfall Way** is an awe-inspiring drive from inland Armidale to coasty Coffs Harbour. Not only does it traverse the gamut of spectacular World Heritage–listed national parks full of magnificent gorges, waterfalls and rare plants and animals, it passes through characteristic old towns including sleepy hillside Dorrigo and charm-your-socks-off Bellingen.

From Armidale the road heads east 40km to **Wollomombi Falls**, one of Australia's highest. Tame paths lead to lookouts and more strenuous multiday tracks head into the wilderness gorges of **Oxley Wild Rivers National Park**. On the southwest edge of the park is **Apsley Falls**.

Near Ebor township, **Ebor Falls** is a spectacular part of **Guy Fawkes River National Park**, deep in gorge country that's popular for canoeing and bushwalking.

Things you need to know www.visitwaterfallway.com.au

lunch & dinner) Save this exquisite restaurant with a terrace overlooking the ocean for a very special occasion. With the sound of surf providing ambience and the seafood platter providing the impetus, this is one to remember.

GETTING THERE & AWAY

The closest commercial airport is at Ballina (p122), but most people use the larger Coolangatta airport on the Gold Coast (p164).

Long-distance buses stop along Jonson St. **Greyhound** (☎ 1300 GREYHOUND/1300 473 946; www.greyhound.com.au) has daily services to Brisbane ($45, 3¼ hours), Coffs Harbour ($65, 4¼ hours) and Sydney ($130, 13½ hours).

FAR NORTH COAST HINTERLAND

Beach bums and surfers might not credit it, but there are people who not so secretly regard the hinterland – as opposed to Byron Bay – as the jewel in the Far North Coast crown.

Characteristic towns hide among the foliage, offering an eclectic take on small-town life. The hinterland also boasts The Border Ranges, Mt Warning and Nightcap National Parks, which form part of the World Heritage–listed rainforests of the Central Eastern Rainforest Reserves.

BANGALOW

Boutiques, fine eateries, bookshops and an excellent pub – a mere 14km from Byron Bay. Beautiful Bangalow, with its character-laden main street, is the kind of place that turns Sydneysiders into country-dwellers.

There's a good weekly **farmers market** (Byron St; 8-11am Sat) and a praised **cooking school** (☎ 02-6687 2799; www.bangalowcookingschool.com).

Stately old **Riverview Guesthouse** (☎ 02-6687 1317; www.riverviewguesthouse.com.au; 99 Byron St; r with/without bathroom $195/180) sits on the river's edge ensuring guests see platypuses and oversized lizards as they take on breakfast. It's the stuff of B&B dreams.

LISMORE

Lismore, the hinterland's commercial centre, appears to have been dropped into its green surroundings without ruffling the feathers of the pristine hinterland. The town itself sits on the Wilson River, though it has yet to take advantage of this, and is otherwise beautified by a liberal supply of heritage and art deco buildings, and a thriving artistic community.

The **Koala Care & Research Centre** (☎ 02-6622 1233; Rifle Range Rd; admission $3; tours 10am & 2pm Mon-Fri, 10am Sat) is home to recovering koalas and well worth a visit. To get a glimpse of platypuses, head to the northern end of Kadina St and walk up to **Tucki Tucki Creek** at dawn or sunset.

NIMBIN

A trip in Nimbin, or rather, a trip *to* Nimbin – is, erm, *high*-ly recommended for anyone visiting the Far North Coast. Wordplays aside, this strange little place, a hangover from an experimental 'Aquarius Festival' in the '70s, still feels like a social experiment where anything goes. Reefers included. But it's not all dreadlocks and tie-dye. A day or two here will reveal a growing artist community, a New Age culture and welcoming locals.

The wacky and wonderful **Nimbin Museum** (☎ 02-6689 1123; 62 Cullen St; admission free; 9am-5pm) pays homage to crashed kombis in psychedelic garb and the pursuit of 'loving the child within yourself'. Across the street, the **Hemp Embassy** (☎ 02-6689 1842; Cullen St; 9am-5pm) features none-too-subtle displays about hemp and marijuana, and might be banned under (more) despotic regimes.

NEW ENGLAND

The verdant scenery prompted the original settlers to name the area New England in 1839. The region has a string of national parks including Bald Rock and Washpool National Parks in the north. On the Waterfall Way linking Armidale and Coffs Harbour, Guy Fawkes River, Cathedral Rock, New England and Oxley Wild Rivers National Parks feature granite outcrops, unforgettably deep gorges and waterfalls.

TAMWORTH

pop 42,499

Country music kicks this town along like a line of boot-scooters but don't expect Nashville-style roadhouses and Route 66 scenery. The country-music capital of Oz has a vibrant nightlife and an emerging wine scene, as well as the rather large golden guitar. They may not wear chaps but you'll sure see some boots.

INFORMATION

To get into the string of things, drop into the guitar-shaped **visitor centre** (☎ 02-6767 5300; www.visittamworth.com.au; cnr Peel & Murray Sts) and check out the **Walk a Country Mile Museum** (adult/child $5/4.50).

SIGHTS

If the names Tex Morton, Buddy Williams and Smoky Dawson mean anything to you, then the **Australian Country Music Foundation** (☎ 02-6766 9696; www.acmf.org.au; 93 Brisbane St; adult/child $6/4; 10am-4pm Mon-Fri, to 1pm Sat) will too. This is a country music great Hall of Fame (in the making) with photographs, historic video and film footage, music and souvenirs.

CLAVER CARROLL

The Big Golden Guitar, Tamworth (p129)

The **Big Golden Guitar Tourist Centre** (☎ 02-6765 2688; www.biggoldenguitar.com.au; New England Hwy; 9am-5pm) has a cafe and a shop where you can stock up on all-important golden-guitar snow cones.

FESTIVALS & EVENTS

Held at the end of January, New England's biggest annual party, the **Country Music Festival**, lasts 10 days. There are over 800 acts, of which 75% are free. If you missed it, get along to **Hats Off to Country Music** in July.

SOUTH COAST

If a road trip takes your fancy you've come to the right place. The South Coast, breathtaking in the extreme, stretches 400km by road to the Victorian border through rolling dairy country, blast-from-the-past heritage towns, stunning national parks and rugged coastline. Though the main thoroughfare, the Princes Hwy, projects a lot of this scenery onto your windscreen, the South Coast is undoubtedly best experienced by dipping on and off the road well travelled. It's on the backroads and byways that isolated beaches, pristine campsites and remote lighthouses reveal themselves.

WOLLONGONG

pop 277,972

The 'Gong', 80km south of Sydney, is the envy of many cities. Sure, it has restaurants, bars, arts, culture and entertainment, that's easy enough. But it also enjoys a laid-back, beachside lifestyle impossible to match anywhere inland. Just to rub it in, Sydney is easily accessible by local rail.

There are 17 patrolled beaches – all unique – and a spectacular sandstone escarpment that runs from the Royal National Park south past Wollongong and Port Kembla. The **Grand Pacific Drive** makes the most of the landscape and the whole combination makes for a host of outdoor activities: excellent surf, safe beaches, bushwalks and sky-high adventures to name a few.

North Beach and **Wollongong City Beach** have breaks suitable for all visitors and are walking distance from the city centre. Look for the Acids Reef break on North Beach for more of a challenge. Up the coast, the options are varied and less crowded, with fun beach breaks at **Coledale** and **Bulli** beaches, and reef breaks at **Sharkies** (also at Coledale) and **Headlands**.

The risk of meeting a finned friend at Sharkies is minimal, but surfers have occasionally encountered humpback whales surfacing close to shore.

ACTIVITIES

Taupu Surf School (☎ 02-4268 0088; www.taupusurfschool.com; 1/3 lessons $59/$159; Mon-Sat) runs courses at Thirroul and North Wollongong.

A bird's-eye view of the coastline is perhaps the best. **Sydney Hang Gliding Centre** (☎ 02-4294 4294; www.hanggliding.com.au; 8am-8pm) has tandem flights ($195) from breathtaking Bald Hill at Stanwell Park. If the adrenalin still hasn't kicked in, you can skydive from 14,000ft and land in the sand with **Skydive the Beach** (☎ 1300 663 634; www.skydivethebeach.com; Stuart Park; tandem jumps from $275; 8am-6pm Mon-Fri, to 2pm Sat & Sun).

SLEEPING

The visitor centre can make accommodation reservations.

Wollongong YHA & Kieraview Accommodation (☎ 02-4229 9700; www.yha.com.au; 75-79 Keira St; dm/d $30/110;) This complex contains the well-equipped and friendly YHA hostel, which caters to students and backpackers in tidy four-bed dorms. It's also home to Kieraview, which has double and family rooms with verandahs and kitchenettes. They are clean but soulless and a tad overpriced.

Novotel Northbeach (☎ 02-4226 3555; www.novotel.com.au; 2-14 Cliff Rd; r from $199;) Wollongong's flashiest joint is all class. The spacious and comfortable rooms have balconies with ocean or escarpment views. Breakfast is included.

WOLLONGONG TO NOWRA

KIAMA & AROUND

Right on the water's edge with good beaches and surf, **Kiama** (population 12,286) hasn't had to work hard for glory. What it has done is admirable and tasteful, making it one of the best stops on the South Coast. The **visitor centre** (☎ 02-4232 3322, 1300 654 262; www.kiama.com.au) is on Blowhole Point, so called because of a **blowhole** that can spurt water 60m.

ROSS BARNETT

Lighthouse, Wollongong

NEW SOUTH WALES

SOUTH COAST

Amid the flora and fauna of the Southern Highlands, about 14km inland from Kiama, the brand-new **Illawarra Fly Tree Top Walk** (☎ 1300 362 881; www.illawarrafly.com; 182 Knights Hill Rd, Knights Hill; adult/child/family $19/9/49; ⏰ 9am-7pm) takes visitors on a 500m elevated walk to the edge of the forest with spectacular Illawarra and ocean views.

South along the coast, **Gerringong** and **Gerroa** have their fair share of picture-postcard scenery. There's good surf at **Werri Beach**, 10km south in Gerringong, and **Surf Camp Australia** (☎ 1800 888 732; www.surfcamp.com.au; 2 lessons $90) gives surf lessons on beautiful Seven Mile Beach in Gerroa.

The modern **Kiama Harbour Cabins** (☎ 1800 823 824; Blowhole Point, Kiama; 1-bedroom cabins from $185) are in the best position in town and have barbecues on the front verandahs, which overlook the beach and the ocean pool.

KANGAROO VALLEY

Unbelievably picturesque Kangaroo Valley is pegged in by a fortress of rainforest-covered cliffs and the valley floor is carpeted by cow-dotted pasturelands, river gums and gurgling creeks. The slow country town of Kangaroo Valley itself has an excellent pub, bakery and general store, plus the odd feel-good shop and gallery to satiate wealthy Sydneysiders who populate the town at the weekend.

If you want to get a little more personal with the landscape, go canoeing, mountain biking and bushwalking in and around the Shoalhaven and Kangaroo Rivers. **Kangaroo Valley Escapes** (☎ 0400 651 170; Moss Vale Rd; half-day tours $50-80, overnight $65-180) offers environmentally conscious guided tours that you design yourself, combining various rigorous activities.

NOWRA

Nowra sits about 17km from the coast and is the largest town in the Shoalhaven area. Although it's not top of the pops in terms of beach holidays, it is a handy base for excursions to beaches and villages around the region.

The **Shoalhaven visitor centre** (☎ 1300 662 808; www.shoalhavenholidays.com.au; Princes Hwy; 💻) is just south of the bridge. There's also a **NPWS office** (☎ 02-4423 2170; 55 Graham St).

Shoalhaven River Cruises (☎ 0429 981 007; www.shoalhavenrivercruise.com; 2hr cruise $22) has great river tours that leave from the wharf, near the visitor centre.

JERVIS BAY

South of Nowra, Jervis Bay is a scenically opulent and unmissable stretch of coastline with white sandy beaches, bushland, forest and a protected marine park. **Huskisson** (population 1593), one of the oldest towns on the bay, has a handful of excellent eating venues, plenty of adventure-based activity and delightful surrounds that make it a great place to spend a night or two.

June to November is prime whale time in Jervis Bay, and **Dolphin Watch Cruises** (☎ 1800 246 010t; www.dolphinwatch.com.au; 50 Owen S) has the best reputation for dolphin (adult/child $25/15, two hours) and whale-watching (adult/child $65/35, three hours, May to November) tours.

Paperbark Camp (☎ 1300 668 167; www.paperbarkcamp.com.au; 571 Woollamia Rd; d from $320; ⏰ Sep-Jun) is ecotourism at its luxury best: five-star accommodation in 12 safari-style tents with outdoor showers. The camp's **Gunyah Restaurant** (☎ 02-4441 7299; entrées $25, mains $35; ⏰ dinner) sits among the treetops, attracting romantics, and the odd possum.

MTMEDIA

Casey's Beach, Batemans Bay

BATEMANS BAY

The good beaches and a luscious estuary in this fishing port have given it a leg up to become one of the South Coast's largest holiday centres.

Corrigans Beach is the closest patch of sand to the town centre. South of here is a series of small beaches nibbled into the rocky shore. Surfers flock to **Surf Beach**, **Malua Bay** and **Broulee**, which has a small wave when everywhere else is flat. For the experienced, the best surfing in the area is at **Pink Rocks** (near Broulee). For amateurs **Soulrider Surf School** (☎ 02-4478 6297; www.soulrider.com.au; 1hr adult/child $40/35) conducts lessons on Surf Beach.

Several boats offer cruises up the estuary from the ferry wharf just east of the bridge, including **Merinda Cruises** (☎ 02-4472 4052; 3hr cruise adult/child $27/14; 11.30am).

The central **Clyde River Motor Inn** (☎ 02-4472 6444; www.clydemotel.com.au; 3 Clyde St; s/d from $85/89) is excellent value, with good river rooms and townhouses.

NAROOMA

Narooma is a sleepy little seaside town with a large number of retiree residents adding to its snail-paced leisurely atmosphere. It's also one of the prettier coastal towns boasting the attractive Wagonga River inlet, a picturesque bridge and relatively little development.

Island Charters Narooma (☎ 02-4476 1047; www.islandchartersnarooma.com) offers diving ($85), snorkelling ($75), kayaking (adult/child $45/40) and whale watching ($80/55). Attractions in the area include grey nurse sharks, fur seals and the wreck of the SS *Lady Darling*.

AROUND NAROOMA

About 10km offshore from Narooma, **Montague Island** was once an important source of food for local Aborigines (who called it Barunguba) and is now a nature reserve. **Little penguins** nest here; the best time to see them is spring. Many other seabirds and hundreds of fur seals also call the island home, and there's a historic **lighthouse**.

Narooma Charters (☎ **0407 909 111; adult/child/family $130/99/430**) operates a daily four-hour boat trip to Montague Island including a NPWS tour. Take the afternoon trip if you want to see the little penguins.

Off the highway, 15km south of Narooma, **Central Tilba** is perched on the side of **Gulaga** (Mt Dromedary; 797m). It's a delightful 19th-century gold-mining boomtown.

SOUTH TO THE VICTORIAN BORDER

MERIMBULA

The surplus of nondescript hotels and holiday apartments lining the sloping main street of Merimbula still manage to play second fiddle to the town's impressive inlet (or lake).

The rocking boat masts and sky-blue water – catering to fisherfolk throwing in a line wherever they please – make this popular holiday place very easy on the eye.

EDEN

Eden lives up to its namesake. Once a haven for fisherfolk and woodchippers, this charming seaside town is now squarely on the itinerary for those looking to laze a day away on the town's 1.5km beach or explore the surrounding national parks and wilderness areas. Whale watching is big on the agenda and you're likely to hear a bit about former resident Benjamin Boyd, a 19th-century entrepreneur, landowner and magnate whose failed whaling boom enterprise – Boydtown – can still be visited.

The **Killer Whale Museum** (☎ **02-6496 2094; 94 Imlay St; adult/child $8/2;** 🕒 **9.15am-4.45pm Mon-Sat, 11am-5pm Sun**) is often derided as a little old hat. You decide. The skeleton of Old Tom, a killer whale and local legend is housed there.

In October and November, **Cat Balou Cruises** (☎ **0427 962 027; www.catbalou.com.au; Main Wharf; adult/child $65/55**) has whale-spotting cruises. At other times, dolphins,

SIMON FOALE

Estuary, Merimbula

fur seals and seabirds can usually be seen during the shorter bay cruise ($30/17).

Boydtown, off the highway 10km south of Eden, has relics of Ben Boyd's stillborn empire.

KOSCIUSZKO NATIONAL PARK

The Snowy Mountains, or Snowies, as they are known, form part of the Great Dividing Range where it straddles the NSW–Victorian border and also the Australian Alps stretching north to the ACT border and south to the Victorian Alps. This larger region boasts five of the highest peaks on the mainland, and the Snowies themselves lay claim to *numero uno*, Mt Kosciuszko (koz-zy-*os*-ko), at 2228m. In its entirety, the region is mainland Australia's only true Alpine area, and as such can expect snow falls from early June to late August.

It would be short-sighted to visit the jewel in NSW's national-park crown – home to Australia's highest mountain, **Mt Kosciuszko** (2228m) – and to focus purely on the snow. Sure the mountain welcomes throngs of ski bunnies in winter, but this natural park, covering 673,492 hectares and stretching 150km from north to south, has so many varied attractions that it takes visits in all seasons to really gauge its full potential.

Entry to the national park costs $27 a day per car in winter and $16 at other times.

With a short season and unpredictable snowfalls, this is not the Swiss Alps. But don't be put off. Thredbo has forked out a fortune to automate its snowmaking machines (ensuring 25% of rideable terrain is covered), and Perisher Blue has upgraded its facilities to enable more reliable connections between major chairlifts.

ROB BLAKERS

Kosciuszko National Park

Off the slopes there's lively nightlife, excellent restaurants, and a plethora of facilities and activities catering for families.

THREDBO

Thredbo (☎ **1300 020 589; www.thredbo.com.au**) is oft lauded as Australia's number-one ski resort. At 1370m it not only has the longest runs and some of the best skiing, the village itself is eye candy compared with other Australian ski villages, the blue, green and grey tones ensuring chalets and lodges blend with the surrounding snow gums and alpine flora.

Thredbo YHA Lodge (☎ **02-6457 6376; www.yha.com.au; 8 Jack Adams Path; winter dm/**

JOHN BANAGAN

Thredbo (p135), Kosciuszko National Park

d, $145/163, r with bathroom $179, summer dm/d $30/69, r with bathroom $80; 💻) The best-value on the mountain, this YHA is well appointed, with great common areas, a good kitchen and a balcony. Peak-season adults must be full YHA members.

Aneeki Lodge (☎ 0417 479 581; www.aneeki.com.au; 9 Bobuck Lane, winter 2-night d per person $170-340, summer d $190) One of the cheapest lodges on the mountain.

Thredbo Alpine Hotel (☎ 1800 026 333; Friday Dr; winter s/d from $190/270, summer r from $105; ❄ 💻 🏊) The only hotel on the mountain has suitably flash rooms. Breakfast is included.

PERISHER BLUE

Perisher Valley, Smiggin Holes, Mt Blue Cow and Guthega make up the massive resort of **Perisher Blue** (☎ 02-6459 4495, 1300 655 811; www.perisherblue.com.au). Guthega (1640m) and Mt Blue Cow (1640m) are mainly day resorts, so they're smaller and less crowded.

Mt Blue Cow is accessible via the **Skitube** (☎ 1300 655 822; same-day return adult/child/family $42/23/99, open return $55/37/141), Perisher Blue's most underrated draw-card. Simply park the car at **Bullocks Flat** (Alpine Way), buy a ticket, board the train and within 15 minutes you're on the slopes.

Sundeck Hotel (☎ 02-6457 5222; www.sundeckhotel.com.au; Kosciuszko Rd; 2-night d/tw per person from $375-645) Australia's highest hotel, and one of Perisher's oldest lodges, has a comfy bar and great views over the Quad 8 Express.

↘ BRISBANE & QUEENSLAND

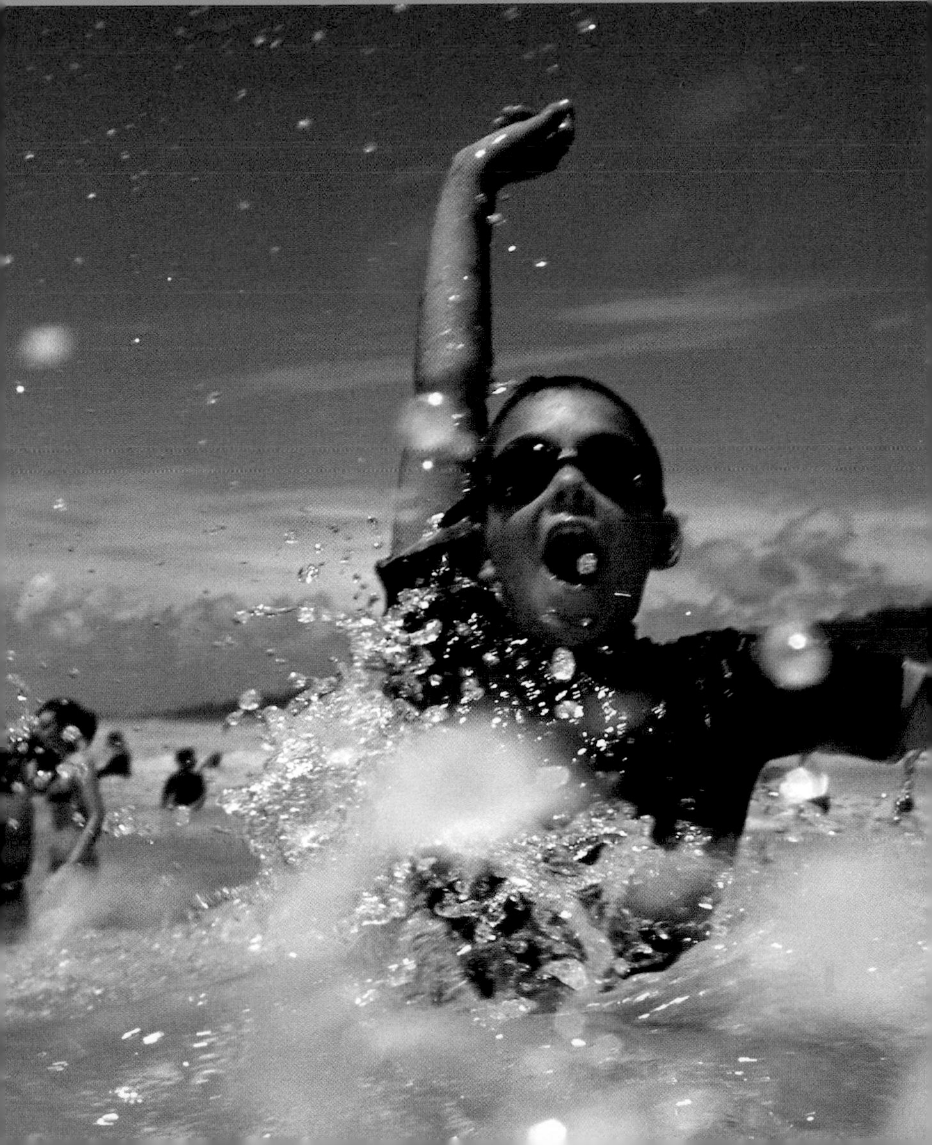

QUEENSLAND

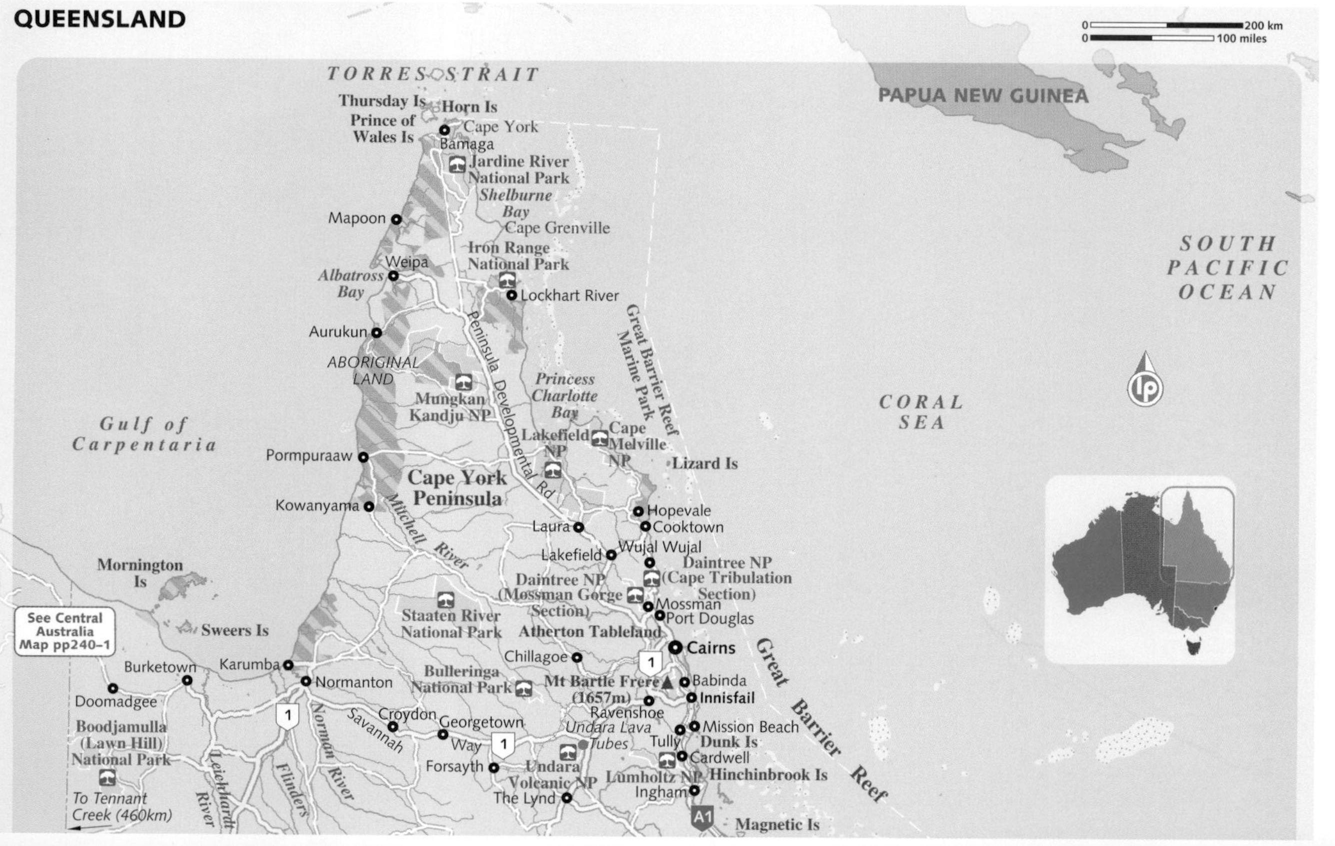

See Central Australia Map pp240–1

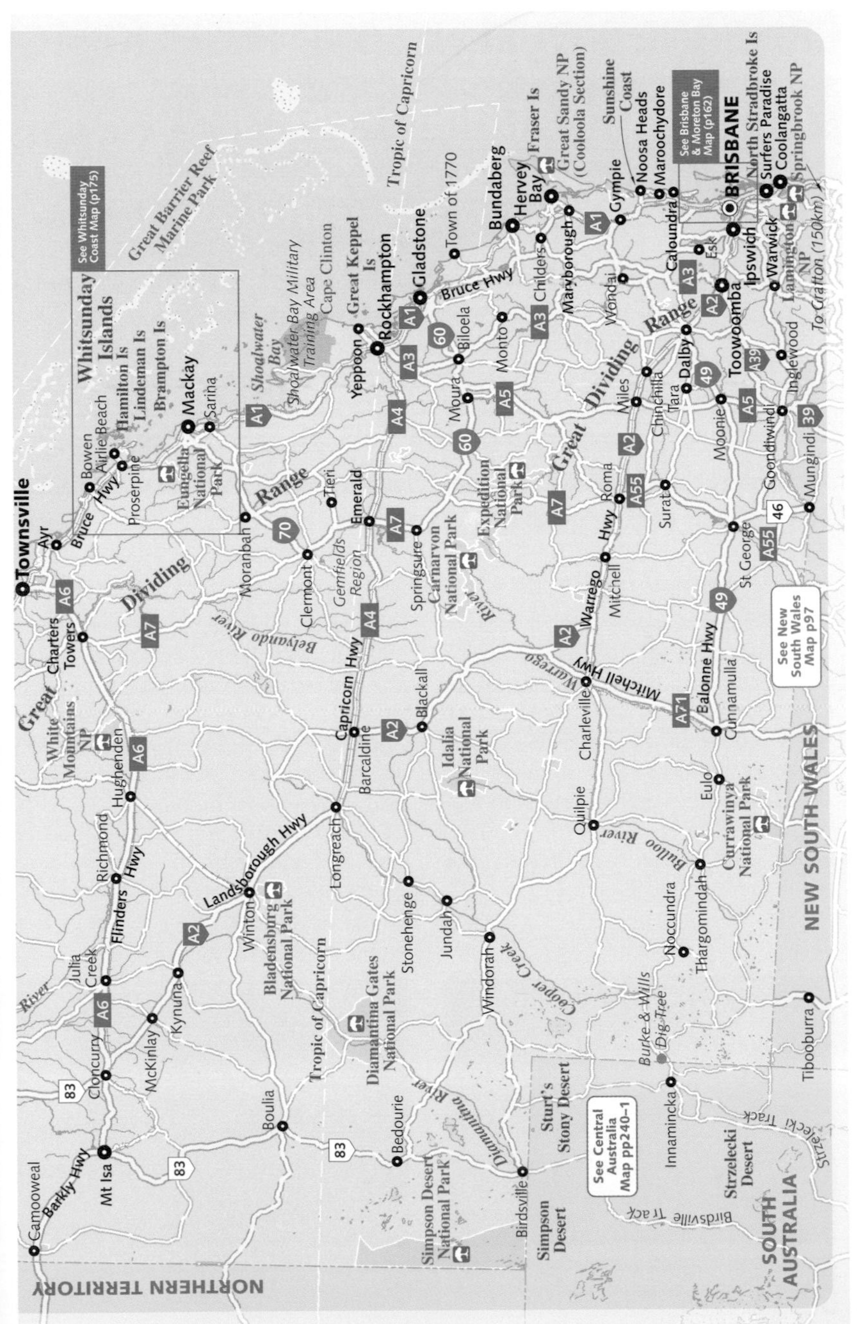

Townsville
Ayr
Bowen
Airlie Beach
Proserpine
Whitsunday Islands
Hamilton Is
Lindeman Is
Brampton Is
Mackay
Sarina
Eungella National Park
See Whitsunday Coast Map (p175)
Great Barrier Reef Marine Park
Shoalwater Bay
Shoalwater Bay Military Training Area
Cape Clinton
Yeppoon
Great Keppel Is
Rockhampton
Gladstone
Tropic of Capricorn
Town of 1770
Bundaberg
Hervey Bay
Fraser Is
Great Sandy NP (Cooloola Section)
Sunshine Coast
Noosa Heads
Maroochydore
Caloundra
Gympie
Maryborough
Childers
Biloela
Moura
Monto
Wondai
Bruce Hwy
See Brisbane & Moreton Bay Map (p162)
BRISBANE
North Stradbroke Is
Surfers Paradise
Coolangatta
Springbrook NP
Ipswich
Esk
Toowoomba
Warwick
Lamington NP
To Grafton (150km)
Dalby
Tara
Chinchilla
Miles
Great Dividing Range
Inglewood
Goondiwindi
Moonie
Mungindi
Roma
Surat
St George
Expedition National Park
Carnarvon National Park
Springsure
Emerald
Tieri
Clermont
Moranbah
Gemfields Region
Charters Towers
Belyando River
Warrego Hwy
Mitchell
Charleville
Mitchell Hwy
Warrego River
Balonne Hwy
Cunnamulla
See New South Wales Map p97
Capricorn Hwy
Barcaldine
Blackall
Idalia National Park
Longreach
Landsborough Hwy
Winton
Bladensburg National Park
Hughenden
White Mountains NP
Richmond
Flinders Hwy
Julia Creek
Cloncurry
McKinlay
Kynuna
Mt Isa
Camooweal
Barkly Hwy
Boulia
Bedourie
Birdsville
Diamantina Gates National Park
Diamantina River
Tropic of Capricorn
Stonehenge
Jundah
Windorah
Cooper Creek
Quilpie
Bulloo River
Eulo
Currawinya National Park
Thargomindah
Noccundra
Burke & Wills Dig Tree
Innamincka
Tiboobura
Sturt's Stony Desert
See Central Australia Map pp240-1
Strzelecki Desert
Strzelecki Track
Birdsville Track
Simpson Desert
Simpson Desert National Park
NORTHERN TERRITORY
SOUTH AUSTRALIA
NEW SOUTH WALES

BRISBANE & QUEENSLAND HIGHLIGHTS

1 GREAT BARRIER REEF

BY LEN ZELL, GREAT BARRIER REEF GUIDE & AUTHOR – WWW.LENZELL.COM

I have been 'discovering' this very special place – the Great Barrier Reef (GBR or Reef) – since 1969. On every visit to a popular or remote site I discover something new. I am amazed at the reef's resilience after being battered by natural and now chronic human impacts, which are causing a continuing decline.

➘ LEN ZELL'S DON'T MISS LIST

❶ THE REEF BY NIGHT

If possible, take an extended dive charter or stay overnight on a sand cay resort or camping ground. An overnight stay allows you to 'feel' some of the many moods of this gigantic system, especially during an atmospheric night dive. During the summer breeding seasons of sea turtles and birds, the fish, worms and corals turn the waters into a thriving 'gamete soup'.

❷ GETTING WET

Staff at all snorkelling and diving destinations will assist you to get wet in the best way for your ability or, best of all, take you way beyond your imagined ability – safely. Having seen an 80-year-old Scottish woman who had never gone beyond knee-deep, be led into the water with snorkelling gear and stay there for more than an hour until she was shivering with cold, shows anyone can do it. Once in you won't want to come out!

Clockwise from top: Humpback whale; Pink anemone fish; Freckled hawkfish; Snorkellers exploring the Great Barrier Reef; Green turtle at Briggs Reef, Great Barrier Reef

CLOCKWISE FROM TOP: LEONARD ZELL; DAVID WALL; BOB CHARLTON; MICHAEL AW; MICHAEL AW

❸ WATERY WILDLIFE ENCOUNTERS

Don't miss the magnificent manta rays at **Lady Elliot Island** (p184), the most southerly of the reef's islands. Tranquil **Heron Island** (p184) is a nesting ground for birds, and green and loggerhead turtles, and features the 'Bommie', a fish-filled mini-reef or coral head. Snorkel with minke whales midyear between Cairns and Lizard Island, eyeball massive cod at the Cod Hole on No 10 Ribbon Reef, and dive with sea snakes in the Swain Reefs.

❹ THE CHANCE TO EXPLORE

Take a deeper look into this magnificent ecosystem by exploring beyond the well-known cays. Seek out the remote and the less-visited reefs to witness the unexpected, which may include reefs recently smashed by cyclones, devoured by crown of thorns sea stars, or reefs in recovery mode. Check out the fascinating wreck of the *Yongala* (p184), between Bowen and Townsville, the outer reefs far off **Cairns** (p188), and the rarely visited islands and reefs north of **Lizard Island** (p184), towards Torres Strait.

↘ THINGS YOU NEED TO KNOW

Mainland gateways Numerous operators in Airlie Beach (p174) and Cairns (p179) can arrange your reef visit **Best true reef island resorts** Heron, Lady Elliot and Lizard Islands (all on p184) or Green Island (p188) **Best camping** Lady Musgrave Island, Northwest Island and East Hope Island

BRISBANE & QUEENSLAND HIGHLIGHTS

2 WHITSUNDAY ISLANDS

BY MICHAEL O'CONNOR, WHITSUNDAY BOOKINGS MANAGER & SKYDIVING & SCUBA DIVING INSTRUCTOR

There is no better way to experience the breathtaking Whitsunday Islands than to set sail on an overnight sailing adventure. Get out there and explore the best of the 74 Whitsunday Islands and make the most of your time. Be one with the crystal clear waters and amazing marine life.

↘ MICHAEL O'CONNOR'S DON'T MISS LIST

❶ THE WHITSUNDAY NGARO SEA TRAIL

Follow in the footsteps of the Ngaro people, the traditional owners of the Whitsunday area, and undertake a journey through a region of unsurpassed natural beauty and rich cultural history. Blending seaways with a range of walks, the Whitsunday Ngaro Sea Trail highlights many iconic features that have made the area famous. Walk pure white sands, sail turquoise waters, see ancient rock art, rugged headlands, dry rainforest, rolling grasslands, and experience breathtaking views.

❷ BAIT REEF

Having been a dive instructor for over 15 years and diving my way around the world, Bait Reef is still one of my favourite dive sites. It is one of the most pristine and spectacular diving sites on the Great Barrier Reef and is classed as a Special Management Area. Limited numbers of boats are allowed to visit Bait Reef and no fishing is

Clockwise from top: Boats moored off Airlie Beach (p174); Hayman Island Resort, Whitsunday Islands (p177); Whitehaven Beach (p178); Acropora coral and spotfin lionfish; Relaxing in the Whitsunday Islands

CLOCKWISE FROM TOP: MICAH WRIGHT; MICHAEL AW; RICHARD I'ANSON; HOLGER LEUE; CHRISTOPHER GROENHOUT

allowed. The best dive sites are Manta Ray Drop Off, The Stepping Stones and Paradise Lagoon.

❸ CRAYFISH BEACH, HOOK ISLAND

Crayfish is my favourite camping getaway in the Whitsundays. It is at the top of **Hook Island** (p178) and offers fantastic snorkelling, a beautiful beach and a secluded campsite that takes a maximum of 12 people. If you want a few days away from the rat race this is the place.

❹ THE ESPLANADE, AIRLIE BEACH

The Esplanade at **Airlie Beach** (p174) is a great spot to just relax and watch people pass by while enjoying great food and drinks at one of the many restaurants. The Airlie Beach markets are at the end of the Esplanade every Saturday morning, and Sunday sessions are a great way to end the week: from around 2pm there is live music on the beachfront opposite the Esplanade restaurants.

↘ THINGS YOU NEED TO KNOW

Best photo opportunity Take to the air for a fabulous angle on world-famous Whitehaven Beach (p178) **Best snorkelling** Hook (p178) and Whitsunday Islands (p177) **Best island camping** Hook and Whitsunday Islands (both p178) and South Molle Island **See our author's review on p177**

BRISBANE & QUEENSLAND HIGHLIGHTS

3

➘ BRISBANE

Australia's third-largest city is a booming metropolis engraved with a graceful meandering river. Exploring **Brisbane** by river ferry, and passing under the mighty **Story Bridge** (p155), will give you a wonderful appreciation of this prosperous city. On its banks are lush subtropical gardens and magnificent vestiges of colonial architecture as well as vibrant cafes, galleries, theatres and restaurants.

4

➘ NOOSA

It just keeps getting better at **Noosa** (p168), the Sunshine Coast's premier resort town, where style meets surf, or chic meets surfie chick. Noosa is developed, but the little luxuries of the well-heeled mingle effortlessly with the free-of-charge natural attributes – the beach and the bush. Enjoy the culinary and shopping delights of Hastings St, take a lesson in surfboard riding or just lie back and sip a cafe latte.

5

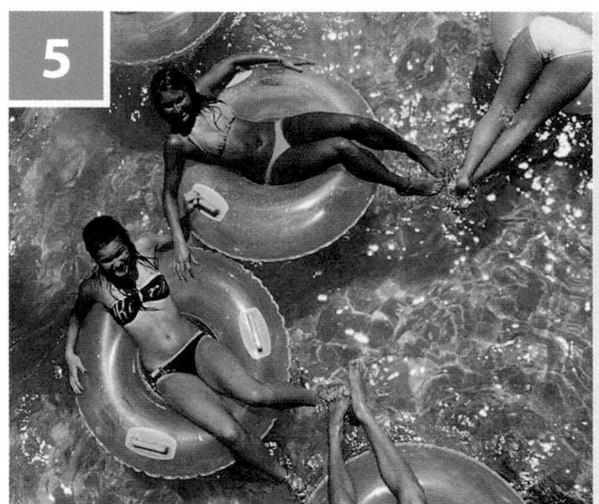

BLITZ THE GOLD COAST

Sparkling high-rise buildings parade along the beachfront of the aptly named **Gold Coast** (p164). Stretching for 35km, this ribbon of manufactured tourist attractions – casinos, **theme parks** (p165), shopping malls and glitzy accommodation – faces the original natural attraction: superb golden sand beaches and blue Pacific rollers.

6

MORETON BAY

Where the Brisbane River meets the sea, magnificent **Moreton Bay** (p161) is brimming with marine life, including whales, dolphins and dugongs. Feed wild dolphins and snorkel in crystal-clear water at Tangalooma or join Brisbane families on holiday on the pristine sandy beaches and freshwater lakes of North Stradbroke Island.

7

CAIRNS

Far North Queensland's tourism hub is a tropical hive of activity, and there's no limit to the capers you can organise in **Cairns** (p179), from bungee jumps to white-water rafting. But it's the excellent diving and snorkelling that keeps this town humming. An armada of slick craft whisk adventurers out to the Great Barrier Reef and then back to their stylish base station.

3 Queen St Mall, Brisbane (p150); 4 Tea Tree Bay (p170), Noosa; 5 Gold Coast (p164); 6 Tangalooma Wild Dolphin Resort (p164), Moreton Island; 7 Green Island (p188), off Cairns

BRISBANE & QUEENSLAND'S BEST...

ISLAND ESCAPES

- **Hamilton Island** (p178) Not for Robinson Crusoes, this luxury resort has abundant activities and entertainment options.
- **North Stradbroke Island** (p163) A laid-back resort with natural attractions, just a skip from Brisbane.
- **Green Island** (p188) Day trippers from Cairns pile in to enjoy the beaches and snorkelling, or you can opt for a luxury overnight stay.

ADRENALIN THERAPY

- **Gold Coast theme parks** (p165) Adventure is on tap for thrill seekers and parents of restless teens.
- **Diving the Great Barrier Reef** (p182) Take a course and enjoy the buzz of an extended underwater swim over a deep water drop-off.
- **Surfing and kitesurfing** (p166) Catch the Gold Coast surf with just a board or, for an extra kick, attach a kite and power over the waves.

DIVING & SNORKELLING

- **Green Island** (p188) Quick and easy access from Cairns with super offshore snorkelling.
- **Hook Island** (p178) Superb access to coral coupled with fabulous camping or simple budget digs.
- **Frankland Islands National Park** (p189) Fabulous coral reef surrounds these uninhabited, national park islands off Cairns.

BEACHES

- **Gold Coast** (p164) From Coolangatta in the south all the way to the Surfers Paradise glitter strip, there's sand and surf galore.
- **Whitehaven** (p178) Postcard-perfect Whitehaven is as dazzlingly beautiful as the brochures promise.
- **Noosa** (p168) Tranquil and tasteful Noosa inevitably tops the list of Queensland's beach holiday destinations.

LEFT: HOLGER LEUE; RIGHT: DAVID WALL

Left: Snorkelling; Right: Surfing the Gold Coast

THINGS YOU NEED TO KNOW

VITAL STATISTICS

- **Population** 4.3 million
- **Telephone code** ☎ 07
- **Best time to visit** April to November

LOCALITIES IN A NUTSHELL

- **Brisbane** (p150) Friendly, enriching and energetic capital
- **Gold Coast** (p164) Extravagant and just a bit tacky
- **Sunshine Coast** (p167) Enchanting beaches and hinterland
- **Whitsunday Coast** (p174) Sailing nirvana among tropical islands
- **Far North Queensland** (p179) Cairns and Great Barrier Reef adventures

ADVANCE PLANNING

- **One month before** Organise and book internal flights and resort accommodation.
- **Two weeks before** Reserve places on live-aboard boats and sailing or dive charters.
- **One week before** Book surf riding or diving courses.

RESOURCES

- **Queensland Holidays** (www.queenslandholidays.com.au) A great resource for planning your trip. The travel information section of its website is a decent source for visitors with disabilities.
- **Royal Automobile Club of Queensland** (RACQ; ☎ 13 19 05; www.racq.com.au) Maps and information on road conditions, and 24-hour roadside assistance for members of affiliated clubs.
- **Sunlover Holidays** (☎ 13 88 33; www.sunloverholidays.com) Book accommodation and tours – offices are located in state capitals.
- **Tourism Queensland** (☎ 07-3535 3535; www.tq.com.au) A government-run body responsible for promoting Queensland.
- **Tourism Tropical North Queensland** (☎ 07-4051 3588; www.tropicalaustralia.com.au; 51 the Esplanade, Cairns; 8.30am-6.30pm) Accredited and helpful office for north Queensland.

EMERGENCY NUMBER

- **Police, fire and ambulance** (☎ 000)

GETTING AROUND

- **Walk** the esplanades of Cairns and Airlie Beach.
- **Train** on the *Tilt Train* to Cairns, and from there on the scenic railway to Kuranda.
- **Ferry** to the Moreton Bay escapes of Moreton and North Stradbroke Islands.
- **Fast Cat** to the reef and islands on superfast catamarans.

BE FOREWARNED

- **Box jellyfish** (p367) occur in coastal waters north of Agnes Water from October to April and are potentially deadly.
- **Saltwater crocodiles** (p367) are a real danger in Far North Queensland and can be found in estuaries, creeks and rivers. Observe signs.

BRISBANE & QUEENSLAND ITINERARIES

KOALAS & ROLLERCOASTERS Three Days

Start in the Queensland capital of **(1) Brisbane** (p150) where you can take in a show or two and explore the sights along the Brisbane River. Board a leisurely river cruise to the **(2) Lone Pine Koala Sanctuary** (p155), where you can cuddle a cute and furry koala and get photographic proof of the event.

You could cool off on a hinterland tour, but if you want to get wet then head to the coast and take a ferry across Moreton Bay to Tangalooma or **(3) North Stradbroke Island** (p163), where you can spend a night and wake for an early morning surf.

When it's time to move on head back towards Brisbane but take a turn to the south to the glitzy **(4) Gold Coast** (p164) and succumb to the party atmosphere of Surfers Paradise. If you have the kids or enjoy the rush of a roller coaster, try the range of adrenalin-surging rides at a suite of theme parks.

GLITTER & SURF Five Days

Start in **(1) Surfers Paradise** (p165) and take a lesson or three on how to catch and ride a wave. Spend a few days wandering up and down the Gold Coast Hwy exploring the various resort towns and their respective beaches, enjoying the surf, the shopping and the glitz. For wild rides and other artificial gravity-defying antics head to one or all of the **(2) Gold Coast theme parks** (p165) to loosen a few cobwebs.

When you've had enough, strike north up the Pacific Hwy to Queensland's first city, **(3) Brisbane** (p150), for its stylish galleries, theatres and restaurants. Take time for a river cruise and a gourmet dinner. Still heading north, veer onto Glass House Mountains Rd and snake your way through the **(4) Glass House Mountains** (p167), enjoying the verdant hinterland and visiting world-famous Australia Zoo.

Continue through languid Sunshine Coast towns to the elegant beachside haven of **(5) Noosa** (p168), where you can resurrect those board-riding skills and gorge on first-class multicultural cuisine.

REEF MADNESS One Week

Begin this coral-themed escapade in the hub of Great Barrier Reef adventure, **(1) Cairns** (p179). Spend a couple of days enjoying the lagoon, bars and restaurants of the tropical city, and explore the hinterland by taking the scenic railway to **(2) Kuranda** (p189). No visit to Cairns is complete without a trip to the nearby coral-fringed islands, such as **(3) Green Island** (p188) or the pristine outer reef.

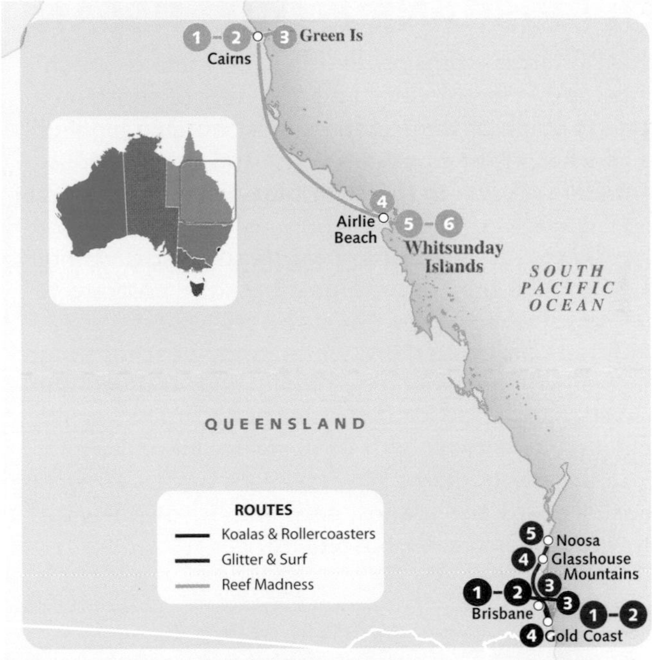

From Cairns head down to **(4) Airlie Beach** (p174), which has a great range of accommodation and water-based activities, and is an ideal base for exploring the numerous **(5) Whitsunday Islands** (p177). You can catch a ferry from Shute Harbour, near Airlie, or fly directly to **(6) Hamilton Island** (p178), where you can start the resort lifestyle as soon as you step off the plane. Spend a few days experimenting with watercraft or just lazing by the pool then explore other islands in the group such as Whitsunday Island, with dazzling Whitehaven Beach, or the laid-back and naturally beautiful Hook or South Molle Islands.

DISCOVER BRISBANE & QUEENSLAND

Occupying Australia's northeastern corner, this vast state is awash with dazzling landscapes, vibrant cities and 300 days of sunshine a year. It's also home to some of the country's most notable highlights, from the golden beaches of the Sunshine Coast and the luminous green of the Daintree rainforest to the clear blue waters of the Great Barrier Reef.

It hides some of the country's lesser-known treasures, delivering wow-factor with gusto. You only have to peel back the postcard to find corners seemingly untouched by other visitors – spectacular national parks with tumbling waterfalls, white sandy beaches fringed by kaleidoscopic coral, vibrant and unique Indigenous festivals and jaw-dropping sunsets.

Brisbane will delight city slickers with its lively, cosmopolitan atmosphere and, in the north, Cairns is a travellers' mecca. Between the two are strings of towns and islands, each with its own flavour but all brimming with Queenslander hospitality.

BRISBANE

pop 1.9 million

Blessed with an abundance of sunshine and spectacular waterways, Brisbane is surging as a modern metropolis with a new air of confidence and style. Rapid inner-city development, a swelling population and a cosmopolitan upswing have given it greater stature in recent times, yet it retains the friendliness and relaxed attitude it has always been praised for.

INFORMATION

EMERGENCY

Ambulance (☎ 000)

Fire (☎ 000)

Police (☎ 000) City centre (☎ 07-3258 2582; 46 Charlotte St); Fortitude Valley (☎ 07-3131 1055; cnr Brookes & Wickham Sts); headquarters (☎ 07-3364 6464; 200 Roma St)

MEDICAL SERVICES

Royal Brisbane Hospital (☎ 07-3636 8111; cnr Butterfield St & Bowen Bridge Rd, Herston; 24hr switchboard & casualty ward)

MONEY

There are foreign-exchange bureaus in the domestic and international terminals at Brisbane airport, as well as ATMs that take most international credit cards.

Amex (☎ 1300 139 060, 07-3229 3926; 260 Queen St, Brisbane) Located within the Westpac bank.

Commonwealth Bank (☎ 13 22 21, 07-3237 3499; 240 Queen St, Brisbane)

Travelex (☎ 07-3210 6325; Shop 149F, Myer Centre, Queen St Mall, Brisbane)

POST

Main post office (GPO; ☎ 13 13 18; 261 Queen St, Brisbane; 7am-6pm Mon-Fri);

Post office (Post Shop; ☎ 13 13 18; 2nd fl, Wintergarden Centre, Queen St Mall, Brisbane; 9am-5pm Mon-Fri, 9am-12.30pm Sat)

RICHARD I'ANSON

Brisbane Sq

TOURIST INFORMATION

Brisbane Transit Visitor Information (☎ 07-3236 2020; 3rd fl, Roma St Transit Centre, Roma St, Brisbane; 7am-6.30pm Mon-Fri, 7.30am-6pm Sat & Sun) Information counter specialising in backpacker travel, tours and accommodation in Queensland.

Brisbane Visitor Information & Booking Centre (☎ 07-3006 6290; www.visitbrisbane.com.au; Queen St Mall, Brisbane; 9am-5.30pm Mon-Thu, to 7pm Fri, to 5pm Sat, 9.30am-4.30pm Sun) Great one-stop information centre in the middle of the mall near Wintergarden has all you'll need to know about Brisbane.

South Bank visitor information centre (☎ 07-3867 2051; Stanley St Plaza, South Bank Parklands; 9am-5pm) Information on South Bank activities and the place to buy tickets for entertainment events.

SIGHTS

CITY CENTRE

CITY HALL & AROUND

The majestic old **Brisbane City Hall** (☎ 07-3403 8888; www.brisbane.qld.gov.au/cityhall; btwn Ann & Adelaide Sts, Brisbane; admission free; lift & viewing tower 10am-3pm), opened in 1930, is slowly sinking and suffering concrete cancer. Savour what you can from the outside; the four clock faces on each side of the tower are the largest in Australia and, until the Sydney Opera House was completed in 1971, Brisbane's City Hall was the most expensive building in the country.

Next to City Hall is the recently redeveloped **King George Sq**, a popular CBD meeting place with an underground bus station.

Housed within the old School of Arts, a short walk east of King George Sq, is the **Footsteps Gallery** (☎ 07-3229 0395; 166 Ann St, Brisbane; admission free; 8am-5pm Mon-Fri), established to support emerging artists from the Aboriginal and Torres Strait Islander communities.

TREASURY BUILDING & AROUND

The most grand and impressive of the city's historical architecture is the state

CENTRAL BRISBANE

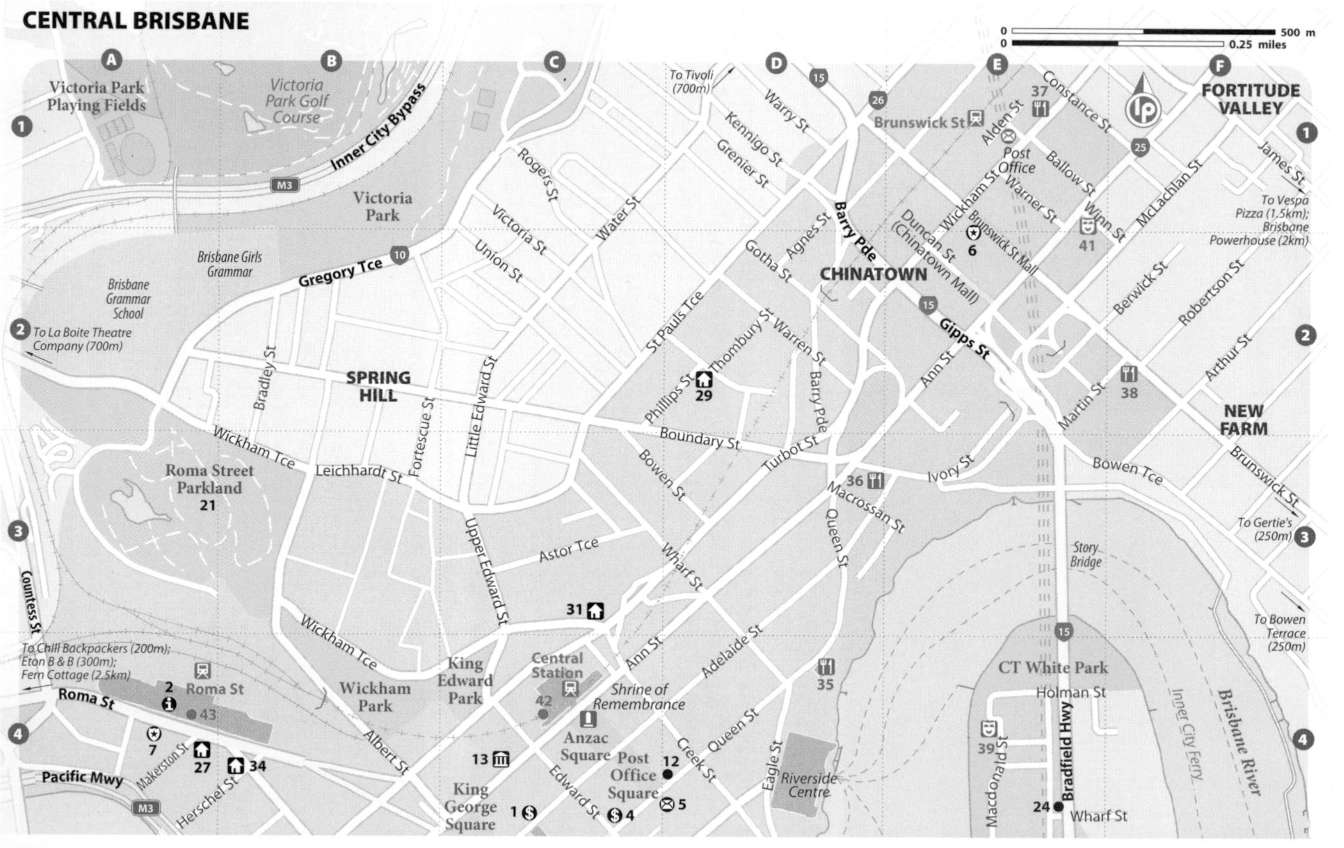

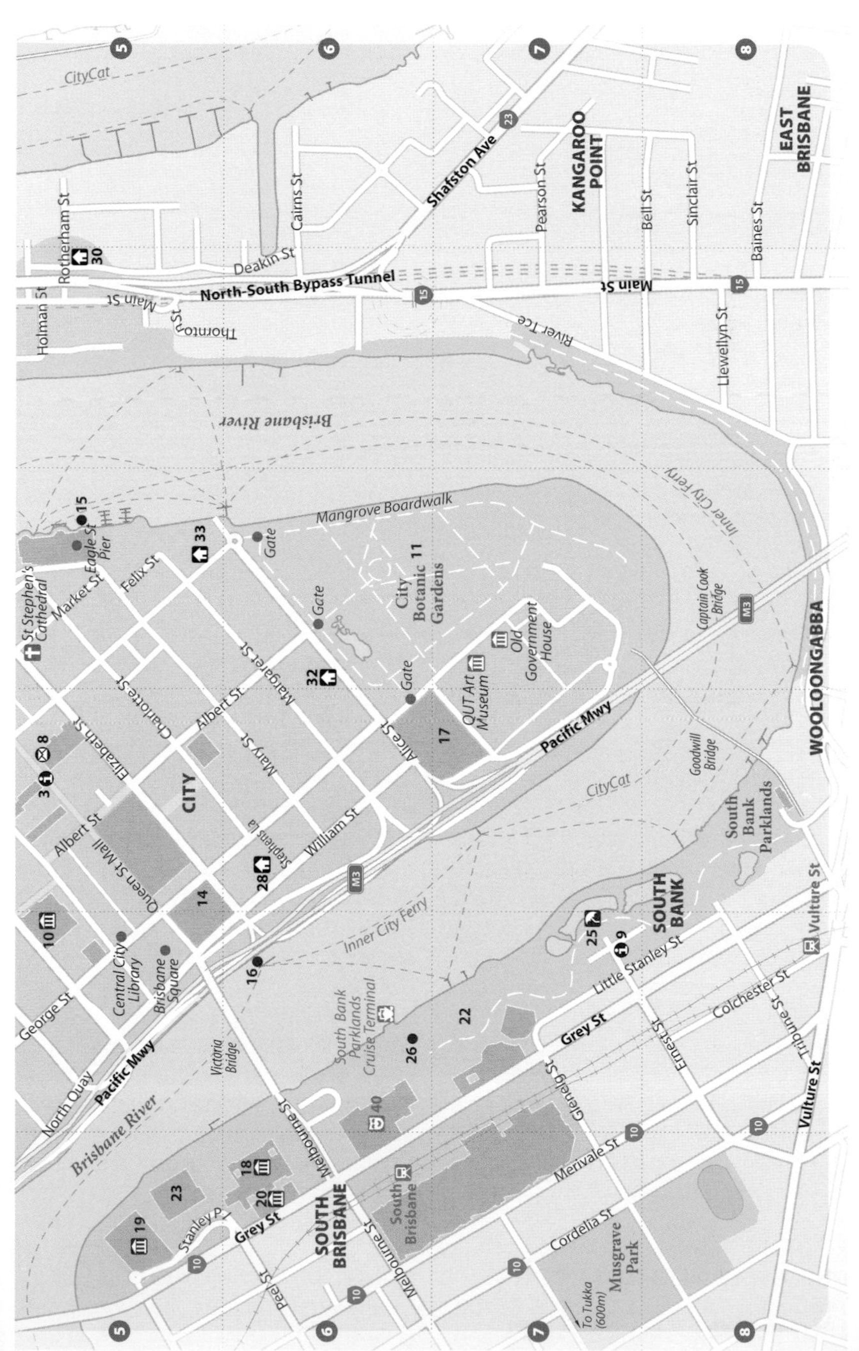
CityCat
Rotherham St
Holman St
Main St
Thornton St
Deakin St
Cairns St
North-South Bypass Tunnel
Shafston Ave
Pearson St
KANGAROO POINT
Bell St
Sinclair St
Baines St
EAST BRISBANE
Llewellyn St
River Tce
Brisbane River
Inner City Ferry
Mangrove Boardwalk
St Stephen's Cathedral
Market St
Eagle St Pier
Felix St
Gate
City Botanic Gardens
Old Government House
QUT Art Museum
Captain Cook Bridge
M3
WOOLOONGABBA
Charlotte St
Albert St
Margaret St
Elizabeth St
Mary St
CITY
Alice St
Pacific Mwy
Goodwill Bridge
CityCat
South Bank Parklands
William St
Stephens La
Queen St Mall
Central City Library
Brisbane Square
George St
Inner City Ferry
SOUTH BANK
Vulture St
Little Stanley St
Colchester St
Ernest St
Tribune St
South Bank Parklands Cruise Terminal
Grey St
Glenelg St
Victoria Bridge
North Quay
Brisbane River
Melbourne St
Merivale St
South Brisbane
SOUTH BRISBANE
Stanley Pl
Cordelia St
Musgrave Park
Peel St
To Tukka (600m)
5
6
7
8

INFORMATION
Amex 1 C4
Brisbane Transit Visitor Information 2 A4
Brisbane Visitor Information & Booking Centre 3 C5
Commonwealth Bank 4 C4
Main Post Office 5 D4
Police 6 E2
Police 7 A4
Post Office 8 C5
South Bank Visitor Information Centre 9 B7

SIGHTS & ACTIVITIES
Brisbane City Hall 10 B5
City Botanic Gardens 11 D6
City Sights Bus Tour Departure Point 12 D4
Footsteps Gallery 13 C4
Former Treasury Building 14 C5
Kookaburra River Queens 15 D5
Land Administration Building .... (see 28)
Mirimar Cruises 16 B6
Parliament House 17 C7
Queensland Art Gallery 18 A6
Queensland Gallery of Modern Art 19 A5
Queensland Museum 20 A6
Roma Street Parkland 21 A3
South Bank Parklands 22 B7
State Library of Queensland 23 A5
Story Bridge Adventure Climb 24 E4
Streets Beach 25 B7
Wheel of Brisbane 26 B6

SLEEPING
Abbey Apartments 27 A4
Conrad Treasury 28 C6
Dahrl Court Apartments 29 D2
Il Mondo 30 E5
Inchcolm Hotel 31 C3
Quay West Suites Brisbane 32 D6
Stamford Plaza Brisbane 33 D5
Tinbilly 34 B4

EATING
Customs House Brasserie 35 D4
E'cco 36 D3
Garuva Hidden Tranquillity Restaurant & Bar 37 E1
Lucky's Trattoria 38 F2

ENTERTAINMENT
Brisbane Jazz Club 39 E4
Queensland Performing Arts Centre 40 B6
Zoo 41 E1

TRANSPORT
Queensland Rail Travel Centre .... (see 43)
Queensland Rail Travel Centre 42 C4
Roma St Transit Centre 43 A4

government's **Former Treasury Building**, now Conrad Treasury casino.

In the block southeast of the casino is the equally magnificent former **Land Administration Building**, which has been transformed into a luxury five-star hotel under the Conrad Treasury banner (p158).

PARLIAMENT HOUSE & BOTANIC GARDENS

With its unique roof made from Mt Isa copper, **Parliament House** (☎ 07-3406 7111; www.parliament.qld.gov.au; cnr Alice & George Sts, Brisbane; admission free; ⏰ 9am-5pm Mon-Fri) is where you can watch state politicians trade legislation and insults from the public balcony on sitting days.

The spacious **City Botanic Gardens** (☎ 07-3403 0666; Albert St, Brisbane; admission free; ⏰ 24hr, free guided tours 11am & 1pm Mon-Sat) is a regular chill-out spot for CBD workers and students craving fresh air and beautiful views of the Kangaroo Point cliffs.

SOUTH BANK

QUEENSLAND CULTURAL CENTRE

The vast Queensland Cultural Centre forms the city's cultural backbone and comprises two art galleries, a performing arts centre, museum, and state library.

The most recent addition to this group of buildings is the world-class **Queensland Gallery of Modern Art** (GoMA; ☎ 07-3840 7303; www.qag.qld.gov.au; Stanley Pl, South Brisbane; admission free; ⏰ 10am-5pm Mon-Fri, 9am-5pm Sat & Sun). It opened in 2006 and is the nation's largest modern art gallery, focusing on art, including cinematic and multimedia, from the last 30 years.

Standing beside GoMA is the impressive **State Library of Queensland** and the **Queensland Art Gallery** (☎ 07-3840 7303; Stanley Pl, South Brisbane; admission free; ⏰ 10am-5pm Mon-Fri, 9am-5pm Sat & Sun).

An entrée to Queensland's history and cultural identity, the **Queensland Museum** (☎ 07-3840 7555; www.southbank.qm.qld.gov.au; cnr Grey & Melbourne Sts, South Brisbane; admission free; ⏰ 9.30am-5pm) houses a diverse range of displays including the Discover Queensland exhibition and the Museum Zoo, which houses over 700 prehistoric and modern animals from dung beetles to dinosaurs.

SOUTH BANK PARKLANDS

Swarming with locals and day-trippers is **South Bank Parklands** (☎ 07-3867

2051; www.visitsouthbank.com.au; admission free; ⌚ sunrise-sunset) on the banks of the Brisbane River, an enormously popular family area with blooming arbours, cafes and restaurants, picnic spots, tropical gardens and walkways.

LONE PINE KOALA SANCTUARY

Cuddling a koala at Lone Pine (**☎ 07-3378 1366; www.koala.net; Jesmond Rd, Fig Tree Pocket; adult/child/family $20/15/52, photo with koala $15; ⌚ 8.30am-5pm**) and getting your photo taken with one of the cute, fuzzy creatures has long been a must-do when in southeast Queensland. Situated 11km southwest of the city centre, Lone Pine was established in 1927 as the world's first koala sanctuary with just two koalas; these days there are 130 and it's still the world's largest sanctuary of its kind.

The most enjoyable way to get here is with Mirimar Cruises (**☎ 1300 729 742; adult/child/family incl park entry $50/30/145**), which depart daily at 10am from the Queensland Cultural Centre pontoon on the boardwalk outside the State Library, next to Victoria Bridge, returning at 2.45pm.

BRISBANE FOR CHILDREN

The spacious inner-city parks are your best place to start. South Bank Parklands (p154) have a smattering of playgrounds and the Wheel of Brisbane would be the highlight of any kids' day out. Streets Beach is also located here with a shallow paddling pool for really small tots. In the Roma Street Parkland there are free *Out and About with Bub* guided walks for parents and under fives every Wednesday and Friday at 10am, leaving from the Melange Café.

You can't go wrong taking the kids to South Bank. Always a big hit with the little ones is the Sciencentre, in the Queensland Museum (p154), with its mind-boggling fun displays.

Departing from outside the State Library at South Bank, a river cruise to the Lone Pine Koala Sanctuary (p155) is guaranteed to win parents brownie points.

For child-care listings see www.ourbrisbane.com/businesses/browse/all/6308

DAVID WALL

Story Bridge

↘ STORY BRIDGE ADVENTURE CLIMB

Fast becoming a Brisbane must-do, the bridge climb offers breath-taking views of the city. Established in 2005, it is only the third licensed bridge climb experience in the world (the other two being in Sydney and Auckland) and you can climb at dawn, during the day, or at the recommended twilight time slot. The 900m climb takes place on the southern half of Story Bridge and reaches heights of 80m above the Brisbane River. Tours last 2½ hours and bookings are essential. Prices differ according to time of day with twilight tours being the most expensive.

Things you need to know **☎ 1300 254 627; www.sbac.net.au; 170 Main St, Kangaroo Point; adult $89-130, child $75-110**

or contact the Child Care Information Service.

TOURS

CITY TOURS

Brisbane Lights Tours (☎ 07-3822 6028; adult/child from $60/25) The tour departs at 6.30pm each night (pick-up from your hotel is included in the price) and covers a dozen city landmarks, dinner or refreshments at Mt Coot-tha Lookout and a CityCat cruise.

City Sights bus tour (☎ 13 12 30; adult/child day ticket $25/20; every 45min 9am-3.45pm) Hop-on, hop-off bus departs from outside Post Office Sq (Queen St) and shuttles around 19 of the city's major landmarks. Day tickets can be bought on the bus. The same ticket covers you for unlimited use of CityCat services.

RIVER CRUISES

Kookaburra River Queens (☎ 07-3221 1300; www.kookaburrariverqueens.com; lunch/dinner cruise per person $55/75) Enjoy a seafood buffet lunch (two hours) or an evening meal (2½ hours) on a paddle wheeler as it coasts lazily up and down the river. Cruises depart from Eagle St Pier, on the eastern side of the city. Boarding happens at 11.45am daily for the lunch cruise and then at 7pm Sunday to Thursday (and public holidays) for the dinner cruise. On Friday and Saturday nights the evening cruise departs at 6.45pm ($10 extra).

Mirimar Cruises (☎ 1300 729 742; www.mirimar.com; 90min cruise per adult/child/family $25/12/70, wildlife cruise $50/30/145) The Mirimar cruises 19km upstream to the Lone Pine Koala Sanctuary (see p155) departing from the Queensland Cultural Centre pontoon outside the State Library at South Bank daily at 10am. You can take the one-way 90-minute cruise, or the return trip including entry to the sanctuary.

HINTERLAND TOURS

Aries Tours (☎ 07-5594 9933; www.ariestours.com; adult/child from $80/40) The pick of the offerings from this eco-certified company is the glow-worm tour to Natural Bridge in Springbrook National Park.

DAVID HALL

Story Bridge (p155), over the Brisbane River

Bushwacker Ecotours (☎ 1300 559 355, 07-3871 0057; www.bushwacker-ecotours.com.au; adult/child from $115/95) Day tours and overnight trips to southeast Queensland national parks.

SLEEPING

The Brisbane Visitor Information & Booking Centre (p151) has brochures and information on accommodation in Brisbane and up and down the coast.

BUDGET

our pick **Chill Backpackers** (☎ 1800 851 875, 07-3236 0088; www.chillbackpackers.com; 328 Upper Roma St, Brisbane; dm $28-35, d & tw $89, tr $105; P) This garish aqua building on the CBD fringe delivers city and river views from its sun-lounge deck like no other Brisbane hostel. All rooms are super clean and modern, have shared bathrooms and the kitchen is fully equipped.

Tinbilly (☎ 1800 446 646, 07-3238 5888; www.tinbilly.com; 466 George St, Brisbane; dm $30-34, d & tw $115;) Right across from the Roma St Transit Centre, this brightly coloured party hostel has modern interiors and soundproof windows in rooms to block out traffic noise.

Bowen Terrace (☎ 07-3254 0458; www.bowentceaccommodation.com; 365 Bowen Tce, New Farm; s $38-40, d $60-70; deluxe $80-90 P) A beautifully restored old home, this hotel is tucked away in a quiet area of New Farm. Excellent value for money.

MIDRANGE

Eton B&B (☎ 07-3236 0115; www.eton.com.au; 436 Upper Roma St, Petrie Tce; s $115, d & tw $125-145, 1-bedroom apt per week $595-700; P) If Upper Roma St's party hostels are not really your cup of tea, head further along to this colonial-style home. There are five bedrooms (with en suites) and an attic apartment all decorated in heritage style. Travellers with laptops can use the wireless internet ($5 per day); the back courtyard garden is a relaxing spot to log on.

Fern Cottage (☎ 07-3511 6685; www.ferncottage.net; 89 Fernberg Rd, Paddington; s/d from $120/$150;) Those preferring green suburban surrounds will adore this very homely B&B within a charming Queenslander house. There's a range of pretty bedrooms with individual outdoor patios. Your hosts, Geoff and Mary, also offer free wireless internet access.

Il Mondo (☎ 07-3392 0111; www.ilmondo.com.au; 23-35 Rotherham St, Kangaroo Point; r $129-169, apt from $189; P) Corporate clientele shack up at Il Mondo where self-contained units have been tastefully decorated with contemporary furniture and bold lashings of colour. Oddly enough, there's complimentary bicycle hire, but you won't need it to get to one of Brisbane's best pubs – the Story Bridge Hotel is just across the street.

Ridge Haven B&B (☎ 07-3391 7702; 374 Annerley Rd, Annerley; s $130-190, d $140-200; P) Located 10 minutes south of the city, Ridge Haven B&B is set in a gorgeous Victorian home filled with old-world character. The owner, Morna, will make you feel welcome and loves to cook gourmet breakfasts. Free wireless internet access is a bonus.

Dahrl Court Apartments (☎ 07-3830 3400; www.dahrlcourt.com.au; 45 Phillips St, Spring Hill; apt $135, 1-/2-bed townhouse $150/165; P) These elegant self-contained apartments tucked away in a leafy corner of Spring Hill are some of the best in town. Tastefully decorated with modern kitchen appliances and designer bathrooms, they offer incredible value for money. For a private balcony or courtyard, upgrade to one of the town houses.

Inchcolm Hotel (☎ 07-3226 8888; www.inchcolmhotel.com.au; 73 Wickham Tce, Spring Hill; r from $160;) This renovated block of medical offices has been restored into a very classy boutique hotel. The building is heritage listed – even the doors for the rooms are originals from the 1920s. All rooms have a TV, minibar, ultra-modern bathroom, and wireless internet is available on request. And you've got to love a hotel with a rooftop swimming pool.

TOP END

Quay West Suites Brisbane (☎ 1800 672 726, 07-3853 6000; reservations@qwsb.mirvac.com.au; 132 Alice St, Brisbane; apt from $189; P) Half of the five-star apartments here are privately owned and have been finished to a standard worthy of the price tag. Every luxury imaginable is at your fingertips and the unobstructed views of the City Botanic Gardens are a special touch.

Conrad Treasury (☎ 1800 506 889, 07-3306 8888; www.conradtreasury.com.au; 130 William St, Brisbane; r from $295; P) One for the high rollers, Conrad Treasury is as posh as they make them. This beautiful building, next to the casino, once housed the Land Administration Offices and has been carefully restored to its former opulent grandeur. Now darling, would you prefer the park or city view?

Also recommended:

Abbey Apartments (☎ 07-3236 0600; www.abbeyhotel.com.au; 160 Roma St, Brisbane; 1-bed apt per night/week $200/980; P) Plush CBD apartments; call for last-minute deals.

Stamford Plaza Brisbane (☎ 07-3221 1999; www.stamford.com.au/spb; cnr Edward & Margaret Sts, Brisbane; r from $250; P) Five-star luxury rooms plus a gymnasium, business centre and three restaurants.

EATING

No need to drag the tables and chairs inside for winter: Brisbane's climate allows year-round outdoor dining.

Gertie's (☎ 07-3358 5088; www.gerties.com.au; 699 Brunswick St, New Farm; dishes $6-16; dinner Tue-Thu, lunch & dinner Fri-Sun) A super-cool tapas bar and lounge, the massive bi-fold windows here offer a fabulous breezy feel. Best bets on the menu include the beef and oregano meatballs, and Peking duck rolls.

Lucky's Trattoria (☎ 07-3252 2353; Shop 14, Central Brunswick, 455 Brunswick St, Fortitude Valley; dishes $10-29; dinner 6pm-late) This gritty diner has been serving up authentic pasta and pizza in the Valley since 1974 and the original Italian owners still run the business. It's BYO and there's a bottle shop right next door.

Vespa Pizza (☎ 07-3358 4100; 148 Merthyr Rd, New Farm; mains $18-20; lunch Fri, dinner daily) No chance of a boring selection like the big pizza chains here, Vespa's wood-fired varieties are certainly unique. Big sellers include the streaky bacon and red currant with camembert, and the cinnamon roast butternut pumpkin with dried chilli and fetta.

our pick **Garuva Hidden Tranquillity Restaurant & Bar** (☎ 07-3216 0124; www.garuva.com.au; 324 Wickham St, Fortitude Valley; mains $20; dinner) This genuine gem of the Valley restaurant scene has the ultimate chilled-out vibe; dimly-lit private booths with cushioned seating are partitioned with white silk curtains. All dishes are the same price including the delicious lamb curry and warm Thai beef salad. The cocktail bar out the back is a good option if you missed out on a booking (essential).

Customs House Brasserie (☎ 07-3365 8921; 399 Queen St; mains $29-34; breakfast Sun, lunch daily, dinner Tue-Sat) Few restaurants in

OLIVER STREWE

Queensland Gallery of Modern Art (p154)

Brisbane have open-air settings quite like the majestic Customs House, overlooking the Brisbane River and Story Bridge. The Queensland prawn and crab tian with roasted tomato and avocado, and the seared scallops are divine options. Go on, splash out.

Tukka (**☎ 07-3846 6333; www.tukkarestaurant.com.au; 145b Boundary St; mains $30; ⏲ dinner**) If you don't mind eating animals that are on Australia's coat of arms, this upmarket restaurant serves them up with flair. Emu and kangaroo fillet are mains, or for something lighter, chow down on the Tasmanian possum entrée. Tried crocodile? Here's your chance.

E'cco (**☎ 07-3831 8344; 100 Boundary St; mains $39-43; ⏲ lunch Tue-Fri, dinner Tue-Sat**) A slick bistro set within a converted tea warehouse near the Story Bridge, E'cco has won dozens of awards for its innovative, gourmet cuisine. Field mushrooms with olive toast, rocket, parmesan, truffle oil and lemon is the staff's recommendation from the menu.

ENTERTAINMENT

THEATRE

South Bank's venues stage most of the mainstream productions, but there are some excellent more intimate theatres around the inner city. The **Queensland Cultural Centre** (**☎ 13 62 46**) has a 24-hour phone line that handles bookings for events at South Bank theatres and other venues and events nationally.

Queensland Performing Arts Centre (**☎ 07-3840 7444; www.qpac.com.au; cnr Grey & Melbourne Sts, South Bank; Ⓟ**) Blockbuster musicals, orchestral performances, dance and other theatre is staged at this colossal centre. There are four world-class concert venues for everything from French ballet to *Chicago*.

Brisbane Powerhouse (**☎ 07-3358 8622, box office 3358 8600; www.brisbanepowerhouse.org; 119 Lamington St, New Farm; Ⓟ**) Emerging theatre and visual arts are performed within the graffitied walls of the robust Powerhouse building. Photography displays, cabaret feasts, live comedy and experimental music are regular features here.

La Boite Theatre Company (☎ 07-3007 8600; www.laboite.com.au; Roundhouse Theatre, 6-8 Musk Ave, Kelvin Grove) This intimate venue was purpose-built for theatre in the round. The company produces plays by Australian and international playwrights; ask about discounts for under-30s.

LIVE MUSIC

Fortitude Valley has the majority of Brisbane's rock and dance venues, though there are a few others in West End, New Farm and Kangaroo Point.

Zoo (☎ 07-3854 1381; 711 Ann St, Fortitude Valley) A long-standing supporter of independent music, most touring Australian bands have earned their stripes playing the Zoo at some stage in their career.

Tivoli (☎ 07-3852 1711; 52 Costin St, Fortitude Valley) International artists such as Nick Cave and Noel Gallagher have graced the stage at this elegant old art deco venue built in the early 20th century. Hosting a range of touring acts, you're likely to see quality comedy here too.

Brisbane Jazz Club (☎ 07-3391 2006; 1 Annie St, Kangaroo Point; cover $10-15) Perched on the riverside, this little old wooden boatshed comes alive at night as Brisbane's best port for traditional, swing and contemporary jazz. Known for its friendly atmosphere and lively gigs, the Brisbane Jazz Club hosts all the big names in jazz. Views from the river deck are magnificent.

GETTING THERE & AWAY

AIR

Brisbane's main airport is about 16km northeast of the city centre at Eagle Farm and has separate international and domestic terminals about 2km apart, linked by the **Airtrain** (☎ 07-3215 5000; www.airtrain.com.au; per person $4; ⏲ every 30min, 6am-8pm).

BUS

Brisbane's main terminus and booking office for all long-distance buses and trains is the **Roma St Transit Centre** (Roma St, Brisbane), about 500m west of the city centre.

CAR & MOTORCYCLE

All of the major companies – **Hertz** (☎ 13 30 39), **Avis** (☎ 13 63 33), **Budget** (☎ 1300 362 848), **Europcar** (☎ 1300 131 390) and **Thrifty** (☎ 1300 367 227) – have offices at the Brisbane airport terminals and throughout the city.

TRAIN

The **Roma St Transit Centre** (Roma St, Brisbane) is Brisbane's main station for long-distance trains. For any information and reservations, call into the **Queensland Rail Travel Centre** (☎ 13 16 17; www.qr.com.au; Central Station ☎ 07-3235 1323; ground fl, Central Station, 305 Edward St, Brisbane; ⏲ 8am-5pm Mon-Fri; Roma St Transit Centre ☎ 07-3235 1331; Roma St, Brisbane; ⏲ 6.30am-5pm Mon-Fri, 6.30am-1pm Sat, 6.30-11am Sun). It is also possible to make reservations online or over the phone.

CountryLink (☎ 13 22 32; www.countrylink.info.au) has a daily XPT (express passenger train) service between Sydney and Brisbane (economy/1st class/sleeper $135/155/235). The northbound service runs overnight, and the southbound service runs during the day. Each one takes 14 hours.

Services within Queensland:

Spirit of the Outback Brisbane to Longreach via Rockhampton twice weekly (economy seat/economy sleeper/1st-class sleeper $185/240/375, 24 hours).

Sunlander Brisbane to Cairns via Townsville (economy seat/economy sleeper/1st-class sleeper/Queenslander class $210/270/415/760, 30 hours). The exclusive Queenslander class includes restaurant meals and historical commentary.

Tilt Train Brisbane to Cairns (business seat only $310, 24 hours) and Brisbane to Rockhampton (economy seat/business seat $100/155, eight hours).

GETTING AROUND

Brisbane boasts an efficient public transport network. Information on bus, train and ferry routes and connections can be obtained by calling **TransLink** (☎ 13 12 30; www.translink.com.au; 24hr).

The two major taxi companies here are **Black & White Cabs** (☎ 133 222) and **Yellow Cab Co** (☎ 13 19 24).

MORETON BAY

The Brisbane River winds its way east of the city centre for about 20km and enters Moreton Bay, which stretches from Caloundra in the north to the Gold Coast in the south. Few marine parks have an island for every day of the year but with some 365, this one has the perfect number.

Moreton Bay is separated from the Pacific Ocean by four sand islands: Moreton Island and Bribie Island to the north, and North and South Stradbroke Islands towards the south. The most popular of these is North Stradbroke Island with its great surfing beaches, visible marine life and a new wave of sophisticated dining and accommodation options. On Moreton Island, wild dolphin feeding is the major attraction.

TOURS

Humpback whales are a regular sight in the bay between June and November when they migrate to and from their southern feeding grounds. Moreton Bay also has the largest resident population of bottlenose dolphins in the world (more than 300).

Dolphin Wild (☎ 07 3880 4444; www.dolphinwild.com.au; per adult/child/family incl lunch $110/60/290) Departing from Redcliffe,

BOB CHARLTON

Humpback whale

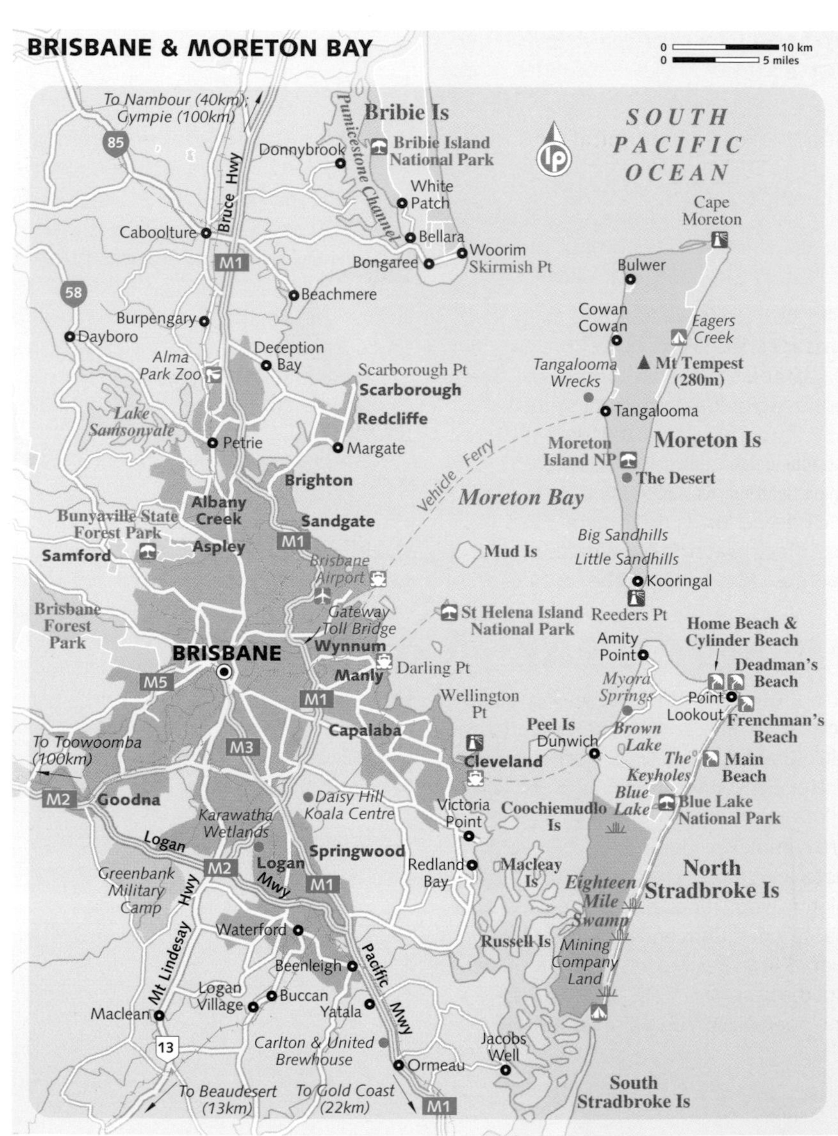

these full-day ecotours include a cruise to Moreton Island with commentary from a marine naturalist and guided snorkel tours (adult/child $20/10) around the Tangalooma wrecks.

Manly Eco Cruises (☎ **07-3396 9400; www.manlyecocruises.net; per adult/child $99/44**) Ride on the catamaran boom nets, enjoy free canoe rides or sit back on the MV *Getaway* and spot marine life.

NORTH STRADBROKE ISLAND

Saturated with natural beauty, North Stradbroke is a subtropical sand island close to Brisbane that feels a world away from the mainland.

TOURS

Stradbroke Island 4WD Tours (☎ 07-3409 8051; straddie4wd@bigpond.com; half-day tours adult/child $35/20, full-day tours adult/child $85/55) Tours to beaches and lakes with an option to go beach fishing.

Straddie Guides (☎ 07-3415 3106; www.straddieguides.com; half-day tours $49, full-day whale-watching tours $69) Half-day 4WD tours include exploring the beaches and a trip to a freshwater lake. Whale-watching tours are May to November only.

SLEEPING

Stradbroke Island Beach Hotel & Spa Resort (☎ 07-3409 8188; www.stradbrokehotel.com.au; East Coast Rd, Point Lookout; r from $165) The daggy, old brown-brick Straddie Pub at Point Lookout was knocked down in 2006 and replaced with this dazzling modern complex comprising a bar, restaurant, hotel and spa. Spotlessly clean rooms have blonde wood tones, top-grade kitchen and bathroom fittings and flat-screen TVs. The extra $40 for sea views is money well spent but the best view of all is free downstairs at the open-air bar. Be there for sunset!

GETTING THERE & AWAY

The gateway to North Stradbroke Island is the seaside town of Cleveland. Regular city train services run from Central or Roma St stations in Brisbane to Cleveland station ($4.80, one hour), from where you can get a bus (free if you show your train ticket) to the ferry terminal. Buses to the terminal are infrequent so a taxi is a good option (five minutes).

MICHAEL AW

Minke whale

IF YOU LIKE...

If you like **spotting whales** in Moreton Bay (p161), you might like these other amazing locations with whale-watching opportunities:

- **Hervey Bay** Sightings of migrating humpback whales are guaranteed from 1 August to 1 November – you get a free subsequent trip if the whales don't show. Among the many available tours are Blue Dolphin Marine Tours (☎ 07-4124 9600; www.bluedolphintours.com.au), which takes a maximum 20 passengers on a 10m catamaran; and MV *Tasman Venture* (☎ 1800 620 322; www.tasmanventure.com.au), which takes a maximum of 80 passengers, and offers underwater microphones and viewing windows.
- **Sunshine Coast** Whale-watching cruises are run by Steve Irwin's Whale One (☎ 1300 274 539; www.whaleone.com.au; Mooloolaba; adult/child/family $125/75/320) in September and October.
- **Fraser Island** From July to October you can spot migrating humpback whales from the beaches and headlands.

Stradbroke Ferries (☎ **07-3286 2666; www.stradbrokeferries.com.au**) runs a water taxi to Dunwich almost every hour from about 6am to 6.30pm (adult/child $17/10 return, 25 minutes).

MORETON ISLAND

City life rapidly fades from memory when you're cruising on the ferry from Brisbane out to this sand island north of Stradbroke.

The main attraction is the **wild dolphin feeding**, which takes place every evening around sunset at the Tangalooma resort. Between five and nine dolphins swim in from the ocean to take fish from the hands of volunteer feeders, but you need to be a guest at the resort with a 'dolphin feeding package' to be involved. Day visitors to Tangalooma are welcome to watch from the jetty.

SLEEPING

Tangalooma Wild Dolphin Resort (☎ **1300 652 250, 07-3268 6333; www.tangalooma.com; r from $290;**) Situated at the old whaling station on the waterfront, there's a huge range of ritzy rooms here including some particularly posh new serviced apartments. Some rooms are noticeably older, but all have modern facilities and contemporary decor.

GETTING THERE & AROUND

The **Tangalooma Flyer** (☎ **1300 652 250; 07-3268 6333; www.tangalooma.com; adult/child return day-trip from $40/25; 7.30am, 10am & 5pm daily, plus 12.30pm Mon, Sat & Sun**) is the resort's fast catamaran. It departs from Holt St, off Kingsford Smith Dr in Eagle Farm, Brisbane. A bus ($14) departs Brisbane's Roma St Transit Centre at 9am to catch the 10am boat. Bookings are essential.

GOLD COAST

Be prepared to show plenty of skin and wear your finest 'bling', the Gold Coast is southeast Queensland's glitzy beach-holiday hot spot. The 70km stretch of coastline from South Stradbroke Island to

LEFT: RICHARD I'ANSON; RIGHT: DAVID WALL

Left: Warner Bros Movie World; Right: Surfers Paradise

GOLD COAST THEME PARKS

The roller coasters and waterslides at these American-style theme parks offer so much dizzying action, keeping your lunch down can be a constant battle. Discount tickets are sold in most tourist offices. The Fun Pass (adult/child $147/93) allows one single-day entry into Movie World, Sea World and Wet 'n' Wild over a five-day period.

Australian Outback Spectacular (☎ 13 33 86, 07-5519 6200; www.myfun.com.au; Entertainment Rd, Oxenford; adult/child incl dinner $99/65; 6.15pm Tue-Sun) Between Movie World and Wet 'n' Wild, this is not actually a theme park but rather a 1½-hour dinner and show in a 1000-seat arena. The venue captures the spirit of the Australian outback with displays of brilliant horsemanship, stampeding cattle and even a little boot scootin' to music written by Australian country singer Lee Kernaghan. You're given a stockman's hat to keep; dinner is three courses of outback tucker.

Dreamworld (☎ 07-5588 1111; www.dreamworld.com.au; Pacific Hwy, Coomera; adult/child $67/43; 10am-5pm) Home to the Big 6 Thrill Rides, including the Giant Drop and Tower of Terror. Get your photo taken with a Bengal tiger at Tiger Island.

Sea World (☎ 07-5588 2222, show times 07-5588 2205; www.myfun.com.au; Sea World Dr, The Spit, Main Beach; adult/child $67/43; 10am-5pm) See polar bears, sharks and performing dolphins at this aquatic park, or ride one of the original Gold Coast roller coasters, the Corkscrew. Catch up with Bert and Ernie at the new Sesame Street Beach.

Warner Bros Movie World (☎ 07-5573 8485; www.myfun.com.au; Pacific Hwy, Oxenford; adult/child $67/43; 10am-5pm) Movie-themed shows, rides and attractions including the Batwing Spaceshot and Lethal Weapon roller coaster.

Wet 'n' Wild (☎ 07-5573 2255; www.myfun.com.au; Pacific Hwy, Oxenford; adult/child $47/30; 10am-5pm Feb-Apr & Sep-Dec, 10am-4pm May-Aug, 10am-9pm 27 Dec-25 Jan) The ultimate waterslide here is the Kamikaze where you plunge down an 11m drop in a two-person tube at 50km/h. This vast water fun park also has slippery slides, white-water rapids, tube rides and latest-release films are shown at Dive'n'Movies.

WhiteWater World (☎ 1800 073 300, 07-5588 1111; www.whitewaterworld.com.au; Dreamworld Parkway, Coomera; adult/child $43/28; 10.30am-4.30pm) Connected to Dreamworld; features the Cave of Waves, Pipeline Plunge and more than 140 water activities and slides. A World Pass (adult/child $77/55 for one day, adult/child $99/$66 for two days) ensures entry to Dreamworld and WhiteWater World.

Rainbow Bay on the NSW border attracts a staggering four million sun-seeking visitors every year.

The coastline is studded with high-rise apartment blocks, has a Las Vegas-style flashy feel and is famous for million-dollar theme parks where tourists get their thrills on roller coasters and waterslides.

SURFERS PARADISE & BROADBEACH

Some say the 'Surfers' prefer other beaches and the 'Paradise' is tragically lost, but there's no denying this wild and trashy party zone attracts phenomenal visitor numbers all year round.

Directly south is Broadbeach (population 3800) where the decibel level is considerably lower, but it offers some chic restaurants and a gorgeous stretch of golden beach.

ACTIVITIES

Most surf schools aim to have you standing up and catching waves in your first lesson. They charge between $45 and $55 for a two-hour group lesson. Surfboard and wetsuit hire is also available.

Cheyne Horan School of Surf (☎ **1800 227 873, 0403 080 484; www.cheynehoran.com.au; lessons 10am & 2pm**) Lessons for beginners held daily. Coaches are trained by Cheyne, a former world champion surfer.

Go Ride a Wave (☎ **1300 132 441; www.goridea wave.com.au; shop 189, Centro Centre, Cavill Ave, Surfers Paradise**) Also a popular place for surfboard hire.

Kamikaze Kites (☎ **07-5592 5171; www.kamikazekites.com; group lesson $80, private $150**) Three-hour lessons including radio contact with instructor.

SLEEPING

Cosmopolitan Apartments (☎ **1300 553 800, 07-5570 2311; 3142 Gold Coast Hwy, Surfers Paradise; apt from $105**) The apartments here are all privately owned so some have a fresh modern feel, while others are still stuck in the '80s. The location is primo (close to Cavill Ave) and you can fry yourself on the rooftop sun deck.

our pick **Vibe Hotel** (☎ **07-5539 0444; www.vibehotels.com.au; 42 Ferny Ave, Surfers Paradise; d/tr/ste from $125/169/385;**) A high-rise on the Nerang River, Vibe's lime-and-chocolate-brown exterior and bright seaside-themed lobby decor make surrounding hotels seem bland. The luxurious rooms are tastefully decorated, have all mod cons, and the poolside bar rocks. Reception staff? Outstanding.

Marriott Resort (☎ **07-5592 9800; www.marriott.com/oolsp; 158 Ferny Ave, Surfers Paradise; d/ste from $275/460;** P) Five-star accommodation with immaculate rooms and decadent extras such as the resort's private beach with saltwater lagoon and artificial coral reef for snorkelling (among 400 fish!). Restaurants on site include a Japanese steakhouse.

BURLEIGH HEADS

Directly in between Surfers Paradise and Coolangatta lies gorgeous Burleigh Heads, a rocky headland linked to a strip of coastline popular with holidaying families and hard-core surfers.

The town itself has some of the Gold Coast's best dining options with sunny cafes and open-air beachfront restaurants.

SIGHTS & ACTIVITIES

A walk around the headland through **Burleigh Heads National Park** is a must for any visitor – it's a 27-hectare eucalypt forest reserve with plenty of birdlife and several walking trails. The natural rock slides and water cascades at the **Currumbin Rock Pools** are wonderful in the summer months.

The **Currumbin Wildlife Sanctuary** (☎ **1300 886 511, 07-5534 0803; www.cws.org.au; Gold Coast Hwy, Currumbin; adult/child $39/21; 8am-5pm**) has Australia's biggest rainforest aviary where you can hand feed rainbow lorikeets. There's also kangaroo feeding, photo opportunities with koalas, Aboriginal dance displays and a Snakes Alive show.

Opened by the doctor who first succeeded in breeding platypuses, the **David Fleay Wildlife Park** (☎ **07-5576 2411; West**

Burleigh Rd; adult/child/family $16.60/7.75/42.15; 9am-5pm) is an important education and conservation centre for the duck-billed creatures.

SLEEPING & EATING

Burleigh Palms (**07-5576 3955; www.burleighpalms.com; 1849 Gold Coast Hwy; 1-bedroom apt per night/week from $120/490, 2-bedroom apt from $150/600;**) These self-contained family units are ideally located near the local shops and there's a private walkway through to Burleigh Beach. Rooms have open-plan living/kitchen/dining and large TVs; ask the owner Kae about wireless internet for a small charge.

our pick **Mermaids Dining Room & Bar** (**07-5520 1177; 31 Goodwin Tce, Burleigh Heads; dishes $14-36; breakfast, lunch & dinner)** So close to the waves you could almost reach out and pluck a surfer from their board, this restaurant with a stunning sea-view terrace is located on the rocks at the southern end of Burleigh Beach. Breakfasts include a 'Queensland fruit plate' or classic eggs Benedict; feast on fresh king prawns, reef fish or scallops for mains.

SUNSHINE COAST

A seemingly endless summer and waxed-down surfer chic make life a breeze on the Sunshine Coast. A short drive north of Brisbane, this fast-growing region, which includes classic beach suburbs Caloundra, Maroochydore and Mooloolaba, is a permanent home for lucky locals and retirees, and a thriving holiday spot for Aussie families from further south.

GLASS HOUSE MOUNTAINS

Rising above the green subtropical hinterland are the 16 volcanic crags known as the Glass House Mountains. Mt Beerwah (556m), the highest of these ethereal cornices, is the mother according to Indigenous Dreamtime mythology. These stunning natural formations lend an eerie otherworldliness to a region brimming with life.

OLIVER STREWE

Glass House Mountains

PETER HENDRIE

Noosa Heads

Just north of Beerwah is the justifiably famous **Australia Zoo** (☎ **07-5494 1134; www.australiazoo.com.au; Steve Irwin Way, Beerwah; adult/child/family $49/29/146; 9am-4.30pm**) a homage to wildlife super-enthusiast Steve Irwin and home to a remarkable assortment of critters. This is not the usual passive zoo experience, but rather an exotic animal extravaganza featuring the 'Crocoseum', Tiger Temple, armfuls of Australian natives and enough slimy-faced, beady-eyed beauties to keep the kids busy all day long. Courtesy buses are available from throughout the Sunshine Coast.

NOOSA

If Noosa isn't the hippest beachside destination in Australia, then we give up! The brightest light on the Sunshine Coast has bloody close to the lot: superb north-facing surf beaches; a pristine waterway in Noosa Sound; haute couture on Hastings St; beds for all budgets; fab local markets, and all encircled by a resplendent national park.

ORIENTATION

It's easy to get disoriented when driving in Noosa – over 100 roundabouts mean more than 300 choices to make! In short, get a map.

A number of communities surround Noosa River yet Noosa, to many, still means Hastings St. Further west is Noosa Spit, reached via a footpath from the far west end of Hastings St.

Tucked around the headland to the east in Noosa National Park are superb walking tracks and quiet stretches of sand ending at funky little Sunshine Beach, which is ideal for longer stays.

Most of the accommodation options are a few minutes' drive from Noosa Heads along the mouth of the Noosa River in Noosaville or Tewantin.

You'll also find restaurants clustered around Gympie Tce and Thomas St in Noosaville.

Uphill from Noosa Heads is Noosa Junction, home to the post office, supermarkets, shops and a cinema.

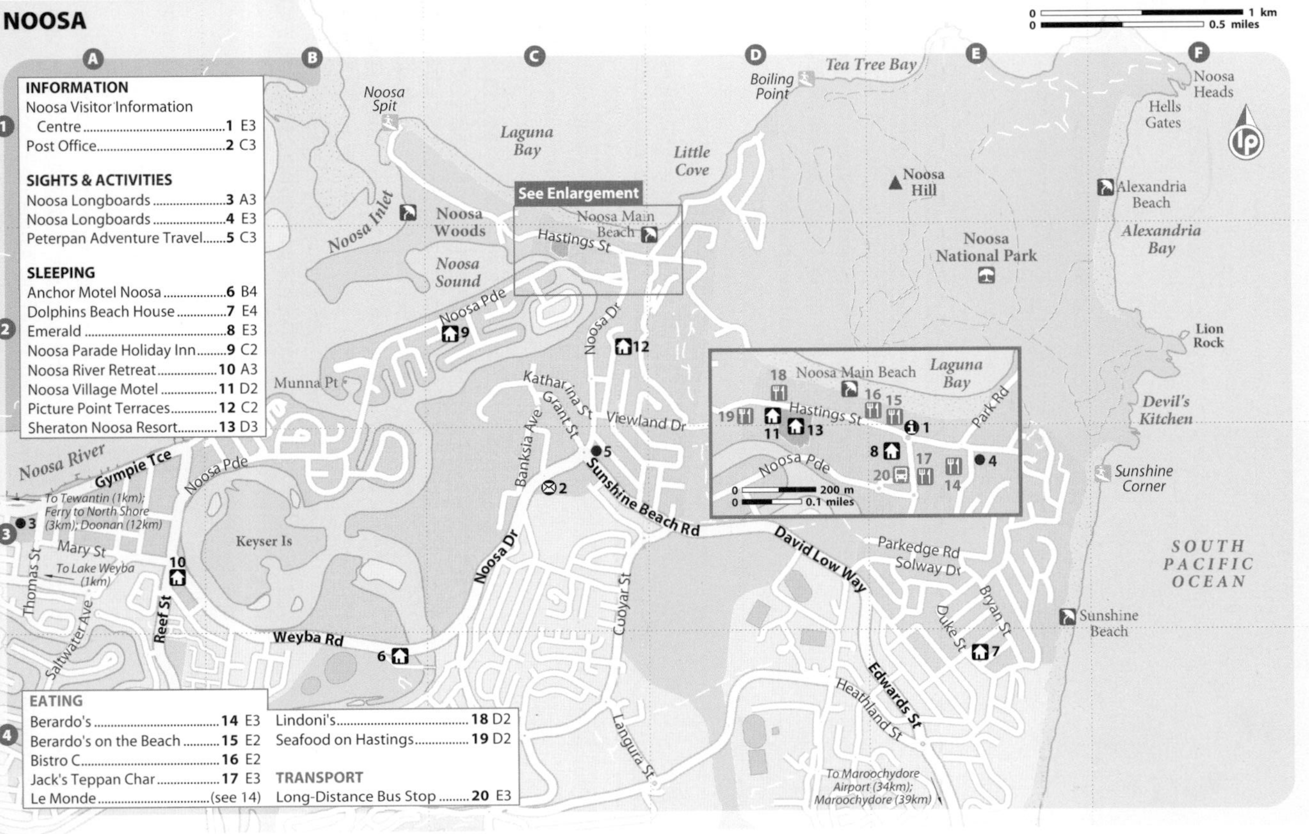
NOOSA
INFORMATION
Noosa Visitor Information Centre.....1 E3
Post Office.....2 C3
SIGHTS & ACTIVITIES
Noosa Longboards.....3 A3
Noosa Longboards.....4 E3
Peterpan Adventure Travel.....5 C3
SLEEPING
Anchor Motel Noosa.....6 B4
Dolphins Beach House.....7 E4
Emerald.....8 E3
Noosa Parade Holiday Inn.....9 C2
Noosa River Retreat.....10 A3
Noosa Village Motel.....11 D2
Picture Point Terraces.....12 C2
Sheraton Noosa Resort.....13 D3
EATING
Berardo's.....14 E3
Berardo's on the Beach.....15 E2
Bistro C.....16 E2
Jack's Teppan Char.....17 E3
Le Monde.....(see 14)
Lindoni's.....18 D2
Seafood on Hastings.....19 D2
TRANSPORT
Long-Distance Bus Stop.....20 E3
0 1 km
0 0.5 miles
See Enlargement
0 200 m
0 0.1 miles
Noosa Spit
Laguna Bay
Little Cove
Boiling Point
Tea Tree Bay
Noosa Heads
Hells Gates
Noosa Hill
Alexandria Beach
Alexandria Bay
Noosa National Park
Lion Rock
Devil's Kitchen
Sunshine Corner
SOUTH PACIFIC OCEAN
Sunshine Beach
Noosa Inlet
Noosa Woods
Noosa Sound
Noosa Main Beach
Hastings St
Noosa Pde
Noosa Dr
Munna Pt
Katharina St
Grant St
Viewland Dr
Banksia Ave
Sunshine Beach Rd
David Low Way
Parkedge Rd
Solway Dr
Bryan St
Duke St
Edwards St
Heathland St
Cooyar St
Langura St
Park Rd
Noosa River
Gympie Tce
To Tewantin (1km); Ferry to North Shore (3km); Doonan (12km)
Mary St
Thomas St
To Lake Weyba (1km)
Saltwater Ave
Reef St
Keyser Is
Weyba Rd
To Maroochydore Airport (34km); Maroochydore (39km)

ANDREW BAIN
Kayaking, Noosa River

INFORMATION

Noosa Visitor Information Centre (☎ 1800 448 833, 07-5447 4988; www.tourismnoosa.com.au; Hastings St; ⏰ 9am-5pm) A helpful service.

Post office (☎ 07-5473 8591; 91 Noosa Dr)

SIGHTS

Boutique shopping is found on **Hastings St** in Noosa Heads. Here you'll also find **Noosa Main Beach** and the main entrance to **Noosa National Park** (☎ 07-5447 3243; ⏰ 9am-3pm). The 2km-long park has fine walks, great coastal scenery and a string of popular bays for surfing on the northern side – when there's good swell, don't miss an iconic Australian afternoon at Tea Tree Bay or Little Cove. **Sunshine Beach** is a popular destination for a morning stroll – the monstrous shore-break and bluebottles will keep the kids giddily on their toes. Charming **Alexandria Bay**, on the eastern side of the national park, is for both naturalists and nature enthusiasts.

Art lovers can pick up information on the excellent **Sunshine Coast Gallery Trail** from the visitors centre.

ACTIVITIES

Noosa River is excellent for canoeing and kayaking. It's possible to follow it past beautiful homes to Lakes Cooroibah and Cootharaba, and the Cooloola Section of the Great Sandy National Park to just south of Rainbow Beach Rd. **Ocean & River Kayak Tours** (☎ 0418 787 577; www.learntosurf.com) offers two-hour sea-kayaking tours ($66) around Noosa National Park and Noosa River – if you're lucky, you'll see turtles and dolphins.

For the hard-core paddler, **Peterpan Adventure Travel** (☎ 1800 777 115; www.peterpans.com; shop 3, 75 Noosa Dr, Noosa Junction; per person $160) offers three-day canoe tours into the national park, including tents and equipment.

For a more sedate experience, hop aboard **Noosa Ferry Cruises** (☎ 07 5449 8442; all day pass adult/child/family $20/5.50/45, departs 10 times daily), which chugs (or, rather, motors) the 40 minutes between the Sheraton Hotel and Tewantin. Guides are friendly and knowledgeable. The sunset cruise ($20) is a thirst-quenching BYO affair.

TOURS

A number of tour operators offer trips from Noosa to Fraser Island via the Cooloola Coast.

Beyond Noosa (☎ 1800 657 666; www.beyondnoosa.com.au; afternoon tours from adult/child $69/45; 💻 🚌) Relaxed ecotours of the Noosa everglades.

Fraser Island Adventure Tours (☎ 07-5444 6957; www.fraserislandadventuretours.com.au; adult/child $159/115) An industry award-winner that includes a delicious barbecue lunch.

Fraser Island Excursions (☎ 07-5449 0393; www.fraserislandexcursions.com.au; tours $189) Small day tours take place in comfortable 4WD minibuses, and include a gourmet lunch and a glass of tipple.

SLEEPING

our pick **Dolphins Beach House** (☎ 07-5447 2100; www.dolphinsbeachhouse.com; 14 Duke St, Sunshine Beach; dm/d/apt $27/65/70; 💻 📶) Up there with the better backpacker joints on the east coast, Dolphins is a peaceful

GOOFY OR NATURAL? SURFING'S NOT FOR KOOKS

TOM SPURLING

Marching down to Noosa's Little Cove, the conditions are officially 'cranking' – the best in six months. We paddle out the back (I can do that bit easily enough), and join 30-odd locals. One seven-year-old punk does a 360 turn that nearly rips my head off then a silver bearded senior citizen walks the plank of his bright yellow longboard and gives me a wave from deep inside a curling tube. Everyone's throwing long-distance high-fives and patting themselves on the back just for being here, out in the ocean, on this cloudless January day.

My deltoids are burning, my lower back aching, but this is a day to savour. For the record, I catch four waves, stand up twice, nosedive thrice and love every single minute. Give me a week, and I'll be hangin' (something) loose.

Unspoilt Noosa National Park offers peaceful, peeling right-hand waves for all levels, though it can be fickle in winter. On the northern coast of the headland, good surfers look to Boiling Point and Tea Tree. Little Cove and Granite Bay are the pick of the point breaks for grommets. Sunshine Beach, and in particular Sunshine Corner, is a heavy wave best left to the experts, while Noosa Spit, on the far end of Hastings St, is protected from the rips and makes an ideal place to 'un-kook' yourself (ie learn to surf).

The luxury surfing travel company, **Tropic Surf** (www.tropicsurf.net) is based in Noosa, and its offshoot **Wave Sense** (☎ 07-5474 9076, 1800 249 076; www.wavesense.com.au) runs private lessons for $150 for two hours – a great option for families or those looking to really improve their surfing. Mostly based around Noosa Spit, other options include **Go Ride a Wave** (☎; www.gorideawave.com.au), **Noosa Surf Lessons** (☎ 0412 330 850; www.noosasurflessons.com.au) and **Merrick's Learn to Surf** (☎ 0418 787 577; www.learntosurf.com.au). Two-hour group lessons on longboards cost around $55. They all meet at Noosa Woods, just off Hastings St.

For something extra soulful, have a go at self-explanatory **Standup Paddle Surfing** (☎ 0412 175 233; www.standuppaddlesurfing.com.au) – or look for the dude surfing Main Beach with his pet dog beside him!

If you want to hire equipment, **Noosa Longboards** (www.noosalongboards.com; Noosa Heads ☎ 07-5447 2828; 64 Hastings St; Noosaville ☎ 07-5474 2722; 187 Gympie Tce) has boards for $35/50 per half/full day. You can also grab a boogie board ($15/20).

retreat set in lush tropical gardens. The self-contained dorms are neat and spacious, with their own share of a large Queenslander balcony, while the doubles are decked for travelling lovers. A very short walk to the beach or the Sunshine cafe strip, the real difference here is the absence of a bar – lo-fi days await. The travel-savvy owners know it all in a good way.

Anchor Motel Noosa (☎ **07-5449 8055; www.anchormotelnoosa.com.au; cnr Anchor St & Weyba Rd, Noosaville; r from $100;**) Motel ahoy! The Anchor pushes the nautical theme hard and starboard, with porthole windows, blue sailor-striped doonas and various underwater motifs. Rooms are neat and still new enough, plus there's a small pool with a real jacuzzi! It's centrally located between Hastings St and Noosa Junction.

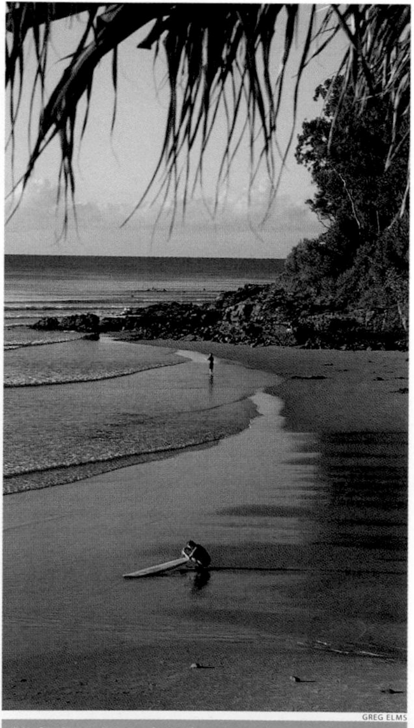

Little Cove, Noosa (p168)

GREG ELMS

Noosa River Retreat (☎ **07-5474 2811; www.noosariverretreat.net; cnr Weyba Rd & Reef St, Noosaville; 1-bedroom units $130;**) Your buck goes a long way at this orderly complex, which houses spick, span and spacious units. On-site are a central barbecue and laundry and the corner units are almost entirely protected by small native gardens.

Noosa Village Motel (☎ **07-5447 5800; www.noosavillage.com; 10 Hastings St; r from $130;**) Save your pennies for a few Noosa iced teas by staying at this good-value joint right on Hastings St. Set inside a bright-blue-and-yellow, boxlike motel, rooms are large, if a little plain, and feature wall-length windows.

Noosa Parade Holiday Inn (☎ **07-5447 4177; www.noosaparadeholidayinn.com; 51 Noosa Pde, Noosa Heads; r $190;**) Close to Hastings St, this is a surprisingly bright and spacious motel, with cool, tiled rooms offering some of the better value in this part of town.

Sheraton Noosa Resort (☎ **07-5449 4888; www.starwoodhotels.com/sheraton; 14-16 Hastings St, Noosa Heads; r $290-540;**) No surprises in this superb downtown five-star hotel that has stylish suede suites (no seriously, they're stylish), with extra-special beds. There are four bars, three restaurants (start your day at Cato's), and state-of-the-nation gym facilities. Book online or get fleeced.

Emerald (☎ **1800 803 899, 07-5449 6100; www.emeraldnoosa.com.au; 42 Hastings St, Noosa Heads; r from $370;**) The ethereal white, angular rooms at Emerald are smoother than a Noosa iced tea. The self-contained rooms are magazine-cover cool, and suit newlyweds and long-time lovers. Dine downstairs on seafood at

Rococo (mains $25 to $38), just because you can.

Picture Point Terraces (☎ 07-5449 2433; www.picturepointterraces.com.au; 47 Picture Point Cres, Noosa Heads; 2-/3-bedroom apt from $475/575;) Peer over the rainforest and down to Laguna Bay from these modern apartments up high behind the Reef Hotel. It's perfect for families or a group of young party pirates who should make full use of the private spa bath on the balcony.

EATING

Hastings St and the Noosa Head area is where to head for sophisticated dining.

Bistro C (☎ 07-5447 2855; On the Beach, Hastings St; mains $16-32) Even the patrons look edible at the famed little Bistro C right on Noosa Main Beach. The whole baby barramundi fried in lime and palm sugar ($23) is suitably sumptuous. For vegies, slurp on the linguini with baby bocconcini, pine nuts, rocket and basil oil ($17). It's that place with the famous people sculptures.

Jack's Teppan Char (☎ 07-5474 9555; 50 Hastings St; mains $18-28; lunch & dinner Tue-Sun) Noosa's very own brewery – Laguna Bay – now has its very own teppanyaki restaurant serving char-grilled goodness in a hip cocktail-induced atmosphere. The vegetarian udon ($18) is deliciously crunchy and the noodles perfectly sweet and sticky, while the chicken teriyaki ($24) is outstanding.

Le Monde (☎ 07-5449 2366; Hastings St; mains $18-32) A recent facelift has merely fixed a permanent smile on Noosa's beloved Le Monde, still the cafe of choice for those who know about those kinds of things! An extraordinarily long menu – juicy burgers, fine pasta, all manner of seafood and curries – hides the secret agenda of this open-air glam spot, which is to simply sip the day away. Regular live music means you can often sip the night away too.

Berardo's (☎ 07-5447 5666; Hastings St, Noosa Heads; mains $26-33; dinner) Find subtropical sex appeal dished up in slithers of truffle polenta and quail crépinette. The seafood hotpot is fragrant, the beach just across the road. There's a grand piano in the centre of the rooftop garden and enough style to sink some *petits fours* from the elegant dessert menu.

Also recommended:

Seafood on Hastings (☎ 07-5474 5210; 2 Hastings St, Noosa Heads; mains $10-18; lunch & dinner) Brand new takeaway fish and chip joint, with fresh and local written all over it.

Berardo's on the Beach (☎ 07-5477 5666; On the Beach, Hastings St; mains $15-30) The more relaxed Berardo's.

Lindoni's (☎ 07-5447 5111; Hastings St, Noosa Heads; mains $25-35; dinner) Australian-style Italian.

GETTING THERE & AROUND

Long-distance buses stop at the bus stop near the corner of Noosa Dr and Noosa Pde.

Sunbus has frequent services to Maroochydore ($5, one hour), and links up with the major parts of Noosa. From Christmas until early January, and over Easter, free shuttle buses run every 10 to 15 minutes between Noosa Junction, Noosa Heads and Tewantin.

SUNSHINE COAST HINTERLAND

When the rain hits Noosa, or the tourists get restless, many make the short trip inland to **Eumundi**, a charming artsy town 18km to the west. Try to time your visit for the world-famous **market** (8am-2pm Wed, 6am-2pm Sat), where you'll find everything from homemade cheese graters to aromatic sneeze abaters, plus clothing, food and music in the 200-plus stalls.

The largest town in the region is **Maleny**, a green and scenic mountain town famous for its 'co-op' spirit. Midway between Mapleton and Maleny is **Montville**, a dinky trinket town popular with short-term visitors escaping the steamy coast. There's an antique clock emporium, candy-making display centre, cafes, pubs and a contender for 'best view from a car park'.

WHITSUNDAY COAST

When Lieutenant James Cook sailed along this coast 50 days after Easter (on White Sunday) in 1770, he must have gargled with resplendent joy. The Whitsunday Islands are a travellers' wonderland where a great southern experience of sun, sand, and sailing is an outstretched arm away.

AIRLIE BEACH

Tacky and tremendous, exploited and exploitative, Airlie Beach is not so much a stepping off point for the Whitsunday Islands, as a high-voltage launching pad. Airlie is the kind of town where humanity celebrates its close proximity to natural beauty by partying very hard, fast and frequently.

ACTIVITIES

Sailing is the leisure activity of choice here, in all its nautical variations. Do-it-yourselfers will appreciate how easy it is to set sail unsupervised.

The Great Barrier Reef is roughly 70km offshore from Airlie Beach – most sailing trips are to a mere fringe. If you came here to see the reef (and aren't going north to Cairns) then check out the eco-certified **Fantasea Adventure Cruising** (☎ 07-5494 6 5111; www.fantasea.com.au; trips $209; plus dm/king r $409/570), which runs trips out to a floating pontoon at Hardy Reef.

SLEEPING

Airlie Waterfront Backpackers (☎ 1800 089 000, 07-4948 1300; www.airliewaterfront.com; 6 the Esplanade; dm $25-30; d & tw with/without bathroom $60/110;) Completely overhauled in 2008, this centrally located hostel is a smart, relaxed choice. The communal areas are spacious and bright, and the dorms are freshly painted and spotlessly clean. Exiting your premises via the shopping arcade is a little postmodern for some, but overall the Waterfront is right back in business.

Backpackers by the Bay (☎ 1800 646 994, 07-4946 7267; www.backpackersbythebay.com; 12 Hermitage Dr; dm/d $26/62;) On the road to Shute Harbour is this warm and friendly backpackers perched high above the sea. Dorms are spacious with just four beds per room. While the emphasis is on guest interaction, quiet time is equally valued. Reception closes at 7.30pm.

Airlie Beach Hotel (☎ 1800 466 233, 07-4964 1999; www.airliebeachhotel.com.au; cnr the Esplanade & Coconut Grove; r $129-259;) The ABH is an icon: a sharply presented, no-nonsense establishment, with spacious sea-facing suites, a world-class restaurant and a robust poolside social scene. Popular with professional sporting teams and amateur talent scouts, it's a generation away from the backpacker indulgence. Facilities for those with disabilities are good.

Shingley Beach Resort (☎ 07-4948 8300; www.shingleybeachresort.com; 1 Shingley Dr; studios from $150;) Managed by an astute and charming couple, these smart apartments make an ideal Whitsundays base. On a grassy patch past Abel Point

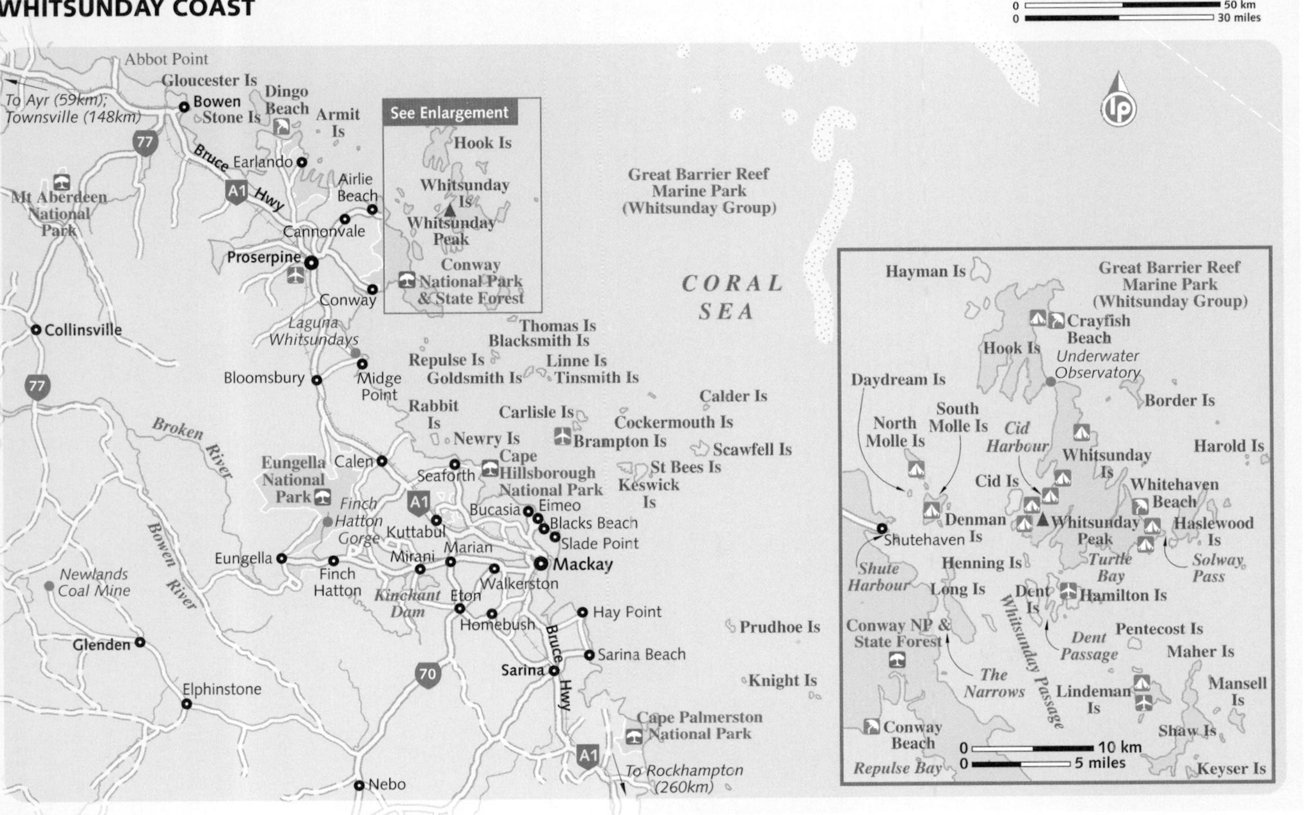
WHITSUNDAY COAST
0 50 km
0 30 miles
Abbot Point
Gloucester Is
To Ayr (59km); Townsville (148km)
Bowen
Stone Is
Dingo Beach
Armit Is
See Enlargement
Hook Is
Whitsunday Is
Whitsunday Peak
Conway National Park & State Forest
Bruce Hwy
Earlando
Airlie Beach
Cannonvale
Mt Aberdeen National Park
Proserpine
Conway
Great Barrier Reef Marine Park (Whitsunday Group)
CORAL SEA
Collinsville
Laguna Whitsundays
Thomas Is
Blacksmith Is
Repulse Is
Linne Is
Bloomsbury
Midge Point
Goldsmith Is
Tinsmith Is
Calder Is
Rabbit Is
Carlisle Is
Cockermouth Is
Newry Is
Brampton Is
Scawfell Is
Broken River
Eungella National Park
Calen
Seaforth
Cape Hillsborough National Park
St Bees Is
Keswick Is
Finch Hatton Gorge
Bucasia
Eimeo
Blacks Beach
Kuttabul
Slade Point
Marian
Mirani
Eungella
Mackay
Newlands Coal Mine
Bowen River
Finch Hatton
Walkerston
Kinchant Dam
Eton
Hay Point
Homebush
Prudhoe Is
Glenden
Sarina Beach
Sarina
Knight Is
Elphinstone
Cape Palmerston National Park
To Rockhampton (260km)
Nebo
Hayman Is
Great Barrier Reef Marine Park (Whitsunday Group)
Crayfish Beach
Hook Is
Underwater Observatory
Daydream Is
Border Is
South Molle Is
North Molle Is
Cid Harbour
Harold Is
Whitsunday Is
Cid Is
Whitehaven Beach
Denman
Whitsunday Peak
Haslewood Is
Shutehaven Is
Henning Is
Turtle Bay
Solway Pass
Shute Harbour
Long Is
Dent Is
Hamilton Is
Whitsunday Passage
Conway NP & State Forest
Pentecost Is
Dent Passage
Maher Is
The Narrows
Lindeman Is
Mansell Is
Conway Beach
Shaw Is
0 10 km
0 5 miles
Repulse Bay
Keyser Is
WHITSUNDAY COAST
BRISBANE & QUEENSLAND

SAILING THE WHITSUNDAYS

Walk down Airlie's main drag and you'll be assaulted by signed specials: 'Two-night sailing trips just $179, includes free dive!' Don't book the first thing you see. Cheaper companies generally have crowded boats, bland food and cramped quarters. Unfortunately no matter what price bracket you go with, bed bugs can be a reality.

The usual package is three days/two nights – really just two days, as trips depart in the afternoon of the first day and return early on the third.

Most companies offer a considerably lower standby rate for last minute bookings, so it's actually best not to book ahead unless you have your heart set on a particular boat and date. And be sure to check the weather before you commit.

Most vessels follow the fringing reef and Whitsunday Island-hopping route. Snorkelling along the fringing reef is as good, if not better (the fish are confined to a smaller space), than the real thing. Divers not able to visit the main reef elsewhere may want to book one of the trips visiting Bait Reef. Reaching Bait Reef requires 1½ hours of sailing across open water – consider seasickness tablets. Boats won't make the trip if it's too windy.

Once you've figured out what boat you'd like to sail on, you'll need to book through a travel agency like **Whitsunday Bookings** (**☎ 07-4948 2201; www.whitsundaybookings.com.au; shop 1, 346 Shute Harbour Rd, Airlie Beach**) or a management company like **Oz Adventure Sailing** (**☎ 1800 359 554; www.aussiesailing.com.au; 293 Shute Harbour Rd, Airlie Beach**). Both can sell berths on most vessels and will offer the same standby rates.

Marina, the views from Shingley are worthy of a far steeper price tag. Two saltwater pools enhance the generous guest amenities.

EATING

Airlie is developing a reputation for fine seafood restaurants, and there are plenty of good cheap eats too.

our pick **Shipwrecked** (**☎ 07-4946 6713; cnr Shute Harbour Rd & the Esplanade; lunch mains $20-25, dinner mains $30-45**) An exceptional wine list accompanies the best seafood menu in town. The barramundi and coral trout are always safe bets, but you're on holidays, for crying out loud, so try the sweet and sultry Penang seafood curry ($31) or the Shipwrecked Platter ($135 at last count) that will easily please three fussy pescatarians.

Capers (**☎ 07-4964 1777; Airlie Beachfront Hotel, the Esplanade; mains $22-40**) This casual, though classy restaurant gets a huge rap from locals and tourists alike. Lots of fresh seafood along with steaks, fine cheeses and a mouth-watering array of desserts complement a good wine list and a prime people-watching locale. Grab a plump couch and get stuck right in (just like Matthew McConaughey and Kate Hudson famously did back in 2007).

Déjà Vu (**☎ 07-4948 4309; Waters Edge Resort, 4 Golden Orchid Dr; lunch $12-20, dinner $25-40; 🕑 lunch & dinner Tue-Sat**) In an airy Polynesian-style thatched building

RICHARD I'ANSON

Hamilton Island (p178)

overlooking a pool, the Déjà Vu sets the standard in Airlie. The menu is modern, but unpretentious, and takes its flavours from Asian and Mediterranean cuisine. The scallop Pad Thai ($32) is genius and the tiki torches are always firing. The slow-burning Sunday lunch (just $36 for eight courses) starts at noon; book ahead for ocean views.

GETTING THERE & AROUND

The closest major airports are at Proserpine and on Hamilton Island.

WHITSUNDAY ISLANDS

These 90-plus islands, most of which are uninhabited, have long sat atop Australian travellers' must-do lists. More than 60 companies jostle to grant travellers access to these continental isles, only four of which have not been accorded national park status. Akin to the tips of coral mountains, the Whitsundays fall within the Great Barrier Reef World Heritage Area that stretches from Cape York in the north to Bundaberg in the south.

GETTING THERE & AWAY

Both Virgin Blue (☎ **13 67 89; www.virginblue.com.au**) and Jetstar (☎ **13 15 38; www.jetstar.com.au**) connect Hamilton Island with Brisbane, Sydney and Melbourne. QantasLink (☎ **13 13 13; www.qantas.com.au**) flies there from Cairns.

Fantasea Ferries (☎ **07-4946 5111; www.fantasea.com.au**) has return fares to Hamilton Island or Daydream Island (adult/child $72/44) via high-speed catamaran. Ferries depart from the pier at 11 Shute Harbour Rd, Airlie Beach. Tickets can be purchased at the airport on Hamilton Island, resorts or directly from the pier at Airlie Beach. A return ticket to Airlie Beach from Hamilton Island airport costs $120.

LONG ISLAND

Some of the best walking in the Whitsundays is found on this little gem. With the majority of the island deemed national park, days here are spent wandering around the 13km of marked tracks and peering across the narrow strait from one of many fine lookouts.

Sadly, camping is no longer available, but there are still three resorts, the best of which is by far **Peppers Palm Bay** (☎ 1800 095 025, 07-4946 9233; www.peppers.com.au/palm-bay; d from $460;). The Whitsundays version of the reputed Peppers boutique resort group is no exception – indulgent, Thai-style cabins snuggled around blissful Palm Bay, topped off with exceptional cuisine and service. Check for standby rates.

DAYDREAM ISLAND

Daydream Island is more manufactured than dreamy, but at just 1km long and a 15-minute ferry ride from Shute Harbour, it's a good compromise for busy families. A usual day sees hordes of kids getting touchy-feely with marine life in a small lagoon, while parents and cheap singles swivel cocktail umbrellas at the bar. Loads of water-sports gear is available for hire.

Daydream Island Resort & Spa (☎ 1800 075 040, 07-4948 8488; www.daydreamisland.com; 3-night package d $910;) is the tackier side of the Whitsundays, with five grades of accommodation. Still, it's efficiently operated and set in beautifully landscaped tropical gardens. There are three swimming pools, tennis courts, catamarans and faux-beaches. There's also a heaven-sent kids' club.

HOOK ISLAND

Just quietly, Hook Island is a magical place. Rugged enough to keep the crowds away, but easy to get around, Hook is perhaps the finest island in the Whitsundays.

At 53 sq km, Hook Island is mainly national park and blessed with great beaches and camping grounds. The underwater traffic is stunning and light on humans. Those you do meet are usually cruising through the weekdays with chilled-out smiles. **Crayfish Beach** (campsites per person $4.50) is a gorgeous camping spot with just 12 secluded campsites. Bookings are essential. Camping Whitsundays offers a spot on a two-night shared camping deal ($329) that includes boat transfers from Shute Harbour, food and camping equipment.

For those who prefer a more solid ceiling, you can stay at **Hook Island Wilderness Resort** (☎ 07-4946 9380; www.hookislandresort.com; sites per person $25, dm $35, d with/without bathroom $150/100;). It's clean though basic, with tiny bathrooms and a licensed restaurant (mains $15 to $25) that serves seafood, steak and pasta.

WHITSUNDAY ISLAND

Whitsunday Island is the largest and most celebrated of the islands, and home to **Whitehaven Beach**, arguably Australia's finest tropical beach. Boats of young and old tourists day trip here daily, but the smart ones stick around until morning. The island comprises 109 sq km and rises to 438m at **Whitsunday Peak**.

HAMILTON ISLAND

Hamilton Island Resort (☎ 1800 075 110, 07-4946 9999; www.hamiltonisland.com.au; d $305-595) manages this superbusy island, which feels more like a friendly film-set town than an established resort. There's also an airport, a deluxe marina full of smiling yuppie sea cats and ageless retirees. There are excellent restaurants, bars, shops and a huge range of accommodation, from the five-star Beach Club down to the relaxed Palm Bunglaows.

Hamilton is a ready-made day trip from Shute Harbour, and you can use some of the resort's facilities – see p177 for transport details.

LINDEMAN ISLAND

Lovely Lindeman is mostly national park, with empty bays and 20km of impressive walking trails. Nature photographers descend for the varied island tree life and the sublime view from Mt Oldfield (210m).

Club Med Resort (☎ **1800 258 2633, 07-4946 9333; www.clubmed.com; packages per person per night $492;**) is a fun all-inclusive option. It has its own launch that connects with flights from the airport at Hamilton Island.

FAR NORTH QUEENSLAND

Far North Queensland is an intoxicating mix of rainforest, strings of islands, outback, farmland and of course the amazing but, thanks to global warming, slowly vanishing, 345,000-sq-km Great Barrier Reef Marine Park.

CAIRNS

pop 122,700

Mangrove boardwalks and croc-infested rivers by the airport, busy retail areas bursting with Ken Done clothes and stuffed koalas and a unique tropical air make Cairns a spread-out city of surprises. The beautifully designed and perfectly located lagoon on the Esplanade is an attempt to make up for the fact that waterfront Cairns doesn't actually have a beach, and when the sun comes out so do locals and backpackers, creating a bikini-clad mirage in the city centre. It's a city where the casino doubles as a rainforest, and you can walk straight from the nightclub to the pier and catch one of the many morning boats that make the daily island or reef, diving or snorkelling pilgrimage.

INFORMATION

EMERGENCY

Police Station (☎ **000, 07-4030 7000; Sheridan St)**

MEDICAL SERVICES

Cairns Base Hospital (☎ **07-4050 6333; the Esplanade)** Has a 24-hour emergency service.

Cairns City 24 Hour Medical Centre (☎ **07-4052 1119; cnr Florence & Grafton Sts)**

WAYNE WALTON

Mission Beach, south of Cairns

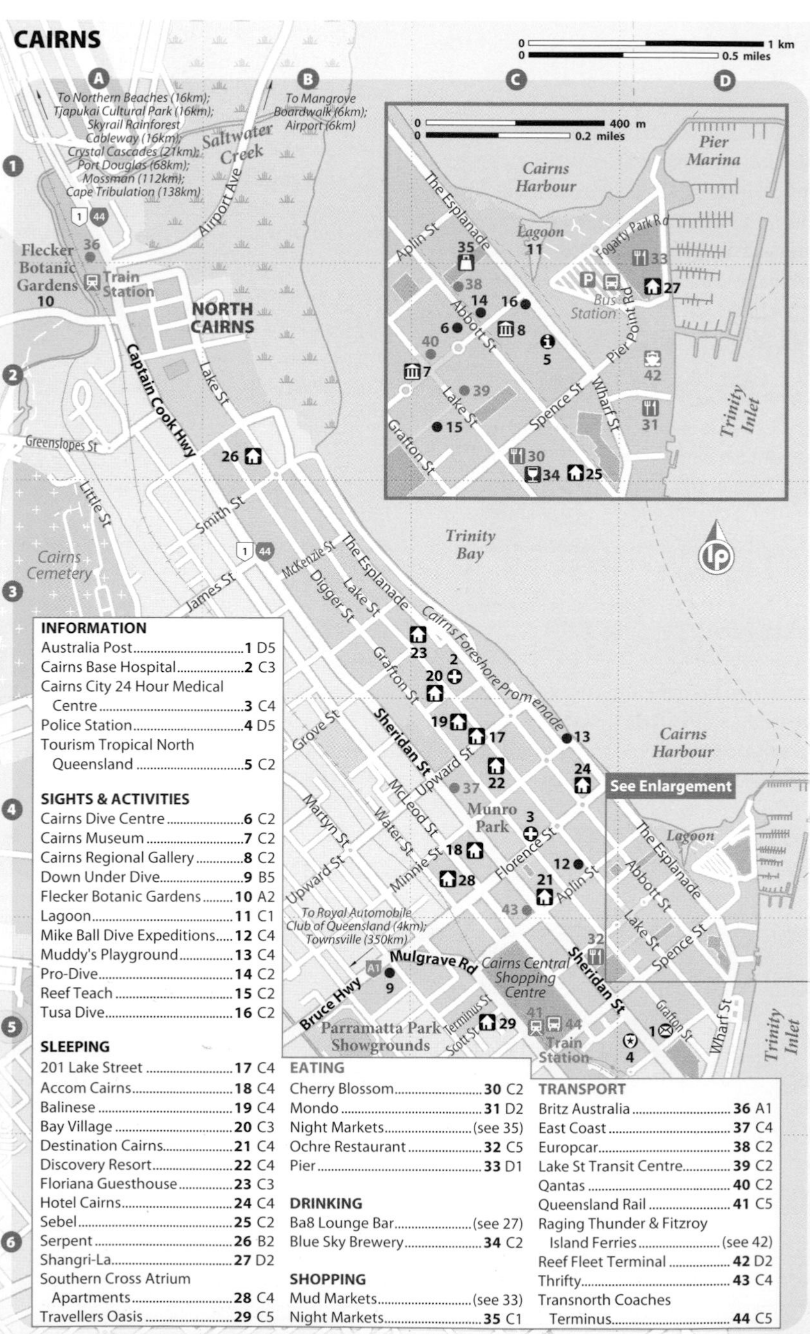

CAIRNS
To Northern Beaches (16km); Tjapukai Cultural Park (16km); Skyrail Rainforest Cableway (16km); Crystal Cascades (21km); Port Douglas (68km); Mossman (112km); Cape Tribulation (138km)
To Mangrove Boardwalk (6km); Airport (6km)
Saltwater Creek
Airport Ave
Flecker Botanic Gardens
Train Station
NORTH CAIRNS
Captain Cook Hwy
Lake St
Greenslopes St
Little St
Cairns Cemetery
Smith St
James St
McKenzie St
Digger St
The Esplanade
Cairns Foreshore Promenade
Trinity Bay
Cairns Harbour
Grafton St
Grove St
Sheridan St
Upward St
McLeod St
Martyn St
Water St
Minnie St
Munro Park
Florence St
Aplin St
See Enlargement
Lagoon
Abbott St
Spence St
To Royal Automobile Club of Queensland (4km); Townsville (350km)
Mulgrave Rd
Bruce Hwy
Cairns Central Shopping Centre
Parramatta Park Showgrounds
Terminus St
Scott St
Wharf St
Trinity Inlet
Pier Marina
Fogarty Park Rd
Bus Station
Pier Point Rd
1 km
0.5 miles
400 m
0.2 miles

INFORMATION
Australia Post 1 D5
Cairns Base Hospital 2 C3
Cairns City 24 Hour Medical Centre 3 C4
Police Station 4 D5
Tourism Tropical North Queensland 5 C2

SIGHTS & ACTIVITIES
Cairns Dive Centre 6 C2
Cairns Museum 7 C2
Cairns Regional Gallery 8 C2
Down Under Dive 9 B5
Flecker Botanic Gardens 10 A2
Lagoon 11 C1
Mike Ball Dive Expeditions 12 C4
Muddy's Playground 13 C4
Pro-Dive 14 C2
Reef Teach 15 C2
Tusa Dive 16 C2

SLEEPING
201 Lake Street 17 C4
Accom Cairns 18 C4
Balinese 19 C4
Bay Village 20 C3
Destination Cairns 21 C4
Discovery Resort 22 C4
Floriana Guesthouse 23 C3
Hotel Cairns 24 C4
Sebel 25 C2
Serpent 26 B2
Shangri-La 27 D2
Southern Cross Atrium Apartments 28 C4
Travellers Oasis 29 C5

EATING
Cherry Blossom 30 C2
Mondo 31 D2
Night Markets (see 35)
Ochre Restaurant 32 C5
Pier 33 D1

DRINKING
Ba8 Lounge Bar (see 27)
Blue Sky Brewery 34 C2

SHOPPING
Mud Markets (see 33)
Night Markets 35 C1

TRANSPORT
Britz Australia 36 A1
East Coast 37 C4
Europcar 38 C2
Lake St Transit Centre 39 C2
Qantas 40 C2
Queensland Rail 41 C5
Raging Thunder & Fitzroy Island Ferries (see 42)
Reef Fleet Terminal 42 D2
Thrifty 43 C4
Transnorth Coaches Terminus 44 C5

POST

Australia Post (☎ 13 13 18; www.auspost.com; 13 Grafton St)

TOURIST INFORMATION

Royal Automobile Club of Queensland (RACQ; ☎ 07-4033 6433; www.racq.com.au; Stockland Shopping Centre, 537 Mulgrave Rd, Earlville) Maps and information on road conditions up to Cape York. Also has a 24-hour road-report service (☎ 1300 130 595).

Tourism Tropical North Queensland (☎ 07-4051 3588; www.tropicalaustralia.com.au; 51 the Esplanade; 8.30am-6.30pm) Accredited and displays the authentic yellow 'i'.

SIGHTS

You can't beat the **Cairns Foreshore Promenade** for some chilled-out Cairns fun: its main feature is a 4800-sq-m saltwater swimming lagoon and, boy, is it popular when the sun comes out. When evening descends, the night market takes over the central zone, offering cheap souvenirs, magic honey and $15 massages.

Flecker Botanic Gardens (☎ 07-4044 3398; Collins Ave, Edge Hill; 7.30am-5.30pm Mon-Fri, 8.30am-5.30pm Sat & Sun), northwest of the city centre, is dominated by the magnificent rainforest, but there are also plots of bush-tucker plants and the Gondwanan Evolutionary Trail, which begins with 415-million-year-old blue-green algae (Quaternary) and reaches its standing ovation in the Age of Angiosperms (now).

Two hour-long **guided walks** (admission free; 10am & 1pm Tue & Thu) through the gardens are available, or pick up a brochure and take yourself on a self-guided walk. The licensed cafe serves not-to-be-outdone mango smoothies, while the info centre has a stinging tree in captivity. Ouch.

Opposite the gardens the **Rainforest Boardwalk** leads to **Saltwater Creek** and **Centenary Lakes**. For more serious walkers, the trails throughout **Mt Whitfield Conservation Park** have several lookouts offering views of Cairns and Trinity Inlet, and there is a terrific **mangrove boardwalk** (Airport Ave) 200m before the airport.

Owned and run by Indigenous Australians, the wonderful **Tjapukai Cultural Park** (☎ 07-4042 9999; www.tjapukai.com.au; Kamerunga Rd, Carevonica; adult/child/family $31/16/78, incl transfers $50/25/126; 9am-5pm) combines interesting aspects of Indigenous culture with show biz. It includes the creation theatre, which tells the story of creation using giant holograms and actors; there's also a dance theatre, and boomerang- and spear-throwing demonstrations (have a go!).

Cairns Regional Gallery (☎ 07-4046 4800; www.cairnsregionalgallery.com.au; cnr Abbott & Shields Sts; adult $5; 10am-5pm Mon-Sat, 1-5pm Sun), in a gorgeous heritage building, is worth a wander. Exhibitions reflect the consciousness of the region, with an emphasis on Indigenous art. Head loft-wards to see work from local emerging artists.

The **Cairns Museum** (☎ 07-4051 5582; www.cairnsmuseum.org.au; cnr Lake & Shields Sts; adult/child/family $5/2/12; 10am-4pm Mon-Sat) is an old-school museum housed in the former School of Arts building. If you have an interest in the history of dentistry and a love of aviation, you'll love this.

Take your knowledge of the reef to greater depths at **Reef Teach** (☎ 07-4031 7794; 85 Lake St; adult/child $15/8; 10am-9pm Mon-Sat, show 6.30-8.30pm Mon-Sat). The lecturer explains how to identify specific types of coral and fish, and, more importantly, how to respect the reef.

ACTIVITIES

Cairns is the undisputed scuba-diving mecca of the Great Barrier Reef and a popular place to attain PADI open-water certification. There's a plethora of courses on offer, from budget four-day courses that combine pool training and reef dives (around $500), to four-day open-water courses ($595). Five-day courses ($540 to $715) include two days' pool theory and three days' living aboard a boat, and are generally more rewarding. Before making a booking, find out whether prices include a medical check (around $55), daily reef tax ($5), passport photos (around $8), plus environmental management charges (around $10).

A selection of reputable schools:

Cairns Dive Centre (☎ 07-4051 0294; www.cairnsdive.com.au; 121 Abbott St; ⌚ 7am-5pm)

Down Under Dive (☎ 1800 079 099, 07-4052 8300; www.downunderdive.com.au; 287 Draper St; ⌚ 7am-7pm) English and Japanese-speaking instructors.

Pro-Dive (☎ 07-4031 5255; www.prodive-cairns.com.au; cnr Shields & Grafton St; ⌚ 8.30am-9pm) Japanese, German and English-speaking instructors.

Tusa Dive (☎ 07-4031 1028; www.tusadive.com; cnr Shields St & the Esplanade; ⌚ 7.30am-9pm)

More comprehensive reef trips last one to 11 days and cost roughly $200 to $3700. Live-aboard trips explore the outer and northern reefs, including Cod Hole, Homes Reef and Osprey Reef in the Coral Sea.

Operators specialising in trips for certified divers:

Mike Ball Dive Expeditions (☎ 07-4053 0500; www.mikeball.com; 143 Lake St; ⌚ 8am-5pm) Three-, four- and seven-night fly-dive trips and open-water dive courses ($385).

Reef Encounter (☎ 1800 815 811, 07-4051 5777; www.reeftrip.com) Live-aboard operator, plus open-water learn-to-dive courses (from $737) and trips from $220.

ReefQuest (☎ 1800 612 223, 07-4046 7333; www.diversden.com.au) Live-aboard dive trips ($330-570) depart daily; learn-to-dive courses from $435; snorkelling trips $120 to $480. Japanese and German tuition available.

Rum Runner (☎ 07-4031 2920; www.rum-runner.com.au; ⌚ 9am-5pm) Two-day/one-night 'sleep on the reef' adventures.

CAIRNS FOR CHILDREN

Muddy's playground (the Esplanade) is a great place to get saturated and it's suitable for all ages, with climbing nets, playgrounds and plenty of water-play areas. Also on the Esplanade, the **Lagoon** (⌚ 6am-10pm Oct-Mar, 7am-9pm Apr-Sep) is popular with kids and is patrolled all day.

TOURS

GREAT BARRIER REEF & ISLANDS

Reef tours usually include lunch, snorkelling gear (with dives an optional extra) and transfers. Rates quoted here are mostly for snorkelling.

Ocean Spirit (☎ 1800 644 227, 07-4031 2920; adult/child incl tax & pick-up $189/95) A fast catamaran whips you out for a full day at Michaelmas Cay.

Reef Magic (☎ 1300 666 700, 07-4031 1588; www.reefmagiccruises.com; adult/child/family $175/90/440) Goes to Moore Reef, one of the best outer reef sites with an observatory, fish feeding and stable platform suitable for those prone to seasickness. Recommended.

Reef Quest (☎ 1800 612 223, 07-4046 7333; www.diversden.com.au; adult/child/family from $120/85/355) One of the longstayers in the industry; has daily trips.

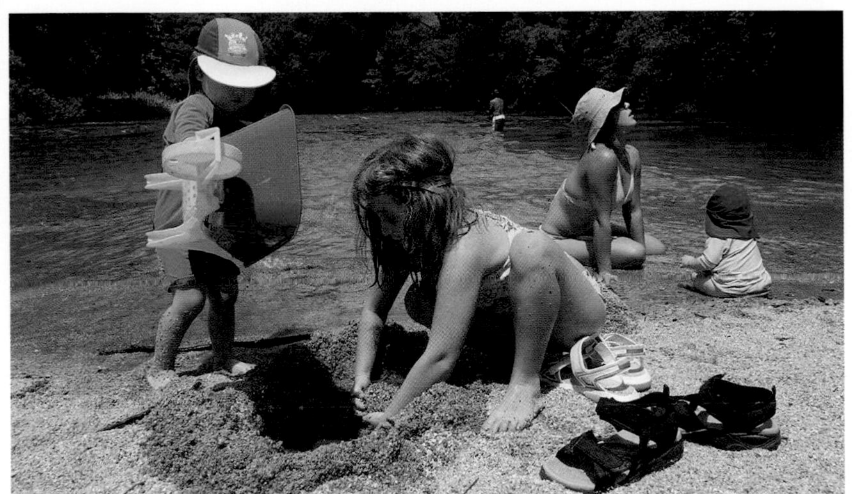

PAUL DYMOND

Mulgrave River, Cairns (p179)

Seastar (☎ 07-4041 6218, 4033 0333; www.seastarcruises.com.au; adult/child $165/110, intro dive from $240) Heads to Michaelmas Cay, where you can walk off the cay and onto reef, and Hastings Reef.

Silverswift (☎ 07-4044 9944; www.quicksilver-cruises.com; adult/child $163/123; certified scuba dive incl gear from $210, 2 dives $235) A quick and new boat visits two sites close to the edge of the continental shelf where's there's plenty of coloured coral. Recommended.

DAINTREE RIVER & CAPE TRIBULATION

Cape Tribulation is one of the most popular day-trip destinations from Cairns.

Back Country Bliss Adventures (☎ 0420 101 757; www.backcountryblissadventures.com.au; Bloomfield Falls trip $199) A funky outfit that offers various 4WD tours plus mountain biking, bushwalking, sea-kayaking and river-drift snorkelling trips.

Billy Tea Bush Safaris (☎ 07-4032 0077; www.billytea.com.au; day trip adult/child $150/100; 7.10am-6.30pm) This operation heads into the Daintree for walks, a tropical barbecue lunch, creek-swimming and time in Cape Trib.

COOKTOWN & CAPE YORK

Adventure North (☎ 07-4040 7500; www.adventurenorthaustralia.com; tours $209-469) Offers one- to three-day tours to Cooktown incorporating the best Indigenous tours along the way. A range of accommodation is available, as is a one-day drive-fly option.

Oz Tours (☎ 1800 079 006, 07-4055 9535; www.oztours.com.au) Purpose-built 4WDs travel to Cape York and the Gulf Savannah. Seven-day drive-fly trips from $1949, or you can return with the more expensive cargo ship option. Has advanced ecocertification.

Wilderness Challenge (☎ 07-4035 4488; www.wilderness-challenge.com.au; 3-day tours adult/child from $895/795; May-Nov) Another advanced ecocertification option with three-day rock-art, rainforest and Cooktown tours.

BOB CHARLTON

A wreck off Heron Island

IF YOU LIKE...

If you like diving the coral reefs off **Cairns** (p179), we think you might like these other amazing diving locations in Queensland:

- **Heron Island** (Map pp138–9) This exclusive and tranquil coral cay sits amid a huge spread of reef. You can step straight off the beach and join a crowd of colourful fish.
- **Lady Elliot Island** (Map pp138–9) The most southerly of the Great Barrier Reef islands, and also a coral cay, is home to 19 highly regarded dive sites, so it's hard to know where to begin.
- **Lizard Island** (Map pp138–9) Remote and rugged, Lizard Island boasts what are arguably Australia's best-known dive sites – Cod Hole, famous for its resident giant and docile potato cod, and Pixie Bommie.
- **HMAS *Brisbane*** This sunk, old Australian warship is the hottest dive spot in Queensland. Easily accessible off the Sunshine Coast, it has a flourishing artificial reef teeming with marine life. Scuba World (www.scubaworld.com.au) arranges a popular wreck dive of the *Brisbane*.
- **SS *Yongala*** Rated as one of Australia's best wreck dives and bristling with abundant marine life, this site is accessible from Townsville.

SLEEPING

Accommodation agencies have up-to-date listings and can assist in locating suitable accommodation. **Destination Cairns** (☎ 1800 807 730, 07-4051 4055; www.accomcentre.com.au; cnr Sheridan & Aplin Sts) has wheelchair access and information. **Accom Cairns** (☎ 1800 079 031; www.accom-cairns.com.au; 127 Sheridan St) gives advice on midrange, top-end and three-to-six-month rental options.

BUDGET

Serpent (☎ 1800 737 736, 07-4040 7777; www.serpenthostel.com; 341 Lake St; dm $14-23, d & tw from $50; 🖳 🏊) Part of the Nomads chain, Serpent has a huge pool, beach volleyball court, bar with meals and a gathering of comfy day beds in the breezy TV area. Rooms are brightly painted, clean and have good mattresses.

our pick **Travellers Oasis** (☎ 1800 621 353, 07-4052 1377; www.travoasis.com.au; 8 Scott St; dm/s/d $25/42/59;) Expect fantastic staff, fresh-smelling homely doubles (complete with bedside tables, fridges and fans), and a small central pool area surrounded by hammocks. The double rooms are great value, the dorms have single beds and it'll make you feel like you're in your own timber Queenslander.

Floriana Guesthouse (☎ 07-4051 7886; maggie@florianaguesthouse.com; 183 the Esplanade; s $69, d & tw $79-120;) Oozing charm, the charismatic Floriana Guesthouse is caught in a 1960s time warp but that's why we love it. The matriarch is piano-playing Maggie and she's a wealth of information about Cairns, as well as a native wildlife carer (her charges are often on site). The sweeping staircase is fit for a debutante, and lined with images of a glam Maggie and her family. It leads guests to bright, personalised rooms and self-contained flats; some have balconies with views out to sea.

MIDRANGE

Southern Cross Atrium Apartments (☎ 07-4031 4000; www.southerncrossapartments .com; 3-11 Water St; d $99-290;) If you find yourself in one of these cool, modern self-contained apartments you'll thank yourself. Enjoy the designer kitchen in the studios, and direct access to the lap pool (one of three) from ground floor apartments. Delux apartments have outdoor dining rooms, living areas and a swinging TV. It's very close to Cairns Central Shopping Centre. There's a three-night minimum stay.

Balinese (☎ 1800 023 331, 07-4051 9922; www.balinese.com.au; 215 Lake St; s, tw & d $100;) It doesn't look like Balin from the outside, but some timber wall hangings do give it a slight Balinese air. The basic rooms are clean, there's a communal kitchen, laundry, minipool and internet access. Room rates include a basic breakfast and return airport transfers (7am to 7pm).

Discovery Resort (☎ 1800 672 753, 07-4044 9777; www.discoveryresort.com.au; 183-185 Lake St; d/tr $105/124;) The folks here have done an excellent job refurbishing this hotel, and some rooms have extras like wine glasses and tasteful pictures on the wall. Superior rooms look out onto saltwater pool number two. Its licensed restaurant, Rimini, serves breakfast and dinner.

Bay Village (☎ 07-4051 4622; www.bay village.com.au; cnr Lake & Gatton Sts; r/apt $145/165;) Owned by the same folks who own Balinese, this has more character and much more space – the central atrium is particularly good looking. Rooms are simple but with Balinese touches, and look out over the pool. Downstairs, the romantic Balinese-inspired Bay Leaf restaurant gets good reviews and serves breakfast, lunch and dinner. Super-dooper staff will organise free airport pickups and tours.

Hotel Cairns (☎ 07-4051 6188; www.the hotelcairns.com; cnr Florence & Abbot Sts; r $165;) The swish of the fan above your bed and the whispering palms outside your door will lull you to sleep, while fat showerheads will wake you up in the morning. Timber slat blinds over floor-to-ceiling windows add to the colonial look of this unique four-star hotel.

TOP END

201 Lake Street (☎ 1800 628 929, 07-4053 0100; www.201lakestreet.com.au; 201 Lake St; r/apt from $140/360;) Lifted from the pages of a trendy magazine, this new apartment complex has a stellar pool and a whiff of

PAUL DYMOND

Cherry Blosson, Cairns

exclusivity. Grecian white predominates and guests can choose from a smooth hotel room or contemporary apartments with an entertainment area, a plasma-screen TV and a balcony.

Sebel (☎ 07-4031 1300; www.mirvachotels.com.au; 17 Abbott St; r $230-330;) This classic 1980s hotel still shines, with fab bathrooms, an on-site day spa and rooms with harbour or city views.

Shangri-La (☎ 07-4031 1411; www.shangri-la.com; Pierpoint Rd; d from $235-362;) Ever-so-slightly too conference-oriented, this hotel nonetheless has outstanding rooms filled to the brim with luxury – from the carpet to the full-wall doors and high ceilings, it's quite extraordinary, especially if you're a lucky bunny and get an exclusive 'horizon lounge' room.

EATING

Pier (☎ 07-4031 4677; Pier Complex, Pier Point Rd; mains $18; lunch & dinner) The Pier's fires burn brightly on the wooden deck that surrounds this waterfront bar-restaurant. The ice machine mesmerises as it moves ice along a Perspex pipe above the bar, but if you can focus your eyes on the menu you'll find a smattering of snacks, finger foods, pizza and fish. There's a band every Sunday night from 8pm.

Mondo (☎ 07-4052 6781; Hilton Hotel, 34 the Esplanade; meals $20) The place to go if you're allergy prone, or fancy some casual waterfront dining under fairy lights. The menu is varied, from Mexican fajitas to wagyu burgers and Indo classics, and reasonably priced. Great for filling up when you've returned from a reef trip.

Ochre Restaurant (☎ 07-4051 0100; 43 Shields St; mains $26-30; lunch Mon-Fri, dinner daily) Red Ochre's certainly creative with its dishes: expect goodies like emu and vermicelli spring rolls, Australian antipasto, crocodile wanton and salt-and-native-pepper crocodile and prawns. It sounds good and it is good. The Australian game platter is $48 per person, while a slice of amazing wattleseed pavlova or quandong pie with macadamia crumble costs $14. Not sure if it's Australian, but chocolate slut is also on the menu.

Cherry Blossom (☎ 07-4052 1050; cnr Spence & Lake Sts; mains $27-45; ⏰ lunch Wed-Fri, dinner Mon-Sat) Teppanyaki reigns supreme at this upstairs Japanese restaurant reminiscent of an *Iron Chef* cook-off, with two chefs working at opposite ends of the restaurant floor. Among the authentic dishes you'll find 'Aussie animals', and they taste good.

The **night markets** (the Esplanade) are busy come dinner time, and self-service is all the rage.

DRINKING

our pick **Blue Sky Brewery** (☎ 07-4051 7290; 34-42 Lake St; meals $20; ⏰ 10am-midnight Sun-Thu, 10am-2am Fri & Sat) Here's a sparkling new drinking hall and brewery that caters for foodies *and* beer-lovers. A 'snow rail' keeps the average barflies' beer cool, and you can try all seven premises-made brews on a taster-tray for $16. Foodwise, the malt from the brewery goes to the tablelands cattle, which end up in the kitchen. True blue beery beef.

Ba8 Lounge Bar (☎ 07-4052 7670; Shangri La Hotel, Pierpoint Rd; ⏰ 11am-midnight) It's all off-white couches, Indian head statues and a sparkling clean clientele here.

SHOPPING

Two-dollar souvenir shops rule the Cairns roost, and there's also a sure supply of opals, Coogi, Ken Done and made-in-Korea didgeridoos and boomerangs. For an authentic termite-made didgeridoo and other Indigenous items, your best bet is Tjapukai Cultural Park (p181).

Head to the **night markets** (the Esplanade; ⏰ 4.30-11pm) and **mud markets** (Pier Marketplace; ⏰ Sat morning) for the mandatory 'Cairns Australia' T-shirt, or if you need a $15 massage or your name on a grain of rice.

GETTING THERE & AWAY

TO/FROM THE AIRPORT

Qantas (☎ 13 13 13, 07-4050 4000; www.qantas.com.au; cnr Lake & Shields Sts), **Virgin Blue** (☎ 13 67 89; www.virginblue.com.au) and **Jetstar** (☎ 13 15 38; www.jetstar.com.au) all service Cairns, with flights to/from Brisbane, Sydney, Melbourne, Darwin (including via Alice Springs) and Townsville.

The airport is about 7km from central Cairns. **Sun Palm** (☎ 07-4087 2900; www.sunpalmtransport.com; adult/child $10/5) has airport services from Cairns city to the airport from 4am to 7pm.

BUS

John's Kuranda Bus (☎ 0418 772 953; tickets $4) runs between Cairns and Kuranda at least twice per day, and up to five times Wednesday to Friday. Buses depart from Cairns' Lake St Transit Centre. **Kuranda Shuttle** (☎ 07-4061-7944; tickets $4) departs Lake St Transit Centre roughly every two hours from 10am to 3pm, and Kuranda (Therwine St) at 10am, 12.15pm, 2pm and 3.45pm (the latter service does not operate on Saturday). **Transnorth** (☎ 07-4061 7944; www.transnorthbus.com; tickets $4) departs Spence St, Cairns for Kuranda at 6.45am, 8.30am, 11.30am, 1.30pm and 3pm daily.

Long-distance buses arrive and depart at Reef Fleet Terminal. **Greyhound Australia** (☎ 1300 GREYHOUND, 1300 4739 46863; www.greyhound.com.au; Reef Fleet Terminal) connects Cairns with Brisbane ($253, 30 hours), Rockhampton ($175, 18 hours), Airlie Beach ($113, 11 hours) and Townsville ($66, five hours).

Premier Motor Service (☎ 13 34 10; www.premierms.com.au) has buses to/from Innisfail ($17, 1½ hours), Mission Beach ($17, two hours), Tully ($24, 2½ hours), Ingham ($32, four hours) and Townsville ($53, 5½ hours).

CHRISTOPHER GROENHOUT

Green Island

Sun Palm Express (☎ **07-4087 2900; www.sunpalmtransport.com**) connects Cairns with Port Douglas ($35, 1½ hours, six daily services), Mossman ($45, 1¾ hours) and Cape Tribulation ($75, 3¼ hours, departs Cairns 7am and 1.15pm daily).

Coral Reef Coaches (☎ **07-4098 2800; www.coralreefcoaches.com.au**) has four services daily to Palm Cove ($20), Port Douglas ($32) and Mossman ($35, two hours).

CAR & MOTORCYCLE

Hiring a car or motorcycle is the best way to travel around Far North Queensland. There's a mind-numbing number of rental companies in Cairns:

Britz Australia (☎ **07-4032 2611; www.britz.com.au; 411 Sheridan St**) Hires out campervans.

East Coast (☎ **1800 028 881, 07-4031 6055; www.eastcoastcarrentals.com.au; 146 Sheridan St**)

Europcar (☎ **07-4051 4600; www.europcar.com.au; 9/40 Abbott St**) Also has an airport desk.

Thrifty (☎ **1300 367 277; www.thrifty.com.au; cnr Sheridan & Aplin Sts**)

TRAIN

The **Queensland Rail** (☎ **1800 872 467, 07-4036 9250; www.traveltrain.com.au; Cairns Central Shopping Centre, Bunda St; 9am-4.30pm Mon, 8am-4.30pm Tue-Fri, 8am-10am Sat & Sun**) *Tilt Train* runs between Cairns and Brisbane ($311, 24 hours), as does the *Sunlander* (economy seat/sleeper $212/271, 31 hours).

ISLANDS OFF CAIRNS

Cairns day trippers can easily head out to Green Island, as well as Fitzroy Island and Frankland Islands National Parks for a bit of sunning, snorkelling and indulging.

GREEN ISLAND

The island itself is a small, flat coral cay with boardwalks through rainforest, a luxury resort with facilities for day visitors (you can jump into their tired-looking pool, relax on their sunbeds and buy food and souvenirs from their shops) and some easily accessible coral to snorkel around.

The luxurious **Green Island Resort** (☎ **07-4031 3300; www.greenislandresort.com.au; r $495-595;**) is a polished-floorboards kind of place, with recently refurbished split-level rooms complete with king beds.

Great Adventures (☎ **07-4051 0455; www.greatadventures.com.au; 1 Spence St, Cairns**) has regular catamaran services to Green Island ($69), departing Cairns at 8.30am, 10.30am and 1pm and returning at noon, 2.30pm and 4.30pm. **Big Cat** (☎ **07-4051 0444; www.bigcat-cruises.com.au; adult/child $69/39**) runs half- and full-day tours, which depart

Cairns at 9am, 11am and 1pm. Prices include the use of either snorkelling gear or a spin in a glass-bottom boat. **Ocean Free** (☎ 07-4050 0550; www.oceanfree.com.au; adult/child/family schooner trips $129/85/379) sends a boutique 16.5m schooner off to Green Island and Pinnacle Reef.

FITZROY ISLAND NATIONAL PARK

You'll be lucky to find a scrap of coral-free sand on the two main beaches, but the fringing coral around the island is worth donning the snorkel to see, and you don't have to do much to attract the attention of turtles. In winter (June to August) whales are spotted from the lighthouse. There's a brand new **resort** (☎ 07-4051 9588; www.fitzroyisland.com.au) on the island, but check availability before making plans.

At the time of research, **Raging Thunder and Fitzroy Island Ferries** (☎ 07-4030 7907; www.ragingthunder.com.au; Reef Fleet terminal, Cairns; adult/child/family return ferry $68/37/163, full-day trip $93/52) was running day trips leaving Cairns daily departing 8.30am and returning at 5.15pm, with BYO food and drinks.

FRANKLAND ISLANDS NATIONAL PARK

For a resort-free island experience try this group of five islands surrounded by little but coral and vibrant marine life.

Frankland Islands Cruise & Dive (☎ 07-4031 6300; www.franklandislands.com.au; adult/child cruise & lunch only $135/95, full-day tour $165/105) runs excellent day tours, and throws in a seafood buffet, stinger/sun suits, snorkelling equipment and sun shades for families.

KURANDA

pop 1610

Kuranda is a hop, skip and jump from Cairns, or make that an historic train journey, sky rail adventure or winding bus trip, from Cairns. The village itself is basically sprawling sets of markets nestled in a spectacular tropical rainforest setting and selling everything from made-in-China Aboriginal art to emu oil. The locals are a friendly bunch, well prepared for the hordes of tourists that arrive in the morning and depart with full bellies, bags and memory cards at almost precisely 3.30pm. There's little reason to stay overnight as this is really a day-trippers' domain.

The **Kuranda visitor information centre** (☎ 07-4093 9311; www.kuranda.org; 🕑 10am-4pm) is in Centenary Park.

SIGHTS & ACTIVITIES

Kuranda's markets are throbbing by midday, and the **Original Kuranda Rainforest Markets** (7 Therwine St; 🕑 10am-3pm) has incense sticks burning in the ground and a more authentic vibe than either the **Heritage Markets** (Rob Veivers Dr; 🕑 9.30am-3.30pm) or the **New Kuranda Markets** (23 Coondoo St). The creative heart of Kuranda exists at the **Kuranda Arts Co-op** (☎ 07-4093 9026; www.artskuranda.asn.au; Shop 6/12 Rob Veivers Dr; 🕑 10am-4pm).

Behind the train station, **Kuranda Rainforest Tours** (☎ 07-4093 7476; adult/child $14/7; 🕑 hourly 10.30am-2.30pm) runs 45-minute calm-water cruises along the Barron River and you might spot a freshwater croc. Check opening times from October to March, as it doesn't operate after heavy rain.

There are several signed walks in the markets, and a short walking track through **Jumrum Creek Environmental Park**, which is off Barron Falls Rd, leads you to a big population of fruit bats.

Further down, Barron Falls Rd divides: the left fork takes you to a wheelchair accessible **lookout** over the Barron Falls, while further along the right fork brings you to **Wrights Lookout**, which looks down at Barron Gorge National Park.

There's loads of 'wildlife' in Kuranda – albeit in zoos. **Rainforestation** (☎ 07-4085 5008; www.rainforest.com.au; Kennedy Hwy; adult/child $39/20; ⏲ 9am-4pm) is an enormous tourist park with a wildlife section, river cruises and an Aboriginal show. For lions, hippos and more, visit **Cairns Wildlife Safari Reserve** (☎ 07-4093 7777; www.cairnswildlifesafarireserve.com.au; Kennedy Hwy; adult/child $28/14; ⏲ 9am-4.30pm).

The **Australian Butterfly Sanctuary** (☎ 07-4093 7575; www.australianbutterflies.com; 8 Rob Veivers Dr; adult/child $16/8; ⏲ 10am-4pm) offers half-hour tours through its butterfly aviary or head next door to **Birdworld** (☎ 07-4093 9188; www.birdworldkuranda.com; Heritage Markets; adult/child $15/8; ⏲ 9am-4pm), which displays 75 species of bird. The **Australian Venom Zoo** (☎ 07-4093 8905; 8 Coondoo St; adult/child $16/10; ⏲ 9am-5pm) won't take up much of your time, and is a no-go zone for an arachnophobe.

GETTING THERE & AWAY

Buses are by far the cheapest way to get to Kuranda, costing $4 and departing Cairns hourly from 10.20am to 4.15pm (see p187), though the other options are more spectacular.

Kuranda Scenic Railway (☎ 1800 620 324, 07-4036 9288; www.traveltrain.com.au; adult/child/student $40/20/33) winds 34km from Cairns to Kuranda through picturesque mountains and no fewer than 15 tunnels. The trip takes 1¾ hours and trains depart from Cairns at 8.30am and 9.30am daily, returning from pretty Kuranda station at 2pm and 3.30pm.

At 7.5km long, **Skyrail Rainforest Cableway** (☎ 07-4038 1555; www.skyrail.com.au; one way adult/child/family $40/20/100, return adult/child $58/29; ⏲ 8.15am-3.45pm) is one of the world's longest gondola cableways and provides a bird's-eye view over the tropical rainforest. It runs from the corner of Cairns Western Arterial Rd and the Cook Hwy in Smithfield, a northern suburb of Cairns, to Kuranda (Arara St). The journey takes about 90 minutes. It includes two stops along the way and features boardwalks that have interpretive panels and passes Barron Falls (which is reduced to a small stream in the Dry). The last departure from Cairns and Kuranda is at 3.45pm; transfers to and from the terminal (15 minutes' drive north of Cairns) and combination deals (Scenic Railway and Skyrail) are available. As space is limited, only daypacks are allowed on board.

↘ MELBOURNE & VICTORIA

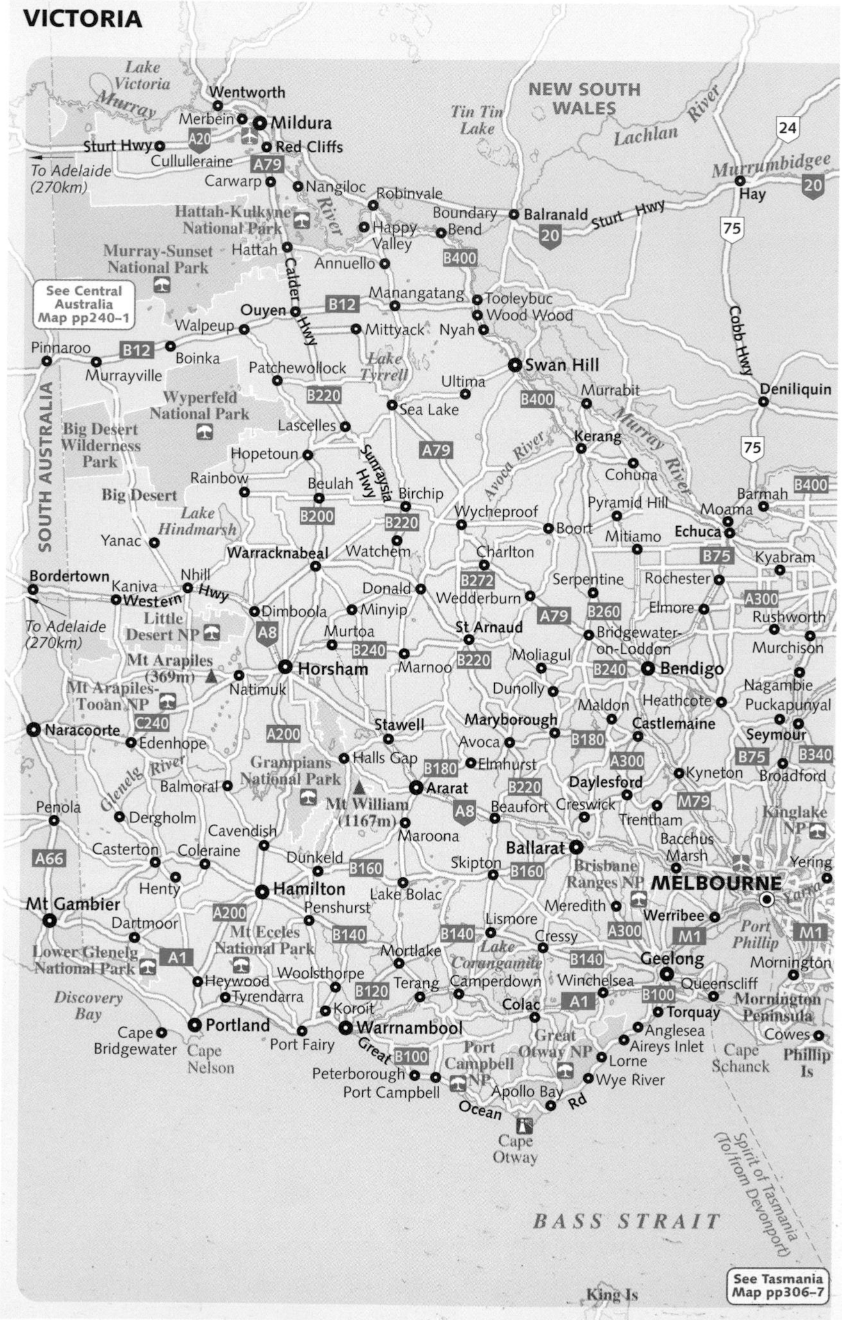

VICTORIA

Lake Victoria
Murray
Wentworth
Merbein
Mildura
Sturt Hwy
Red Cliffs
Cullulleraine
To Adelaide (270km)
Carwarp
Nangiloc
River
Robinvale
Hattah-Kulkyne National Park
Happy Valley
Boundary Bend
Balranald
Sturt Hwy
Murray-Sunset National Park
Hattah
Annuello
Calder Hwy
NEW SOUTH WALES
Tin Tin Lake
Lachlan River
Murrumbidgee
Hay
Cobb Hwy
See Central Australia Map pp240–1
Ouyen
Manangatang
Tooleybuc
Wood Wood
Walpeup
Mittyack
Nyah
Pinnaroo
Boinka
Murrayville
Patchewollock
Lake Tyrrell
Swan Hill
Ultima
Murrabit
Deniliquin
Wyperfeld National Park
Sea Lake
Big Desert Wilderness Park
Lascelles
Kerang
Murray River
SOUTH AUSTRALIA
Hopetoun
Sunraysia Hwy
Avoca River
Cohuna
Rainbow
Beulah
Big Desert
Birchip
Barmah
Lake Hindmarsh
Wycheproof
Pyramid Hill
Moama
Boort
Mitiamo
Echuca
Yanac
Watchem
Warracknabeal
Charlton
Kyabram
Bordertown
Kaniva
Nhill
Western Hwy
Serpentine
Rochester
Donald
Wedderburn
Elmore
To Adelaide (270km)
Little Desert NP
Dimboola
Minyip
Rushworth
Murtoa
St Arnaud
Bridgewater-on-Loddon
Murchison
Mt Arapiles (369m)
Natimuk
Horsham
Marnoo
Moliagul
Bendigo
Mt Arapiles-Tooan NP
Dunolly
Nagambie
Maldon
Heathcote
Puckapunyal
Naracoorte
Edenhope
Stawell
Maryborough
Castlemaine
Seymour
Grampians National Park
Halls Gap
Avoca
Elmhurst
Glenelg River
Kyneton
Broadford
Balmoral
Ararat
Daylesford
Penola
Mt William (1167m)
Beaufort
Creswick
Trentham
Kinglake NP
Dergholm
Cavendish
Maroona
Bacchus Marsh
Casterton
Coleraine
Ballarat
Dunkeld
Skipton
Brisbane Ranges NP
Yering
Henty
Hamilton
Lake Bolac
MELBOURNE
Yarra
Mt Gambier
Penshurst
Meredith
Werribee
Dartmoor
Lismore
Port Phillip
Mt Eccles National Park
Cressy
Lower Glenelg National Park
Mortlake
Lake Corangamite
Geelong
Mornington
Heywood
Woolsthorpe
Terang
Camperdown
Winchelsea
Queenscliff
Tyrendarra
Mornington Peninsula
Discovery Bay
Koroit
Colac
Torquay
Cape Bridgewater
Portland
Warrnambool
Great Otway NP
Anglesea
Cowes
Cape Nelson
Port Fairy
Great Ocean Rd
Port Campbell NP
Aireys Inlet
Cape Schanck
Phillip Is
Lorne
Peterborough
Wye River
Port Campbell
Apollo Bay
Cape Otway
Spirit of Tasmania (To/from Devonport)
BASS STRAIT
King Is
See Tasmania Map pp306–7

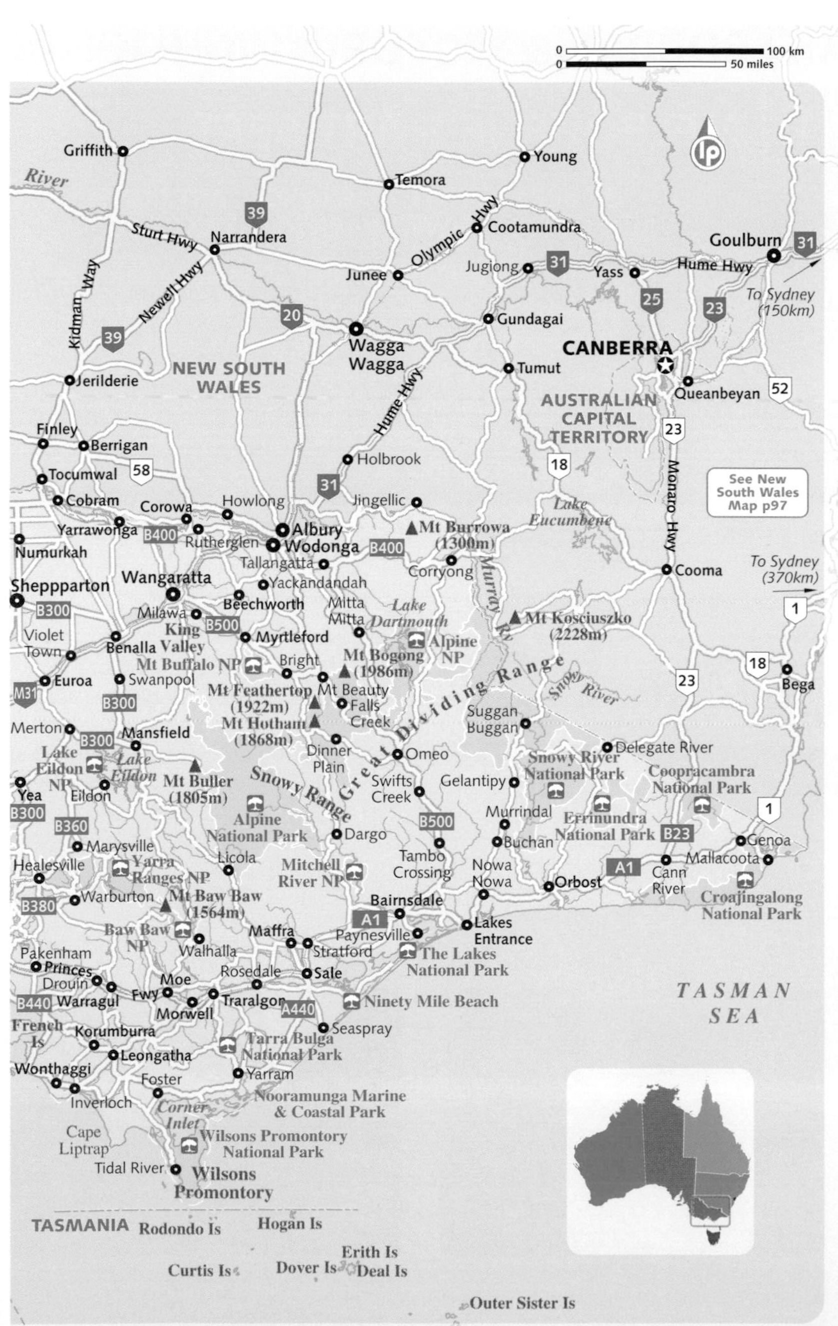
0 100 km
0 50 miles
Griffith
River
Young
Temora
Cootamundra
Olympic Hwy
Sturt Hwy
Narrandera
Newell Hwy
Kidman Way
Junee
Jugiong
Yass
Goulburn
Hume Hwy
To Sydney (150km)
Gundagai
Wagga Wagga
CANBERRA
Tumut
Queanbeyan
Jerilderie
NEW SOUTH WALES
AUSTRALIAN CAPITAL TERRITORY
Hume Hwy
Finley
Berrigan
Holbrook
Tocumwal
See New South Wales Map p97
Monaro Hwy
Cobram
Corowa
Howlong
Jingellic
Lake Eucumbene
Yarrawonga
Albury
Mt Burrowa (1300m)
Numurkah
Rutherglen
Wodonga
Tallangatta
Corryong
Murray R
Cooma
To Sydney (370km)
Shepparton
Wangaratta
Yackandandah
Beechworth
Mitta Mitta
Lake Dartmouth
Mt Kosciuszko (2228m)
Milawa
King Valley
Violet Town
Benalla
Myrtleford
Alpine NP
Mt Buffalo NP
Bright
Mt Bogong (1986m)
Great Dividing Range
Snowy River
Euroa
Swanpool
Mt Beauty
Falls Creek
Bega
Mt Feathertop (1922m)
Mt Hotham (1868m)
Suggan Buggan
Merton
Mansfield
Dinner Plain
Omeo
Delegate River
Lake Eildon NP
Lake Eildon
Mt Buller (1805m)
Snowy Range
Snowy River National Park
Coopracambra National Park
Yea
Eildon
Swifts Creek
Gelantipy
Alpine National Park
Murrindal
Errinundra National Park
Marysville
Dargo
Buchan
Genoa
Healesville
Yarra Ranges NP
Licola
Mitchell River NP
Tambo Crossing
Nowa Nowa
Orbost
Cann River
Mallacoota
Warburton
Mt Baw Baw (1564m)
Bairnsdale
Croajingalong National Park
Baw Baw NP
Walhalla
Maffra
Paynesville
Lakes Entrance
Pakenham
Stratford
The Lakes National Park
Princes Fwy
Drouin
Moe
Rosedale
Sale
Warragul
Morwell
Traralgon
Ninety Mile Beach
TASMAN SEA
French Is
Korumburra
Seaspray
Leongatha
Tarra Bulga National Park
Wonthaggi
Foster
Yarram
Inverloch
Nooramunga Marine & Coastal Park
Corner Inlet
Cape Liptrap
Wilsons Promontory National Park
Tidal River
Wilsons Promontory
TASMANIA
Rodondo Is
Hogan Is
Erith Is
Curtis Is
Dover Is
Deal Is
Outer Sister Is

MELBOURNE & VICTORIA HIGHLIGHTS

1 MELBOURNE'S ART BEAT

BY BERNADETTE ALIBRANDO, ART CONSULTANT & GUIDE – WWW.WALKTOART.COM.AU

People ask me what makes Melbourne tick and I suppose it's the fact that we do have a lot of creative spaces available for artists on a public level. For me, Melbourne is about quirky space and it is about going into those spaces off the beaten track – going down the side alley or into the anonymous building.

➘ BERNADETTE ALIBRANDO'S DON'T MISS LIST

❶ COMMISSIONED LANEWAY ART

The Melbourne City Council started the Laneways Commissions project in 2001. Pick up a **Laneways Commissions map** and explore – for locals it's a bit like being a tourist in your own city. There are several lanes that you really should search out and have a look at. It's always changing. It's really about whenever you are running around town just taking a moment to look up and about and see what's happening.

❷ PLATFORM

Beneath **Flinders St**, in a pink-tiled pedestrian subway called Campbell Arcade, is a great space run by a group called Platform Artists Group, which is supported by the City of Melbourne, Arts Victoria and the Australia Council. Platform is a great space of ever-changing exhibits behind glass windows – the last window is always used for video media and can be quite idiosyncratic.

Clockwise from top: Centre Pl; Graffiti in Union Lane, a designated graffiti laneway; Hosier Lane; Platform gallery, in Campbell Arcade; Graffiti and kegs in a Melbourne laneway

CLOCKWISE FROM TOP: JOHN BANAGAN; GERARD WALKER; RACHEL LEWIS; GREG ELMS; GREG ELMS

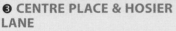

❸ CENTRE PLACE & HOSIER LANE

Melbourne is rated in the top five street-art cities of the world, with New York, London, Berlin and Barcelona. In some lanes, such as Hosier and Union, the city has sanctioned the colourful and political stencil art and graffiti. A lot of credit for the vibrancy and legitimacy of Melbourne's street-art scene goes to Andy Mac – check out the street art, light boxes and Mac's **Until Never Gallery** in Hosier Lane. Platform also has three windows on the beautiful **Majorca Building** in Centre Place, which are used for emerging artists to show their work.

❹ GALLERIES

It's not all about street art. Go to **Australian Centre for Contemporary Art** (p211), a big rusty red building on Sturt St in the arts precinct of Southbank. It's free, it's not really on the tourist maps and it's a great space for contemporary art. Also go to **Stephen McLaughlin Gallery** (☎ 0407 317 323; Level 8, Room 16, Nicholas Bldg, 37 Swanston St; ⏲ Wed-Fri 1-5pm Sat 11am-5pm) for the great art and views.

➘ THINGS YOU NEED TO KNOW

Forms of street art Stencil, freehand spray, tagging, paste-ups **Best photo opportunity** Around Chinatown (p210) you will see some really great paste-ups by Miso and ghostpatrol, two extremely fashionable kids

MELBOURNE & VICTORIA HIGHLIGHTS

2 GREAT OCEAN ROAD

BY CRAIG BAIRD, CURATOR, SURF WORLD MUSEUM

The ocean beaches around Torquay are where we would holiday as kids and I consider myself lucky to now live and work surrounded by spectacular beaches and the natural beauty of nearby bushland. Torquay is Victoria's surf city and gateway to the Great Ocean Road and I am always amazed at the inspirational combination of beach and bush.

↘ CRAIG BAIRD'S DON'T MISS LIST

❶ TORQUAY

Torquay (p227) offers a chance to immerse yourself in surf culture. The **Surf World Museum** (p227) is recognised as the world's largest, and is dedicated to telling the story of Australian surfing. Torquay's surf shops can provide you with all the latest gear and fashion, local surfing schools offer the chance to learn how to get on board, and there are funky galleries encapsulating surfing cool.

❷ BELLS BEACH

The Great Ocean Road heads slightly inland between Torquay and Anglesea, with a turn-off about 7km from Torquay to the famous **Bells Beach** (p228). Bells is a spectacular surf beach with a rich history and is home to the world's longest running surfing competition, the Rip Curl Pro. It's worth a detour as cliff-top platforms provide great views of the waves and surfers.

Clockwise from top: Phantom Falls, near Lorne (p229); Rock stacks near the Twelve Apostles (p232); Great Ocean Road near Wye River (p230); Bells Beach (p228); A beach at Torquay (p227)

❸ LORNE

It's not all about the beaches – exquisite natural beauty extends inland as well, and there are a number of waterfalls and bushwalks around **Lorne** (p229) that can give you a chance to unwind and plug back into nature. If you can tug yourself away from Lorne's pretty bay, head to the **Qdos Gallery** (☎ 03-5289 1989; www.qdosarts.com; 35 Allenvale Rd), amongst the trees just out of Lorne, which features some great contemporary art.

❹ THE RIDE

There is a beautiful rhythm to the **Great Ocean Road**. At a number of spots you are only metres from the water and there are some great sandy beaches and secluded little coves that can be accessed by simply parking and walking to.

❺ PORT CAMPBELL NP

The rugged and beautiful coastline beyond **Cape Otway** (p231) is known as the Shipwreck Coast. At **Port Campbell National Park** (p232), sheer 70m cliffs confront relentless seas, which have carved out spectacular arches, blow holes and stacks, such as the **Twelve Apostles**, from the soft limestone.

➘ THINGS YOU NEED TO KNOW

Only a few hours? Take a helicopter tour (p232) over the Twelve Apostles **Avoid** Standing beneath the soft, crumbly cliffs behind the beaches and on the top edges of the cliffs **See our author's review on p227**

MELBOURNE & VICTORIA HIGHLIGHTS

3

QUEEN VICTORIA MARKET

The largest open-air market in the southern hemisphere, **Queen Victoria Market** (p211) boasts more than 600 traders and a history dating over 130 years. Saturdays are hectic with thousands of Melburnians shopping for fresh produce. Clothing stalls dominate on Sunday, and while much of the merchandise is of questionable style you won't quibble about the price.

4

MELBOURNE CRICKET GROUND

Melbourne hosts internationally renowned events such as the Australian Open tennis tournament, yet it is the home-grown Australian Rules football that dominates this city. Between March and September, arenas reverberate to the roar of thousands of passionate spectators. And the number one stadium to participate in this spectacle is the **Melbourne Cricket Ground** (p212), or MCG, or just 'the G'.

PHILLIP ISLAND

Phillip Island (p225) lies at the entrance to Westernport Bay, 140km southeast of Melbourne. It is most famous for staging the Penguin Parade, one of the state's biggest tourist drawcards. Thousands come down from Melbourne on a day trip to watch the tiny wet birds waddle back to their burrows after a day's fishing.

THE GRAMPIANS (GARIWERD)

The **Grampians** (Gariwerd to local Koories; p232) is a majestic range rising from the flat plains west of Melbourne. They shelter a diverse assortment of flora and fauna as well as Indigenous rock art. It's the showy springtime burst of wildflowers, as well as the dramatic rock formations, that keep bushwalkers returning to the trails.

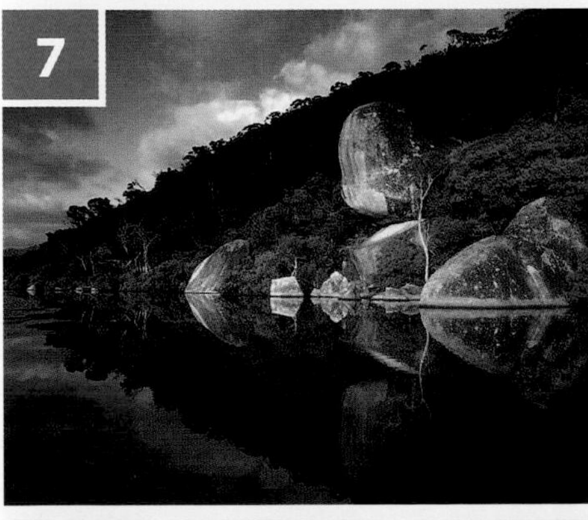

WILSONS PROMONTORY NATIONAL PARK

Close enough to Melbourne for a day trip, the untamed **Wilsons Promontory** (p237), or 'Prom', features squeaky clean beaches, curious wildlife, ferny gullies and exceptional walks. The southern tip of the mainland also boasts over 80km of trails for experienced bushwalkers.

3 JAMES BRAUND; 4 JEFF YATES; 5 PHILIP GAME; 6 RICHARD I'ANSON; 7 RICHARD I'ANSON

3 Queen Victoria Market (p211); 4 Australian Rules football at the Melbourne Cricket Ground (p212); 5 Fairy penguins at Phillip Island (p225); 6 Redman Bluff, Grampians National Park (p232); 7 Wilsons Promontory (p237)

MELBOURNE & VICTORIA'S BEST...

PLACES WITH A VIEW

- **Otway Fly** (p232) This 25m-high treetop walk offers superb canopy views, or go even higher by ascending the 47m lookout tower.
- **Twelve Apostles** (p232) There may only be six left, but these rocky stacks battling the ocean make for a magnificent cliff-top view.
- **Grampians** (p232) This ancient eroded range features several lookouts with breathtaking views of rugged grandeur.

NATURE ESCAPES

- **Wilsons Promontory** (p237) Golden beaches, verdant gullies of tree ferns and inquisitive wombats.
- **Phillip Island** (p225) After observing the antics of fur seals, rug up for the famous Penguin Parade.
- **High Country** (p234) The Victorian Alps, winter playground for snow bunnies, is a year-round adventure, with bushwalking and horse treks.

PLACES TO LUNCH

- **Yarra Valley** (p223) The rows of vineyards make the perfect backdrop to a leisurely liquid lunch.
- **Melbourne Cricket Ground** (p212) Marshal the courage to tackle a pie and sauce while barracking for your team.
- **Chinatown** (p210) Numerous restaurants entice you to yum cha.

ART & CULTURE

- **Arts Precinct** (p211) Under the spectacular spire in Southbank is Melbourne's cultural heart, with a concert hall, theatres and the state's premier art gallery.
- **Federation Square** (p205) Striking 'Fed Square' is Melbourne's favourite meeting point and home to galleries and cultural venues.
- **Melbourne Museum** (p213) In a remarkable modern building is a broad collection of Victoria's natural and cultural heritage.

LEFT: MICHAEL COYNE; RIGHT: JOHN BANAGAN

Left: Twelve Apostles (p232); Right: Chinatown (p210)

THINGS YOU NEED TO KNOW

VITAL STATISTICS

- **Population** 5.3 million
- **Telephone code** ☎ 03
- **Best time to visit** September to May

LOCALITIES IN A NUTSHELL

- **Melbourne** (p204) Multifaceted, with multicultural flair and charm
- **Great Ocean Road** (p227) A great drive along spectacular rugged coastline
- **The Wimmera** (p232) Taste the outback, with walks, wildflowers and rock art
- **The High Country** (p234) Outdoors adventure playground for nature lovers
- **Gippsland** (p237) Victoria's verdant east, boasting beautiful national parks

ADVANCE PLANNING

- **One month before** Reserve Melbourne theatre seats
- **Two weeks before** Plan your Great Ocean Road journey and book a hire car
- **One week before** Book a table at a top-notch restaurant

RESOURCES

Lonely Planet's *Melbourne & Victoria* guide is an excellent resource for getting the most out of your time.

- **Information Victoria** (Map pp208-9; ☎ 1300 366 356; www.information.vic.gov.au; 505 Little Collins St, Melbourne) A government-run bookshop stocking a wide variety of publications about Melbourne and Victoria
- **Melbourne Visitor Information Booth** (Map pp208-9; Bourke St Mall)
- **Melbourne Visitor Information Centre** (Map pp208-9; ☎ 03-9658 9658; www.visitmelbourne.com; Federation Sq, Melbourne; 9am-6pm)
- **Tourism Victoria** (☎ 13 28 42; www.visitvictoria.com) A good source for information, ideas and contacts
- **Parks Victoria** (☎ 13 19 63; www.parkweb.vic.gov.au) Managers of Victoria's national parks
- **Royal Automobile Club of Victoria** (RACV; Map pp208-9; ☎ 13 72 28; www.racv.com.au; 438 Little Collins St, Melbourne) Produces the excellent *Experience Victoria* guide, full of accommodation and touring info

EMERGENCY NUMBER

- **Police, fire and ambulance** (☎ 000)

GETTING AROUND

- **Walk** the caffeine infused laneways of inner Melbourne
- **Bus** to the Phillip Island Penguin Parade (p225)
- **Drive** the Great Ocean Road (p227)

BE FOREWARNED

- **Driving in Melbourne** Watch out for passengers alighting from trams, and for the 'hook turn' at many city intersections – to turn right, pull into the *left* lane, wait until the *other* light turns green, then complete the turn
- **Phillip Island's Penguin Parade** (p225) It kicks off *after* sunset

MELBOURNE & VICTORIA ITINERARIES

NIGHTLIFE & WILDLIFE Three Days

Start your trip in Victoria's multicultural capital **(1) Melbourne** (p204), where you can savour a melting pot of global cuisines and eclectic and creative live theatre. Once you have had your fill of nightlife, overdosed on cafe lattes or long blacks, seen a show or even cheered on a footy team, it's time to leave the city lights behind and experience Victoria's wild side.

It's easy to organise a tour or hire your own set of wheels to visit quiet little **(2) Phillip Island** (p225) at the entrance to Westernport Bay. Phillip Island is home to the famous Penguin Parade, where cute little penguins march up the beach in a floodlit spectacle. And there's more to the Island, including a colony of Australian fur seals and several excellent beaches.

From Phillip Island head to **(3) Wilsons Promontory** (p237), or the 'Prom' as it is affectionately known. The Prom is renowned for its abundant wildlife, pristine beaches and excellent bushwalking tracks. Take the two-hour stroll to Squeaky Beach, a sensational white-sand beach. Go barefoot on the sand to find out where the name comes from.

COASTAL CRUISIN' Five Days

Pick up a set of wheels in **(1) Melbourne** (p204) and head down towards the regional hub of Geelong. On the way you should detour to the **(2) Werribee Open Range Zoo** (p223) for an African-style safari experience.

The fabulous Great Ocean Road officially starts at **(3) Torquay** (p227), the hub of Victoria's surf coast. Here you can visit a surfing museum, shop for surf fashions and pick up a board and have a go at surfing. There are gentle breaks and surf schools, and nearby is the famous Bells Beach. **(4) Anglesea** (p228) promotes a more relaxed surf culture, while **(5) Lorne** (p229) offers wonderful bushwalks and waterfalls as well as delightful beaches. There are more quiet towns, secluded beaches and the wonderfully winding road with spectacular views all the way to **(6) Cape Otway** (p231), a rugged part of the coast that earned the moniker 'the Shipwreck Coast'. Beyond the cape is the stunning **(7) Port Campbell National Park** (p232), where crumbling limestone cliffs retreat from the pounding surf, leaving eerie rock stacks, such as the Twelve Apostles, and natural arches and blowholes.

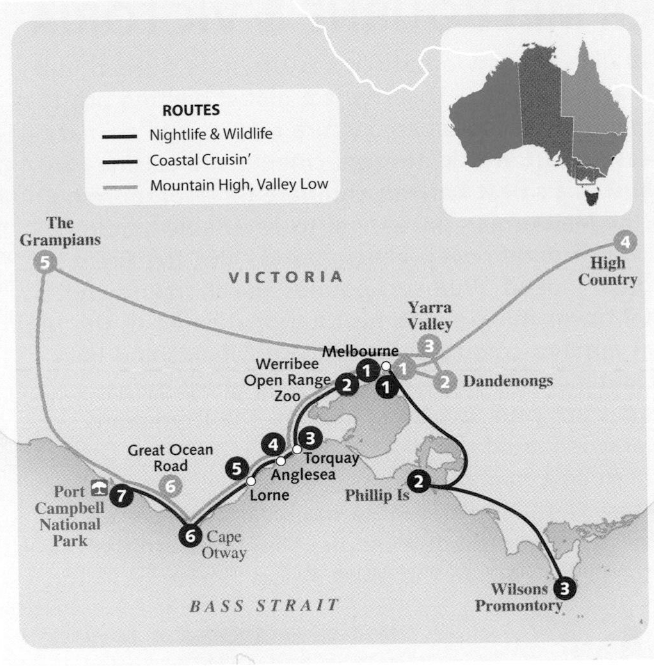

MOUNTAIN HIGH, VALLEY LOW One Week

Again starting from the capital of **(1) Melbourne** (p204), explore the **(2) Dandenongs** (p224), a compact, low and lush range on the city outskirts, where tall forests shelter cool ferny enclaves and low-key tourism such as the Puffing Billy steam train. Descend to the vineyards, wineries and restaurants of the **(3) Yarra Valley** (p223), still only a stone's throw from the city.

Continue east (there are several picturesque routes) to Victoria's **(4) High Country** (p234) where, depending on the season, you can ski, snowboard, bushwalk or horse trek the magnificent mountainous countryside. Next head west to the outstanding **(5) Grampians** (p232), where craggy peaks conceal Indigenous rock art and feature stupendous views. After a day or two exploring these mountains, head south to return to Melbourne along the winding **(6) Great Ocean Road** (p227).

DISCOVER MELBOURNE & VICTORIA

Melbourne, Australia's second-largest city, is the state's urban hub and the nation's artistic centre. This city is a global melting pot that has retained community spirit, where culture junkies and culinary perfectionists feast on art, music, theatre, cinema and cuisine for every budget. Australia's best baristas compete for your morning trade here, but the Melburnian pace is set to an affable amble.

Scalloping its way around coves, beaches and cliffs, the Great Ocean Road is great indeed. Wild surf pounds the shoreline and enigmatic coastal towns mingle with lush national parks. In the High Country, brilliant autumn colours segue into snowfields and back again to sleepy summer towns, haunted by pale ghost gums.

If wild landscapes are your weakness head to the Grampians National Park, sprawled amid the dry plains of the Western District. Australia's southernmost mainland tip is the spiritually reviving Wilsons Promontory National Park. More of a cosmopolitan tourist? Duck just outside of Melbourne and sample some of Australia's finest wines in the Yarra Valley and on the Mornington Peninsula.

MELBOURNE

pop 3.7 million

Ornate Victorian-era architecture and leafy boulevards reflect the city's history, and cutting-edge developments such as Federation Square, the Docklands and the Eureka Tower exemplify its enigmatic contemporary style. Trams lumber back and forth on routes radiating out like spokes from central Melbourne, and bike lanes throughout reflect the city's love affair with cycling.

INFORMATION

EMERGENCY

Dial ☎ 000 for ambulance, fire or police.

Police station (Map pp208-9; ☎ 03-9637 1100; 226 Flinders Lane; 24hr)

POST

All suburbs have an Australia Post branch.

Melbourne GPO (General Post Office; Map pp208-9; ☎ 13 13 18; 250 Elizabeth St, Melbourne; 8.30am-5.30pm Mon-Fri, 9am-4pm Sat, 10am-4pm Sun) Poste restante available.

TOURIST INFORMATION

Melbourne Visitor Information Booth (Map pp208-9; Bourke St Mall, Melbourne)

Melbourne Visitor Information Centre (Map pp208-9; ☎ 03-9658 9658; www.visitmelbourne.com; Federation Sq, Melbourne; 9am-6pm) Comprehensive tourist information including excellent resources for mobility impaired travellers.

SIGHTS

Most of Melbourne's best-known sights are clustered around the city centre, but the surrounding suburbs are thick with their own character. In the alternative north you'll find Fitzroy with its fashionable Brunswick St, and Collingwood the edgier sibling. Seaside St Kilda lures weekend day trippers for lattes and people. Carlton is the Italian district where Alpha Romeos growl along Lygon St, and Williamstown is a village-style seaside port.

CITY CENTRE

FEDERATION SQUARE

A riotous explosion of steel, glass and abstract geometry, **Federation Square** (Map pp208-9; ☎ 03-9655 1900; www.federationsquare.com.au; cnr Flinders & Swanston Sts) is Melbourne's meeting hub, where thousands of locals and visitors gather in the undulating forecourt each year for regular cultural events, sporting telecasts, t'ai chi classes, twilight jazz, Afrobeats and much more. When they're not here to celebrate, protest, party or watch sport on the big telly, people fill the bars, restaurants, galleries and public lecture halls.

The **Ian Potter Centre: National Gallery of Victoria Australia** (NGVA; Map pp208-9; ☎ 03-8620 2222; www.ngv.vic.gov.au/ngvaustralia; Federation Sq; admission free; 10am-5pm Tue-Sun) is devoted to Australian art, featuring works from the colonial to contemporary periods by celebrated artists including Sidney Nolan, Arthur Boyd, Joy Hester, Clifford Possum Tjapaltjarri, Albert Tucker, Jenny Watson, Bill Henson, Howard Arkley, Tony Clark, John Brack and Gordon Bennett.

COLLINS STREET

Collins St is one of Melbourne's most elegant streetscapes. Its fashionable 'Paris end' is lined with plane trees (lit up beautifully with fairy lights at night), grand buildings and upmarket European boutiques (Chanel, Bally, Hermés etc).

Block Arcade (Map pp208–9), which runs between Collins and Elizabeth Sts, was built in 1891 and is a beautifully intact 19th-century shopping arcade. It features etched-glass ceilings and mosaic floors, and magnificently detailed plasterwork. Connecting Block Arcade with Little Collins St, **Block Place** (Map pp208–9) keeps hip city cats topped up with lattes and cafe fare.

RODNEY HYETT

Federation Square

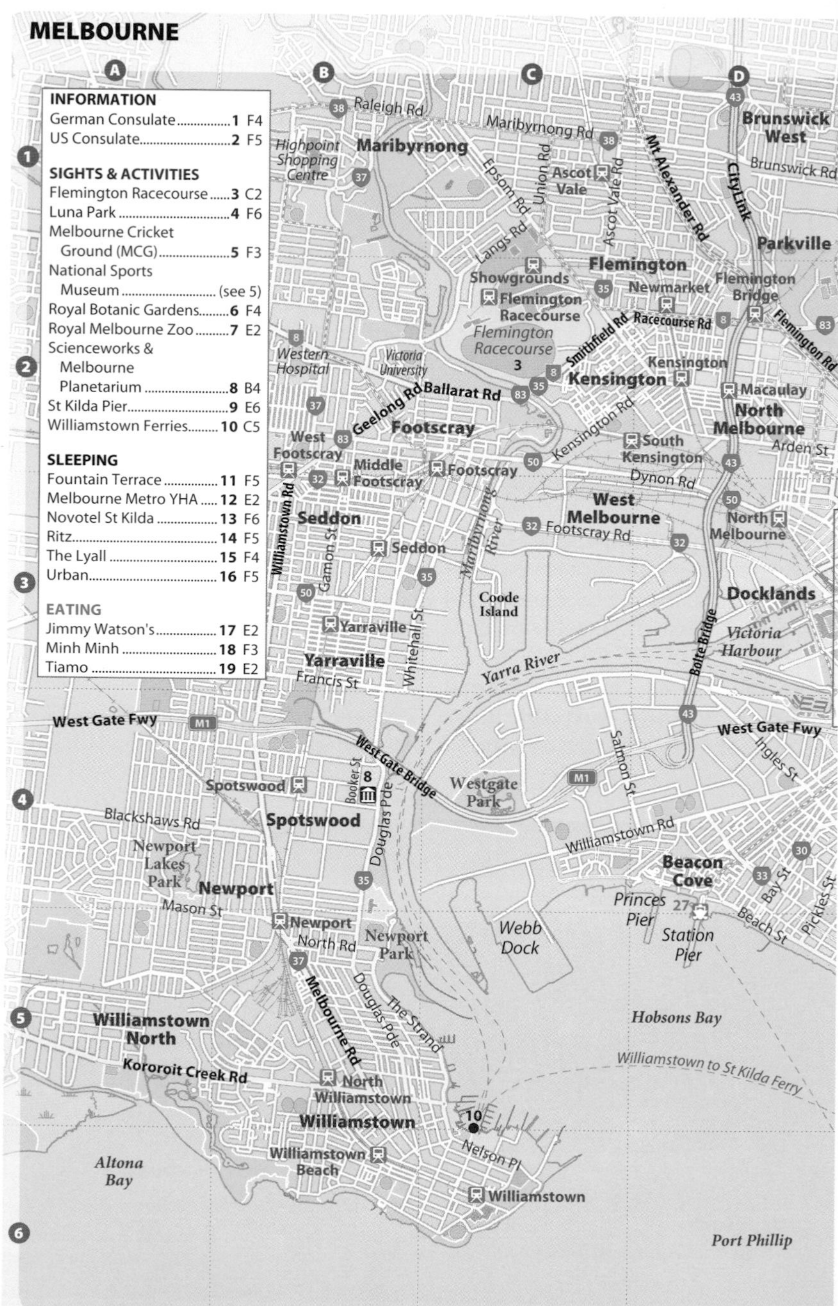
MELBOURNE
INFORMATION
German Consulate 1 F4
US Consulate 2 F5
SIGHTS & ACTIVITIES
Flemington Racecourse 3 C2
Luna Park 4 F6
Melbourne Cricket Ground (MCG) 5 F3
National Sports Museum (see 5)
Royal Botanic Gardens 6 F4
Royal Melbourne Zoo 7 E2
Scienceworks & Melbourne Planetarium 8 B4
St Kilda Pier 9 E6
Williamstown Ferries 10 C5
SLEEPING
Fountain Terrace 11 F5
Melbourne Metro YHA 12 E2
Novotel St Kilda 13 F6
Ritz 14 F5
The Lyall 15 F4
Urban 16 F5
EATING
Jimmy Watson's 17 E2
Minh Minh 18 F3
Tiamo 19 E2
A
B
C
D
1
2
3
4
5
6
Raleigh Rd
Maribyrnong Rd
Highpoint Shopping Centre
Maribyrnong
Brunswick West
Brunswick Rd
Epsom Rd
Union Rd
Ascot Vale
Ascot Vale Rd
Mt Alexander Rd
CityLink
Parkville
Langs Rd
Showgrounds
Flemington
Newmarket
Flemington Bridge
Flemington Racecourse
Racecourse Rd
Smithfield Rd
Flemington Rd
Western Hospital
Victoria University
Kensington
Macaulay
North Melbourne
Arden St
Geelong Rd
Ballarat Rd
Footscray
Kensington Rd
South Kensington
West Footscray
Middle Footscray
Dynon Rd
West Melbourne
Seddon
Williamstown Rd
Gamon St
Maribyrnong River
Footscray Rd
Coode Island
Docklands
Yarraville
Whitehall St
Bolte Bridge
Victoria Harbour
Francis St
Yarra River
West Gate Fwy
M1
West Gate Bridge
Ingles St
Spotswood
Booker St
Douglas Pde
Westgate Park
Salmon St
Blackshaws Rd
Williamstown Rd
Newport Lakes Park
Newport
Beacon Cove
Mason St
North Rd
Newport Park
Webb Dock
Princes Pier
Station Pier
Bay St
Beach St
Pickles St
Melbourne Rd
The Strand
Hobsons Bay
Williamstown North
Kororoit Creek Rd
North Williamstown
Williamstown to St Kilda Ferry
Williamstown
Nelson Pl
Altona Bay
Williamstown Beach
Port Phillip

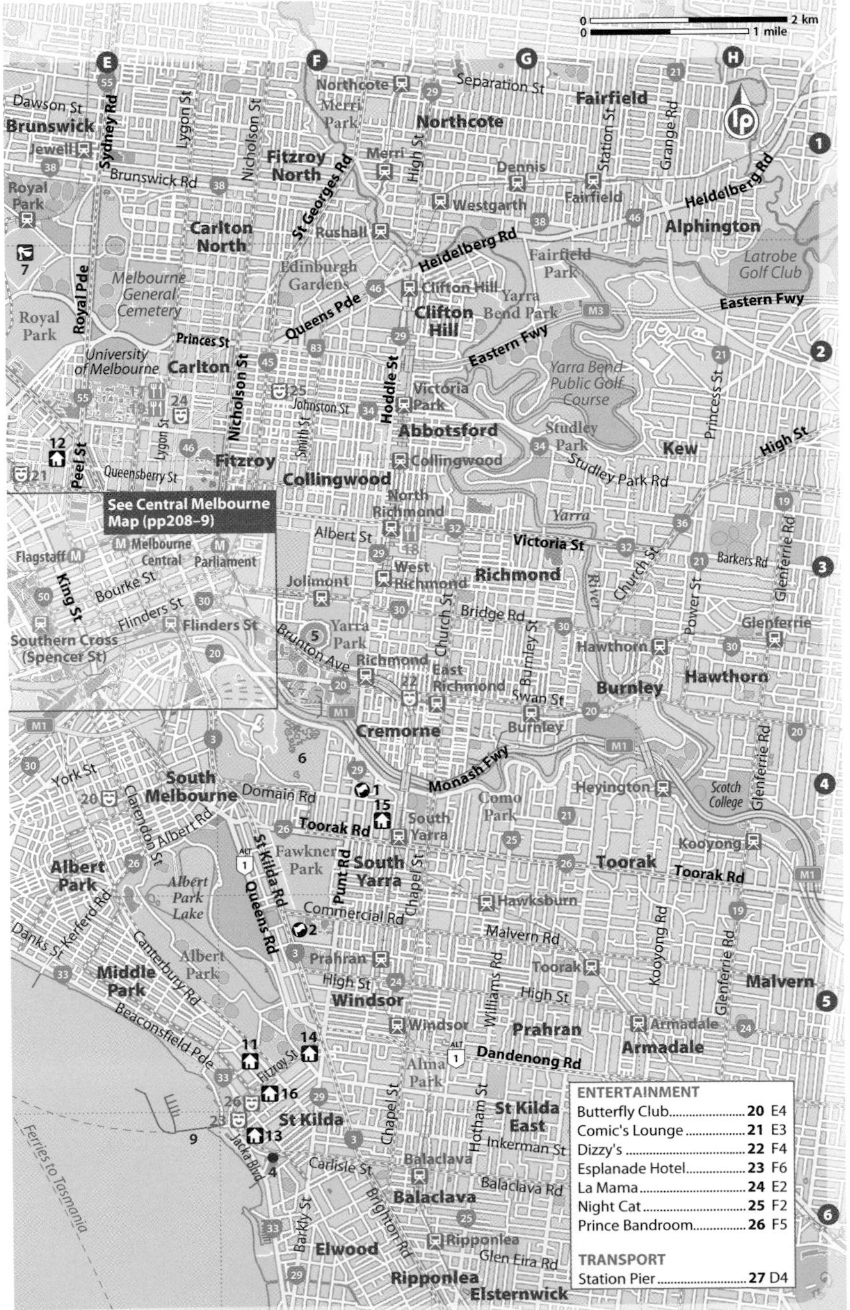

Brunswick
Fitzroy North
Northcote
Fairfield
Alphington
Carlton North
Carlton
Fitzroy
Collingwood
Clifton Hill
Abbotsford
Kew
Richmond
Hawthorn
Burnley
Cremorne
South Melbourne
South Yarra
Toorak
Albert Park
Middle Park
Windsor
Prahran
Armadale
Malvern
St Kilda
St Kilda East
Balaclava
Elwood
Ripponlea
Elsternwick
See Central Melbourne Map (pp208–9)
Ferries to Tasmania
ENTERTAINMENT
Butterfly Club 20 E4
Comic's Lounge 21 E3
Dizzy's 22 F4
Esplanade Hotel 23 F6
La Mama 24 E2
Night Cat 25 F2
Prince Bandroom 26 F5
TRANSPORT
Station Pier 27 D4

CENTRAL MELBOURNE

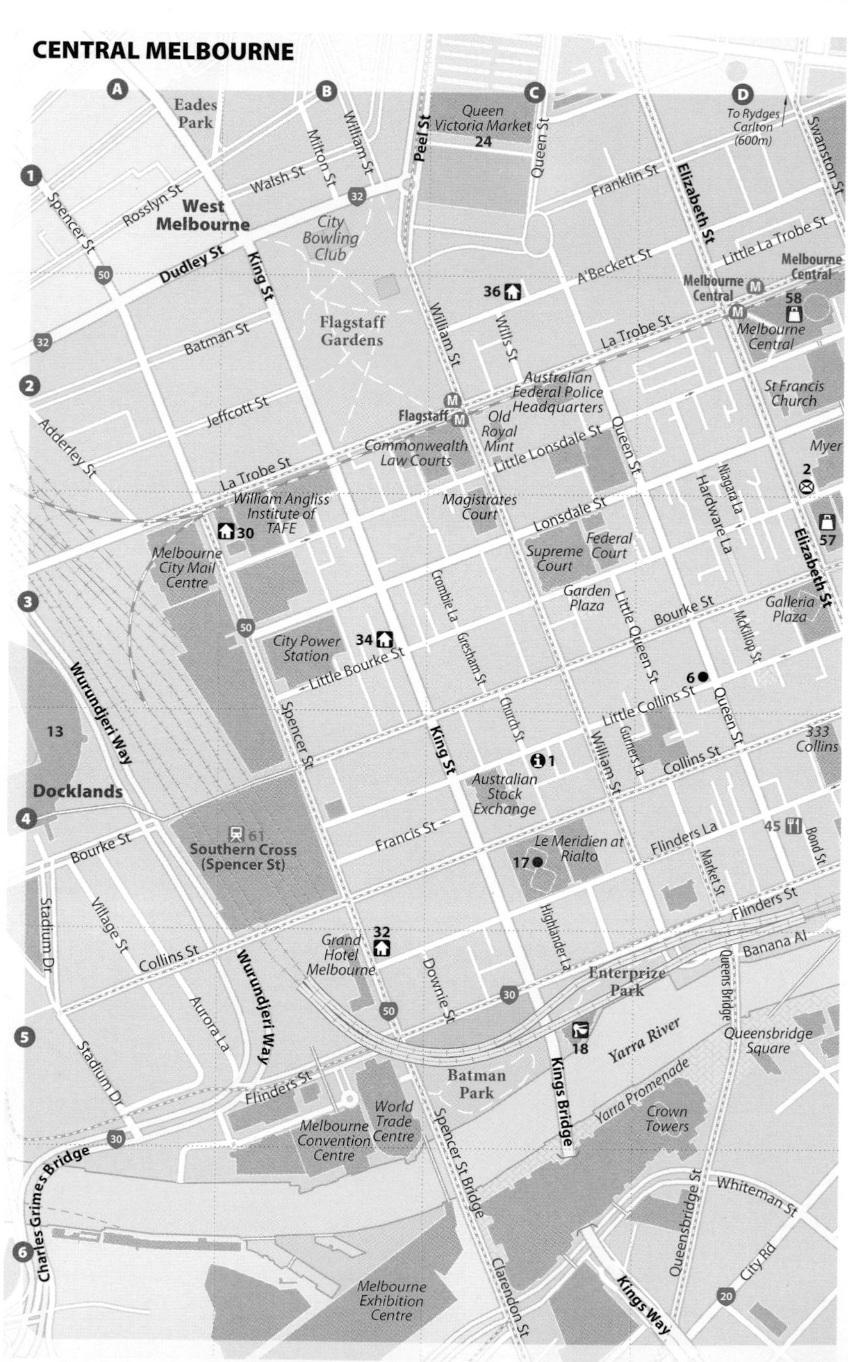

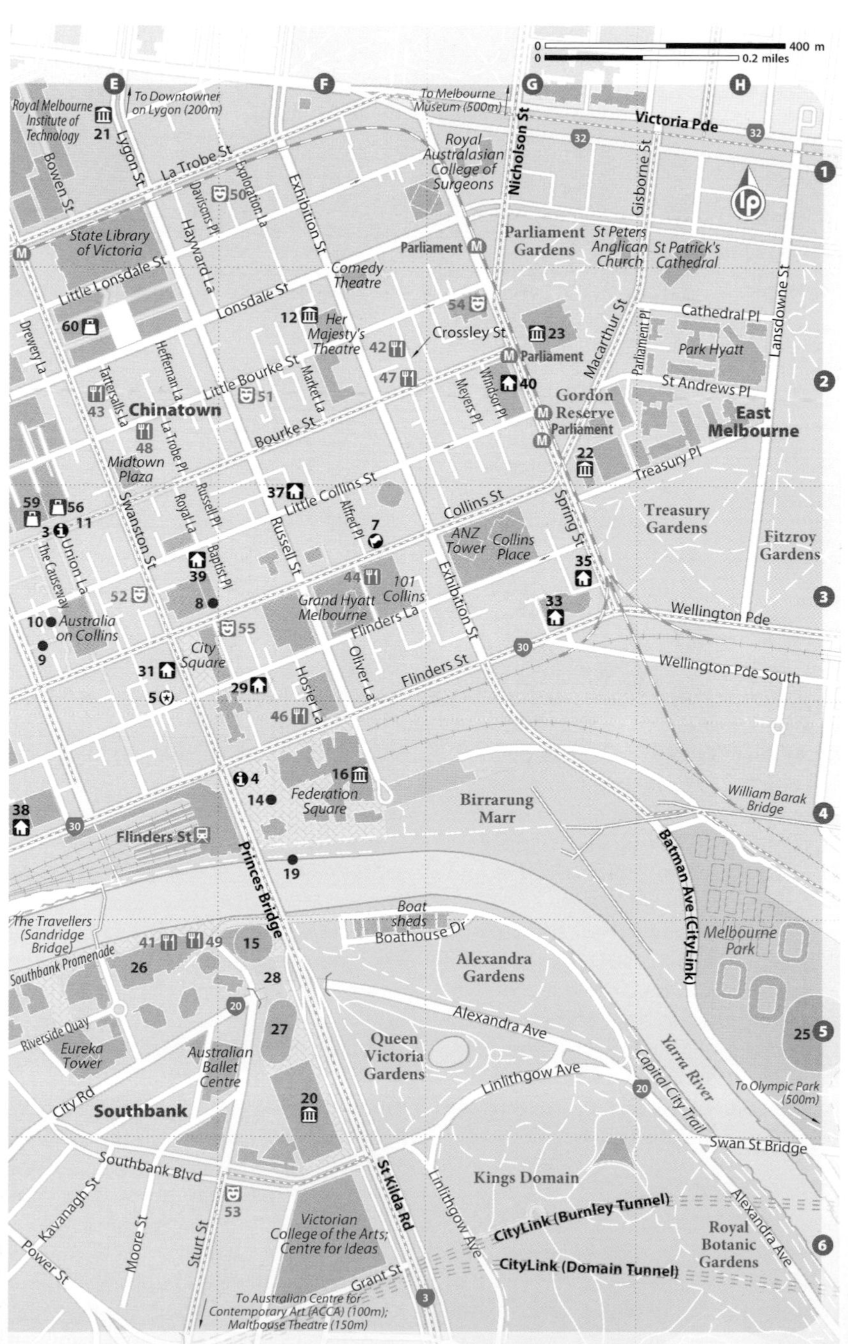
400 m
0.2 miles
To Downtowner on Lygon (200m)
To Melbourne Museum (500m)
Royal Melbourne Institute of Technology
Victoria Pde
Nicholson St
Royal Australasian College of Surgeons
La Trobe St
Lygon St
Bowen St
Exhibition St
Gisborne St
State Library of Victoria
Little Lonsdale St
Lonsdale St
Parliament
Parliament Gardens
St Peters Anglican Church
St Patrick's Cathedral
Comedy Theatre
Her Majesty's Theatre
Crossley St
Cathedral Pl
Lansdowne St
Park Hyatt
Chinatown
Little Bourke St
Bourke St
Gordon Reserve
St Andrews Pl
East Melbourne
Midtown Plaza
Treasury Pl
Little Collins St
Collins St
Treasury Gardens
Fitzroy Gardens
ANZ Tower
Collins Place
Spring St
Australia on Collins
Grand Hyatt Melbourne
101 Collins
Flinders La
Wellington Pde
Wellington Pde South
City Square
Flinders St
Federation Square
Birrarung Marr
William Barak Bridge
Batman Ave (CityLink)
Princes Bridge
The Travellers (Sandridge Bridge)
Boat sheds
Boathouse Dr
Alexandra Gardens
Melbourne Park
Southbank Promenade
Alexandra Ave
Riverside Quay
Eureka Tower
Australian Ballet Centre
Queen Victoria Gardens
Linlithgow Ave
Yarra River
Capital City Trail
To Olympic Park (500m)
City Rd
Southbank
Swan St Bridge
Southbank Blvd
Kings Domain
St Kilda Rd
CityLink (Burnley Tunnel)
CityLink (Domain Tunnel)
Royal Botanic Gardens
Kavanagh St
Moore St
Sturt St
Power St
Victorian College of the Arts; Centre for Ideas
Grant St
To Australian Centre for Contemporary Art (ACCA) (100m); Malthouse Theatre (150m)

INFORMATION
- Information Victoria ... 1 C4
- Melbourne GPO ... 2 D2
- Melbourne Visitor Information Booth ... 3 E3
- Melbourne Visitor Information Centre ... 4 F4
- Police Station ... 5 E3
- RACV ... 6 D3
- UK Consulate ... 7 F3

SIGHTS & ACTIVITIES
- Athenaeum Theatre ... 8 E3
- Block Arcade ... 9 E3
- Block Place ... 10 E3
- Bourke St Mall ... 11 E3
- Chinatown Heritage Walk ... (see 12)
- Chinese Museum ... 12 F2
- Etihad Stadium ... 13 A4
- Federation Square ... 14 F4
- Hamer Hall (Melbourne Concert Hall) ... 15 F5
- Ian Potter Centre: National Gallery of Victoria Australia (NGVA) ... 16 F4
- Le Meridien at Rialto ... 17 C4
- Melbourne Aquarium ... 18 C5
- Melbourne River Cruises ... 19 F4
- National Gallery of Victoria International (NGVI) ... 20 F5
- Old Melbourne Gaol ... 21 E1
- Old Treasury ... 22 G2
- Parliament House of Victoria ... 23 G2
- Queen Victoria Market ... 24 C1
- Rod Laver Arena ... 25 H5
- Southgate ... 26 E5
- Theatres Building ... 27 F5
- Victorian Arts Centre ... 28 F5

SLEEPING
- Adelphi ... 29 F3
- Atlantis Hotel ... 30 B3
- City Square Motel ... 31 E3
- Hotel Enterprize ... 32 B5
- Hotel Lindrum ... 33 G3
- Melbourne Connection Travellers Hostel ... 34 B3
- Mercure Hotel Melbourne ... 35 G3
- Nomad's Industry ... 36 C2
- Quest Hero ... 37 F3
- Rendezvous Hotel ... 38 E4
- Victoria Hotel ... 39 E3
- Windsor Hotel ... 40 G2

EATING
- Bearbrass ... 41 E5
- Becco ... 42 F2
- Camy Shanghai Dumpling Restaurant ... 43 E2
- Il Solito Posto ... 44 F3
- Maha ... 45 D4
- MoVida ... 46 F4
- MoVida Next Door ... (see 46)
- Pellegrini's Espresso Bar ... 47 F2
- Spicy Fish Restaurant ... 48 E2
- Walter's Wine Bar ... 49 E5

ENTERTAINMENT
- Bennetts Lane ... 50 F1
- Billboard The Venue ... 51 F2
- Hi-Fi Bar ... 52 E3
- Last Laugh Comedy Club ... (see 8)
- Melbourne Theatre Company ... 53 F6
- Princess Theatre ... 54 G2
- Regent Theatre ... 55 F3

SHOPPING
- David Jones ... 56 E3
- GPO ... 57 D3
- Melbourne Central ... 58 D2
- Myer ... 59 E3
- QV ... 60 E2
- RM Williams ... (see 58)

TRANSPORT
- Southern Cross Station ... 61 B4

SPRING STREET

The **Old Treasury** (**Map pp208-9; ☎ 03-9651 2233; www.citymuseummelbourne.org; Spring St; adult/concession/family $8.50/5/18; ⌚ 9am-5pm Mon-Fri, 10am-4pm Sat & Sun**) is an elegant edifice built in 1862 with basement vaults to store much of the £200 million worth of gold mined from the Victorian goldfields. The **City Museum**, housed within, has three permanent exhibitions.

The 1856 **Parliament House of Victoria** (**Map pp208-9; ☎ 03-9651 8911; www.parliament.vic.gov.au; Spring St**) is a striking monolith of a structure preceded by a grand flourish of steps. Free half-hour **tours** (**⌚ 10am, 11am, 2pm, 3pm, 3.45pm weekdays when parliament is in recess; bookings required**) take you through both houses and the library.

CHINATOWN

Between Exhibition and Swanston Sts on Little Bourke St, ruby-hued archways usher city-goers into a bustling strip of clattering woks, glowing neon, exotic shopfronts laced with juicy, florid ducks, and floor-to-ceiling chambers of medicinal herbs and tinctures. Melbourne's Chinatown has thrived since the 1850s, and although the opium dens, brothels and boarding houses have long made way for more salubrious enterprises, the area still maintains its entrepreneurial air.

The interesting **Chinese Museum** (**Map pp208-9; ☎ 03-9662 2888; www.chinesemuseum.com.au; 22 Cohen Pl; adult/concession $7.50/5.50; ⌚ 10am-5pm**) documents the long history of Chinese people in Australia over five levels.

OLD MELBOURNE GAOL

Behind its bluestone facade, this penal **museum** (**Map pp208-9; ☎ 03-8663 7228; Russell St; adult/child/family $18/9.50/44; ⌚ 9.30am-5pm**) is a study in the small leaps humankind has made towards enlightenment. The dark, dank and tiny cells display plaster casts of some of the 135 prisoners who were hanged here. Ned Kelly's iconic armour and the very gallows from which he was hanged are also here. Night tours include **Ghostseekers** (**www.ghostseekers.com.au; adult/child $30/22.50; monthly**), which include paranormal investigations of the building. It's not recommended for children under 12; book through **Ticketek** (**☎ 13 28 49; http://premier.ticketek.com.au**).

SOUTHBANK

ARTS PRECINCT

This small area on St Kilda Rd is the high-culture heart of Melbourne.

Behind an iconic waterwall, the **National Gallery of Victoria International** (**NGVI; Map pp208-9; ☎ 03-8620 2222; www.ngv.vic.gov.au; 180 St Kilda Rd; general admission free, call for exhibition prices; 10am-5pm Wed-Mon**) boasts an international collection that is world renowned and arguably Australia's finest. Permanent members include Rembrandt, Tiepolo, Bonnard, Monet and Modigliani. Temporary exhibitions are provocative and dynamic, and tours, talks and workshops are regular features.

The **Victorian Arts Centre** (**VAC; Map pp208-9; ☎ 03-9281 8000; www.theartscentre.net.au; 100 St Kilda Rd**) is made up of two separate buildings: Hamer Hall and the Theatres Building. The interiors of both buildings are stunning. **Hamer Hall** (Map pp208–9) is a major performance venue and base for the Melbourne Symphony Orchestra (MSO). The **Theatres Building** (Map pp208–9) is topped by a distinctive Eiffel-inspired spire (illuminated at night), underneath which are housed the State Theatre, the Playhouse and the George Fairfax Studio. Here you'll also find the **George Adams Gallery** and the **St Kilda Road Foyer Gallery**; both are free and have changing exhibitions. One-hour **tours** (**adult/concession/family $11/8/28**) of the centre are offered at noon and 2.30pm from Monday to Saturday, and a special backstage tour for over-12s only ($14) is offered at 12.15pm on Sunday.

GLENN BEANLAND

Queen Victoria Market

QUEEN VICTORIA MARKET

Chaotic, friendly, multicultural – the **Queen Victoria Market** is one of the largest open-air markets in the southern hemisphere and the grand dame of all Melbourne markets. Over 600 traders hock their wares here and it's been pushing trade for more than 125 years. The bustling **night market** runs between late November and mid-February. The **Queen Victoria Market Cooking School** also holds excellent and diverse cooking classes that change with the seasons.

Things you need to know Queen Victoria Market (**Map pp208-9; ☎ 03-9320 5822; www.qvm.com.au; 513 Elizabeth St; 6am-2pm Tue & Thu, 6am-6pm Fri, 6am-3pm Sat, 9am-4pm Sun**); night market (**5.30-10pm Wed**); Queen Victoria Market Cooking School (**☎ 03-9320 5835**)

The **Australian Centre for Contemporary Art** (**off Map pp208-9; ☎ 03-9697 9999; www.accaonline.org.au; 111 Sturt St; admission free; 10am-5pm Tue-Fri, 11am-6pm Sat & Sun**) is one of Australia's most exciting

RICHARD I'ANSON

Boxing Day Test cricket, Melbourne Cricket Ground

MELBOURNE CRICKET GROUND

The **MCG**, affectionately known as 'the G', is the temple in which sports-mad Melburnians worship their heroes. The devoted come regularly, filled with hope, to watch their contemporary gladiators triumph or fall. It's one of the world's great sporting venues, and is imbued with an indefinable combination of tradition and atmosphere. You scoff? The stadium seats almost 100,000 and at a full-house AFL match or the Boxing Day Test cricket match the atmosphere is electric and the crowd deafening.

The first Australian Rules football game was played here in 1858, and in 1877 it hosted the first Test cricket match between Australia and England. Half-hour **tours** are conducted on nonmatch days. Also housed within 'the G' is the **National Sports Museum**, which contains Australia's largest collection of sporting artefacts and memorabilia in themed exhibitions.

Things you need to know MCG (**Map pp206-7; ☎ 03-9657 8888; www.mcg.org.au; Brunton Ave**); tours (**☎ 03-9657 8879; adult/concession/family $15/11/12; 10am-3pm non-event days**); National Sports Museum (**☎ 03-9657 8879; www.nsm.org.au; adult/child/family $15/8/45; 10am-5pm**)

contemporary galleries. The rust-coloured and cathedralesque structure houses works especially commissioned for the space, plus an impressive range of works by local and international artists.

MELBOURNE AQUARIUM

A mesmerising marine menagerie slinks within the crystal ball of this waterside **aquarium** (**Map pp208-9; ☎ 03-9620 0999; www.melbourneaquarium.com.au; King St; adult/child/concession/family $31.50/18/19.50/79; 9.30am-6pm Feb-Dec, 9.30am-9pm Jan**). Get an eyeful of moray eels, giant cuttlefish, delicate sea dragons, sharks, starfish and much more. Vivid tropical fish flirt with onlookers and majestic rays soar above the domed perspex tunnel. The Antarctic section is home to King and gorgeous little Gentoo penguins and a breeding program promises tiny versions of both. It's hard to beat a dive with the sharks ($150 to $350, depending on your experience and equipment needs).

PARKVILLE & CARLTON

ROYAL MELBOURNE ZOO

The **Royal Melbourne Zoo** (**Map pp206-7; ☎ 03-9285 9300; www.zoo.org.au; Elliot Ave, Parkville; adult/child/concession/family $24/12/18/54; 9am-5pm**) has been operating for more than 140 years, making it the oldest zoo in Australia, and one of the oldest in the world. Set in spacious and attractively landscaped gardens, the enclosures are simulations of the animals' natural habitats and the zoo is home to more than 320 species. Walkways pass through towering bird aviaries, a wide-open lion park, a tropical hothouse full of colourful butterflies and a gorillas' rainforest. There's also a large collection of native animals in a bush setting, a platypus aquarium, fur seals, tigers, plenty of reptiles and lots more.

MELBOURNE MUSEUM

In the middle of Carlton Gardens, **Melbourne Museum** (**off Map pp208-9; ☎ 13 11 02; www.melbourne.museum.vic.gov.au; 11 Nicholson St, Carlton; adult/concession & child $8/free; 10am-5pm**) provides a grand sweep of Victoria's natural and cultural histories. The emphasis is on education and interaction, and the main attractions include Bunjilaka, the Aboriginal Centre; a living forest gallery; and the Australia gallery, with an exhibit dedicated to that great Aussie icon Phar Lap, and another dedicated to the TV show *Neighbours* (filmed in Melbourne).

ST KILDA

Melbourne's most famous seaside suburb maintains a perpetual state of fascinating flux. Home to Russian and Polish émigrés in the 1940s, it shifted from a prestigious address for colonial entrepreneurs to the haunt of the raffish, unkempt and experimental in the 1960s and '70s. By the '90s the suburban-macchiato crowd had begun to muscle in and a dingy flat suddenly became Melbourne's hottest property.

Fitzroy St and **Acland St** are the main strips, and are packed with cafes, bars, sprawling old-school pubs and pavement tables. Acland St is particularly famed for its continental cake shops. Following **Carlisle St**, across St Kilda Rd and into

JOHN BANAGAN

Luna Park (p214)

RICHARD I'ANSON

Australian Open tennis match, Rod Laver Arena

IF YOU LIKE...

If you like joining the fans at big stadiums like the **Melbourne Cricket Ground** (p212), we think you will like these other sporting venues:

- **Etihad Stadium** (**Map pp208-9; ☎ 03-8625 7700; www.etihadstadium.com.au; Docklands**) This 52,000-seat stadium is the city's alternative footy arena, with a state-of-the-art sliding roof. Other sporting (A-league soccer) and entertainment events take place here on a regular basis, and **tours** (**☎ 03-8625 7277; adult/child/family $14/7/37; 11am, 1pm & 3pm**) of the stadium are conducted on weekdays.
- **Flemington Racecourse** (Map pp206–7) The horse race that stops the nation, the Melbourne Cup (www.vrc.net.au), is always run here and always on the first Tuesday in November.
- **Olympic Park** (**off Map pp208-9; ☎ 03-9286 1600; www.mopt.com.au; Batman Ave, Jolimont**) This is the home ground for the Melbourne Storm (www.melbournestorm.com.au), the only Melbourne side in the National Rugby League competition.
- **Rod Laver Arena** (**Map pp208-9; ☎ 03-9286 1600; www.mopt.com.au; Batman Ave, Jolimont**) This arena hosts the Australian Open (www.ausopen.org) – the top tennis players from around the world come to compete in the first of each year's four Grand Slam tournaments. It features a retractable roof, so weather is not an issue.

Balaclava, you'll find some great Jewish bakeries and some natty boutiques and cafes.

St Kilda pier (Map pp206–7) is a favourite spot for strollers, who reward themselves with a coffee or a snack at **St Kilda Pier Pavilion**, a replica of the original 19th-century tearoom at the junction of the pier, which burnt down in 2003.

Luna Park (**Map pp206-7; ☎ 03-9525 5033; www.lunapark.com.au; Lower Esplanade; unlimited ride ticket adult/child/family $38/28/116;**

11am-6pm Sat & Sun winter; 7-11pm Fri, 11am-11pm Sat, 11am-6pm Sun summer; 11am-6pm Sun-Thu, 11am-11pm Sat & Sun school holidays year-round), a St Kilda symbol since 1912, is an old-fashioned amusement park that maintains a whiff of carny atmosphere. The old wooden roller coaster and beautifully crafted carousel are highlights, but the famous facade of a laughing Mr Moon has been the object of many a nightmare.

WILLIAMSTOWN

'Willy' (Map pp206–7) is a gracious seafaring town with scenic promenades heaving with day trippers on the weekend.

Scienceworks & Melbourne Planetarium **(Map pp206-7; 03-9392 4800; http://museumvictoria.com.au/Scienceworks; 2 Booker St, Spotswood; Scienceworks adult/concession/child $8/free/free, planetarium $5/4/3.50; 10am-4.30pm)** incorporates three historic buildings and keeps inquisitive grey matter occupied with interactive displays. Figure out the mysteries of the universe (or your own anatomy) by poking buttons, pulling levers, lifting flaps and learning all sorts of weird facts. The planetarium splashes the universe onto a 16m-domed ceiling.

Williamstown Ferries **(Map pp206-7; 03-9517 9444, 9682 9555; www.williamstownferries.com.au)** runs ferries between Gem Pier and Southgate, stopping at sites along the way.

MELBOURNE FOR CHILDREN

Sights that give 'What I did on my holiday' stories backbone include the **Royal Melbourne Zoo** (p213), where meerkats cause great hilarity; the **Werribee Open Range Zoo** (p223), with its spot-the-zebra/rhino/giraffe/etc open vehicle safari; and **Healesville Sanctuary** (p223), the best option for getting up close to Australian native animals.

Overnight camps at the zoos, such as Melbourne's 'Roar 'n' Snore' and the Open Range's 'Slumber Safari', are also lots of spooky fun.

Other educational options include **Scienceworks** (p215), with lots of hands-on activities, and the **Melbourne Aquarium** (p212), where sharks hovering overhead in the 360-degree aquarium may add weight to parental threats.

TOURS

Aboriginal Heritage Walk **(03-9252 2429; www.rbg.vic.gov.au; Royal Botanic Gardens; adult/child/concession $18/9/14; tours 11am Thu & Fri Dec & Feb)** This 90-minute tour takes you through the story of the Boonerwrung and Woiwurrung peoples, the ancestral owners of the Royal Botanic Gardens.

Chinatown Heritage Walk **(Map pp208-9; 03-9662 2888; www.chinesemuseum.com.au/whatson.html; 22 Cohen Pl; adult/concession from $18/15)** Tours of historic Chinatown, with its atmospheric alleys and bustling vibe.

City Circle trams **(www.metlinkmelbourne.com.au; admission free; 10am-6pm daily, to 9pm Thu-Sat)** Free trams with informative commentary running every 10 minutes around the city centre.

Hidden Secrets Tours **(03-9329 9665; www.hiddensecretstours.com; tours $60-135)** Insider tours of the city's bars, boutiques, laneways, cafes and architectural highlights.

Melbourne City Tourist Shuttle **(www.thatsmelbourne.com.au/shuttle; 9.30am-4.30pm)** Free and informative 90-minute tour that loops around 13 inner-city sights, including the Melbourne Museum, the Royal Botanic Gardens and Chinatown.

DAVID WALL

Southbank (p211), on the Yarra River

Melbourne River Cruises (Map pp208-9; ☎ 03-8610 2600; www.melbcruises.com.au; Federation Wharf; adult/child/family $22/11/50) Yarra cruises.

SLEEPING

During major festivals and events accommodation is scarce, so book in advance. Similar to Sydney and other well-touristed areas, midrange listings in Melbourne cost between $100 and $200 for a double room with bathroom. Anything higher than $200 is regarded as top end; anything less than $100 is classified as budget. Prices listed in this chapter are for nonpeak seasons. Expect to pay a little more in summer.

BUDGET

There are backpacker hostels in the city centre and most of the inner suburbs. Several of the larger hostels have courtesy buses that will pick you up from the bus and train terminals.

Nomad's Industry (Map pp208-9; ☎ 03-9328 4383, 1800 447 762; 198 A'Beckett St, Melbourne; bookings@nomadsindustry.com; dm/d from $20/90; 💻) The latest flashpackers to open in Melbourne caters well to savvy travellers looking for a cut above your average hostel and a cut below hotel prices. This refurbished building has polished surfaces throughout and a range of modern six- to 14-bed dorms, en suite dorms and en suite doubles. Flash as it is (and it is!) it's a hostel, so you won't be guaranteed the quiet of a hotel.

Ritz (Map pp206-7; ☎ 03-9525 3501, 1800 670 364; www.ritzbackpackers.com; 169 Fitzroy St, St Kilda; dm $20-25, d from $50; 💻) A backpacker institution, this hostel is five minutes' walk from St Kilda's heart. All rooms have wi-fi and private rooms have complimentary towels. There are freebies galore and the whole lot sits on top of a 'traditional' British pub (well, the ales are in any case).

Melbourne Connection Travellers Hostel (Map pp208-9; ☎ 03-9642 4464; www.melbourneconnection.com; 205 King St, Melbourne; dm $23-27, d from $70) This friendly hostel sticks to the smaller-is-better mandate, and comes up trumps. Simple, clean and uncluttered dorms, twins and doubles all come with linen and shared bathrooms; the basement lounge provides a comfy night.

Melbourne Metro YHA (Map pp206-7; ☎ 03-9329 8599; www.yha.com.au; 78 Howard St, North Melbourne; dm $26-35, tw & d with/without bathroom $90/80, apt $125; P 💻) A YHA showpiece, this huge hostel is an award-winner and everyone – *everyone* – raves about it. The generous rooms and common areas provide ample space, the rooftop area is breathtaking and facilities include barbecues, a pool table and superfriendly staff.

MIDRANGE

Hotel Enterprize (Map pp208-9; ☎ 03-9629 6991; www.hotelenterprize.com.au; 44 Spencer St, Melbourne; r $90-180; P ❄) The Enterprize is a small and reasonably priced hotel. Don't expect fireworks – the budget rooms are plain and well maintained and the 'business' rooms have faux-antique furnishings, baths and more space. Aim for a room on the 4th floor.

Victoria Hotel (Map pp208-9; ☎ 03-9699 0000, 1800 331 147; www.victoriahotel.com.au; 215 Little Collins St, Melbourne; s/d from $110/180; ❄ 💻 ♿) The iconic 'Vic' opened its doors in 1880, but numerous makeovers have replaced any heritage on the inside with a massive warren of reasonable and clean rooms. The cheapest are as snug as closets, but the Bellerive rooms are spacious and bright with newish bathrooms.

Fountain Terrace (Map pp206-7; ☎ 03-9593 8123; www.fountainterrace.com.au; 28 Mary St, St Kilda; r incl breakfast from $140) This glorious old Victorian terrace on a residential street has seven boutique rooms lavished in brocades, silks and frills. All have been spectacularly appointed in honour of famous Aussies (top billing goes to the Melba Suite, after diva Dame Nellie) with three rooms accessing the front verandah. Book ahead.

Downtowner on Lygon (off Map pp208-9; ☎ 03-9663 5555; www.downtowner.com.au; 66 Lygon St, Carlton; r from $140; P ❄ 💻) This popular, amicable and perpetually busy hotel is perched at the edge of Melbourne's Little Italy. It's pleasantly innocuous and has a variety of rooms; the adjoining versions are good for families.

Atlantis Hotel (Map pp208-9; ☎ 03-9600 2900; www.atlantishotel.com.au; 300 Spencer St, Melbourne; r from $150; P ❄ 💻) The rooms at this conveniently situated hotel are an ocean of vanilla-sponge beige with subtle lighting and soothing decor. Spend a wise $20 to upgrade from a standard room and aim high for gobsmacking views of Telstra Dome and the Docklands.

Rydges Carlton (off Map pp208-9; ☎ 03-9347 7811; www.rydges.com; 701 Swanston St, Carlton; r from $150; P ❄ 💻 ♿) Polished, no-nonsense and four-star, Rydges prides itself on good amenities and justly so. Rooms are semirenovated and sleep up to three. The pricier 'Parkview' versions have views and more space, and there's a heated rooftop pool and spa-sauna room.

Quest Hero (Map pp208-9; ☎ 03-8664 8500; www.questapartments.com.au; 140 Little Collins St, Melbourne; apt from $190; ❄ 💻) These apartments are so well equipped that the dishwashers, beautifully kitted kitchens, stereos and videos will dazzle you into ignoring the utterly nondescript decor. Fabulous value for families.

Rendezvous Hotel (Map pp208-9; ☎ 03-9250 1888; www.rendezvoushotels.com; 328 Flinders St, Melbourne; r $240-330; ❄) Built in 1913, this regal property occupies a plum position on Flinders St and has the exclusive and personal ambience of a boutique hotel but the convenience of more than 300 contemporary rooms. Heritage-listed charm and excellent internet package deals get the thumbs up.

Also available:

City Square Motel (Map pp208-9; ☎ 03-9654 7011; www.citysquaremotel.com.au; 67 Swanston St, Melbourne; r $105-185) Central, no-frills motel.

Mercure Hotel Melbourne (Map pp208-9; ☎ 03-9205 9999; www.accorhotels.com.au; 13 Spring St, Melbourne; r from $145; P ✈) Clinical, functional and comfortable hotel in the 'Paris' end of town.

Urban (Map pp206-7; ☎ 03-8530 8888; www.urbanstkilda.com.au; 35-37 Fitzroy St, St Kilda; r from $199; P ✈ 💻) A sea of blond wood, cream fabric and white tiles; comfortably corporate without breaking new style ground.

Novotel St Kilda (Map pp206-7; ☎ 03-9525 5522; www.novotel.com; 14-16 The Esplanade, St Kilda; r from $200; P ✈ 💻) Generic and dependable chain hotel in a superb location.

TOP END

Windsor Hotel (Map pp208-9; ☎ 03-9633 6000; www.thewindsor.com.au; 103 Spring St, Melbourne; r $200-550; P ✈ 💻) The queen of the scene is the stately Windsor, Melbourne's 'Grand Lady', graced by old-fashioned, haute-luxe embellishments. Built in 1883 she has hosted the who's who of royalty – from Buckingham Palace to the West End to heavy metal. Her five-star rooms are simply fabulous, and no request is too great.

Hotel Lindrum (Map pp208-9; ☎ 03-9668 1111; www.hotellindrum.com.au; 26 Flinders St, Melbourne; r $425-515; P ✈ 💻) This opulent establishment is bathed in rich tones, suede furnishings and deliciously low lighting. Once the pool hall of legendary player Walter Lindrum, it now boasts a range of indulgent rooms, some of which have wheelchair access. Exclusive to the hilt, it's devoid of attitude or pretension.

Adelphi (Map pp208-9; ☎ 03-8080 8888; www.adelphi.com.au; 187 Flinders Lane, Melbourne; r $560-1250; P ✈ 💻 🏊) The landmark Adelphi is a study in minimalism and the open plan rooms contain furnishings and fittings by internationally acclaimed architects. The effect is cutting-edge, verging on clinical. On the top floor a cantilevered lap pool allows you to swim right past the edge of the building and suspend yourself over Collins St.

The Lyall (Map pp206-7; ☎ 03-9868 8222; www.thelyall.com; 14 Murphy St, South Yarra; r from $525; P ✈ 💻) This slick and elegant boutique property sits in a quiet, leafy street in one of Melbourne's priciest pockets. The earthy colour scheme is offset by dramatic art and the commodious rooms are appointed with fine mod cons and five-star luxuries. Discounts of as much as 50% are available on last-minute accommodation booking sites, so shop around.

EATING

In this country of fabulous dining, Melbourne is unsurpassed – not only for the diversity of cuisines, restaurants, cafes, delicatessens, markets, bistros, brasseries and takeaways, but the sheer value for your buck.

CITY CENTRE

Melbourne's Chinatown runs along Little Bourke St from Exhibition St to Swanston St. Chinese restaurants predominate, but you can also find Greek, Indian, Japanese and Mod Oz cuisines.

Flinders Lane, Centre Pl, Degraves St, Hardware Lane and their adjoining alleyways are packed with cafes, hole-in-the-wall favourites, restaurants and wonderful little bars.

Camy Shanghai Dumpling Restaurant (Map pp208-9; ☎ 03-9663 8555; 23-25 Tattersalls Lane, Melbourne; mains $6.50-10; 🕑 lunch & dinner)

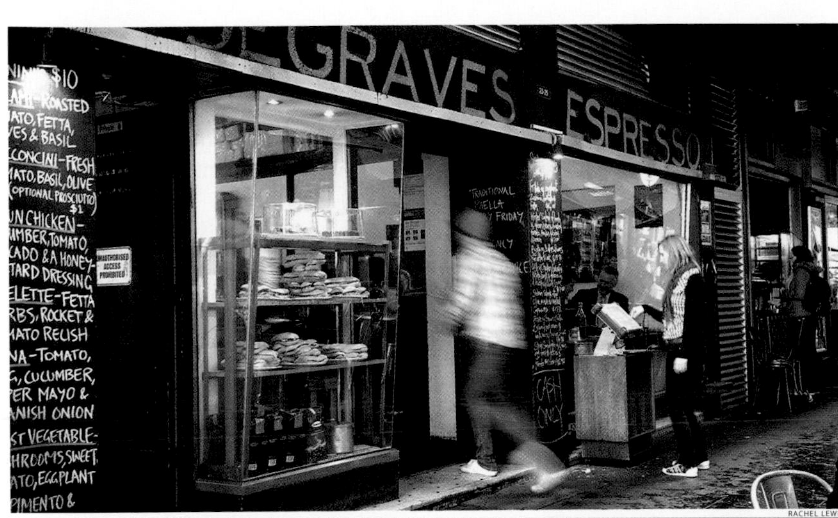

RACHEL LEWIS

Cafe in Degraves St

If you like your dumplings hot and plentiful, your service simple, your surrounds no-nonsense and your bill bottom dollar, the Shanghai is your Shangri-La. Fifteen dumplings for six bucks is hard to beat – it's as Chinatown as it gets.

MoVida (Map pp208-9; ☎ 03-9663 3038; 1 Hosier Lane, Melbourne; tapas $4-8, raciones $10-18; ⌚ lunch & dinner) Pull together a small group, book a table and share a round of the innovative tapas this subtly slick restaurant is known for, such as artichokes with almond sauce and manchego cheese, and Galician-cooked octopus *(pulpo)* with kipfler potatoes and paprika. MoVida is a consistent award-winner and reservations are a must. Fortunately MoVida Next Door (open for dinner Tuesday to Saturday) caters to the unorganised, with similarly divine fare and a no-bookings rule.

Pellegrini's Espresso Bar (Map pp208-9; ☎ 03-9662 1885; 66 Bourke St, Melbourne; mains $12-16) This family-run 1950s-style espresso bar hasn't changed in years. A gleaming coffee machine (allegedly the first in Melbourne) churns out the good stuff and mama brews good honest pasta and sauces from scratch out the back.

Spicy Fish Restaurant (Map pp208-9; ☎ 03-9639 1885; 209 Little Bourke St, Melbourne; mains $15-25; ⌚ lunch & dinner) In true Chinatown tradition the ambience at this busy Szechuan and Shanghai restaurant simmers somewhere between snappy and hectic. But the food has them lining up at the door, and justifiably so. Tables are peppered with large and steaming portions of dumplings, hot, dry and spicy chicken and squid dishes, and stir-fried vegetables. Great value and authentic flavours.

Maha (Map pp208-9; ☎ 03-9629 5900; 21 Bond St, Melbourne, mains $28-38; ⌚ lunch Mon-Fri, dinner Mon-Sat) This sophisticated bar and grill occupies a subterranean pocket on unassuming Bond St and fuses tangy Middle Eastern flavours with Mediterranean overtones and local produce. The result is delicious. Make a booking for lunch or dinner and dine on 12-hour lamb rump, onion, chick pea, mint and fazoulia salatet (salad) or park yourself at the bar for inexpensive meze – the slow-cooked tuna with capers and olives is spectacular.

More good central eats:

Il Solito Posto (Map pp208-9; ☎ 03-9654 4466; 113 Collins St, Melbourne; mains $24-35) A basement favourite serving sensational Italian staples.

Becco (Map pp208-9; ☎ 03-9663 3000; 11-25 Crossley St, Melbourne; mains $25-30; lunch & dinner Mon-Sat) Sexy little Italian bar-restaurant package.

SOUTHBANK

Southgate's river and city skyline views make it a prime eating destination for visitors to Melbourne. It's also close to galleries, theatres and gardens.

Bearbrass (Map pp208-9; ☎ 03-9682 3799; Ground fl, Southgate; mains $15) This casual riverside snug has the full complement for beautifully boozy afternoons: long bench seating for groups, outdoor tables with river and promenade views, global bar bites and inventive mains, laid-back staff and a delicious selection of local and imported beers.

Walter's Wine Bar (Map pp208-9; ☎ 03-9690 9211; Upper Level, Southgate; mains $25-35) Wine is Walter's passion and there's over 20 pages of it on the menu. You can complement that glass of Grange Hermitage with moreish Italian fare and a delicious bar menu.

CARLTON

Tagged 'Little Italy' many moons ago, Lygon St now infuses a host of multicultural flavours alongside the pasta bars and Italian restaurants.

Tiamo (Map pp206-7; ☎ 03-9347 5759; 303 Lygon St, Carlton; mains $11-16) This historic Lygon St institution dishes up generous portions of tasty pasta and traditional Italian cuisine. The older Italian gentlemen fastened to their espressos at the front window aren't part of the decor but they certainly add to it.

Jimmy Watson's (Map pp206-7; ☎ 03-9347 3985; 333 Lygon St, Carlton; mains $25-30; lunch Mon-Sat, dinner Tue-Sat) Wine and talk are the order of the day at this long-running wine bar-restaurant. The fare is European, Middle Eastern and a dash of Mod Oz, with a nod to ingredients such as kangaroo.

RICHMOND

Victoria St is Melbourne's 'Little Saigon' and the turf between Hoddle and Church Sts is packed with Asian grocers, discount shops, fishmongers and myriad places to clack your chopsticks.

Minh Minh (Map pp206-7; ☎ 03-9427 7891; 94 Victoria St, Richmond; mains $12-17; lunch & dinner) Minh Minh's service varies from warm and cheeky to outright rude. If it's the latter, dish it right back and concentrate on the spicy and fragrant food. The menu here is long and authentic and includes the best *laab nuea* (Lao beef salad) in Melbourne.

ENTERTAINMENT

Melbourne has a thriving nightlife and a lively cultural scene. The best source of 'what's on' is the *Entertainment Guide (EG)* in Friday's *Age* newspaper. Also check online at www.melbourne.vic.gov.au/events and **Citysearch** (http://melbourne.citysearch.com.au).

LIVE MUSIC

JAZZ & ACOUSTIC

Jazz cats and blues hounds will be pleased to hear that Melbourne's jazz scene is jumpin'.

Bennetts Lane (Map pp208-9; ☎ 03-9663 2856; www.bennettslane.com; 25 Bennetts Lane, Melbourne; 8.30pm-late) Hidden down a narrow city lane, this dimly lit jazz joint is the preferred choice for the cream of local and international talent, from old-school horns and drum brushes to contemporary electronica.

Dizzy's (Map pp206-7; ☎ 03-9428 1233; www.dizzys.com.au; 381 Burnley St, Richmond; 5.30pm-late Tue-Sun) Dizzy's offers jazz Wednesday to Sunday nights and attracts some pretty big names.

Night Cat (Map pp206-7; ☎ 03-9417 0090; www.thenightcat.com.au; 141 Johnston St, Fitzroy; 9pm-late Thu-Sun) The Cat is a large, comfortable space with a great atmosphere and skewiff 1950s decor (a Melbourne trademark). Bands here are big and play anything from jazz to salsa.

During January, February and March, the Royal Melbourne Zoo (p213) hosts the extremely popular 'Twilights' season of open-air sessions, with jazz or big bands performing on Friday, Saturday and Sunday evenings.

ROCK

Hi-Fi Bar (Map pp208-9; ☎ 03-9654 7617; www.thehifi.com.au; 125 Swanston St, Melbourne) Another fine spot to dress down for indie and alternative rock.

Billboard the Venue (Map pp208-9; ☎ 03-9639 4000; www.billboardthevenue.com.au; 170 Russell St, Melbourne; 6pm-late) This place has been in the business for more than 40 years and has hosted everyone from Tina Turner to Carl Cox.

Esplanade Hotel (Map pp206-7; ☎ 03-9534 0211; www.espy.com.au; 11 The Esplanade, St Kilda; noon-1am Mon-Wed, noon-3am Thu-Fri, 8am-3am Sat, noon-1am Sun) A die-hard rock-pig institution, the Espy is a must for lovers of cheap pots, loud live music and fabulously grungy crowds.

Prince Bandroom (Map pp206-7; ☎ 03-9536 1168; www.princebandroom.com.au; 29 Fitzroy St, St Kilda; for shows) Check out the massive blackboard out front to see who's taking stage; you'll find the calibre is high.

DAWN DELANEY

Paul Kelly performs at the Esplanade Hotel

THEATRE & DANCE

The **Victorian Arts Centre** (p211) is Melbourne's major venue for performing arts and where the **Melbourne Theatre Company** (MTC; Map pp208-9; ☎ 03-9684 4500; www.mtc.com.au) stages around 15 productions, from contemporary to Shakespearean, each year.

The following are noteworthy venues around town for live theatre.

La Mama (Map pp206-7; ☎ 03-9347 6142; 205 Faraday St, Carlton) This tiny, intimate forum produces new Australian works and experimental theatre, and has a reputation for developing emerging playwrights.

Malthouse Theatre (off Map pp208-9; ☎ 03-9685 5111; www.malthousetheatre.com.au; 113 Sturt St, South Melbourne) An outstanding company that stages predominantly Australian works by established and new playwrights.

Princess Theatre (Map pp208-9; ☎ 03-9299 9800; 163 Spring St, Melbourne) This beautifully renovated landmark theatre is the venue for superslick musicals.

Regent Theatre (Map pp208-9; ☎ 03-9299 9500; 191 Collins St, Melbourne) A grand old venue for musicals.

COMEDY & CABARET

The following venues showcase quality comedy and some of Melbourne's most eccentric cabaret.

Butterfly Club (Map pp206-7; ☎ 03-9690 2000; 204 Bank St, South Melbourne) This adorable terrace house holds a small theatre that hosts regular cabaret performances. Show over, head out the back or upstairs to a uniquely decorated bar, where surfaces are bedecked with the kitsch, the cool and the cute.

Comic's Lounge (Map pp206-7; ☎ 03-9348 9488; www.thecomicslounge.com.au; 26 Errol St, North Melbourne) The only place in town which features daily comedy performances; acts range across the comedy spectrum and tickets cost around $25.

Last Laugh Comedy Club (Map pp208-9; ☎ 03-9650 6668; www.thecomedyclub.com.au; Athenaeum Theatre, 188 Collins St, Melbourne) Professional stand-up on Friday and Saturday nights, with dinner-and-show packages available.

SHOPPING

This city loooooves to shop. Stores are most dense in the city centre, but South Yarra, Toorak and Fitzroy are also good for unique purchases.

Bourke St Mall is home to the city's two main department stores: **David Jones** (Map pp208-9; ☎ 03-9643 2222; 310 Bourke St, Melbourne) and **Myer** (Map pp208-9; ☎ 03-9661 1111; 314 Bourke St, Melbourne). **Melbourne Central** (Map pp208-9; ☎ 03-9922 1100; cnr Elizabeth & La Trobe Sts, Melbourne) is a shopping centre with lots of mainstream shops, especially clothing. In an imposing modern complex, **QV** (Map pp208-9; ☎ 03-9658 0100; cnr Swanston & Lonsdale Sts, Melbourne) is Melbourne's freshest contender and features populist commercial options and a supermarket. **GPO** (Map pp208-9; ☎ 03-9663 0066; cnr Elizabeth & Bourke St Mall, Melbourne) houses fabulous boutiques including Akira and Veronika Maine, plus the ABC shop. **RM Williams** (Map pp208-9; ☎ 03-9663 7126; Melbourne Central, Lonsdale St, Melbourne) is an Aussie icon, even for city slickers, this brand will kit you up with stylish essentials for working the land, including a pair of those famous boots.

GETTING THERE & AWAY

Most of the major airlines have direct international flights to **Melbourne airport** (☎ 03-9297 1600; www.melbourneairport.com.au) in Tullamarine, 22km northwest of the city centre. The wheelchair-accessible **Skybus** (☎ 03-9335 2811; www.skybus.com.au) operates a 24-hour shuttle bus to/from the airport and Southern Cross Station (one way $16, every 20 minutes).

The **Spirit of Tasmania** (☎ 1800 634 906; www.spiritoftasmania.com.au) sails between Melbourne and Tasmania at 8pm nightly year-round, departing from Port Melbourne's Station Pier (Map pp206–7) and the Esplanade in Devonport – both arrive at around 7am.

The long-distance bus terminal in the city centre is at **Southern Cross Station** (Map pp208-9; Spencer St, Melbourne). **Skybus**

(☎ 03-9335 2811; www.skybus.com.au) airport buses also operate from here.

Long-distance trains also operate to/from Southern Cross station. Victoria's **V/Line** (☎ 13 61 96; www.vline.com.au) runs train services between Melbourne and regional Victoria.

CountryLink (☎ 13 22 32; www.countrylink.info) runs daily XPT trains between Melbourne and Sydney ($95, 11 hours).

GETTING AROUND

For public transport timetables, maps and fares call the **Met Information Centre** (☎ 13 16 38; www.metlinkmelbourne.com.au).

AROUND MELBOURNE

MELBOURNE TO GEELONG

The one-hour drive down the Princes Fwy (M1) from Melbourne to Geelong takes you over the soaring West Gate Bridge, which provides super views over the city and Port Phillip Bay.

Werribee Open Range Zoo (☎ 03-9731 9600; www.zoo.org.au; K Rd; adult/child/family $24/12/54, combined zoo & mansion ticket $33/17/77; 9am-5pm, last entry 3.30pm) is a 225ha African safari-style experience about 30 minutes southwest of Melbourne. Meerkats greet you at the entrance and admission includes the safari tour: plenty of emus, bison, Mongolian wild horses, hippos, rhinos, zebras and giraffes grazing on the savannah.

THE YARRA VALLEY

An hour from Melbourne, the Yarra Valley is one of Victoria's premier wine regions and a superb area for walking and cycling. **Yarra Valley Winery Tours** (☎ 03-5962 3870; www.yarravalleywinerytours.com.au; tours $90-100) offers tastings at five wineries and lunch.

Beloved of day trippers and weekenders from the city, **Healesville** is the gateway to the Yarra Valley wineries, Yarra Ranges forest drive and north to the High Country.

One of the best places to see Australian native fauna is the **Healesville Sanctuary** (☎ 03-5957 2800; www.zoo.org.au; Badger Creek Rd, Healesville; adult/child/family $24/12/54; 9am-5pm), a wildlife park set in native bushland. The Platypus House is a top spot to see these shy creatures underwater, and you'll see koalas, kangaroos and Tasmanian devils, but the real star is the exciting **Birds of Prey** (show noon & 2pm) display where predatory birds swoop, dive and attack.

JULIET COOMBE

Hot air ballooning over the Yarra Valley

YARRA VALLEY WINERIES

The **Yarra Valley** (www.wineyarravalley.com) has more than 80 wineries scattered around its rolling hills, and it is recognised as Victoria's oldest wine region – the first vines were planted at Yering Station in 1838. The region produces cool-climate, food-friendly drops such as Chardonnay, Pinot Noir and Pinot Gris. A small percentage of vines were damaged in the February 2009 bushfires.

Of the many food and wine festivals in the region, our favourite is **Grape Grazing** (www.grapegrazing.com.au) in February, celebrating the beginning of the grape harvest.

Most wineries offer cellar door sales and tastings from 10am to 5pm daily. These four are worth a visit:

TarraWarra Estate (☎ 03-5957 3510; www.tarrawarra.com.au; Healesville Rd, Yarra Glen) This striking building combines an art gallery and rowdy bistro for lunch.

Coldstream Hills (☎ 03-5964 9410; www.coldstreamhills.com.au; 31 Maddens Lane, Coldstream) Chardonnay, effusive Pinot Noir and velvety Merlot are the star picks.

Rochford (☎ 03-5962 2119; www.rochfordwines.com.au; cnr Maroondah Hwy & Hill Rd, Coldstream) Large winery with restaurant and gallery, plus fine Cabernet Sauvignon and Pinot Noir.

Yering Station (☎ 03-9730 0100; www.yering.com; 38 Melba Hwy, Yering) A massive, modern complex with a fine-dining restaurant, produce store and bar; it's home to the heady Shiraz-Viognier blend and a sparkling white wine, as well as Pinot Noir, Rosé and Chardonnay. The Yarra Valley Farmers' Market is held here every third Sunday.

THE DANDENONGS

On a clear day, the Dandenong Ranges and their highest peak, Mt Dandenong (633m), can be seen from Melbourne. The landscape is a patchwork of exotics and natives with a lush understorey of tree ferns – it's the most accessible bushwalking in Melbourne's backyard.

Puffing Billy (☎ 03-9754 6800; www.puffingbilly.com.au; Old Monbulk Rd, Belgrave; adult/child/family return $51/26/103) is an immensely popular steam train that snakes through lush fern gullies and bush while kids dangle arms and legs out the window. There are up to six departures between Belgrave and Gembrook during holidays, and three or four on other days; you can also ride shorter sections of line or travel one way.

Dandenong Ranges National Park, a combination of five parks, offers short walks and four-hour trails. **Sherbrooke Forest** has a towering cover of mountain ash trees. Reach the start of its eastern loop walk (10km, three hours), just 1km or so from Belgrave station, by walking to the end of Old Monbulk Rd past Puffing Billy's station. Combining this walk with a ride on *Puffing Billy* makes a great day out.

William Ricketts Sanctuary (☎ 13 19 63; www.parkweb.vic.gov.au; Mt Dandenong Tourist Rd, Mt Dandenong; adult/child/family $7/5/17; 🕓 10am-4.30pm, closed on total fire ban days) features sculptures blended beautifully with damp fern gardens. Ricketts' work was inspired by nature and the years he spent living with Indigenous people.

PHILLIP ISLAND

Penguins and petrol heads have made Phillip Island what it is today. This small island was originally settled by the Boonwurrung people, who are probably the only people in history not to have attended the island's penguin parade. Instead they came for the diet of seafood and short-tailed shearwaters, both of which can still be seen on the island.

Of course, most tourists come to see those cute little penguins waddle up the beach to their burrows in the dunes every night, but the island is ruggedly handsome and has plenty to offer, including seal colonies and wild surf beaches.

The island also revs up for the Motorcycle Grand Prix; it's also a popular getaway in summer, when the population more than quadruples.

SIGHTS & ACTIVITIES

PHILLIP ISLAND NATURE PARKS

The nature parks comprises three of the islands biggest attractions: the **Penguin Parade** (☎ 03-5951 2800; www.penguins.org.au; Summerland Beach; adult/child/family $20/10/50; ⌚ 10am-dusk); the **Koala Conservation Centre** (☎ 03-5952 1307; adult/child/family $10/5/25; ⌚ 10am-5pm, extended hr in summer), off Phillip Island Rd, with elevated boardwalks; and trips to **Churchill Island** (☎ 03-5956 7214; adult/child/family $10/5/25; ⌚ 10am-4.30pm, extended hrs in summer), a working farm also off Phillip Island Rd, where Victoria's first crops were planted and today features historic displays, including butter churning and blacksmithing (call ahead for times).

If you're keen on all three attractions buy the **Three Parks Pass** (adult/child/family $34/17/85), which is valid for six months (you can only visit the penguin parade once though) and is available at the visitors centre.

Most people come for the **Little Penguins**, the world's smallest and probably cutest of their kind. The penguin complex includes concrete amphitheatres that hold up to 3800 spectators who visit to see the little fellas just after sunset as they waddle from the sea to

CHRISTOPHER GROENHOUT

Puffing Billy steams through the Dandenongs

GREG ELMS

A Mornington Peninsula winery

IF YOU LIKE...

If you like tasting the results of the vignerons and winemakers of the **Yarra Valley** (p223), we think you'll like these other local wine regions:

- **King Valley** On the back road between Mansfield and Wangaratta, the King Valley is a prosperous wine region noted for its Italian varietals and cool-climate wines such as Sangiovese, Barbera, sparkling Prosecco and Pinot Grigio.
- **Milawa** Tiny Milawa, in the state's northeast, has had a renaissance as a regional gourmet centre, boasting notable wineries, fine restaurants and several local food producers – a perfect stop on the way to the snowfields.
- **Mornington Peninsula** Just southeast of Melbourne, the peninsula produces famous Pinot Noir and Chardonnay and features numerous winery-restaurants.
- **Rutherglen** Rutherglen wineries, north of Milawa, produce superb fortifieds (Port, Muscat and Tokay) and some potent Durifs and Shirazs – among the biggest, beefiest and strongest reds.

their land-based nests. Penguin numbers swell in summer, after breeding, but they parade year-round. You usually get a closer view from the boardwalks as they search for their burrows and mates. Bring warm clothing. There are a variety of specialised **tours** (adult $35-70) so you can be accompanied by rangers or see them from the vantage of a Skybox (an elevated platform). Be sure to book well in advance in summer.

SEAL ROCKS & THE NOBBIES

The extreme southwestern tip of Phillip Island leads to the Nobbies and beyond them is **Seal Rocks**, inhabited by Australia's largest colony of fur seals. The **Nobbies Centre** (☎ 03-5951 2816; admission free; tours adult/child $10/5; 10am-8pm summer, 10am-5pm autumn, 10am-4pm winter; 10am-6pm spring) is a sort of gigantic cafe and souvenir shop with an interpretive centre tacked on, but there are some great interactive panels and games, and the huge windows afford great views of the 6000 Australian fur seals who loll here during the October–December breeding season.

TOURS

Go West (☎ 1300 736 551; www.gowest.com.au; tour $109) These folks run a one-day tour from Melbourne that includes lunch, entry fees and iPod commentary in several languages.

Wildlife Coast Cruises (☎ 03-5952 3501; www.wildlifecoastcruises.com.au; Rotunda Bldg, Jetty, Cowes; Nov-May) There is a two-hour cruise from Cowes jetty around Seal Rocks (adult/child $60/40), a half-day cruise and tour of French Island ($65/45) and a one-hour bay cruise ($25/16).

GETTING THERE & AROUND

The best service from Melbourne to Cowes is the direct **V/Line** (☎ 13 61 96) bus departing at 3.50pm from Southern Cross station, Monday to Friday ($11, 3½ hours).

There's no public transport around Phillip Island. You can hire bicycles from **Ride On Bikes** (☎ 03-5952 2533; www.rideonbikes.com.au; 85-87 Thompson Ave, Cowes; per hr/half-/full day $15/25/35).

GREAT OCEAN ROAD

Australia's most famous stretch of road winds its way almost 250km from Torquay to Warrnambool, and for once it lives up to the hype. The famous rock stacks known as the Twelve Apostles are only part of the story as you pass dramatic views of the wild coastline, classic surf beaches and seaside towns, much of it backed by lush temperate rainforest. Wind down the windows and you'll cop a unique perfume of bush and beach, gums and salt water.

TOURS

Several tour companies will take you out on the Great Ocean Road, many leaving from Melbourne.

Go West Tours (☎ 1300 736 551; www.gowest.com.au) Takes trips along the Great Ocean Road and to Phillip Island. Full-day Great Ocean Road tour is $105.

Groovy Grape (☎ 1800 66 11 77; www.groovygrape.com.au) Three-day Great Ocean Road and Grampians trips between Melbourne and Adelaide ($345).

Ride Tours (☎ 1800 605 120; www.ridetours.com.au; Mon, Thu & Sat) Two-day bus tours in summer for $165.

Wayward Bus (☎ 1300 653 510; www.waywardbus.com.au) Follows the southwest coast to South Australia (SA) as part of its Melbourne to Adelaide trip; you can do stopovers, too. Three-day Melbourne to Adelaide is $395.

TORQUAY

Victoria's undisputed surf capital heaves under the weight of surf shops and surf gear factory outlets – this is the spiritual home of Rip Curl, but all the major names are represented here in a sort of mall for wave-lovers.

SIGHTS & ACTIVITIES

Next to the visitor centre, **Surf World Museum** (☎ 03-5261 4606; adult/child/family $9/6/20; 9am-5pm) is a must for would-be waxheads with boards through the ages, a board-shaping workshop and plenty of footage of mountainous waves.

Torquay revolves around gorgeous local beaches: **Fisherman's Beach**, protected from ocean swells, and **Front Beach**, ringed by shady pines and sloping lawns, are ideal for families. Surf lifesavers patrol the frothing **Back Beach** during summer. **Bells Beach**, 7km southwest of Torquay, is legendary among surfers the world over for its powerful break and hosts a world-championship surfing contest every Easter.

There are plenty of opportunities in Torquay to learn to surf, hire gear and get involved in other adventure activities such as snorkelling and kayaking.

Go Ride a Wave (☎ 1300 132 441; www.gorideawave.com.au; Bell St; 2hr lessons incl hire $70, 2hr hire from $25) Hires surfing gear, sells secondhand equipment and offers lessons (cheaper with advance booking).

SLEEPING

Summer and Easter are peak times for Torquay so book well ahead, even for campsites. **Torquay Holiday Rentals** (☎ 03-5261 5579; www.torquayholidays.com.au) can help find accommodation.

Mossop's Beach Shack (☎ 0422 989 837; 21 Zeally Bay Rd; d low/high season from $80/140) Colourful self-contained beach houses close to town.

Torquay Foreshore Caravan Park (☎ 03-5261 2496; 35 Bell St; powered sites 1/2 people $15/30, cabins $75-130) Just behind Back Beach, this sprawling caravan park is the best place to pitch a tent or park a camper.

ANGLESEA

This sweet little seaside village has long been a family favourite for its terrific beaches and low-key holiday feel. The town winds around the gum-green Anglesea River, and accommodation makes the most of tranquil bush settings. The town is oddly well known for

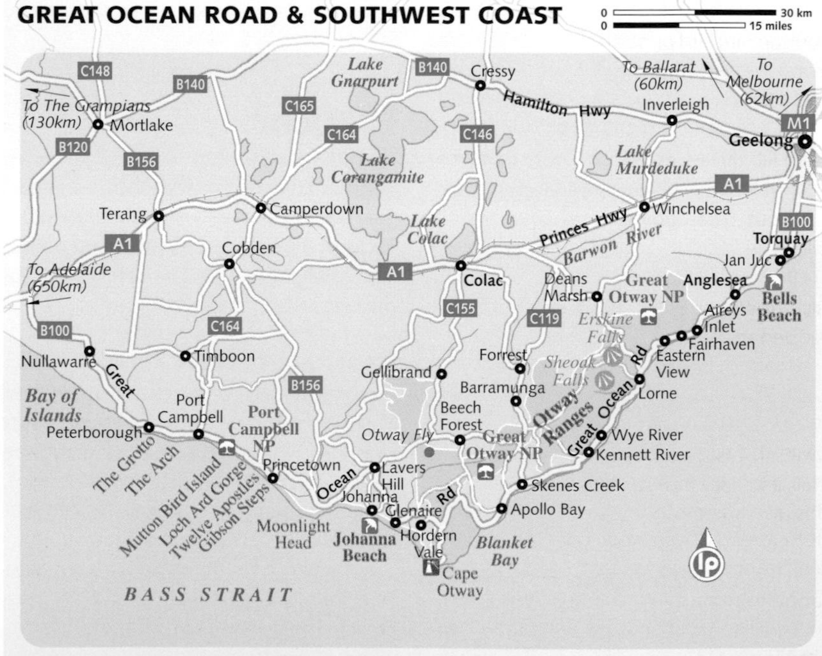

HOLGER LEUE

Surf class run by Go Ride a Wave

the kangaroos that graze on the local golf course.

ACTIVITIES

You can hire surf or beach-play equipment from the **Anglesea Surf Centre** (☎ 03-5263 1530; cnr Great Ocean Rd & McMillan St) or **Go Ride a Wave** (☎ 1300 132 441; 143b Great Ocean Rd; 2hr lessons incl hire $70, 2hr hire from $25), which also gives surfing lessons.

About 10km down the road at Aireys Inlet, the **Split Point Lighthouse** (☎ 1800 174 045; www.splitpointlighthouse.com.au; tours adult/child/family $12/7/35; hourly 10am-4pm) is open for guided tours.

SLEEPING

Surf Coast Spa Resort (☎ 03-5263 3363; www.surfcoastspa.com.au; 105 Great Ocean Rd; d $160, d with spa from $200) Get pampered at this upmarket resort, which offers all sorts of health-spa add-ons to enhance your stay, from a mud wrap to full facial. Rooms range from motel-style to spa units.

Anglesea Beachfront Caravan Park (☎ 03-5263 1583; www.angleseabeachfront.com.au; 35 Cameron St; powered sites $32, cabins from $80;) Lovely beachfront park with bush camping sites (all powered) and a range of cabins. Wireless internet.

LORNE

With lots of good cafes, nightlife, pier fishing, bushwalks and accommodation, Lorne is a good place to start exploring the Great Ocean Road. Over the peak Christmas/New Year season, parking, footpath space and accommodation are scarce, but out of season it's a laid-back beach town that quietly hums along with the locals and retirees who love the good life out here.

SIGHTS & ACTIVITIES

Lorne is a good base for more than 50km of walking tracks in the eastern extremity of Great Otway National Park. **Teddy's Lookout**, just above town, has good views of the coast. **Erskine Falls**, about 10km northwest of town, is the most impressive waterfall in the area and it's an easy walk to the viewing platform or 250 steps down to the base.

SLEEPING & EATING

Locals seem to have thrown a B&B sign up on every backyard loo to create 'boutique' accommodation, but some represent poor value. Most places are booked solid during summer holidays, but it's worth enquiring at the Lorne visitor information centre (p231), which offers frank advice on places around town. Prices vary considerably in low and high seasons.

Mountjoy Parade is lined with cafes and some quality restaurants catering to the summer tourist crowds. For fresh seafood off the boat, head to Lorne Seafoods at the pier.

Great Ocean Road Backpackers YHA (☎ 03-5289 1809; www.yha.com.au; 10 Erskine Ave; dm/d/f $25/75/100) Snuggled away in the bush just across the Erskine River, this relaxed two-storey timber lodge has spacious dorms, top-value doubles and the secluded scrub offering cockatoo and the odd koala sightings.

Surfers, Apollo Bay

WILL SALTER

Great Ocean Road Cottages (☎ 03-5289 1070; www.greatoceanroadcottages.com; Erskine Ave; d $150-170) These comfy self-contained timber cottages enjoy a bush setting at the same location as the YHA. They're roomy, with a mezzanine level, full kitchen and verandah. In peak holiday season minimum rental is a week ($1575).

LORNE TO APOLLO BAY

Driving west out of Lorne, the Great Ocean Road really starts to get interesting with twists and turns revealing spectacular coastal views from lookout points and koalas hanging out of roadside trees. If you're busy rubber-necking or driving a slow vehicle, respect the traffic behind you and use the slow vehicle turn-outs!

About 3km from Lorne (signposted) is the easy 20-minute walk to the base of pretty **Sheoak Falls**. A further 13km on, the cute little hamlet of **Wye River** is well worth a stop for a swim, and more importantly a beer and lunch on the timber deck of the **Wye Beach Hotel** (☎ 03-5289 0240; Great Ocean Rd; mains $16-30; 🕑 lunch & dinner). There's also a sprawling caravan park taking up much of the beachfront area here. Keep going another 5km to **Kennett River**, the best place to spot koalas on the Great Ocean Road. Park your car and wander up Grey River Rd with your neck craned.

APOLLO BAY

Once a fishing town, beautiful Apollo Bay was never going to remain a secret for long, but despite creeping development it has kept its charm, with rolling hills looming over ribbons of surf beach. It's more low key than Lorne, but has a good range of accommodation and restaurants and is a jumping-off point for exploring the surrounding Great Otway National Park.

The **Great Ocean Road visitor information centre** (☎ 03-5237 6529; 100 Great Ocean Rd; 9am-5pm;) is on the left as you arrive from Lorne and has displays on Aboriginal history, rainforests, shipwrecks and the building of the Great Ocean Road.

SIGHTS & ACTIVITIES

Apollo Bay Surf & Kayak (☎ 0405 495 909; www.apollobaysurfkayak.com.au; Great Ocean Rd), opposite the visitor centre, has surfing lessons ($45), excellent seal kayak tours to the Marengo Reef Seal Colony ($55) and guided bushwalks, and also hires out boards, wetsuits, fishing rods and camping gear.

Otway Expeditions (☎ 03-5237 6341; www.otwayexpeditions.tripod.com; 3hr mountain-bike tours min 6 people $65, Argo buggies $45) runs mountain-bike tours through the Otways, as well as gentle bush-bashing adventures in cross-terrain-and-water Argo buggies.

A marked multiday hike, the **Great Ocean Walk** (www.greatoceanwalk.com.au), starts at Apollo Bay and runs about 100km all the way to the Twelve Apostles. You can hop on and off the trail to do shorter walks or take on the whole trek in six days; see the website for suggestions about different legs.

SLEEPING

Apollo Bay is blessed with some excellent budget accommodation, including four backpackers and plenty of motels and B&Bs.

YHA Eco Beach (☎ 03-5237 7899; 5 Pascoe St; dm/s/d $38/80/95;) The lounge and communal areas of this architect-designed hostel are like something out of a *Home Beautiful* magazine. It's definitely one for the flashpacker – not only luxurious but eco-designed.

Haley Reef Views B&B (☎ 03-5237 7885; www.haleyreefviews.com.au; 31 Noel St; d low/high season $110/140;) The immaculate English garden gives you an idea of the care taken with guests at this sweet little spot. It's just a short stroll to the beach, but there's an indulgent spa to relax in.

Sandpiper Motel (☎ 03-5237 6732; www.sandpiper.net.au; 3 Murray St; d low/high season from $130/165) Simple beach-style rooms in sea blues and sandy tones make for a relaxing stay at this stylish modern motel. Go for a view of the ocean or a garden deck room. Some are self-contained and there's a deluxe spa unit.

CAPE OTWAY

The 14km drive down to the lighthouse at Cape Otway passes through beautiful tall-timbered forest – keep an eye out for koalas hanging out of trees close to the roadside. Cape Otway's rugged coastline smashed several ships wide open in its history, but today it's a magnificent area where bushland meets the coast and forms part of the Great Otway National Park.

About 8km along Lighthouse Rd, a signpost points down an unsealed road to **Parker Hill**, **Point Franklin** and **Crayfish Beach**, all gorgeous, secluded spots for beach ambling, swimming and snorkelling. Further along, **Blanket Bay** is a national parks camping ground.

At the end of Lighthouse Rd is the **Cape Otway Lighthouse** (☎ 03-5237 9240; www.lightstation.com.au; Lighthouse Rd; adult/child/family $15/8/38; 9am-5pm), Australia's oldest, dating back to 1848. The historic complex includes the old telegraph station, lightkeeper's house and a cafe with shipwreck gallery, and you can climb the decommissioned lighthouse for fine views along the coast.

Deep in the rainforest north of the Great Ocean Road (take the turn-off towards Lavers Hill), the **Otway Fly** (☎ 1800 300 477; www.otwayfly.com.au; adult/child/family $20/9/50; 9am-5.30pm, last admission 4.30pm) is a 25m-high elevated tree-top walk. The views of the forest canopy are wonderful and you can go even higher by ascending the spiral staircase to the 47m-high lookout tower. There's a visitor centre and cafe.

PORT CAMPBELL NATIONAL PARK

The most photographed stretch of the Great Ocean Road offers sheer limestone cliffs towering over fierce seas. For thousands of years, waves and tides have relentlessly sculpted the soft rock into a fascinating series of rock stacks, gorges, arches and blowholes.

The **Gibson Steps**, hand-carved into the cliffs in the 19th century (and later replaced with concrete steps), lead down to foaming Gibson Beach. This beach, and others along this stretch of coast, are unpatrolled and not recommended for swimming – you can walk along the beach, but be wary of high-tide strandings.

The **Twelve Apostles** are the best-known rock formations in Victoria. These lonely rocky stacks have been abandoned to the ocean by the eroding headland. Today their number has been whittled down to six apostles, visible from the snaking viewing platforms. There's a rather pointless walk-through visitor centre leading to boardwalks that ring the cliff tops, providing viewing platforms and seats – don't stop at the first place you come to. Sunrise is a good time for photography and to beat the crowds.

At **Loch Ard Gorge** haunting tales of woe await. It's one of the Shipwreck Coast's most notorious sections. You can find out more at the **Port Campbell visitor information centre** (☎ 1300 137 255; www.visit12apostles.com; 26 Morris St, Port Campbell; 9am-5pm).

West of Port Campbell, the next piece of ocean sculpture is the **Arch**, a rocky archway offshore from Point Hesse. Nearby is **London Bridge**, albeit fallen down. It was once a double-arched rock platform linked to the mainland, but in 1990 one of the arches collapsed into the sea. Further west, beyond Peterborough, is the scenic **Bay of Islands Coastal Park**.

TOURS

You can tour the coastline from the air or sea. The cheapest chopper flights last around 10 minutes.

12 Apostles Helicopters (☎ 03-5598 6161; www.12ah.com; 9400 Great Ocean Rd, Port Campbell; flights per person $100-215) Flights over the Twelve Apostles, London Bridge and Bay of Islands, recorded on a 'Skycam' video as a souvenir.

Port Campbell Boat Charters (☎ 0428 986 366; 155 Rounds Rd, Port Campbell; tours $50) Scenic boat tours to Twelve Apostles (four daily), plus diving, snorkelling and fishing trips.

The Edge Helicopters (☎ 03-5598 8283; www.theedgehelicopters.com.au; flights per person $90-195) Based at the Twelve Apostles centre.

THE WIMMERA & GRAMPIANS NATIONAL PARK

The Wimmera is an endless expanse of wheat fields, grain silos and sheep properties bisected by the Western Hwy (A8), the main route between Melbourne and Adelaide.

The major attractions in the region are the Grampians National Park, Mt Arapiles

State Park – Australia's most famous rock-climbing venue (known as Djurite to Koories) – and the Little Desert National Park.

The **Grampians** (known as Gariwerd to local Koories) is a bushwalkers' paradise and one of Victoria's most outstanding natural features. The rich diversity of flora and fauna, unique rock formations, Aboriginal rock art, accessible walking trails and rock-climbing sites offer something for everyone, regardless of your energy levels. The mountains are at their best in spring, when the wildflowers (including 20 species that don't exist anywhere else in the world) are at their peak. The Grampians lie west of Ararat and Stawell, and stretch 90km from Dunkeld in the south almost to Horsham in the north.

Sealed access roads in the park run from Halls Gap south to Dunkeld and northwest to Horsham. Off these roads are side trips to car parks and some of the park's most notable sights such as McKenzies Falls, Reed Lookout for walks to the Balconies, and Boroka Lookout.

There is a lot of **Aboriginal rock art** in the park, but not all is publicised or accessible. In the northern Grampians, near Mt Stapylton, the main sites are **Gulgurn Manja Shelter** and **Ngamadjidj Shelter**. In the western Grampians, near the Buandik camping ground, the main sites are **Billimina Shelter** and **Manja Shelter**.

Close to Halls Gap, the **Wonderland Range** has some spectacular and accessible scenery. There are scenic drives and walks, from an easy stroll to Venus Bath (30 minutes) to a walk up to the Pinnacles Lookout (five hours). Walking tracks start from Halls Gap, and the Wonderland and Sundial car parks.

There are two tracks from the **Zumstein picnic area**, northwest of Halls Gap, to the spectacular **McKenzie Falls**.

Pretty **Halls Gap**, in the heart of the Grampians, is the base for exploring the region. It gets very busy on weekends and holiday periods, but midweek it calms down and it's a delightful place, where kangaroos come to graze on the front lawns of the town's houses and where the

ROSS BARNETT

The Balconies rock formation, Grampians National Park

air is thick with the songs of kookaburras and parrots.

INFORMATION

Halls Gap visitor information centre (☎ 03-5356 4616, 1800 065 599; www.grampianstravel.com.au, www.visithallsgap.com.au; Grampians Rd; 9am-5pm) In the village centre; information and accommodation bookings.

TOURS

Brambuk Cultural Centre (☎ 03-5356 4452; Grampians Rd; 9am-5pm) Offers a two-hour cultural and rock art tour ($35/22). Bookings essential.

Eco Platypus Tours (☎ 1800 819 091; www.ecoplatypustours.com) Offers day trips to the Grampians from Melbourne for $99 per person.

Grampians Mountain Adventure Company (☎ 03-5383 9218, www.grampiansadventure.com.au; half-/full-day instruction $75/125) Rock-climbing and abseiling adventures tailored to suit those who fancy the vertical world, assisted by accredited instructors.

Grampians Personalised Tours & Adventures (☎ 0429 954 686, 03-5356 4654; www.grampianstours.com; half-/full-day tours $79/149) Offers a range of 4WD tours and guided bushwalks, as well as multiday walks.

SLEEPING

our pick **D'Altons Resort** (☎ 03-5356 4666; www.daltonsresort.com.au; 48 Glen St; standard/deluxe cottages from $100/120;) These delightful timber cottages spread up the hill, away from the main road, between the gums and kangaroos. They have cosy fires, big lounge chairs and little verandahs. There's a tennis court and laundry.

Boronia Peak Villas (☎ 03-5356 4500; www.boroniapeakvillas.com.au; cnr Grampians & Tandara Rds; 2-/3-bed villas from $130/220;) With a lovely bush setting, these cottages offer excellent self-contained accommodation from standard and family units to super-deluxe spa units.

Mountain Grand Guesthouse (☎ 03-5356 4232; www.mountaingrand.com; Grampians Rd; s/d incl breakfast & dinner $160/206) This gracious timber guest house prides itself on being an old-fashioned lodge, where breakfast and dinner is included, encouraging guests to mingle and relax. The bedrooms are fresh and colourful with their own spacious bathrooms.

THE HIGH COUNTRY

The Great Dividing Range – Australia's eastern spine – curls around Victoria from the Snowy Mountains to the Grampians, peaking in the spectacular High Country. This is Victoria's mountain playground, attracting skiers and snowboarders in winter and bushwalkers and mountain-bikers in summer. Although not particularly high – the highest point, Mt Bogong, only reaches 1986m – the mountain air is clear and invigorating and the scenery spectacular.

MANSFIELD

pop 2840

Gateway to Mt Buller, Mansfield is a vibrant all-seasons base where you can organise winter skiing trips, or go horse riding or mountain-biking through some fabulous high country in spring and summer. With plenty of accommodation, good restaurants and regional wineries, it makes a great base for a weekend or a longer stay.

The helpful visitor information centre, **Mansfield-Mt Buller High Country Reservations** (☎ 03-5775 7000, 1800 039 049;

www.mansfield-mtbuller.com.au; Old Railway Station, Maroondah Hwy; 9am-5pm), has a free accommodation booking service.

ACTIVITIES

In winter ski hire shops rent out ski and snowboard equipment and chains for trips to Mt Buller. At other times, horse riding and mountain-biking are the most popular organised activities from Mansfield.

High Country Horses (**03-5777 5590; www.highcountryhorses.com.au; 10 McCormacks Rd, Merrijig; 2hr rides $65, half-day $90, full-day from $160, overnight from $450**) offers rides around Merrijig and overnight trips across Mt Stirling, camping in a cattleman's hut at Razorback.

High Country Scenic Tours (**03-5777 5101; www.highcountryscenictours.com.au; Nov-May**) has a range of specialised off-road vehicles taking groups on exciting day and overnight tours of Victoria's high country, priced from $200 per person.

SLEEPING

Mansfield Backpackers' Inn & Travellers Lodge (**03-5775 1800; www.mansfieldtravel lodge.com; 112 High St; dm summer/winter $25/30, d $95/105, f $160/180;**) This restored heritage building has a spotless backpacker section with a well-equipped kitchen, lounge, laundry and drying room. Adjacent motel rooms are modern and neat (prices drop midweek).

Highton Manor (**03-5775 2700; www .hightonmanor.com.au; 140 Highton Lane; stable/manor d $120/225;**) Built in 1896, this stately two-storey manor has motel-style rooms in the former stables and lavish period rooms in the main house. The impressive gardens are great for a stroll.

GETTING THERE & AWAY

V/Line (**13 61 96**) buses run twice daily (once Sunday) from Melbourne ($21, three hours). **Mansfield-Mt Buller Bus Lines** (**03-5775 2606; www.mmbl.com.au**) runs seven times daily buses for skiers from Mansfield to Mt Buller (adult/child return $50/34).

JOHN HAY

High Country, near Mansfield

MT BULLER

elev 1805m

Three hours' drive from Melbourne, Mt Buller is Victoria's largest ski resort and most popular year-round mountain destination. There's an extensive lift network, including a chairlift that takes you from the day car park directly to the slopes. Cross-country trails link Mt Buller and Mt Stirling.

The downhill skiing area is 180 hectares (snow-making covers 44 hectares), and runs are divided into 25% beginner, 45%

intermediate and 30% advanced, with a vertical drop of 400m.

There are over 7000 beds on the mountain. **High Country Reservations** (☎ 1800 039 049) and **Mt Buller Alpine Reservations** (☎ 03-5777 6633; www.mtbullerreservations.com.au) book lodge accommodation.

FALLS CREEK

elev 1780m

Falls Creek is the most fashion-conscious and upmarket ski resort in Australia, combining a picturesque alpine setting among the snow gums with impressive skiing and infamous après-ski entertainment. Hordes of city folk make the 4½-hour journey from Melbourne at weekends during the ski season.

DANIEL BOAG

Mt Hotham ski village

The skiing is spread over two main areas, the **Village Bowl** and **Sun Valley**. There are 19 lifts: 17% beginner, 60% intermediate and 23% advanced runs. The downhill area covers 451 hectares with a vertical drop of 267m. Night skiing in the Village Bowl operates several times a week.

INFORMATION

Falls Creek visitor information centre (☎ 03-5758 3224; www.fallscreek.com.au) On the right-hand side at the bottom of the Falls Express chairlift, it has plenty of information on the whole alpine region. The daily admission fee is $31 per car, $10/5 adult/child for bus passenger during the ski season only. There are full-day lift tickets (adult/child/youth $97/49/82), and combined lift-and-lesson packages ($146/99/124). One-day cross-country trail fees are adult/child/family $12/6/30.

SLEEPING

Accommodation can be booked through **Falls Creek Central Reservations** (☎ 03-5758 3733, 1800 033 079; www.fallscreek.com.au; Bogong High Plains Rd) and **Mountain Multiservice** (☎ 03-5758 3499, 1800 465 666; www.mountainmultiservice.com.au; Schuss St).

GETTING THERE & AROUND

Falls Creek is 375km and a 4½-hour drive from Melbourne. During the winter, **Falls Creek Coach Service** (☎ 03-5754 4024; www.fallscreekcoachservice.com.au) operates daily buses between Falls Creek and Melbourne (one way/return $95/154) and also runs services to and from Albury ($54/86) and Mt Beauty ($33/52).

MOUNT HOTHAM

elev 1868m

Serious hikers, skiers and snowboarders head to Mt Hotham, the starting point for some stunning alpine walks between

November and May, and home to 320 hectares of downhill runs, with a vertical drop of 428m. About 80% of the ski trails are intermediate or advanced. The Big D is open for **night skiing** every Wednesday and Saturday.

Off-piste skiing in steep and narrow valleys is good. **Cross-country skiing** is also good, with 35km of trails winding through tree-lined glades.

INFORMATION

Mt Hotham Alpine Resort Management (☎ 03-5759 3550; www.mthotham.com.au; ⏲ 8am-5pm daily ski season, Mon-Fri other times) At the village administration centre. The ski-season admission fee is $34 per car and $11.50/6.25 per adult/child bus passenger. Lift tickets per adult/child/youth cost $97/49/82. Lift-and-lesson packages start from $146 for adults. Rates are slightly cheaper in June and September.

SLEEPING

Only a handful of lodges are open year-round. There are three booking agencies: **Mt Hotham Reservation Centre** (☎ 1800 354 555; www.hotham.com.au; Hotham Central) operates year-round; **Mt Hotham Accommodation Service** (☎ 03-5759 3636, 1800 032 061; www.mthothamaccommodation.com.au; Lawlers Apartments) operates during ski season only; and **Mt Hotham Central Reservations** (☎ 03-5759 3522, 1800 657 547; www.mthotham-centralres.com.au) can book local and off-mountain accommodation throughout the year.

GETTING THERE & AROUND

Mt Hotham is 373km northeast of Melbourne and reached via the Hume Fwy (M31) and Harrietville (4½ hours), or via the Princes Hwy (A1) and Omeo (5½ hours).

In winter, **Snowball Express** (☎ 03-9370 9055, 1800 659 009; www.snowballexpress.com.au) has daily buses from Melbourne to Mt Hotham ($160 return, 6½ hours), via Wangaratta, Myrtleford, Bright and Harrietville.

GIPPSLAND & WILSONS PROMONTORY NATIONAL PARK

Sprawling across the southeastern corner of Australia, this diverse region is packed full of national parks, lakes, deserted coastline and some of the most absorbing wilderness, scenery and wildlife on the continent.

With some of Victoria's best bushwalking country, wonderful beaches and abundant wildlife, 'the Prom' is one of the most popular national parks in all of Australia. Much of it is true wilderness, with only one sealed road on the park's western side. The wildlife around Tidal River is very tame: kookaburras and rosellas lurk expectantly (resist the urge to feed them), and wombats waddle out of the undergrowth seemingly oblivious to the campers and day trippers.

The only access road leads to **Tidal River** on the western coast, which has the Parks Victoria office and education centre, a petrol station, general store (with internet access), open-air cinema (summer only), camp sites, cabins, lodges and facilities.

INFORMATION

Parks Victoria (☎ 03-5680 9555, 1800 350 552; www.parkweb.vic.gov.au; Tidal River; ⏲ 8am-4.30pm) Takes accommodation reservations and issues camping permits for outside the Tidal River area.

TOP FIVE PROM WALKS

From November to Easter a free shuttle bus operates between the Tidal River visitors' car park and the Mt Oberon car park (a nice way to start the Prom Circuit Walk).

Great Prom Walk This is the most popular long-distance hike, a moderate 45km circuit across to Sealers Cove from Tidal River, down to Refuge Cove, Waterloo Bay, the lighthouse and back to Tidal River via Oberon Bay. Allow two to three days, and coordinate your walks with tide times, as creek crossings can be hazardous. It's possible to visit or stay at the lighthouse by prior arrangement with the park office.

Lilly Pilly Gully Nature Walk An easy 5km (two-hour) walk through heathland and eucalypt forests, with lots of wildlife.

Mt Oberon Summit Starting from the Mt Oberon car park, this moderate-to-hard 7km (2½-hour) walk is an ideal introduction to the Prom with panoramic views from the summit. The free Mt Oberon shuttle bus can take you to the car park and back.

Little Oberon Bay An easy-to-moderate 8km (three-hour) walk over sand dunes covered in coastal tea trees with beautiful views over Little Oberon Bay.

Squeaky Beach Nature Walk Another easy 5km return stroll through coastal tea trees and banksias to a sensational white-sand beach.

Day entry to the park is $10, which is included in camping fees.

ACTIVITIES

The Prom's diverse walking tracks will take you through swamps, forests, marshes, valleys of tree ferns and long beaches lined with sand dunes. The park office has details of walks, from 15-minute strolls to overnight and longer hikes. For some serious exploration, buy a copy of *Discovering the Prom* ($15).

SLEEPING

Apart from bush camping, the only accommodation in the park is at Tidal River and it must be booked well in advance in summer through **Parks Victoria** (☎ 03-5680 9555, 13 19 63). There are basic huts (four to six beds from $62 to $95) in the park, units ($118), self-contained two-bedroom cabins ($163) and safari tents ($250).

Nearby Yanakie offers several comfortable accommodation options for those day-tripping into the Prom.

Black Cockatoo Cottages (☎ 03-5687 1306; www.blackcockatoo.com; 60 Foley Rd, Yanakie; d $140) Black Cockatoo Cottages offers glorious views of the Prom without leaving your very comfortable bed. These self-contained cottages are private and stylish.

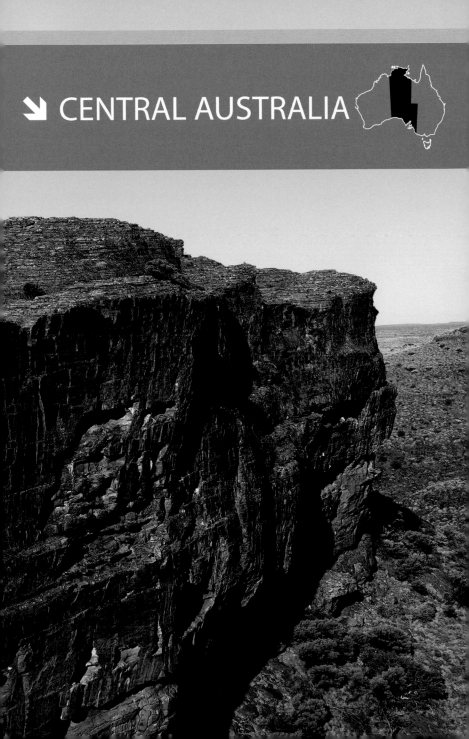

↘ CENTRAL AUSTRALIA

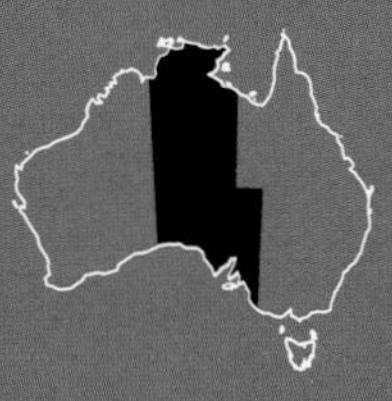

CENTRAL AUSTRALIA

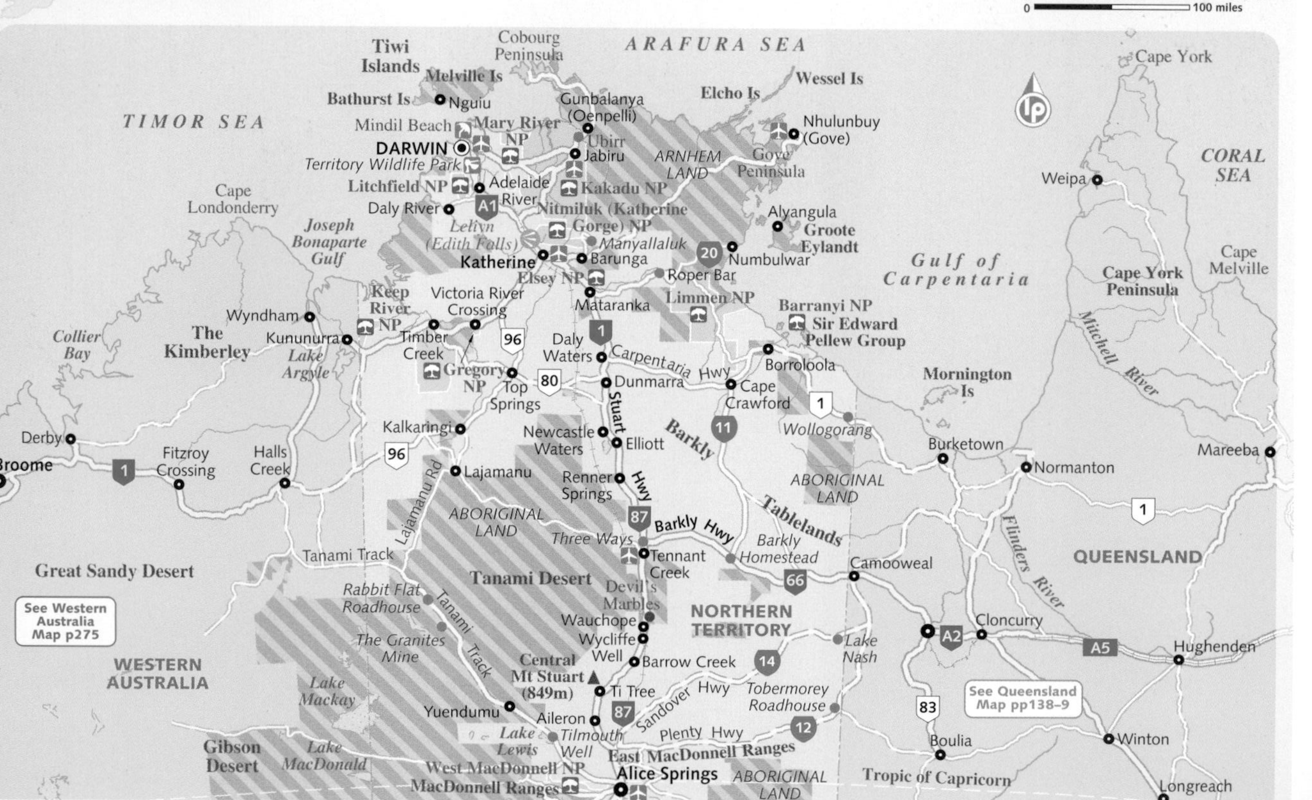

CENTRAL AUSTRALIA

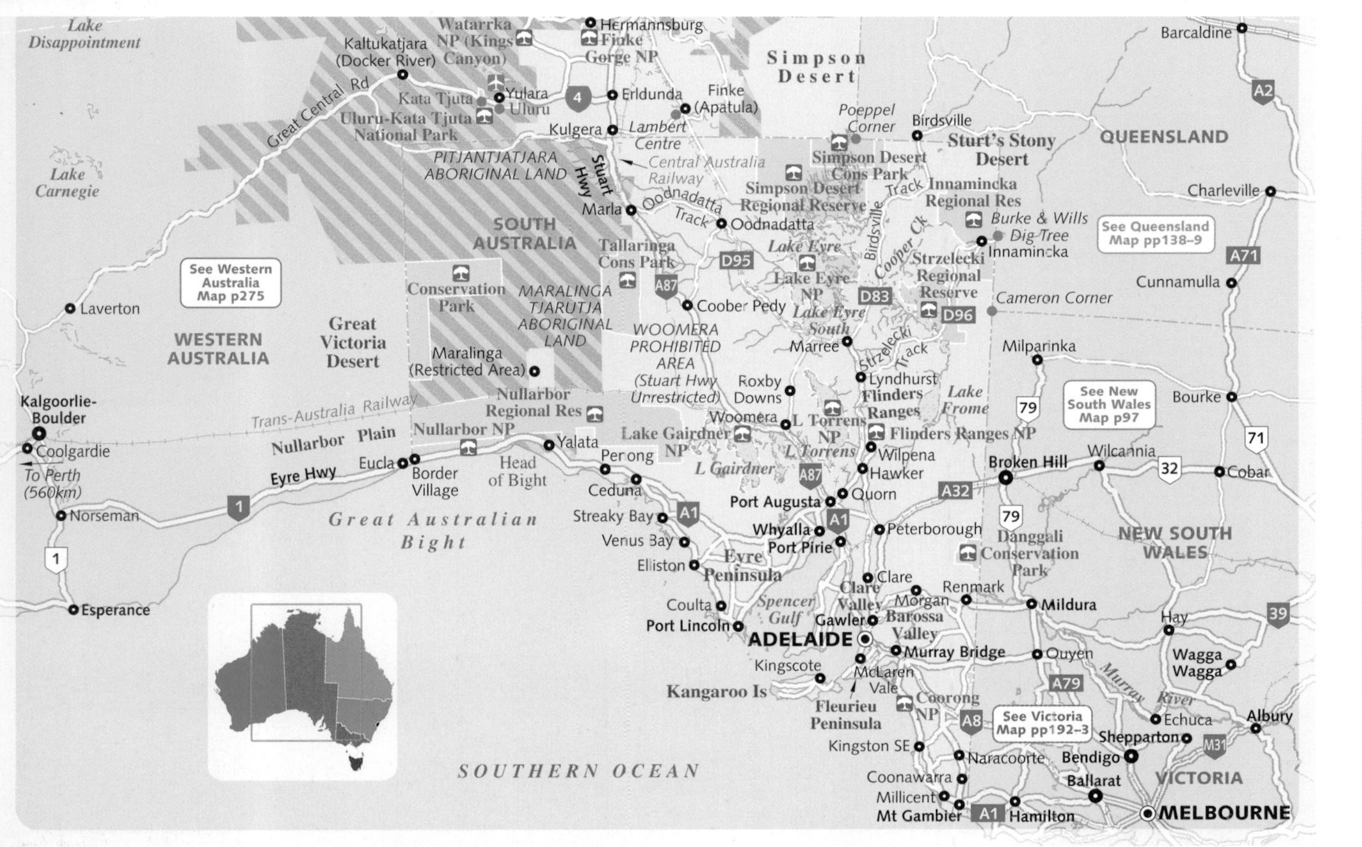

CENTRAL AUSTRALIA HIGHLIGHTS

1 ULURU-KATA TJUTA NATIONAL PARK

BY TIM ROGERS, VISITOR SERVICES OFFICER, ULURU-KATA TJUTA NATIONAL PARK

Come and see the sun rising to unveil an ancient and spectacular rock in the middle of the continent, just as it has done every day for more than 3000 million years. Wonder at how this rock has provided water to a resourceful people for tens of thousands of years.

↘ TIM ROGERS' DON'T MISS LIST

❶ ANANGU TOUR

Make sure you go on **tour** (p263) with a traditional owner and learn to see the landscape through Anangu eyes. You'll experience a land that's been sung through story and law for generations, and hear a true Australian language that's been spoken throughout the desert regions for thousands of years. You'll begin to see how everything is interconnected and how this land has always provided everything the people need.

❷ ULURU'S CHANGING MOODS

I'm a keen photographer, so here are my tips. Winter months are best for great sunrise shots. If you come in summer, then sunset shots are your best bet. If you're really lucky you'll get a rainbow with sun showers. When the heavens open and rain falls, Uluru suddenly has over 60 waterfalls cascading down – but only one in a hundred visitors gets to see this remarkable event.

Clockwise from top: Uluru (Ayers Rock; p263); Kata Tjuta (the Olgas; p264); 'We Don't Climb' sign at the base of Uluru; Viewing site, Uluru; The landscape of Uluru-Kata Tjuta National Park (p262)

CLOCKWISE FROM TOP: JULIET COOMBE; RICHARD I'ANSON; RICHARD I'ANSON; JOHN BANAGAN; BETHUNE CARMICHAEL

❸ YOUR OWN CONNECTION

If you want to be on your own at Uluru, slip off to one of the waterholes along the base walk an hour before sunset. While all the other guests are scrabbling for sunset photos, you'll have the whole rock to yourself. If you sit quietly the birds will come in to drink and just on dusk the micro bats will come out and snatch insects out of the air.

❹ KATA TJUTA

My favourite activity is a sunrise walk at Kata Tjuta (p264). As the sun comes up it casts an array of hues, and you'll see the wildlife among the domes. Or, contrary to the crowd, you can visit the car sunset viewing area at sunrise. It's a nice spot to have breakfast, and you have a fantastic view of the mysterious silhouette of Uluru as dawn awakens.

➘ THINGS YOU NEED TO KNOW

Best bird-watching time From May to September **Best bird-watching spot** Along the Valley of the Winds walk or Walpa Gorge at Kata Tjuta, sit next to one of the many creek beds and you'll see a variety of birds **See our author's review on p262**

CENTRAL AUSTRALIA HIGHLIGHTS

2

↘ KAKADU NATIONAL PARK

Kakadu National Park (p257) showcases the remarkable landscape, wildlife and cultural heritage of the Top End. It is so much more than just a nature reserve; it is a celebration of the enduring link between the Indigenous custodians and the country they have nurtured for thousands of years. Visit wondrous and enigmatic rock-art sites and explore spectacular wildlife-teeming wetlands with local guides.

3

↘ BAROSSA VALLEY

South Australia's **Barossa Valley** (p270) is an indulgence that should be savoured slowly, like the famous and fabulous wines that it produces. The Barossa Valley is compact, yet it manages to turn out 21% of the country's wine – mostly big, luscious reds. The 80-plus wineries here are within easy reach of one another and make a straightforward day trip from Adelaide.

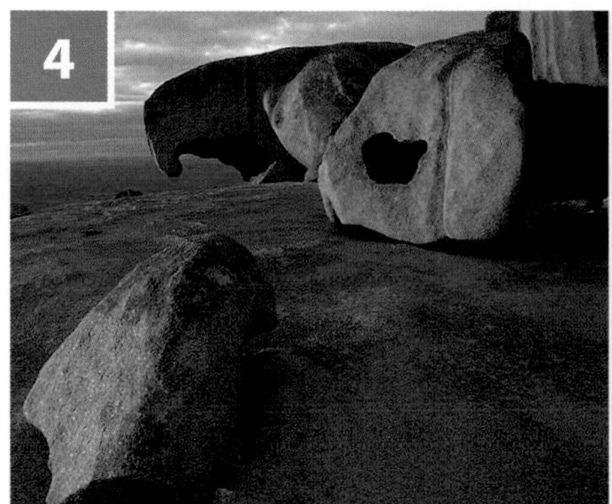

4

KANGAROO ISLAND

Rugged and serene **Kangaroo Island** (KI; p269) lies 13km off the bottom of the Fleurieu Peninsula. Its isolation has been a boon for its flora and fauna: seals, penguins, echidnas and, of course, roos are a drawcard, as are the clear turquoise waters lapping photogenic beaches. KI has also developed into a gourmet traveller destination within reach of Adelaide.

5

MINDIL BEACH SUNSET MARKET

Just follow your nose, and the many Darwin locals, to the fabulous **Mindil Beach Sunset Market** (p254), held every Thursday and Sunday from May to October. The relaxed tropical vibe is accompanied by a concoction of sweet aromas from multicultural food stalls. There are always a few bands, craft stalls and a masseur or two.

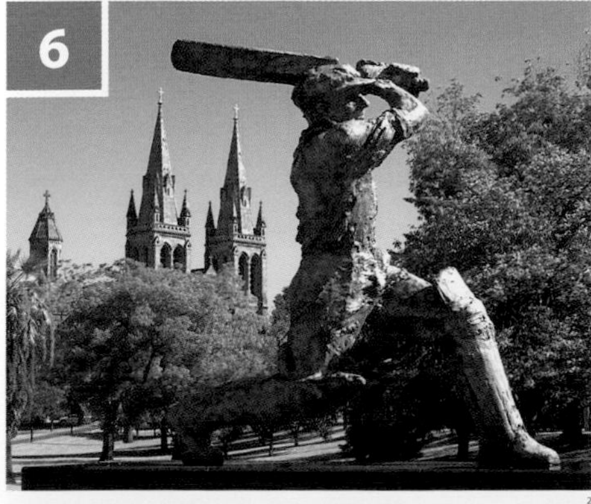

6

ADELAIDE

The European-inspired capital of South Australia, **Adelaide** (p265), is a vibrant mix of 'old-money' establishment, the artistic avant garde and multiculturalism. Though geographically isolated, colourful festivals are a sign of its progressive spirit. There's also a healthy live music scene and epicureans can sample innovative cuisine and wine.

2 BETHUNE CARMICHAEL; 3 CHRIS MELLOR; 4 PAUL SINCLAIR; 5 HOLGER LEUE; 6 DIANA MAYFIELD

2 Jim Jim Falls, Kakadu National Park (p257); 3 Harvesting in the Barossa Valley (270); 4 The Remarkable Rocks, Kangaroo Island (p269); 5 Mindil Beach Sunset Market (p254); 6 Sir Donald Bradman statue, Adelaide (p265)

CENTRAL AUSTRALIA'S BEST...

INDIGENOUS CULTURE EXPERIENCES

- **Kakadu National Park** (p257) Amazing rock art and informative tours
- **Darwin** (p250) Excellent Top End museum and art gallery
- **Uluru-Kata Tjuta National Park** (p262) Anangu-led tours reveal the true spirituality of the amazing rock formations
- **Alice Springs** (p259) Explore Alice and the MacDonnell Ranges with a local Warlpiri guide

WILDLIFE ENCOUNTERS

- **Kakadu National Park** (p257) Amazing rock art and informative tours
- **Alice Springs Desert Park** (p259) The best place to see the mostly cryptic and shy desert wildlife
- **Territory Wildlife Park** (p258) A showcase of Top End animals and birds

SHOPPING

- **Mindil Beach Sunset Market** (p254) Glorious multicultural food and Asian crafts
- **Darwin's Galleries** (p251) 'X-ray art', didgeridoos and craft from the Tiwi Islands
- **Alice Springs Galleries** (p261) From close to the source of Central Desert art, including 'dot paintings'
- **Adelaide** (p267) For hand-crafted wine, beer and chocolate

WINING & DINING

- **Darwin** (p250) From amazing food stalls to Asian-influenced fusion
- **Kakadu National Park** (p257) Try bush tucker on an stimulating tour
- **Barossa Valley** (p270) Australia's top drops can be sipped along with excellent fare

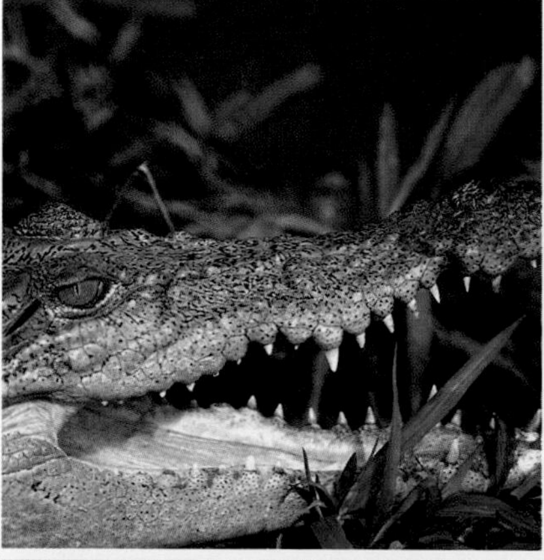

LEFT: CHRIS MELLOR; RIGHT: RICHARD I'ANSON

Left: A Kakadu croc; Right: Food stalls at the Mindil Beach Sunset Market (p254)

THINGS YOU NEED TO KNOW

VITAL STATISTICS

- **Population** South Australia 1.6 million; Northern Territory 202,800
- **Telephone code** ☎ 08
- **Best time to visit** May to September

ADVANCE PLANNING

- **One month before** At least a month before in peak times, book your room at Yulara (p264)
- **Two weeks before** Reserve a seat on the *Ghan* railway (p257)
- **One week before** Book a tour of Kakadu National Park (p257)

RESOURCES

- **Automobile Association of the Northern Territory** (AANT; ☎ 08-8981 3837; www.aant.com.au; 79-81 Smith St, Darwin; 9am-5pm Mon-Fri) Members of automobile associations in other states have reciprocal rights
- **Department of Environment & Heritage** (DEH; ☎ 08-8463 3999; www.environment.sa.gov.au; Level 1, 100 Pirie St; 9am-5pm Mon-Fri) Maps and comprehensive parks information
- **Parks & Wildlife Service** (www.nt.gov.au/nreta/parks) Details on Northern Territory parks and reserves
- **Royal Automobile Association of South Australia** (RAA; ☎ 08-8202 4600; www.raa.net; 55 Hindmarsh Sq; 8.30am-5pm Mon-Fri, 9am-noon Sat) Auto advice and plenty of maps
- **South Australian Visitor & Travel Centre** (SATC; ☎ 1300 655 276; www.southaustralia.com; 18 King William St; 8.30am-5pm Mon-Fri, 9am-2pm Sat & Sun) Abundantly stocked with leaflets and publications on Adelaide and South Australia
- **Tourism Top End** (www.tourismtopend.com.au) Darwin-based tourism body
- **Travel NT** (http://en.travelnt.com) Official tourism site

EMERGENCY NUMBERS

- **Ambulance, fire & police** (☎ 000)
- **AANT Roadside Assistance** (☎ 13 11 11)
- **RAA Roadside Assistance** (☎ 13 11 11)

GETTING AROUND

- **Walk** around the base of Uluru (p263)
- **Bus** to Barossa (p270) so you don't drink and drive!
- **Train** from Darwin to Adelaide on the *Ghan* (p257)
- **Ferry** to Kangaroo Island (p269)

BE FOREWARNED

- **Crocodiles** can move a long way inland – respect the safety signs
- **Yulara** accommodation gets mightily stretched in the peak (winter) months so book well in advance

CENTRAL AUSTRALIA ITINERARIES

TOP END TASTER Three Days

Start this tour at the Top End capital of **(1) Darwin** (p250), where you can savour the delights of Asia and other cuisines from around the globe as you wander the stalls of the Mindil Beach Sunset Market. You will also come across crocodile, emu, kangaroo and barramundi on the menus at many of the relaxed restaurants.

Moving east head towards **(2) Kakadu National Park** (p257), via the croc-jumping attraction at Adelaide River Crossing. You can drop a line to catch your own barramundi at Kakadu or join a bush tucker–themed Indigenous tour. Learn about the hunt, the seasonal migrations of animals and the vegetation changes. Watch bush food being prepared, join in and, of course, taste the results.

Head back to the Stuart Highway at Pine Creek (look out for mangoes in season) and then head towards **(3) Litchfield National Park** (p258), which boasts some of the best natural swimming holes in the entire Top End. If you don't intend to camp, nearby Batchelor has numerous accommodation options.

CULTURAL LANDSCAPE Five Days

The amazing Indigenous culture of Australia is as varied as the country. Begin this journey in the heart of Australia at **(1) Uluru-Kata Tjuta National Park** (p264). The many colours and moods of Uluru change with the hours of the day, and full appreciation of this amazing region requires a couple of days. A tour guided by an Anangu person will reveal the true nature and spirituality of the Rock. Also take some time to converse with the country by yourself – walking around Uluru and among the eerie domes of Kata Tjuta.

From here head to **(2) Alice Springs** (p259), the base for exploring the rugged **(3) West MacDonnell National Park** (p258), as well as for encountering Central Desert culture and maybe purchasing a dot painting.

After Alice, fly north to tropical **(4) Darwin** (p250), where you can pick up a didgeridoo and other Top End arts and crafts. Darwin is also your base for exploring the fascinating Tiwi Islands, Arnhem Land and **(5) Kakadu National Park** (p257).

TOP TO BOTTOM One Week

Leave the multicultural, breezy and laid-back vibe of **(1) Darwin** (p250) and take to the road to explore the Top End's scenic and cultural delights. There's great swimming to be had at **(2) Litchfield National**

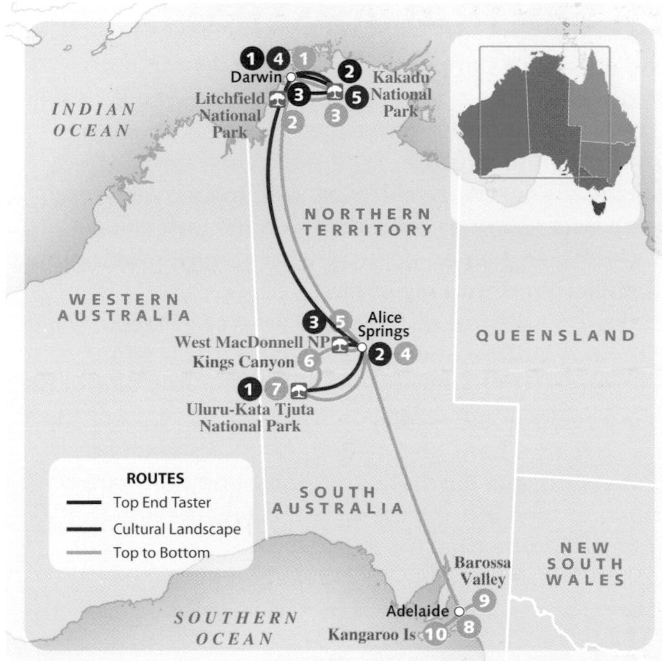

Park (p258) and amazing rock art, wildlife and Indigenous culture experiences at **(3) Kakadu National Park** (p257).

Return to Darwin and catch a flight or hop on the *Ghan* train to barrel across the desert country to **(4) Alice Springs** (p259), the frontier hub of central Australia. If you can manage it, take time out to explore **(5) West MacDonnell National Park** and **(6) Kings Canyon** (both p258) before continuing the journey south to **(7) Uluru-Kata Tjuta National Park** (p262).

From here you may have to return to Alice to catch a plane to South Australia's capital city, **(8) Adelaide** (p265), because Yulara's airport may not support services to Adelaide. The 'city of churches' makes a good base for exploring the wine region of the **(9) Barossa Valley** (p270), and you can dip a toe in the Southern Ocean at **(10) Kangaroo Island** (p269).

DISCOVER CENTRAL AUSTRALIA

From the Top End capital of Darwin to the leafy parks of South Australia's Adelaide there runs a road (for most of the way it's called the Stuart Hwy) and a railway (the passenger service is the famous *Ghan*). They pass through an ancient, little-populated land, which for many travellers is the real Australia: vast and apparently empty country, locals with wits as dry as their dusty boots, unfamiliar customs and landforms, and an ancient spiritual culture rubbing up against a more familiar Western way of life.

Darwin looks towards Asia and at the same time celebrates the region's Indigenous culture and amazing natural splendour. Kakadu offers an unsurpassed education in both. The Red Centre of Australia – the sand really is red – offers a different story. Here the harsh climate has shaped a bare beauty and deep spirituality that is lost on few who visit Uluru. Further south the pendulum swings back to the familiar; to wonderful wine-growing regions and that prescribed amount of Europe that is Adelaide.

NORTHERN TERRITORY

DARWIN

pop 70,005

Australia's only tropical capital, Darwin gazes out confidently across the Timor Sea. It's closer to Bali than to Bondi, and many from the southern states still see it as some strange frontier outpost or jumping-off point for Kakadu National Park.

Darwin's cosmopolitan mix – more than 50 nationalities are seamlessly represented – is typified by the wonderful Asian markets held throughout the dry season.

INFORMATION

Tourism Top End (☎ 08-8980 6000; www.tourismtopend.com.au; 6 Bennett St; 8.30am-5.30pm Mon-Fri, 9am-3pm Sat, 10am-3pm Sun) Stocks hundreds of brochures and can book tours or accommodation for businesses within its association.

SIGHTS

THE ESPLANADE

Bicentennial Park runs the length of Darwin's waterfront and Lameroo Beach – a sheltered cove popular in the '20s when it housed the saltwater baths, and traditionally a Larrakia camp area.

At Doctors Gully there's a remarkable fish-feeding frenzy daily at **Aquascene** (☎ 08-8981 7837; www.aquascene.com.au; 28 Doctors Gully Rd; adult/child/family $8/5/20; high tide, check website). Visitors, young and old, wade into the water and hand-feed hordes of mullet, catfish, batfish and big milkfish.

CROCOSAURUS COVE

If the tourists won't go out to see the crocs, then bring the crocs to the tourists. Right in the middle of Mitchell St, **Crocosaurus Cove** (☎ 08-8981 7522; www.crocosauruscove.com; 58 Mitchell St; adult/child $28/16; 8am-8pm, last admission 6pm) is as up close and personal as you'll ever want to get to these amazing creatures. Six of the largest crocs in captivity can be seen in state-of-the-art aquariums and pools. You can be lowered right into a pool with Snowy, a 600kg 'albino' saltie, in the transparent 'Cage of Death' (one/two people $120/160).

WHARF PRECINCT

Bold development of the Darwin Harbour is well underway. The first stage of the billion-dollar Darwin City Waterfront development features a new cruise-ship terminal, luxury hotels, boutique restaurants and shopping, and a wave pool. The old **Stokes Hill Wharf** is well worth an afternoon promenade.

MUSEUM & ART GALLERY OF THE NORTHERN TERRITORY

This superb **museum** and **gallery** (MAGNT; ☎ 08-8999 8201; Conacher St, Fannie Bay; admission free; ⌚ 9am-5pm Mon-Fri, 10am-5pm Sat & Sun) boasts beautifully presented galleries of Top End–centric exhibits. The Indigenous art collection is a highlight, with Tiwi Island carvings, Arnhem Land bark paintings and dot paintings from the desert.

GALLERIES

Darwin's commercial and public galleries are a fabulous (and free) way to appreciate the spirit of the Top End, both non-Indigenous and Indigenous.

Aboriginal Fine Arts (☎ 08-8981 1315; www.aaia.com.au; 1st fl, cnr Mitchell & Knuckey Sts; ⌚ 9am-5pm) Displays and sells art from Arnhem Land and the Central Desert region, including the work of high-profile artists such as 'Lofty' Bardayal Nadjamerrek.

Karen Brown Gallery (☎ 08-8981 9985; www.karenbrowngallery.com; 1/22 Mitchell St; ⌚ 9am-5pm Mon-Fri, to 3pm Sat) Commercial gallery specialising in changing exhibitions of contemporary Indigenous art.

Maningrida Arts & Culture (☎ 08-8981 4122; www.maningrida.com; Shop 1, 32 Mitchell St; ⌚ 9am-5pm Mon-Sat, 9am-3pm Sun) Features didgeridoos, weavings and paintings from the Kunibidji community at Maningrida on the banks of the Liverpool River, Arnhem Land.

Tiwi Art Network (☎ 08-8941 3593; www.tiwiart.com; 3/3 Vickers St, Parap; ⌚ 10am-5pm

GRANT DIXON

Mindil Beach, Darwin

CENTRAL DARWIN

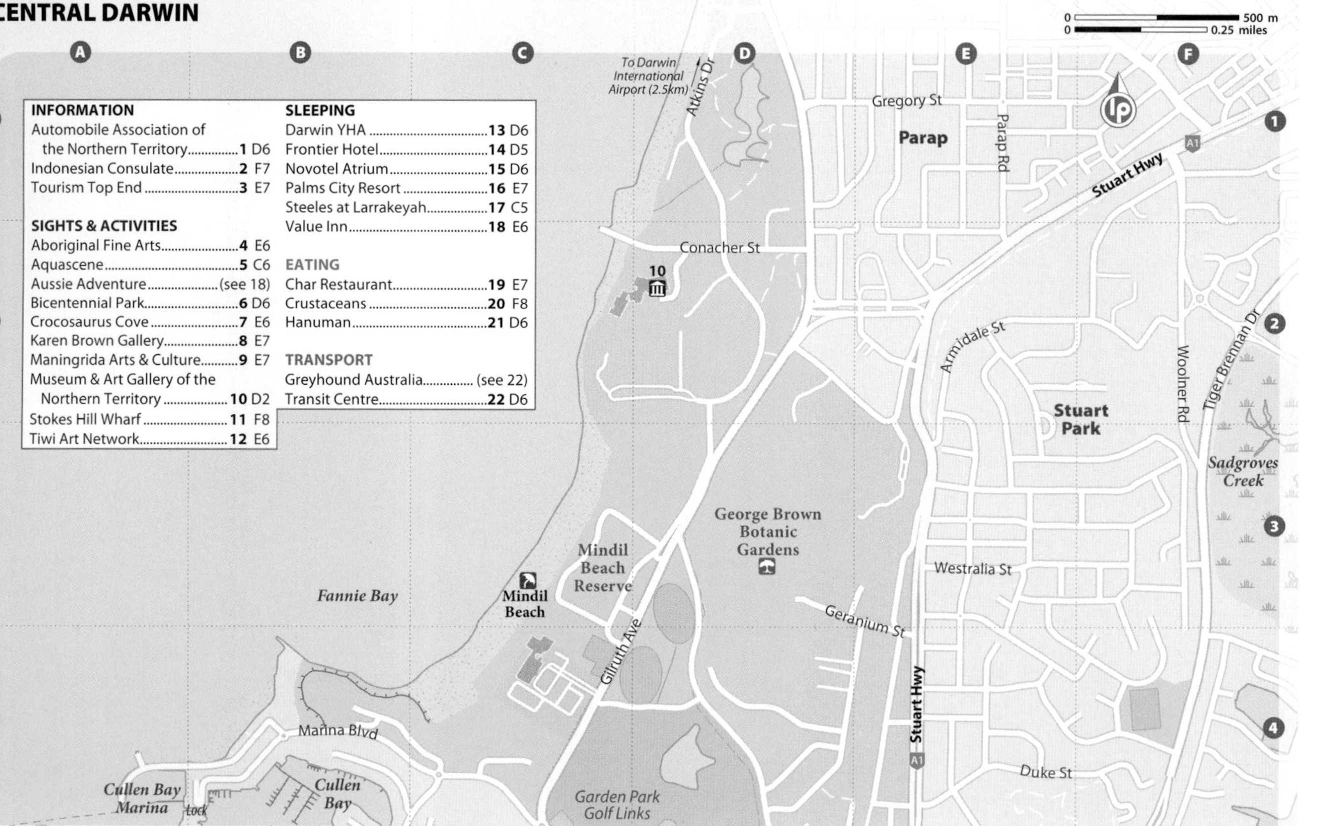

INFORMATION
Automobile Association of the Northern Territory........**1** D6
Indonesian Consulate........**2** F7
Tourism Top End........**3** E7

SIGHTS & ACTIVITIES
Aboriginal Fine Arts........**4** E6
Aquascene........**5** C6
Aussie Adventure........(see 18)
Bicentennial Park........**6** D6
Crocosaurus Cove........**7** E6
Karen Brown Gallery........**8** E7
Maningrida Arts & Culture........**9** E7
Museum & Art Gallery of the Northern Territory........**10** D2
Stokes Hill Wharf........**11** F8
Tiwi Art Network........**12** E6

SLEEPING
Darwin YHA........**13** D6
Frontier Hotel........**14** D5
Novotel Atrium........**15** D6
Palms City Resort........**16** E7
Steeles at Larrakeyah........**17** C5
Value Inn........**18** E6

EATING
Char Restaurant........**19** E7
Crustaceans........**20** F8
Hanuman........**21** D6

TRANSPORT
Greyhound Australia........(see 22)
Transit Centre........**22** D6

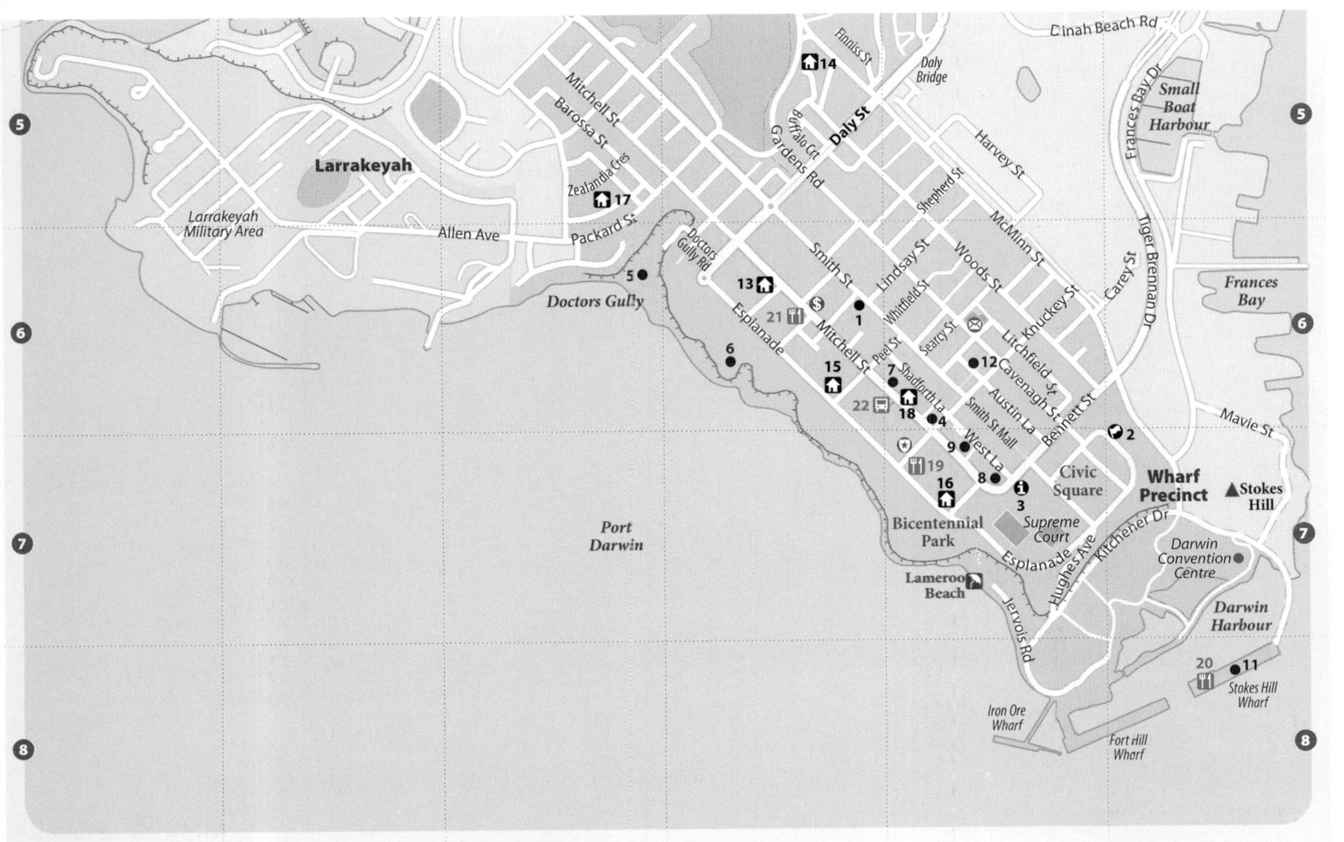
Larrakeyah
Larrakeyah Military Area
Allen Ave
Mitchell St
Barossa St
Zealandia Cres
Packard St
Doctors Gully Rd
Doctors Gully
Finniss St
Daly Bridge
Daly St
Buffalo Crt
Gardens Rd
Harvey St
Shepherd St
McMinn St
Smith St
Lindsay St
Woods St
Whitfield St
Searcy St
Knuckey St
Litchfield St
Cavenagh St
Austin La
Smith St Mall
West La
Bennett St
Peel St
Shadforth La
Mitchell St
Esplanade
Carey St
Tiger Brennan Dr
Dinah Beach Rd
Frances Bay Dr
Small Boat Harbour
Frances Bay
Mavie St
Civic Square
Wharf Precinct
Stokes Hill
Bicentennial Park
Supreme Court
Esplanade
Hughes Ave
Kitchener Dr
Darwin Convention Centre
Lameroo Beach
Jervois Rd
Darwin Harbour
Stokes Hill Wharf
Iron Ore Wharf
Fort Hill Wharf
Port Darwin
CENTRAL DARWIN
CENTRAL AUSTRALIA

Darwin Day Tours (☎ 1300 721 365; www.aussieadventure.com.au; afternoon city tour adult/child $59/30) Runs an afternoon city tour at 2pm that takes in all the major attractions, including Stokes Hill Wharf, the Museum & Art Gallery and East Point Reserve, and can be linked with a sunset harbour cruise ($99/48).

Sacred Earth Safaris (☎ 08-8981 8420; www.sacredearthsafaris.com.au) Multiday, small group camping tours to Kakadu, Arnhem Land and the Kimberley. Two-day 4WD Kakadu tour starts at $645; the five-day Top End tour is $1850.

Wallaroo Eco Tours (☎ 08-8983 2699; www.litchfielddaytours.com) Small-group tours to Litchfield National Park ($120).

Wilderness 4WD Adventures (☎ 1800 808 288, 08-8941 2161; www.wildernessadventures.com.au; 2/3 days $370/485) Small-group 4WD camping tours into Kakadu and further afield, visiting some out-of-the-way spots; all meals included.

SLEEPING

Darwin YHA (☎ 08-8981 5385; www.yha.com.au; 97 Mitchell St; dm $28-32, d $87;) One of the newer additions to the hostel scene, the YHA is in a converted motel, so all rooms (including dorms) have an en suite, and they're built around a decent pool. The kitchen and TV room are tiny, but there's the Brit pub-style Globetrotters Bar, with cheap meals and entertainment, next door.

Value Inn (☎ 08-8981 4733; www.valueinn.com.au; 50 Mitchell St; d from $140;) Also in the thick of the Mitchell St action but quiet and comfortable, Value Inn lives up to its name, especially out of season. En-suite rooms are small but sleep up to three and have fridge and TV.

our pick **Steeles at Larrakeyah** (☎ 08-8941 3636; www.steeles-at-larrakeyah.com.au; 4 Zealandia Cres, Larrakeyah; d $150-190, apt from $250;) With a perfect residential location midway between the city centre, Cullen Bay and Mindil Beach, the three rooms in this pleasant Spanish Mission–style home are equipped with air-con, TV, fridge and private entrance.

Palms City Resort (☎ 1800 829 211, 08-8982 9200; www.citypalms.com; 64 The Esplanade; motel d $175-185, villas d $190-285;) With palm-filled gardens and a fabulous location at the southern end of the Esplanade, Palms City lives up to its name. The villas, with solid timber finishes and louvred windows orbit a central pool, while the executive villas with outdoor spa are pure luxury.

Frontier Hotel (☎ 08-8981 5333; www.frontierdarwin.com.au; 3 Buffalo Crt; d $185, apt $225;) Towering above other places on the northern edge of town, this block of spacious, stylish rooms boasts excellent views, particularly from the 6th-floor apartments. The rooftop restaurant has stunning harbour views across the golf course.

Novotel Atrium (☎ 08-8941 0755; www.novoteldarwin.com.au; 100 The Esplanade; d $200-275, 2-bedroom apt from $295;) This four-star tower of contemporary style has slick hotel rooms and fine views from the upper floors.

EATING

our pick **Hanuman** (☎ 08-8941 3500; 28 Mitchell St; mains $16-32; lunch Mon-Fri, dinner daily) Sophisticated but not stuffy or pretentious, enticing aromas of innovative Indian and Thai Nonya dishes waft from the kitchen to the stylish open dining room and deck.

Char Restaurant (☎ 08-8981 4544; www.charrestaurant.com.au; cnr The Esplanade & Knuckey St; mains $25-40; lunch & dinner Mon-Fri, dinner Sat & Sun) In the historic Admiralty House on the Esplanade, Char is the latest

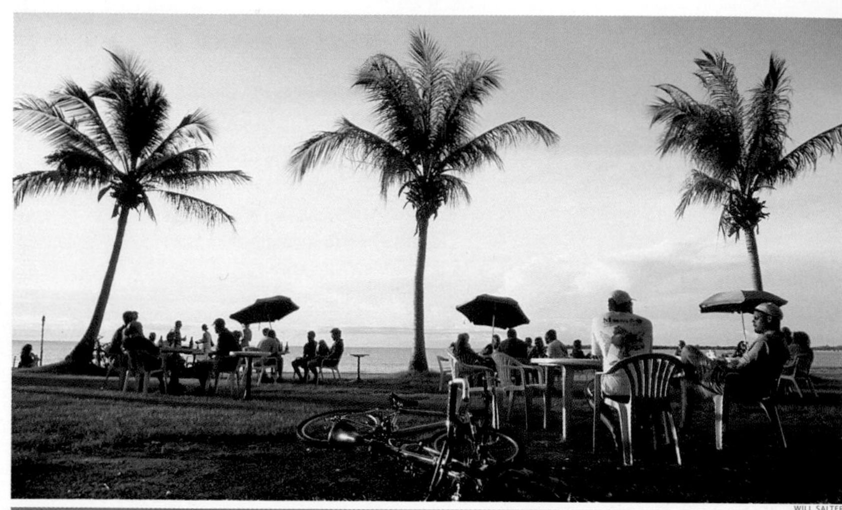
WILL SALTER

A Darwin sunset

addition to Darwin's culinary landscape. The speciality here is char-grilled steaks – aged, grain-fed and cooked to perfection – but there's also a range of seafood, a crab-and-croc lasagne and a thoughtful vegetarian menu.

Crustaceans (☎ 08-8981 8658; Stokes Hill Wharf; mains $25-55; 🕑 dinner Mon-Sat) This highly regarded but rather touristy seafood restaurant perches on the end of Stokes Hill Wharf, where diners can enjoy the sunset and views over fresh fish, mud crabs, lobster, crocodile and oysters.

DRINKING & ENTERTAINMENT

Drinking is big business in tropical Darwin and the city has dozens of pubs and terrace bars that make the most of sunny afternoons and balmy evenings. Virtually all bars double as restaurants. Mitchell St has the densest concentration of bars popular with travellers, all within a short walk of each other. While there is only a handful of nightclubs, you'll find something on every night of the week.

There's also a thriving arts and entertainment scene of theatre, film and concerts. Find up-to-date entertainment listings for live music and other attractions in the free guide *Off the Leash. Top End Arts* (www.topendarts.com.au) and *Darwin Community Arts* (www.darwincommunityarts.org.au) list events happening around town. Just about every pub/bar in town has some form of live music, mostly on Friday and Saturday nights.

GETTING THERE & AWAY

AIR

Domestic flights connect Darwin with all other Australian capital cities, as well as Alice Springs, Broome, Cairns, Kununurra and various regions throughout the Top End. A few international flights to Asian destinations also leave Darwin.

BUS

There's only one road in and out of Darwin and long-distance bus services are operated by **Greyhound Australia** (☎ 1300

473 946; www.greyhound.com.au; Transit Centre, 69 Mitchell St).

For Kakadu, there's a daily return service from Darwin to Cooinda ($74, 4½ hours) via Jabiru ($53, 3½ hours).

TRAIN

The famous *Ghan* train operates weekly (twice weekly May to July) between Adelaide and Darwin via Alice Springs. The Darwin terminus is located on Berrimah Rd, about 15km or 20 minutes from the city centre. Bookings (recommended) can be made through **Trainways** (☎ 13 21 47; www.trainways.com.au).

GETTING TO/FROM THE AIRPORT

Darwin International Airport (☎ 08-8920 1805) is about 12km northeast of the centre of town, and handles both international and domestic flights. **Darwin Airport Shuttle** (☎ 1800 358 945, 08-8981 5066; www.darwinairportshuttle.com.au) will pick up or drop off almost anywhere in the centre for $11. When leaving Darwin book a day before departure. A taxi fare into the centre is about $25.

KAKADU & ARNHEM LAND

Kakadu is much more than just a national park. It's an adventure into a natural and cultural landscape that almost defies description. Encompassing almost 20,000 sq km, it holds in its boundaries a spectacular ecosystem and a mind-blowing concentration of ancient rock art.

INFORMATION

Admission to the park is free: pick up an excellent *Visitor Guide & Maps* booklet from Bowali visitor information centre, or check online at www.environment.gov.au/parks/kakadu or www.kakadunationalpark.com. Fuel is available at Kakadu Resort, Cooinda and Jabiru. Jabiru has a shopping complex with a supermarket, post office, a Westpac bank and newsagency.

The excellent **Bowali Visitor Information Centre** (☎ 08-8938 1121; Kakadu Hwy, Jabiru; 8am-5pm) has walk-through displays that sweep you across the land, explaining Kakadu's ecology from both Indigenous and non-Indigenous perspectives.

TOURS

Most trips require some notification that you'll be joining them, so book at least a day ahead if possible; operators generally collect you from your accommodation. For tours departing Darwin, see p254.

Guluyambi (☎ 1800 089 113; www.guluyambi.com.au; adult/child $45/25; 9am, 11am, 1pm & 3pm May-Nov) Launch into an Aboriginal-led river cruise from the upstream boat ramp on the East Alligator River near Cahill's Crossing.

Kakadu Air (☎ 1800 089 113; www.kakaduair.com.au) Offers 30-minute/one-hour fixed-wing flights for $100/175 per person. Helicopter tours, though more expensive, give a more exciting aerial perspective. They cost from $195 (20 minutes) to $425 (70 minutes) per person.

Kakadu Animal Tracks (☎ 08-8979 0145; www.animaltracks.com.au; adult/child $165/125) Based at Cooinda, this outfit runs highly recommended tours combining a wildlife safari and Aboriginal cultural tour with an Indigenous guide. You'll see thousands of birds on the floodplains in the Dry, and get to hunt and gather, prepare and consume bush tucker and crunch on some green ants.

Kakadu Culture Camp (☎ 0428 792 048; www.kakaduculturecamp.com) Indigenous-owned and -operated cruises on Djarradjin

JOHN BANAGAN

Nourlangie Rock, Kakadu National Park

IF YOU LIKE...

If you like **Kakadu National Park** (p257) we think you will also like:

- **Litchfield National Park** (www.nt.gov.au/nreta/parks/find/litchfield.html) The waterfalls that pour off the edge of spectacular Tabletop Range are a highlight of this 1500-sq-km national park, feeding crystal-clear cascades and croc-free plunge pools.
- **Nitmiluk (Katherine Gorge) National Park** (www.nt.gov.au/nreta/parks/find/nitmiluk.html) Spectacular Katherine Gorge forms the backbone of this 2920-sq-km park, about 30km from Katherine. A series of 13 deep sandstone gorges have been carved out by the Katherine River on its journey from Arnhem Land to the Timor Sea. Take a guided cruise or paddle your own canoe.
- **Territory Wildlife Park** (☎ 08-8988 7200; www.territorywildlifepark.com.au; Cox Peninsula Rd; adult/child/concession/family $20/10/14/55; 🕑 8.30am-6pm, last admission 4pm) Much like the Alice Springs Desert Park, this showcases the best of Aussie wildlife in a state-of-the-art open-air zoo. Near Darwin.
- **West MacDonnell National Park** (www.nt.gov.au/nreta/parks/find/westmacdonnell.html) Spectacular gorge country west of Alice Springs offers excellent camping and bushwalking, including the renowned Larapinta Trail.
- **Watarrka (Kings Canyon) National Park** (www.nt.gov.au/nreta/parks/find/watarrka.html) This park is centred on the grand Kings Canyon (north of Uluru) – one of the best short walks in the Territory.

Billabong; two-hour night cruise ($49/30 per adult/child, at 6.20pm daily) and bush tucker and boat cruise ($179/119 per adult/child, from 5pm to 10pm Tuesday). Tours depart from Muirella Park camping ground.

Kakadu Gorge & Waterfall Tours (☎ 08-8979 0111; www.gagudju-dreaming.com;

adult/child $170/145) Operates 4WD tours to Jim Jim Falls.

Lord's Kakadu & Arnhemland Safaris (☎ **08-8948 2200; www.lords-safaris.com; adult/child $195/155)** One-day trip into Arnhem Land (Gunbalanya) from Jabiru visits Oenpelli with a guided walk around Injalak Hill. Lord's also has a range of multiday trips covering Kakadu and Arnhem Land departing from Darwin.

Magela Cultural & Heritage Tours (☎ **08-8979 2548; www.kakadutours.com.au; adult/child $235/188)** Aboriginal-owned and -operated day tour into northern Kakadu and Arnhem Land, including Injalak Hill and a cruise on Inkiyu Billabong. Pick-up from Jabiru.

Murdudjurl Kakadu (☎ **08-8979 0145; www.murdudjurlkakadu.com.au; tours $75)** Aboriginal-owned and -run cultural tour that takes you onto private land where you can interact with the traditional owners and learn about bush tucker, basket weaving and painting.

Yellow Water Cruises (☎ **08-8979 0145; www.gagudju-dreaming.com)** This is a highlight for many – cruise the South Alligator River and Yellow Water Billabong spotting wildlife. Purchase tickets from Gagudju Lodge, Cooinda, where a shuttle bus will deliver you to the departure point. Two-hour cruises ($70/49 per adult/child) depart at 6.45am, 9am and 4.30pm; 1½ hour cruises ($50/35) leave at 11.30am, 1.15pm and 2.45pm.

ALICE SPRINGS

pop 26,305

The iconic outback town of Alice Springs is no longer the rough-and-ready frontier settlement of legend, yet the vast surroundings of red desert and barren rocky ranges still underscore its remoteness. No matter where you arrive from, or how you get here, this thriving town makes a welcome halt to a long journey.

INFORMATION

Tourism Central Australia Visitor Information Centre (☎ **1800 645 199, 08-8952 5199; www.centralaustraliantourism.com; 60 Gregory Tce;** ⏲ **8.30am-5.30pm Mon-Fri, 9am-4pm Sat & Sun)** This very helpful centre can load you up with stacks of brochures and the free visitors guide.

SIGHTS

Like a kind of Noah's Ark, the **Alice Springs Desert Park** (☎ **08-8951 8788; www.alicespringsdesertpark.com.au; Larapinta Dr; adult/child/family $20/10/55;** ⏲ **7.30am-6pm, last entry 4.30pm)** has gathered up all the creatures of central Australia and put them on display in one accessible location. So, should the travel itinerary not allow weeks of camping in desert, woodlands and river ecologies to glimpse a spangled grunter or splendid fairy-wren, come here, where the sightings are guaranteed.

The **Araluen Cultural Precinct** (☎ **08-8951 1120; www.nt.gov.au/nreta/arts/ascp; cnr Larapinta Dr & Memorial Ave; precinct pass adult/child/family $10/7/30;** ⏲ **most attractions 10am-5pm)** combines a natural-history collection, a stellar arts centre, a cemetery, a sculpture garden, sacred sites and an aviation museum, all connected by a walking path. You can wander around freely outside, accessing the cemetery and grounds, but a precinct pass provides entry to the exhibitions and displays.

TOURS

AROUND ALICE & MACDONNELL RANGES

Alice Wanderer (☎ **1800 722 111; www.alicewanderer.com.au)** Runs day tours into the West MacDonnell Ranges as far as Glen

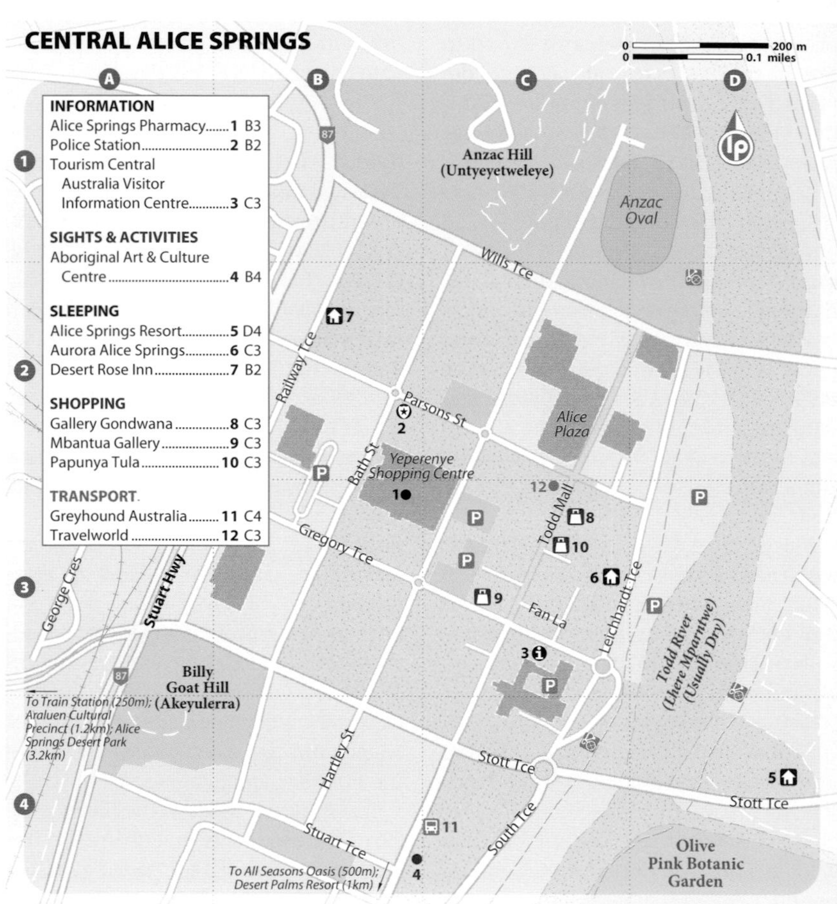

Helen Gorge, including morning tea and lunch (adult/child $105/75), and a half-day trip to Simpsons Gap and Standley Chasm ($62/42).

Dreamtime Tours (☎ 08-8955 5095; www.rstours.com.au; adult/child $84/42, self-drive $66/33; 🕑 8.30-11.30am) Runs the popular three-hour Dreamtime & Bushtucker Tour, where you meet Warlpiri Aboriginal people and learn a little about their traditions.

Foot Falcon (☎ 0427 569 531; www.footfalcon.com; 2hr guided walking tour $30) Excellent morning, evening and afternoon walking tours of the Alice covering Aboriginal history, historical buildings and tales of the early days.

ULURU, KINGS CANYON & PALM VALLEY

Ossies Outback 4WD Tours (☎ 08-8952 2308; www.ossies.com.au) Ossies promises to get you further off the beaten track than most other tours. There are several excellent 4WD tours, including a three-day trip that goes through Finke Gorge National Park to Kings Canyon and Uluru. It costs from $1650 depending on the accommodation option selected.

Palm Valley Tours (☎ 08-8952 0022; www.palmvalleytours.com.au) Day tours depart daily, taking in Palm Valley National Park and Hermannsburg ($135 including lunch); better two-day tours depart weekly ($325), spending longer in Palm Valley and traversing the Mereenie Loop.

Wayoutback (☎ 1300 551 510, 08-8952 4324; www.wayoutback.com.au) Runs three-day 4WD safaris that traverse 4WD tracks to Uluru and Kings Canyon for $565, and five-day safaris that top it up with the Palm Valley and West MacDonnells for $885.

SLEEPING

Desert Rose Inn (☎ 08-8952 1411; www.desertroseinn.com.au; 15 Railway Tce; budget s/d $45/50, motel r from $85;) Centrally located, the Desert Rose is a great alternative to the backpacker hostels with spotless budget rooms, a communal kitchen and lounge. Budget rooms are two share, with beds (no bunks) and a shower. There are other rooms with double beds, fridges and TVs, and motel rooms with full bathrooms.

All Seasons Oasis (☎ 08-8952 1444; www.allseasons.com.au; 10 Gap Rd; d from $110;) The well-appointed rooms here are conventional and comfortable and the numerous tour groups coming and going attest to its popularity. Facilities include a sports-themed bar, restaurant and wheelchair-accessible rooms. The large, sail-shaded pool surrounded by palms convincingly recreates the oasis experience.

Desert Palms Resort (☎ 08-8952 5977; 1800 678 037; www.desertpalms.com.au; 74 Barrett Dr; s/d villas from $120/135;) True to its name, this resort is padded with palms positioned for seclusion. The rows of Indonesian-style villas add to the exotic feel, with cathedral ceilings and tropical-style furnishings. Each has a kitchenette, tiny bathroom, TV, breakfast bar and private balcony.

Alice Springs Resort (☎ 08-8951 4545; www.voyages.com.au; 34 Stott Tce; d standard/superior/deluxe $150/180/240;) With a circle of double-storey buildings arranged around a swathe of lawns and gum trees, Alice Springs Resort has a relaxed country-club vibe.

Aurora Alice Springs (☎ 1800 089 644; 08-8950 6666; www.auroraresorts.com.au; 11 Leichhardt Tce; d standard/deluxe/executive $160/180/250;) Right in the town centre (the 'back' door opens out onto Todd Mall), this modern hotel has a relaxed atmosphere and an excellent restaurant, the Red Ochre Grill. Standard rooms are nondescript but well-appointed with fridge, phone and free in-house movies.

EATING & ENTERTAINMENT

Alice has a reasonable diversity of eateries, with most making an effort to cater for vegetarians. For fine dining the top-end hotel restaurants can't be beaten, and for a range of options for casual breakfasts, brunches and lunches, Todd Mall is the place to head. The gig guide in the entertainment section of the *Centralian Advocate* lists what's on in and around town.

SHOPPING

Alice is the centre for Indigenous arts from all over central Australia. The places owned and run by community art centres ensure that a better slice of the proceeds goes to the artist and artist's community.

Gallery Gondwana (☎ 08-8953 1577; www.gallerygondwana.com.au; 43 Todd Mall; 9.30am-6pm Mon-Fri, 10am-5pm Sat) Gondwana is a well-established private gallery, recognised for dealing directly with community art centres and artists.

Mbantua Gallery (☎ 08-8952 5571; www.mbantua.com.au; 71 Gregory Tce; 9am-6pm

Mon-Fri, 9.30am-5pm Sat) This privately owned gallery, which extends through to Todd Mall, includes a cafe and extensive exhibits of works from the renowned Utopia region, as well as watercolour landscapes from the Namatjira school.

Papunya Tula Artists (☎ **08-8952 4731; www.papunyatula.com.au; 78 Todd Mall;** 🕑 **9am-5pm Mon-Fri, 10am-2pm Sat)** The Western Desert art movement began at Papunya Tula in 1971, and today this Aboriginal-owned gallery displays some of this most sought-after art.

GETTING THERE & AWAY

AIR

Alice Springs is well connected with **Qantas** (☎ **13 13 13, 08-8950 5211; www.qantas.com.au)** and **Tiger Airways** (☎ **08-9335 3033; www.tigerairways.com.au)** operating daily flights to/from capital cities.

BUS

Greyhound Australia (☎ **1300 473 946; www.greyhound.com.au; Shop 3, 113 Todd St;** 🕑 **office 8.30-11.30am, 1.30-4pm Mon-Fri)** has regular services from Alice Springs (check website for timetables). Buses arrive at, and depart from, the Greyhound office in Todd St.

Austour (☎ **1800 335009; www.austour.com.au)** runs the cheapest daily connections between Alice Springs and Yulara ($120/60 per adult/child) and Kings Canyon ($110/60). **AAT Kings** (☎ **08-8952 1700; www.aatkings.com)** also run between Alice Springs and Yulara (adult/child $135/68), and between Kings Canyon and Alice Springs ($138/69).

TRAIN

In Alice, tickets for the classic, Australia-crossing *Ghan* can be booked through **Trainways** (☎ **13 21 47; www.trainways.com.au)** or **Travelworld** (☎ **08-8953 0488; 40 Todd Mall).**

The train station is at the end of George Cres off Larapinta Dr.

ULURU-KATA TJUTA NATIONAL PARK

One of the world's most recognised natural attractions holds pride of place in this fascinating national park. Fascinating, because no picture conveys entirely the multidimensional grandeur of Uluru, or the equally impressive Kata Tjuta (the Olgas). And fascinating because this entire area is of cultural significance to the traditional owners, the Pitjantjatjara and Yankuntjatjara Aboriginal peoples (who refer to themselves as Anangu). The Anangu officially own the national park, which is leased to Parks Australia and jointly administered.

INFORMATION

The **park (www.environment.gov.au/parks/uluru; adult/child $25/free)** is open from half an hour before sunrise to sunset daily (varying between 5am to 9pm November to March and 6.30am to 7.30pm April to October). Entry permits are valid for three days and available at the drive-through entry station on the road from Yulara.

Uluru-Kata Tjuta Cultural Centre (☎ **08-8956 3138;** 🕑 **7am-6pm, information desk 8am-noon & 1-5pm)** is 1km before Uluru on the road from Yulara and should be your first stop.

TOURS

Most tour operators have desks at Yulara's Tour & Information Centre (p264) and depart from the resort unless otherwise stated.

BUS TOURS

The small-group operator **Discovery Ecotours** (☎ **08-8956 2563; www.ecotours.com.au)** runs a five-hour Uluru circum-

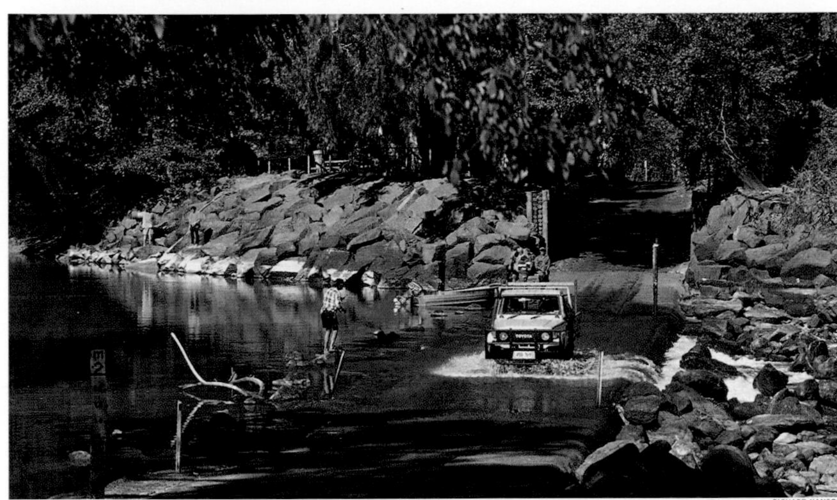

RICHARD I'ANSON

Four-wheel driving in Kakadu National Park

ambulation and breakfast for $115/86 per adult/child; Spirit of Uluru is a four-hour, vehicle-based version for the same price. The Kata Tjuta & Dunes Tour includes a walk into Olga Gorge and sunset at Kata Tjuta for $97/73.

CAMEL TOURS

Uluru Camel Tours (**☎ 08-8956 2444; www.ananguwaai.com.au; short rides adult/child $10/5; ⌚ 10.30am-2.30pm**) provides the opportunity to view Uluru and Kata Tjuta from a distance in a novel way: atop a camel ($65, 45 minutes). Most popular, though, are the Camel to Sunrise tours ($99, 2½ hours) and the sunset equivalent with champagne or beer ($99).

CULTURAL TOURS

Anangu Tours (**☎ 08-8956 2123; www.ananguwaai.com.au**), owned and operated by Anangu from the Mutitjulu community, offers a range of trips led by an Anangu guide and gives an insight into the land through Anangu eyes; tours depart from the cultural centre (p262).

ULURU (AYERS ROCK)

Nothing in Australia is as readily identifiable as Uluru (Ayers Rock). No matter how many times you've seen it on postcards, nothing prepares you for the hulk on the horizon – so solitary and impressive. Closer inspection reveals a wondrous pitted and contoured surface concealing numerous sacred sites of particular significance to the Anangu people.

There are **walking tracks** around Uluru, and ranger-led walks explain the area's plants, wildlife, geology and mythology. All the walks are flat and suitable for wheelchairs. Several areas of spiritual significance to Anangu people are off limits; these are marked with fences and signs.

About halfway between Yulara and Uluru, the **sunset viewing area** has plenty of car and coach parking for that familiar postcard view. The **Talnguru Nyakunytjaku viewing area** should be operational by the time you read this. This new area provides a different perspective of Uluru to the postcard profile, and will be of interest for more than just sunrise.

RICHARD I'ANSON

Kata Tjuta (The Olgas)

KATA TJUTA (THE OLGAS)

A striking group of domed rocks huddle together about 35km west of Uluru to form Kata Tjuta (the Olgas). There are 36 domed rocks shoulder to shoulder forming deep valleys and steep-sided gorges. Most visitors find them as captivating as their prominent neighbour.

The main walking track here is the **Valley of the Winds**, a 7.4km loop trail (two to four hours) that traverses varying desert terrain and yields wonderful views of surreal boulders. It's not particularly arduous, but wear sturdy shoes, and take plenty of water and sun protection.

The short signposted track beneath towering rock walls into pretty **Walpa Gorge** (2.6km return, 45 minutes) is especially beautiful in the afternoon, when sunlight floods the gorge.

There's a picnic and sunset-viewing area with toilet facilities just off the access road a few kilometres west of the base of Kata Tjuta. Like Uluru, the Olgas are at their glorious, blood-red best at sunset.

YULARA (AYERS ROCK RESORT)

pop 2080 (including Mutitjulu)

Yulara is the service village for the Uluru-Kata Tjuta National Park and has effectively turned one of the world's least hospitable regions into an easy and comfortable place to visit. Lying just outside the national park, 20km from Uluru and 53km from Kata Tjuta, the complex is the closest base for exploring the area's renowned attractions. The village includes a bank, a petrol station, emergency services, the resort's four hotels, apartments, a lodge, a camping ground and a supermarket.

Even though there are almost 5000 beds, it's wise to make a reservation, especially during school holidays. Bookings can be made through **central reservations** (☎ 1300 134 044; www.ayersrockresort.com.au).

GETTING THERE & AWAY

Connellan airport is about 4km north from Yulara. **Qantas** (☎ 13 13 13; www.qantas.com.au) has direct flights from Alice Springs, Melbourne, Perth, Adelaide and Sydney.

Daily shuttle connections (listed as mini-tours) between Alice Springs and Yulara are run by **AAT Kings** (☎ 1300 556100; www.aatkings.com) and cost adult/child $135/68. **Austour** (☎ 1800 335009; www.austour.com.au) run the cheapest daily connections between Alice Springs and Uluru ($120/60).

The road from Alice to Yulara is sealed, with regular food and petrol stops along the way. Yulara is 441km from Alice Springs (241km west of Erldunda on the Stuart Hwy), and the direct journey takes four to five hours.

SOUTH AUSTRALIA

ADELAIDE

pop 1.2 million

Sophisticated, cultured, neat casual – this is the self-image Adelaide projects, a nod to the days of free colonisation without the 'penal colony' taint.

INFORMATION

Adelaide Visitor Information Kiosk (☎ 08-8203 7611; Rundle Mall; 10am-5pm Mon-Thu, to 8pm Fri, to 3pm Sat & Sun) Adelaide-specific information, and free city-centre walking tours at 9.30am Monday to Friday; at the King William St end of the mall.

SIGHTS

Spend a few hushed hours in the vaulted, parquetry-floored **Art Gallery of South Australia** (☎ 08-8207 7000; www.artgallery.sa.gov.au; North Tce; admission free; 10am-5pm), which represents the big names in Australian art. Permanent exhibitions include Australian, modern Australian, contemporary Indigenous, Asian, Islamic and European art (with 20 bronze Rodins!).

The **South Australian Museum** (☎ 08-8207 7368; www.samuseum.sa.gov.au; North Tce; admission free; 10am-5pm) digs into Australia's natural history, with special exhibits on whales and Antarctic explorer Sir Douglas Mawson, and an Aboriginal Cultures Gallery displaying artefacts of the Ngarrindjeri people of the Coorong and lower Murray.

SLEEPING

our pick **My Place** (☎ 08-8221 5299; www.adelaidehostel.com.au; 257 Waymouth St; dm incl breakfast $24, d incl breakfast & TV $64) The antithesis of the big formal operations, My Place has a welcoming, personal vibe and is just a stumble from the Grace Emily, arguably Adelaide's best pub!

Jasper Motor Inn (☎ 08-8271 0377; www.jaspermotorinn.com.au; 17 Jasper St, Hyde Park; s & d $85-120) Just beyond the city (3.5km), Jasper is off King William Rd in upper-crust Hyde Park. It's a low-slung '70s number without much style, but on a super-quiet street – far preferable to the traffic rumble of Glen Osmond Rd's 'Motel Alley'. Great value.

City Parklands Motel (☎ 08-8223 1444; www.citypark.com.au; 471 Pulteney St; d with/without bathroom from $120/99, tr/f from $130/150) Immaculate bathrooms, leather lounges, winsome French prints and an easy walk to the Hutt St restaurants. Free parking, bike hire, DVDs and wireless internet, too.

Mercure Grosvenor Hotel (☎ 08-8407 8888; www.mercuregrosvenorhotel.com.au; 125 North Tce; d $110-270) This place was built in 1918, but there's not much old-world vibe left inside – slick modern rooms and friendly staff compensate. Kids under 16 stay free.

Royal Coach Motor Inn (☎ 08-8362 5676; www.royalcoach.com.au; 24 Dequetteville Tce, Kent Town; d from $155, extra adult/child $15/10) Three-storey brick motel

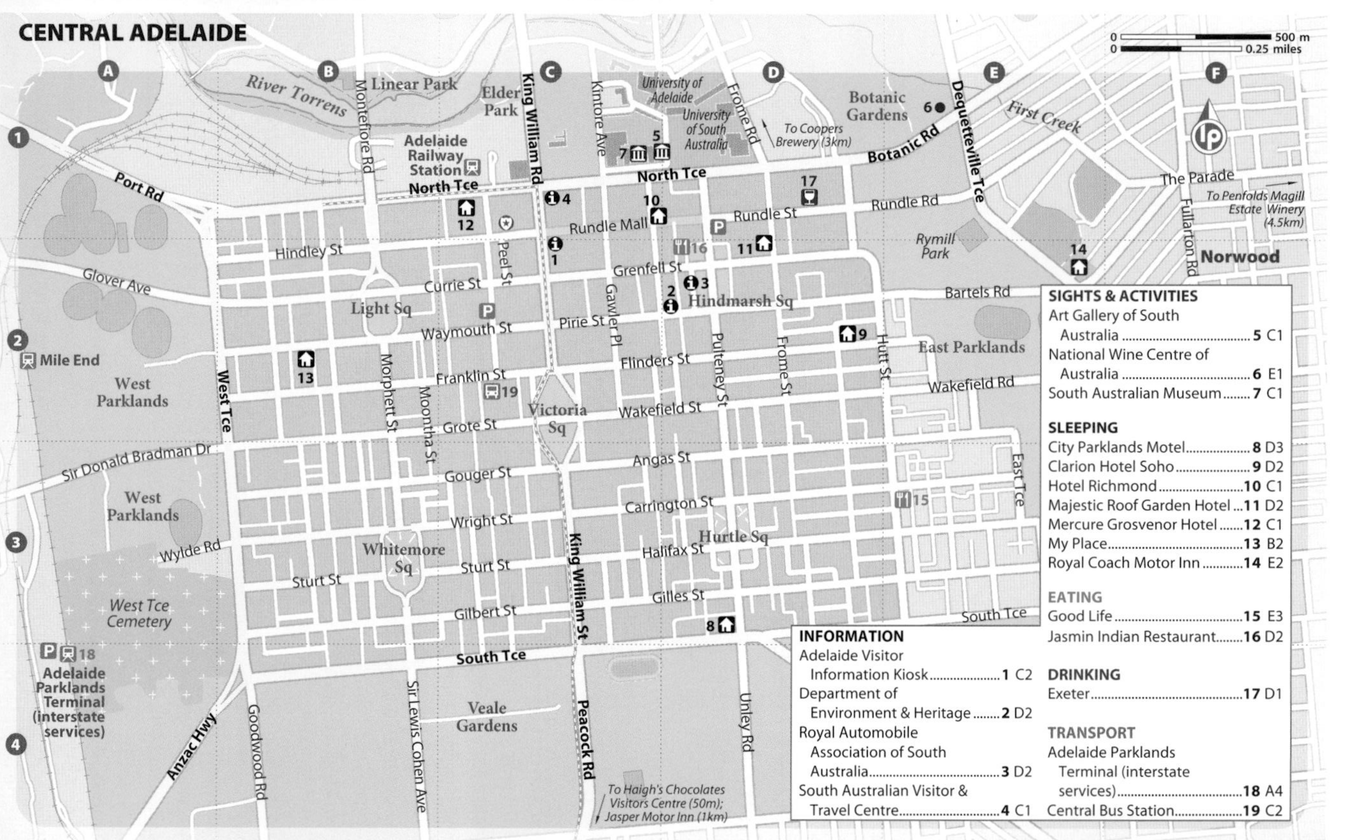
CENTRAL ADELAIDE
0 500 m
0 0.25 miles
SIGHTS & ACTIVITIES
Art Gallery of South Australia 5 C1
National Wine Centre of Australia 6 E1
South Australian Museum 7 C1
SLEEPING
City Parklands Motel 8 D3
Clarion Hotel Soho 9 D2
Hotel Richmond 10 C1
Majestic Roof Garden Hotel 11 D2
Mercure Grosvenor Hotel 12 C1
My Place 13 B2
Royal Coach Motor Inn 14 E2
EATING
Good Life 15 E3
Jasmin Indian Restaurant 16 D2
DRINKING
Exeter 17 D1
TRANSPORT
Adelaide Parklands Terminal (interstate services) 18 A4
Central Bus Station 19 C2
INFORMATION
Adelaide Visitor Information Kiosk 1 C2
Department of Environment & Heritage 2 D2
Royal Automobile Association of South Australia 3 D2
South Australian Visitor & Travel Centre 4 C1
River Torrens
Linear Park
Elder Park
Montefiore Rd
King William Rd
Kintore Ave
University of Adelaide
University of South Australia
Frome Rd
To Coopers Brewery (3km)
Botanic Gardens
Botanic Rd
Dequetteville Tce
First Creek
The Parade
To Penfolds Magill Estate Winery (4.5km)
Fullarton Rd
Norwood
Port Rd
Adelaide Railway Station
North Tce
Rundle Mall
Rundle St
Rundle Rd
Rymill Park
Hindley St
Glover Ave
Currie St
Peel St
Grenfell St
Hindmarsh Sq
Bartels Rd
Light Sq
Waymouth St
Pirie St
Gawler Pl
Pulteney St
Frome St
Hutt St
East Parklands
Mile End
West Parklands
West Tce
Morphett St
Moontha St
Franklin St
Flinders St
Wakefield Rd
Victoria Sq
Grote St
Wakefield St
Sir Donald Bradman Dr
Angas St
Gouger St
East Tce
Carrington St
Wright St
Whitemore Sq
Hurtle Sq
Wylde Rd
Halifax St
Sturt St
King William St
West Tce Cemetery
Gilles St
Gilbert St
South Tce
Adelaide Parklands Terminal (interstate services)
Veale Gardens
Anzac Hwy
Goodwood Rd
Sir Lewis Cohen Ave
Peacock Rd
Unley Rd
To Haigh's Chocolates Visitors Centre (50m); Jasper Motor Inn (1km)

JOHN HAY

Wine country, Barossa Valley (p270)

↘ WINE, BEER & CHOCOLATE

Check out the self-guided, interactive 'Wine Discovery Journey' exhibition, paired with tastings of Australian wines, at the very sexy **National Wine Centre of Australia**.

The 100-year-old **Penfolds Magill Estate Winery** is home to Australia's best known wine – the legendary Grange.

You can't possibly come to Adelaide without entertaining thoughts of touring the **Coopers Brewery**. Bookings required; minimum age 18.

If you've got a chocolate problem, get guilty at the iconic **Haigh's Chocolates Visitors Centre**. Tours run at 11am, 1pm and 2pm Monday to Saturday; bookings essential.

Things you need to know National Wine Centre of Australia (☎ **08-8303 3355; www.wineaustralia.com.au; cnr Botanic & Hackney Rds; exhibition free, tastings $8-16;** ⏰ **10am-5pm**); Penfolds Magill Estate Winery (☎ **08-8301 5569; www.penfolds.com.au; 78 Penfolds Rd, Magill; tastings free, mains $42-45;** ⏰ **tastings 10am-5pm, lunch Fri, dinner Tue-Sun**); Coopers Brewery (☎ **08-8440 1800; www.coopers.com.au; 461 South Rd, Regency Park; 1½hr tours per person $20;** ⏰ **tours 1pm Tue-Fri**); Haigh's Chocolates Visitors Centre (☎ **08-8372 7070; www.haighschocolates.com; 154 Greenhill Rd, Parkside; admission free;** ⏰ **8.30am-5.30pm Mon-Fri, 9am-5pm Sat**)

monster just beyond the parklands at the eastern end of town, with good facilities and late-'90s decor. There's a restaurant downstairs, but Rundle St is just a 10-minute walk away.

Hotel Richmond (☎ **08-8223 4044; www.hotelrichmond.com.au; 128 Rundle Mall; d from $165;** ❄ 💻) This opulent hotel in a grand 1920s building in the middle of Rundle Mall has mod-minimalist rooms with king-sized beds, marble bathrooms and American oak and Italian furnishings. Rates include breakfast, movies, papers and gym passes. Great value!

our pick Clarion Hotel Soho (☎ 08-8412 5600; www.clarionhotelsoho.com.au; 264 Flinders St; d $170-590;) Thirty very plush suites (some with spas, most with balconies) are complemented by sumptuous linen, 24-hour room service, iPod docks, Italian marble bathrooms, jet pool, a fab restaurant… Rates take a tumble midweek.

Majestic Roof Garden Hotel (☎ 08-8100 4400; www.majestichotels.com.au; 55 Frome St; d from $199, extra person $30, parking per day $24;) Everything looks new in this place – a speck of dirt would feel lonely. Book a room facing Frome St for a balcony and the best views, or take a bottle of wine up to the rooftop garden to watch the sunset.

EATING

Eating out in Adelaide is a divine pleasure, with reasonable prices, multicultural offerings and high standards. Foodies flock to Gouger St for **Chinatown**, the food-filled corridors of Central Market, and eclectic international eateries. Rundle St in the East End is the place for all-day alfresco cafes and people watching; nearby Hutt St has some quality food rooms. Artsy-alternative Hindley St – Adelaide's dirty little secret – has a smattering of good eateries and some great pubs (see www.beerand burger.info for reviews of pub meals).

Good Life (☎ 08-8376 5900; 1st fl, cnr Jetty Rd & Moseley St; pizzas $13-37; lunch Tue-Fri & Sun, dinner daily) At this brilliant organic pizzeria above the Jetty Rd tram-scape, thin crusts are stacked with tasty toppings like free-range roast duck, Spencer Gulf 'monster' prawns and spicy Angaston salami. Also at 170 Hutt St in the city (☎ 08-8223 2618).

Jasmin Indian Restaurant (☎ 08-8223 7837; basement, 31 Hindmarsh Sq; mains $24- 26; lunch Thu & Fri, dinner Tue-Sat) Magical North Indian curries and consummately professional staff (they might remember your name from when you ate here in 1997). There's nothing too surprising about the menu, but it's done to absolute perfection. Bookings essential.

DRINKING & ENTERTAINMENT

For a true Adelaide experience, head for the bar and order a schooner of Coopers – the local brew – or a glass of South Australia's impressive wine. Rundle St has a few iconic pubs, while along Hindley St in the West End, grunge and sleaze collides with student energy and groovy bars. Most bars are closed on Mondays.

The free monthly **Adelaide Review** (www.adelaidereview.com) features theatre and gallery listings, and on Thursday and Saturday the **Advertiser** (www.theadvertiser .news.com.au) lists events, cinema programs and gallery details.

Exeter (☎ 08-8223 2623; 246 Rundle St; 11am-1am Mon, to 2am Tue & Wed, to 3am Thu-Sat, to midnight Sun) The best pub in the city, this legendary boozer attracts a kooky mix of postwork, punk and uni drinkers, shaking the day off their backs. Music most nights; curry nights Wednesday and Thursday.

GETTING THERE & AWAY

Adelaide is connected by regular air services to all Australian capitals.

Adelaide's new **Central Bus Station** (85 Franklin St) has ticket offices and terminals for all major interstate and statewide services. For online bus timetables see the **Bus SA** (www.bussa.com.au) website.

The interstate train terminal is **Adelaide Parklands Terminal** (☎ 13 21 47; www.gsr .com.au; Railway Tce, Keswick), 1km southwest of the city centre.

GETTING TO/FROM THE AIRPORT & TRAIN STATION

Skylink (☎ 08-8413 6196; www.skylinkadelaide.com; one way adult/child $8/3) runs around 20 shuttles between 5.50am and 9.15pm to/from Adelaide airport via Adelaide Parklands interstate train station (adult/child one way $5/3). Bookings essential for all city pick-up locations other than the Central Bus Station.

KANGAROO ISLAND

From Cape Jervis, car ferries chug across the swells of the Backstairs Passage to Kangaroo Island. Long devoid of tourist trappings, the island these days is a booming destination for fans of wilderness and wildlife – it's a veritable zoo of seals, birds, dolphins, echidnas and roos.

INFORMATION

Kangaroo Island Gateway visitors centre (☎ 08-8553 1185; www.tourkangarooisland.com.au; Howard Dr; 9am-5pm Mon-Fri, 10am-4pm Sat & Sun) Just outside Penneshaw on the road to Kingscote, this centre is stocked with brochures and maps. It also books accommodation and sells park entry tickets and passes.

ACTIVITIES

The safest **swimming** is along the north coast, where the water is warmer and there are fewer rips than down south. The easiest beaches to access are Emu Bay, Stokes Bay, Snelling Beach and Western River Cove.

For **surfing**, hit the uncrowded swells along the south coast. Pennington Bay has strong, reliable breaks; Vivonne Bay and Hanson Bay in the southwest also serve up some tasty waves.

There's plenty to see under your own steam on KI. Check out www.tourkangarooisland.com.au/wildlife/walks.aspx for info on **bushwalks** from 1km to 18km.

The waters around KI harbour 230 species of fish, soft and hard corals and around 60 shipwrecks – perfect for **snorkelling** and **diving**. For charters, contact **Kangaroo Island Diving Safaris** (☎ 0427

ROSS BARNETT

Australian sea lions, Seal Bay, Kangaroo Island

102 387; www.kidivingsafaris.com), which runs boat dives with equipment ($290 per day) and boat-based snorkelling ($137 per day).

Kangaroo Island Outdoor Action (☎ 08-8559 4296, 0428 822 260; www.kioutdooraction.com.au; Jetty Rd, Vivonne Bay) rents out sandboards ($29 for four hours) and toboggans ($39) to skid down the dunes at Little Sahara, plus single/double kayaks ($39/69).

TOURS

See the Kangaroo Island Gateway visitors centre or www.tourkangarooisland.com.au for comprehensive tour listings. Day tours from Adelaide are hectic – stay at least one night on the island if you can. Multiday tours generally include meals and accommodation. A few operators:

Adventure Tours (☎ 1300 654 604; www.adventuretours.com.au) Popular two-day tours ($425) ex-Adelaide with lots of walking and wildlife.

Exceptional Kangaroo Island (☎ 08-8553 9119; www.exceptionalkangarooisland.com) Small group, deluxe 4WD day tours ($348), with a wildlife or Flinders Chase focus. Tours depart KI.

Kangaroo Island Marine Tours (☎ 0427 315 286; www.kimarinetours.com) Water tours from one hour ($55) to a full day ($275), including swimming with dolphins, visiting seal colonies and access to remote areas of KI.

Sealink (☎ 13 13 01; www.sealink.com.au) The ferry company runs a range of KI-highlight day tours ($62 to $131) departing Adelaide or Kingscote. Overnight backpacker tours, self-drive tours and multiday tours also available.

SLEEPING

Self-contained cottages, B&Bs and beach houses abound, most charging $150 per night or more per double, and most require guests stay a minimum of two-nights.

Accommodation booking resources include the Kangaroo Island Gateway visitors centre (p269), Sealink (below) and **Century 21** (☎ 08-8553 2688; www.century21.com.au/kangarooisland; 66 Dauncey St, Kingscote).

GETTING THERE & AWAY

For daily flights (one way from $77 online) between Adelaide and Kingscote, contact **Regional Express Airlines** (Rex; ☎ 13 17 13; www.regionalexpress.com.au) or **Air South** (☎ 1300 247 768, 08-8234 4988; www.airsouth.com.au).

A car ferry operates between Cape Jervis and Penneshaw. **Sealink** (☎ 13 13 01; www.sealink.com.au) runs at least three ferries each way daily (one-way adult/child/concession $43/24/36, bicycles/motorcycles/cars $15/30/84, 45 minutes).

BAROSSA VALLEY

With hot, dry summers and cool, moderate winters, the Barossa is one of the world's great wine regions – an absolute must for anyone with even the slightest interest in a good drop. It's a compact valley – just 25km long – yet it manages to produce 21% of Australia's wine, mostly big, luscious reds. The 80-plus wineries here are within easy reach of one another, and make a no-fuss day trip from Adelaide, just 65km to the southwest.

INFORMATION

Barossa visitor centre (☎ 1300 852 982, 08-8563 0600; www.barossa.com; 66-68 Murray St, Tanunda; 9am-5pm Mon-Fri, 10am-4pm Sat & Sun;) Has the lowdown on the valley, plus internet access, bike hire and accommodation bookings.

MTMEDIA

Seppeltsfield vineyard,

IF YOU LIKE...

If you like the **Barossa Valley** (p270) we think you might also like:

- **Adelaide Hills** One of South Australia's (SA) cooler climates, just east of Adelaide, is perfect for producing some complex and truly top-notch white wines, especially Chardonnay and Sauvignon Blanc.
- **McLaren Vale** Flanked by the wheat-coloured Willunga Scarp, 'The Vale' rivals the Barossa as SA's most-visited wine region. Just 40 minutes south of Adelaide, it's an easy cruise to SA's version of the Mediterranean.
- **Coonawarra** When it comes to spicy Cabernet Sauvignon, it's just plain foolish to dispute the virtues of the Coonawarra Wine Region – the *terra rossa* (red earth) region between Penola and Naracoorte. The climate also produces some irresistible Shiraz and Chardonnay.
- **Clare Valley** Despite a warm climate, the Clare Valley's cool microclimates (around rivers, creeks and gullies) noticeably affect the wines, enabling Clare Valley whites to be laid down for long periods and still be brilliant. The valley produces some of the best Riesling going around, plus grand Semillon and Shiraz.

TOURS

The Barossa visitor centre has details on organised tours, including the following.

Barossa Epicurean Tours (☎ 08-8564 2191, 0402 989 647; www.barossatours.com.au; full-/half-day tours $90/60) These folk offer good-value, small-group tours visiting the wineries of your choice and Mengler Hill Lookout.

Barossa Experience Tours (☎ 08-8563 3248, 0418 809 313; www.barossavalleytours.com; full-/half-day tours $105/75) A local small-group operator who will whisk you around the major sites. The Food & Wine Experience ($210) includes lunch, cheese tastings and a glass of plonk.

Barossa Wine Lovers Tours (☎ 08-8263 1633; tours incl lunch from $65) This tour takes

TOP FIVE BAROSSA VALLEY WINERIES

From the moment Johann Gramp planted the valley's first grapes on his property at Jacob's Creek in 1847, the Barossa Valley was destined to become a major Australian wine region. The valley is best known for Shiraz, with Riesling the dominant white. There are around 80 vineyards here and 60 cellar doors, ranging from boutique wine rooms to monstrous complexes. Five of the best:

- **Henschke** (☎ 08-8564 8223; www.henschke.com.au; Henschke Rd, Keyneton; 9am-4.30pm Mon-Fri, to noon Sat) Henschke, 11km southeast of Angaston in the Eden Valley, is known for its iconic Hill of Grace red, but most of the wines here are classics.
- **Penfolds** (☎ 08-8568 9408; www.penfolds.com.au; Tanunda Rd, Nuriootpa; 10am-5pm) You know the name. Book ahead for the 'Make your own Blend' tour ($55) or 'Taste of Grange' tour ($150), which allows you to slide some Grange Hermitage across your lips.
- **Peter Lehmann Wines** (☎ 08-8563 2100; www.peterlehmannwines.com.au; Para Rd, Tanunda; 9.30am-5pm Mon-Fri, 10.30am-4.30pm Sat & Sun) The multiaward-winning Shiraz and Riesling vintages here (oh, and the Semillon) are probably the most consistent and affordable wines in the Barossa. Buy a bottle and have a picnic in the grounds.
- **Rockford Wines** (☎ 08-8563 2720; www.rockfordwines.com.au; Krondorf Rd, Tanunda; 11am-5pm) This 1850s winery uses traditional winemaking methods and produces a small range of superb wines, including sparkling reds. The Black Shiraz is a smooth and spicy killer; the cellar door in a beautiful old stable is picturesque.
- **St Hallett** (☎ 08-8563 7000; www.sthallett.com.au; St Halletts Rd, Tanunda; 10am-5pm) Using only Barossa grapes, St Hallet produces reasonably priced but consistently good whites (try the Poacher's Blend) and the excellent Gamekeeper's Reserve Shiraz-Grenache. Unpretentious and great value for money.

in several wineries, lookouts, shops and heritage buildings – a good blend.

GETTING THERE & AROUND

There are several routes from Adelaide; the most direct is along Main North Rd through Elizabeth and Gawler. If you're coming from the east and want to tour the wineries before hitting Adelaide, the scenic route via Springton and Eden Valley to Angaston is a sure bet.

Barossa Valley Coaches (☎ 08-8564 3022; www.bvcoach.com) runs services between Adelaide and Angaston. Buses ply the return route twice daily (once on Sunday), stopping at Tanunda ($18, 1¾ hours), Nuriootpa ($20, two hours) and Angaston ($21, 2¼ hours).

↘ WESTERN AUSTRALIA

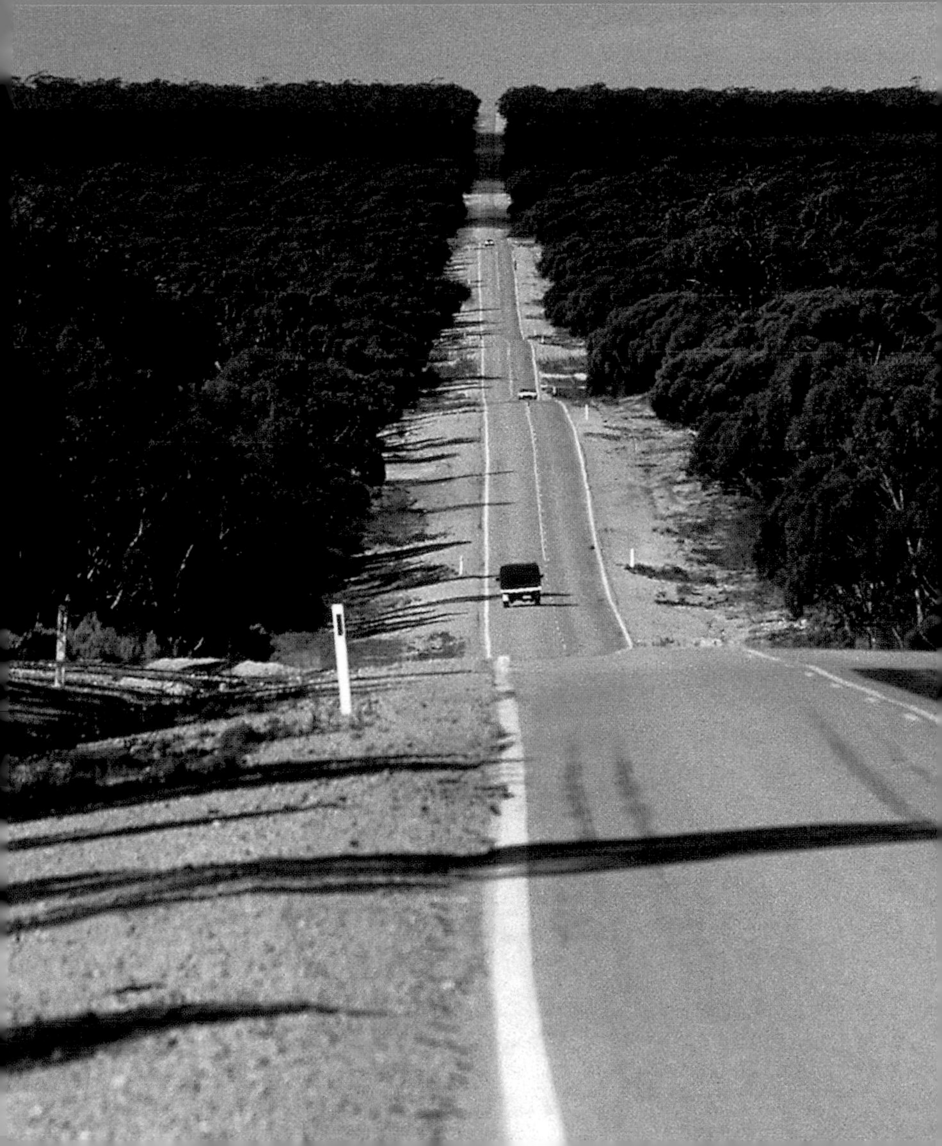

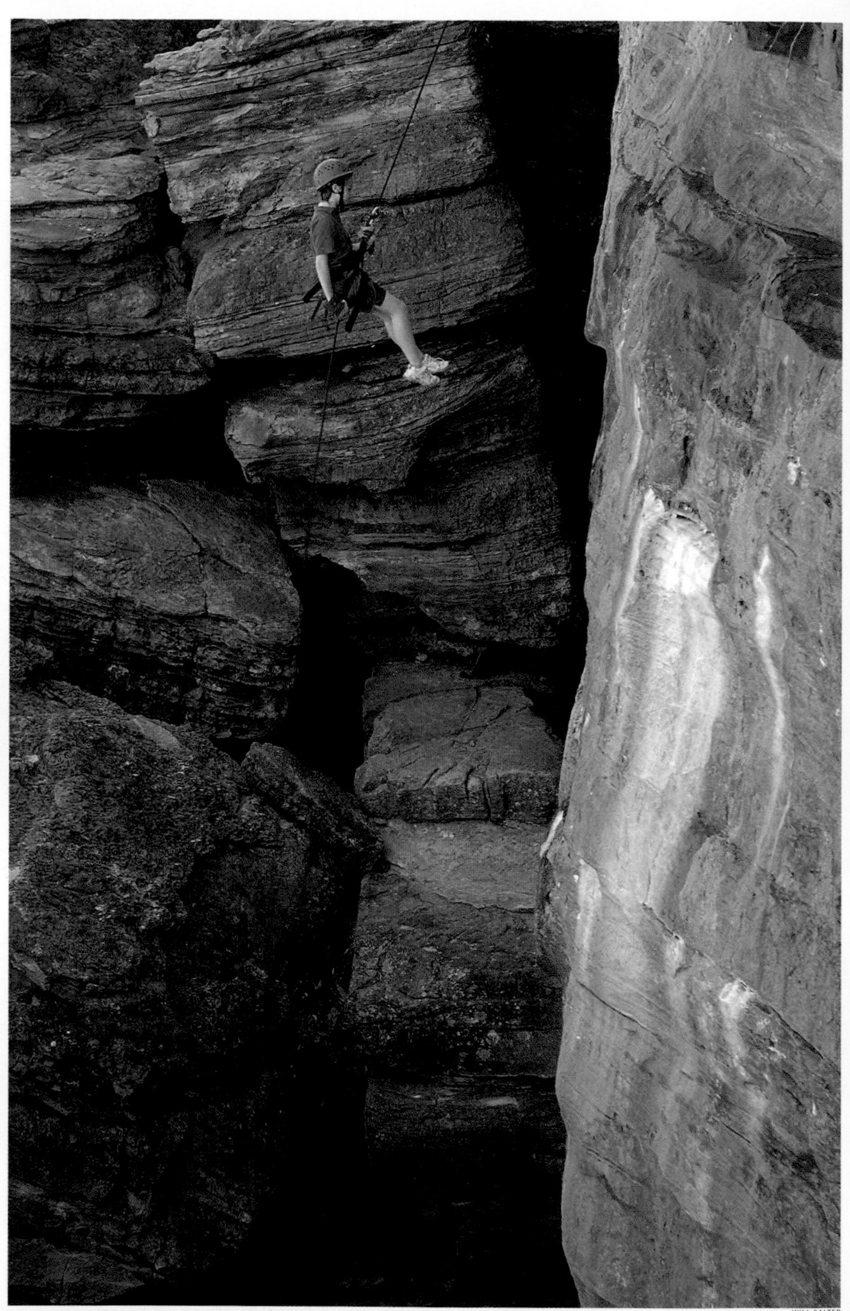

WILL SALTER

Kalbarri National Park (p294)

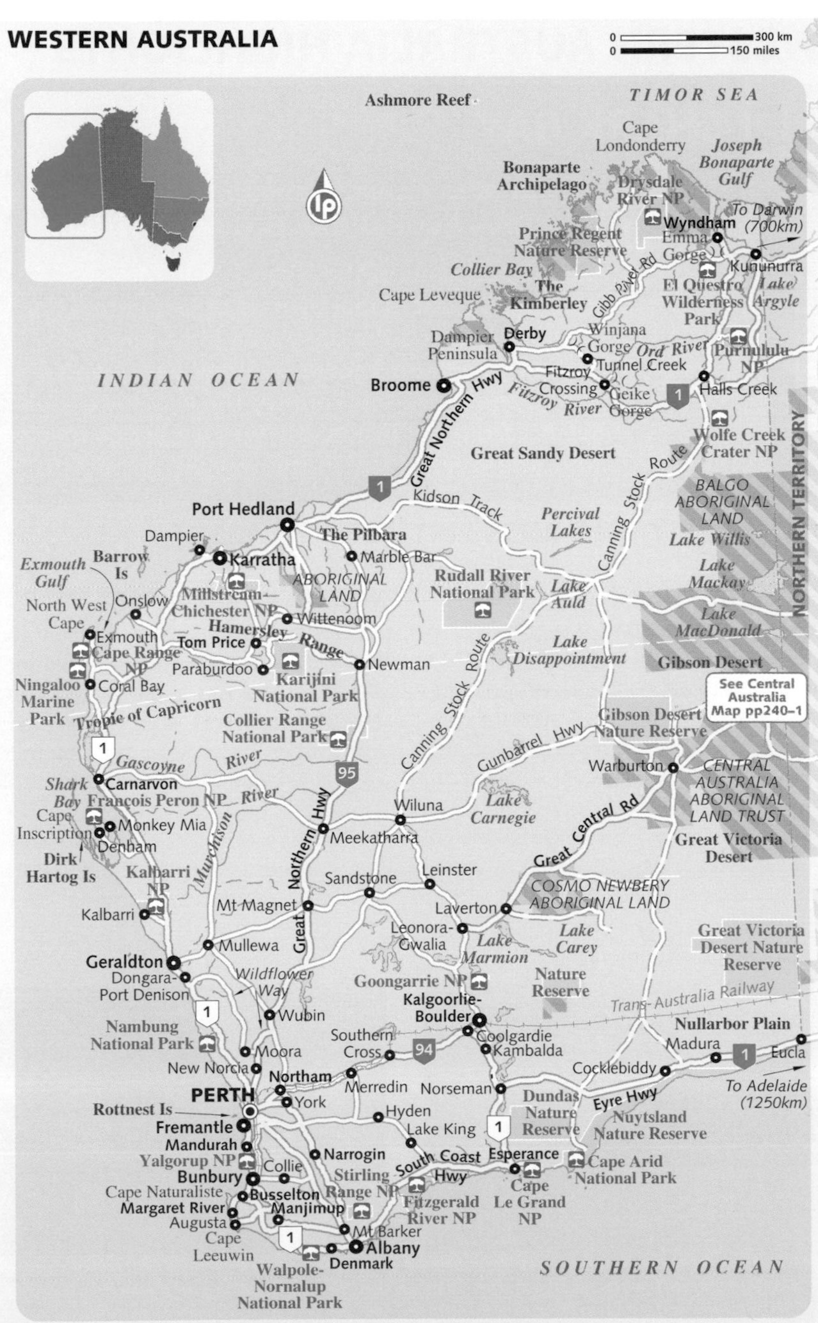
WESTERN AUSTRALIA
0 300 km
0 150 miles
TIMOR SEA
Ashmore Reef
Cape Londonderry
Joseph Bonaparte Gulf
Bonaparte Archipelago
Drysdale River NP
To Darwin (700km)
Wyndham
Emma Gorge
Kununurra
Prince Regent Nature Reserve
Collier Bay
Gibb River Rd
El Questro Wilderness Park
Lake Argyle
Cape Leveque
The Kimberley
Dampier Peninsula
Derby
Winjana Gorge
Ord River
Purnululu NP
Tunnel Creek
Fitzroy Crossing
Geike Gorge
Fitzroy River
Halls Creek
INDIAN OCEAN
Broome
Great Northern Hwy
Wolfe Creek Crater NP
Great Sandy Desert
Canning Stock Route
BALGO ABORIGINAL LAND
NORTHERN TERRITORY
Kidson Track
Percival Lakes
Lake Willis
Port Hedland
The Pilbara
Dampier
Barrow Is
Karratha
Marble Bar
Exmouth Gulf
ABORIGINAL LAND
Rudall River National Park
Lake Mackay
Lake Auld
North West Cape
Onslow
Millstream-Chichester NP
Wittenoom
Lake MacDonald
Exmouth
Hamersley Range
Tom Price
Cape Range NP
Lake Disappointment
Gibson Desert
Paraburdoo
Newman
Karijini National Park
Ningaloo Marine Park
Coral Bay
See Central Australia Map pp240–1
Tropic of Capricorn
Collier Range National Park
Gibson Desert Nature Reserve
Gunbarrel Hwy
Gascoyne River
95
Warburton
CENTRAL AUSTRALIA ABORIGINAL LAND TRUST
Shark Bay
Carnarvon
Francois Peron NP
Wiluna
Lake Carnegie
Cape Inscription
Monkey Mia
Meekatharra
Great Central Rd
Denham
Great Victoria Desert
Dirk Hartog Is
Murchison River
Leinster
Kalbarri NP
Sandstone
COSMO NEWBERY ABORIGINAL LAND
Kalbarri
Mt Magnet
Laverton
Leonora-Gwalia
Lake Carey
Great Victoria Desert Nature Reserve
Lake Marmion
Geraldton
Mullewa
Dongara-Port Denison
Wildflower Way
Goongarrie NP
Nature Reserve
Trans-Australia Railway
Kalgoorlie-Boulder
Wubin
Nullarbor Plain
Nambung National Park
Southern Cross
Coolgardie
Madura
Eucla
Kambalda
94
Moora
New Norcia
Cocklebiddy
Northam
Merredin
Norseman
To Adelaide (1250km)
PERTH
York
Dundas Nature Reserve
Eyre Hwy
Rottnest Is
Hyden
Nuytsland Nature Reserve
Fremantle
Lake King
Mandurah
South Coast Hwy
Esperance
Cape Arid National Park
Yalgorup NP
Narrogin
Collie
Stirling Range NP
Bunbury
Cape Le Grand NP
Cape Naturaliste
Busselton
Fitzgerald River NP
Margaret River
Manjimup
Augusta
Mt Barker
Cape Leeuwin
Albany
Denmark
Walpole-Nornalup National Park
SOUTHERN OCEAN

WESTERN AUSTRALIA HIGHLIGHTS

1 SHARK BAY

BY DARREN 'CAPES' CAPEWELL, WULA GUDA NYINDA – ABORIGINAL ECO ADVENTURES

I am descendant of the Nhanda and Malgana people, the traditional owners of Gutharraguda, pronounced Goo-tha-da-gooda (meaning 'Two Waters'), and also known as Shark Bay. I would like to show you this country the way my people see it…from the inside, the way we are connected to it, the way we feel it, the way we respect it.

CAPES' DON'T MISS LIST

❶ MONKEY MIA

Monkey Mia (p296) needs no formal introduction, as it is world renowned for the friendly wild dolphins that visit the beach daily. Dolphins started interacting with humans when local Aboriginal fishers Jimmy Poland and Laurie Bellotti began handing them fish as they swam around their boats after fishing expeditions. In the 1960s, Nin Watts, a visitor to the area, began feeding the dolphins from the beach and thus cemented the dolphin–human interaction.

❷ OCEAN PARK

Ocean Park (p295) is located on the Shark Bay World Heritage Drive into Denham and was established in the 1990s. Ocean Park is open daily and introduces visitors to the magnificent Shark Bay marine playground. It offers guided tours allowing visitors the chance to get up close to Shark Bay marine wildlife, including shark-feeding experiences.

Clockwise from top: Thorny devil, Francois Peron National Park (p296); Stromatolites in Hamelin Pool, Shark Bay (294); Salt lakes, Francois Peron National Park; Shark Bay; Southern bottlenose dolphins, Monkey Mia (p296)

CLOCKWISE FROM TOP: MARTIN COHEN; MICHAEL AW; MITCH REARDON; JOHN BANAGAN; RACHEL LEWIS

❸ PERON HOMESTEAD & HOT TUB

Take a pleasant drive out to the Peron Homestead and visitor centre in the **Francois Peron National Park** (p296), accessible to 2WD vehicles. Take a walk around the visitor centre and various trails discovering local flora and fauna – a fantastic opportunity to learn more about the Project Eden Conservation Program, which is aiming to restore native animal species. In a picturesque setting, there is also a chance to have a barbecue and a soak in the artesian fed 'hot tub', ideal for families or anyone wanting to soothe away aches and pains after a day of exploring.

❹ DIRK HARTOG ISLAND

Former pastoral station Dirk Hartog is the largest island on the west coast. Recognised as the first European landing site, it has recently been earmarked to become a national park. The island offers overnight stays in camp-style accommodation, fishing charters, surfing trips and much more.

➘ THINGS YOU NEED TO KNOW

First stop The Shark Bay Visitors Centre is in the Shark Bay World Heritage Discovery Centre (p295), on the Denham foreshore **Dirk Hartog Island** Visit www.dirkhartogisland.com **Avoid** Fishing or collecting material from sanctuary zones within the marine park **See our author's review on p294**

WESTERN AUSTRALIA HIGHLIGHTS

2

↘ FREMANTLE

Breezy and relaxed, the old historic port town of **Fremantle** (p289) enjoys a bohemian reputation and alternative *joie de vivre*. As well as solid colonial architecture and a maritime heritage, 'Freo' mixes museums with a caffeine-infused restaurant scene and several monumental pubs. It's a heady mix which gets all the more interesting when kids from the suburbs come to party on the weekend.

3

↘ NINGALOO MARINE PARK

The stunning **Ningaloo Marine Park** (p300) is a natural wonder that is perhaps Western Australia's most precious natural resource. The reef is amazingly accessible, lying only 100m offshore from some parts of the peninsula. You can literally swim out to a dazzling display of coral gardens teeming with colourful fish. Ningaloo is also justifiably famous for its whale shark encounters.

4

↘ MARGARET RIVER

Hugely popular **Margaret River** (p292) serves up some of the best surfing in Australia, along with wild coastal caves, sophisticated restaurants and internationally acclaimed vineyards scattered throughout richly forested land. The town itself, known as 'Margs', is an affable enclave of cafes and accommodation that satisfies both surfies and the slickest 'suits'.

5

↘ VALLEY OF THE GIANTS

Tingle trees live for up to 400 years, can grow to 60m tall and 16m around the base, and are unique to this region of Western Australia. For years folks would come to the **Valley of the Giants** (p294) eager to see the amazing 'Ancient Empire' stand of trees. Now you can enter the elevated realm of the canopy on the spectacular Tree Top Walk.

6

↘ BROOME

Broome (p302) looms large in the Australian psyche as the perfect get-away-from-it-all destination. This remote town on the vast Kimberley coast has emerged as a tourism hub with gourmet restaurants and luxury resorts. Yet Broome retains much of its exotic frontier feel, and the broad sandy beaches, sapphire waters and cosmopolitan heritage will always appeal.

2 RICHARD I'ANSON; 3 PETER PTSCHELINZEW; 4 ORIEN HARVEY; 5 ANDREW BAIN; 6 JOHN BANAGAN

2 Fremantle Markets (p291); 3 Turquoise Bay, Ningaloo Marine Park (p300); 4 Grape vines, Margaret River (p292); 5 Valley of the Giants (p294); 6 Camel trek along Cable Beach, Broome (p302)

WESTERN AUSTRALIA'S BEST...

NATURAL RETREATS

- **Shark Bay** (p294) A fascinating marine wonderland surrounded by starkly beautiful landforms in a remote, peaceful setting
- **Ningaloo Marine Park** (p300) This highly accessible coral reef supports an abundance of colourful marine life
- **Valley of the Giants** (p294) Be humbled by the natural grandeur of the mighty tingle trees in this ancient forest

PLACES TO RELAX

- **Margaret River** (p292) Lose the kids and treat yourself to wining and dining and quiet country drives
- **Rottnest Island** (p291) Join the locals for an old-fashioned swimmin' and fishin' beach holiday
- **Broome** (p302) Change down a gear at the old pearling port and rest the soul at Cable Beach

DIVING & SNORKELLING

- **Monkey Mia** (p296) Go snorkelling here and Monkey Mia's famous friendly dolphins may join you
- **Ningaloo Marine Park** (p300) One of the world's best locations to dive with whale sharks and manta rays
- **Rottnest Island** (p291) Family friendly, with protected snorkelling sites and dive lessons, and handy to Perth

DINING SCENES

- **Broome** (p302) Superb seafood and a magnificent setting, with bay views and an Indian Ocean sunset
- **Margaret River** (p292) A succulent blend of excellent regional wines with romantic restaurants
- **Fremantle** (p289) Sip on a cafe latte, munch on an organic muffin and watch the parade on South Tce

LEFT: ANDREW BAIN; RIGHT: ANDREW WATSON

Left: Stark Bay, Rottnest Island (p291); Right: Wine bottles, Saracen Estates winery, Margaret River (p292)

THINGS YOU NEED TO KNOW

VITAL STATISTICS

- **Population** 2.5 million
- **Telephone code** ☎ 08
- **Best time to visit** The South – any time; Far North – May to September

ADVANCE PLANNING

- **One month before** Reserve accommodation and hire vehicles
- **Two weeks before** Book regional flights to Broome, Exmouth or Denham
- **One week before** Book a diving lesson or whale swim tour

RESOURCES

- **Royal Automobile Club of Western Australia** (RACWA; ☎ 13 17 03; www.rac.com.au; 832 Wellington St, Perth) The RACWA produces the terrific *Western Australia Experience Guide*, full of accommodation and touring information. Download free basic maps (with distances, en route facilities and road conditions) from its website.
- **Western Australian Tourism Commission** (www.westernaustralia.com) A website for general statewide information. Most country towns have their own helpful visitors centres.
- **Western Australian Visitors Centre** (☎ 1300 361 351; www.westernaustralia.net; cnr Forrest Pl & Wellington St; 8.30am-5.30pm Mon-Thu, 8.30am-6pm Fri, 9.30am-4.30pm Sat, noon-4.30pm Sun) A good resource for a trip anywhere in Western Australia.
- **Department of Environment & Conservation** (DEC; ☎ 08-6467 5000; www.naturebase.net; 168 St Georges Tce, Perth) The department manages the state's important national parks.

EMERGENCY NUMBER

- **Ambulance, fire and police** (☎ 000)

GETTING AROUND

- **Walk** beneath the giant tingle trees (p294) or amidst the wildflower blooms (p294)
- **Swim** with whale sharks (p300) and dolphins (p296)
- **Train** across the continent to Sydney (p289)
- **Fly** to Broome, Denham (for Monkey Mia) and Exmouth (for Ningaloo)
- **Ferry** to Rottnest Island (p291)

BE FOREWARNED

- **Rottnest Island** (p291) is booked out in summer and school holidays for months in advance
- **Ningaloo Marine Park's** (p300) whale sharks arrive in May and depart in July

WESTERN AUSTRALIA ITINERARIES

SURF, SAND & VINE Three Days

After you have seen the sights of **(1) Perth** (p284) and taken a dip at Cottesloe Beach, head out to nearby **(2) Fremantle** (p289) for a taste of maritime history or just a chance to drink a cool beer with the Fremantle Doctor (the afternoon sea breeze that arrives like clockwork in summer).

From Fremantle you can ferry to pedal-powered **(3) Rottnest Island** (p291) for a car-free, care-free holiday atmosphere.

Back on the mainland take a drive down to **(4) Margaret River** (p292), a richly forested region interspersed with vineyards and award-winning wineries. Here you can find romantic accommodation and a cosy restaurant and settle in with a chilled Sauvignon Blanc and a marinated marron (freshwater crayfish).

CAMELS, PEARLS & SHARKS Five Days

Start this trip in the Kimberley. You can arrive in **(1) Broome** (p302) by road from the Northern Territory via Kununurra, by air, or even by the odd cruise ship. Cosmopolitan and laid-back Broome offers a history in pearling and the opportunity to ride a camel on the sweeping sandy swathes of Cable Beach. There's a lot to do in and around Broome and it is also the perfect place to spend time doing not much.

Broome is a long way from anywhere, so if time is in short supply catch a flight (regular but not daily) to **(2) Exmouth** (p299) for a few days enjoying the stunning marine life of **(3) Ningaloo Marine Park** (p300). Exmouth offers the chance to cruise over the reef in glass-bottomed boats, to learn to scuba dive, and even the possibility to swim or dive with the largest shark in the world – the whale shark.

From Exmouth you could move on to the nearby base of **(4) Coral Bay** (p298) for exploring the southern reaches of Ningaloo Reef with a number of excellent tour operators. You can also go it alone and swim off the beach to view exceptional coral.

NATURE'S BOUNTY One Week

This route gives you the best of the country's lush southwest and then takes you up to the dramatic Central West Coast, where you can swim with dolphins.

Start in **(1) Perth** (p284) and exhaust all of your urban urges in the great pubs, galleries, bars and restaurants. In season you can also do a whale-watching cruise. After a short visit to **(2) Fremantle** (p289) to savour the heritage and cafe scene, snake your way south

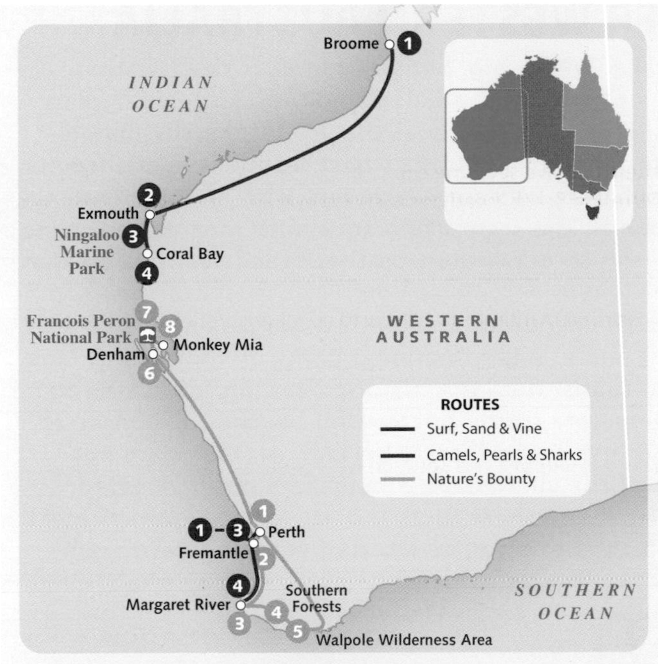

via the stunning beaches of Cape Naturaliste, before settling in at **(3) Margaret River** (p292).

Go surfing, explore a cave and taste-test the quality wines before continuing south and east through the fertile **(4) Southern Forests** (p293) region to view the magnificent karri forests. Next stop is the pretty **(5) Walpole Wilderness Area** (p294), where you can walk among the treetops in a forest of magnificent tingle trees.

Loop back to Perth, via the Albany Hwy, to catch a flight to **(6) Denham** (p295), the gateway to the astonishing marine splendour of Shark Bay. Here you can explore the remote **(7) Francois Peron National Park** (p296), take an eye-opening Aboriginal cultural tour and mingle with wild dolphins at **(8) Monkey Mia** (p296).

DISCOVER WESTERN AUSTRALIA

Western Australia (WA) is big. Seriously big. Its size, swathes of gloriously empty outback, small population largely hugging the coast and Perth's distinction as the world's most isolated capital city offer perhaps Australia's best frontier experience. Its residents are defiantly *Western* Australian, with an independence shaped by distance. The state's mining wealth means a booming economy that isn't so dependent on that other Australia on the east coast.

'Up north' you'll encounter unexpected gorges and waterfalls along the coast and in inland national parks on Indigenous land, and a colourful tourist hub, the historic pearling town of Broome. In the more temperate south, uncrowded beaches, expanses of wildflowers and lush green forests beckon. Around Margaret River, the fruit of the vine keeps winemakers busy, vineyard restaurants offer the freshest food and artisans of all sorts make inspired craft from the salvaged wood of stunning karri, marri and jarrah trees.

PERTH

pop 1.5 million

Laid-back, liveable Perth has wonderful weather, beautiful beaches and an easygoing character. About as close to Southeast Asia as to Australia's eastern state capitals, Perth's combination of big-city attractions with relaxed and informal surrounds offers an appealing lifestyle for locals and a variety of things for visitors to do.

INFORMATION

EMERGENCY

Dial ☎ 000 for ambulance, fire or police.

Police station (☎ 08-9222 1111; Curtin House, 60 Beaufort St)

POST

Main post office (GPO; ☎ 08-9237 5460, info line 13 13 18; 3 Forrest Pl; 8.30am-5pm Mon-Fri, 9am-12.30pm Sat)

TOURIST INFORMATION

i-City Information Kiosk (Murray St Mall; 9.30am-4.30pm Mon-Thu & Sat, 9.30am-8pm Fri, 11am-3.30pm Sun) Volunteers answer questions and lead walking tours.

SIGHTS

PERTH CULTURAL CENTRE

Just north of the Perth train station, between James St Mall and Roe St in Northbridge, you'll find the state museum, art gallery, library and the Perth Institute of Contemporary Arts.

The **Western Australian Museum** (☎ 08-9212 3700; www.museum.wa.gov.au; James St; admission by donation; 9.30am-5pm, tours 11am & 2pm) includes an excellent 'land and people' display that examines both ancient history and the more recent past; a gallery of dinosaur casts; a good collection of meteorites; and galleries dedicated to mammals, butterflies and birds.

The **Art Gallery of Western Australia** (☎ 08-9492 6600; www.artgallery.wa.gov.au;

James St Mall; admission free; 10am-5pm, tours 11am & 1pm Tue-Thu, 12.30pm & 2pm Fri, 1pm Sat, 11am & 1pm Sun) has a brilliant collection of Aboriginal artworks and a fine permanent exhibition of early Europeans-in-Australia paintings.

Cutting-edge contemporary art – installations, performance, sculpture, video works – lives at **Perth Institute of Contemporary Arts** (PICA; 08-9227 6144; www.pica.org.au; James St; admission free; 11am-6pm Tue-Sun).

AQUARIUM OF WESTERN AUSTRALIA

For all things fishy, head to the **Aquarium of Western Australia** (AQWA; 08-9447 7500; www.aqwa.com.au; Hillarys Boat Harbour, West Coast Dr, Hillarys; adult/child $26/14.50; 10am-5pm). Here you can wander through a 98m underwater tunnel as gargantuan turtles, stingrays, fish and sharks stealthily glide over the top of you.

PERTH FOR CHILDREN

There's plenty of free kids' entertainment in Perth: **Cottesloe Beach** has long been a family favourite and **Leighton Beach** is fairly sheltered and shallow. **Kings Park** (right) has numerous playgrounds, walking tracks and gardens. And there's always the bike tracks stretching along the river and the coast, long enough to tire out any young 'un.

Many of Perth's big attractions, such as the **Aquarium of Western Australia** (above), the **Western Australian Museum** (p284) and the **Art Gallery of Western Australia** (p284), cater well for young audiences.

TOURS

Several cruise companies run tours from Barrack St Jetty, including **Captain Cook Cruises** (08-9325 3341; www.captaincook cruises.com.au), **Oceanic Cruises** (08-9325 1191; www.oceaniccruises.com.au) and the cheaper and less-frills **Golden Sun Cruises** (08-9325 9916; goldensuncruises@arach.net.au). All offer lunch and dinner cruises on the Swan River, winery visits and trips to Fremantle and Rottnest Island.

Rottnest Express (1300 467 688; www.rottnestexpress.com.au) specialises in transport to and packages on Rottnest Island (p291).

ORIEN HARVEY

Kings Park and Perth skyline

KINGS PARK

The green hilltop crown of **Kings Park & Botanic Garden** is set amid 4 sq km of natural bushland. The garden boasts over 2000 Western Australian plant species, which bloom during the September **Perth Wildflower Festival**.

Kings Park Visitors Centre is opposite the war memorial on Fraser Ave. Free guided walks leave at 10am and 2pm. If you are laden with picnic gear, take the free bus (number 37) from the city to the park entrance.

Things you need to know Kings Park & Botanic Garden (08-9480 3600; www.bgpa.wa.gov.au; Kings Park Rd, West Perth); Kings Park Visitors Centre (9.30am-4pm)

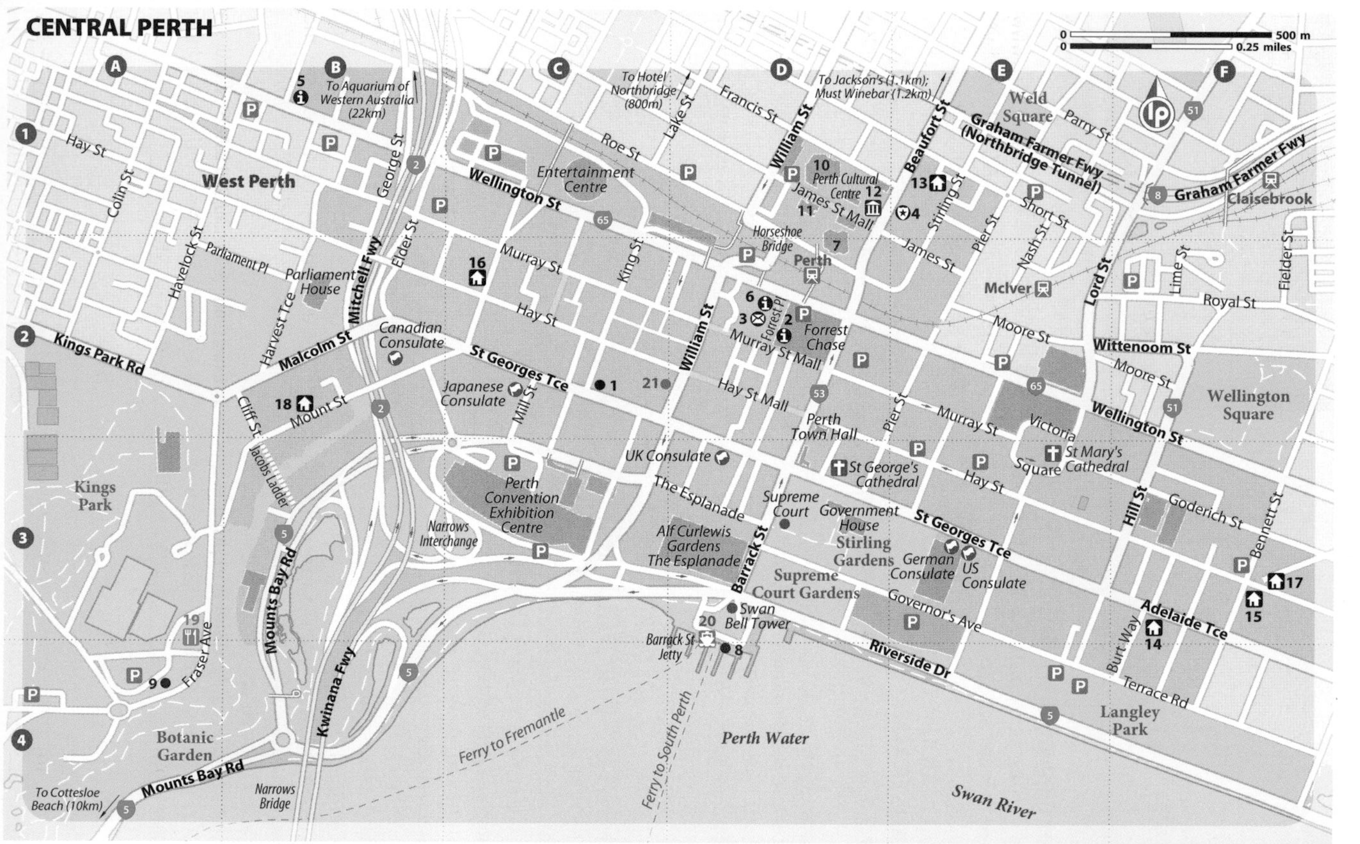
CENTRAL PERTH
0 500 m
0 0.25 miles
West Perth
Kings Park
Botanic Garden
Wellington Square
Weld Square
Stirling Gardens
Supreme Court Gardens
Alf Curlewis Gardens The Esplanade
Langley Park
Perth Water
Swan River
Ferry to South Perth
Ferry to Fremantle
Barrack St Jetty
Swan Bell Tower
Narrows Bridge
Narrows Interchange
Perth Convention Exhibition Centre
Entertainment Centre
Perth Cultural Centre
Parliament House
Government House
Supreme Court
Perth Town Hall
St George's Cathedral
St Mary's Cathedral
Forrest Chase
Horseshoe Bridge
Perth
McIver
Claisebrook
UK Consulate
US Consulate
German Consulate
Japanese Consulate
Canadian Consulate
Jacobs Ladder
To Aquarium of Western Australia (22km)
To Hotel Northbridge (800m)
To Jackson's (1.1km); Must Winebar (1.2km)
To Cottesloe Beach (10km)
Graham Farmer Fwy
Graham Farmer Fwy (Northbridge Tunnel)
Mitchell Fwy
Kwinana Fwy
Mounts Bay Rd
Riverside Dr
Kings Park Rd
Malcolm St
Mount St
Cliff St
Fraser Ave
Harvest Tce
Parliament Pl
Havelock St
Colin St
Hay St
George St
Elder St
Wellington St
Murray St
St Georges Tce
Mill St
King St
Roe St
Lake St
Francis St
William St
James St Mall
James St
Forrest Pl
Murray St Mall
Hay St Mall
Barrack St
The Esplanade
Beaufort St
Stirling St
Pier St
Short St
Nash St
Parry St
Moore St
Lord St
Wittenoom St
Lime St
Royal St
Fielder St
Victoria Square
Hill St
Goderich St
Bennett St
Adelaide Tce
Terrace Rd
Burt Way
Governor's Ave

INFORMATION
Department of Environment & Conservation ... 1 C2
i-City Information Kiosk ... 2 D2
Main Post Office ... 3 D2
Police Station ... 4 E1
RACWA ... 5 B1
Western Australian Visitors Centre ... 6 D2

SIGHTS & ACTIVITIES
Art Gallery of Western Australia ... 7 D2
Captain Cook Cruises ... 8 D4
Golden Sun Cruises ... (see 8)
Kings Park Visitors Centre ... 9 A4
Oceanic Cruises ... (see 8)
Perth Cultural Centre ... 10 D1
Perth Institute of Contemporary Arts ... 11 D1
Rottnest Express ... (see 8)
Western Australian Museum ... 12 D1

SLEEPING
Emperor's Crown ... 13 E1
Goodearth Hotel ... 14 F3
Mantra on Hay ... 15 F3
Melbourne ... 16 C2
Mont Clare Apartments ... 17 F3
Riverview on Mount Street ... 18 B2

EATING
Fraser's Restaurant ... 19 A3

TRANSPORT
Ferries to South Perth, Fremantle ... 20 D3
Qantas ... 21 C2

A ferry leaves from Barrack St Jetty for the few minutes' trip to the zoo ($3.20 return, at least every half hour).

SLEEPING

Perth is very spread out so choose your location carefully. The CBD and Northbridge are close to all forms of public transport, while the beachside Cottesloe and Scarborough are better for those who just want to loll on the beach.

CITY CENTRE

Riverview on Mount Street (☎ 08-9321 8963; www.riverviewperth.com.au; 42 Mount St; d from $130;) Riverview stands out as the best personality on this block below Kings Park. The refurbished 1960s bachelor pads are self- contained, spacious, sunny and simple, and there's (limited) free on-site parking.

Mont Clare Apartments (☎ 08-9225 4300; www.montclareapartments.com; 190 Hay St, East Perth; 1-bedroom apt $145, 2-bedroom apt from $160;) Friendly and unfussy, with somewhat casual housekeeping, the self-contained apartments here are spacious and, notably, quiet and private.

Melbourne (☎ 08-9320 3333; www.melbournehotel.com.au; cnr Hay & Milligan Sts; d from $160;) Classic country charm wafts through this gold-rush-era, heritage-listed hotel. Inside you'll find a stylish and serious dining room, and a polished bar and cafe buzzing with office workers.

Goodearth Hotel (☎ 08-9494 7777; www.goodearthhotel.com.au; 195 Adelaide Tce; studio/1-bedroom apt from $175/200;) Popular with country folk coming to town, these self- contained units have (tiny) balconies, some with views of the river just a block away, secure parking and a great location near the CAT bus route.

Mantra on Hay (☎ 08-9267 4888; www.mantraresorts.com.au; 201 Hay St; studio/1-bedroom apt from $207/230;) With a Tuscan-orange outside, and muted, urban-chic greys and purples inside, the Mantra is low-key and classy. Apartments are roomy, with laundries, dishwashers and good-sized benches and great utensils – plenty of room to prepare some local rock lobster here.

NORTHBRIDGE & AROUND

Emperor's Crown (☎ 08-9227 1400; www.emperorscrown.com.au; 85 Stirling St; dm $30, r with/without bathroom $102/92;) A minimalist and stylish taste of urban chic for midrange and budget travellers. It has multilanguage internet, a chilled-out movie lounge and decent access for disabled guests.

Hotel Northbridge (☎ 08-9328 5254; www.hotelnorthbridge.com.au; 210 Lake St; d with spa $125-170;) The Northbridge has long been the star attraction for couples and country folk with its good-value rooms and old-fashioned charm. A recent refurbishment has dropped a spa in every single room, and considering its smack-bang location it's a great midrange choice.

COTTESLOE & SCARBOROUGH

Ocean Beach Hotel (☎ 08-9384 2555; www.obh.com.au; cnr Marine Pde & Eric St, Cottesloe; d $145-185;) Overlooking the water, the only boutique-style hotel on Cottesloe Beach features smart, playful colours and contemporary furnishings that bring this art deco building to life. Rooms are big, but get a deluxe or spa room if you want to watch the waves.

Sun Moon Resort (☎ 08-9245 8000; www.arcadiahospitality.com.au; 200 West Coast Hwy, Scarborough; r from $160;) While this Bali-style resort and Scarborough marriage might appear a mismatch, the two make a lovely couple. Batik furnishings complement the otherwise minimalist rooms, but note there's a busy main road between hotel and beach.

EATING

Fraser's Restaurant (☎ 08-9481 7100; Fraser Ave, Kings Park; mains $35-55) Atop Kings Park, overlooking the city and the glittering Swan River, Fraser's location is unrivalled. And the food has enjoyed a good reputation for years, with Mod Oz standards such as chargrilled rock lobster and roast 'roo on beetroot rösti and polenta.

Must Winebar (☎ 08-9328 8255; 519 Beaufort St, Mt Lawley; mains $38; noon-late) Arguably Perth's best wine bar, this is a fine restaurant as well. Tuck into local WA speciality produce such as Margaret River *wagyu* beef shanks, or simply stop by for a glass of something delicious.

Jackson's (☎ 08-9328 1177; 483 Beaufort St, Highgate; mains $44, 7-course tasting menu $115, with wine $170; dinner Mon-Sat) Foodies flock to what is one of Perth's top dining experiences: Neal Jackson's tasting menu. Á-la-carte highlights include seasonal specials – for example, in winter you might see gamey dishes involving meats such as venison, rabbit and partridge.

DRINKING

While the city has a few popular watering holes, the gems of Perth's drinking scene are sprinkled throughout the suburbs. Generally, the mainstream drink-

RACHEL LEWIS

Cottesloe Beach and pavilion (p285)

ing venues are in Northbridge; smaller, more laid-back clubs and bars are in Mt Lawley, Leederville and Subiaco; and big beer gardens are strewn around the suburbs, notably in Cottesloe.

GETTING THERE & AWAY

AIR

Qantas (☎ 13 13 13; www.qantas.com.au; 55 William St) and **Virgin Blue** (☎ 13 67 89; www.virginblue.com.au) fly between Perth and other Australian state capitals.

Skywest (☎ 1300 660 088; www.skywest.com.au) flies between Perth and regional destinations such as Esperance and Broome. Qantas also flies to Broome and Kalgoorlie.

BUS

Greyhound Australia (☎ 13 14 99; www.greyhound.com.au; East Perth terminal, West Pde) has daily services from the East Perth terminal to Darwin via Broome.

Transwa (☎ 1300 662 205; www.transwa.wa.gov.au) operates services from the bus terminal at East Perth train station to many destinations around the state.

South West Coach Lines (☎ 08-9324 2333) focuses on the southwestern corner of WA, doing trips from the Esplanade Busport to most towns in the region, including Bunbury, Busselton and Margaret River.

TRAIN

There is only one interstate rail link: the famous *Indian Pacific* transcontinental train journey, run by **Great Southern Railway** (☎ 13 21 47; www.trainways.com.au), which leaves from East Perth station. One-way fares between Sydney and Perth are about $690 (seat only), $315 (seat only, backpacker rate) or $1350 (sleeper cabin).

GETTING TO/FROM THE AIRPORT

The domestic and international terminals of Perth's airport are 10km and 13km east of Perth respectively. Taxi fares to the city are around $25/35 from the domestic/international terminal.

The **Perth Airport City Shuttle** (☎ 08-9277 7958; www.perthshuttle.com.au) provides transport to the city centre, hotels and hostels. The shuttle costs $15/20 from the domestic/international terminal.

FREMANTLE

pop 26,800

'Freo' lies at the mouth of the Swan River, 19km from Perth but a world away in terms of atmosphere. Creative and relaxed, clean-and-green Freo makes a cosy home for performers, professionals, artists, hippies and more than a few eccentrics. There's a lot to enjoy here – Freo is also home to some fantastic museums, historic buildings, galleries, pubs and a thriving coffee culture.

INFORMATION

Visitors centre (☎ 08-9431 7878; www.fremantlewa.com.au; Kings Sq; 🕓 9am-5pm Mon-Fri, 10am-3pm Sat, 11.30am-2.30pm Sun) Nongovernment visitors centre with excellent online accommodation booking service.

SIGHTS & ACTIVITIES

Housed in a stunning, architect-designed building on the harbour, just west of the city centre, the **Western Australian Maritime Museum** (☎ 08-9431 8444; www.museum.wa.gov.au; Victoria Quay; museum adult/child $10/3, submarine $8/3, combined ticket $15/5; 🕓 9.30am-5pm) explores WA's relationship with the ocean. It faces the sea, which

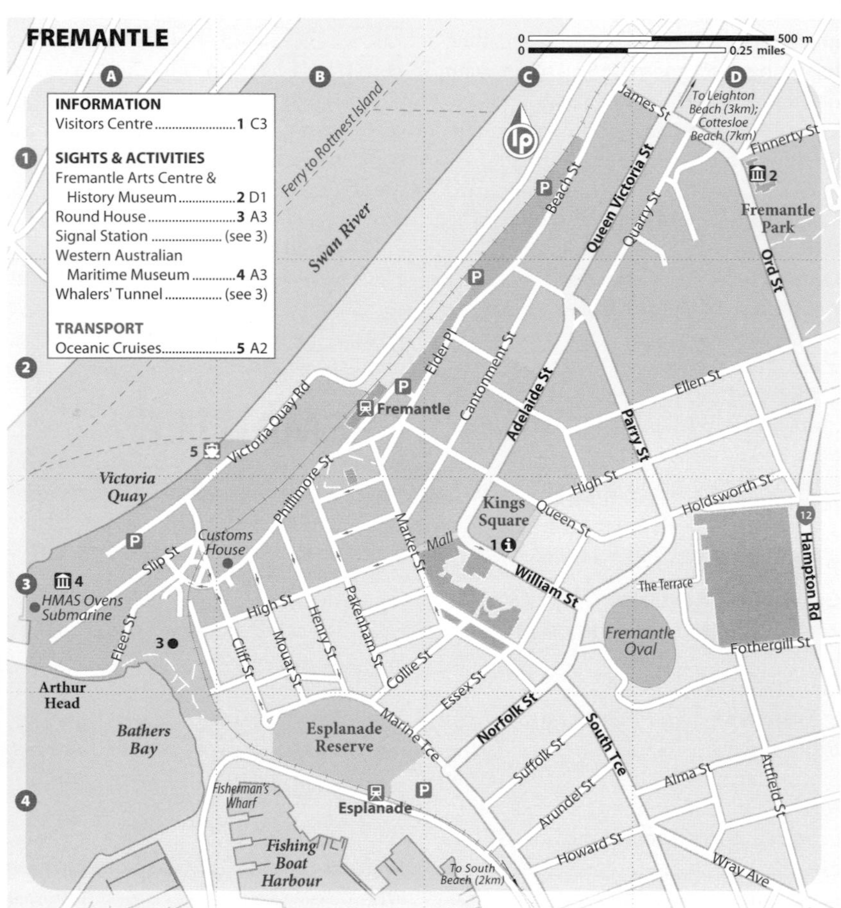

has shaped so much of the state's, and Fremantle's, destiny.

An impressive neo-Gothic building, the **Fremantle Arts Centre** (☎ **08-9432 9555; www.fac.org.au; cnr Ord & Finnerty Sts;** 🕒 **10am-5pm**) was constructed by convict labourers as a lunatic asylum in the 1860s. Saved from demolition in the late 1960s, the building now also houses the excellent **Fremantle History Museum** (☎ **08-9430 7966**). Admission to both is free.

Out on **Arthur Head**, the western end of High St near the Maritime Museum, is the **Round House** (☎ **08-9336 6897; admission by donation;** 🕒 **10.30am-3.30pm**). Built in 1831, it's the oldest public building in WA. It was originally a local prison and the site of the colony's first hanging. On the hilltop outside is the **Signal Station**, where at 1pm daily a time ball and cannon blast were used to alert seamen to the correct time – the ceremony is re-enacted daily. Later, the building was used for holding Aborigines before they were taken away to Rottnest Island. To the Noongar people, the Round House is a sacred site because of the number of their people killed while incarcerated here. Beneath it is an impressive 1837 **Whalers' Tunnel** carved through sandstone and used for moving goods from the port into town.

Originally opened in 1897, the colourful **Fremantle Markets** (☎ 08-9335 2515; cnr South Tce & Henderson St; ⏲ Fri-Sun) reopened in 1975 and today draws slow-moving crowds combing over souvenirs and depleting the food and fresh produce stalls to the accompaniment of rotating buskers.

EATING

Eating and drinking your way around town are two of the great pleasures of Freo. The three main areas to browse before you graze are around the town centre, around Fishing Boat Harbour, and around East Freo's George St and riverbank.

GETTING THERE & AROUND

The **Fremantle Airport Shuttle** (☎ 08-9457 7150; www.fremantleairportshuttle.com.au) travels to and from the airport several times daily ($35 per person).

The train between Perth and Fremantle runs every 10 minutes or so throughout the day ($3.50). There are countless buses between Perth city and Fremantle train station; they include buses 103, 106, 111, 158 and 107.

Oceanic Cruises (☎ 08-9325 1191; www.oceaniccruises.com.au) runs several ferries a day from Perth's Barrack St Jetty to Freo (adult/child $21/13, return $31/20).

ROTTNEST ISLAND

pop 475

'Rotto' is the family holiday playground of choice for Perth locals. About 19km from Fremantle, it's ringed by secluded tropical beaches and bays. Outdoor activities rule, and swimming, snorkelling, fishing, surfing and diving are just some of the popular things to do here. Cycling round the 11km-long, 4.5km-wide car-free island is a real pleasure; just ride around and pick your own bit of beach to spend the day on.

INFORMATION

Rottnest Island website (www.rottnestisland.com)

Visitors centre (☎ 08-9372 9752; ⏲ 7.30am-5pm Sat-Thu, to 7pm Fri) At the main jetty.

SIGHTS & ACTIVITIES

All year round, the small but informative **Rottnest Museum** (☎ 08-9372 9753; Kitson St; admission by donation; ⏲ 11am-3.30pm) has exhibits about the natural and human history of the island.

Most visitors come for Rottnest's **beaches** and water activities. **Surfing** is big at Strickland, Salmon and Stark Bays at the west end of the island, while **swimmers** prefer the Basin (protected by a ring of reefs) and Longreach and Geordie Bays. Excellent visibility in the temperate waters, coral and shipwrecks appeal to **scuba divers** and **snorkellers**; snorkel trails are at Little Salmon Bay and Parker Point. When we visited, tenders were out for a new island-based dive operator; check the island website for updates.

GETTING THERE & AWAY

Apart from their points of departure, all ferry services are basically the same. Return trips are around $53/24 per adult/child from Fremantle (25 minutes), $69/34 from Perth (1½ hours) and $72/33 (40 minutes) from Hillarys Boat Harbour. Each company offers transfers only, or transfer and accommodation packages.

Rottnest Express (☎ 1300 467 688; www.rottnestexpress.com.au) departs Fremantle (C Shed, Victoria Quay) about five times

JENNY JONES

Hay Shed Hill winery, Margaret River

daily, and Northport terminal, Fremantle, about four times daily. There's a thrice-daily service from Perth. Secure parking is available at Northport.

GETTING AROUND

Bicycles are the time-honoured way of getting around the island. Rotto is just big enough (and with enough hills) to make a day's ride good exercise. Hire a bike from one of the ferry companies or on the island.

THE SOUTHWEST

The farmland, forests, rivers and coast of the lush, green southwestern corner of WA are simply magnificent. Bottlenose dolphins and whales frolic offshore while devoted surfers search for the perfect line on perfect waves. On land, world-class wineries beckon and tall trees provide enticing shade for walking trails and scenic drives.

MARGARET RIVER

The ample attractions of Margaret River – top surf, undulating bushland, some of Australia's best wineries and gourmet local produce – make it one of WA's most popular destinations, and a place where travellers can often find seasonal harvest work.

INFORMATION

Visitors centre (☎ 08-9757 2911; www.margaretriver.com; Bussell Hwy; ⏲ 9am-5pm) This sleek visitors centre has wads of information, as well as an on-site wine centre.

SIGHTS & ACTIVITIES

Drop by the **Margaret River Regional Wine Centre** (☎ 08-9755 5501; www.mrwines.com; 9 Bussell Hwy, Cowaramup; ⏲ 10am-7pm Mon-Sat, to 6pm Sun), where the knowledgeable staff can plan a vineyard itinerary for you and will ship wine to almost anywhere in the world.

Caveworks visitor centre (☎ 08-9757 7411; www.margaretriver.com; Caves Rd; ⏲ 9am-5pm), about 25km from Margaret River, has excellent screen displays about the many caves of the region and cave conservation, a 'cave crawl' experience, and cave tours. Fees apply to some of these.

Margaret River Tours (☎ 0419 917 166; www.margaretrivertours.com) One of the longest-standing local operators; runs combined wineries-sightseeing tours (half/full day $70/110) or can arrange charters.

SLEEPING

Surfpoint Resort (☎ 1800 071 777, 08-9757 1777; www.surfpoint.com.au; Gnarabup Beach;

WINING & DINING

A number of great vineyards in Margaret River are equally renowned for their dining. The region produces highly regarded Cabernets and dry whites. Here's some winemakers that do both very well:

- **Leeuwin Estate** (☎ 08-9759 0000; www.leeuwinestate.com.au; Stevens Rd, Margaret River) A brilliant estate, with excellent wines (taste the Art Series Chardonnay), a stylish cellar door, a highly regarded restaurant and an annual sell-out concert series.
- **Vasse Felix** (☎ 08-9756 5000; www.vassefelix.com.au; cnr Caves & Harmans Rds, South Cowaramup) A good all-round winery with a fabulous art collection.
- **Voyager Estate** (☎ 08-9757 6354; www.voyagerestate.com.au; Stevens Rd, Margaret River) A true gem, with great wines across the board and an elegant cellar door and restaurant.
- **Xanadu Estate** (☎ 08-9757 2581; www.xanaduwines.com; Terry Rd, Margaret River) A broad range (including its popular Secession label) and a decent cellar door and restaurant.

dm/d $25/95;) Offers the beach on a budget, rents boogie boards and surfboards, and offers lessons from an expert.

Riverglen Chalets (☎ 08-9757 2101; www.riverglenchalets.com.au; Carters Rd; chalets $115-220;) Just north of town, these timber chalets are spacious and fully self-contained, with verandahs looking out onto bushland; there's full disabled access to a couple of them.

Margaret River Resort Knight's Inn (☎ 08-9757 0000; www.mrresort.com.au; 40 Wallcliffe Rd; motel/hotel/villas $130/140/230;) Ignore the dinky exterior: the jarrah-dense hotel rooms here are big and gorgeous, and the motel rooms luxurious.

SOUTHERN FORESTS

The tall forests of WA's southwest are world famous, and rightly so. They are simply superb, with a musical combination of karri, jarrah and marri trees sheltering cool undergrowth.

The area of 'tall trees' lies between the Vasse Hwy and the South Western Hwy, and includes the timber towns of Bridgetown, Manjimup, Nannup, Pemberton and Northcliffe.

The forests around Pemberton are simply stunning. Aim to spend at least a day, or preferably two, driving the well-marked **Karri Forest Explorer** tracks, walking the trails and picnicking in the green depths. Popular attractions include the **Gloucester Tree**, laddered with a daunting metal spiral stairway that winds 60m to the top, and the **Dave Evans Bicentennial Tree**, tallest of the 'climbing trees' at 68m, in Warren National Park, 11km south of Pemberton. The Karri Forest Explorer track makes a one-way driving loop via **Maiden Bush** to the **Heartbreak Trail**, passing through 400-year-old karri stands; nearby **Drafty's Camp** and **Warren Campsite** are delightful for overnighting or bush picnics. Take a short scenic walk at **Beedelup National Park**, 15km west of town, where the bridge that crosses Beedelup Brook near **Beedelup Falls** was built from a single karri log.

Wend through marri and karri forests on the scenic **Pemberton Tramway** (☎ 08-9776 1322; www.pemtram.com.au; Pemberton Railway Station; adult/child $18/9) daily at 10.45am and 2pm.

SOUTH COAST

The South Coast, or 'Great Southern', offers all things to all people. Almost everywhere you look is stunning coastline, interspersed with 386,000 hectares of tall forest, including the famous Valley of the Giants; early colonial history and heritage in Albany; and artisanal food, wine and craft.

The peaceful twin inlets of **Walpole** and **Nornalup** make good bases from which to explore the heavily forested Walpole Wilderness Area.

The **Tree Top Walk** (☎ 08-9840 8263; adult/child $8/4; 9am-4.15pm, Christmas school holidays 8am-5.15pm) has become Walpole's main drawcard. A 600m-long ramp gently rises from the floor of the **Valley of the Giants**, allowing visitors access high into the canopy of the giant tingle trees. At its highest point, the ramp is 40m above the ground and the views are simply stunning. The ramp is an engineering feat in itself, though vertigo sufferers might have a few problems; it's designed to sway gently in the breeze, mimicking life in the tree tops. At ground level, the **Ancient Empire** boardwalk meanders around and through the base of veteran red tingles, some of which are 16m in circumference.

The Valley of the Giants is part of the **Walpole Wilderness Area**, which comprises several national parks. Old forests fringe granite peaks, calm rivers and wetlands, sandy beaches and wild coast. Look for *Exploring the Walpole Wilderness and Surrounding Area,* a terrific booklet produced by DEC.

SHARK BAY

The sun-kissed Central West Coast is a 550km stretch from the sedate fishing town of Dongara-Port Denison on the Batavia Coast in the south to the agriculturally lush Gascoyne region surrounding Carnarvon in the north. Jagged sea cliffs, historic settlements, craggy national parks and lovely beaches set the stage for some fascinating exploring.

The spectacular World Heritage–listed site of Shark Bay contains more than 1500km of coastline stretching along two jagged peninsulas and numerous

BLOOMING WILDFLOWERS

Western Australia is famed for its 8000 species of wildflower, which bloom between August and November. Even some of the driest regions put on a colourful display after a little rainfall at any time of the year.

The southwest has over 3000 species, many of which are unique to this region. They're commonly known as everlastings because the petals stay attached after the flowers have died. You can find flowers almost everywhere in the state, but the jarrah forests in the southwest are particularly rich. Coastal national parks such as Fitzgerald River and Kalbarri also have brilliant displays, as do the Stirling Ranges. Near Perth, the Badgingarra, Alexander Morrison, Yanchep and John Forrest national parks are excellent choices. There's also a wildflower display in Kings Park, Perth. As you go further north, they tend to flower earlier in the season. Common flowering plants include mountain bell, Sturt's desert pea and various species of banksia, wattle, kangaroo paw and orchid.

islands. Its natural beauty – white-sand beaches, fiery red cliffs and turquoise lagoons – is only one part of its allure. This is also one of WA's most biologically rich habitats with an array of plant and animal life found nowhere else on earth. Lush beds of seagrass and sheltered bays nourish dugongs, sea turtles, humpback whales, dolphins, rays, sharks and other aquatic life.

DENHAM

Australia's most westerly town, laid-back Denham, with its crystal-clear water and charming beachfront, makes a decent base for visiting the marine park, nearby Francois Peron National Park and Monkey Mia, 26km away. Originally established as a pearling town, Denham was paved with pearl shell, according to old-timers. These days, all you'll see is bitumen, but some shell-brick buildings still stand.

INFORMATION

Shark Bay visitors centre (**☎ 08-9948 1590; 53 Knight Tce; ⌚ 8am-5pm Mon-Fri**) Has plenty of information on the World Heritage area and national park.

SIGHTS & ACTIVITIES

In a striking contemporary building, the cutting- edge **Shark Bay World Heritage Discovery Centre** (**☎ 08-9948 1590; www.sharkbayinterpretivecentre.com.au; 53 Knight Tce; adult/child $10/6; ⌚ 9am-6pm**) is one of WA's best museums, with compelling exhibitions on Shark Bay's natural environment, its Indigenous people, the many explorers who've ventured here and how understanding these entanglements can help us experience a sense of place.

On the way into town, **Ocean Park** (**☎ 08-9948 1765; www.oceanpark.com.au; Shark Bay Rd; adult/child $15/10; ⌚ 10am-3.30pm**) is a locally run aquaculture farm featuring

JOHN HAY

Australian eucalyptus, Margaret River (p292)

an artificial lagoon where you can observe sharks, turtles, stingrays and fish on guided 45-minute tours. The cafe has panoramic views.

TOURS

Majestic Tours (**☎ 08-9948 1627; www.sharkbayholiday.com.au; tours $75-170**) has various full-day 4WD tours, including Francois Peron National Park and Shell Beach. **Shark Bay Scenic Flights** (**☎ 08-9948 1773; www.sharkbayair.com.au**) offers seven different scenic flights including 15-minute Monkey Mia flyovers ($55), 40-minute trips over Zuytdorp Cliffs ($150) and half-day flying/4WD excursions visiting Dirk Hartog Island ($255). **Shark Bay Coaches & Tours** (**☎ 08-9948 1081; www.sbcoaches.com; tours $70**) runs half-day tours to all key sights.

SLEEPING & EATING

Denham Villas (☎ 08-9948 1264; www.denhamvillas.com; 4 Durlacher St; villas $140-155;) The spacious, fully self-contained villas (with proper kitchen and laundry) are excellent value and ideal for families.

Oceanside Village (☎ 08-9948 3003; www.oceanside.com.au; 117 Knight Tce; houses $135-175;) The friendly, Dutch-owned Oceanside Village consists of trim freestanding blue-and-white cottages, most with waterfront views. All have kitchen units, free wi-fi access and small balconies.

Seaside Tourist Village (☎ 1300 133 733, 08-9948 1242; www.sharkbayfun.com; Knight Tce; unpowered/powered sites $25/30, cabins d $70, 1-/2-bedroom chalets $110/125;) This big beachside park has good facilities, including barbecues and self- contained chalets with verandahs overlooking the sea.

Old Pearler Restaurant (☎ 08-9948 1373; Knight Tce; mains $29-45) Built from seashell bricks, this splendid building houses one of WA's most atmospheric old restaurants.

GETTING THERE & AROUND

Skywest (☎ 1300 660 088; www.skywest.com.au) has flights from Geraldton and Carnarvon, linking to Perth, Exmouth and Karratha.

Daily shuttle buses from Denham ($67, 1½ hours) and Monkey Mia ($68, two hours) connect with the north- and south-bound **Greyhound** (☎ 1300 473 946; www.greyhound.com.au) services at the Overlander Roadhouse on the main highway, including Denham to Carnarvon ($115, four hours).

Bay Lodge (☎ 08-9948 1278) runs a shuttle bus to Monkey Mia (Monday, Wednesday, Friday and Saturday; return for nonguests $20) that leaves from the Shell service station on Knight Tce; bookings essential.

FRANCOIS PERON NATIONAL PARK

Renowned for its dramatic golden cliffs, pristine white-sand beaches, salt lakes and rare marsupial species, this **national park** (per bus passenger/car $4/10), 4km from Denham on Monkey Mia Rd, will reward those with 4WD vehicles and an adventurous spirit. There's a visitors centre at the old **Péron Homestead**, 6km from the main road, where a former artesian bore has been converted to a 35°C **hot tub**, a novel spot for a sunset soak. There are **campsites** ($7) with limited facilities at Big Lagoon, Gregories, Bottle Bay and Herald Bight. If you don't have your own wheels, take a tour to the park (see p295).

MONKEY MIA

World-famous for the wild dolphins that turn up in the shallow water for feeding each day, the beach resort of **Monkey Mia** (admission adult/child/family $6/2/12), 26km northeast of Denham, now tops many travellers' list of things to do. The morning feeding session (around 7.45am) can get packed, but often the dolphins return for a second feeding later in the morning. Aside from dolphins, the resort offers plenty of other diversions, including Aboriginal heritage walks, sailing, camel trips, diving and stargazing.

The **Monkey Mia Visitors Centre** (☎ 08-9948 1366; 7.30am-4pm) has lots of info, as well as showing videos and hosting presentations. There are great books for sale in the shop and you can also buy tour tickets here.

TOURS

Aristocat II (☎ 08-9948 1446; 1½-3½hr tours $54-89) On these wonderful wildlife-spotting cruises on the *Shotover* catamaran you'll get to see dugongs, dolphins,

JOHN BANAGAN

Locals at Monkey Mia

loggerhead turtles, sea snakes and perhaps even tiger sharks.

Wula Guda Nyinda Aboriginal Cultural Tours (☎ 0429 708 847, 9948 1320; www.monkeymia.com.au; daytime tour adult/child $30/15, dusk tour $35/17, night tour $30/15) Local Aboriginal guide Darren 'Capes' Capewell (see p276) leads excellent bushwalks where he teaches you 'how to let the bush talk to you'. You'll learn some local Malgana language, and identify bush tucker and native medicine. The evening 'Didgeridoo Dreaming' walks are magical.

SLEEPING & EATING

Monkey Mia is a resort and not a town, so eating and sleeping options are limited. Self-catering is a good option.

Monkey Mia Dolphin Resort (☎ 1800 653 611, 08-9948 1320; www.monkeymia.com.au; tent sites $14, van sites $31-37, dm/d $25/80, garden units $233, beachfront villas $285;) This leafy resort offers a range of accommodation, from popular tent and van sites to top-end villas with verandahs overlooking the beach. Backpackers can overnight in dorms or in simple doubles with shared bathrooms. You can rent kayaks and snorkelling gear, play tennis, watch free films playing daily or just soak up rays on the pretty beach.

Bough Shed Restaurant (☎ 08-9948 1171; mains $15-34) Boasting splendid waterfront views, the Bough Shed offers a tasty selection of seafood and grill items, including Shark Bay snapper, sesame-toasted prawns, Moroccan lamb and vegetarian quesadillas.

CORAL COAST & PILBARA

Western Australia's great reef system may lack the size of the Great Barrier Reef, but it holds some spectacular marine riches. Brilliant coral gardens bloom all around the Ningaloo Reef, while divers and snorkellers can swim with whale sharks and manta rays, and seek dugongs, sea turtles and numerous tropical fish species on sailing tours.

ROSS BARNETT

Pinnacles Desert, Nambung National Park

IF YOU LIKE...

If you like **Francois Peron National Park** (p296) we think you will also like:

- **Cape Range National Park** (admission per vehicle $10) The park covers 510 sq km, about a third of the North-West Cape peninsula, and is rich in wildlife – kangaroos, emus, echidnas – and spectacular scenery. Rugged red stone gorges dramatically cut into the range and flow with deep blue water. The gorges give way to white sand and the sparkling waters of Ningaloo Reef.
- **Nambung National Park** (bus passenger/car $4/10) Seventeen kilometres from Cervantes, Nambung is home to the spectacular and otherworldly Pinnacles Desert, where thousands of limestone pillars are scattered across a moonlike landscape on a golden desert floor.
- **Yalgorup National Park** This beautiful coastal region of woodlands, lakes and sand dunes is 50km south of Mandurah. The park is recognised as a wetland of international significance for seasonally migrating waterbirds, so bird watching here can be rewarding. Amateur scientists can visit the rock-like thrombalites of Lake Clifton, descendants of some of the earliest living organisms on earth.
- **Purnululu National Park** (per car $10) The 3000 sq km of ancient country of this park in the north of the state is home to the wonderful ochre and black striped 'beehive' domes of the Bungle Bungle Range.

CORAL BAY

pop 190

The tiny community of Coral Bay overlooks a picturesque bay in the southern reaches of Ningaloo Marine Park. The town consists of one street, down which you amble to the white-sand beach to swim and snorkel on the reef just offshore. It's a superb base for outer-reef activities as well, such as swimming with (harmless) whale sharks, scuba diving, fishing and whale watching (from June to November).

TOURS

Coral Bay tours include snorkelling, diving, swimming with whale sharks, whale watching, marine-life-spotting tours to search for dolphins, dugongs, turtles and manta rays, and coral viewing from glass-bottom boats. Most trips include equipment and refreshments. Tour operators have offices in the shopping centre.

Coral Bay Adventures (☎ 08-9942 5955; www.coralbayadventures.com.au) This excellent company offers half-day and full-day trips to go wildlife watching ($190), swimming with whale sharks ($345) or manta rays ($150), whale watching ($110) and coral viewing on a glass-bottom boat ($32).

Coral Bay Ecotours (☎ 08-9942 5870; www.coralbayecotours.com.au) This respected ecocertified outfit offers popular glass-bottom boat cruises (one-/two-hour cruise $30/45) with stops for snorkelling, as well as five-hour wildlife-watching cruises ($140) where you can swim with manta rays. They also have sunset cruises ($40), whale-watching cruises in season ($125), and you can book scenic flights here.

Ningaloo Reef Dive (☎ 08-9942 5824; www.ningalooreefdive.com) This outfit specialises in diving and snorkelling, and offers snorkelling with whale sharks ($365, from late March to June), reef dives ($160) and PADI courses from $445.

SLEEPING & EATING

our pick **Ningaloo Club** (☎ 08-9948 5100; www.ningalooclub.com; dm $24-26, d/tr without bathroom $80/100, d/tr with bathroom $100/120;) This excellent and well-maintained hostel boasts a festive ambience, with its central pool a focal point. It also has a well-equipped kitchen, big lounge area with bar and table tennis.

Bayview Coral Bay Resort (☎ 08-9385 7411; www.coralbaywa.com; unpowered/powered sites $30/33, cabins d from $95, chalets $125-270;) Offers an enormous range of quality accommodation, including grassy sites for camping or parking the van, along with comfortable self-contained villas, units, chalets and cabins. The resort facilities are far-ranging: swimming pool, barbecues, tennis courts, kid's playground, and you can book discount tours here.

Ningaloo Reef Resort (☎ 08-9942 5934; www.ningalooreefresort.com.au; d/apt from $191/243;) On a fine grassy site above the beach, this laid-back resort, pub and bottle shop has a range of accommodation, from motel-style rooms to spacious apartments. The pub, Coral Bay's only drinking spot, is particularly popular on Thursdays when there's live music.

GETTING THERE & AWAY

Skywest Airlines (☎ 1300 660 088; www.skywest.com.au) flies into Exmouth's Learmonth airport, about a 75-minute drive from Coral Bay; most Coral Bay resorts can arrange a private taxi service on request. **Greyhound** (☎ 1300 473 946; www.greyhound.com.au) has regular bus services via Exmouth and, along with **Easyrider** and **Western Exposure** buses, stop at the Ningaloo Club.

EXMOUTH

pop 2500

Gateway to the magnificent Ningaloo Marine Park and Cape Range National Park, Exmouth is a lively little place where the natural world frequently interacts with small-town life. Emus still wander through the main streets and parks of Exmouth, while pink-breasted galahs rule the skies and kangaroos and goannas keep watch over the highway leading into town.

INFORMATION

Visitors centre (☎ 1800 287 328, 08-9949 1176; www.exmouthwa.com.au; Murat Rd;

ANDREW BAIN

Snorkelling the waters of the Ningaloo reef

↘ NINGALOO MARINE PARK

The spectacular **Ningaloo Marine Park** protects more than 250km of waters and foreshore areas from Bundegi Reef in the northeast of the North-West Cape peninsula to Amherst Point in the southwest. The Ningaloo reef lies only 100m offshore and is home to a staggering array of marine life: sharks, manta rays, humpback whales, turtles, dugongs and more than 500 species of fish.

There's wonderful marine activity to enjoy year-round:

November to February Turtles – four species are known to nestle and hatch in the sands.

March & April Coral spawning – a dazzling event 10–12 days after a full moon.

May to July Whale sharks – these behemoths follow the coral spawning.

May to November Manta rays – dramatic migrations in big schools.

July to November Humpback whales – they have fun splashing about on their migration south.

What also makes Ningaloo special is its **coral**. Over 220 species of hard coral have been recorded, from the slow-growing bommies to delicate branching varieties. It's this coral that attracts the park's biggest drawcard, the speckled **whale shark** *(Rhiniodon typus)*. Ningaloo is the only place in the world where these solitary gentle giants arrive like clockwork each year to feed on plankton and small fish, making the area a mecca for marine biologists and tourists alike.

Most people visit Ningaloo to snorkel. Stop at the **Milyering visitors centre** to get maps, information and an eyeful of dangerous critters in glass bottles. Staff can tell you which beaches are best for snorkelling and where to avoid dangerous currents off the reefs. The shop sells and rents snorkelling equipment.

Things you need to know Visitors centre (☎ 08-9949 2808; 🕑 9am-3.45pm)

9am-5pm Mon-Fri, 9am-noon Sat & Sun) Has lots of info on the national parks and good fishing spots, and can book tours, flights, bus tickets and accommodation.

TOURS

Memorable tours from Exmouth include swimming with whale sharks, whale watching, wildlife spotting, scuba diving, sea kayaking, fishing and coral viewing from glass-bottom boats.

Ningaloo Dreaming (**08-9949 4777; www.ningaloodreaming.com; Exmouth Shopping Centre, Maidstone Cres; from $135**) This eco-certified company offers whale-shark cruises, wildlife spotting, trips to Muiron Islands, scuba-diving courses and dives off biologically rich Exmouth Navy Pier.

Ningaloo Ecology Cruises (**08-9949 2255; www.ecology.com.au; tours from $60**) Operates one- to 2½-hour glass-bottom boat trips to view coral in the Ningaloo Reef, leaving from Tatabiddi on the west coast of the cape (free bus transfers).

SLEEPING

Potshot Hotel Resort (**08-9949 1200; www.potshotresort.com; Murat Rd; dm/d $28/65, motel d $68, studio $164, apt from $175;**) This bustling resort, with several bars, two eateries, a swimming pool and a bottle shop, offers a range of clean and comfortable sleeps, from simple motel rooms to the trim and stylish Osprey Apartments across the road.

Novotel Ningaloo Resort (**08-9949 0000; www.novotelningaloo.com.au; Madaffari Dr; d/apt from $275/355;**) Opened in 2006, the Novotel Ningaloo Resort, has brought a new level of sophistication (and expense) to Exmouth. Handsomely designed rooms feature tasteful fabrics and ample natural light, and even the standards are spacious and well equipped. All have balconies, while the best rooms sport ocean views. There's a private beach, a large pool, and an excellent restaurant.

ORIEN HARVEY

Surfers at Salmon Holes, near Albany

IF YOU LIKE...

If you like diving **Ningaloo Marine Park** (opposite) we think you might also like:

- **Geraldton** The Houtman Abrolhos archipelago of 122 coral islands is about 60km off the coast of Geraldton. Here *Acropora* genus corals abound and, thanks to the warm Leeuwin Current, a rare and spectacular mix of tropical and temperate fish species thrives.
- **Busselton** On the shores of Geographe Bay, 230km south of Perth, diving is popular, especially on Four Mile Reef (a 40km limestone ledge about 6.5km off the coast) and on the scuttled navy vessel HMAS *Swan* off Dunsborough.
- **Albany** It's been a top-class diving destination since the warship HMAS *Perth* was scuttled in 2001 to create an artificial reef. Its natural reefs feature temperate corals that are home to the bizarre and wonderful leafy and weedy sea dragons.

GETTING THERE & AWAY

Exmouth's Learmonth airport is 37km south of town and there are daily **Skywest** (☎ 1300 660 088; www.skywest.com.au) flights to and from Perth.

Buses stop at the visitors centre. **Greyhound** (☎ 1300 473 946; www.greyhound.com.au) has three services a week from Perth ($252, 20 hours).

THE KIMBERLEY & BROOME

The vast and rugged Kimberley holds some of Australia's most spectacular – and remote – scenery. With just two opposing seasons, the Wet and the Dry, the Kimberley is a land of extremes: semi-arid plains dotted with spinifex, outback roads that flow like rivers, panoramic ranges cut by steep stony gorges and dramatic waterfalls surrounded by tropical rainforest.

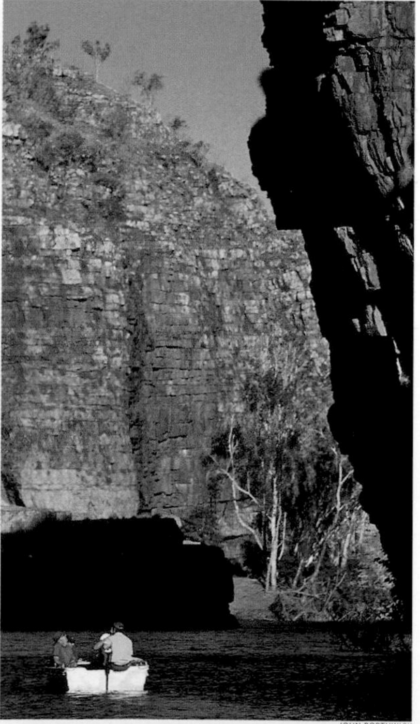

JOHN BORTHWICK

Crusing though a gorge in the Kimberley

Broome's peninsula setting is undoubtedly dramatic, from the powdery white sands of its famous Cable Beach to the deep aquamarine hues of Roebuck Bay. Surrounding the town is the arid clay-baked landscape of the Kimberley, which turns lush when the thundering storms of the Wet arrive. The natural world is very much a part of Broome's allure, from fiery red sunsets over the beach to enchanting full-moon rises over the mud flats.

INFORMATION

Visitors centre (☎ 08-9192 2222; www.broomevisitorcentre.com.au; 1 Hamersley St; 8.30am-4.30pm Mon-Fri, 9.30am-2.30pm Sat & Sun Apr-Nov, 9am-4pm Mon-Fri, 10am-2pm Sat & Sun Dec-Mar) Just off the first roundabout on the way into town, the visitors centre has masses of info on the Kimberley and Broome, and books transport, accommodation and tours.

SIGHTS & ACTIVITIES

About 4km west of town, **Cable Beach** is one of Australia's finest beaches, with azure waters and a wide, unblemished stretch of white sand as far as the eye can see. Red dunes rise behind the beach, with marked walking paths leading to **Gantheaume Point**, 7km south of Broome.

Enchanting **Chinatown** is Broome's historical and commercial heart; there's scant evidence of the Chinese now, its atmosphere coming from the vernacular architecture. Corrugated-iron buildings with lattice, louvres and verandahs line Carnarvon St, Short St, Dampier Tce and Napier Tce.

JOHN BANAGAN

Camel ride, Broome

Pearl Luggers (☎ 08-9192 2059; www.pearlluggers.com.au; 31 Dampier Tce; admission free; 75min tours adult/child $19/free; ⏰ tours 9am, 11am, 1pm & 3pm) offers compelling tours covering Broome's pearling past, including a glimpse of restored sailing vessels, rare archival footage of divers at work, and a taster of flavourful pearl meat. Equally fascinating is **Broome Museum** (☎ 08-9192 2075; 67 Robinson St; adult/child/concession $5/1/3; ⏰ 10am-4pm Mon-Fri, 10am-1pm Sat & Sun Jun-Oct; 10am-1pm Nov-May), with a collection of early photos documenting the town's multicultural history and exhibits on pearling and luggers.

Tiny **Town Beach** is fine for a dip, while the **port** has a pleasant sandy beach from where you can swim across to the rocks, and good fishing from the jetty.

TOURS

Broome Sightseeing Tours (☎ 08-9192 5041; www.broomesightseeingtours.com; adult/child $90/70) An award-winning, comprehensive four-hour guided multimedia tour.

Red Sun Camels (☎ 08-9193 7423; www.redsuncamels.com.au; 40min morning ride adult/child $45/30, 1hr sunset ride $60/40) Seeing Cable Beach from atop a slow-moving dromedary is an essential Broome experience, particularly for the youngest of travellers.

Willie Creek Pearl Farm (☎ 08-9192 0000; www.williecreekpearls.com.au) A fascinating insight into modern pearl farming with compelling presentations on oyster insemination, plus a boat ride on the azure-coloured estuary to see a pearl farm. Half-day bus tour from Broome (adult/child $80/40) or self-drive (4WD recommended) then join the two-hour tour at the farm ($40/20). You can also sign up for a helicopter tour over the coastline.

SLEEPING

Prices skyrocket during the Dry. If you're here in the Wet, compare deals, as many places slash their rates (some by 50%). Prices listed in this section are for the high season (June to October).

Broome Motel (☎ 08-9192 7775; www.broomemotel.com.au; 51-57 Frederick St; d $175, self-contained r $225;) This pleasant two-storey motel has clean, comfortable rooms with TV, fridge and tea and coffee facilities; it's just a short stroll into Chinatown.

Seashells Resort (☎ 08-9192 6111; www.seashells.com.au; 4 Challenor Dr; 1-/2-/3-bedroom apt $295/345/425;) A short walk to Cable Beach, Seashells has spacious, attractive apartments and bungalows, each with a verandah and a fully equipped kitchen.

Cable Beach Club Resort (☎ 08-9192 0400; www.cablebeachclub.com; Cable Beach Rd; d/bungalow/villa from $376/529/846;) Broome architecture plus touches of Eastern exoticism create an idyllic retreat at this beautifully set resort near the edge of Cable Beach. Lush gardens, serene swimming pools, fine restaurants, a spa and numerous other facilities add to the appeal.

EATING

Broome has the only serious dining scene between Perth and Darwin. During the Wet some eateries close, keep shorter hours or only offer takeaway. Chinatown has the densest concentration of restaurants, particularly on Napier Tce and neighbouring Carnarvon St. Self-caterers should visit well-stocked supermarkets and bakeries at the Paspaley and Boulevard shopping centres.

GETTING THERE & AWAY

Broome is a regional hub with flights or links to all Australian capitals, including Perth and several towns in the Kimberley. **Greyhound Australia** (☎ 1300 473 946; www.greyhound.com.au) stops at the visitors centre.

TASMANIA

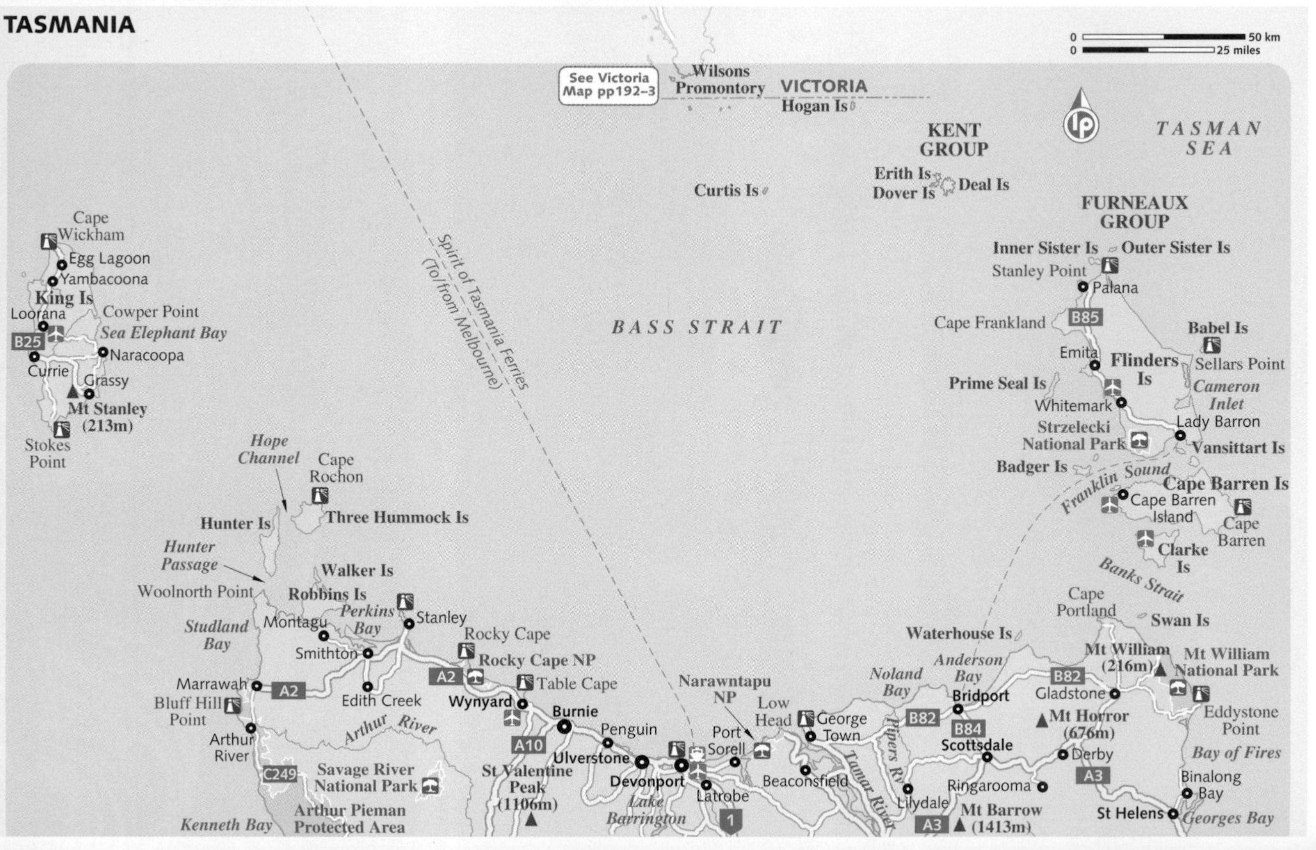
TASMANIA
0 50 km
0 25 miles
See Victoria Map pp192–3
Wilsons Promontory
VICTORIA
Hogan Is
KENT GROUP
Erith Is
Dover Is
Deal Is
Curtis Is
TASMAN SEA
FURNEAUX GROUP
Inner Sister Is
Outer Sister Is
Stanley Point
Palana
Cape Frankland
B85
Babel Is
Emita
Flinders Is
Sellars Point
Cameron Inlet
Prime Seal Is
Whitemark
Lady Barron
Strzelecki National Park
Vansittart Is
Badger Is
Franklin Sound
Cape Barren Is
Cape Barren Island
Cape Barren
Clarke Is
Banks Strait
Cape Portland
Swan Is
Waterhouse Is
Mt William (216m)
Mt William National Park
Anderson Bay
Noland Bay
B82
Gladstone
Eddystone Point
Bridport
Mt Horror (676m)
B84
Scottsdale
Derby
Bay of Fires
A3
Binalong Bay
St Helens
Georges Bay
Ringarooma
Lilydale
Mt Barrow (1413m)
Pipers Rv
Tamar River
Beaconsfield
George Town
Low Head
Narawntapu NP
Port Sorell
Latrobe
1
Devonport
Lake Barrington
Ulverstone
Penguin
Burnie
A10
St Valentine Peak (1106m)
Wynyard
Table Cape
Rocky Cape NP
Rocky Cape
A2
Stanley
Perkins Bay
Smithton
Montagu
Edith Creek
Arthur River
Savage River National Park
Arthur Pieman Protected Area
C249
Kenneth Bay
Arthur River
Bluff Hill Point
Marrawah
Studland Bay
Woolnorth Point
Robbins Is
Walker Is
Hunter Passage
Hunter Is
Hope Channel
Cape Rochon
Three Hummock Is
BASS STRAIT
Spirit of Tasmania Ferries (To/from Melbourne)
Cape Wickham
Egg Lagoon
Yambacoona
King Is
Loorana
Cowper Point
Sea Elephant Bay
B25
Naracoopa
Currie
Grassy
Mt Stanley (213m)
Stokes Point

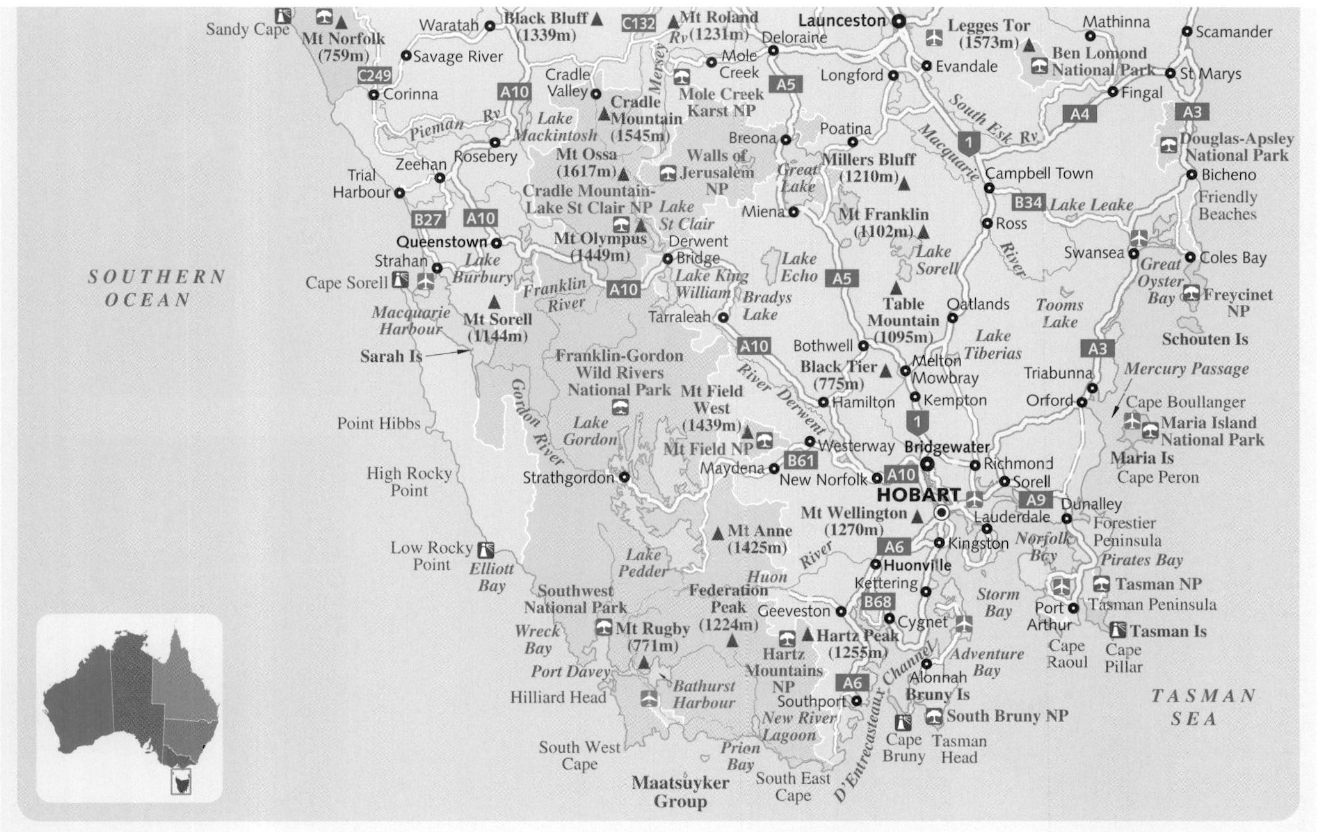
SOUTHERN OCEAN
TASMAN SEA
Sandy Cape
Mt Norfolk (759m)
Corinna
Savage River
Waratah
Black Bluff (1339m)
Cradle Valley
Cradle Mountain (1545m)
Mt Roland (1231m)
Mole Creek
Mole Creek Karst NP
Deloraine
Launceston
Legges Tor (1573m)
Evandale
Ben Lomond National Park
Mathinna
Fingal
St Marys
Scamander
Douglas-Apsley National Park
Bicheno
Friendly Beaches
Coles Bay
Freycinet NP
Schouten Is
Great Oyster Bay
Swansea
Lake Leake
Campbell Town
Ross
South Esk Rv
Macquarie River
Longford
Poatina
Millers Bluff (1210m)
Mt Franklin (1102m)
Lake Sorell
Tooms Lake
Oatlands
Lake Tiberias
Melton Mowbray
Kempton
Bridgewater
Richmond
Sorell
Triabunna
Orford
Mercury Passage
Cape Boullanger
Maria Island National Park
Maria Is
Cape Peron
Dunalley
Forestier Peninsula
Pirates Bay
Tasman NP
Tasman Peninsula
Tasman Is
Cape Pillar
Port Arthur
Cape Raoul
Norfolk Bay
Lauderdale
Kingston
Storm Bay
HOBART
Mt Wellington (1270m)
Huonville
Kettering
Cygnet
Adventure Bay
Alonnah
Bruny Is
South Bruny NP
Cape Bruny
Tasman Head
D'Entrecasteaux Channel
Southport
Hartz Peak (1255m)
Hartz Mountains NP
Geeveston
Huon River
South East Cape
New River Lagoon
Prion Bay
Maatsuyker Group
Bathurst Harbour
Mt Rugby (771m)
Southwest National Park
Port Davey
Hilliard Head
South West Cape
Wreck Bay
Federation Peak (1224m)
Mt Anne (1425m)
Lake Pedder
Maydena
Mt Field NP
Mt Field West (1439m)
New Norfolk
Westerway
Hamilton
Black Tier (775m)
Bothwell
Table Mountain (1095m)
River Derwent
Bradys Lake
Lake Echo
Miena
Great Lake
Walls of Jerusalem NP
Breona
Tarraleah
Lake King William
Derwent Bridge
Lake St Clair
Cradle Mountain-Lake St Clair NP
Mt Ossa (1617m)
Mt Olympus (1449m)
Lake Mackintosh
Mersey Rv
Franklin River
Franklin-Gordon Wild Rivers National Park
Lake Gordon
Strathgordon
Gordon River
Mt Sorell (1144m)
Sarah Is
Macquarie Harbour
Lake Burbury
Queenstown
Strahan
Cape Sorell
Rosebery
Zeehan
Pieman Rv
Trial Harbour
Point Hibbs
High Rocky Point
Low Rocky Point
Elliott Bay
A10
A5
A4
A3
A9
A6
B34
B27
B61
B68
C132
C249
1

TASMANIA

TASMANIA HIGHLIGHTS

1 HOBART WATERFRONT

BY MICHAEL TATLOW, HISTORIAN & CO-AUTHOR OF *A WALK IN OLD HOBART*

Curled like a horseshoe around majestic Sullivans Cove, Hobart's waterfront is a captivating working fishing, shipping and recreational port right in the city, and was the cradle of white settlement in 1804. It offers a few hours of entertainment, marvellous restaurants, an iconic museum and gracious buildings of sandstone recalling the area's colourful past.

↘ MICHAEL TATLOW'S DON'T MISS LIST

❶ VICTORIA DOCK

I recommend you begin your waterfront sojourn beside old **Victoria Dock**, packed with fishing boats, on the cove's northeastern shore. The stone, multistorey former warehouses facing Hunter St house restaurants and shops and the five-star **Henry Jones Art Hotel** (p322). Stroll southwest over the swing-bridge and past, on the River Derwent side, an array of bronze sculptures of seals, birds and heroes of Antarctic exploration who set out from here.

❷ CONSTITUTION DOCK

Fishing and recreational boats fill **Constitution Dock**. Beside **Mures** seafood restaurant (p323) there is a row of punts in the water selling fresh fish and fried fish and chips. The dock and pier are the destination for yachts that arrive every December after the classic Sydney to Hobart ocean classic, which fills the waterfront with people. One of the stately queens of the dock is the restored 1867 sailing ship *May Queen*.

Clockwise from top: Tasmanian Museum & Art Gallery (p320); Crowds at the Salamanca Market (p317); Salamanca Market browsers; Buying fish from a floating punt, Constitution Dock; Victoria Dock

CLOCKWISE FROM TOP: RICHARD I'ANSON; GRANT DIXON; GRANT DIXON; RICHARD I'ANSON; MANFRED GOTTSCHALK

❸ MUSEUMS

Facing Constitution Dock is the ornate former Customs House, now part of the outstanding **Tasmanian Museum & Art Gallery** (p320). The museum has a splendid collection of Indigenous memorabilia, and showpieces from the days when the island was a penal colony for convicts transported from Britain and Ireland. Do not miss the museum's Antarctic display and collections of fauna and of colonial and contemporary art. Also by the dock, on Argyle St, is a fine showcase of the island's seafaring past in the **Maritime Museum of Tasmania** (p320).

❹ SALAMANCA PLACE

On the southern shore of Sullivan's Cove is breathtaking Salamanca Place, with a long row of sandstone former warehouses that once bordered the river. This was home to a generation of whaling clipper ships. The **Salamanca Market** (p317), the nation's top street market, operates here every Saturday at the dining, wining and entertainment hub of Hobart.

➘ THINGS YOU NEED TO KNOW

Best photo opportunity Reflections of boats, colonial buildings and Mt Wellington in the mirrorlike waters **Best time to visit** From late December to early January the waterfront hosts the Taste Festival (p49); sample culinary delights including seafood, wine and cheese

TASMANIA HIGHLIGHTS

2

↘ PORT ARTHUR HISTORIC SITE

Just an hour or so from Hobart lies the rugged and dramatic Tasman Peninsula, and cradled on one of its verdant shorelines is Australia's most poignant historical location. The **Port Arthur Historic Site** (p326) is a serenely beautiful if desperately sad reminder of Tasmania's brutal convict past. A guided tour of the restored buildings, complete with anecdotes, is a must; the ghost tour is only for the brave!

3

↘ CRADLE MOUNTAIN-LAKE ST CLAIR NATIONAL PARK

The glacier-sculpted, twin-peak majesty of Cradle Mountain is the crowning glory of renowned **Cradle Mountain-Lake St Clair National Park** (p329). The legendary adventure within this rugged park is the week-long Overland Track. Alternatively, at the foot of Cradle Mountain are atmospheric short walks to charge the spirit, postcard-perfect scenery to soothe the eyes and cosy lodgings to warm the heart.

4

STRAHAN

Take a tour on the wild side. Tasmania's wet and windy west coast faces the Roaring Forties and provides a true wilderness experience. The cheery little village of **Strahan** (p328) is your base for exploring the lonely beaches and rain-soaked forests. The highlight of any trip here is a Gordon River cruise into the heart of the eerie and magnificent west coast wilderness.

5

FREYCINET NATIONAL PARK

Basking in the east coast's sun-dappled waters is the gorgeous Freycinet Peninsula and popular **Freycinet National Park** (p326). Taking centre stage is famous Wineglass Bay, a perfect arc of sugar-white sand embracing sapphire-blue waters. Other pristine beaches, energetic hikes and furry wildlife will keep you enthralled.

6

MOUNT WELLINGTON

Keeping a comforting eye over the environs of Hobart, **Mt Wellington** (p321) vividly displays the changing climatic moods of the city – be that dusted in snow on a crystal-clear winter morning or quietly vanishing in the clouds on a stormy afternoon. The summit lookout over Hobart and the Derwent River is simply a must-do when in town.

2 GRANT DIXON; 3 GRANT DIXON; 4 RICHARD I'ANSON; 5 PETER HENDRIE; 6 GRANT DIXON

2 Port Arthur (p326); 3 Cradle Mountain (p329) reflected in Dove Lake; 4 Strahan (p328); 5 Canoeing on the Freycinet Peninsula (p326); 6 Hobart sits below Mt Wellington (p321)

TASMANIA'S BEST...

WILDLIFE ENCOUNTERS

- **Freycinet National Park** (p326) Wildlife abounds in this coastal park, though early morning or evening and nights reveal the true numbers of marsupials
- **Tasmanian Devil Conservation Park** (p325) This important devil conservation centre also show-cases other Tasmanian wildlife
- **Cradle Mountain** (p329) The many short hikes feature cute and curious wallabies

PLACES WITH A VIEW

- **Mt Wellington** (p321) The view from the summit is unbelievable
- **Wineglass Bay** (p327) Take an energetic uphill hike to look down on this picturesque bay
- **Cradle Mountain** (p329) It may be rare to get a sunny day, but the reflection of the mountain in placid Dove Lake is divine

GHOSTLY EXPERIENCES

- **Port Arthur** (p326) The sombre ruins have stories to tell – take a ghost tour to bring them alive
- **Hobart** (p316) Historic Hobart has a remarkable collection of colonial buildings and another ghost tour
- **Strahan** (p328) This wild west-coast town hosts the wonderful, interactive play, *The Ship that Never Was*. Every night!

TASTE TEMPTATIONS

- **Hobart waterfront** (p308) Home to several superb restaurants, this is the place to sample Tassie's excellent seafood
- **Cascade Brewery** (p320) Some of Australia's finest lagers are brewed in this imposing Gothic brewery, Australia's oldest
- **Taste Festival** (p49) Tasmania celebrates its culinary flair with a week-long festival centred on the Hobart waterfront

LEFT: JOHN BANAGAN; RIGHT: LINDSAY BROWN

Left: Tasmanian devils (p362); Right: Port Arthur (p326)

THINGS YOU NEED TO KNOW

VITAL STATISTICS

- **Population** 497,500
- **Telephone code** ☎ 03
- **Best time to visit** October to May

ADVANCE PLANNING

- **One month before** Book flights and/or berths on *Spirit of Tasmania* (p316)
- **Two weeks before** Book your Gordon River cruise (p328)
- **One week before** Book a table at Mures (p323) and a place on a Hobart Ghost Tour (p322)

RESOURCES

There are helpful visitor information centres in most major towns. They are generally overflowing with brochures, including the free publications *Tasmanian Travelways, Treasure Island* and *Explore Tasmania,* all containing statewide listings of accommodation, events, public transport and vehicle hire.

- **Tourism Tasmania** (☎ 1300 827 743, 03-6230 8235; www.discovertasmania.com) The government-operated tourism authority has a good website and provides loads of travel information.
- **Parks & Wildlife Service** (☎ 1300 315 513; www.parks.tas.gov.au) This service has detailed information on walks, camp sites, activities and facilities in the state's magical national parks and reserves.
- **Royal Automobile Club of Tasmania** (RACT; ☎ 13 27 22; www.ract.com.au) The RACT offers roadside automotive assistance, road weather updates and general travel information.

EMERGENCY NUMBERS

- **Police, fire and ambulance** (☎ 000)
- **Hobart Police Station** (☎ 03-6230 2111; www.police.tas.gov.au; 43 Liverpool St; 24hr)
- **Royal Hobart Hospital** (☎ 03-6222 8423; www.dhhs.tas.gov.au; 48 Liverpool St; 24hr) Argyle St emergency entry.

GETTING AROUND

- **Walk** around the Hobart waterfront and Battery Point
- **Bus** (p324) around the island
- **Airporter Shuttle Bus** (p324) will take you to/from the airport

BE FOREWARNED

- **Cradle Mountain** (p329) is cloudy eight days out of 10.
- **Port Arthur Historic Site** (p326) staff won't speak of the 1996 massacre.
- **Salamanca Place** (p317) becomes a buzzing market each and every Saturday – don't miss it!

TASMANIA ITINERARIES

HERITAGE JAUNT Three days

After arriving in **(1) Hobart** (p316) stretch the legs on a leisurely walk around the historic port, soaking up the maritime atmosphere and colonial past. Don't miss the Tasmanian Museum & Art Gallery (p320) or the Maritime Museum of Tasmania.

Take a stroll up Kellys Steps to revive early life in Battery Point (p319), and enjoy a seafood meal at one of the many impressive seafood restaurants on the waterfront. Experience the erstwhile colony's early days with a guided tour and, if you are game, join a ghost tour (p320) to add an extra edge to your first night in Hobart.

The next day head out along the forbidding **(2) Tasman Peninsula** (p324) to experience the solemn beauty of **(3) Port Arthur Historic Site** (p326). A guided tour is a must, and so is a harbour cruise to the Isle of the Dead with a stop at the tragic Point Puer Boys' Prison. Aficionados will spend the night at Port Arthur and inflict the Historic Ghost Tour on their already rattled nerves. It's fun! After a restless night you can return to Hobart where (of course) there are far fewer ghosts...

SUNNYSIDE UP Five days

Tasmania's east coast is the sunny side of this 40-degree-south island. Spend a couple of days roaming the charming city of **(1) Hobart** (p316). Hobart has a surprisingly cosmopolitan vibe with good coffee, contemporary arts and wonderful restaurants fused with its colonial inheritance.

If the sky is clear head to the summit of Mt Wellington (p321) for stupendous views over the city and beyond. The next destination is the dramatic **(2) Tasman Peninsula** (p324), where the brutal grandeur of the coastline hints at the cruel human history at Port Arthur Historic Site (p326).

History lesson over, wind your way north, stopping to talk to the devil (Tasmanian devil, that is) at Taranna (p325). Near Copping, look out for the short-cut to the east coast via the winding Wielangta Forest Drive.

Take a break in Swansea before landing at Coles Bay and the beautiful **(3) Freycinet National Park** (p326). You need at least two days to explore the park on foot, experiencing the wildlife and, of course, the beauty of pristine Wineglass Bay (p327).

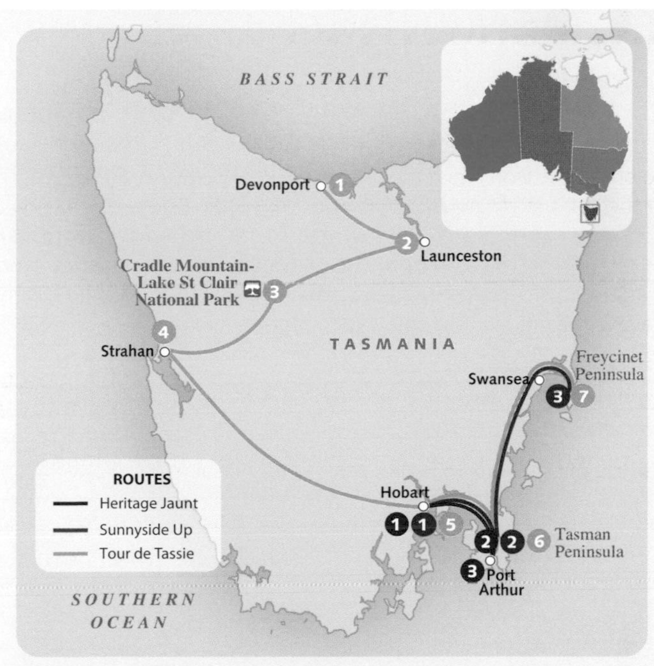

TOUR DE TASSIE One week

Compact Tasmania is perfect for a whirlwind tour where the theme is to fit in as much as possible. A great way to arrive in Tassie is on the *Spirit of Tasmania* from Melbourne. Drive straight off the boat or pick up a hire car in **(1) Devonport**.

Take lunch in Tasmania's second city, **(2) Launceston**, before heading up through rolling countryside to **(3) Cradle Mountain-Lake St Clair National Park** (p329). After taking the mountain air and stretching the legs on a few mountain walks, head down to **(4) Strahan** (p328), the historical port on the wild west coast.

Take a Gordon River cruise before heading east over the mountains to **(5) Hobart** (p316). Take your time in the relaxed capital; ideally you will have timed your visit to coincide with Saturday's Salamanca Market (p317).

From Hobart you should wend your way along the east coast, via historic **(6) Port Arthur** (p326) and picturesque **(7) Freycinet National Park** (p326), before heading back to your departure point of Devonport, Launceston or Hobart.

DISCOVER TASMANIA

Dazzlin' Tassie is brilliant, beautiful and accessible. It's compact enough to 'do' in a few weeks and layered enough to keep bringing you back. The island state has exquisite beaches, jagged mountain ranges, rarefied alpine plateaus, plentiful wildlife and vast tracts of virgin wilderness, much of it within a World Heritage area. Tasmania produces some of the world's great gourmet food and wine, and has a flourishing arts scene and a burgeoning urban cool.

For too long Australian mainlanders derided their compatriots across Bass Strait, partly because Tasmania took a long time to emerge from the ignominy of its grim past.

Tassie's bushwalking, cycling, rafting and kayaking opportunities rank among the best on the planet. See voluptuous Wineglass Bay, brilliant Bay of Fires and the ragged craggy glory of Cradle Mountain. Come and camp out, or doss down in some superb boutique hotel accommodation. Tasmania is still Australia, but beguilingly, bewitchingly, a little different.

GETTING THERE & AWAY

Airlines flying between Tasmania and mainland Australia:

Jetstar (☎ 13 15 38; www.jetstar.com.au) Direct flights from Melbourne, Sydney and Brisbane to Hobart and Launceston.

Qantas (☎ 13 13 13; www.qantas.com.au) Direct flights from Sydney and Melbourne to Hobart, and from Melbourne to Launceston. QantasLink (the regional subsidiary) flies between Melbourne and Devonport.

Virgin Blue (☎ 13 67 89; www.virginblue.com.au) Direct flights from Melbourne, Sydney, Brisbane and Adelaide to Hobart, and from Melbourne and Sydney to Launceston.

The **Spirit of Tasmania** (☎ 1800 634 906; www.spiritoftasmania.com.au) operates two ferries that cruise nightly between Melbourne and Devonport in both directions, usually departing at 9pm and taking about 10 hours shore to shore. Additional daytime sailings are scheduled during peak and shoulder seasons. There's a range of cabin and seat options, and child, student, pensioner and senior discounts apply. Some cabins are wheelchair-accessible. And you can bring your car!

HOBART

pop 200,525

Hobart rocks! It's Australia's second-oldest city and southernmost capital, lying at the foothills of Mt Wellington on the banks of the Derwent River. The waterfront areas around Sullivans Cove – Macquarie Wharf, Constitution Dock, Salamanca Place and Battery Point – are simply gorgeous with their neat Georgian buildings and the towering bulk of Mt Wellington behind.

Hobart visitor information centre (☎ 03-6230 8233; www.hobarttravelcentre.com.au; cnr Davey & Elizabeth Sts; 8.30am-5.30pm Mon-Fri, 9am-5pm Sat, Sun & public holidays) has brochures, maps, information and statewide tour and accommodation bookings.

GRANT DIXON

Outdoor dining, Salamanca Place

↘ SALAMANCA PLACE

This picturesque row of four-storey sandstone warehouses on Sullivans Cove is a wonderful example of Australian colonial architecture and the best-preserved and most cohesive historic urban precinct in the country. Salamanca Place was the hub of old Hobart Town's trade and commerce, but by the mid–20th century many of these 1830s whaling-era buildings had become decrepit ruins. The 1970s saw the dawning of Tasmania's sense of 'heritage', from which flowed a push to revive the warehouses as home to restaurants, cafes, bars and shops – an evolution that continues today. The development of the quarry behind the warehouses into **Salamanca Square** has bolstered the atmosphere.

Operating behind the scenes here is a vibrant and creative arts community. The nonprofit **Salamanca Arts Centre** occupies seven Salamanca warehouses and is home to 75-plus arts organisations and individuals, including shops, galleries, studios, performing arts venues and public spaces.

Colourful hippies and crazy craftspeople have been coming to sell their wares at **Salamanca Market** on Saturday mornings since 1972. They come from all over the state's southern reaches with their fresh produce, secondhand clothes and books, tacky tourist souvenirs, CDs, cheap sunglasses, antiques and bric-a-brac. The buskers and jugglers also come, as do the purveyors of fine food and snake-oil treatments, and everyone enjoys the street-party love-in atmosphere. Rain or shine – don't miss it!

To reach Salamanca Place from Battery Point, descend the well-weathered **Kellys Steps**, wedged between warehouses halfway along the main block of buildings.

Things you need to know Salamanca Arts Centre (☎ 03-6234 8414; www.salarts.org.au; 77 Salamanca Pl; ⏰ shops & galleries 9am-6pm); Salamanca Market (☎ 03-6238 2843; www.hobartcity.com.au; ⏰ 8.30am-3pm Sat)

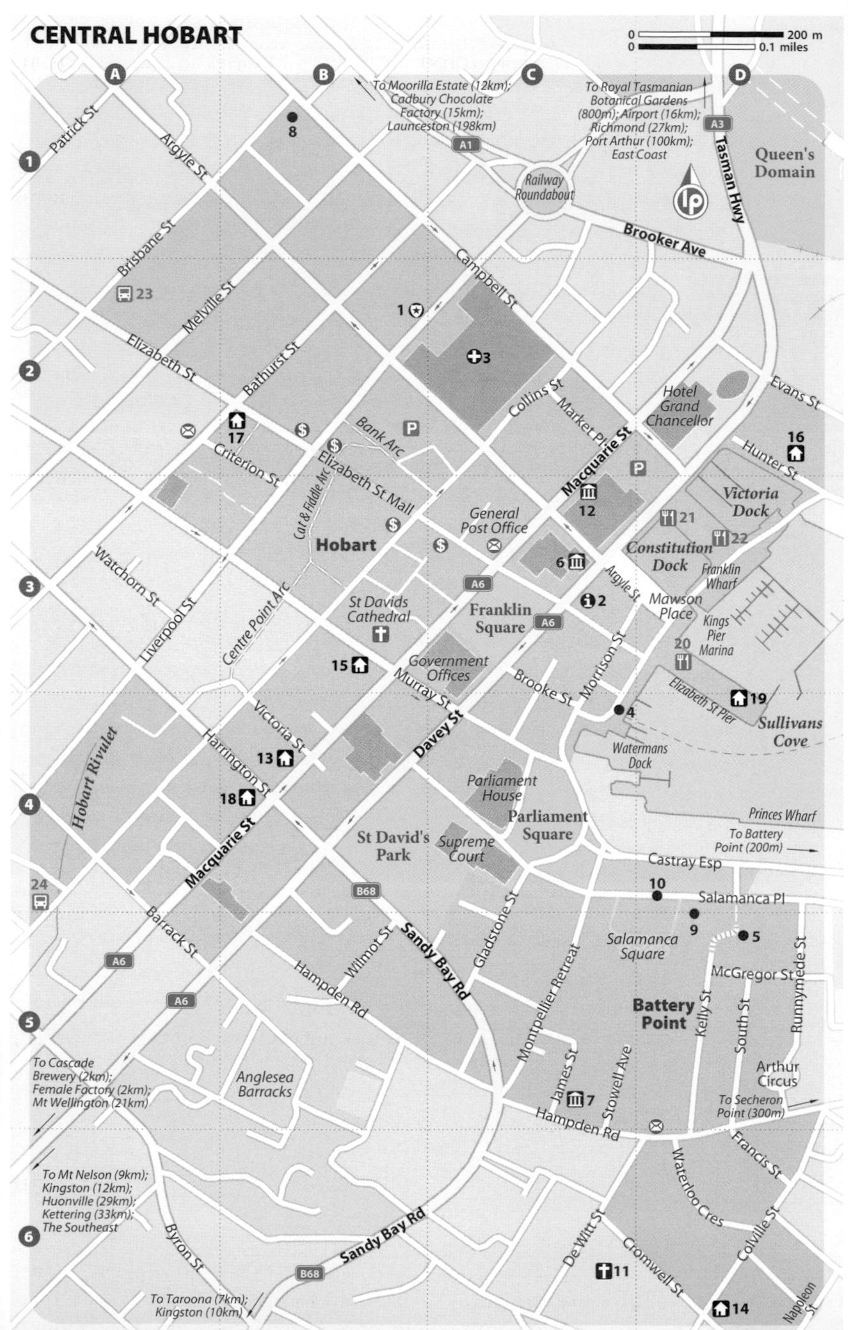
CENTRAL HOBART
0 200 m
0 0.1 miles
To Moorilla Estate (12km); Cadbury Chocolate Factory (15km); Launceston (198km)
To Royal Tasmanian Botanical Gardens (800m); Airport (16km); Richmond (27km); Port Arthur (100km); East Coast
Queen's Domain
Railway Roundabout
Tasman Hwy
Brooker Ave
Patrick St
Argyle St
Brisbane St
Melville St
Campbell St
Elizabeth St
Bathurst St
Collins St
Market Pl
Macquarie St
Hotel Grand Chancellor
Evans St
Hunter St
Bank Arc
Criterion St
Elizabeth St Mall
Cat & Fiddle Arc
Hobart
General Post Office
Victoria Dock
Constitution Dock
Franklin Wharf
Watchorn St
Liverpool St
Centre Point Arc
St Davids Cathedral
Franklin Square
Argyle St
Mawson Place
Kings Pier Marina
Government Offices
Murray St
Brooke St
Morrison St
Elizabeth St Pier
Sullivans Cove
Watermans Dock
Davey St
Victoria St
Harrington St
Hobart Rivulet
Parliament House
Parliament Square
Princes Wharf
To Battery Point (200m)
St David's Park
Supreme Court
Castray Esp
Salamanca Pl
Salamanca Square
McGregor St
Barrack St
Wilmot St
Sandy Bay Rd
Gladstone St
Hampden Rd
Montpellier Retreat
Battery Point
Kelly St
South St
Runnymede St
Arthur Circus
To Secheron Point (300m)
To Cascade Brewery (2km); Female Factory (2km); Mt Wellington (21km)
Anglesea Barracks
James St
Stowell Ave
Francis St
Waterloo Cres
To Mt Nelson (9km); Kingston (12km); Huonville (29km); Kettering (33km); The Southeast
Byron St
De Witt St
Cromwell St
Colville St
Napoleon St
To Taroona (7km); Kingston (10km)

INFORMATION
Hobart Police Station 1 B2
Hobart Visitor Information Centre 2 C3
Royal Hobart Hospital 3 C2

SIGHTS & ACTIVITIES
Captain Fell's Historic Ferries .... (see 4)
Carnegie Gallery .... (see 6)
Cruise Company Booking Offices 4 C4
Kellys Steps 5 D5
Maritime Museum of Tasmania 6 C3
Narryna Heritage Museum 7 C5
National Trust .... (see 8)
Navigators .... (see 4)
Penintentiary Chapel Historic Site 8 B1
Salamanca Arts Centre 9 D5
Salamanca Market 10 D4
St George's Anglican Church 11 C6
Tasmanian Museum & Art Gallery 12 C3

SLEEPING
Astor Private Hotel 13 B4
Battery Point Manor 14 D6
Grand Mercure Hadleys Hotel 15 B3
Henry Jones Art Hotel 16 D2
Hobart Midcity Hotel 17 B2
Leisure Inn Hobart Macquarie 18 B4
Somerset on the Pier 19 D4

EATING
Fish Frenzy 20 D3
Flippers Fish Punt 21 D3
Jam Packed .... (see 16)
Mures 22 D3

TRANSPORT
Airporter Shuttle Bus .... (see 24)
Redline Coaches .... (see 24)
TassieLink 23 A2
Transit Centre 24 A4

SIGHTS

The city centre and waterfront areas of Hobart are very picturesque, and all the places of interest are in easy walking distance of each other. You'll need wheels to explore the city outskirts and visit the historic houses and wineries of the Hobart environs.

BATTERY POINT

An empty rum bottle's throw from the once notorious Sullivans Cove waterfront is a nest of tiny 19th-century cottages and laneways, packed together like herring fillets in a can. This is the old maritime village of **Battery Point** (www.batterypoint.net) – its name derives from the 1818 gun battery that stood on the promontory, protecting Hobart Town from nautical threats both real and imagined.

Battery Point's liquored-up ale houses on **Hampden Rd** have been refitted as groovy cafes and classy restaurants, and cater to a rather more gracious and dignified clientele. Stumble up Kellys Steps from Salamanca Place and dogleg into **South St** where red lights once burned night and day and many a lonesome sailor sought the refuge of a buxom maiden. Spin around the picturesque **Arthur Circus**, check out **St George's Anglican Church** on Cromwell St or shamble down **Napoleon St** to the waterfront where the rigging of tethered yachts' sings and clatters with the wind.

Narryna Heritage Museum (☎ 03-6234 2791; www.nationaltrust.org.au; 103 Hampden Rd; adult/concession/child/family $6/3/5/12; ⏲ 10.30am-5pm Tue-Fri, 2-5pm Sat & Sun, closed Jul) is a stately Georgian sandstone-fronted mansion (pronounced 'Narinna') built in 1836, set in beautiful grounds with a wonderful collection of artefacts.

HISTORIC BUILDINGS

Hobart has more than 90 buildings classified by the National Trust – 60 of these are on Macquarie and Davey Sts. This stock of amazingly well-preserved old buildings makes Hobart exceptional among Australian cities. The intersection of Macquarie and Murray Sts features a gorgeous sandstone edifice on each corner. For detailed information contact the **National Trust** (☎ 03-6223 5200; www.nationaltrust.org.au; cnr Brisbane & Campbell Sts; ⏲ 9am-1pm Mon-Fri) or pick up the *Hobart's Historic Places* brochure from the visitor information centre.

See the court rooms, and grim cells and gallows of the **Penitentiary Chapel Historic Site** (☎ 03-6231 0911; www.penitentiarychapel.com; cnr Brisbane & Campbell Sts; tours adult/concession/child/family $8/6/6/16; ⏲ tours 10am, 11.30am, 1pm & 2.30pm). Writer TG Ford mused: 'As the Devil was going through

Hobart Gaol, he saw a solitary cell; and the Devil was pleased for it gave him a hint, for improving the prisons in hell'. For extra frisson take the excellent one-hour National Trust–run **Ghost Tour** (☎ **0417 361 392; www.hobartghosts.com; adult/concession/family $10/8/25; ⌚ 8.30pm**) held most nights (bookings essential).

MUSEUMS

The excellent **Tasmanian Museum & Art Gallery** (☎ **03-6211 4177; www.tmag.tas.gov.au; 40 Macquarie St; admission free; ⌚ 10am-5pm**) is installed in Hobart's oldest building, the Commissariat Store (1808). The museum features Aboriginal displays, colonial relics and shifting exhibitions, while the gallery curates a collection of Tasmanian colonial art. There are free guided tours at 2.30pm from Wednesday to Sunday.

Hobart is still the staging post for many voyages into the Southern Ocean and Antarctic, and its unbreakable bond with the sea is celebrated at the fascinating **Maritime Museum of Tasmania** (☎ **03-6234 1427; www.maritimetas.org; 16 Argyle St; adult/concession/child/under 12/family $7/5/4/free/16; ⌚ 9am-5pm**). There are wonderful collections of old photos, paintings, models and relics – just try resisting ringing the huge brass bell from the *Rhexenor*. Upstairs you'll find the **Carnegie Gallery** (**admission free; ⌚ 9am-5pm**) with its exhibitions of contemporary Tasmanian art, craft, design and photography.

TASTES OF HOBART

The **Cascade Brewery** (☎ **03-6224 1117; www.cascadebrewery.com.au; 140 Cascade Rd, South Hobart; 1½hr tours adult/concession/child/family $20/15/10/45; ⌚ tours 9.30am, 10am, 1pm & 1.30pm Mon-Fri except public holidays, additional summer tours**), in South Hobart is a grand Gothic edifice. It's Australia's oldest brewery, established in 1832 (the building dates from 1824) next to the clean-running Hobart Rivulet, and still pumps out superb beer and soft drinks. Tours involve plenty of stair climbing with beer tastings at the end. Visitors must wear flat, enclosed shoes and long trousers (no shorts or skirts), and book in advance. You

GRANT DIXON

Cascade Brewery

can take a tour on weekends, but none of the machinery will be operating (brewers have weekends, too).

Moorilla Estate (☎ 03-6277 9900; www.moorilla.com.au; 655 Main Rd, Berriedale; tastings free; 10am-5pm) sits on a saucepan-shaped peninsula on the Derwent River 12km north of Hobart's centre. Since its founding in the 1950s, the winery has played a prominent role in Hobart society. Stop by for wine and beer tastings, have lunch or dinner at the outstanding restaurant **The Source** (mains $25-33; lunch & dinner) or splash some cash for a night in the deluxe accommodation (doubles $395).

OUTDOOR STUFF

Cloaked in winter snow, **Mt Wellington** (www.wellingtonpark.tas.gov.au) peaks at 1270m, towering above Hobart like a benevolent overlord. The citizens find reassurance in its constant, solid presence, while outdoorsy types find the space to hike and bike on its leafy flanks. And the view from the top is unbelievable! Don't be deterred if the sky is overcast – often the peak rises above cloud level and looks out over a magical ocean of rolling white cloud tops.

HOBART FOR CHILDREN

There's always something interesting going on around the waterfront – fishing boats chugging in and out of Victoria Dock, yachts tacking and jibing in Sullivans Cove – and you can feed the family on a budget at the **floating fish punts** (p323) at Constitution Dock. There's free Friday-night music in the courtyard at the **Salamanca Arts Centre** (p317) and the street performers, buskers and sights of **Salamanca Market** (p317) captivate kids of all ages.

Rainy-day attractions include the **Tasmanian Museum & Art Gallery** (p320), the **Maritime Museum of Tasmania** (p320), the **Cadbury Chocolate Factory** (☎ 1800 627 367, 03-6249 0333; www.cadbury.com.au; 100 Cadbury Rd, Claremont; adult/child under 13 $7.50/free; 8am-4pm Mon-Fri except public holidays, 9am-3pm Jun-Aug), and the Discovery Centre at the **Royal Tasmanian Botanical Gardens** (north of the CBD).

There are crews spruiking boat cruises on the river. Or you might assail the heights of Mt Wellington or Mt Nelson or rent a bike and explore the cycling paths.

TOURS

BUS TOURS

Gray Line (☎ 1300 858 687, 03-6234 3336; www.grayline.com.au) City tours in an idiotic bus-dressed-as-tram (adult/child $40/20), plus longer tours to destinations including Mt Wellington ($45/22.50), Mt Field National Park ($134/67) and the Huon Valley ($139/69.50). Free hotel pick-ups.

Red Decker (☎ 03-6236 9116; www.reddecker.com.au) Commentated sightseeing on an old London double-decker bus (sigh). Buy a 20-stop, hop-on-hop-off pass (adult/concession/child $25/23/15) or do the tour as a 90-minute loop. Pay a bit more and add a Cascade Brewery tour ($44/42/25) or river cruise ($48/46/37) to the deal.

Tasman Island Cruises (☎ 03-6250 2200; www.tasmancruises.com.au; full-day tour adult/child $220/150) Take a bus to Port Arthur for a three-hour ecocruise around Tasman Island, then explore the Port Arthur Historic Site and bus back to town. Includes morning tea, lunch and Port Arthur admission.

TassieLink (☎ 1300 300 520, 03-6230 8900; www.tassielink.com.au) Full-day trips including to Lake St Clair (adult/child $75/38) and Freycinet National Park (adult/child $85/51), or a half-day trip to Huonville and Franklin ($16/8). Tours depart the terminal at 64 Brisbane St.

CRUISES

Captain Fell's Historic Ferries (☎ **03-6223 6893; www.captainfellshistoricferries.com.au**) Good-value cruises on cute old ferries (adult/child/family $28/14/70) that can incorporate lunch (from $30/45/100) and dinner ($53/27/140). They also run coach or double-decker bus sightseeing trips around town and to Mt Wellington and Richmond.

Hobart Harbour Jet Boat (☎ **0404 078 687; www.hobartharbourjet.com.au**) Water-taxi rides to Hobart locales (Moorilla, Bellerive and Wrest Point Casino) from $10 per person, plus adrenaline-fuelled jet-boat river tours from adult/child $35/20.

Navigators (☎ **03-6223 1914; www.navigators.net.au**) Slick ships sailing north to Moorilla Estate (adult/child $22/11) and south to Port Arthur ($149/110, including site entry and return coach trip) and Storm Bay ($35/18). Also Derwent River cruises ($22/12).

WALKING TOURS

Ghost Tours of Hobart (☎ **0439 335 696; www.ghosttoursofhobart.com.au; adult/child/family $25/15/70**) Walking tours with ghoulish commentaries departing the Bakehouse in Salamanca Sq at dusk. Bookings are essential.

Hobart Historic Tours (☎ **03-6278 3338; www.hobarthistorictours.com.au; adult/child $27.50/12**) A highly informative 1½-hour Hobart Historic Walk (10am) and a beery Old Hobart Pub Tour (5pm).

SLEEPING

our pick Astor Private Hotel (☎ **03-6234 6611; www.astorprivatehotel.com.au; 157 Macquarie St; dm $42, s $63-80, tw/d $76/90, d with bathroom $115-140, all incl breakfast;** 💻) The Astor's an authentic old-school 1920s hotel in a great central location retaining much of its original decor and charm, including wonderful old furniture, stained-glass windows and ornate ceilings. Older-style rooms share facilities.

Battery Point Manor (☎ **03-6224 0888; www.batterypointmanor.com.au; 13-15 Cromwell St, Battery Point; s/d incl breakfast from $85/95;** ❄) With sweeping views from the outdoor terrace, this pearly-white 1834 Georgian building offers a range of comfortable rooms, all with en suites and some with king-size beds, and a separate two-bedroom cottage.

Leisure Inn Hobart Macquarie (☎ **03-6220 7100; www.leisureinnhotels.com; 167 Macquarie St; d from $105;** 💻 ❄) The original facade was an interesting 1968 edifice, but a recent makeover has 'modernised' the exterior and made over the inside with coffee-and-cream colours, dark timber floors, flat-screen TVs and natty bathrooms. It's comfortable, good value and in a great location close to the city and waterfront (views to either from most rooms).

Hobart Midcity Hotel (☎ **03-6234 6333, 1800 030 966; www.hobartmidcity.com.au; cnr Elizabeth & Bathurst Sts; r $135-215;** 💻 ❄) Don't be put off by the Midcity's graceless '70s stance, because the staff and rooms are great, the location's peerless, there's 24-hour reception and an on-site restaurant and bar. A good all-rounder.

Grand Mercure Hadleys Hotel (☎ **1800 131 689, 03-6223 4355; www.grandmercure.com.au; 34 Murray St; d from $180;** 💻 ❄) This National Trust-listed hotel in the heart of the city was constructed by convicts in 1834 and has been hosting guests ever since. It's acquired many modern accoutrements along the way, including a restaurant and bar, but retained much of its colonial grandeur.

Henry Jones Art Hotel (☎ **03-6210 7700; www.thehenryjones.com; 25 Hunter St; d $220-320, ste $490-850;** 💻) Since opening

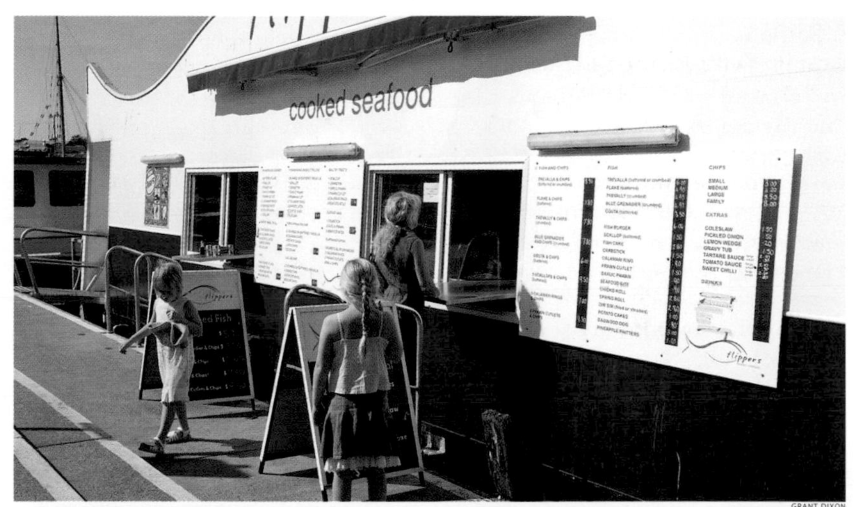

GRANT DIXON

Takeaway seafood from a punt on Constition Dock (p308)

in 2004, superswish HJs has become famous around Australia as the paradigm of modern style and sophistication. Absolute waterfront in a restored jam factory, it oozes class but is far from intimidating (this is Hobart after all, not Sydney). Modern art enlivens the walls, while facilities and downstairs distractions (bar, restaurant and cafe) are world class.

Somerset on the Pier (☎ **1800 766 377, 03-6220 6600; www.somerset.com; Elizabeth St Pier; apt from $270;** 💻) These luxuriously appointed apartments occupy perhaps Hobart's most prestigious address on the upper level of Elizabeth Pier, and come with glorious harbour views and slick contemporary decor.

EATING

The waterfront streets, docks and piers are the main areas of the city's culinary scene and quality seafood is the main theme. Salamanca Place is an almost unbroken string of excellent cafes and restaurants, and Battery Point's Hampden Rd restaurants are always splendid, too. Elizabeth St in North Hobart has evolved into a diverse collation of cosmopolitan cafes, multicultural eateries and pubs.

Flippers Fish Punt (☎ **03-6234 3101; Constitution Dock; meals $7-15;** ⏲ **lunch & dinner)** Flippers Fish Punt, with its voluptuous fish-shaped profile and sea-blue exterior, has been floating at Constitution Dock for as long as anyone can remember. Fillets of flathead and curls of calamari – straight from the deep blue sea and into the deep fryer.

Mures (☎ **03-6231 2121; www.mures.com.au; Victoria Dock;** ⏲ **lunch & dinner)** Mures is the name in Hobart seafood with its own fishing fleet serving this restaurant as well as local markets. On the ground level is the fishmonger, a sushi bar, ice-cream parlour and the hectic, family-focused bistro Lower Deck (mains $7 to $13), serving fish and chips and salmon burgers to the masses. The Upper Deck (mains $20 to $28) is a sassier affair, with expansive dockside views and à la carte seafood dishes.

Jam Packed (☎ 03-6231 3454; 27 Hunter St; mains $8-18; breakfast & lunch) This trendy cafe inside the brilliant redeveloped IXL Jam Factory atrium next to the Henry Jones Art Hotel is jam-packed at breakfast time. The BLT is the perfect hangover salve and the prawn spaghetti puttanesca, simmered in olive oil, tomato and caper sauce, makes a filling lunch.

our pick **Fish Frenzy** (☎ 03-6231 2134; Elizabeth St Pier; meals $11-32; lunch & dinner) This casual place at a great location on Elizabeth Pier has a slightly upmarket take on the humble fish and chip, and keeps bringing us back for its waterfront outdoor tables, seafood platters, fishy salads (spicy calamari, smoked salmon and brie), wine by the glass and perky service. The eponymous 'Fish Frenzy' ($16) delivers a bit of everything. It's ridiculously popular, but doesn't take bookings.

GETTING THERE & AWAY

There are no direct international flights to/from Tasmania. Airlines with services between Hobart and the mainland are **Qantas** (☎ 13 13 13; www.qantas.com.au), **Jetstar** (☎ 13 15 38; www.jetstar.com.au) and **Virgin Blue** (☎ 13 67 89; www.virginblue.com.au).

The main bus companies (and their terminals) operating to/from Hobart are **Redline Coaches** (☎ 1300 360 000; www.tasredline.com.au; Transit Centre, 199 Collins St; 9am-5.30pm Mon-Fri, to 3pm Sat, to 4pm Sun) and **TassieLink** (☎ 1300 300 520; www.tassielink.com.au; Hobart Bus Terminal, 64 Brisbane St; 7am-6pm Sun-Fri, to 4pm Sat).

GETTING TO/FROM THE AIRPORT

The airport is 16km east of the city centre. The **Airporter Shuttle Bus** (☎ 0419 382 240; 199 Collins St; one-way adult/concession/child $15/6/7.50) scoots between the Transit Centre and the airport (via various city pick-up points), connecting with all flights. Bookings are essential.

A taxi between the airport and the city centre will cost around $33 between 6am and 8pm weekdays, or $38 at other times.

TASMAN PENINSULA

Port Arthur Historic Site, Tassie's single biggest tourist attraction, is the Tasman Peninsula's centre of activity. However, the ruins of convict settlement are only part of the peninsula's story. Here, too, are astonishing 300m-high sea cliffs, empty surf beaches, sandy bays and stunning bushwalks through thickly wooded forests and isolated coastlines.

See the websites www.tasmanregion.com.au and www.portarthur.org.au for more information.

GETTING THERE & AROUND

TassieLink (☎ 1300 300 520; www.tassielink.com.au) runs a 3.55pm weekday bus from Hobart Bus Terminal to Port Arthur ($26.60, 2¼ hours) during school terms; the Port Arthur–Hobart bus leaves at 6am. The service is reduced to Monday, Wednesday and Friday during school holidays. Buses stop at the main towns en route.

Redline Coaches (☎ 1300 360 000; www.redlinecoaches.com.au) also operates some weekday services between Hobart, Sorell and Dunalley, but go no further.

TOURS

Gray Line (☎ 1300 858 687, 03-6234 3336; www.grayline.com.au; adult/child $98/49) Coach tours including Isle of the Dead harbour cruise, Port Arthur admission and guided tour,

RICHARD I'ANSON

Tessellated Pavement, Eaglehawk Neck

and pit stops at Tasman Arch and the Devils' Kitchen.

Navigators (☎ 03-6223 1914; www.navigators.net.au; Brooke St Pier, Hobart; adult/child $229/183) Boat cruises from Hobart returning by bus, departing Wednesday, Friday and Sunday. Includes site entrance, guided tour, morning tea and cruise around Tasman Island.

Port Arthur Bus Service (☎ 03-6250 2200; www.tasmancruises.com.au; adult/child $85/55) Tasman Island Cruises run this return bus service that includes site admission. Departs Hobart visitor information centre at 7.45am.

Tasman Island Cruises (☎ 03-6250 2200; www.tasmancruises.com.au; adult/child $165/110) Take a bus to Port Arthur for a three-hour ecocruise around Tasman Island, then explore the Port Arthur Historic Site and bus back to town. Includes morning tea, lunch and Port Arthur admission. Departs Hobart visitors centre at 8am. You can also take the three-hour ecocruise from Port Arthur (adult/child $100/55).

EAGLEHAWK NECK TO PORT ARTHUR

Most tourists associate the Tasman Peninsula only with Port Arthur, but there are many attractions (natural and otherwise) down this way. Hit the bookshops for *Peninsula Tracks* by Peter and Shirley Storey ($18) for track notes on 35 walks in the area. The *Convict Trail* booklet, available from visitor information centres, covers the peninsula's historic sites.

Approach Eaglehawk Neck from the north, then turn east onto Pirates Bay Dr for the **lookout** – the Pirates Bay views extending to the rugged coastline beyond are truly incredible. Also clearly signposted around Eaglehawk Neck are some bizarre and precipitous coastal formations: **Tessellated Pavement**, the **Blowhole**, **Tasmans Arch** and **Waterfall Bay**. South of Port Arthur is the sea-gouged **Remarkable Cave**.

The **Tasmanian Devil Conservation Park** (☎ 03-6250 3230; www.tasmaniandevilpark.com; 5990 Arthur Hwy, Taranna; adult/child/

family $26/14/64; 9am-6pm) functions as a quarantined breeding centre for devils to help protect against devil facila tumour disease (DFTD). There are plenty of other native animals and birds here, with feedings throughout the day.

PORT ARTHUR

In 1830 Lieutenant-Governor George Arthur chose the Tasman Peninsula to confine prisoners who had committed further crimes in the colony. A 'natural penitentiary', the peninsula is connected to the mainland by a strip of land less than 100m wide – Eaglehawk Neck. To deter escape, ferocious guard dogs were chained across the isthmus.

Although Port Arthur is a hugely popular tourist site – over 300,000 visitors annually – it remains a sombre, confronting and haunting place. Don't come expecting to remain unaffected by what you see – there's a palpable sadness and sense of woe that clouds your senses on the sunniest of days. What makes it all the more poignant is the scale of the penal settlement and its genuine beauty – the stonemasonry work, Gothic architecture, lawns and gardens are exquisite – and visitors leave feeling profoundly moved and conflicted by the experience.

The visitor centre at the **Port Arthur Historic Site** (**☎ 03-6251 2310, 1800 659 101; www.portarthur.org.au; Arthur Hwy, Port Arthur; adult/child/concession/family $28/14/23/62; tours & buildings 9am-5pm, grounds 8.30am-dusk)** includes an information counter, cafe, restaurant and gift shop. Downstairs is an excellent interpretation gallery, where you can follow the convicts' journey from England to Tasmania. Buggy transport around the site can be arranged for people with restricted mobility; ask at the information counter.

Worthwhile guided tours (included in admission) leave regularly from the visitor centre. You can visit all the restored buildings, including the Old Asylum (now a museum and cafe) and the Model Prison. Admission tickets, valid for two consecutive days, also entitle you to a short harbour cruise circumnavigating (but not stopping at) the **Isle of the Dead**. For an additional $12/8/34 per adult/child/family, you can visit the island on 40-minute guided tours – count headstones and listen to some stories. You can also tour to **Point Puer** boys' prison for the same additional prices.

Another extremely popular tour is the 90-minute, lantern-lit **Historic Ghost Tour** (**☎ 1800 659 101; adult/child/family $20/12/55)**, which leaves from the visitor centre nightly at dusk (rain or shine) and visits a number of historic buildings, with guides relating spine-chilling occurrences. Bookings are essential.

EAST COAST

Tasmania's laid-back east coast is drop-dead gorgeous. Hardy types will find superb opportunities for swimming in clean, clear water, while the rest can enjoy walking barefoot along the white-sand beaches, letting the waves lick at their ankles and shins.

COLES BAY & FREYCINET NATIONAL PARK

The spectacular 485m-high pinky-orange granite outcrops known as the Hazards dominate the tiny town of **Coles Bay** (population 473). Brilliant Freycinet Peninsula (pronounced *fray*-sin-ay) is one of Tasmania's principal tourism drawcards, and Coles Bay exists as the gateway and service town for its national park. Check out www.freycinetcolesbay.com.

INFORMATION

At the park entrance is the professionally run **Freycinet National Park Visitor Centre** (☎ 03-6256 7000; Freycinet Dr; www.parks.tas.gov.au; 8am-5pm Nov-Apr, 9am-4pm May-Oct) – pay your park fees or catch free ranger-led activities in summer.

SIGHTS & ACTIVITIES

Sheathed in coastal heaths, orchids and wildflowers, **Freycinet National Park** (www.parks.tas.gov.au) incorporates Freycinet Peninsula, people-free Schouten Island and the lesser-known Friendly Beaches north of Coles Bay. Black cockatoos, yellow wattlebirds, honeyeaters and Bennett's wallabies flap and bounce between the bushes.

For bushwalkers it's nirvana, with long hikes including the two-day, 31km peninsula circuit. Shorter tracks include the up-and-over saddle climb to the majestic white bowl of **Wineglass Bay**. Ascend the saddle as far as **Wineglass Bay Lookout** (one to 1½ hours return, 600 steps each way) or continue down the other side to the beach (2½ to three hours return). Alternatively, the 500m wheelchair- and pram-friendly lighthouse boardwalk at **Cape Tourville** affords sweeping coastal panoramas and a less-strenuous glimpse of Wineglass Bay. On longer walks, sign in (and out) at the registration booth at the car park; national park fees apply.

SLEEPING

Freycinet Lodge (☎ 03-6257 0101; www.freycinetlodge.com.au; d cabins $247-389; 💻) This is the plush Freycinet arm of the giant Federal Hotels' 'Pure Tasmania' enterprise and managed super professionally. It's inside the national park at the southern end of Richardsons Beach with 60 deluxe bushland cabins with balconies, some with self-catering facilities and/or spas, and several with disabled access. Activities and walks are organised and there are two on-site restaurants.

GLENN BEANLAND

Ross Bridge

↘ IF YOU LIKE...

If you like **Port Arthur** (p326) we think you might like these other examples of Tasmania's colonial past:

- **Sarah Island** In the middle of Macquarie Harbour and accessed by tour boat from Strahan, Sarah Island isolated the colony's worst convicts.
- **Maria Island** (www.parks.tas.gov.au) Accessed by boat from Triabunna, this island boasts some interesting convict and industrial ruins among exquisite natural features.
- **Ross** The midland town of Ross is famous for the superbly constructed and whimsically carved Ross Bridge (1836), the third-oldest bridge in Australia.
- **Richmond** Pride of place here goes to another bridge, Richmond Bridge, built by convicts in 1823 and purportedly haunted by the 'Flagellator of Richmond', George Grover, who died here in 1832. Only 27km northeast of Hobart.

GETTING THERE & AWAY

Bicheno Coach Service runs between Bicheno, Coles Bay and Freycinet National Park, connecting with east coast Redline and TassieLink coaches at the Coles Bay turn-off.

THE WEST

Primeval, tempestuous and elemental – this region of Tasmania is unlike anywhere else in Australia. Towering, jagged mountains, button grass–covered alpine plateaus, raging tannin-stained rivers, impenetrable rainforest and unyielding rain. This western wilderness has never been tamed and today much of the region comprises Tasmania's World Heritage area. Tourist-centric Strahan aside, the few towns and settlements are rough and primitive, weathered and hardened by wilderness.

STRAHAN

Strahan (pronounced 'Strawn'), 40km southwest of Queenstown on the Macquarie Harbour, is the only vestige of civilisation on Tasmania's wild west coast and the epicentre of west-coast tourism. Visitors come in droves seeking a taste of Tasmania's famous wilderness, whether by seaplane, a Gordon River cruise or the Wilderness Railway.

INFORMATION

The architecturally innovative **West Coast visitor information centre** (☎ 03-6472 6800; www.westcoast.tas.gov.au; The Esplanade; 10am-7pm Dec-Mar, to 6pm Apr-Nov;) provides information on accommodation, attractions and activities around town.

SIGHTS & ACTIVITIES

Beyond the Huon pine reception desk at the visitor information centre is **West Coast Reflections** (☎ 03-6472 6800; The Esplanade), a creative, thought-provoking display on west-coast history, including a refreshingly blunt appraisal of environmental disappointments and achievements.

Nearby is **Strahan Woodworks** (☎ 03-6471 7244; 12 Esplanade; 8.30am-5pm) with old machine-powered saws and lathes.

The Ship That Never Was (☎ 03-6472 6800; www.roundearth.com.au; The Esplanade; adult/child/concession $17.50/gold-coin donation/12.50; 5.30pm, also 8.30pm in Jan) is a pantomime-style show (Australia's longest-running play!) staged daily at the visitor information centre's amphitheatre. It tells the story of the last ship built at Sarah Island, and the convicts who stole it and escaped.

Hogarth Falls is at the end of a rainforest walk (40 minutes return) alongside the platypus-inhabited Botanical Creek, starting from People's Park south of town.

TOURS

Both cruises include a rainforest walk at Heritage Landing; views of (or passage through) Hells Gates, Macquarie Harbour's narrow entrance; and a land tour of Sarah Island.

Gordon River Cruises (☎ 1800 628 288, 03-6471 4300; www.puretasmania.com.au; The Esplanade) Offers 5½-hour cruises departing 8.30am daily, and also at 2.45pm over summer. Cost depends on where you sit. Standard seats with an excellent buffet lunch cost from $90/35/235 per adult/child/family. You can pay more for window recliner seats, but the windows fog up and people wander around anyway, and they're not worth the extra. Or you can pay $195 (all tickets) for the Captain's Premier Upper Deck with a swisho lunch, wine and all beverages (no, you're not allowed to drive).

World Heritage Cruises (☎ 1800 611 796, 03-6471 7174; www.worldheritagecruises.com.au; The Esplanade) Take a 5¾-hour morning or afternoon cruise daily costing per adult/child/family $85/45/235 including a fine buffet lunch, or pay $110/60/295 for premium window seats. You can buy Gold Pass tickets that cost $130 (all tickets) and include a few extras like a glass of wine, *Story of Sarah Island* booklet, premium window seats…wouldn't bother.

SLEEPING

The sprawling **Strahan Village** (☎ **1800 628 286, 03-6471 4200; www.puretasmania.com.au**) takes up most of the town centre and is a(nother) Federal Hotels enterprise. The booking office is under the clock tower on the Esplanade. Book well ahead.

CRADLE MOUNTAIN-LAKE ST CLAIR NATIONAL PARK

Tasmania is world famous for the stunning 168,000-hectare World Heritage area of Cradle Mountain-Lake St Clair. Mountain peaks, dank gorges, pristine lakes, tarns and wild moorlands extend triumphantly from the Great Western Tiers in the north to Derwent Bridge on the Lyell Hwy in the south. It was one of Australia most heavily glaciated areas, and includes Mt Ossa (1617m) – Tasmania's highest peak – and Lake St Clair, Australia's deepest natural freshwater lake (167m).

There are fabulous day walks at both Cradle Valley in the north and Cynthia Bay (Lake St Clair) in the south, but it's the outstanding 80.5km Overland Track between the two that has turned this park into a bushwalkers' mecca.

INFORMATION

All walking tracks in the park are signposted, well defined and easy to follow, but it's prudent to carry a map – pick one up at park visitor information centres.

Adjacent to Discovery Holiday Parks Cradle Valley, 3km north of the park's northern boundary, is the privately run **Cradle Information Centre** (☎ **03-6492 1590; Cradle Mountain Rd;** **8am-5pm**) with its vast car park. This is the starting point for the national-park shuttle-bus service (p331). The centre provides bushwalking information and sells park passes, food and fuel.

GRANT DIXON

Du Cane Range, Cradle Mountain-Lake St Clair National Park

It's more worthwhile to go to the mega-helpful Parks & Wildlife Service's **Cradle Mountain visitor information centre** (☎ 03-6492 1110; www.parks.tas.gov.au; Cradle Mountain Rd; 🕑 8am-5pm Jun-Aug, 8am-6pm Sep-May), within the park itself, which provides extensive bushwalking information (including national park and Overland Track passes and registration), and informative flora, fauna and park history displays.

Regardless of the season, be prepared for cold, wet weather around Cradle Valley. On average it rains here seven days out of 10, is cloudy eight days in 10, the sun shines all day only one day in 10 and it snows on 54 days each year!

SIGHTS & ACTIVITIES

Bushwalking is the primary lure of this national park. Aside from the **Overland Track**, there are dozens of short walks here. For Cradle Valley visitors, behind the Cradle Mountain visitor information centre (above) there is an easy but first-rate 20-minute circular boardwalk through the adjacent rainforest, called the **Pencil Pine Falls & Rainforest Walk**, suitable for wheelchairs and prams. Nearby is another trail leading to **Knyvet Falls** (45 minutes return), as well as the **Enchanted Walk** alongside Pencil Pine Creek (20 minutes return), and the **King Billy Walk** (one hour return). The **Cradle Valley Walk** (2½ hours one way) is an 8.5km-long boardwalk linking the Cradle Mountain visitor information centre and **Dove Lake**. The **Dove Lake Walk** is a 6km lap of the lake, which takes around two hours.

TOURS

Most travellers to Tasmania consider Cradle Mountain a must-see, so almost every tour operator in the state offers day trips or longer tours to the area (including guided walks along the Overland Track). Some recommendations:

Craclair (☎ 03-6339 4488; www.craclair.com.au) Craclair has among its many offerings a seven-day/six-night Overland Track tour ($2150 per person including packs, sleeping bags, tents, jackets and over-trousers) and also runs shorter trips.

KAREN TRIST

Cradle Mountain and Dove Lake

Cradle Mountain Huts (☎ 03-6391 9339; www.cradlehuts.com.au) If camping isn't your bag, from November to May you can take a six-day/five-night, small-group guided walk along the Overland Track with accommodation in plush private huts and others carrying your pack. The fee (from $2500 per person) includes meals, national park fees and transfers to/from Launceston.

SLEEPING & EATING

Cradle Mountain Highlanders Cottages (☎ 03-6492 1116; www.cradlehighlander.com.au; Cradle Mountain Rd; d $120-180) Hospitable Highlanders is a cluster of 10 Germanic, shingle-clad timber cottages straight out of *The Sound of Music*. It's an easy-going, family-run operation. All cottages have a kitchen and lounge; the more luxurious ones have a wood heater and spa. Yodel-lay-hee-hoo…

Cradle Mountain Lodge (☎ 1300 134 044, 02-8296 8010; www.cradlemountainlodge.com.au; Cradle Mountain Rd; d $270-750; 💻) This huge stone-and-timber resort near the national park entrance has nearly 100 cabins surrounding the main chalet lodge. Four types of cabin each have tea- and coffee-making facilities and fridge, but no kitchens. Prices include buffet breakfast. There's good eating at the house restaurants – the neat-casual Highland (mains $19 to $28; open for breakfast, lunch and dinner) and the laid-back Tavern (mains $12 to $19; open for lunch and dinner), with pub-style meals and ski-lodge vibes. There's a spa retreat here, too, and heaps of organised activities.

GRANT DIXON

Cradle Mountain seen from Mt Campbell

IF YOU LIKE...

If you like **Cradle Mountain-Lake St Clair National Park** (p329) we think you might also like these other national parks and reserves:

- **Mt Field National Park** (www.parks.tas.gov.au) Mt Field is famed for its spectacular mountain scenery, alpine moorlands and lakes, rainforest, waterfalls and abundant wildlife. It's 80km northwest of Hobart and makes a terrific day trip.
- **Hartz Mountains National Park** (www.parks.tas.gov.au) Part of Tasmania's World Heritage area and only 84km from Hobart, this park is also ideal for day trippers. It's renowned for its jagged peaks, glacial tarns, gorges and dense rainforest.
- **Bay of Fires Conservation Area** (www.parks.tas.gov.au) This pristine coastline hosts the luxurious wilderness experience of the four-day Bay of Fires Walk (☎ 03-6391 9339; www.bayoffires.com.au).

GETTING AROUND

Leave your car at the Cradle Information Centre (p329) and jump on a **shuttle bus**, departing at 10-minute intervals (mid-September to late May) and stopping at the visitor information centre inside the park, Snake Hill, Ronny Creek (the Overland Track departure point) and Dove Lake. The service is free, but national park fees apply. Visitors can alight at any bus stop along the way.

➘ AUSTRALIA IN FOCUS

ACTIVITIES

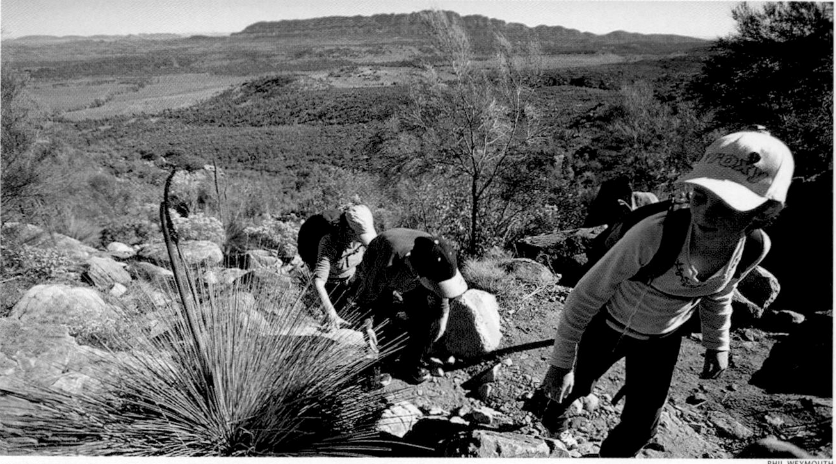

PHIL WEYMOUTH

Walking Rawnsley Bluff Track, Flinders Ranges National Park, South Australia

Australia is a natural adventure playground and its sheer size alone means there is an incredible range of outdoor activities. The easy-on-the-eye landscape, so much of it still refreshingly free from the pressures of overpopulation, lends itself to any number of energetic pursuits and pure natural fun, whether you're on a wilderness trail or ski slope, under the sea beside a coral reef, or catching a wave.

BUSHWALKING

Bushwalking is supremely popular in Australia and almost every national park has marked trails or wilderness walking opportunities, ranging from short hikes of a few hours to multiday, more challenging treks. Don't be put off by the thought of a lengthy trek because many of these longer walks can be broken up into stages or even sampled as day walks. The best time to go varies significantly from state to state, but a general rule is that the further north you go the more tropical and humid the climate gets; June to August are the best walking months up top and in the south, summer – December to March – is better.

In Sydney, it's worth picking up *Sydney's Best Harbour & Coastal Walks*, published by the *Sydney Morning Herald*. It includes the must-do 6km Bondi to Coogee Coastal Walk (p750) and the beautiful 10km Manly Scenic Walkway, in addition to wilder walks.

Elsewhere in New South Wales (NSW) you can trek between Sydney and Newcastle on the Great North Walk, tackle the Royal National Park's Bundeena-Maianbar Heritage Walk, or trek Mt Kosciuszko (p135) to reach the highest point in Australia.

In Victoria there's the Australian Alps Walking Track, a 655km walk that traverses the Alpine National Park. If coastal treks are more your pace, head south to Wilsons Promontory National Park (p237), with marked trails that can take anywhere from a few hours to a couple of days. Other popular areas to flex your calf muscles are the Otway Ranges (p231) and the Grampians National Park (Gariwerd; p232), with more than 150km of well-marked walking tracks past waterfalls and sacred Aboriginal rock-art sites.

Other notable walks include the Overland Track (p329) and the South Coast Track in Tasmania, the romantic heartland of Australian bushwalking. In Western Australia (WA) there's the Bibbulmun Track and, in Queensland, the Thorsborne Trail across Hinchinbrook Island, and the Gold Coast Hinterland's Great Walk. In South Australia (SA) there's the epic 1200km Heysen Trail, and in the Northern Territory (NT) there are the majestic, 234km Larapinta Trail, the 39km Tabletop Track, and beautifully remote tracks in Nitmiluk (Katherine Gorge) National Park (p258).

Outdoor stockists are good sources of bushwalking information. For national park information and detailed descriptions of national park trails, visit the websites of the various state government national parks departments. *Walking in Australia* by Lonely Planet provides detailed information and trail notes for Australia's best bushwalks.

SAFETY GUIDELINES FOR WALKING

Before embarking on a walk, consider the following to ensure a safe and enjoyable experience:

- Pay any fees and make sure you have any permits required by authorities.
- Be sure to sign in at the start and remember to sign out at the end of monitored walks.
- Tell someone where you are going and when you expect to return.
- Obtain reliable information about the weather and terrain along your intended route.

CYCLING

Avid cyclists have access to lots of great routes and can tour the country for days, weekends or even on multiweek trips.

Victoria is a great state for on- and off-road cycling and mountain biking. Standout routes for longer rides in this state include the Murray to the Mountains Rail Trail and the East Gippsland Rail Trail. There is a whole network of routes that follow disused railway lines; **Railtrails Australia** (☎ **03-9306 4846; www.railtrails.org.au**) describes these and other routes.

In WA, the Munda Biddi Mountain Bike Trail offers 900km of pedal power and you can tackle the same distance on the Mawson Trail in SA.

Rates charged by most bike hire companies for renting road or mountain bikes are anywhere from $8 to $14 per hour, and $18 to $40 per day. Security deposits can range from $50 to $200.

The **Bicycles Network Australia** (**www.bicycles.net.au**) website is useful, as is Lonely Planet's *Cycling Australia*.

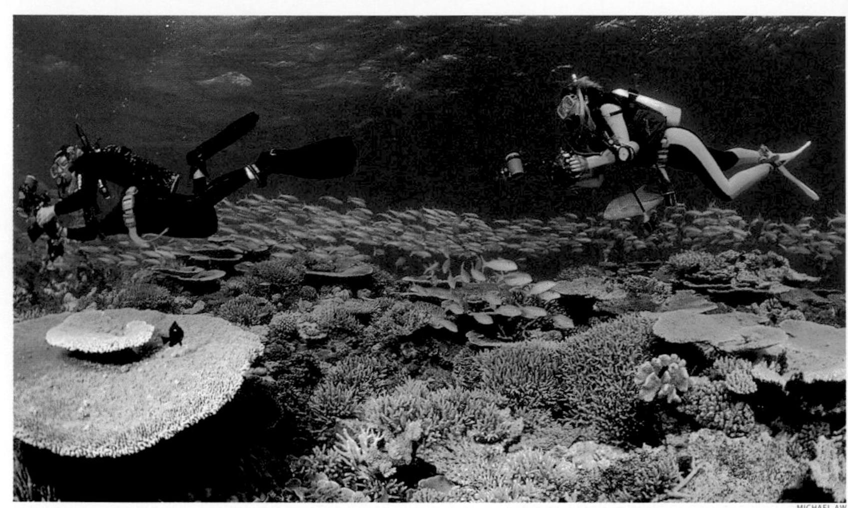

MICHAEL AW

Divers photograph the Great Barrier Reef (p140)

DIVING & SNORKELLING

Professional Association of Diving Instructors (PADI) dive courses are offered throughout the country; on the east coast you don't have to travel far before stumbling across one. Learning here is fairly inexpensive: PADI courses range from two to five days and cost anything between $300 and $700. Also, don't forget you can enjoy the marine life by snorkelling; hiring a mask, snorkel and fins is cheap.

North of Sydney try Broughton Island near Port Stephens, and further north, Fish Rock Cave off South West Rocks is renowned for its excellent diving, with shells, schools of clownfish and humpback whales. Swim with grey nurse sharks at The Pinnacles near Forster, and leopard sharks at Julian Rocks Marine Reserve off Byron Bay. Good dive schools can be found at Coffs Harbour (p120) and Byron Bay (p122). On the south coast popular diving spots include Jervis Bay (p132), Montague Island and Merimbula (p134).

The Great Barrier Reef has more dazzling dive sites than you can poke a fin at (see p140). For more outstanding diving in Queensland, see the boxed text, p184. There are coral reefs off some mainland beaches and around several of the islands, and many day trips to the Great Barrier Reef provide snorkelling gear free.

In WA the Ningaloo Reef (p300) is every bit as interesting as the east-coast coral reefs, without the tourist numbers.

SKIING & SNOWBOARDING

Australia has a small but enthusiastic skiing industry, with snowfields straddling the NSW–Victoria border. The season is relatively short, running from about mid-June to early September, and snowfalls can be unpredictable. The top resorts to ski in NSW are within Kosciuszko National Park, (see p135) in the Snowy Mountains, including Charlotte Pass, Perisher Blue, Selwyn and Thredbo.

Victoria's snowfields are scattered around the High Country northeast and east of Melbourne. The two largest ski resorts are Mt Buller (p235) and Falls Creek (p236). Mt Hotham (p236) is smaller but has equally good skiing, while Mt Baw Baw and Mt Buffalo are small resorts that are popular with families and less-experienced skiers. Cross-country skiing is popular and most resorts offer lessons and equipment.

Skiing Australia (www.skiingaustralia.org.au) has links to the major resorts and race clubs.

SURFING

World-class waves can be ridden all around Australia, from Queensland's subtropical Gold Coast, along the entire NSW coast and at cool-water beaches in Victoria and Tasmania. Surf shops in all these areas generally offer board hire and have information on surf schools. If you've never hit the surf before, it's a good idea to have a lesson or two.

NSW has some 2137km of coastline and 721 ocean beaches, so it goes without saying that practically any coastal town can satisfy the need of surfers. For the low-down on Sydney's top surfing and swimming spots, see p78. Crescent Head (p119) is the long-board capital of Australia and further north you can hang ten at Lennox Head (p122) and Byron Bay (p122). The NSW South Coast is literally awash with great surf beaches, particularly around Wollongong (p130), Ulladulla and Merimbula.

There are some fantastic breaks along Queensland's southeastern coast, most notably at Coolangatta, Burleigh Heads (p166), Surfers Paradise (p165), North Stradbroke Island (p163) and Noosa (p168).

Exposed to the chilly Southern Ocean swell, Victoria's coastline provides quality surf. Local and international surfers gravitate to Torquay (p227), while nearby Bells Beach plays host to the Rip Curl Pro festival every Easter. For the less experienced, popular places with surf schools in Victoria include Anglesea (p228), Lorne (p229) and Phillip Island (p225). Elsewhere, southern WA is a surfing mecca, and Margaret River is the heartland.

ENVIRONMENT Dr Tim Flannery

MARTIN COHEN

Sturt's desert pea, Alice Springs (p259)

Australia's plants and animals are just about the closest things to alien life you are likely to encounter on earth. That's because Australia has been isolated from the other continents for a very long time – at least 45 million years. The other habitable continents have been able to exchange species at different times because they've been linked by land bridges. Just 15,000 years ago it was possible to walk from Africa right through Asia and the Americas to Tierra del Fuego. Not Australia, however. Its birds, mammals, reptiles and plants have taken their own separate and very different evolutionary journey, and the result is the world's most distinct natural realm.

The first naturalists to investigate Australia were astonished by what they found. Here the swans were black – to Europeans this was a metaphor for the impossible – while mammals such as the platypus and echidna laid eggs. It really was an upside-down world, where many of the larger animals hopped, where each year the trees shed their bark rather than their leaves, and where the 'pears' were made of wood.

If you are visiting Australia for a short time, you might need to go out of your way to experience some of the richness of the environment. That's because Australia is a subtle place, and some of the natural environment – especially around the cities – has been damaged or replaced by trees and creatures from Europe. Places like Sydney, however, have preserved extraordinary fragments of their original environment that are relatively easy to access. Before you enjoy them though, it's worthwhile understanding the basics about how nature operates in Australia. This is important because there's nowhere like Australia, and once you have an insight into its origins and natural rhythms, you will appreciate the place so much more.

FUNDAMENTALLY DIFFERENT

There are two really big factors that go a long way towards explaining nature in Australia: its soils and its climate. Both are unique. It may not be obvious but Australian soils have been fundamental in shaping life here. On other continents in recent geological times, processes such as volcanism, mountain building and glacial activity have been busy creating new soil. Just think of the glacier-derived soils of North America, north Asia and Europe, made by glaciers grinding up rock of differing chemical composition over the last two million years. They feed the world today. The rich soils of India and parts of South America were made by rivers eroding mountains, while Java in Indonesia owes its extraordinary richness to volcanoes.

All of these soil-forming processes have been almost absent from Australia in more recent times. Only volcanoes have made a contribution, and they cover less than 2% of the continent's land area. In fact, for the last 90 million years, beginning deep in the age of dinosaurs, Australia has been geologically comatose. It was too flat, warm and dry to attract glaciers, and its crust too ancient and thick to be punctured by volcanoes or folded into mountains. Look at Uluru (p263) and Kata Tjuta (p264). They are the stumps of mountains that 350 million years ago were the height of the Andes. Yet for hundreds of millions of years they've been nothing but nubs.

Under such conditions no new soil is created and the old soil is leached of all its goodness by the rain, and is blown and washed away. Almost all of Australia's mountain ranges are more than 90 million years old, so you will see a lot of sand, and a lot of country where the rocky 'bones' of the land stick up through the soil. It is an old, infertile landscape, and life in Australia has been adapting to these conditions for aeons.

Australia's misfortune in respect to soils is echoed in its climate. In most parts of the world outside the wet tropics, life

ENVIRONMENTAL CHALLENGES

The European colonisation of Australia heralded a period of catastrophic environmental upheaval, with the result that Australians today are struggling with some of the most severe environmental problems to be found anywhere. It may seem strange that a population of just 20 million, living in a continent the size of the USA (minus Alaska), could inflict such damage, but Australia's long isolation, fragile soils and difficult climate have made it particularly vulnerable to human-induced change.

Damage to Australia's environment has been inflicted in several ways, the most important being the introduction of pest species, destruction of forests, overstocking rangelands, inappropriate agriculture and interference with water flows.

responds to the rhythm of the seasons – summer to winter, or wet to dry. Most of Australia experiences seasons – sometimes very severe ones – yet life does not respond solely to them. This can clearly be seen by the fact that although there's plenty of snow and cold country in Australia, there are almost no trees that shed their leaves in winter, nor do any Australian animals hibernate. Instead there is a far more potent climatic force that Australian life must obey: El Niño.

The cycle of flood and drought that El Niño brings is profound. Australia's rivers – even the mighty Murray River, the nation's largest river, which runs through the southeast – can be miles wide one year, yet you can literally step over its flow the next. This is the power of El Niño, and its effect, when combined with Australia's poor soils, manifests itself compellingly. As you might expect from this, relatively few of Australia's birds are seasonal breeders, and few migrate. Instead, they breed when the rain comes, and a large percentage are nomads, following the rain across the breadth of the continent.

FUEL-EFFICIENT FAUNA

Australia is, of course, famous as the home of the kangaroo (roo) and other marsupials. Unless you visit a wildlife park, such creatures are not easy to see as most are nocturnal. Their lifestyles are exquisitely attuned to Australia's harsh conditions. Have you ever wondered why kangaroos, alone among the world's larger mammals, hop? It turns out that hopping is the most efficient way of getting about at medium speeds. This is because the energy of the bounce is stored in the tendons of the legs – much like in a pogo stick – while the intestines bounce up and down like a piston, emptying and filling the lungs without needing to activate the chest muscles. When you travel long distances to find meagre feed, such efficiency is a must.

MITCH REARDON

Eastern grey kangaroos, Pebbly Beach, New South Wales

Marsupials are so energy-efficient that they need to eat one-fifth less food than equivalent-sized placental mammals (everything from bats to rats, whales and ourselves). But some marsupials have taken energy efficiency much further. If you visit a wildlife park or zoo you might notice that faraway look in a koala's eyes. It seems as if nobody is home – and this is near the truth. Several years ago biologists announced that koalas are the only living creatures that have brains that don't fit their skulls. Instead they have a shrivelled walnut of a brain that rattles around in a fluid-filled cranium. Other researchers have contested this finding, pointing out that the brains of the koalas examined for the study may have shrunk because these organs are so soft. Whether soft-brained or empty-headed, there is no doubt that the koala is not the Einstein of the animal world, and we now believe that it has sacrificed its brain to energy efficiency. Brains cost a lot to run – our brains typically weigh 2% of our body weight, but use 20% of the energy we consume. Koalas eat gum leaves, which are so toxic that koalas use 20% of their energy just detoxifying this food, leaving little energy for the brain. Living in the treetops where there are so few predators means that koalas can get by with few wits at all.

The peculiar constraints of the Australian environment have not made everything dumb. The koala's nearest relative, the wombat (of which there are three species), has a large brain for a marsupial. These creatures live in complex burrows and can weigh up to 35kg, making them the largest herbivorous burrowers on Earth. Because their burrows are effectively air-conditioned, they have the neat trick of turning down their metabolic activity when they are in residence. A physiologist who studied their thyroid hormones found that biological activity ceased to such an extent in sleeping wombats that, from a hormonal point of view, they appeared to be dead! Wombats can remain underground for a week at a time, and can get by on just a third of the food needed by a sheep of equivalent size. One day, perhaps, efficiency-minded farmers will keep wombats instead of sheep. At the moment, however, that isn't possible; the largest of the wombat species, the northern hairy-nose, is one of the world's rarest creatures, with only around 100 surviving in a remote nature reserve in central Queensland.

FLORAL TRIBUTES

Australia's plants are irresistibly fascinating. Even if your visit extends only as far as Sydney, you can be rewarded with showy native blossom. The sandstone country that extends approximately 150km around Sydney – from the Blue Mountains to the Gap – is one of the most recognisable and diverse regions in Australia. In springtime, brilliant red waratahs abound in the region's parks.

If you happen to be in the Perth area in spring it's well worth taking a wildflower tour. The blaze of colour produced by the kangaroo paws, banksias and other native plants can be dizzying. The sheer variety of flowers is amazing, with 4000 species crowded into the southwestern corner of the continent.

FAMILY TRAVEL

ORIEN HARVEY

Floreat Beach, Perth (p284)

Are we there yet? The key to hassle-minimised travel with kids is good planning. Don't underestimate distances if planning a road trip. The wide yonder may be just the tonic for stressed-out parents, but it is probably not numero uno on the kids' menu. The big cities and the populated east coast, however, abound with attractions and distractions designed for bright young minds and bodies of limitless energy.

Lonely Planet's *Travel with Children* contains plenty of useful information. All cities and most major towns have centrally located public rooms where mothers (and sometimes fathers) can go to nurse their baby or change its nappy; check with the local tourist office or city council for details. While most Australians have a relaxed attitude about breastfeeding or nappy changing in public, some do frown on it.

Most motels and the better-equipped caravan parks have playgrounds and swimming pools, and can supply cots and baby baths – motels may also have in-house children's videos and child-minding services. Top-end hotels and many (but not all) midrange hotels are well versed in the needs of guests with children. B&Bs, on the other hand, often market themselves as sanctuaries from all things child related. Many cafes and restaurants have a specialised kid's menu, or will provide small serves from the main menu.

If you want to leave Junior behind for a few hours, some of Australia's numerous licensed childcare agencies offer casual care. Check under 'Baby Sitters' and 'Child Care Centres' in the *Yellow Pages* telephone directory, or phone the local council for a list. Licensed centres are subject to government regulations and usually adhere to high standards; to be on the safe side, avoid unlicensed ones.

Child concessions (and family rates) often apply to accommodation, tours, admission fees and transport, with some discounts as high as 50% of the adult rate. However, the definition of 'child' varies from under 12 to under 18 years. Accommodation concessions generally apply to children under 12 years sharing the same room as adults. On the major airlines, infants travel free provided they don't occupy a seat – child fares usually apply between the ages of two and 11 years.

Australia has high-standard medical services and facilities, and items such as baby formula and disposable nappies are widely available in urban and regional centres. Major hire-car companies will supply and fit booster seats, charging around $18 for up to three days' use, with an additional daily fee for longer periods.

THE NITTY GRITTY

- **Change Facilities** Found in most towns and large shopping malls in cities
- **Cots** Available in midrange and top-end establishments
- **Health** See the general health section (p370)
- **Highchairs** Widely available in restaurants, as are booster seats
- **Nappies (diapers)** Widely available
- **Strollers** Even on public transport you will get a helping hand
- **Transport** All public transport caters for young passengers

SIGHTS & ACTIVITIES

There's no shortage of active, interesting or amusing things for children to focus on in Australia. Plenty of museums, zoos, aquariums, interactive technology centres and pioneer villages have historical, natural or science-based exhibits to get kids thinking. And of course outdoor destinations are always a winner. This guide has hot tips for keeping kids occupied in Sydney (p79), Melbourne (p215), Perth (p285), Brisbane (p155), Cairns (p182) and Hobart (p321).

In Victoria, Wilsons Promontory National Park (p237) is a favourite family haunt and keeps knee-biters occupied with bushwalks, swimming, surfing and wildlife spotting. The Penguin Parade of Phillip Island (p225) is also a must for families. In NSW, some surf schools in Byron Bay (p125) run camps specifically for kids during school holidays, and the Art Gallery of NSW (p72) runs the excellent GalleryKids program on Sundays. In the NT you can take kids wildlife spotting in Territory Wildlife Park (p258). Not quite as wild, but a family-must nevertheless, is the world-famous Australia Zoo (p168) in Queensland, and the Alice Springs Desert Park (p259), in the NT.

For synthetic but scintillating fun spend a day at the Gold Coast theme parks (p165), in Queensland.

FOOD & DRINK

JAMES BRAUND

Diners in one of Melbourne's many superb restaurants (p218)

Once upon a time in a decade not so far away Australians proudly survived and thrived on a diet of 'meat and three veg'. Fine fare was a Sunday roast cooked to carcinogenic stages and lasagne was considered exotic. Fortunately the country's culinary sophistication has evolved and, mirroring the population's cheeky and disobedient disposition, contemporary Australian cuisine now thrives on breaking rules and conventions.

Australian cuisine may not have a high international profile, but visitors will find a huge range and wealth of food available in city restaurants, markets, delicatessens and cafes. Competition for the custom of savvy-tastebud owners is increasingly high and so too are standards. This is most evident in Sydney and Melbourne, but also in all large urban areas and tourist destinations. In regional areas variety diminishes along with the population.

MOD OZ?

The Australian propensity to absorb global influences is spurred by an inquisitive public willing to give anything new a go. The result is dynamic and constantly surprising cuisine, and what's hot this morning may be dated by tomorrow – or reinvented and improved.

Immigration has been the key to Australia's culinary bloom. A significant influx of migrants from Europe, Asia, the Middle East and, increasingly, Africa in the last 60 years has introduced new ingredients and new ways to use existing staples. But urban Australians have become culinary snobs along the way, and in order to wow the socks off diners, restaurants must succeed in fusing contrasting ingredients and traditions into ever more innovative fare. The phrase Modern Australian (Mod Oz) has been coined to describe the cuisine. Laksas, curries and marinara pastas are now old-school 'pub grub'. If it's a melange of East and West, it's Mod Oz. If it's not authentically French or Italian, it's Mod Oz. As Australians' appetite for diversity and invention grows, so do the avenues of discovery.

If this sounds overwhelming, fear not. Dishes are characterised by bold and interesting flavours and fresh ingredients rather than fuss or clutter. Spicing ranges from gentle to extreme, coffee is great (it still reaches its heights in cities), wine is world renowned, seafood is plentiful and meats are tender and full flavoured. The range of food in Australia is its greatest culinary asset – all palates, timid or brave, shy or inquisitive, are well catered for.

CHEERS

No matter what your poison, you're in the right country if you're after a drink. Long recognised as some of the finest in the world, wine is now one of Australia's top exports. In fact, if you're in the country's southern climes, you're probably not far from a wine region. Some regions have been producing wines from the earliest days of settlement – almost 200 years ago. Most wineries have small cellar door sales where you can taste for free or a minimal fee. Although plenty of good wine comes from big producers with economies of scale on their side, the most interesting wines are usually made by smaller, family-run wineries.

As the public develops a more demanding palate, local beers are rising to the occasion, with a growing wealth of flavours and varieties available. Most beers have an alcohol content between 3.5% and 5.5%. That's less than many European beers but more than most in North America. Light beers contain under 3% alcohol and are finding favour with people observing the stringent drink-driving laws.

The term for ordering beer varies with the state. In NSW you ask for a 'schooner' (425mL) if you're thirsty and a 'middy' (285mL) if you're not quite so dry. In Victoria and Tasmania it's a 'pot' (285mL), and in most of the country you can just ask for a beer and wait to see what turns up. Pints (425mL or 568mL, depending on where you are) aren't as common, though Irish- and English-theme pubs tend to pour them.

Coffee has become an Australian addiction; there are Italian-style espresso machines in virtually every cafe, boutique roasters are all the rage and, in urban areas, the qualified barista (coffee-maker) is virtually the norm. Sydney and Melbourne have borne a whole generation of coffee snobs, but Melbourne easily takes top billing as Australia's coffee-obsessed capital. The cafe scene there rivals the most vibrant in the world – the best way to immerse yourself is by wandering the city centre's cafe-lined lanes.

THE BEST

DIANA MAYFIELD

Grape vines, Margaret River (p292)

WINE REGIONS

- **Barossa Valley, South Australia** (p270)
- **Hunter Valley, New South Wales** (p116)
- **Margaret River, Western Australia** (p292)
- **Yarra Valley, Victoria** (p223)

HISTORY Dr Michael Cathcart

JOHN BORTHWICK

Kurnell Peninsula, at Botany Bay in Sydney's south, is where Captain Cook first stepped ashore in Australia

By sunrise the storm had passed. Zachary Hicks was keeping sleepy watch on the British ship *Endeavour* when suddenly he was wide awake. He summoned his commander, First Lieutenant James Cook, who climbed into the brisk morning air to a miraculous sight. Ahead lay an uncharted country of wooded hills and gentle valleys. It was 19 April 1770. In the coming days Cook began to draw the first European map of Australia's eastern coast. He was mapping the end of Aboriginal supremacy.

Two weeks later Cook led a party of men onto a narrow beach. As they waded ashore, two Aboriginal men stepped onto the sand, and challenged the intruders with spears. Cook drove the men off with musket fire. For the rest of that week, the Aborigines and the intruders watched each other warily.

Cook's ship *Endeavour* was a floating annexe of London's leading scientific organisation, the Royal Society. The ship's gentlemen passengers included technical artists,

60,000–35,000 BC	1606	1770
The first Australians arrive by sea to northern Australia.	Dutch Navigator Willem Janszoon makes the first authenticated European landing on Australian soil.	First Lieutenant James Cook claims the entire east coast of Australia for England.

scientists, an astronomer and a wealthy botanist named Joseph Banks. As Banks and his colleagues strode about the Aborigines' territory, they were delighted by the mass of new plants they collected.

The local Aborigines called the place Kurnell, but Cook gave it a foreign name: he called it 'Stingray Bay' and later 'Botany Bay'.

When the *Endeavour* reached the northern tip of Cape York, Cook and his men could smell the sea-route home. And on a small, hilly island (Possession Island), Cook raised the Union Jack. Amid volleys of gunfire, he claimed the eastern half of the continent for King George III.

Cook's intention was not to steal land from the Aborigines. In fact he rather idealised them. 'They are far more happier than we Europeans', he wrote. 'They think themselves provided with all the necessaries of Life and that they have no superfluities.' At most, his patriotic ceremony was intended to contain the territorial ambitions of the French, and of the Dutch, who had visited and mapped much of the western and southern coast over the previous two centuries. Indeed, Cook knew the western half of Australia as 'New Holland'.

CONVICT BEGINNINGS

Eighteen years after Cook's arrival, in 1788, the English were back to stay. They arrived in a fleet of 11 ships, packed with supplies including weapons, tools, building materials and livestock. The ships also contained 751 convicts and over 250 soldiers, officials and their wives. This motley 'First Fleet' was under the command of a humane and diligent naval captain, Arthur Phillip. As his orders dictated, Phillip dropped anchor at Botany Bay. But the paradise that had so delighted Joseph Banks filled Phillip with dismay. So he left his floating prison and embarked in a small boat to search for a better location. Just a short way up the coast his heart leapt as he sailed into the finest harbour in the world. There, in a small cove, in the idyllic lands of the Eora people, he established a British penal settlement. He renamed the place after the British Home Secretary, Lord Sydney.

The intruders set about clearing the trees and building shelters and were soon trying to grow crops. Phillip's official instructions urged him to colonise the land without doing violence to the local inhabitants. Among the Aborigines he used as intermediaries was an Eora man named Bennelong, who adopted many of the white people's customs and manners. For many years Bennelong lived in a hut on the finger of land now known as Bennelong Point, the site of the Sydney Opera House. But his people were shattered by the loss of their lands. Hundreds died of smallpox, and many of the survivors, including Bennelong himself, succumbed to alcoholism and despair.

1788	1803	1835
Captain Arthur Phillip and the First Fleet, 11 ships and about 1350 people, arrive at Botany Bay.	A second convict settlement is established at Risdon Cove in Van Diemen's Land.	John Batman negotiates a land deal with the Kulin nation; Melbourne is settled that same year.

HISTORY HEALING

So miserable were the country's convict beginnings, that Australians long regarded them as a period of shame. But things have changed: today most white Australians are inclined to brag a little if they find a convict in their family tree. Indeed, Australians annually celebrate the arrival of the First Fleet at Sydney Cove, on 26 January 1788, as 'Australia Day'.

In 1803, English officers established a second convict settlement in Van Diemen's Land (later called Tasmania). Soon, re-offenders filled the grim prison at Port Arthur (p326) on the beautiful and wild coast near Hobart.

FROM SHACKLES TO FREEDOM

At first, Sydney and the smaller colonies depended on supplies brought in by ship. Anxious to develop productive farms, the government granted land to soldiers, officers and settlers. After 30 years of trial and error, the farms began to flourish. The most irascible and ruthless of these new landholders was John Macarthur. Along with his spirited wife, Elizabeth, Macarthur pioneered the breeding of merino sheep on his property near Sydney.

Macarthur was also a leading member of the 'Rum Corps', a clique of powerful officers who bullied successive governors (including William Bligh of *Bounty* fame) and grew rich by controlling much of Sydney's trade, notably rum. But the Corps' racketeering was ended in 1810 by a tough new governor named Lachlan Macquarie. Macquarie laid out the major roads of modern-day Sydney, built some fine public buildings (many of which were designed by talented convict-architect Francis Greenway) and helped to lay the foundations for a more civil society.

Macquarie also championed the rights of freed convicts, granting them land and appointing several to public office. By now, word was reaching England that Australia offered cheap land and plenty of work, and adventurous migrants took to the oceans in search of their fortunes.

MELBOURNE & ADELAIDE

In the cooler grasslands of Tasmania, the sheep farmers were also thriving. In the 1820s they waged a bloody war against the island's Aborigines, driving them to the brink of extinction. Now these settlers were hungry for more land. In 1835 an ambitious young man named John Batman sailed to Port Phillip Bay on the mainland. On the banks of the Yarra River, he chose the location for Melbourne, famously announcing 'This is the place for a village'. Batman persuaded local Aborigines to 'sell' him their traditional lands (a whopping 250,000 hectares) for a crate of blankets, knives and knick-knacks.

1836	1851	1854
Colonel William Light chooses a site for Adelaide. All the settlers are free immigrants, many Christian.	A gold rush in central Victoria brings settlers from across the world. Democracy is introduced in the eastern colonies.	Angered by the cost of gold-mining licences, miners protest at the Eureka Stockade.

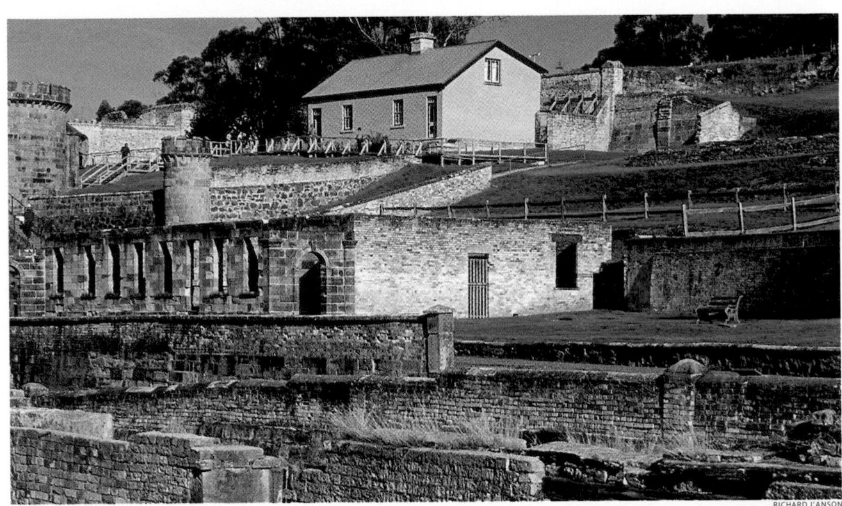
RICHARD I'ANSON

Port Arthur (p326), Tasmania

Back in Sydney, Governor Bourke declared the contract void, not because it was unfair, but because the land officially belonged to the British Crown.

At the same time, a private British company settled Adelaide in South Australia. Proud to have no links with convicts, these God-fearing folk instituted a scheme under which their company sold land to well-heeled settlers, and used the revenue to assist poor British labourers to emigrate. When these worthies earned enough to buy land from the company, that revenue would in turn pay the fare of another shipload of labourers.

GOLD & REBELLION

Transportation of convicts to eastern Australia ceased in the 1840s. This was just as well: in 1851, prospectors discovered gold in NSW and central Victoria, including at Ballarat. The news hit the colonies with the force of a cyclone. Young men and some adventurous women from every social class headed for the diggings. Soon they were caught up in a great rush of prospectors, publicans and prostitutes. In Victoria the British governor was alarmed – both by the way the Victorian class system had been thrown into disarray, and by the need to finance the imposition of law and order on the goldfields. His solution was to compel all miners to buy an expensive monthly licence.

But the lure of gold was too great and in the reckless excitement of the goldfields, the miners initially endured the thuggish troopers who enforced the government licence.

1861

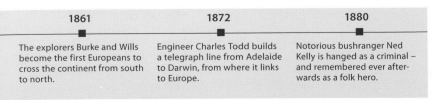

The explorers Burke and Wills become the first Europeans to cross the continent from south to north.

1872

Engineer Charles Todd builds a telegraph line from Adelaide to Darwin, from where it links to Europe.

1880

Notorious bushranger Ned Kelly is hanged as a criminal – and remembered ever afterwards as a folk hero.

RICHARD I'ANSON

Sovereign Hill, a recreation of a gold rush town, in Ballarat, Victoria

After three years, though, the easy gold at Ballarat was gone, and miners were toiling in deep, water-sodden shafts. They were now infuriated by a corrupt and brutal system of law which held them in contempt. Under the leadership of a charismatic Irishman named Peter Lalor, they raised their own flag, the Southern Cross, and swore to defend their rights and liberties. They armed themselves and gathered inside a rough stockade at Eureka, where they waited for the government to make its move.

In the predawn of Sunday 3 December 1854, a force of troopers attacked the stockade. It was all over in 15 terrifying minutes. The brutal and one-sided battle claimed the lives of 30 miners and five soldiers. But democracy was in the air and public opinion sided with the miners. The eastern colonies were already in the process of establishing democratic parliaments, with the full support of the British authorities.

NATIONHOOD

On 1 January 1901 Australia became a federation. When the bewhiskered members of the new national parliament met in Melbourne, their first aim was to protect the identity and values of a European Australia from an influx of Asians and Pacific Islanders. Their solution was a law which became known as the White Australia Policy. It became a racial tenet of faith in Australia for the next 70 years.

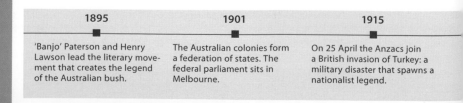

1895

'Banjo' Paterson and Henry Lawson lead the literary movement that creates the legend of the Australian bush.

1901

The Australian colonies form a federation of states. The federal parliament sits in Melbourne.

1915

On 25 April the Anzacs join a British invasion of Turkey: a military disaster that spawns a nationalist legend.

For whites who lived inside the charmed circle of citizenship, this was to be a model society, nestled in the skirts of the British Empire. Just one year later, white women won the right to vote in federal elections. In a series of radical innovations, the government introduced a broad social welfare scheme and it protected Australian wage levels with import tariffs. Its radical mixture of capitalist dynamism and socialist compassion became known as the 'Australian settlement'.

THE CHINESE

The gold rush also attracted boatloads of prospectors from China, who sometimes endured serious hostility from whites, and were the victims of ugly race riots on the goldfields at Lambing Flat (now called Young) in NSW in 1860–61. Chinese precincts soon developed in the backstreets of Sydney and Melbourne, and popular literature indulged in tales of Chinese opium dens, dingy gambling parlours and brothels. But many Chinese went on to establish themselves in business and, particularly, in market gardening. Today the vibrant and busy Chinatowns of the capital cities and the presence of Chinese restaurants in towns across the country are reminders of the vigorous role of the Chinese in Australia since the 1850s.

ENTERING THE WORLD STAGE

Living on the edge of a dry and forbidding land, and isolated from the rest of the world, most Australians took comfort in the knowledge that they were a dominion of the British Empire. When war broke out in Europe in 1914, thousands of Australian men rallied to the Empire's call. They had their first taste of death on 25 April 1915, when the Australian and New Zealand Army Corps (the Anzacs) joined thousands of other British and French troops in an assault on the Gallipoli Peninsula in Turkey. It was eight months before the British commanders acknowledged that the tactic had failed. By then 8141 young Australians were dead. Before long the Australian Imperial Force was fighting in the killing fields of Europe. By the time the war ended, 60,000 Australians had died. Ever since, on 25 April, Australians have gathered at war memorials around the country for the sad and solemn services of Anzac Day.

In the 1920s Australia embarked on a decade of chaotic change. The country careered wildly through the 1920s until it collapsed into the abyss of the Great Depression in 1929. World prices for wheat and wool plunged. Unemployment brought its shame and misery to one in three households.

1919

Australian aviators Ross and Keith Smith become national heroes after they fly from England to Australia.

1932

Right-wing activist Francis de Groot cuts the ribbon to open the Sydney Harbour Bridge.

1939

Prime Minister Robert Menzies announces that Britain has gone to war; 'as a result, Australia is also at war'.

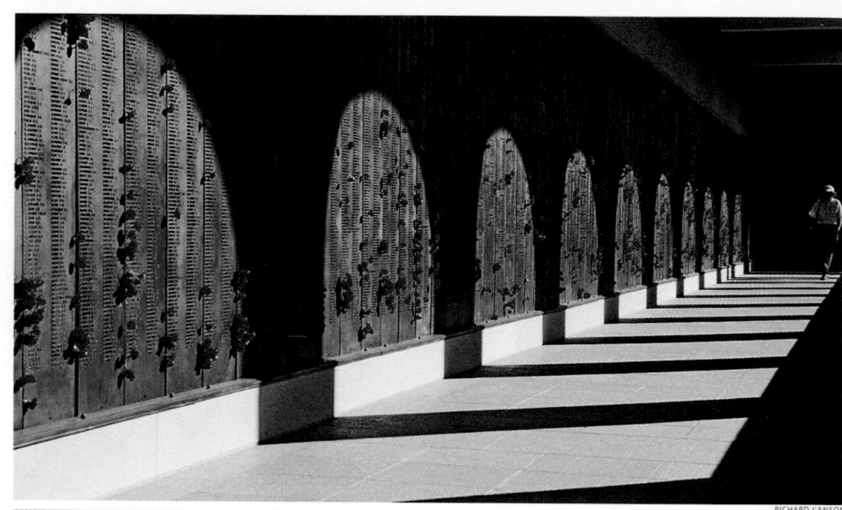

RICHARD I'ANSON

Australian War Memorial, Canberra

WAR WITH JAPAN

After 1933 the economy began to recover. The whirl of daily life was hardly dampened when Hitler hurled Europe into a new war in 1939. Though Australians had long feared Japan, they took it for granted that the British navy would keep them safe. In December 1941, Japan bombed the US Fleet at Pearl Harbor. Weeks later, the 'impregnable' British naval base in Singapore crumbled, and before long thousands of Australians and other Allied troops were enduring the savagery of Japanese prisoner-of-war camps.

As the Japanese swept through Southeast Asia and into Papua New Guinea, the British announced that they could not spare any resources to defend Australia. But the legendary US commander General Douglas MacArthur saw that Australia was the perfect base for American operations in the Pacific. In a series of fierce battles on sea and land, Allied forces gradually turned back the Japanese advance. Importantly, it was the USA, not the British Empire, which saved Australia.

VISIONARY PEACE

When WWII ended, a new slogan rang through the land: 'Populate or Perish!' The Australian government embarked on an ambitious scheme to attract thousands of immigrants. With government assistance, people flocked from Britain and from non-English speaking countries. They included Greeks, Italians, Slavs, Serbs, Croatians, Dutch

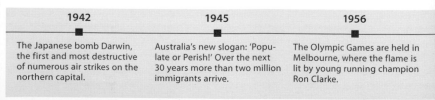

1942
The Japanese bomb Darwin, the first and most destructive of numerous air strikes on the northern capital.

1945
Australia's new slogan: 'Populate or Perish!' Over the next 30 years more than two million immigrants arrive.

1956
The Olympic Games are held in Melbourne, where the flame is lit by young running champion Ron Clarke.

and Poles, followed by Turks, Lebanese and many others.

In addition to growing world demand for Australia's primary products – metals, wool, meat and wheat – there were jobs waiting in manufacturing and on major public works, notably the mighty Snowy Mountains Hydro-Electric Scheme in the mountains near Canberra.

This era of growth and prosperity was dominated by Robert Menzies, the founder of the Liberal Party of Australia, and Australia's longest-serving prime minister. Menzies was steeped in British tradition, and was also a vigilant opponent of communism. As Asia succumbed to the chill of the Cold War, Australia and New Zealand entered a formal military alliance with the USA – the 1951 Anzus security pact. When the USA jumped into a civil war in Vietnam, Menzies committed Australian forces to battle. The following year Menzies retired, leaving his successors a bitter legacy.

STICKY WICKET

The year 1932 saw accusations of treachery on the cricket field. The English team, under captain Douglas Jardine, employed a violent new bowling tactic known as 'bodyline'. The aim was to unnerve Australia's star batsman, the devastatingly efficient Donald Bradman. The bitterness of the tour provoked a diplomatic crisis with Britain and became part of Australian legend. Bradman batted on. When he retired in 1948 he had an unsurpassed career average of 99.94 runs.

In an atmosphere of youthful rebellion and new-found nationalism, the Labor Party was elected to power in 1972 under an idealistic lawyer named Gough Whitlam. In four short years his government transformed the country, ending conscription and abolishing university fees. He introduced a free universal health scheme, no-fault divorce, the principle of Indigenous land rights and equal pay for women. By now, around one million migrants had arrived from non-English speaking countries, filling Australia with new languages, cultures, foods and ideas.

By 1975, the Whitlam government was rocked by a tempest of inflation and scandal. At the end of 1975 his government was controversially dismissed from office by the governor general.

TODAY

Today Australia faces new challenges. After two centuries of development and population growth, the strains on the environment are starting to show – on water supplies, forests, soils, air quality and the oceans.

Under the conservative John Howard, Australia's second-longest-serving prime minister (1996–2007), the country grew closer than ever to the USA, joining that country's

1965

Menzies commits Australian troops to the American war in Vietnam, and divides the nation.

1967

In a national referendum, white Australians vote overwhelmingly to give citizenship to Indigenous people.

1975

Against a background of radical reform and uncontrolled inflation, Governor-General Sir John Kerr sacks Labor's Whitlam government.

KAREN TRIST

Parliament House, Canberra

war in Iraq. The Australian government's harsh treatment of asylum seekers, its refusal to acknowledge climate change, its anti-union reforms and the prime minister's lack of empathy with Indigenous people dismayed many liberal-minded Australians. But Howard presided over a period of economic growth that emphasised the values of self-reliance, and won him continuing support in middle Australia.

By 2007 Howard was losing touch with a changing society. In December that year he was defeated in a bid to win a fifth term in office, suffering the indignity of losing his own seat. The victorious Labor Government, led by Kevin Rudd, immediately set a tone of reform and reconciliation when the new prime minister issued a formal apology to Indigenous people for the injustices they had suffered over the past two centuries. Though it promised sweeping environment and education reforms, the Rudd government found itself faced with a crisis when the world economy crashed in 2008. What comes next, for Australia and for the world, remains to be seen.

1992

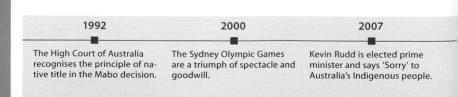

The High Court of Australia recognises the principle of native title in the Mabo decision.

2000

The Sydney Olympic Games are a triumph of spectacle and goodwill.

2007

Kevin Rudd is elected prime minister and says 'Sorry' to Australia's Indigenous people.

SHOPPING

MICHAEL COYNE

Browsers at a Melbourne bookshop

Australians are fond of spending money, a fact evidenced by the huge variety of local- and international-brand shops, and the feverish crowds that gather at every clearance sale. Big cities can satisfy most consumer appetites with everything from high-fashion boutiques to second-hand emporia, while many smaller places tend towards speciality retail, be it home-grown produce, antiques or arts and crafts. Markets are a great place to shop and most cities have at least one permanent bazaar. You may be able to get a refund on the tax you pay on goods; see p375.

INDIGENOUS ART & ARTEFACTS

An Indigenous artwork or artefact makes an evocative reminder of your trip. By buying authentic items you are supporting Indigenous culture and helping to ensure that traditional and contemporary expertise and designs continue to be of economic and cultural benefit for Indigenous individuals and their communities. Unfortunately, much of the so-called Aboriginal art sold as souvenirs is ripped off, consisting of appropriated designs illegally taken from Indigenous people; or it's just plain fake, and usually made overseas by underpaid workers.

The best place to buy artefacts is either directly from the communities that have art-and-craft centres or from galleries and outlets that are owned, operated or supported by Indigenous communities. There are also many reputable galleries that have long supported the Indigenous arts industry, that will offer certificates of authenticity with their goods (see the boxed text, below, for more information).

Didgeridoos are in high demand, but you should decide whether you want a decorative piece or a functional musical instrument. The didgeridoos on the market are not always made by Indigenous people, which means that at a nonsupportive souvenir shop in Darwin or Cairns you could pay anything from $250 to $400 or more for something that looks pretty but is little more than a painted bit of wood. Buying from a community outlet such as Manyallaluk or Julalikari in the Northern Territory is your best opportunity to purchase a functional, authentic didgeridoo painted with natural pigments such as ochre.

AUSTRALIANA

The cheapest souvenirs, usually mass-produced and with little to distinguish them, are known collectively by the euphemism 'Australiana'. They are supposedly representative of Australia and its culture but in reality are just lowest-common-denominator trinkets, often made in China (check the label).

You could instead consider a bottle of fine Australian wine, honey (Tasmanian leatherwood honey is one of many powerful local varieties), macadamia nuts (native to Queensland), Bundaberg Rum with its unusual sweet flavour, or genuine Ugg boots (sheepskin boots that conquer any winter).

BUYING INDIGENOUS ART

Taking home a piece of Indigenous art can create an enduring connection with Australia. For Indigenous artists, painting is an important cultural and economic enterprise.

An authentic piece will come with a certificate indicating the artist's name, language group and community, and the work's title, its story, and when it was made. You may also check that the selling gallery is associated with a regulatory body, such as the Australian Commercial Galleries Association (www.acga.com.au) or Art Trade (www.arttrade.com.au).

Where possible, buy direct from Indigenous arts centres or their outlets (see www.ankaaa.org.au or www.aboriginalart.org); this ensures authenticity and that the money goes directly to the artist and their community. You also get to view the works in the context in which they were created.

There is incredible Indigenous art to be found in urban centres such as Sydney and Melbourne; most of which comes from elsewhere in Australia. To ensure you're not perpetuating non-Indigenous cash-ins on Aboriginal art's popularity, make sure you're buying from an authentic dealer selling original art. If the gallery doesn't pay their artists up front, ask exactly how much of your money will make it back to the artist or community. Another good test is to request some biographical info on the artists – if the vendor can't produce it, keep walking.

PAUL DYMOND

Classic souvenir? Stuffed cane toads, Queensland

OPALS & GEMSTONES

The opal, Australia's national gemstone, is a popular souvenir, as is the jewellery made with it. It's a beautiful stone but buy wisely and shop around, as quality and price varies widely from place to place. Coober Pedy, in SA, and Lightning Ridge and White Cliffs in NSW are opal-mining towns where you can buy the stones or fossick for your own.

On the Torres Strait Islands look out for South Sea pearls, while in Broome, in WA, cultured pearls are sold in many local shops.

Australia is a mineral-rich country and semiprecious gemstones such as topaz, garnets, sapphires, rubies, zircon and others can sometimes be found lying around in piles of dirt at various locations. There are sites around rural and outback Australia where you can pay a few dollars and fossick for your own stones. The gem fields around Emerald, Anakie and Rubyvale in Queensland's Capricorn Hinterland are a good place to shop for jewellery and gemstones.

SPORT

RICHARD I'ANSON

Australian Rules football, Etihad Stadium (p214), Melbourne

Although Australia is a relatively new nation, its inhabitants constantly vie for kudos by challenging formidable and well-established sporting opponents around the globe in just about any event they can attempt. This has resulted in some extraordinary successes on the world stage for a country of 20 odd million. But it's the local football codes that excite Aussies and tap primal passions.

FOOTBALL, FOOTBALL & SOCCER

Australia's everyday heroes are found in the number-one-watched sport: Australian Rules football. Originally exclusive to Victoria, the Australian Football League (AFL; www.afl.com.au) is over-represented in Melbourne (with nine of the 16 teams). There are no teams from Tasmania, the Northern Territory or the Australian Capital Territory. Some teams run Indigenous programs designed to promote the sport in communities across the country, and all teams recruit Indigenous players. The most spectac-

A DAY AT THE RACES

On the first Tuesday in November the nation stops for a horse race, the **Melbourne Cup** (www.racingvictoria.net.au). In Victoria it's cause to have a day off. Australia's most famous cup winner was Phar Lap, who won in 1930, then died of a mystery illness in the USA. Phar Lap is now a prize exhibit in the Melbourne Museum (p213). Makybe Diva is the event's most recent star for winning three in a row before retiring in 2005.

ular aspects of the game are the long kicking, high marking and brutal collisions. Crowd participation is high, with 'Carn the [insert team nickname]' and '[insert expletive]; you're [insert expletive] joking umpire' screamed by over 50,000 sore throats and merging into a primal roar.

While Melburnians refuse to acknowledge it (or do so with a scowl akin to that directed at an unfaithful spouse), there are other football codes. The National Rugby League (NRL; www.nrl.com.au) is the most popular sporting competition north of the Murray River. Undoubtedly the highlight of the season is the annual State of Origin series. To see one of these games is to acquire a grim appreciation of Newton's laws of motion: a force travelling in one direction can only be stopped with the application of an equal and opposite force. It's terrifying stuff. If Newton had been hit by a Queensland second-rower rather than an apple, science would have been very much the poorer.

FAIR DINKUM

We're not sure if it is a sport or not, let alone a source of national pride, but the town of Wooli, near Coffs Harbour on the NSW north coast, has revived the oddly named activity of **goanna pulling**, where grown men and women wearing leather harnesses try to pull each other's heads off.

Australians who play rugby union argue that theirs is the dominant code. The national team, the Wallabies, has won the William Webb Ellis trophy (or Rugby World Cup trophy) with sufficient frequency for Australians to refer to it as 'Bill'. The glory days are beginning to look like a distant memory, though. In between times, the Bledisloe Cup (www.rugby.com.au) games against New Zealand are the most anticipated fixtures and form part of a Tri Nations tournament that also includes South Africa. The same countries also share a club competition, the ever-popular Super 14, which includes four Australian teams: the Waratahs (Sydney), the Reds (Brisbane), the Brumbies (ACT) and the Western Force (Perth).

The Socceroos finally qualified for the World Cup in 2006 after a 32-year history of almost-but-not-quite getting there. For years local soccer floundered as young players chose the better competition and contracts on offer in Europe, but the national A-League (www.a-league.com.au) has enjoyed increased support and attention in recent years and seems to be an effective vehicle to develop home-grown talent for home-grown competition.

CREAMS & BAGGY GREENS

The Australian cricket team dominated both test and one-day cricket for much of the naughties, holding the number-one world ranking for the best part of a decade. This lack of competition had many Aussies barracking for Australia's opponents – until early 2007. Australian cricket began reeling from several losses. And joining the hat trick of players exiting the game in 2007 – once-in-a-lifetime legend Shane Warne, Glenn McGrath and Damien Martyn – was the Mexican wave. Cricket Australia, which instituted the ban, acknowledged that it could be construed as 'the fun police gone wrong' but explained that it was the only way to stop people throwing things.

PHIL WEYMOUTH

Men's final, 2001 Australian Open, Rod Laver Arena (p214)

A dismal performance in early 2009 saw the Australian team lose convincingly at home against an impressive South Africa, and flounder against New Zealand – once considered good only for batting practice. The loss to the English in the 2009 Ashes series has unquestionably verified that the once-formidable Australian team is in the 'developmental stage' of team building.

OPEN LOVE

Come January, tennis shoes melt to the outer courts and games get cancelled because of the heat. The Australian Open (www.ausopen.com.au) is one of four tennis tournaments that comprise the Grand Slam, and it attracts more people to Australia than does any other sporting event. In the men's competition, last won by an Australian back in 1976, Lleyton Hewitt has been Australia's great hope in recent years. In the women's game, Sam Stosur has been climbing the ranks but the celebrated comeback kid is Jelena Dokic. Vilified for her erratic departure from Australia in 2001 under the influence of her father, Jelena was once ranked number four in the world but spiralled out of competition. In 2009 she recaptured Australians' hearts after ditching Dad and fighting her way back into top competition in true Little Aussie Battler style.

WATCHING WILDLIFE

MARTIN COHEN

Short-beaked echidna, Queensland

Wildlife is one of Australia's top selling points and justifiably so. A network of national parks, state forests and reserves is home to unique and fascinating native fauna, and although many of the furry mammals are nocturnal the birdlife is vibrant, noisy and colourful. Zoos and wildlife parks have come a long way from the miserable cement enclosures of yore and, so, when time is of the essence, these created environments provide unparalleled opportunities to observe Australia's rare and cryptic animals.

In NSW there are platypuses and gliders to be found in New England National Park, not far from the Waterfall Way (p128), and 120 bird species in nearby Dorrigo National Park. The Border Ranges National Park is home to a quarter of Australia's bird species, while Willandra National Park is World Heritage–listed and encompasses dense temperate wetlands and wildlife. If your visit extends only as far as Sydney, don't give up on seeing Australian wildlife. Even in a Sydney backyard you're likely to see more reptile species (mostly skinks) than can be found in all of Great Britain – so keep an eye out!

HOT TROPICS

The fantastic diversity of Queensland's Great Barrier Reef (p182) is legendary, and a diving or snorkelling trip out to the reef is unforgettable. For those intrigued by the lush diversity of tropical rainforests, Queensland's World Heritage sites are well worth visiting. Birds of paradise, cassowaries and a variety of other birds can be seen by day, while at night you can search for tree-kangaroos (yes, some kinds of kangaroo live in trees). In your nocturnal wanderings you are highly likely to see curious possums, some of which look like skunks, and other marsupials that today are restricted to a small area of northeast Queensland. Fossils from as far afield as western Queensland and southern Victoria indicate that such creatures, and their rainforest habitat, were once widespread. Head to Magnetic Island in Queensland for superb koala spotting.

For spectacular bird-watching opportunities, head to Kakadu National Park (p257), especially towards the end of the dry season, around November. You're also guaranteed to spot crocodiles in the Top End, in places such as Cahill's Crossing or Yellow Waters in Kakadu. The best place for guaranteed sighting of a great range of the Top End's fauna is the excellent Territory Wildlife Park (p258), outside Darwin.

DESERT CREATURES

Australia's deserts can be a real hit-and-miss affair as far as wildlife is concerned. In a drought year, all you might see are dusty plains, the odd mob of kangaroos and emus, and a few struggling trees. Return after big rains and you'll encounter something close to a Garden of Eden. Fields of white and gold daisies stretch endlessly, perfuming the air. The salt lakes fill with fresh water, and millions of water birds – pelicans, stilts, shags and gulls – can be seen feeding on the superabundant fish and insect life. It all seems like a mirage, and as such it will vanish as the land dries out, only to spring to life again in a few years or a decade's time. For guaranteed encounters and a wonderful introduction to the arid zone take advantage of the beautifully executed Alice Springs Desert Park (p259).

LAND OF THE DEVIL

One of the most fruitful regions for seeing Australian wildlife is Tasmania. The island is jam-packed with wallabies, wombats and possums, principally because foxes, which have decimated marsupial populations on the mainland, were slow to reach the island (the first fox was found in Tasmania only as recently as 2001). It is also home to the Tasmanian devil – the Australian hyena, less than one-third the size of its African ecological counterpart. Devils are common on the island, and in some national parks you can watch them tear apart road-killed wombats. Their squabbling is fearsome, the shrieks ear-splitting. It's the nearest thing Australia can offer to experiencing a lion kill on the Masai Mara. Unfortunately, Tassie devil populations are being decimated by the facial tumour disease; which infects up to 75% of the wild population. Quarantined populations have been established but efforts to find a cure have been depressingly fruitless. In the meantime, you can check them out at wildlife parks around the country.

THE BEST

BOB CHARLTON

Humpback whale, Queensland

PLACES TO WATCH WHALES

- **Eden, New South Wales** (p134)
- **Moreton Bay, Queensland** (p161)
- **Narooma** (p133)
- **Ningaloo Marine Park, Western Australia** (p300)
- **Great Ocean Road, Victoria** (p227)

DIRECTORY & TRANSPORT

BOOK YOUR STAY ONLINE

For more accommodation reviews and recommendations by Lonely Planet authors, check out the online booking service at www.lonelyplanet.com. You'll find the true, insider lowdown on the best places to stay. Reviews are thorough and independent. Best of all, you can book online.

DIRECTORY

ACCOMMODATION

The accommodation listings in this book are organised into budget, midrange and top-end sections. Places that primarily offer tent and campervan sites (eg camping grounds and holiday parks) appear at the tail of the accommodation section.

We generally treat any place that charges up to $90 per double as budget accommodation. Midrange facilities are usually in the range of $90 to $180 per double, although B&Bs (considered midrange) often go for as much as $200 for a double. The top-end tag is mostly applied to places charging more than $180 per double. In more expensive areas, however, such as Far North Queensland, Kangaroo Island, metropolitan Sydney and Melbourne, and the tourist towns surrounding these cities, budget can mean paying up to $110 per double, and midrange places can charge up to $200 for a double.

In most areas you'll find seasonal price variations. During the high season over summer (December to February) and at other peak times, particularly school and public holidays, prices are usually at their highest, whereas outside these times you will find useful discounts and lower walk-in rates. An exception is the Top End, where the wet season (roughly October to March) is the low season, and prices can drop substantially. Another exception is the ski resorts whose high season is winter.

Low or normal-season prices (as opposed to high-season prices) are quoted in this guidebook unless otherwise indicated. High season generally encompasses Christmas to New Year and school holidays (see p373).

B&BS

The local 'bed and breakfast' (guest house) industry is thriving. Options include everything from restored miners' cottages, converted barns, rambling old houses, upmarket country manors and beachside bungalows to a simple bedroom in a family home.

Local tourist offices can usually provide a list of places.

Online resources:

australianbandb.com.au (www.australianbandb.com.au)
babs.com.au (www.babs.com.au)
OZBedandBreakfast.com (www.ozbedandbreakfast.com)

HOTELS & MOTELS

Except for pubs, the hotels that exist in cities or well-touristed places are generally of the business or luxury variety (insert the name of your favourite chain here), where you get a comfortable, anonymous and mod con-filled room in a multistorey block. These places tend to have a pool, restaurant/cafe, room service and various other facilities. For these hotels we quote 'rack rates' (official advertised rates), though significant discounts can be offered when business is quiet.

Motels (or motor inns) offer comfortable budget to midrange accommodation and are found all over Australia. Prices vary and there's rarely a cheaper rate for singles, so motels are better for couples or groups of three. Most motels are modern, low rise, and have similar facilities (tea- and coffee-making, fridge, TV, air-con, bathroom) but the price will indicate the standard. You'll mostly pay between $70 and $130 for a room.

Useful booking agencies that can save you some dosh:

Lastminute.com (www.lastminute.com.au)
Quickbeds.com (www.quickbeds.com.au)
Wotif.com (www.wotif.com.au)

CLIMATE CHARTS

The southern third of the country has cold (though generally not freezing) winters (June to August). Tasmania and the alpine country in Victoria and NSW get particularly chilly. Summers (December to February) range from pleasantly warm to sweltering.

As you head north, the climate changes dramatically. Seasonal variations become fewer until, in the far north, around Darwin and Cairns, you're in the monsoon belt with just two seasons: hot and wet, and hot and dry. The Dry lasts roughly from April to September, and the Wet from October to March; the build-up to the Wet (from early October) is when the humidity is at its highest and when the locals confess to being at their most irritable. The centre of the country is arid – hot and dry during the day, but often bitterly cold at night.

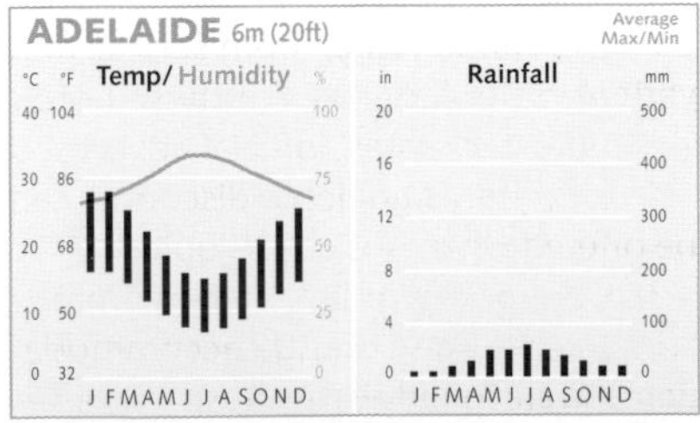

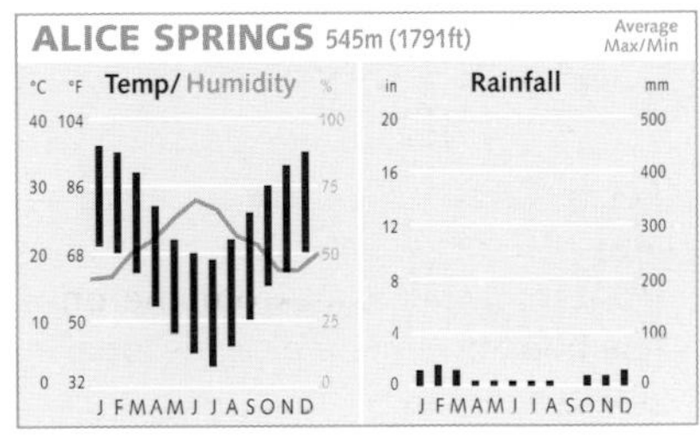

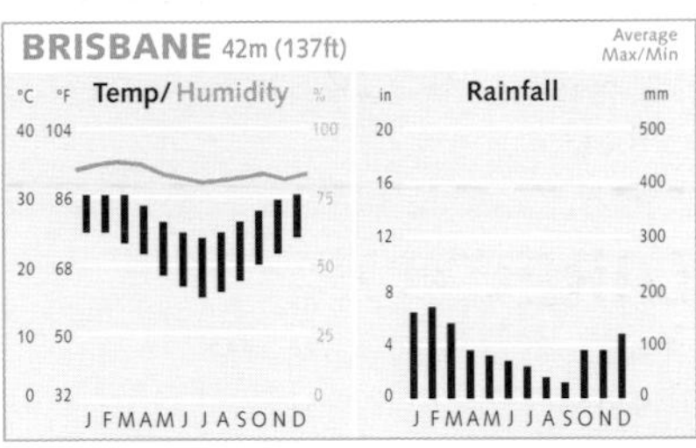

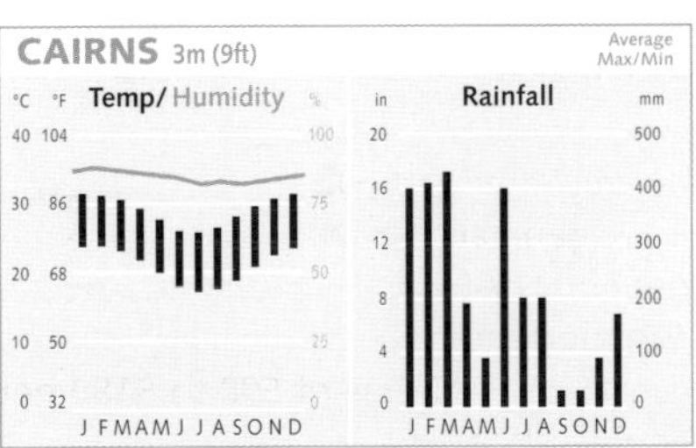

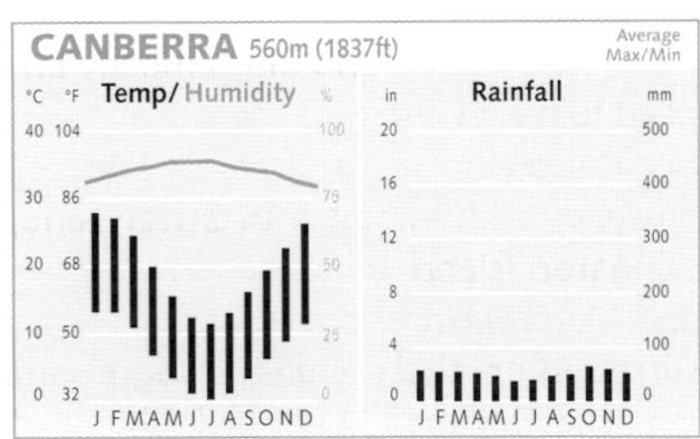

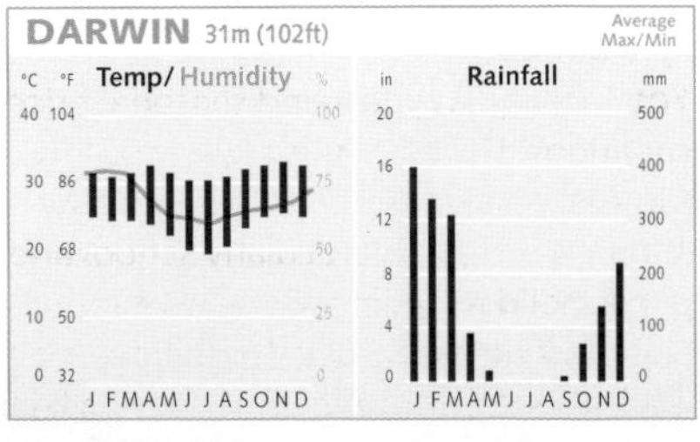

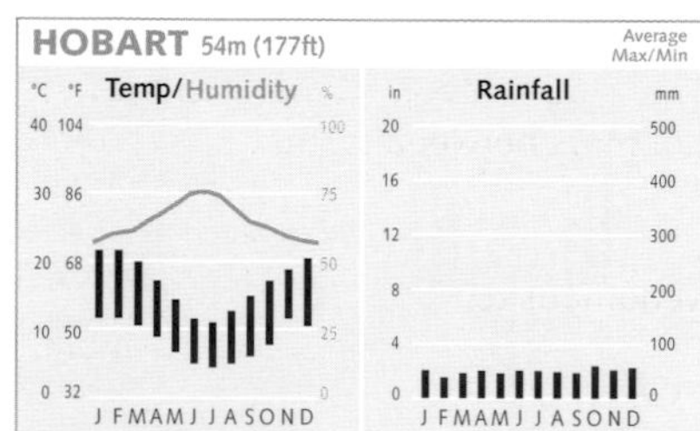

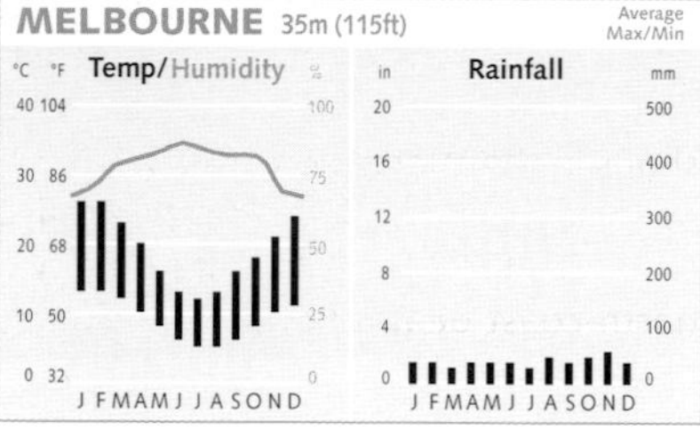

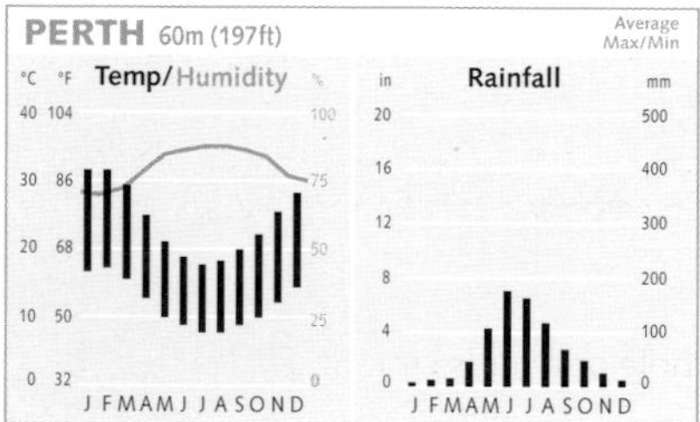

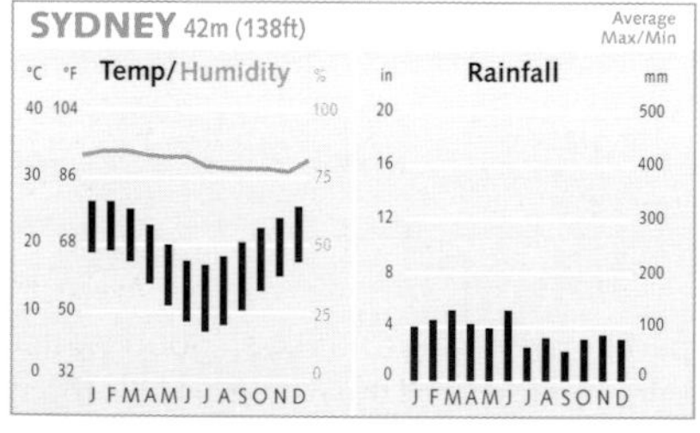

COURSES

You can learn how to dive around the country, with open-water and shore diving courses available at coastal locations in nearly every state and territory. You could also learn how to stand up on a thin piece of fibreglass while it's sliding down the face of a wave by taking a surfing lesson or two. There are surf schools around the country, though the east coast has the greatest concentration.

Well-fed cosmopolitan habitats such as Melbourne and Sydney offer plenty of opportunities for you to learn how to cook up a storm by utilising the wonderful array of local produce and the skilled cookery of Australia's many imported ethnic cuisines.

CUSTOMS & QUARANTINE

For information on customs regulations, contact the **Australian Customs Service** (☎ **1300 363 263, 02-6275 6666; www.customs.gov.au**).

When entering Australia you can bring most articles in free of duty provided that customs is satisfied they are for personal use and that you'll be taking them with you when you leave. There's a duty-free quota per person (over the age of 18) of 2.25L of alcohol, 250 cigarettes and dutiable goods up to the value of $900 ($450 for people under 18).

When arriving or departing the country, you'll need to declare all animal and plant material (wooden spoons, straw hats, the lot) and show them to a quarantine officer. And if you lug in a souvenir, such as a drum with animal hide for a skin, or a wooden article (though these items are not strictly prohibited, they are subject to inspection) that shows signs of insect damage, it won't get through. Some items may require treatment to make them safe before they are allowed in. The authorities are naturally keen to protect Australia's unique environment and important agricultural industries by preventing weeds, pests or diseases from getting into the country. Food is also prohibited, particularly meat, cheese, fruit, vegetables and flowers; plus, there are restrictions on taking fruit and vegetables between states.

You also need to declare currency in excess of $10,000 (including foreign currency) and all medicines.

There are strong restrictions on the possession and use of weapons in Australia. If you plan to travel with weapons of any sort contact the customs service or consult their website well before departure, as permits may be required.

Unless you want to make a first-hand investigation of conditions in Australian jails, don't bring illegal drugs in with you. Customs authorities are adept at searching for them and those cute sniffer dogs are a permanent fixture in arrival and baggage halls.

Australia takes quarantine very seriously. All luggage is screened or X-rayed – if you fail to declare quarantine items on arrival and are caught, you risk a hefty on-the-spot fine or prosecution, which may result in much more significant fines and up to 10 years imprisonment. For more information on quarantine regulations contact the **Australian Quarantine and Inspection Service** (AQIS; ☎ 1800 020 504, 02-6272 3933; www.aqis.gov.au).

DANGERS & ANNOYANCES

ANIMAL HAZARDS

Australia's profusion of dangerous creatures is legendary. Apart from the presence of poisonous snakes and spiders, the country has its share of shark and crocodile attacks and, to top it off, it's home to the world's deadliest creature, the box jellyfish (right). Travellers don't need to be constantly alarmed, however – you're unlikely to see many of these creatures in the wild, much less be attacked by one.

Hospitals have antivenin on hand for all common snake and spider bites, but it helps to know what it was that bit you.

BOX JELLYFISH

There have been numerous fatal encounters between swimmers and these large jellyfish on the northern coast. Also known as the sea wasp or 'stinger', their venomous tentacles can grow up to 3m long. You can be stung during any month, but the worst time is from November to the end of April, when you should stay out of the water unless you're wearing protective clothing such as a 'stinger suit', available from swimwear and sporting shops in the stinger zone. The box jellyfish also has a tiny, lethal relative called an irukandji, though to date only two north-coast deaths have been directly attributed to it.

CROCODILES

In northern Australia, saltwater crocodiles ('salties') are a real danger. As well as living around the coast they can be found in estuaries, creeks and rivers, sometimes a long way inland. Observe safety signs or ask locals whether an inviting water hole or river is croc-free before plunging in – these precautions have been fatally ignored in the past.

INSECTS

Flies aren't too bad in the cities but they start getting out of hand in the outback. In central Australia the flies emerge with the warmer spring weather (late August), particularly if there has been good winter rain, and last until the next frost kills them off. Widely available repellents, such as Aerogard and Rid, may also help to deter the little bastards, but don't count on it.

Mozzies are a problem in summer, especially near wetlands in tropical areas, and some species are carriers of viral infections; see p372. Try to keep your arms and legs covered as soon as the sun goes down and make liberal use of insect repellent.

SNAKES

There are many venomous snakes in the Australian bush, the most common being the brown and tiger snakes, but few are aggressive – unless you're interfering with one, or have the misfortune to stand on one, it's extremely unlikely that you'll be bitten. The golden rule if you see a snake is to do a Beatles and *let it be*.

SPIDERS

The deadly funnel-web spider is found in NSW (including Sydney) and its bite is treated in the same way as a snake bite. Another eight-legged critter to stay away from is black with a distinctive red stripe on its body. It's called the redback spider for obvious reasons; if bitten apply ice and seek medical attention. The white tail is a long, thin black spider with, you guessed it, a white tail, and has a fierce bite that can lead to local inflammation and ulceration.

CRIME

Australia is a relatively safe place to visit but you should still take reasonable precautions. Don't leave hotel rooms or cars unlocked, and don't leave your valuables unattended or visible through a car window. Sydney, the Gold Coast, Cairns and Byron Bay all get a dishonourable mention when it comes to theft, so keep a careful eye on your belongings in these areas.

SWIMMING

Popular beaches are patrolled by surf life savers and patrolled areas are marked off by flags. Even so, surf beaches can be dangerous places to swim if you aren't used to the conditions. Undertows (or 'rips') are the main problem. If you find yourself being carried out by a rip, the important thing to do is just keep afloat; don't panic or try to swim against the rip, which will exhaust you. In most cases the current stops within a couple of hundred metres of the shore and you can then swim parallel to the shore for a short way to get out of the rip and make your way back to land.

A number of people are also paralysed every year by diving into waves in shallow water and hitting a sand bar; check the depth of the water before you leap.

DISCOUNT CARDS

Senior travellers with some form of identification are often eligible for concession prices. Overseas pensioners are entitled to discounts of at least 10% on most express bus fares with Greyhound. Travellers over 60 years of age (both Australian residents and visitors) will simply need to present current age-proving identification to be eligible for discounts on full economy air fares.

EMBASSIES & CONSULATES

The main diplomatic representations are in Canberra. There are also representatives in other major cities, particularly from countries with a strong link to Australia, such as the USA, the UK or New Zealand, or in cities with important connections, such as Darwin, which has an Indonesian consulate.

Addresses of major offices include the following. Look in the *Yellow Pages* phone directories of the capital cities for a more complete listing.

Canada Canberra (☎ 02-6270 4000; www.australia.gc.ca; Commonwealth Ave, Yarralumla, ACT 2600); Sydney (Map pp64-5; ☎ 02-9364 3000; Level 5, 111 Harrington St, Sydney, NSW 2000)

China (☎ 02-6273 4780; http://au.china-embassy.org/eng/; 15 Coronation Dr, Yarralumla, Canberra, ACT 2600)

France Canberra (☎ 02-6216 0100; www.ambafrance-au.org; 6 Perth Ave, Yarralumla, ACT 2600); Sydney (Map p64-5; ☎ 02-92668 2400; Level 26, St Martins Tower, 31 Market St, Sydney, NSW 2000)
Germany Canberra (☎ 02-6270 1911; www.canberra.diplo.de; 119 Empire Circuit, Yarralumla, ACT 2600); Sydney (Map p52-3; ☎ 02-9328 7733; 13 Trelawney St, Woollahra, NSW 2025); Melbourne (Map p206-7; ☎ 03-9864 6888; 480 Punt Rd, South Yarra, Vic 3141)
Ireland (☎ 02-6273 3022; www.embassyofireland.au.com; 20 Arkana St, Yarralumla, Canberra, ACT 2600)
Japan Canberra (☎ 02-6273 3244; www.au.emb-japan.go.jp; 112 Empire Circuit, Yarralumla, ACT 2600); Sydney (Map p64-5; ☎ 02-9231 3455; Level 34, Colonial Centre, 52 Martin Pl, Sydney, NSW 2000)
Malaysia (☎ 02-6273 1543; www.malaysia.org.au; 7 Perth Ave, Yarralumla, Canberra, ACT 2600)
Netherlands Canberra (☎ 02-6220 9400; www.netherlands.org.au; 120 Empire Circuit, Yarralumla, ACT 2600); Sydney (Map p52-3; ☎ 02-9387 6644; Level 23, Tower 2, 101 Grafton St, Bondi Junction, NSW 2022)
New Zealand Canberra (☎ 02-6270 4211; www.nzembassy.com/australia; Commonwealth Ave, Canberra, ACT 2600); Sydney (Map p64-5; ☎ 02-8256 2000; Level 10, 55 Hunter St, Sydney, NSW 2001)
Singapore (☎ 02-6271 2000; www.mfa.gov.sg/canberra; 17 Forster Cres, Yarralumla, Canberra, ACT 2600)
South Africa (☎ 02-6272 7300; www.sahc.org.au; cnr Rhodes Pl & State Circle, Yarralumla, Canberra, ACT 2600)
Thailand Canberra (☎ 02-6273 1149; http://canberra.thaiembassy.org; 111 Empire Circuit, Yarralumla, ACT 2600); Sydney (Map p64-5; ☎ 02-9241 2542; http://thaisydney.idx.com.au; Level 8, 131 Macquarie St, Sydney, NSW 2000)
UK Canberra (☎ 02-6270 6666; www.britaus.net; Commonwealth Ave, Yarralumla, ACT 2600); Sydney (Map p64-5; ☎ 02-9247 7521; 16th fl, 1 Macquarie Pl, Sydney, NSW 2000); Melbourne (Map p208-9; ☎ 03-9652 1600; 17th fl, 90 Collins St, Melbourne, Vic 3000)
USA Canberra (☎ 02-6214 5600; http://canberra.usembassy.gov; 1 Moonah Pl, Yarralumla, ACT 2600); Sydney (Map p64-5; ☎ 02-9373 9184; Level 59, 19-29 Martin Pl, Sydney, NSW 2000); Melbourne (Map p206-7; ☎ 03-9526 5900; Level 6, 553 St Kilda Rd, Melbourne, Vic 3004)

It's important to realise what your own embassy – the embassy of the country of which you are a citizen – can and can't do to help you if you get into trouble. Generally speaking, it won't be much help in emergencies if the trouble you're in is even remotely your own fault. Remember that while in Australia you are bound by Australian laws. Your embassy will not be sympathetic if you end up in jail after committing a crime locally, even if such actions are legal in your own country.

In genuine emergencies you might get some assistance, but only if other channels have been exhausted. If you have all your money and documents stolen, it might assist with getting a new passport, but a loan for onward travel is out of the question.

FESTIVALS & EVENTS

Some of the most enjoyable Australian festivals are also the most typically Australian – such as the surf life-saving competitions on beaches all around the country during summer, or outback race meetings, which draw together isolated communities. There are also big city-based street festivals, sporting events and arts festivals that showcase comedy, music and dance, and some important commemorative get-togethers. See p46 for more information on local festivals.

GAY & LESBIAN TRAVELLERS

Australia is a popular destination for gay and lesbian travellers, with the so-called 'pink tourism' appeal of Sydney especially big, thanks largely to the city's annual, high-profile and spectacular Sydney Gay & Lesbian Mardi Gras. Throughout the country, but particularly on the east coast, there are tour operators, travel agents and accommodation places that make a point of welcoming gay men and lesbians.

Major gay and lesbian events include the aforementioned **Sydney Gay & Lesbian Mardi Gras** (www.mardigras.org.au) held annually in February and March, Melbourne's **Midsumma Festival** (www.midsumma.org.au) from mid-January to mid-February, Adelaide's **Feast** (www.feast.org.au) held in November, and Perth's **Pride March** and **Perth Pride** (www.pridewa.asn.au) festival – both held in October.

All major cities have gay newspapers, available from gay and lesbian venues and from newsagents in popular gay and lesbian residential areas. Gay lifestyle magazines include *DNA, Lesbians on the Loose,* the monthly *Queensland Pride* and the bimonthly *Blue*. Perth has the free *OutinPerth* and Adelaide has *Blaze*.

The website of **Gay and Lesbian Tourism Australia** (Galta; www.galta.com.au) has general information, and **Pinkboard** (www.pinkboard.com.au) is also helpful. **Gay and Lesbian Counselling and Community Services of Australia** (GLCCS; www.glccs.org.au) telephone counselling services are often a useful source of general information. It has a switchboard in every capital city and toll-free numbers for rural areas.

HEALTH

Healthwise, Australia is a remarkably safe country in which to travel, considering that such a large portion of it lies in the tropics. Tropical diseases such as malaria and yellow fever are unknown; diseases of insanitation such as cholera and typhoid are unheard of. Thanks to Australia's isolation and quarantine standards, even some animal diseases such as rabies and foot-and-mouth disease have yet to be recorded.

Few travellers to Australia will experience anything worse than an upset stomach or a bad hangover, and, if you do fall ill, the standard of hospitals and health care is high.

BEFORE YOU GO

Since most vaccines don't produce immunity until at least two weeks after they're given, visit a physician four to eight weeks before departure. Ask your doctor for an International Certificate of Vaccination (otherwise known as 'the yellow booklet'), which will list all the vaccinations you've received. This is mandatory for countries that require proof of yellow fever vaccination upon entry (sometimes required in Australia, see Required & Recommended Vaccinations, p371), but it's a good idea to carry a record of all your vaccinations wherever you travel.

Bring medications in their original, clearly labelled containers. A signed and dated letter from your physician describing your medical conditions and medications, including generic names, is also a good idea. If carrying syringes or needles, be sure to have a physician's letter documenting their medical necessity.

INSURANCE

If your health insurance doesn't cover you for medical expenses abroad, consider getting extra insurance – check www

.lonelyplanet.com for more information. Find out in advance if your insurance plan will make payments directly to providers or if it will reimburse you later for overseas health expenditures. In Australia, as in many countries, doctors expect payment at the time of consultation. Make sure you get an itemised receipt detailing the service and keep the contact details of the health provider. See right for details of health care in Australia.

MEDICAL CHECKLIST

- antibiotics
- antidiarrhoeal drugs (eg loperamide)
- acetaminophen (paracetamol) or aspirin
- anti-inflammatory drugs (eg ibuprofen)
- antihistamines (for hay fever and allergic reactions)
- antibacterial ointment in case of cuts or abrasions
- steroid cream or cortisone (for allergic rashes)
- bandages, gauze, gauze rolls
- adhesive or paper tape
- scissors, safety pins, tweezers
- thermometer
- pocket knife
- DEET-containing insect repellent for the skin
- permethrin-containing insect spray for clothing, tents and bed nets
- sun block
- oral rehydration salts
- iodine tablets or water filter (for water purification)

REQUIRED & RECOMMENDED VACCINATIONS

If you're entering Australia within six days of having stayed overnight or longer in a yellow fever-infected country, you'll need proof of yellow fever vaccination. For a full list of these countries visit the **World Health Organization** (**WHO; www.who.int/wer**) or **Centers for Disease Control & Prevention** (**www.cdc.gov/travel**) websites.

If you're really worried about health when travelling, there are a few vaccinations you could consider for Australia. The WHO recommends that all travellers should be covered for diphtheria, tetanus, measles, mumps, rubella, chickenpox and polio, as well as hepatitis B, regardless of their destination. Planning to travel is a great time to ensure that all routine vaccination cover is complete. The consequences of these diseases can be severe, and while Australia has high levels of childhood vaccination coverage, outbreaks of these diseases do occur.

IN AUSTRALIA

AVAILABILITY & COST OF HEALTH CARE

Health insurance is essential for all travellers. While health care in Australia is of a high standard and not overly expensive by international standards, considerable costs can build up and repatriation is extremely expensive. Make sure your existing health insurance will cover you – if not, organise extra insurance.

Australia has an excellent health-care system. It's a mixture of privately run medical clinics and hospitals alongside a system of public hospitals funded by the Australian government. There are excellent specialised, public health facilities for women and children in Australia's major centres.

The Medicare system covers Australian residents for some of their health-care costs. Visitors from countries with which Australia has a reciprocal health-care agreement are eligible for benefits specified under the Medicare program. There are agreements currently in place with Finland, Ireland, Italy, Malta, the Netherlands, New Zealand, Norway, Sweden and the UK – check the details before departing from these countries. In general, the agreements provide for any episode of ill-health that requires prompt medical attention. For further information, visit www.medicareaustralia.gov.au/public/migrants/visitors.

Over-the-counter medications are widely available at privately owned chemists throughout Australia. These include painkillers, antihistamines for allergies, and skin-care products.

You may find that medications readily available over the counter in some countries are only available in Australia by prescription. These include the oral contraceptive pill, most medications for asthma and all antibiotics. If you take medication on a regular basis, bring an adequate supply and ensure you have details of the generic name as brand names may differ between countries.

ENVIRONMENTAL HAZARDS

Heat exhaustion occurs when fluid intake does not keep up with fluid loss. Symptoms include dizziness, fainting, fatigue, nausea or vomiting. The skin is usually pale, cool and clammy. Treatment consists of rest in a cool, shady place and fluid replacement with water or diluted sports drinks.

Heatstroke is a severe form of heat illness that occurs after fluid depletion or extreme heat challenge from heavy exercise. This is a true medical emergency, with heating of the brain leading to disorientation, hallucinations and seizures. Prevent heatstroke by maintaining an adequate fluid intake to ensure the continued passage of clear and copious urine, especially during physical exertion.

A number of unprepared travellers die from dehydration each year in outback Australia. This can be prevented by following some simple rules:

- Carry sufficient water for any trip, including extra in case your vehicle breaks down.
- Always let someone, such as the local police, know where you are going and when you expect to arrive.
- Carry communications equipment of some form.
- Stay with your vehicle rather than walking for help.

Various insects can be a source of irritation and, in Australia, may be the source of specific diseases (dengue fever, Ross River fever, tick typhus, viral encephalitis). Protection from mosquitoes, sandflies, ticks and leeches can be achieved by a combination of the following strategies:

- Wear loose-fitting, long-sleeved clothing.
- Apply 30% DEET to all exposed skin and reapply every three to four hours.
- Impregnate clothing with permethrin (an insecticide that is believed to be safe for humans).

Australia has exceptional surf, particularly on the eastern, southern and western coasts. Beaches vary enormously in their underwater conditions: the slope offshore can result in changeable and often powerful surf. It's a good idea to check with local surf life-saving organisations and be aware of your own expertise and limitations before entering the water.

Australia has one of the highest rates of skin cancer in the world. Monitor your exposure to direct sunlight closely. Ultraviolet (UV) exposure is greatest between 10am and 4pm, so avoid skin exposure during these times. Always use 30+ sunscreen; apply it 30 minutes before going into the sun and repeat applications regularly to minimise damage.

HOLIDAYS

PUBLIC HOLIDAYS

The following is a list of the main national and state public holidays (* indicates holidays that are only observed locally). As the timing can vary from state to state, check locally for precise dates.

NATIONAL

New Year's Day 1 January
Australia Day 26 January
Easter (Good Friday to Easter Monday inclusive) March/April
Anzac Day 25 April
Queen's Birthday (except WA) Second Monday in June
Queen's Birthday (WA) Last Monday in September
Christmas Day 25 December
Boxing Day 26 December

NEW SOUTH WALES

Bank Holiday First Monday in August
Labour Day First Monday in October

NORTHERN TERRITORY

May Day First Monday in May
Show Day* (Alice Springs) First Friday in July; (Tennant Creek) Second Friday in July; (Katherine) Third Friday in July; (Darwin) Fourth Friday in July
Picnic Day First Monday in August

QUEENSLAND

Labour Day First Monday in May
RNA Show Day (Brisbane) August

SOUTH AUSTRALIA

Adelaide Cup Day Third Monday in May
Labour Day First Monday in October
Proclamation Day Last Tuesday in December

TASMANIA

Regatta Day 14 February
Eight Hours Day First Monday in March
Bank Holiday Tuesday following Easter Monday
Hobart Show Day Thursday preceding fourth Saturday in October
Recreation Day* (northern Tasmania only) First Monday in November

VICTORIA

Labour Day Second Monday in March
Melbourne Cup Day First Tuesday in November

WESTERN AUSTRALIA

Labour Day First Monday in March
Foundation Day First Monday in June

SCHOOL HOLIDAYS

The Christmas holiday season, from mid-December to late January, is part of the summer school holidays – it's also the time you are most likely to find transport and accommodation booked out, and long, restless queues at tourist attractions.

INSURANCE

Don't underestimate the importance of a good travel insurance policy that covers theft, loss and medical problems – nothing is guaranteed to ruin your holiday plans quicker than an accident or having that brand new digital camera stolen. Most policies offer lower and higher medical-expense options; the higher ones are chiefly for countries that have extremely high medical costs, such as the USA.

Some policies specifically exclude designated 'dangerous activities' such as scuba diving, bungee jumping, motorcycling, skiing and even bushwalking. If you plan on doing any of these things, make sure the policy you choose fully covers you for your activity of choice.

You may prefer a policy that pays doctors or hospitals directly rather than requiring you to pay on the spot and claim later. If you have to claim later make sure you keep all documentation. Check that the policy covers ambulances and emergency medical evacuations by air.

INTERNET ACCESS

If you've brought your palmtop or notebook computer and want to get connected to a local Internet Service Provider (ISP), there are plenty of options – some ISPs do limit their dial-up areas to major cities or particular regions. Whatever enticements a particular ISP offers, make sure it has local dial-up numbers for the places where you intend to use it – the last thing you want is to be making timed long-distance calls every time you connect to the internet. Another useful tip when dialling up from a hotel room is to put 0 in front of your dial-up number to enable your modem to dial an outside line.

Some major ISPs:

Australia On Line (☎ 1300 650 661; www.ozonline.com.au)
Dodo (☎ 13 24 73; www.dodo.com.au)
iinet (☎ 13 19 17; www.iinet.net.au)
iPrimus (☎ 13 17 89; www.iprimus.com.au)
Optus (☎ 13 33 45; www.optus.com.au)
Telstra BigPond (☎ 13 76 63; www.bigpond.com)

An increasing number of hotels, cafes and bars in cities offer wi-fi (wireless) access. Most internet cafes in Australia now have broadband access, but prices vary significantly depending on where you are. Most public libraries also have internet access, but this is provided primarily for research needs, not for travellers to check their email, so head for an internet cafe first. Some charge a fee so make sure you ask the price before connecting. These locations are most prevalent in Sydney and Melbourne but they're on the rise elsewhere. The following websites are helpful for sourcing locations:

Azure Wireless (www.azure.com.au)
Free WiFi (www.freewifi.com.au)
Wi-Fi HotSpotList (www.wi-fihotspotlist.com/browse/au)

Australia uses RJ-45 telephone plugs and Telstra EXI-160 four-pin plugs, but neither is universal – electronics shops such as Tandy and Dick Smith should be able to help. You'll also need a plug adaptor, and a universal AC adaptor will enable you to plug in without frying the innards of your machine.

Keep in mind that your PC-card modem may not work in Australia. The safest option is to buy a reputable 'global' modem before you leave home or buy a local PC-card modem once you get to Australia.

LEGAL MATTERS

Most travellers will have no contact with the Australian police or legal system. Those that do are likely to experience it while driving. There is a significant police presence on the roads, with the power to stop your car and ask to see your licence (you're required to carry it at all times), check your vehicle for roadworthiness, and insist that you take a breath test for alcohol – needless to say, drink-driving offences are taken very seriously here.

If you remain in Australia beyond the life of your visa, you will officially be an 'overstayer' and could face detention and expulsion, and then be prevented from returning to Australia for up to three years.

If you are arrested, it's your right to telephone a friend, relative or lawyer before any formal questioning begins. Legal Aid is available only in serious cases and only to the truly needy (for links to Legal Aid offices see www.nla.aust.net.au). However, many solicitors do not charge for an initial consultation.

MAPS

Good-quality road and topographical maps are plentiful and readily available. The various state motoring organisations are a dependable source of road maps, while local tourist offices usually supply free maps, though the quality varies.

MONEY

ATMS, EFTPOS & BANK ACCOUNTS

Branches of the ANZ, Commonwealth, National Australia, Westpac and affiliated banks are found all over Australia, and many provide 24-hour automated teller machines (ATMs). But don't expect to find ATMs *everywhere,* certainly not off the beaten track or in very small towns. Most ATMs accept cards issued by other banks and are linked to international networks.

Eftpos (Electronic Funds Transfer at Point of Sale) is a convenient service that most Australian businesses have embraced. It means you can use your bank card (credit or debit) to pay for services or purchases directly, and often withdraw cash as well. Eftpos is available practically everywhere these days, even in outback roadhouses where it's a long way between banks.

CREDIT & DEBIT CARDS

Credit cards such as Visa and MasterCard are widely accepted for everything from a hostel bed or a restaurant meal to an adventure tour, and are pretty much essential (in lieu of a large deposit) for hiring a car. They can also be used to get cash advances over the counter at banks and from many ATMs, depending on the card, though these transactions incur immediate interest. Charge cards such as Diners Club and American Express (Amex) are not as widely accepted.

CURRENCY

Australia's currency is the Australian dollar, made up of 100 cents. There are 5c, 10c, 20c, 50c, $1 and $2 coins, and $5, $10, $20, $50 and $100 notes. Although the smallest coin in circulation is 5c, prices are often still marked in single cents and then rounded to the nearest 5c when you come to pay.

Cash amounts equal to or in excess of the equivalent of A$10,000 (in any currency) must be declared on arrival or departure.

In this book, unless otherwise stated, all prices given in dollars refer to Australian dollars.

EXCHANGING MONEY

Changing foreign currency or travellers cheques is usually no problem at banks throughout Australia or at licensed moneychangers such as Travelex or Amex in cities and major towns.

TAXES & REFUNDS

The Goods and Services Tax (GST) is a flat 10% tax on all goods and services – accommodation, eating out, transport, electrical and other goods, books, furniture, clothing etc. There are exceptions, however, such as basic foods (milk, bread, fruits and vegetables etc). By law the tax is included in the quoted or shelf prices, so all prices in this book are GST-inclusive. International air and sea travel to/from

Australia is GST-free, as is domestic air travel when purchased outside Australia by nonresidents.

If you purchase new or secondhand goods with a total minimum value of $300 from any one supplier no more than 30 days before you leave Australia, you are entitled under the Tourist Refund Scheme (TRS) to a refund of any GST or WET (wine equalisation tax) paid. The scheme doesn't apply to all goods, and those that do qualify you must be able to wear or take as hand luggage onto the plane or ship. Also note that the refund is valid for goods bought from more than one supplier, but only if at least $300 is spent in each. For more details, contact the **Australian Customs Service** (☎ 1300 363 263, 02-6275 6666; www.customs.gov.au).

TRAVELLERS CHEQUES

The ubiquity and convenience of internationally linked credit and debit card facilities in Australia means that travellers cheques are virtually redundant. However Amex and Travelex will exchange their associated travellers cheques, and major banks will change travellers cheques also. In all instances you'll need to present your passport for identification when cashing them.

PHOTOGRAPHY & VIDEO

Digital cameras, memory sticks and batteries are sold prolifically in cities and urban centres. The availability of batteries and memory sticks in more rural or remote areas is far diminished so if you're planning to get trigger happy it's best to stock up in the cities.

As in any country, politeness goes a long way when taking photographs; ask before taking pictures of people. Particularly bear in mind that Indigenous Australians are not objects of curiosity; they are people like you and photography can be highly intrusive. Regardless of whether the purpose is personal or commercial, always ask permission before photographing or videoing a person, group or residence and offer to return copies of photographs or footage (and get an address). Taking photographs of cultural places, practices and images, sites of significance and ceremonies may also be a sensitive matter. Always ask and always respect the right to say no.

Useful Lonely Planet titles for the budding photographer include *Urban Travel Photography Wildlife, Travel Photography,* and *Landscape Photography*.

TELEPHONE

INFORMATION & TOLL-FREE CALLS

Numbers starting with ☎ 190 are usually recorded information services, charged at anything from 35c to $5 or more per minute (more from mobiles and payphones). To make a reverse-charge (collect) call from any public or private phone, dial ☎ 1800 REVERSE (☎ 1800 738 3773), or ☎ 12 550.

Toll-free numbers (prefix ☎ 1800) can be called free of charge from almost anywhere in Australia – they may not be accessible from certain areas or from mobile phones. Calls to numbers beginning with ☎ 13 or ☎ 1300 are charged at the rate of a local call – the numbers can usually be dialled Australia-wide, but may be applicable only to a specific state or STD district. Telephone numbers beginning with either ☎ 1800, ☎ 13 or ☎ 1300 cannot be dialled from outside Australia.

INTERNATIONAL CALLS

Most payphones allow International Subscriber Dialling (ISD) calls, the cost and international dialling code of which will vary depending on which international phone card provider you are using.

International phone cards are readily available from internet cafes and small independent stores. Check the fine print on your phone card to ensure you aren't paying a hefty trunk charge every time you make a call.

The **Country Direct service** (☎ **1800 801 800**) connects callers in Australia with operators in nearly 60 countries to make reverse-charge (collect) or credit-card calls.

When calling overseas you will need to dial the international access code from Australia (☎ 0011 or ☎ 0018), the country code and then the area code (without the initial 0). So for a London telephone number you'll need to dial ☎ 0011-44-20, then the number.

If dialling Australia from overseas, the country code is ☎ 61 and you need to drop the 0 in state/territory area codes.

SOME COUNTRY CODES

Country	International Country Code
France	☎ 33
Germany	☎ 49
Ireland	☎ 353
Japan	☎ 81
Netherlands	☎ 31
New Zealand	☎ 64
UK	☎ 44
USA & Canada	☎ 1

LOCAL CALLS

Calls from private phones cost 15c to 30c, while local calls from public phones cost 50c; both involve unlimited talk time. Calls to mobile phones attract higher rates and are timed.

LONG-DISTANCE CALLS & AREA CODES

Long-distance calls (over around 50km) are timed. Australia uses four Subscriber Trunk Dialling (STD) area codes. These STD calls can be made from any public phone and are cheaper during off-peak hours – generally between 7pm and 7am and on weekends.

Area codes don't necessarily coincide with state borders; for example some parts of NSW use neighbouring states' codes.

AUSTRALIAN AREA CODES

State/Territory	Area code
ACT	☎ 02
NSW	☎ 02
NT	☎ 08
QLD	☎ 07
SA	☎ 08
TAS	☎ 03
VIC	☎ 03
WA	☎ 08

MOBILE (CELL) PHONES

Local numbers with the prefixes ☎ 04xx or ☎ 04xxx belong to mobile phones. Australia's GSM and 3G mobile networks service more than 90% of the population but leaves vast tracts of the country uncovered. The east coast, southeast and southwest get good reception, but elsewhere (apart from major towns) it can be haphazard or nonexistent.

Australia's digital network is compatible with GSM 900 and 1800 (used in Europe), but generally not with the systems used in the USA or Japan. It's easy and cheap enough to get connected short-term, as prepaid mobile systems are offered by providers such as **Telstra** (**www.telstra.com.au**), **Optus** (**www.optus.com.au**), **Vodafone** (**www.vodafone.com.au**), **Virgin** (**www.virginmobile.com.au**) and **3** (**www.three.com.au**).

PHONECARDS

A variety of phonecards can be bought at newsagents, hostels and post offices for a fixed dollar value (usually $10, $20 etc) and can be used with any public or private phone by dialling a toll-free access number and then the PIN number on the card. Some public phones also accept credit cards.

TIME

Australia is divided into three time zones: the Western Standard Time zone (GMT/UTC plus eight hours) covers WA; Central Standard Time (plus 9½ hours) covers the NT and SA; and Eastern Standard Time (plus 10 hours) covers Tasmania, Victoria, NSW, the ACT and Queensland. There are minor exceptions – Broken Hill (NSW) for instance is on Central Standard Time. For international times, see www.timeanddate.com/worldclock.

'Daylight saving', for which clocks are put forward an hour, operates in some states during the warmer months (October to early April). However, things can get pretty confusing, with WA, the NT and Queensland staying on standard time, while in Tasmania daylight saving starts a month earlier than in SA, Victoria, the ACT and NSW.

TIPPING

It's common but by no means obligatory to tip in restaurants and upmarket cafes if the service warrants it – a gratuity of between 5% and 10% of the bill is the norm. Taxi drivers will also appreciate you rounding up the fare.

TOURIST INFORMATION

The **Australian Tourist Commission** (www.australia.com) is the national government tourist body, and has a good website for pretrip research.

LOCAL TOURIST OFFICES

Almost every major town in Australia seems to maintain a tourist office of some type and in many cases they are very good, with friendly staff (often volunteers) providing local info not readily available from the state offices.

TOURIST OFFICES ABROAD

The federal government body charged with improving relationships with foreign tourists is **Tourism Australia** (☎ 02-9360 1111; www.australia.com). A good place to start some pretrip research is on its website, which provides information about many aspects of visiting Australia in 10 languages (including French, German, Japanese and Spanish).

Some countries with Tourism Australia offices:

Germany (☎ 069-274 00622; Neue Mainzer Strasse 22, Frankfurt D 60311)

Japan (☎ 13-5214 0720; Australian Business Centre, New Otani Garden Court Bldg 28F, 4-1 Kioi-cho Chiyoda-ku, Tokyo 102-0094)

New Zealand (☎ 09-915 2826; Level 3, 125 The Strand, Parnell, Auckland)

Singapore (☎ 6255 4555; 101 Thomson Rd, United Sq 08-03, Singapore 307591)

Thailand (☎ 02 670 0640; 16th fl, Unit 1614, Empire Tower, 195 South Sathorn Rd, Yannawa, Sathorn, Bangkok 10120)

UK (☎ 020-7438 4601; 6th fl, Australia House, Melbourne Place/Strand, London WC2B 4LG)

USA (☎ 310-695 3200; Suite 1150, 6100 Center Dr, Los Angeles CA 90045)

TRAVELLERS WITH DISABILITIES

Disability awareness in Australia is pretty high and getting higher. Legislation requires that new accommodation meets accessibility standards for mobility-impaired travellers, and discrimination by tourism operators is illegal.

Many of Australia's key attractions, even including many national parks, provide access for those with limited mobility and a number of sites also address the needs of visitors with visual or aural impairments; contact attractions in advance to confirm the available facilities. Tour operators with vehicles catering to mobility-impaired travellers operate from most capital cities.

VISAS

All visitors to Australia need a visa – only New Zealand nationals are exempt, and even they receive a 'special category' visa on arrival. Application forms for the several types of visa are available from Australian diplomatic missions overseas, travel agents or the website of the **Department of Immigration & Citizenship** (☎ 13 18 81; www.immi.gov.au).

eVISITOR

Many European passport holders are eligible for an eVisitor, which is free and allows visitors to stay in Australia for up to three months. eVisitors must be applied for online and they are electronically stored and linked to individual passport numbers, so no stamp in your passport is required. It's advisable to apply at least 14 days prior to the proposed date of travel to Australia. Applications are made on the Department of Immigration and Citizenship website.

ELECTRONIC TRAVEL AUTHORITY (ETA)

Some visitors who aren't eligible for an eVisitor can get an ETA through any International Air Transport Association (IATA)-registered travel agent, overseas airline or Australian visa office outside Australia. They make the application direct when you buy a ticket and issue the ETA, which replaces the usual visa stamped in your passport – it's common practice for travel agents to charge a fee, in the vicinity of US$25, for issuing an ETA. This system is available to passport holders of eight countries: Brunei, Canada, Hong Kong, Japan, Malaysia, Singapore, South Korea and the USA.

You can also apply for the ETA online (www.eta.immi.gov.au), which attracts a nonrefundable service charge of $20.

TOURIST VISAS

Short-term tourist visas have largely been replaced by the eVisitor and ETA. However, if you are from a country not covered by either, or you want to stay longer than three months, you'll need to apply for a visa. Standard Tourist Visas (which cost $100) allow one (in some cases multiple) entry, for a stay of up to 12 months, and are valid for use within 12 months of issue.

TRANSPORT

GETTING THERE & AWAY

They don't call Australia the land 'down under' for nothing. It's a long way from just about everywhere, and getting here is usually going to mean a long-haul flight. That 'over the horizon' feeling doesn't stop once you're here, either – the distances between key cities (much less opposing coastlines) can be vast, requiring a minimum of an hour or two of air time or up to several days of highway cruising or dirt-road jostling to traverse.

ENTERING THE COUNTRY

Disembarkation in Australia is a straightforward affair, with only the usual customs declarations (p366) and the fight to be first to the luggage carousel to endure. However, global instability in the last few years has resulted in conspicuously increased security in Australian airports, and you may find that customs procedures are now more time-consuming.

There are no restrictions when it comes to citizens of foreign countries entering Australia. If you have a visa (p379), you should be fine.

AIR

The high season for flights into Australia is roughly over the country's summer (December to February), with slightly less of a premium on fares over the shoulder months (October/November and March/April). The low season generally tallies with the winter months (June to August), though this is actually the peak tourist season in central Australia and the Top End.

Australia has several international gateways, with Sydney and Melbourne being the busiest. The full list of international airports follows.

Adelaide (code ADL; ☎ 08-8308 9211; www.aal.com.au)
Brisbane (code BNE; ☎ 07-3406 3000; www.brisbaneairport.com.au)
Cairns (code CNS; ☎ 07-4080 6703; www.cairnsport.com.au/airport)
Darwin (code DRW; ☎ 08-8920 1811; www.ntapl.com.au)
Melbourne (Tullamarine; code MEL; ☎ 03-9297 1600; www.melbourneairport.com.au)
Perth (code PER; ☎ 08-9478 8888; www.perthairport.net.au)
Sydney (Kingsford Smith; code SYD; ☎ 02-9667 9111; www.sydneyairport.com.au)

Australia's international carrier Qantas flies chiefly to runways across Europe, North America, Asia and the Pacific.

GETTING AROUND

AIR

Time pressures combined with the vastness of the Australian continent may lead you to consider taking to the skies at some point in your trip.

Both **STA Travel** (☎ 134 782; www.statravel.com.au) and **Flight Centre** (☎ 133 133; www.flightcentre.com.au) have offices throughout Australia. For online bookings, try www.travel.com.au.

AIR PASSES

With discounting being the norm these days, air passes are not great value. Qantas' **Boomerang Pass** (☎ 13 13 13) can only be purchased overseas and involves buying coupons for either short-haul flights (up to 1200km, eg Hobart to Melbourne) or multizone sectors (including New Zealand and the Pacific). You must purchase a

CLIMATE CHANGE & TRAVEL

Travel – especially air travel – is a significant contributor to global climate change. At Lonely Planet, we believe that all who travel have a responsibility to limit their personal impact. As a result, we have teamed with Rough Guides and other concerned industry partners to support Climate Care, which allows people to offset the greenhouse gases they are responsible for with contributions to energy-saving projects and other climate-friendly initiatives in the developing world. Lonely Planet offsets all staff and author travel.

For more information, turn to the responsible travel pages on www.lonelyplanet.com. For details on offsetting your carbon emissions and a carbon calculator, go to www.climatecare.org.

minimum of two coupons before you arrive in Australia, and once here you can buy more.

AIRLINES IN AUSTRALIA

Qantas is the country's chief domestic airline, represented at the budget end by its subsidiary Jetstar. Another highly competitive carrier that flies all over Australia is Virgin Blue. Keep in mind if flying with Jetstar or Virgin Blue that these no-frills airlines close check-in 30 minutes prior to a flight.

Australia has many smaller operators flying regional routes. In many places, such as remote outback destinations or islands, these are the only viable transport option. Many of these airlines operate as subsidiaries or commercial partners of Qantas.

Some regional airlines:

Jetstar (☎ 13 15 38; www.jetstar.com.au) Budget- oriented Qantas subsidiary flying to all the capital cities and around 15 east-coast destinations from Cairns to Hobart.

Macair (☎ 1300 622 247; www.macair.com.au) Commercially partnered with Qantas, this Townsville-based airline flies throughout western and northern Queensland.

Qantas (☎ 13 13 13; www.qantas.com.au) Australia's chief domestic airline.

QantasLink (☎ 13 13 13; www.qantas.com.au) Flying across Australia under this Qantas subsidiary brand is a collective of regional airlines that includes Eastern Australia Airlines, Airlink and Sunstate Airlines.

Regional Express (Rex; ☎ 13 17 13; www.regionalexpress.com.au) Flies from Sydney, Melbourne, Burnie and Adelaide to around 25 other destinations in New South Wales (NSW), Victoria, South Australia (SA) and Tasmania.

Tasair (☎ 02-6248 5088; www.tasair.com.au) Flies within Tasmania.

Tiger Airways (www.tigerairways.com) A subsidiary of Singapore Airlines, this budget carrier flies between a handful of major capital cities in Australia.

Virgin Blue (☎ 13 67 89; www.virginblue.com.au) Highly competitive, Virgin Blue flies all over Australia – Virgin fares are cheaper if booked online (discount per ticket $10).

BUS

Australia's extensive bus network is a relatively cheap and reliable way to get around, though it can be a tedious means of travel and requires planning if you intend to do more than straightforward city-to-city trips. Most buses are equipped with air-con, toilets and videos, and all are smoke-free zones.

A national bus network is provided by **Greyhound Australia** (☎ 1300 473 946; www.greyhound.com.au). Fares purchased online are roughly 5% cheaper than over-the-counter tickets; fares purchased by phone incur a $4 booking fee.

Small regional operators running key routes or covering a lot of ground include the following:

Firefly Express (☎ 1300 730 740; www.fireflyexpress.com.au) Runs between Sydney, Melbourne and Adelaide.

Northern Rivers Buslines (☎ 02-6626 1499; www.nrbuslines.com.au) Northern NSW.

Premier Motor Service (☎ 13 34 10; www.premierms.com.au) Runs along the east coast between Cairns and Melbourne.

Redline Coaches (☎ 1300 360 000; www.tasredline.com.au) Services Hobart and Tasmania's northern and eastern coasts.

Transwa (☎ 1300 662 205; www.transwa.wa.gov.au) Hauls itself around the southern half of WA.

V/Line (☎ 13 61 96; www.vline.com.au) Runs to most major towns and cities in Victoria.

PRINCIPAL BUS ROUTES & RAILWAYS

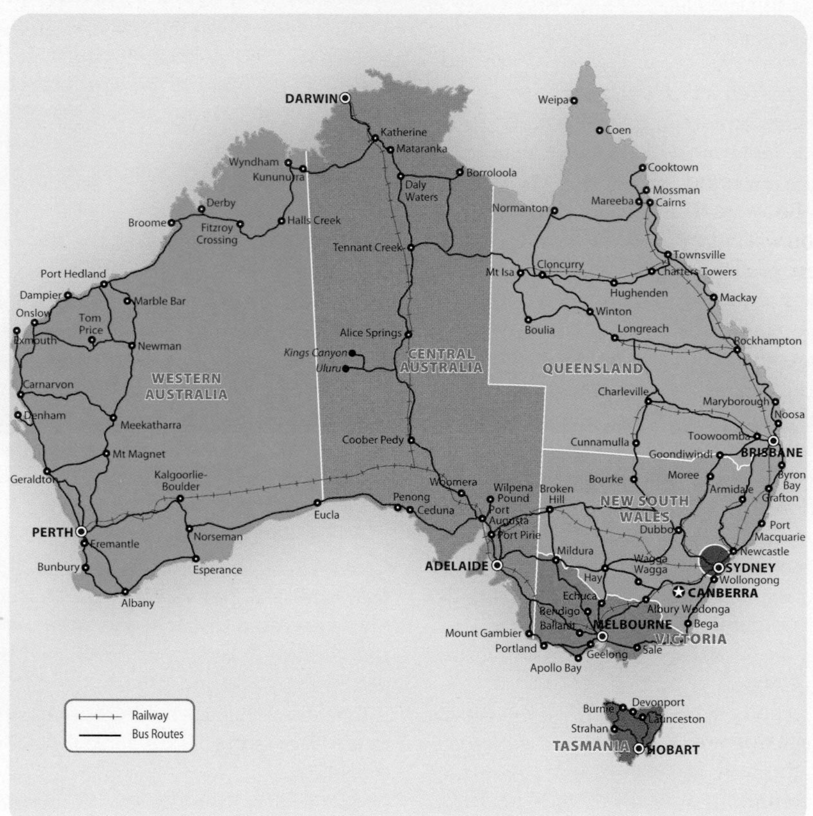

CAR & MOTORCYCLE

With its vast distances, long stretches of road and off-the-beaten-track sights, Australia explored by road guarantees an experience unlike any other. Diverting from the well-serviced east coast will reveal vast tracts of country without comprehensive or convenient public transport and many travellers find that the best way to see the place is to purchase or hire a car. It's certainly the only way to get to those interesting out-of-the-way places without taking a tour.

DRIVING LICENCE

You must hold a current driving licence that has been issued in English from your home country in order to drive in Australia. If the licence from your home country is not issued in English, you will also need to carry an International Driving Permit, issued in your home country, at all times.

INSURANCE

When it comes to hire cars, understand your liability in the event of an accident. Rather than risk paying out thousands of dollars, you can take out your own comprehensive car insurance or (the usual option) pay an additional daily amount to the rental company for an 'insurance excess reduction' policy. This reduces the excess you must pay in the event of an accident from between $2000 and $5000 to a few hundred dollars.

Be aware that if travelling on dirt roads you will not be covered by insurance unless you have a 4WD. Also, most companies' insurance won't cover the cost of damage to glass (including the windscreen) or tyres.

RENTING A VEHICLE

Most companies require the driver to be over the age of 21, though in some cases it may be 18, and in others 25. Some suggestions to assist in the process of hiring a car include the following:

- Get a copy of the contract and read it carefully.
- Check what the bond entails. Some companies may require a signed credit-card slip, others may actually charge your credit card; if this is the case, find out when you'll get a refund.
- Ask if unlimited kilometres are included and if not, what the extra charge per kilometre is.
- Find out what excess you will pay and if this can be lowered by an extra charge per day. Check if your personal travel insurance covers you for motor vehicle accidents and rental insurance excess.
- Check for any exclusions. Some companies won't cover single vehicle accidents (eg if you hit a kangaroo), accidents occurring while the car is being reversed or damage occurring on unsealed roads. Check whether you are covered on unavoidable unsealed roads, such as gaining access to camping grounds. Some companies also exclude parts of the car from cover, such as the underbelly, tyres and windscreen or any damage from immersion in water.
- At pick-up inspect the vehicle for any damage. Make a note of anything on the contract before you sign.
- Ask about procedures in the event of a breakdown or accident.
- If you can, return the vehicle during business hours and insist on an inspection in your presence.
- If you have a complaint, contact the office of consumer affairs of the state or territory you are in.

ROAD RULES

Australians drive on the left-hand side of the road and all cars are right-hand drive. An important road rule is 'give way to the right' – if an intersection is unmarked (unusual), you must give way to vehicles entering the intersection from your right.

The general speed limit in built-up and residential areas is 50km/h, although in many cases it's 40km/h, so keep an eye out for signs. Near schools, the limit is 40km/h in the morning and afternoon. On the open highway it's usually 100km/h or 110km/h. Pay close attention to signage while driving; the police have speed radar guns and cameras and are fond of using them in strategically concealed locations.

All new cars in Australia have seat belts back and front and it's the law to wear them; you're likely to get a fine if you don't. Small children must be belted into an approved safety seat.

Drink-driving is a real problem, especially in country areas. Serious attempts to reduce the resulting road toll are ongoing and random breath-tests are not uncommon in built-up areas. If you're caught with a blood-alcohol level of more than 0.05% expect a hefty fine and the loss of your licence. Note also that talking on a mobile phone while driving is illegal in Australia.

Australian police operate mobile and roadside speed cameras. If you are caught speeding you will be heavily fined. The police also operate breathalyser and drug check-points on Australian roads and penalties for being under the influence of alcohol or drugs while driving are severe. Police can randomly pull any driver over for a breathalyser or drug test.

TRAIN

Long-distance rail travel in Australia is something you do because you really want to – not because it's cheaper or more convenient, and certainly not because it's fast. That said, trains are more comfortable than buses, and on some of Australia's long-distance train journeys the romance of the rails is alive and kicking. The *Indian Pacific* across the Nullarbor Plain and the *Ghan* from Adelaide to Darwin are two of Australia's great rail journeys.

The three major interstate services in Australia are operated by **Great Southern Railways** (**☎ 13 21 47; www.gsr.com.au**), namely the *Indian Pacific* between Sydney and Perth, the *Overland* between Melbourne and Adelaide, and the *Ghan* between Adelaide and Darwin via Alice Springs.

As the railway-booking system is computerised, any station (other than those on metropolitan lines) can make a booking for any journey throughout the country. For reservations call ☎ 13 22 32; this will connect you to the nearest main-line station.

Discounted tickets work on a first-come, first-served quota basis, so it helps to book in advance.

BEHIND THE SCENES

THE AUTHORS

LINDSAY BROWN

Coordinating author; Australia's Top Itineraries; Planning Your Trip; Northern Territory (coauthor)

A former conservation biologist and Publishing Manager of Outdoor Activity Guides at Lonely Planet, Lindsay enjoys nothing more than heading into the outback to explore and photograph Australia's heartland. As a Lonely Planet author and photographer Lindsay has contributed to several titles covering South Asia and Australia including *Central Australia – Adelaide to Darwin*, *Queensland & the Great Barrier Reef*, *East Coast Australia* and *Sydney & NSW*.

Author thanks Thanks to the wonderful 'locals' who enthusiastically shared their highlights of their home towns for this edition. Also thanks to the other Lonely Planet authors who provided the bulk of the text and thanks to the hard-working team at Lonely Planet that helped put this book together.

JUSTINE VAISUTIS

Melbourne; Culture; Food & Drink; Directory & Transport

Despite the world's best efforts, Justine is tragically in love with her own country. Having chartered vast sections of it numerous times in many directions, her wonder at Australia's beauty is ceaseless. This love affair began on a New South Wales beach when she was a tiny tacker – she still returns to her favourite secret there whenever possible. For the most part Melbourne is now home and she revelled in the opportunity to rediscover her own city again, not to mention fuel her passion for beer, coffee, live music and art. Justine has written 13 Lonely Planet titles. She now devotes most of her time to improving her manners (tough ask) and working at the Australian Conservation Foundation with truly inspiring folk.

LONELY PLANET AUTHORS

Why is our travel information the best in the world? It's simple: our authors are passionate, dedicated travellers. They don't take freebies in exchange for positive coverage so you can be sure the advice you're given is impartial. They travel widely to all the popular spots, and off the beaten track. They don't research using just the internet or phone. They discover new places not included in any other guidebook. They personally visit thousands of hotels, restaurants, palaces, trails, galleries, temples and more. They speak with dozens of locals every day to make sure you get the kind of insider knowledge only a local could tell you. They take pride in getting all the details right, and in telling it how it is. Think you can do it? Find out how at **lonelyplanet.com**.

JAYNE D'ARCY
Far North Queensland

Still carrying the juggling skills she picked up from hippies at the Kuranda market as a 12-year-old, Jayne finally got the chance to return to the land of crocs, stingers and laid-back locals as a grown-up, and see who'd changed the most. When she's not discovering her own backyard and teaching her four-year-old how to read maps, Jayne writes on travel, design, the environment and homes for newspapers, magazines and her blog.

KATJA GASKELL
Sydney; New South Wales (coauthor)

Having spent the last three years living in Sydney, Katja jumped at the chance to spend even more time at the beach – all in the name of research, of course. In addition to comparing the surf and sand of the north shore to the eastern suburbs, Katja had the tough task of sampling the many bars, restaurants and cafes that make Sydney such a fabulous city. Add to that magical weekends on the Hawkesbury and wine-soaked trips to the Hunter Valley and she's suddenly beginning to wonder quite why she's leaving Australia... By the time this is published, Katja, along with her boys, Nick and Alfie, will have embarked on a new adventure living in Delhi, India.

PAUL HARDING
Melbourne & Victoria (coauthor), Northern Territory (coauthor),

Melbourne-born, and raised in central Victoria, Paul spent childhood summer holidays in the Gippsland Lakes and indulged in many years of camping and fishing trips along the Murray River. He has since travelled to many parts of Australia and the world, but still finds Australia one of the world's greatest countries to explore and was intrigued to find so many gems in his own backyard of Victoria. He also packed the campervan and travelled to the Northern Territory's Top End. Paul has worked on numerous Lonely Planet titles; when not travelling, he lives by the beach in Melbourne.

VIRGINIA JEALOUS
Western Australia (coauthor)

Virginia was thrilled to hit the road locally from her base in Denmark – that's Denmark on Western Australia's stunning south coast. After years of overseas contracts – with Lonely Planet, aid agencies and development NGOs – it was great to simply pack up the car and go bush. A birder from way back, she's happiest with a pair of binoculars to hand, and over the 6000km travelled enjoyed spotting new birds (emu wrens at last!) and spending time with old ones like the kooky Cape Barren geese, last seen when she contributed to Lonely Planet's *Perth & Western Australia*.

ROWAN MCKINNON
Tasmania

A Melburnian through and through, Rowan got the Tasmania bug on his first trip across Bass Strait decades ago and keeps going back with his partner and children (he'd move to Tassie's northeast coast if he didn't love Melbourne so much). A freelance writer and lapsed rock musician, Rowan has contributed to many Lonely Planet titles on his native Australia as well as the island states of the South Pacific and the Caribbean.

CHARLES RAWLINGS-WAY **South Australia (coauthor)**

As a likely lad, Charles suffered in shorts through Tasmanian winters and in summer counted the days until he visited his grandparents in Adelaide. With desert-hot days, cool swimming pools, pasties with sauce squirted into the middle and four TV stations, this flat city held paradisaical status. In teenage years he realised that girls from Adelaide – with their Teutonic cheekbones and fluoridated teeth – were better looking than anywhere else in Australia. These days he lives with a girl from Adelaide in the Adelaide Hills and has developed an unnatural appreciation for Coopers Pale Ale. An underrated rock guitarist and proud new dad, Charles has written 14 books for Lonely Planet.

ROWAN ROEBIG **Brisbane & Queensland (coauthor)**

A Melbourne-based writer and editor, Rowan jumped at the chance to return to his native southeast Queensland for this book. Raised in Brisbane, his writing career began with a journalism degree at the University of Queensland, followed by stints at various local newspapers. Passion for travel led him around the world and on one occasion to Ireland for a week – but he stayed for two years, working as a scribe for a magazine in Dublin. He eventually moved back to Australia and, with travel obsession intact, worked as a digital content producer for Lonely Planet, then joined the guidebook-author ranks.

TOM SPURLING **Brisbane & Queensland (coauthor)**

It took an anarchic German vegan with a penchant for Bundy Rum to remind Tom that thumbs out, balls 'n' all, Australia is bloody unreal for travel. Tom came to writing guidebooks after reading them cover-to-cover in 30 countries, including Guatemala, Mozambique and Portugal. He's worked on Lonely Planet guides to India and Turkey and spent a year in rural South Africa on a project supported by the Lonely Planet Foundation. For the recent *Australia* guide, he went without socks for six weeks. Back in Melbourne, Tom lives with his wife, Lucy, and their son, Oliver, and teaches high school boys that it pays to have a second job.

REGIS ST LOUIS **Western Australia (coauthor)**

Regis has always been captivated by rugged wilderness and big journeys, which made his 9000km road trip around Western Australia one of his all-time favourites. Memorable moments from his travels include stargazing beside remote billabongs in the Kimberley, watching dramatic sunsets along the Coral Coast and introducing his daughter to emus, galahs and other Australian wildlife. When not out travelling the world for Lonely Planet, he splits his time between New York City and Sydney, but seems increasingly drawn to the big skies out west.

PENNY WATSON **New South Wales (coauthor)**

Penny Watson grew up on the New South Wales–Victoria border in Albury. Her frequent family holidays instilled an early love of New South Wales' many and varied landscapes, from coastal, outback and river country to the hinterlands, highlands and Snowies. Penny covered the South Coast, Riverina and snowfields for Lonely Planet's *Sydney & New South Wales*. For the recent *Australia* guide she chartered more territory, clocking up almost 10,000km twisting and turning around alpine bends, pot-holing through isolated national parks and slip-sliding over the red-earthy roads of the outback. She is a trained journalist and travel writer and her work (www.pennywatson.com.au) appears in magazines, newspapers and guidebooks in Australia, Asia, Europe and the US.

MEG WORBY

South Australia (coauthor)

After six years at Lonely Planet in the languages, editorial and publishing teams, Meg swapped the desktop for a laptop in order to write about her home state, South Australia. After 10 years away, she was stoked to find that King George Whiting is still every bit as fresh on Kangaroo Island, there are the same endless roads to cruise down in the Flinders Ranges, and the Adelaide Hills now has more wineries. In fact, obvious wine analogies aside, she found that most places in South Australia just keep getting better. Meg has written four Australian guidebooks for Lonely Planet.

CONTRIBUTING AUTHORS

Dr Michael Cathcart wrote the History feature. Michael teaches history at the Australian Centre, the University of Melbourne. He is well known as a broadcaster on ABC Radio National and has presented history programs on ABC TV. His most recent book is *The Water Dreamers* (2009), a history of how water shaped the history of Australia.

Dr Tim Flannery wrote the Environment feature. Tim is a naturalist, explorer and writer. He is the author of a number of award-winning books, including *The Future Eaters* and *Throwim Way Leg* (an account of his adventures as a biologist working in New Guinea) and the landmark ecological history of North America, *The Eternal Frontier*. Tim lives in Adelaide, where he is director of the South Australian Museum and a professor at the University of Adelaide.

Dr David Millar wrote the Health section. David is a travel-medicine specialist, diving doctor and lecturer in wilderness medicine who graduated in Hobart, Tasmania. He has worked as an expedition doctor with the Maritime Museum of Western Australia, accompanying a variety of expeditions around Australia. David is currently a medical director with the Travel Doctor in Auckland.

THIS BOOK

This 1st edition of *Discover Australia* was coordinated by Lindsay Brown, and researched and written by Justine Vaisutis, Jayne D'Arcy, Lindsay Brown, Katja Gaskell, Paul Harding, Virginia Jealous, Rowan McKinnon, Charles Rawlings-Way, Rowan Roebig, Tom Spurling, Regis St Louis, Penny Watson and Meg Worby. This guidebook was commissioned in Lonely Planet's Melbourne office and produced by the following:
Commissioning Editors Emma Gilmour, Errol Hunt, Suzannah Shwer
Coordinating Editor Kirsten Rawlings
Assisting Editor Helen Yeates
Coordinating Cartographer Hunor Csutoros
Coordinating Layout Designer Cara Smith
Managing Editor Bruce Evans

SEND US YOUR FEEDBACK

We love to hear from travellers – your comments keep us on our toes and help make our books better. Our well-travelled team reads every word on what you loved or loathed about this book. Although we cannot reply individually to postal submissions, we always guarantee that your feedback goes straight to the appropriate authors in time for the next edition. Each person who sends us information is thanked in the next edition and the most useful submissions are rewarded with a free book.

To send us your updates – and find out about Lonely Planet events, newsletters and travel news – visit our award-winning website: **lonelyplanet.com/contact**.

Note: we may edit, reproduce and incorporate your comments in Lonely Planet products such as guidebooks, websites and digital products, so let us know if you don't want your comments reproduced or your name acknowledged. For a copy of our privacy policy visit **lonelyplanet.com/privacy**.

Managing Cartographer David Connolly
Managing Layout Designer Laura Jane
Assisting Cartographers Xavier Di Toro, Ross Macaw
Cover research Naomi Parker, lonelyplanetimages.com
Internal image research Jane Hart, lonelyplanetimages.com
Project Manager Chris Girdler

Thanks to Sasha Baskett, Glenn Beanland, Yvonne Bischofberger, Sally Darmody, Eoin Dunlevy, Ryan Evans, Suki Gear, Joshua Geoghegan, Mark Germanchis, Michelle Glynn, Brice Gosnell, Imogen Hall, James Hardy, Steve Henderson, Lauren Hunt, Chris Lee Ack, Nic Lehman, Alison Lyall, John Mazzocchi, Jennifer Mullins, Wayne Murphy, Darren O'Connell, Trent Paton, Piers Pickard, Howard Ralley, Lachlan Ross, Julie Sheridan, Jason Shugg, Caroline Sieg, Naomi Stephens, Geoff Stringer, Jane Thompson, Sam Trafford, Stefanie Di Trocchio, Tashi Wheeler, Clifton Wilkinson, Juan Winata, Emily K Wolman, Nick Wood

Internal photographs p4 Cockatoos, Hamilton Island, Queensland, Christopher Groenhout; p10 Nullarbor Plain, Oliver Strewe; p12 Kangaroos at the Anglesea Golf Club, Victoria, Bernard Napthine; p31 Kata Tjuta (The Olgas), Northern Territory, Richard I'Anson; p39 Rock climbing Mt French, Moogerah Peaks National Park, Queensland, Andrew Peacock; p3, p50 Sydney Harbour Bridge and ferry, Milson's Point, Sydney, Greg Elms; p3, p95 Wentworth Falls, Blue Mountains National Park, New South Wales, Grant Dixon; p3, p137 Sunshine Beach, Queensland, Oliver Strewe; p3, p191 Centre Pl, Melbourne, David Hannah; p3, p239 Watarrka (Kings Canyon) National Park, Richard I'Anson; p3, p273 Eyre Hwy on the Nullarbor Plain, Western Australia, Tony Wheeler; p3, p305 Victoria Dock, Hobart, John Banagan; p332 Victorian Alps, Mt Buffalo National Park, Victoria, Glenn van der Knijff; p363 The Pinnacles, Nambung National Park, Western Australia, Richard I'Anson

INDEX

000 Map pages
000 Photograph pages

M

000 Map pages
000 Photograph pages

000 Map pages
000 Photograph pages

000 Map pages
000 Photograph pages

Y

Z

GREENDEX

Choosing ecofriendly tours and accommodation is one of the best ways you can limit your impact on the environment. But what is ecotourism? Basically any tourism venture that is ecologically sustainable, focuses on experiencing natural areas, and fosters environmental and cultural understanding and conservation. In Australia, look for operators sporting the eco-tick assurance, determined by Ecotourism Australia (www.ecotourism.org.au). This accreditation is rigorous and graded.

The following choices have all been selected by Lonely Planet authors because they demonstrate an active sustainable-tourism policy. It's not an exhaustive list and we want to continue developing our sustainable-tourism content. If you have a suggestion or amendment, email us at **talk2us@lonelyplanet.com.au**.

For more information:

Lonely Planet (www.lonelyplanet.com/responsibletravel) Advice on how to travel responsibly.

Sustainable Travel International (www.sustainabletravelinternational.org) Has developed an ecocertification program.

Green Building Council of Australia (www.gbcaus.org) Has a green star rating for buildings (examining design and construction).

Central Australia

New South Wales

Queensland

Tasmania

Victoria

Western Australia

MAP LEGEND

ROUTES

Tollway
Freeway
Primary
Secondary
Tertiary
Lane
Under Construction
Unsealed Road
One-Way Street
Mall/Steps
Tunnel
Pedestrian Overpass
Walking Tour
Walking Tour Detour
Walking Path
Track

TRANSPORT

Ferry
Metro
Monorail
Rail/Underground
Tram
Cable Car, Funicular

HYDROGRAPHY

River, Creek
Intermittent River
Swamp/Mangrove
Reef
Canal
Water
Dry Lake/Salt Lake
Glacier

BOUNDARIES

International
State, Provincial
Disputed
Regional, Suburb
Marine Park
Cliff/Ancient Wall

AREA FEATURES

Area of Interest
Beach, Desert
Building/Urban Area
Cemetery, Christian
Cemetery, Other
Forest
Mall/Market
Park
Restricted Area
Sports

POPULATION

CAPITAL (NATIONAL)
LARGE CITY
Small City
CAPITAL (STATE)
Medium City
Town, Village

SYMBOLS

Sights/Activities

Buddhist
Canoeing, Kayaking
Castle, Fortress
Christian
Confucian
Diving
Hindu
Islamic
Jain
Jewish
Monument
Museum, Gallery
Point of Interest
Pool
Ruin
Sento (Public Hot Baths)
Shinto
Sikh
Skiing
Surfing, Surf Beach
Taoist
Trail Head
Winery, Vineyard
Zoo, Bird Sanctuary

Information

Bank, ATM
Embassy/Consulate
Hospital, Medical
Information
Internet Facilities
Police Station
Post Office, GPO
Telephone
Toilets
Wheelchair Access

Eating

Eating

Drinking

Cafe
Drinking

Entertainment

Entertainment

Shopping

Shopping

Sleeping

Camping
Sleeping

Transport

Airport, Airfield
Border Crossing
Bus Station
Bicycle Path/Cycling
FFCC (Barcelona)
Metro (Barcelona)
Parking Area
Petrol Station
S-Bahn
Taxi Rank
Tube Station
U-Bahn

Geographic

Beach
Lighthouse
Lookout
Mountain, Volcano
National Park
Pass, Canyon
Picnic Area
River Flow
Shelter, Hut
Waterfall

LONELY PLANET OFFICES

Australia
Head Office
Locked Bag 1, Footscray, Victoria 3011
☎ 03 8379 8000, fax 03 8379 8111
talk2us@lonelyplanet.com.au

USA
150 Linden St, Oakland, CA 94607
☎ 510 250 6400, toll free 800 275 8555,
fax 510 893 8572
info@lonelyplanet.com

UK
2nd fl, 186 City Rd,
London EC1V 2NT
☎ 020 7106 2100, fax 020 7106 2101
go@lonelyplanet.co.uk

Published by Lonely Planet
ABN 36 005 607 983

Printed by Markono Print Media Pte Ltd
Printed in Singapore